Seventh Edition

MOSAICS
READING AND WRITING ESSAYS

KIM FLACHMANN
California State University, Bakersfield

Boston Columbus Indianapolis New York San Francisco Amsterdam
Cape Town Dubai London Madrid Milan Munich Paris Montréal Toronto
Delhi Mexico City São Paulo Sydney Hong Kong Seoul Singapore Taipei Tokyo

Executive Editor: Matthew Wright
Program Manager: Katharine Glynn
Marketing Manager: Jennifer Edwards
Executive Media Producer: Jaclyn Reynen
Media Editor: Kelsey Loveday
Associate Multimedia Specialist: Elizabeth Bravo
Content Specialist: Laura Olson
Project Manager: Savoula Amanatidis
Project Coordination, Text Design, and Electronic Page
  Makeup: Integra Software Services Pvt Ltd.

Program Design Lead: Beth Pacquin
Cover Designer: Studio Montage
Cover Image: Fotolia – 65508743
Senior Manufacturing Buyer: Roy L. Pickering, Jr.
Printer and Binder: R. R. Donnelley and Sons Company–
  Crawfordsville
Cover Printer: Lehigh-Phoenix Color Corporation–
  Hagerstown

Credits and acknowledgments borrowed from other sources and reproduced, with permission, in this textbook appear on the appropriate page within text or on page 754.

Library of Congress Cataloging-in-Publication Data
Flachmann, Kim.
  Mosaics: reading and writing essays / Kim Flachmann.—Seventh edition.
    pages cm
  Includes index.
  ISBN 978-0-13-402167-6—ISBN 0-13-402167-3
  1. English language—Rhetoric.   2. English language—Grammar—Problems, exercises, etc.   3. Report writing.   I. Title.
PE1408.F469 2015
808.4—dc23
                                                                                    2015030090

2   16

PEARSON

www.pearsonhighered.com

Student Edition
ISBN-10:   0-13-402167-3
ISBN-13: 978-0-13-402167-6

Annotated Instructor's Edition
ISBN-10:   0-13-404824-5
ISBN-13: 978-0-13-404824-6

For Michael

BRIEF CONTENTS

iv

unt 6 chap 41 p.635

DETAILED CONTENTS

PART IV The Handbook 489

PREFACE

Students have the best chance of succeeding in college if they learn how to analyze ideas and think critically about issues in many different subject areas. *Mosaics: Reading and Writing Essays* is the third in a series of three books that teach the basic skills essential to all good academic writing. This series illustrates how the companion skills of reading and writing are parts of a larger, interrelated process that moves back and forth through the tasks of prereading and reading, prewriting and writing, and revising and editing. In other words, this series demonstrates how these skills are integrated at every stage of the communication process and helps you discover the "mosaics" of your own reading and writing processes.

OVERALL GOAL

Ultimately, each book in the *Mosaics* series portrays writing as a way of thinking and processing information. One by one, these books encourage students to discover how the "mosaics" of their own reading and writing processes work together to form a coherent whole. By demonstrating the interrelationship among thinking, reading, and writing on progressively more difficult levels, these books will help prepare students for success in college throughout the curriculum and in their lives after graduation.

THE *MOSAICS* SERIES

Each of the three books of the *Mosaics* series has a different emphasis: *Reading and Writing Sentences, Reading and Writing Paragraphs,* and *Reading and Writing Essays.* As the titles imply, the first book highlights sentence structure, the second book paragraph development, and the third the composition of essays. *Mosaics: Reading and Writing Sentences* provides instruction and practice on grammar and usage conventions. Then the Paragraph and Essay books move from personal to more academic writing and become gradually more sophisticated in the length and level of their reading selections, the complexity of their writing assignments, the degree of difficulty of their revising and editing strategies, and the content and structure of their student writing samples.

This entire three-book series is based on the following fundamental assumptions:

- Students must think critically or analytically to succeed in college.
- Students build confidence in their ability to read and write by reading and writing.
- Students learn best from discovery and experimentation rather than from instruction and abstract discussions.
- Students profit from studying both professional and student writing.
- Students need to discover their personal reading and writing processes.

- Students learn both individually and collaboratively.
- Students benefit most from assignments that integrate reading and writing.
- Students learn how to revise by following clear guidelines.
- Students learn grammar and usage rules by editing their own writing.
- Students must be able to transfer their writing skills to all their college courses.

NEW IN THIS EDITION

- **Visual Presentation of the Reading/Writing Process:** A modified design introduces a color-coded system throughout the writing process chapters. Purple type signals reading. Then green type alerts students to the "creative/composition" aspect of the writing process, blue type connects students with "revising" elements of the essay, and maroon type signals the important aspects associated with "editing" essays.

- **Writing Across the Curriculum and at the Workplace:** An all-new Chapter 8 provides examples of the kinds of writing students can expect to do in future coursework and on the job.

- **A Deeper Connection Between Print and Media:** Pearson's MyWritingLab (www.mywritinglab.com) is now even more deeply integrated into the writing assignments and activities in the new edition. Once again, students can actually complete and submit the "Writing Prompts" in Chapters 9–17 and the "Write Your Own" activities from the Chapter Review exercise sets in Chapters 25–52 right in the *Mosaics*, Seventh Edition, module in MyWritingLab! These unique activities are clearly identified in the print text by a new icon.

- **New MyWritingLab Prompts:** All new MyWritingLab prompts line up with the new XL MyWritingLab program and give students a unique opportunity to link to more instruction and practice, along with tips on how to succeed with a particular skill or process.

- **Enhanced eText:** The MWL eText Course for *Mosaics: Reading and Writing Essays*, Seventh Edition, includes access to Pearson's "What Every Student Should Know About Critical Reading" and to Pearson's "What Every Student Should Know About Writing Across the Curriculum." This additional content in the MWL eText Course expands upon what is outlined in Chapter 3 "Critical Reading" and Chapter 8 "Writing Across the Curriculum and in the Workplace," respectively, and prepares students more effectively for future coursework.

UNIQUE FEATURES OF THIS BOOK

Several other unique and exciting features define this book.

It teaches and demonstrates the reading-writing connection:

- It integrates reading and writing throughout the text.
- It introduces rhetorical modes as patterns of thought.
- It teaches and demonstrates reading as a process.
- It features culturally diverse reading selections that are of high interest to students.
- It moves students systematically from personal to academic writing.
- It uses both student and professional essays as models.

- It illustrates all aspects of the writing process through student writing.
- It develops a student research paper from assignment to completed paper.
- It helps students discover their own reading and writing processes.
- It includes a complete, color-coded handbook filled with exercises.
- It offers worksheets for peer- and self-evaluation.

This book teaches a different reading strategy in every chapter of Part II:

- Description
- Narration
- Illustration
- Process Analysis
- Comparison/Contrast
- Division/Classification
- Definition
- Cause/Effect
- Argument

Making Personal Associations
Thinking Aloud
Chunking
Graphing the Ideas
Peer Teaching
Summarizing
Reacting Critically
Making Connections
Recognizing Facts and Opinions
Reading with the Author/Against the Author

These strategies are applied to all aspects of the writing process: reading/getting ready to write, reading the prompt, reading another student's essay, and reading their own essays.

The innovative lessons, exercises, and assignments of Pearson's MyWritingLab (www.mywritinglab.com) are strategically integrated into the content of every chapter:

- The instruction in all of the chapters is supplemented by useful exercises, activities, and writing assignments that can be completed in MyWritingLab.
- As in the previous edition, students can complete and submit exercises from the seventh edition of *Mosaics* within MyWritingLab. Students can complete the "Writing Prompts" in Chapters 9–17 and the "Write Your Own" activities from the Chapter Review exercise sets in Chapters 25–52 right in the *Mosaics*, Seventh Edition, module in MyWritingLab! These unique activities are clearly identified in the print text by a new icon.

HOW THIS BOOK WORKS

Mosaics: Reading and Writing Essays teaches students how to read and write critically. For flexibility and easy reference, this book is divided into four parts:

Part I: Reading and Writing: An Overview
All eight chapters in Part I demonstrate the cyclical nature of the reading and writing processes. Each chapter begins with the logistics of getting ready to read and write and then moves systematically through the interlocking stages of the processes by following a student from prereading to rereading and then from prewriting to revising and editing. Part I ends with four review practices that summarize the material and let students practice what they have learned.

Part II: Reading and Writing Effective Essays
Part II, the heart of the instruction in this text, teaches students how to read and write essays by introducing the rhetorical modes as patterns of development. It moves from personal writing to more academic types of writing: describing, narrating, illustrating, analyzing a process, comparing and contrasting, dividing and classifying, defining, analyzing causes and effects, and arguing. Within each chapter, students learn how to read a professional essay critically, write their own essays, and revise and edit another student's essay as well as their own. Finally, two professional writing samples are included in each rhetorical mode chapter so students can actually see the features of each strategy at work in different models. Each professional essay is preceded by prereading activities and then followed by 10 questions that move students from a literal to an analytical understanding as they consider the essay's content, purpose, audience, and paragraph structure.

Part III: The Research Paper
The next section of this text helps students move from writing effective essays to writing a documented paper by following a student through the process of developing a paper with sources. Part III ends with a series of writing assignments and workshops designed to encourage students to write, revise, and edit a term paper and then reflect on their own writing process.

Part IV: The Handbook
Part IV is a complete grammar/usage handbook, including exercises, that covers nine units of instruction: The Basics, Sentences, Verbs, Pronouns, Modifiers, Punctuation, Mechanics, Effective Sentences, and Choosing the Right Word. These categories are coordinated with the Editing Checklist that appears periodically throughout this text. Each chapter starts with five self-test questions so students can determine their strengths and weaknesses in each area. The chapters provide at least three types of practice after each grammar concept, moving the students systematically from identifying grammar concepts to filling in the blanks to writing their own sentences. Each chapter ends with a practical editing workshop that asks students to use the skills they just learned as they work with another student to edit their own writing. Pre- and Post-Unit Tests—including practice with single sentences and paragraphs—are offered for each unit in the *Instructor's Resource Manual*.

APPENDIXES

The appendixes help students keep track of their progress in the various skills they learn in this text. References to these appendixes are interspersed throughout the book so students know when to use them as they study the concepts in each chapter:

- Appendix 1: Critical Thinking Log
- Appendix 2A: Your EQ (Editing Quotient)
- Appendix 2B: Editing Quotient Answers
- Appendix 2C: Editing Quotient Error Chart
- Appendix 3: Test Yourself Answers
- Appendix 4: Revising an Essay (Forms A and B)
- Appendix 5: Revising a Research Paper
- Appendix 6: Editing
- Appendix 7: Error Log
- Appendix 8: Spelling Log

ACKNOWLEDGMENTS

I want to acknowledge the support, encouragement, and sound advice of several people who have helped me through the development of the *Mosaics* series. First, Pearson Higher Education has provided guidance and inspiration for this project through the enduring wisdom of Matt Wright, executive editor of developmental English and Craig Campanella, previous senior acquisitions editor of developmental English; the thoughtful guidance of Eric Stano, editorial director of English; the special creative inspiration of Jennifer Edwards, marketing manager; the unparalleled support of Laura Marenghi, editorial assistant; the exceptional organizational skills of Katharine Glynn, program manager, and Savoula Amanatidis, project manager; the insight and vision of Marta Tomins and Harriett Prentiss, past development editors; the tender loving care of Integra's Kristin Jobe, project manager; the hard work and patience of Joe Croscup, permissions editor; and the leadership of Paul Corey, managing director. Also, this book would not be a reality without the insightful persistence of Phil Miller, former publisher at Pearson.

I want to give very special thanks to Cody Ganger, Keith Keikiro, Sabrina Buie, Tiffany Wong, Tracie Grimes, Veronica Wilson, Laura Harris, Joanie Sahagun, Laraine Rosema, Carlos Tkacz, Julie Paulsen, Kevin Goodwin, Kristen Mercer, and Robyn Thompson, my advisors and sources of endless ideas and solutions to problems. I am also grateful to Lauren Martinez and Cheryl Smith for their inspiration and hard work on previous editions and to Cody Ganger, Isaac Sanchez, Lauren Martinez, Rebecca Hewett, Valerie Turner, and Li'l Pearl for their discipline and hard work—past and present—on the *Instructor's Resource Manuals* and the PowerPoint presentations for each of the books in the series.

Two more groups of consultants and assistants were inspirational in the development of this book: First, I want to thank Brooke Hughes, Randi Brummett, and Isaac Sanchez for their invaluable expertise and vision in crafting and placing the instructional inserts for MyWritingLab. Also, I want to express my gratitude to my students, from whom I have learned so much about the writing process, about teaching, and about life itself. Thanks especially to the students who contributed paragraphs and essays to this series: Josh Ellis, Jolene Christie, Mary Minor, Michael Tiede, Juliana Schweiger, Chris Dison, and Keith Keikiro.

In addition, I am especially indebted to the following reviewers who have guided me through the development and revision of this book: Lisa Berman, Miami-Dade Community College; Patrick Haas, Glendale Community College; Jeanne Campanelli, American River College; Dianne Gregory, Cape Cod Community College; Clara Wilson-Cook, Southern University at New Orleans; Thomas Beery, Lima Technical College; Jean Petrolle, Columbia College; David Cratty, Cuyahoga Community College; Allison Travis, Butte State College; Suellen Meyer, Meramec Community College; Jill Lahnstein, Cape Fear Community College; Stanley Coberly, West Virginia State University at Parkersville; Jamie Moore, Scottsdale Community College; Nancy Hellner, Mesa Community College; Ruth Hatcher, Washtenaw Community College; Thurmond Whatley, Aiken Technical College; W. David Hall, Columbus State Community College; Marilyn Coffee, Fort Hays State University; Teriann Gaston, University of Texas at Arlington; Peggy Karsten, Ridgewater College; Nancy Hayward, Indiana University of Pennsylvania; Carol Ann Britt, San Antonio College; Maria C. Villar-Smith, Miami-Dade Community College; Jami L. Huntsinger, University of New Mexico at Valencia Campus; P. Berniece Longmore, Essex County College; Lee Herrick, Fresno City College; Elaine Chakonas, Northeastern Illinois University; Roy Warner, Montana State University; Chris Morelock, Walters State Community College; Maria Villar-Smith, Miami-Dade College; Angela Bartlett, Chaffey College; Sharisse Turner, Tallahassee CC; Billy Jones, Miami-Dade College; Chrishawn Speller, Seminole CC; Albert Hernandez, SW Texas JC; Greg Zobel, College of the Redwoods; Ben Worth, KCTCS–Bluegrass-Cooper; Jacinth Thomas-Val, Sacramento City College; Liz Ann Aguilar, San Antonio College; James McCormick, Rochester Community and Technical College; Jessica Carroll, Miami-Dade College; Nancy Risch, Caldwell Community College; Anna Schmidt, Lonestar College; Meridith Nelson, Des Moines Area Community College; Mary Geren, Tri-County Technical College; Giano Cromley, Kennedy King College; Sarah Salmons, Linn State Technical College; Dustin Greene, Caldwell Community College; Ember Smith, Tri-County Technical College. Dawn Cable, West Virginia Northern Community College; Vito Gulla, Delaware County Community College; James Scannell McCormick, Augsburg College; Sobia Saleem, Ohlone College; Dianne Zoccola, Delaware County Community College.

Finally, I owe a tremendous personal debt to the people who have lived with this project for the last 21 years; they are my closest companions and my best advisors: Michael, Christopher, Laura, and Abby Flachmann.

Kim Flachmann

SUPPLEMENTS AND ADDITIONAL RESOURCES

Pearson Writing Resources for Instructors and Students

Book-Specific Ancillary Material

Annotated Instructor's Edition for *Mosaics: Reading and Writing Essays*, Seventh Edition
ISBN 0-13-404824-5
The AIE offers in-text answers, marginal annotations for teaching each chapter, links to the *Instructor's Resource Manual*, and MyWritingLab teaching tips. It is a valuable resource for experienced and first-time instructors alike.

Instructor's Resource Manual for *Mosaics: Reading and Writing Essays*, Seventh Edition
ISBN 0-13-394914-1
The material in the IRM is designed to save instructors time and provide them with effective options for teaching their writing classes. It offers suggestions for setting up their course; provides lots of extra practice for students who need it; offers quizzes and grammar tests, including unit tests; furnishes grading rubrics for each rhetorical mode; and supplies answers in case instructors want to print them out and have students grade their own work. This valuable resource is exceptionally useful for adjuncts who might need advice in setting up their initial classes or who might be teaching a variety of writing classes with too many students and not enough time.

PowerPoint Presentation for *Mosaics: Reading and Writing Essays*, Seventh Edition
ISBN 0-13-404839-3
PowerPoint presentations to accompany each chapter consist of classroom-ready lecture outline slides, lecture tips and classroom activities, and review questions. Available for download from the Instructor Resource Center.

Answer Key for *Mosaics: Reading and Writing Essays*, Seventh Edition
ISBN 0-13-404840-7
The Answer Key contains the solutions to the exercises in the student edition of the text. Available for download from the Instructor Resource Center.

Additional Resources

Pearson is pleased to offer a variety of support materials to help make teaching writing easier for teachers and to help students excel in their coursework. Many of our student supplements are available free or at a greatly reduced price when packaged with *Mosaics: Reading and Writing Essays*. Visit www.pearsonhighereducation.com, contact your local Pearson sales representative, or review a detailed listing of the full supplements package in the *Instructor's Resource Manual* for more information.

MyWritingLab™ Online Course (access code required)
for *Mosaics: Reading and Writing Essays,*
Seventh Edition, by Kim Flachmann

MyWritingLab is an online homework, tutorial, and assessment program that provides engaging experiences for today's instructors and students.

Writing Help for Varying Skill Levels

For students who enter the course at widely varying skill levels, MyWritingLab provides unique, targeted instruction that is personalized and adaptive. Starting with a pre-assessment known as the Path Builder, MyWritingLab diagnoses strengths and weaknesses in students' writing skills. The results of the pre-assessment inform each student's Learning Path, a personalized pathway for students to work on requisite skills through multimodal activities. In doing so, students feel supported and ready to succeed in class.

Respond to Student Writing with Targeted Feedback and Instruction

MyWritingLab unites instructor comments and feedback with targeted instruction via rich multimedia activities, allowing students to learn from and through their own writing.

- When giving feedback on student writing, instructors can add links to activities that address issues and strategies needed for review. Instructors may link to multimedia resources in Pearson Writer, which include curated content from Purdue OWL.
- In the Writing Assignments, students can use instructor-created peer review rubrics to evaluate and comment on other students' writing.
- Paper review by specialized tutors through Tutor Services is available, as is plagiarism detection through TurnItIn.

Learning Tools for Student Engagement

Learning Catalytics

Generate class discussion, guide lectures, and promote peer-to-peer learning with real-time analytics. MyLab and Mastering with eText now provides Learning Catalytics—an interactive student response tool that uses students' smartphones, tablets, or laptops to engage them in more sophisticated tasks and thinking.

MediaShare

MediaShare allows students to post multimodal assignments easily—whether they are audio, video, or visual compositions—for peer review and instructor feedback. In both face-to-face and online course settings, MediaShare saves instructors valuable time and enriches the student learning experience by enabling contextual feedback to be provided quickly and easily.

Direct Access to MyLab

Users can link from any Learning Management System (LMS) to Pearson's MyWritingLab. Access MyLab assignments, rosters, and resources, and synchronize MyLab grades with the LMS gradebook. New direct, single sign-on provides access to all the personalized learning MyLab resources that make studying more efficient and effective.

Proven Results

No matter how MyWritingLab is used, instructors have access to powerful gradebook reports. These reports provide visual analytics that give insight to course performance at the student, section, or even program level.

Visit www.mywritinglab.com for more information.

Reading and Writing: An Overview

" There is an art of reading, as well as an art of thinking and an art of writing. "

—Isaac D'Israeli

Reading and writing are so closely related that succeeding in one is directly related to succeeding in the other. So the goal of Part I is to help you develop self-confidence both as a reader *and* as a writer. It will provide you with the basic tools you need to improve your reading and writing. Then, as you move through these eight chapters, you will discover how to adjust these processes to suit your own needs and preferences. As you become more aware of the available choices, you will also develop a better understanding of your strengths and weaknesses as both a reader and a writer. With practice, your personalized reading and writing processes will soon become a routine part of your academic life and will help you confirm your place in the community of college students.

1

Reading and Writing in College

Words help us solve problems, discover new ideas, feel better, make people laugh, and understand the world around us. Reading and writing are companion processes for using words. They let us connect with our immediate environment as we learn from our reading and contribute to society through writing.

WHY LEARN HOW TO READ AND WRITE WELL?

The better you read and write, the more completely you can connect with your environment and the more control you have over your daily routine. Reading and writing well let you understand precisely what issues are important and communicate exactly what you want to say about them. These companion skills actually help you get what you want out of life. So reading and writing well give you power in a variety of ways.

Reading and Writing as Critical Thinking

Critical thinking is the highest form of mental activity that human beings engage in, and it is a major source of success in college and in life beyond college. Thinking critically involves grappling with the ideas, issues, and problems in your immediate environment and in the larger world. It means constantly questioning and analyzing different aspects of life. Because critical thinking is complex, it requires a great deal of concentration and practice. Once you have a sense of how your mind works at this level, you will be able to think critically whenever you want.

Reading and writing are companion activities that engage people in the creation of thought and meaning—either as readers interpreting a text or as writers constructing one. Clear thinking is the pivotal point that joins these two tasks. The traditional rhetorical strategies are presented in this text as ways of processing information that you can use in other academic assignments. We feature one strategy at a time in each chapter so you can understand how it works before you combine it with other techniques. In this way, you will be able to systematically improve your ability to think, read, and write critically.

With some guidance, learning how to read and write according to different rhetorical modes or strategies (such as describing, narrating, or dividing and classifying) can give you the mental workout you need to think critically in much the same way that physical exercise warms you up for various sports. As you move through the chapters in Part II, you will be asked to isolate each rhetorical mode—just as you isolate your abs, thighs, and biceps in a physical workout. Each rhetorical mode offers a slightly different way of seeing the world, processing information, and solving problems. So each rhetorical mode is really a different way of thinking and making sense of the world.

Reading and Writing as Discovery

In both reading and writing, we often start out not knowing specifically where we are going. As we read, we follow another person's line of reasoning and discover our own thoughts and reactions in response to our reading material. Similarly, we often don't know the points we want to make until we start writing. As we write, we discover what we think and want to say.

The physical acts of reading and writing let your mind sort through lots of ideas and help you decide exactly what you think and feel on specific topics. Sometimes new ideas will come out of something you have read, or you might understand an idea better once you start writing about it. Whatever the case, the simple acts of reading and writing lead to understanding of both the subject matter and your own thought processes.

The more you read and write, the more ideas you generate. This is why your instructor might suggest you read and/or write if you are stuck on a topic or don't know what to say next. Reading and writing help you discover and express the good ideas already in your mind.

Reading and Writing as Necessities

Most important, reading and writing are necessary for surviving both in college and on the job. On a daily basis, you have to read and respond to a multitude of documents from endless e-mails to textbooks to professional reports. In addition, you have to write more in today's electronic age than any previous generation has. Some of your writing will be reports or projects that extend over a long period of time. Other writing tasks will have to be completed immediately, such as responses to e-mail messages. Whatever the terms, reading and writing will be significant parts of your life throughout college and beyond.

The better your reading and writing skills, the better grades you will make in college and the further you will get in your chosen career. Everything you learn about reading and writing in this text applies to all your courses. These strategies will also be helpful on the job, especially when you have to read a dense analysis, write a difficult report, or summarize your accomplishments for a professional evaluation. The same reading and writing guidelines apply to all communication tasks.

PRACTICE 1 Answer the following questions.

1. Why should you learn to read and write?

_____

_____

_____

2. Why should you learn to read and write well?

_____

_____

_____

3. How can reading and writing help you think critically?

_____

_____

_____

4. In what ways are reading and writing processes of discovery?

_____

_____

_____

5. Why are reading and writing necessary in today's world?

_____

_____

_____

THINKING OF YOURSELF AS A READER AND A WRITER

Part of this important process is thinking of yourself as both a reader and a writer. You do these tasks every day in a variety of ways. Yet many people don't envision themselves as readers and writers. How we use words tends to be the hallmark of our success—no matter what our field. So learning how to read and write critically—at the highest possible level of performance—is a basic requirement for a meaningful, successful life.

Words are a commodity that you use every day and that can help you get what you want out of life. If you want to enter into an e-mail conversation at work, you first need to read the words that have already been written. Then you must write your response. Any word choices you put forward reflect on you as a person. They are the grounds on which others judge you.

Whether you read a text message, the newest best seller, or a new lease agreement for your apartment, you are a reader. In like manner, if you jot a note to put on the refrigerator, post a message on a friend's Facebook "wall," write a paper for economics class, or draft a report for your boss, you are a writer. Now that you are in college, you are part of a very special community of readers and writers who are trying to perfect these skills and live their lives at a more informed and intellectually stimulating level than your friends who do not attend college.

As you face more complex reading and writing tasks in college, you need to understand the sequence of activities that make up the reading and writing processes. Learning to use these processes so that the work you produce is the best you are capable of is what this book is all about.

Even though each reader and writer is different, some general principles apply to everyone—students and professionals alike. Before you actually begin to read or write, a wise move is to get your surroundings ready. This involves gathering supplies, setting aside a time to study, finding a comfortable place to do your work, and establishing a routine.

1. **Gather your supplies before you begin to study.** Don't risk losing your great ideas by not being able to find a pen and paper or a computer. Some students keep a yellow tablet and a pen or pencil by their sides as they study; others write directly in their books. In like manner, with writing, some students draft their essays on paper, and others write directly on their computers. One of the main advantages of writing on a computer is that once you word process your ideas, changing them or moving them around is easy. As a result, you are more likely to make revisions when you work on a computer, and you will therefore turn in a better paper. Whatever equipment you choose, make sure it is ready at the time you have set aside to study.

2. **Set aside a special time to read and write, and plan to do nothing else during that time.** The bird's cage can wait to be cleaned until tomorrow, the furniture doesn't have to be dusted today, the garage can be hosed down some other time, and the dirt on your kitchen floor won't turn to concrete overnight. When you first get a reading or writing assignment, a little procrastination is natural. In fact, procrastination can actually work in your favor when you are writing because your mind is working on the task subconsciously. The trick is to know when to quit procrastinating and get down to work so that you meet your deadlines with time to spare.

3. **Find a comfortable place with few distractions.** Joyce Carol Oates, a famous contemporary writer, claims that writing is a very private act that requires lots of patience, time, and space. The same principle applies to reading. First, you need to set up a place to read and/or write that suits your specific needs. It should be a place where you are not distracted or interrupted. Some people work best in a straight-backed chair sitting at a table or desk, while others do their best work sitting cross-legged in bed. The exact place doesn't matter, as long as you can think there.

Even if you are fortunate enough to have a private study area, you may find that you want to make some adjustments. You may decide to unplug your phone during your study time. Or you may discover that quiet background music helps you shut out all kinds of noises but doesn't distract you the way talk shows and rock stations would. One student may do her best studying after soaking in a hot tub; another might play jazz when he is getting down to work; and still another may have a Pepsi on one side of his table and a Snickers bar on the other. Whatever your choices, you need a comfortable working environment.

4. **Establish a personal ritual.** As a member of the community of students, acknowledging your own study habits and rituals is a major part of discovering your reading and writing processes. These rituals begin the minute you are given an assignment. What activities help you get ready to read? Some people exercise, others catch up on e-mail, and still others clean their rooms before they study. What activities prepare you to write? Most people follow a routine when they face reading and writing tasks without even realizing it. But they are preparing their minds for studying. So, in the course of validating yourself as a reader and writer, take a moment now to record some of the preferences and rituals connected with your own study time.

PRACTICE 2 Explain the rituals you instinctively follow as you get ready to study. How do you prepare your mind for reading? Where do you write? At what time of day do you produce your best work? Do you like noise? Quiet? What other details describe your study environment? What equipment do you need to read and write?

KEEPING A JOURNAL

The word *journal* refers to a daily log of your thinking. It is a place where you can record ideas, snatches of conversation, dreams, descriptions of people, pictures of places, and thoughts about objects—whatever catches your attention. Keeping a journal to respond to your reading and writing tasks will be very beneficial to your progress as a critical thinker. The more you respond in writing to what you are reading, the more engaged you are in your learning.

A good way to establish the habit of journal writing is to use your journal for answering the questions that accompany the instruction in Parts II and III of this text and the writing exercises in the Handbook (Part IV). You should definitely use your journal to respond to your reading in this text, and you can also use it to jot down ideas and plans for essays as they occur to you. In addition, you might want to complete your prewriting activities in your journal. Keeping track of a journal is much easier than finding notes on assorted scraps of paper.

Making a section of your journal private is also a good idea. Sometimes, when you think freely on paper or screen, you don't want to share the results with anyone. Yet those notes can be very important in finding a subject to write about or in developing a topic.

Your journal in college will essentially be a bank of thoughts and topics for you. If used thoughtfully, it can become an incredible resource—a place to both generate and retrieve your ideas. Writing in your journal can help you discover your thoughts and feelings about specific issues as well as let you think through important choices you have to make. In this way, writing can help you solve problems and work your way through various college projects.

If you use a notebook for your journal, choose one that you really like. You might even keep your journal on your computer. However, unless you have a laptop, you won't have your electronic journal with you all the time. The choice is yours (unless your instructor has specific requirements). Just remember that a journal should be a notebook (paper or electronic) that you enjoy writing in and carrying with you.

The content of your journal entries depends to a great extent on your instructor's directions. But some basic advice applies to all entries, whether on paper or on a computer.

1. Date your entries, and note the time; you may find it useful to see when your best ideas occur.

2. Record anything that comes to your mind, and follow your thoughts wherever they take you (unless your instructor gives you different directions).

3. Glue or somehow attach to your journal anything that stimulates your thinking, reading, or writing—cartoons, magazine ads, poems, pictures, advice columns, and URLs for useful Web sites.

4. Think of your journal as someone to talk to—a friend who will keep your cherished ideas safe and sound and won't talk back or argue with you.

PRACTICE 3 Begin your own journal.

1. Buy a paper notebook that you like, and write in it.

2. Record at least two journal entries on your computer or electronic notebook.

3. Which type of journal do you prefer—paper or electronic? Write an entry explaining your preference.

READING AND WRITING IN TANDEM WITH ANOTHER STUDENT

In the rest of Part I, you will be reading and writing in tandem or along with another student, Beth Olson, who has already completed the assignments you will be doing. In other words, this student will be demonstrating her reading and writing processes as you work on your own. As you consider Beth's words and ideas, concentrate on discovering your own original thoughts as you do each assignment.

PRACTICE 4 Answer the following questions.

1. What does reading and writing in tandem mean in this text?

_____

_____

_____

2. How can this approach help you?

_____

_____

_____

3. Why is it important to discover your own original thoughts for each assignment?

_____

_____

_____

MyWritingLab | ### Understanding Writing in College

To make sure you understand the concepts covered in this chapter, go to **MyWritingLab.com,** and choose **Getting Started** in **The Craft of Writing** module. For this topic, read the **Overview,** watch the three **Animation** videos, and complete the **Recall, Apply,** and **Write** activities. Then check your understanding by taking the **Post-test.**

MyWritingLab™ Visit Chapter 1 "Reading and Writing in College," in MyWritingLab, and complete the Post-test to check your understanding of the chapter's objectives.

The Reading Process

The reading process, like the writing process, consists of "steps" or "stages" that overlap. But unlike writing, reading has to occur in a certain order or you will not be able to understand your material. As you write, you might first decide to develop a paragraph for your second topic, then go back to your first topic, and finally write your introduction and conclusion. Reading, however, dictates its own order. To get the most out of the process, you must start at the beginning and read to the end. What you do during the process is what can raise your level of understanding to the analytical or critical level, which is where you want to be to succeed in college and in life after college. This chapter will introduce you to the entire reading process. But keep in mind that you should adjust the options presented here to your individual preferences.

VISUALIZING THE READING PROCESS

Although we talk about reading in a fairly sequential way, the options you can pursue while reading something from beginning to end can occur and reoccur in any order. The activities you engage in as you read make you an active or passive reader.

The purpose of reading actively (rather than passively) is to make you a critical reader. Once you read critically, your writing will rise to a higher level as well. Passive readers begin a reading assignment on the first page and read to the end without engaging in any recognizable activities as they read. Active readers physically work with their reading material from beginning to end—making it their own, trying to understand it on a more sophisticated level, and constantly reacting to it as they read. Identifying your own opinions and thoughts in reference to your reading material is one of the essential parts of the reading process.

As you work with the reading process in this textbook, the following graphic might help you understand how its various stages can overlap. The rest of this chapter will explain in detail each of these elements.

The Cycle of Reading

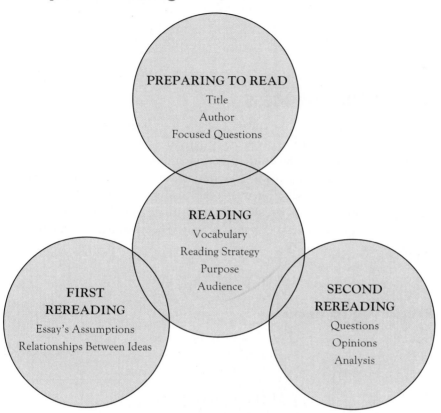

PREPARING TO READ
Title
Author
Focused Questions

READING
Vocabulary
Reading Strategy
Purpose
Audience

FIRST REREADING
Essay's Assumptions
Relationships Between Ideas

SECOND REREADING
Questions
Opinions
Analysis

PRACTICE 1 Answer the following questions.

1. List the three elements of prereading.

    _____

    _____

2. List the four elements of reading.

    _____

    _____

3. List the two elements of the first rereading.

    _____

    _____

4. List the three elements of the second rereading.

_____

_____

THE READING PROCESS

The reading process, like the writing process, begins the minute you get a reading assignment. It involves many activities—from finding your reading material to reading the entire piece, including trips to the library, text messages, and late-night snacks. Understanding the role these personal choices play in the reading process is just as important as knowing how the formal process works because all these rituals have to work together to help you complete your assignment on time. The main parts of the process are discussed in this section.

Preparing to Read

PREPARING TO READ
Title
Author
Focused Questions

Prereading, or preparing to read, refers to activities that help you explore your reading material and its general subject so that you can read as efficiently as possible. It includes surveying your assignment and focusing on the task ahead of you. Your mission at this stage is to stimulate your thinking before and during the act of reading.

The most important tasks at this point include looking closely at the title to see if it reveals any clues about the author and his or her attitude, finding out as much as you can about the author (background, profession, biases, etc.), and responding in this text to some preliminary questions that will focus your attention before you read. All of these activities are demonstrated in Chapter 3 as Beth Olson approaches a reading assignment.

Reading

READING
Vocabulary
Reading Strategy
Purpose
Audience

Once you have previewed your reading material, you can start reading at the beginning of the selection. As you read, mark or look up words you don't understand from the context, and annotate your reading material as you move through it. Writing on the material itself will keep you engaged in the process as the tasks become more difficult. You should also try to figure out the author's primary purpose for writing the selection.

Each chapter in Part II of this book will give you a specific reading strategy to master with a particular essay. These strategies can be applied to any reading material and are especially useful in helping you be an active reader. Once you learn different strategies that will improve your reading comprehension, you can choose your favorites to use in other courses.

First Rereading

**FIRST
REREADING**
Essay's Assumptions
Relationships Between Ideas

Most students don't want to read their assignments more than once, but the second and third readings are the ones that teach you how to read critically. Only after the first reading can you hope to understand your reading material at a deeper level. This second reading allows you to get to the assumptions behind the words on the page and to see relationships between ideas that you didn't notice in the first reading.

With this reading, you are closer to critical reading, but you are not there yet. This reading helps you dig more deeply into what the author is saying and prepares you to go one step farther when you read the essay for the third time. Once again, the details of this reading will be demonstrated by Beth Olson in Chapter 3 as she records her reactions to her reading material.

Second Rereading

SECOND
REREADING
Questions
Opinions
Analysis

Now read the material one more time slowly and carefully to discover your opinions and analysis of the topic. This critical reading is the highest level of comprehension and should be your goal with each essay that you approach in this book. To achieve this level of understanding, you must actually wrestle with the subject matter—ask questions, make associations of your own, and draw conclusions that capture your personal reactions to the reading material.

This reading requires the most energy on your part because you have to produce the questions and argue with the essay as it moves from point to point. Even though this third reading requires the most effort, it is also the most satisfying because your mind exercises and grapples with ideas on a level that helps you understand both your reading and writing assignments more completely. Ultimately, your ability to reach this level of reading will raise your grades in all subjects.

Once you start reading and understand where you are headed, these "stages" can occur in any order that you perform them. You may look up a word, disagree with an idea in the first paragraph, and go back over a passage for a second reading—all in the first few minutes of reading an essay. Although you may never approach any two reading projects in the same way, the chapters in Part I will help you establish a framework for your personal reading process and guide you toward a comfortable ritual as a reader.

PRACTICE 2 Answer the following questions.

1. When does the reading process start?

   _____

   _____

2. Explain "preparing to read" in your own words.

_____

_____

3. Describe your reading environment.

_____

_____

4. What does "reading" consist of?

_____

_____

5. What does rereading accomplish?

_____

_____

SAMPLE READING ASSIGNMENT

This first assignment is much like the reading tasks you will be asked to do throughout this book. As you learn some new techniques for reading at a higher level, you will follow the work of student Beth Olson so you can see how she approaches and completes the same assignment. If you work alongside her and mirror her actions, you too will understand the essay analytically and be able to apply it to all your work in college. By the end of Chapter 3, you will have a feel for the entire reading process, which is essential to strengthening your identity as a reader.

Reading Assignment

Read the essay in Chapter 3 titled "I Just Wanna Be Average" by Mike Rose, following the guidelines in that chapter. Do the prereading activities and follow the directions for all three readings. Be aware of your level of understanding as you apply a specific reading strategy to the essay. Also, try to ask more complex questions with each reading.

MyWritingLab™ Visit Chapter 2, "The Reading Process," in MyWritingLab, and complete the Post-test to check your understanding of the chapter's objectives.

3

Reading Critically

Reading critically is the heart and soul of successful communication. But unfortunately critical reading is not taught at any level. After elementary school, teachers simply assume that students' reading abilities progress with the complexity of their assignments. But we are learning that this assumption is not true. We live in an age of pictures, Xboxes, cell phones with photo capabilities, and iPods, which has created a culture that does not naturally support reading. Reading requires time and reflection. Only then will the imagination be engaged so that you can read analytically and critically and be productive students and citizens in a very fast-moving world. But because our culture does not promote reading, we need to work actively as individuals to become critical readers. Reading critically will positively affect every aspect of your life in and out of college—especially your writing ability. As you read this chapter, record your responses to the exercises in your journal or on a separate piece of paper so that you can refer to them throughout the course.

PREPARING TO READ

Activities that take place before you actually start reading fall into the general category of prereading, or preparing to read. This is a time when you should get your mind ready to interact with new information so that you can make meaning out of the text. You should also consider using the right side (the imaginative, creative side) of your brain over the left (the more linear, sequential side). The right side of your brain thinks up new ideas and sees relationships among old ideas. More specifically, prereading consists of activities that help you do the following tasks:

- Survey and analyze the title.
- Find out what you can about the author.
- Focus your attention on the subject of the reading selection.

Let's begin by looking at activities many writers use to stimulate their minds as they approach a reading task. We will follow the thoughts and activities of a student named Beth Olson.

Title: "I Just Wanna Be Average"

Beth learned that the title of the essay she is about to read is "I Just Wanna Be Average." From the acknowledgments in the back of the book, she discovers that this selection is from a book called *Lives on the Boundary*. This is a surprising title because most people wouldn't admit their desire to be average even if it were true. They would say they want to be better than average. As Beth thinks about this title, she explores the following questions:

At face value, what does the title mean?

On what assumptions is it based?

Why would someone want to focus on this statement in an essay?

Author: Mike Rose

Beth then finds out the author's name (Mike Rose), but she doesn't know anything about him. So she does a Web search of his name to learn why he would write an essay on this topic. Here is a biography she found:

Mike Rose is on the faculty of the UCLA Graduate School of Education and Information Studies, specializing in language and literacy. He has written a number of books and articles on language and literacy and has received awards from the Spencer Foundation, the McDonnell Foundation, and the National Council of Teachers of English. He is the recipient of a Guggenheim Fellowship and is the author of *Lives on the Boundary: The Struggles and Achievements of America's Underprepared* (1989).

One site Beth consulted was web.mac.com/mikerosebooks/Site/Welcome .html. According to this site and the book's jacket, the author is an immigrant who was singled out in school because he couldn't speak English. His experiences in school, in particular, taught him how to fight stereotyping and prejudice. He survived oppression and many hardships by continuing to push forward and by taking risks when he didn't know what the outcome would be. His story is one of determination and survival through education.

Focusing Your Attention

In this book, a set of questions will help you focus your attention on the material you are about to read. When you read material separate from this book, you should try to generate questions on your own—about the author, about the subject matter, about the title. In this way, you begin all your reading with an inquiring mind, which is a basic necessity for active, rather than passive, reading.

Here are some questions to focus on for the Mike Rose essay. Writing your thoughts about these questions in a journal is the most beneficial approach to this exercise. Beth wrote her personal reactions to these questions before she started reading the essay.

1. What do you think about tracking, or separating students by ability level, in high school? What are the advantages and disadvantages of this system of teaching? How would it affect your learning? Did your high school track its students?

2. In the essay you are about to read, the writer claims that students use sophisticated defense mechanisms to get through high school. Have you ever used any defenses in school? How did these defenses make you act? Did they help or hinder your learning?

READING

As you approach a reading task, you should plan to read it three times if you want to understand it critically. To get to the deeper levels of meaning, you need to work through literal and interpretive comprehension first. These readings take time and reflection.

As you read, be aware that you are creating meaning out of a text that someone else has written. To do this, work in partnership with the author and his or her words to make sense of the material. Usually, this does not happen in one reading. Similarly, when someone reads your writing, he or she must work with your words on the page to figure out what you are saying and what your words imply.

Expanding Your Vocabulary

The first task you should undertake in your reading is to identify the general sense of the selection and look up vocabulary words you don't understand. In this book, difficult vocabulary is identified and defined for you. You should keep this list handy and add other words to it as you read.

If you want to increase your vocabulary and actually use these words in your speaking and writing, you should interact with the text and highlight the words, compose your own lists, and create index cards—that is, complete some activity that will make the words your own. In this text, a specific task is suggested in each vocabulary section so you can try a few different activities and then choose those that work best for you to use in your reading outside this class.

Here is a list of difficult words you need to know for the first reading of "I Just Wanna Be Average." Beth looked at the words she knew and circled those that were new for her. Then she put each word she wanted to add to her vocabulary on an index card, with the definition on the other side. That way, she could quiz herself on her new words as she accumulated cards.

vocational: focused on training for a job (paragraph 1)

Horace's Compromise: a novel by Theodore R. Sizer (paragraph 1)

hypotheses: educated guesses (paragraph 1)

disaffected: rebellious, uncooperative (paragraph 1)

skeletal: very basic (paragraph 1)

scuttling: moving quickly (paragraph 1)

somnambulant: walking while asleep (paragraph 2)

wherewithal: ability (paragraph 2)

prowess: strength (paragraph 3)

clique: exclusive social group (paragraph 3)

testament to: proof of (paragraph 3)

dearth: lack (paragraph 3)

much-touted: repeatedly praised (paragraph 4)

salubrious: socially or morally acceptable (paragraph 4)

equivocal: having two or more meanings (paragraph 4)

Argosy: a science-fiction magazine (paragraph 4)

Field and Stream: a hunting and fishing magazine (paragraph 4)

Daily Worker: a Socialist newspaper (paragraph 4)

The Old Man and the Sea: a novel by Ernest Hemingway (paragraph 4)

rough-hewn: unsophisticated, unpolished (paragraph 4)

apocryphal: a story that is not true but is believed by some people anyway (paragraph 4)

ducktail: a hairstyle in which the sides of the hair are swept back to meet at a point in the back (paragraph 5)

parable of the talents: a story from the New Testament (paragraph 5)

restive: restless, fidgety (paragraph 5)

laryngectomize: surgically remove a person's larynx (paragraph 5)

platitudinous: dull, boring, full of unoriginal thoughts (paragraph 5)

melee: battle (paragraph 5)

dissonant: nonconforming, disagreeing (paragraph 6)

elite: privileged individuals (paragraph 6)

gray matter: brain (paragraph 7)

diffuse: scatter (paragraph 7)

cultivate: encourage (paragraph 7)

malady: illness (paragraph 7)

Using a Reading Strategy

As you begin to read, you will be prompted to use a reading strategy with each reading assignment. Here are the 10 reading strategies we introduce in this book:

Making Personal Associations   We all naturally make personal associations with our reading. However, one person's associations are usually quite different from those of someone else. Recording the associations you make with a reading selection lets you "own" the essay. It allows you to connect the author's ideas to your own experiences. To perform this strategy, make notes in the margin that relate some of your specific memories to the details in this essay. Be prepared to explain the connection between your notes and the facts in the essay.

Thinking Aloud   As we read and interpret an author's words, we absorb them on a literal level, bring in any implications the author suggests, think about how the ideas relate to one another, and keep the process going until the entire essay makes sense. These focused thoughts are what help us process the author's writing. On another level, however, we may stray from the essay in a wide variety of ways—thinking about chores we need to do, calls we forgot to return, and plans we are looking forward to on the weekend. These random ideas are only loosely related to the reading. As you might suspect, focused reading is more productive than random reading, but you can teach yourself to apply your stray ideas to a better understanding of the material. To do this strategy, stop and "think aloud" about what is on your mind as you read. Point out confusing passages, connections you make, specific questions you have, related information you know, and personal experiences you associate with the text. In this manner, you can "hear" what your mind does (in both focused and random ways) as you read.

Chunking   Reading essays critically means looking closely at the selection to discover what its purpose is and how it is structured. To understand how an essay works, circle the main idea or thesis. Then draw horizontal lines throughout the essay to separate the various topics that support the thesis. These lines may or may not coincide with paragraph breaks. Finally, in the margins, label the topics of each "chunk." Be prepared to explain the divisions you made.

Graphing the Ideas   To understand their reading material and how it works, students often find that making drawings of its ideas and details is much more effective than outlining. Graphic organizers, or concept maps, let you literally "draw" the relationship of ideas to one another. Figuring out what framework to use for this exercise is part of the process. You can make up a drawing of your own or do a Web search for "graphic organizers" to see some different options. For an essay, show the relationship of the ideas to one another in a graphic form that makes sense to you. Be prepared to explain your drawing.

Peer Teaching   Teaching something to your peers is an excellent way to test your understanding. To practice this technique, the class must first divide an essay into parts. The class members should then get into groups (one for each part of the essay) and choose one of the essay's sections. After identifying the main ideas, the details, and their relationship to one another, each group should teach its section to the rest of the class.

Summarizing   As you read more difficult essays, the ability to summarize is essential. A summary features the main ideas of a selection in a coherent paragraph. First, identify the main ideas in your reading; then fold them into a paragraph with logical transitions so your sentences flow from one to another. After you write your summary, draft three questions for discussion.

Reacting Critically   Forming your own opinions and coming up with new ideas in response to your reading are very important parts of the reading process, but you need to learn how to produce these reactions. As you read an essay, record your notes on a separate piece of paper. First, draw a vertical line down the center of your paper. Then, as you read, write the author's main ideas on the left side of the page and your reactions to those ideas on the right. Be prepared to explain the connection between your notes and the material in the essay.

Making Connections   Separating related ideas is an important part of understanding an essay. After a first reading, divide a sheet of paper into two parts with a vertical line. Then, as you read the essay for a second time, record one set of ideas in the left column and related ideas from the essay on the right. Draw lines from one detail to another (if applicable). Be prepared to explain the connection between your lists and the details in the essay.

Recognizing Facts and Opinions   Reading an argument critically calls for very high-level skills. You need to understand your reading on a literal level, know the difference between opinions and facts, and come up with your own thoughts on the topic by challenging the author's ideas. To do this, highlight facts in one color and the author's opinions in another color. This activity works very well with the next strategy.

Reading with the Author/Against the Author

This approach is a very advanced form of reading. It asks you to consciously figure out which ideas you agree with and which you disagree with. By doing this, you will force yourself to form your own opinions. From the previous highlighting exercise, put an X by any facts or opinions you do not agree with or want to question in some way. Then, record your own thoughts and opinions on a separate sheet of paper. Be prepared to explain any marks you made on the essay.

Beth's Reading   Beth read the following essay by Mike Rose. It stimulated her thoughts about learning in general because she believes the most important part of learning is taking risks. She jotted several personal annotations to herself in the margins as she read.

Yes I agree

Students will float to the mark you set. I and the others in the vocational classes were bobbing in pretty shallow water. Vocational education was aimed at increasing the economic opportunities of students who do not do well in our schools. Some serious programs succeed in doing that, and through exceptional teachers—like Mr. Gross in *Horace's Compromise*—students learn to develop hypotheses and troubleshoot, reason through a problem, and communicate effectively—the true job skills. The vocational track, however, is most often a place for those who are just not making it, a dumping ground for the disaffected. There were a few teachers who worked hard at education; young Brother Slattery, for example, combined a stern voice with weekly quizzes to try to pass along to us a skeletal outline of world

But how does Gross do this?

3 important skills

1

I know

history. But mostly the teachers had no idea of how to engage the imaginations of us kids who were scuttling along at the bottom of the pond.

And the teachers would have needed some inventiveness, for none of us was groomed for the classroom. It wasn't just that I didn't know things—didn't know how to simplify algebraic fractions, couldn't identify different kinds of clauses, bungled Spanish translations—but that I had developed various faulty and inadequate ways of doing algebra and making sense of Spanish. Worse yet, the years of <u>defensive</u> tuning out in elementary school had given me a way to escape quickly while seeming at least half alert. During my time in Voc. Ed., I developed further into a mediocre student and a (somnambulant) problem solver, and that affected the subjects I did have the wherewithal to handle: I detested Shakespeare; I got bored with history. My attention flitted here and there. I fooled around in class and read my books indifferently—the intellectual equivalent of playing with your food. I did what I had to do to get by, and I did it with half a mind.

2

Why defensive?

But I did learn things about people and eventually came into my own socially. I liked the guys in Voc. Ed. Growing up where I did, I understood and admired physical (prowess,) and there was an abundance of muscle here. There was <u>Dave Snyder, a sprinter and halfback of true quality</u>. Dave's ability and his quick wit gave him a natural appeal, and he was welcome in any clique, though he always kept a little independent. He enjoyed acting the fool and could care less about studies, but he possessed a certain maturity and never caused the faculty much trouble. It was a (testament to) his independence that he included me among his friends— I eventually went out for track, but I was no jock. Owing to the Latin alphabet and a (dearth) of *R*'s and *S*'s, Snyder sat behind Rose, and we started exchanging one-liners and became friends.

Max is like this

3

How did learning about people help Rose?

There was <u>Ted Richard, a much-touted Little League pitcher</u>. He was chunky and had a baby face and came to Our Lady of Mercy as a seasoned street fighter. Ted was quick to laugh, and he had a loud, jolly laugh, but when he got angry he'd smile a little smile, the kind that simply raises the corner of the mouth a quarter of an inch. For those who knew, it was an eerie signal. Those who didn't found themselves in big trouble, for Ted was very quick. He loved to carry on what we would come to call philosophical discussions: What is courage? Does God exist? He also loved words, enjoyed picking up big ones

4

like Sam in Intro to Psych

like (salubrious) and (equivocal) and using them in our conversations—laughing at himself as the word hit a chuckhole rolling off his tongue. Ted didn't do all that well in school—baseball and parties and testing the courage he'd speculated about took up his time. His textbooks were (Argosy) and *Field and Stream*, whatever newspapers he'd find on the bus stop—from the *Daily Worker* to pornography—conversations with uncles or hobos or businessmen he'd meet in a coffee shop, *The Old Man and the Sea*. With hindsight, I can see that Ted was developing into one of those rough-hewn intellectuals whose sources are a mix of the learned and the (apocryphal,) whose discussions are both assured and sad.

like
Sasha in
Orientation

And then there was <u>Ken Harvey</u>. Ken was <u>good-looking in a puffy way and had a full and oily ducktail and was a car enthusiast</u>.... One day in religion class, he said the sentence that turned out to be one of the most memorable of the hundreds of thousands I heard in those Voc. Ed. years. We were talking about the (parable of the talents,) about achievement, working hard, doing the best you can do, blah-blah-blah, when the teacher called on the restive Ken Harvey for an opinion. Ken thought about it, but just for a second, and said (with studied, minimal affect), "<u>I just wanna be average.</u>" That woke me up. Average?! Who wants to be average? Then the athletes chimed in with the clichés that make you want to (laryngectomize) them, and the exchange became a (platitudinous) (melee). At the time, I thought Ken's assertion was stupid, and I wrote him off. But his sentence has stayed with me all these years, and I think I am finally coming to understand it.

5

What a great line, but why not "special"?

English
1A!!

so true

How?

Ken Harvey was gasping for air. School can be a tremendously disorienting place. No matter how bad the school, you're going to encounter notions that don't fit with the assumptions and beliefs that you grew up with—maybe you'll hear these dissonant notions from teachers, maybe from the other students, and maybe you'll read them. You'll also be thrown in with all kinds of kids from all kinds of backgrounds, and that can be unsettling—this is especially true in places of rich ethnic and linguistic mix, like the L.A. basin. You'll see a handful of students far excel you in courses that sound exotic and that are only in the curriculum of the elite: French, physics, trigonometry. And all this is happening <u>while you're trying to shape an identity, your body is changing, and your emotions are running wild</u>. If you're a working-class kid in the vocational track, the options you'll have to deal with this will be constrained in certain ways: You're defined by your school as "slow"; you're

6

I hate this feeling

placed in a curriculum that isn't designed to liberate you but to occupy you or, if you're lucky, train you, though the training is for work the society does not esteem; other students are picking up the cues from your school and your curriculum and interacting with you in particular ways. If you're a kid like Ted Richard, you turn your back on all this and let your mind roam where it may. But youngsters like Ted are rare. What Ken and so many others do is protect themselves from such suffocating mad-

putting down what you don't know or under-stand = a defense

ness by taking on with a vengeance the identity implied in the vocational track. Reject the confusion and frustration by openly defining yourself as the Common Joe. Champion the average. Rely on your own good sense. **** this bullshit. Bullshit, of course, is everything you—and the others—fear is beyond you: books, essays, tests, academic scrambling, complexity, scientific reasoning, philosophical inquiry.

The <u>tragedy</u> is that you have to twist the knife in your own gray matter to make this defense work. You'll have to shut down, have to reject intellectual stimuli or (diffuse) them with sarcasm, have to cultivate stupidity, have to convert boredom from a (malady) into a way of confronting the world. Keep your vocabulary simple, act stoned when you're not or act more

Defense = Magic?

stoned than you are, flaunt ignorance, materialize your dreams. It is a powerful and effective defense—it neutralizes the insult and the frustration of being a vocational kid and, when per-

What price?

fected, it drives teachers up the wall, a delightful secondary effect. But like all strong magic, it exacts a price.

7

Why a tragedy?

Learning goes on hold so this "role" can succeed

Your Reading Read Mike Rose's essay, and add your own notes to Beth's comments in the margins.

Discovering Purpose and Audience

Finally, at this stage of the reading process, you should determine the writer's purpose and audience. In Beth's case, she learns from the book jacket that Rose set out to write his autobiography, which ended up focusing on his educational experiences. Teachers had a great effect on Rose and his progress as a child trying to survive in American society. His initial audience was probably educators, but now he has a much broader appeal.

FIRST REREADING

Your first rereading must now focus on raising your level of thinking so that you have a deeper understanding of the essay you just finished. Looking again at the essay with an inquiring mind is the heart of this stage.

This book provides questions on progressively more difficult levels to help you accomplish this goal. But without these questions, you need to ask your own questions as you read. Focusing on questions that wonder "why" or "how" something happened will move you to these higher levels. You also want to focus on assumptions that the writer bases his or her points on and the relationship between the ideas in an essay. These might be either stated or unstated. As you become a more proficient reader, you will be able to see both with ease.

Beth's First Rereading   As Beth read Rose's essay a second time, she saw several relationships she had not previously noticed. She noted these relationships on the essay and then answered the following questions provided in the text. Her answers appear after each question.

Thinking Critically About Content

1. What was vocational education aimed at in Rose's school? Who is this track for?

   Vocational training was aimed at students who were deemed "slow." They were

   "placed in a curriculum that isn't designed to liberate you but occupy you or, if

   you're lucky, train you" (para. 6).

2. What examples from this essay illustrate most clearly what Rose's academic life involved?

   The examples in paragraph 2 illustrate most clearly Rose's academic life. They

   point out his troubles with academics and his desire to retreat somewhat from

   the academic world.

3. Rose says the Voc. Ed. students "were bobbing in pretty shallow water" and then refers to them "scuttling along at the bottom of the pond" (paragraph 1). In these examples, he is comparing people trying to swim and stay above water to students on a vocational track in high school. This comparison is called a *metaphor*. Find another comparison like this in paragraph 7.

   Here are two examples: "The tragedy is that you have to twist the knife in

   your own gray matter to make this defense work" and "But like all strong

   magic, it exacts a price."

Thinking Critically About Purpose and Audience

4. What do you think Rose's purpose is in this essay? Explain your answer.

   Rose's purpose is to inform readers that teachers who expect mediocre work

   from students will receive just that. He wants teachers to set the mark higher

   so that students will reach it.

5. What audience do you think would most understand and appreciate this essay?

   Anyone can appreciate this essay, but students who were perceived to be

   performing at low levels will understand it best.

6. What do you think Ken Harvey meant when he said, "I just wanna be average" (paragraph 5)?

   Harvey probably wanted to go unnoticed. He didn't want to stand out, but at

   the same time, he didn't want to fail. He was content to live his life somewhere

   in the middle.

Thinking Critically About Essays

7. Does Rose give you enough examples to understand his learning environment in high school? Explain your answer.

   His examples do paint a picture about his learning environment because they

   show readers how teachers expected mediocrity from students who were more

   than willing to provide it.

8. Is this essay unified? Does each of the author's topic sentences support the essay's thesis statement? Explain your answer.

   The topic sentences do support Rose's thesis statement, and the essay is uni-

   fied. All the paragraphs focus on proving that if teachers don't expect much

   from their students, they won't get much.

9. What is Rose's thesis in this essay? Where is it located?

   Rose's thesis is the first sentence in the essay: "Students will float to the mark

   you set."

10. Explain your opinion about tracking students. Is tracking a good idea? Does it help some students? Does it hurt anyone? Can you think of any alternatives to tracking? Respond to these questions in detail.

> *I think tracking makes students feel bad. If they're in a low class, they know teachers don't expect much from them. If they're not as strong as Mike Rose, they could be affected by this label beyond school.*

Your First Rereading   Read "I Just Wanna Be Average" a second time, and take more notes about assumptions and relationships among ideas in the margins as you read. Then, in your journal, generate five "why" or "how" questions about ideas in this essay. Then, exchange questions with a class-mate, and answer each other's questions in your journal.

SECOND REREADING

This final reading is the real test of your understanding. It has the potential to raise your grades in all subjects if you complete it for each of your reading assignments. It involves understanding the author's ideas as you form your own opinions and analyze your thoughts.

To accomplish this reading, you should ask more questions that go beyond the words on the page and then answer them in writing. You should also bring your own opinions to the surface. Write them down as they occur to you. Finally, analyze your thoughts so that you end with some form of self-evaluation.

Beth's Second Rereading   Beth took the following notes in her journal as she read Rose's essay for the third time. She asked herself some questions, answered those questions as best she could, recorded her opinions as they occurred to her, and analyzed her thoughts along the way. She covers all of these thought processes in the following journal entry:

Opening yourself up to learning is tough. If you try and don't get it, you feel stupid. I guess that's the advantage of putting up defenses when confronted with something to learn. With a defense, you don't look stupid—you just look cool because you are refusing to try.

I know that feeling. I've dug my heels in before when I thought I wouldn't understand something. And it saved me from embar-rassment, but I'm not sure I came out ahead. My feelings were intact/unruffled, but I realized that with that behavior I would be stuck in the mud forever. The only way to get ahead is to move forward (even a little bit), and the only way to move is to learn, and the only way to learn is to take some risks—risk embarrassment, risk feeling stupid, risk your fragile ego. But defenses are circular. Here's how they work—you get nervous or uncomfortable, you put up a defense of some sort, you save face, and you start all over again. You never learn anything that would help you get out of your rut. You only learn how to save your emotions. That's a form of survival. But I want more.

Your Second Rereading   Take notes in your journal as you read Rose's essay for the third time. Ask yourself more "how" and "why" questions, answer those questions, record your opinions, and analyze your thoughts as they occur.

MyWritingLab™   Visit Chapter 3, "Reading Critically," in MyWritingLab, and complete the Post-test to check your understanding of the chapter's objectives.

4

The Writing Process

The writing process consists of identifiable "stages" that overlap in a number of unique ways. No two people write in the same way, so it is important for you to figure out exactly how your writing process works. In other words, you need to know how to arrange these stages to produce the best writing you are capable of. Knowing each of the stages individually will help you organize them in a way that best suits your lifestyle. This chapter will introduce you to the entire process in the hope that you will tailor it along the way to meet your individual needs.

VISUALIZING THE WRITING PROCESS

Even though we talk about the stages of writing, it is actually a cyclical process, which means that at any point you may loop in and out of other stages. As you work with the writing process in this textbook, the following graphic might help you understand how various stages of the process can overlap. The rest of this chapter will explain each of these elements in detail.

The Cycle of Writing

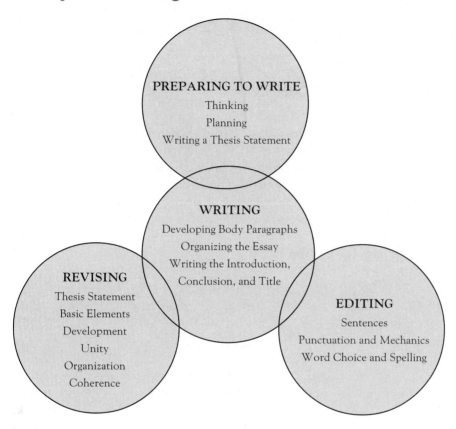

PREPARING TO WRITE
Thinking
Planning
Writing a Thesis Statement

WRITING
Developing Body Paragraphs
Organizing the Essay
Writing the Introduction,
Conclusion, and Title

REVISING
Thesis Statement
Basic Elements
Development
Unity
Organization
Coherence

EDITING
Sentences
Punctuation and Mechanics
Word Choice and Spelling

PRACTICE 1 Answer the following questions.

1. List the three elements of prewriting.

_____

_____

2. List the three elements of writing.

_____

_____

3. List the six elements of revising.

_____

_____

4. List the three elements of editing.

_____

_____

THE WRITING PROCESS

The writing process begins the minute you receive a writing assignment. It involves all the activities you do, from choosing a topic to turning in a final draft, including computer searches, text messages, discussions with classmates, and late-night trips to Starbucks. All aspects of your individual ritual constitute your writing process and must work together throughout your college career to produce a piece of writing by the assigned deadline. The main parts of the process are explained in this section.

Preparing to Write

PREPARING TO WRITE
Thinking
Planning
Writing a Thesis Statement

Preparing to write, or prewriting, refers to activities that help you explore a general subject, generate ideas about it, select a specific topic, establish a purpose, learn as much as possible about your readers, and draft a thesis statement. Chapter 5 will teach you different strategies for accomplishing these goals before you actually begin to write a draft of your essay. Your mission at this stage is to stimulate your thinking before and during the act of writing.

Whenever you generate new material throughout the writing process, you are prewriting. The most common prewriting activities are freewriting, brainstorming, clustering, questioning, and discussing. All of these activities will be demonstrated in Chapter 5 as Beth Olson approaches a writing assignment. The more ideas you generate now and throughout the entire writing process, the more you have to work with as you draft your essay.

Writing

> **WRITING**
> Developing Body Paragraphs
> Organizing the Essay
> Writing the Introduction,
> Conclusion, and Title

As you begin to give your ideas shape, your thesis statement will help you focus your writing. This statement, or controlling idea, should include your purpose for writing or an overview of what you want to accomplish in the essay. Stating your "mission" in this way will help you make important decisions as you begin to actually put your thoughts into essay form. Developing and organizing your ideas will come after you get your thoughts on paper.

You can start writing after you have some ideas to work with. Writing includes developing some of your ideas further, organizing your thoughts with your purpose in mind, and writing a first draft, which we explain in detail in Chapter 6. To begin writing, go back to your notes, journal entries, and other prewriting activities; then mold these ideas into a logical, coherent essay. As you write, concentrate on what you are saying and how your ideas fit together.

Only after you actually generate a draft do you know what you are going to say in an essay. So you might find it easier to add your introduction, conclusion, and title after you compose the body of your essay. Don't let grammar and spelling distract you from your task at this point; just get your ideas out of your head in some logical order. You can correct your grammar and mechanical errors later.

Revising

> **REVISING**
> Thesis Statement
> Basic Elements
> Development
> Unity
> Organization
> Coherence

Most people do not want to take the time to revise their writing. But revising always pays off because it will make your writing stronger. Revising involves rethinking your content and organization so that your words say exactly what you mean. (Editing, the last step, focuses on your grammar, punctuation, mechanics, and spelling.) Your main goal in revising is to make sure that the purpose of your essay is clear to your audience and that your main ideas are supported with adequate details and examples. In addition, you should check that your paper is organized logically and moves smoothly from one idea to the next.

The items listed in the figure above appear on the revising checklist throughout this text. We explain each of these elements in Chapter 7 so you can use them effectively in the revisions of your own essays. If you go through this list each time you rewrite your essays, you will be creating a better draft with each change you make.

Editing

EDITING

Sentences
Punctuation and Mechanics
Word Choice and Spelling

Editing is the final stage of the writing process. After you revise your content, read your writing slowly and carefully to find errors in grammar, punctuation, mechanics, and spelling. Such errors can distract your reader from the message you are trying to convey or can even cause communication to break down. Editing gives you the chance to clean up your draft so that your writing is clear, precise, and effective.

In this text, we have grouped grammar and usage errors into three categories: (1) sentence errors, which include fragments and run-together sentences that need to be corrected for clear communication; (2) punctuation and mechanics, which cover end punctuation (periods, question marks, and exclamation points), internal punctuation (commas, semicolons, colons, apostrophes, quotation marks), capitalization, abbreviations, and numbers; and (3) word choice and spelling, which focus on whether or not you have chosen the right word for what you mean and whether that word is spelled correctly. Checking all these features of your writing will give you the best chance possible to produce an effective essay. We explain these items in detail in Chapter 7.

Once you start writing, these "stages" do not necessarily occur in any specific order. You may change a word (revise) in the very first sentence you write, then think of another detail you want to add to your opening sentence (prewrite), and next cross out and rewrite a misspelled word (edit)—all in the first two minutes of writing. Although you may never approach any two writing projects in the same way, the chapters in Part I will help you establish a framework for your personal writing process and feel comfortable as a writer working within that framework.

PRACTICE 2 Answer the following questions.

1. When does the writing process start?

   _____

   _____

   _____

2. Explain "prewriting" in your own words.

   _____

   _____

   _____

3. Describe your writing environment.

   _____

   _____

   _____

4. What does "writing" consist of?

   _____

   _____

   _____

5. What is the difference between "revising" and "editing"?

   _____

   _____

   _____

WRITING ON A COMPUTER

Most people—in school and at work—compose directly on a computer. This strategy saves them time and energy and helps them meet deadlines. First of all, composing directly on a computer lets you change words and sentences as you develop your essay. It also saves you time because you don't have to write out a draft by hand and then type it later. When you complete a first draft on a computer, you can move your ideas around without having to rewrite your whole paper. Finally, you can correct your grammar and spelling errors right on the final draft.

To compose on your computer, follow some simple rules so you don't lose your work or make word processing more complex than it is. Here are five essential guidelines for writing on a computer:

1. Give your document a name before you start writing.

2. Save your work often (or set the computer to save at short intervals). This will help you avoid losing your writing in a power failure or other accident.

3. Save your work in two different places—for example, your desktop and a travel drive. Then if one becomes damaged, you always have the other.

4. Name and number each draft so you can go back to earlier drafts if you want. For example, you might name and number an assignment this way: Description Essay D1, Description Essay D2, and so forth (D = draft).

5. Print out your work frequently so you can refer to printed copies as well as electronic copies.

PRACTICE 3 Answer the following questions.

1. What are the advantages of writing directly on a computer?

    _____

    _____

    _____

    _____

    _____

2. What five guidelines should you remember if you write on a computer?

    _____

    _____

    _____

    _____

    _____

MyWritingLab | ## Understanding the Writing Process

Test your own knowledge of the writing process! Go to **MyWritingLab.com,** and choose **The Writing Process** in **The Craft of Writing** module. For this topic, read the **Overview,** watch the two **Animation** videos, and complete the **Recall, Apply,** and **Write** activities. Then check your understanding by taking the **Post-test.**

SAMPLE WRITING ASSIGNMENT

This first writing assignment, or "prompt," is much like the writing tasks you will be asked to do throughout this book. You'll be working on this assignment over the next three chapters as you apply what you are learning about the writing process to this task. At the same time, we will follow the work of student Beth Olson so you can see how she approaches and completes the same assignment. By the end of Chapter 7, you will have a feel for the entire writing process, which is essential to strengthening your writing and your identity as a writer.

Writing Prompt

We all learn about life in a variety of ways. These lessons help us become who we are. What have you learned over the years? How did you learn these lessons? What experiences have made you the person you are today? Based on a combination of your observations, your reading, and your personal experiences, write an essay explaining how you learn best.

MyWritingLab
Complete this Writing Prompt assignment in MyWritingLab.

MyWritingLab™ | Visit Chapter 4, "The Writing Process," in MyWritingLab, and complete the Post-test to check your understanding of the chapter's objectives.

5

Preparing to Write

Activities that take place before you actually start writing your paper fall into the general category of prewriting, or preparing to write. This is when you should be generating as many thoughts related to a topic as you can, using the right side of your brain, which is the part of your mind that thinks up new ideas and sees relationships among old ideas. More specifically, prewriting consists of activities that help you do the following tasks:

- Explore a subject
- Generate ideas about a subject
- Settle on a specific topic
- Establish a purpose
- Analyze your audience

Let's begin by looking at activities many writers use to stimulate their minds as they approach a writing task. You will get a chance to try each one. Record your responses to the following exercises in your journal or on a separate piece of paper so you can refer to them throughout the course.

Student Comment:
"My past teachers always had me use outlining as a prewriting strategy. In the video, I learned about all the other ways to prewrite. I tried each one and learned my favorite is clustering."

MyWritingLab | **Understanding Prewriting**

Before you move on, let's make sure you understand the most important elements of prewriting. First, go to **MyWritingLab.com,** and choose **Prewriting** in **The Craft of Writing** module. Next, read the **Overview,** watch the six **Animation** videos, and complete the **Recall, Apply,** and **Write** activities. Once you complete these activities, check your understanding of this material by taking the **Post-test.**

THINKING

Thinking is always the best way to start any writing project. Thinking means exploring your topic and letting your mind run freely over the ideas you generate. We'll demonstrate five activities students often use to stimulate their thoughts: freewriting, brainstorming, clustering, questioning, and discussing. You will see how Beth Olson uses each strategy before you try it yourself.

Freewriting

The strategy of freewriting involves writing about anything that comes to mind. Writing nonstop for five to ten minutes will naturally lead you to other ideas. Do not worry about grammar, punctuation, mechanics, or spelling. If you get stuck, repeat an idea or start rhyming words. Just keep writing.

Beth's Freewriting Beth had trouble freewriting, but she got going and then repeated some words to keep herself writing.

> My English teacher wants us to freewrite about whatever comes to our minds, but I can't think of anything to say. It's hard for me to just start writing. I still can't think of anything to say. And it's hard for me to just write. I don't even know what to write about. Everyone in here is writing furiously in their notebooks; I wonder what they're writing about. How many are writing about their girlfriends? their families? their dreams? I wonder what their dreams are. No one could ever guess that one of my dreams is to someday be my own boss in a company that will make enough money for my family to live comfortably. I suppose that's everyone's dream, really, but I don't think many people would think I had enough guts to go out on my own. But I will someday, and it's going to be a great life.

Focused freewriting follows the same procedure as freewriting, but it focuses on a specific topic—either one your instructor provides or one you choose. Just write without restrictions about a designated topic so you find words for your thoughts and impressions.

Beth's Focused Freewriting Beth produced the following focused freewriting in her journal. She is trying to get ready to write her essay about learning.

> People can learn about life from just about everything they do. It seems that every action can result in some sort of lesson. It's like all those fairy tales that have morals at the end of the story. If we keep our eyes open, everything we do can have a moral at the end. We can learn about how to study when we join a study group. We can decide how to treat our boyfriends or girlfriends when we watch our friends. And we

can even learn from what's on the tube. I also like asking questions and talking to people about problems I'm having. I often get answers that way. Everywhere we look there's something to learn.

Your Freewriting   To prepare for the essay you are going to compose, do a focused freewriting in your journal about the ways you learn.

Brainstorming

Like freewriting, brainstorming is based on free association. When you are brainstorming, you let one thought naturally lead to another, generally in the form of a list. You can brainstorm by yourself, with a friend, or with a group. Regardless of the method, list whatever comes to mind on a topic— ideas, thoughts, examples, facts, anything. As with freewriting, don't worry about grammar, punctuation, mechanics, or spelling.

Beth's Brainstorming   Here is Beth's brainstorming on learning about life:

- everyone learns about life through everyday lessons
- from my parents
- from my brothers and sisters
- from friends
- by watching our friends make mistakes
- by listening to others
- by listening to the radio
- by making my own mistakes
- by asking questions
- by listening to music
- by taking risks
- by succeeding and failing
- by reading books or newspapers
- by studying or going to school
- by observing

Your Brainstorming   Brainstorm in your journal about how you think you learn.

Clustering

Clustering, like brainstorming and freewriting, is also based on free association, but this strategy shows how your thoughts are related to one another. To cluster, take a sheet of blank paper, write a key word or phrase in the center of the page, and draw a circle around it. Next, write down and circle any related ideas that come to your mind. As you add ideas, draw lines to connect them to the thoughts they came from. After two or three minutes, you'll have a map of your ideas that can guide you toward a good essay.

Beth's Cluster   Here is Beth's cluster on learning about life:

Your Cluster   Write "Learning About Life" in the middle of a piece of paper, circle it, and create a cluster of your own associations with this concept.

Questioning

Journalists use questions known as the "five *W*s and one *H*"—*Who? What? When? Where? Why?* and *How?*—to ensure they have covered all the important information in a news story. Other writers use these questions to generate ideas on a writing topic. Ask yourself each question as it relates to a particular topic. Then answer the questions one by one.

Beth's Questions   Here is how Beth used questioning to generate ideas on her topic, learning about life:

Who?	everyone I know learns about life
What?	learning about life
When?	all day, every day
Where?	depends on what's being learned
Why?	to better themselves in life, for fun, for a variety of reasons
How?	by paying attention and taking action I guess we can even learn without realizing it.

Your Questions   In your journal, answer these six questions about learning in preparation for your essay: Who? What? When? Where? Why? How?

Discussing

Discussing involves talking about your ideas with friends, relatives, classmates, tutors, or anyone who will listen. Often someone else will have a completely new perspective on your topic that will help you come up with even more ideas. Be sure to take notes on these conversations so you don't lose the ideas.

Beth's Discussion   Here are Beth's notes from a conversation she had with her running partner concerning how people learn about life.

When I spoke with my friend Alison, I realized that we all learn about life in just about everything we do. I guess it really depends on how much we want to pay attention. Alison talked about the risks I took when I decided to leave my hometown and study nursing at my current college. She also reminded me how much I learned from my cousin when she was involved in gangs. And we even reminisced about some of the bad choices I made and what they taught me. We talked about all the ways we learn in life and realized that we learn by watching what other people do, by taking risks, and by actually making mistakes. We figured these were the best ways to learn about life—for us.

Your Discussion Discuss learning about life with someone, and record notes from your conversation in your journal.

PRACTICE 1 Now that you have been introduced to several prewriting strategies, which is your favorite? Why do you like it best?

PRACTICE 2 Using two prewriting strategies on one assignment is often a good idea. What is your second favorite prewriting strategy? Why do you like this strategy?

PLANNING

In this course, you'll be writing essays. Although they may differ a great deal in design, organization, and content, essays share certain identifying features that distinguish them from other types of writing. An essay usually has a title that names its broad subject. Many longer, more complex essays also have subtitles. When writers move from one topic to another, they indicate this shift by indenting a new paragraph. Most essays include a thesis either stated or implied in the introduction, several body paragraphs explaining or supporting the thesis, and a conclusion.

Essays are nonfiction, as opposed to short stories, poetry, or drama; that is, they deal with real-life subjects rather than made-up ones. Most essays concentrate on a specific subject and focus on a single purpose. For an essay to be successful, most writers choose methods of development that both suit their purpose and appeal to the audience they hope to inform or persuade. A successful essay gets the reaction from the readers that its author hopes for—whether this response is to appreciate a special scene, identify with someone's grief, or leap into action.

If you haven't already discovered it, you will learn in this book that writing an essay takes planning. If you make some decisions about your topic, audience, and purpose before you actually write, the job of writing will be much smoother and less stressful.

- **What is your subject (person, event, object, idea, etc.)?** An essay focuses on a single subject, along with related thoughts and details. In approaching an essay assignment, then, deciding what you are going to write about is very important. Sometimes your topic is provided, as when your sociology instructor assigns a paper on abused children. But other times, you choose your own subject. In such cases, selecting a subject that interests you is best. You will have more to say, and you will enjoy writing much more if you know something about your topic.

- **What is your purpose?** Your purpose is your reason for writing an essay. Your purpose could be to explore your feelings on a topic (*personal writing*), to tell a friend about something funny that happened to you (*entertain*), to explain something or share information (*inform*), or to convince others of your position on a controversial issue (*persuade*). Whatever your purpose, deciding on it in advance makes writing the rest of your essay easier.

- **Who is your audience?** Your audience consists of the people for whom your message is intended. The more you know about your audience, the more likely you are to accomplish your purpose. The audience for your writing in college is usually your instructor, who represents a "general audience"—people with an average amount of knowledge on most subjects. Unless you are given other directions, a general audience is a good group to aim for in all your writing.

PRACTICE 3 Identify the subject, purpose, and audience of each of the following paragraphs.

1. Schools have been dealing with the issue of bilingual education for many years. The debate centers on whether or not students should be allowed to study in their native language in order to learn English. Many people believe students should learn in English, even if they don't know the language. Other people believe this method of instruction will prevent students from learning and are fairly sure bilingual education programs will not succeed. Obviously, a compromise must be reached in order to help the students.

   Subject: _____

   Purpose: _____

   Audience: _____

2. The world of computers has reached a point when people can conduct all of their business transactions from the comfort of their homes. Online companies have made it possible for people to shop and do all of their business online. While most people using these services enjoy the convenience of having a business meeting in their bathrobes, the idea of never needing to leave the house worries other computer users: If everything

is done from home and people stop interacting with each other face to face, human interaction could eventually be lost.

Subject: _____

Purpose: _____

Audience: _____

3. Playing sports came naturally to me and taught me a valuable lesson. I began playing soccer and T-ball when I was five years old and continued playing different types of sports through high school. Sometimes I would get tired of constantly having to be at practices for one sport or another. Having a social life became very difficult because I was always busy with sports or trying to stay caught up in my classes. However, through the years of playing sports, I realized I had learned something that none of the teachers in my classes could ever teach me. I had learned how to deal with people. Competing against people taught me how to play with a team and how to keep calm when something wasn't going my way.

Subject: _____

Purpose: _____

Audience: _____

4. Reading a good book can be a fine substitute for a vacation. Every once in a while, people feel like getting away from their normal routine and taking a trip. Unfortunately, dropping everything and leaving town is not always possible. In this case, reading a book about somewhere far away can make people feel as if they have actually left their normal surroundings. People can become so involved in a book that they are completely oblivious to the world around them. Sometimes reading a book is just what people need to get away.

Subject: _____

Purpose: _____

Audience: _____

5. Last summer, my family and I went on a two-day rafting trip. The morning our trip began, we loaded all the camping equipment and food into the gear trailer and were on our way. The first day, the rapids were Class 2 and 3, which meant they were moderate rapids and perfect for beginners. Everyone had fun playing in the rapids, swimming, and jumping off the rocks on the side of the river. That night in camp, the entire group was tired

from such a full day on the river, so everyone went to bed early. On the second day, the rapids were Class 4 because they had large holes and waves and were considered intermediate. I have to admit that the second day was more exciting than the first day. At the end of the trip, everyone was ready to get a good night's sleep but eager to come back and do it all again.

Subject: _____

Purpose: _____

Audience: _____

Beth's Plans   Beth made the following decisions before beginning to write on learning about life:

Subject: Learning about life

Purpose: Informative—to talk about different ways of learning

Audience: General—anyone from the general population

Your Plans   Identify the subject, purpose, and audience of the essay you will write on learning about life.

Subject: _____

Purpose: _____

Audience: _____

WRITING A THESIS STATEMENT

By now, you have a subject (learning about life), and you have used several prewriting techniques with this subject, which means you have generated a number of thoughts you can use in your essay. You have also decided on a purpose and an audience. Next, you will learn how to write a thesis statement, which you will develop into an essay in the next two chapters. Again, you will be writing alongside Beth Olson as she works through her writing process.

To compose a good essay, you need to narrow a broad subject to an idea you can discuss in a limited number of pages. Your thesis statement limits your subject and is the controlling idea of an essay. It is the main point that all other sentences relate to. Like a high-powered telescope, your thesis statement zooms in on the specific topic you will discuss in the body of your essay. The decisions you made earlier in this chapter about subject, purpose, and audience will lead you to your thesis.

A thesis statement usually appears in the first paragraph of an essay and works best as the last sentence of this paragraph. Ending the introductory paragraph with the thesis lets the writer use the beginning of the paragraph to capture the reader's interest or provide background information.

A thesis has two parts: a topic and your opinion on that topic.

Subject	Limited Subject	+	Opinion	=	Thesis Statement
Sports	Playing a team sport		has lots of benefits		Playing a team sport teaches a person self-discipline, cooperation, and leadership.
Anger	Road rage		is very dangerous		Road rage is dangerous because it puts the driver, the victim, and the surrounding cars at risk.
Writing	College writing		is similar to writing in the business world		College writing is similar to writing in the business world in three important ways: Both types of writing must be logical, well developed, and clear.

MyWritingLab | **Understanding Thesis Statements**

To make sure you understand thesis statements, go to **MyWritingLab.com,** and choose **Thesis Statement** in the **Essay Development** module. From there, read the **Overview,** watch the three **Animation** videos, and complete the **Recall, Apply,** and **Write** activities. Finally, check your understanding of this topic by taking the **Post-test.**

Student Comment:
"The most helpful MyWriting-Lab topic for me was **Thesis Statement,** because it made me think about how my thesis must connect to the ideas in my essays."

PRACTICE 4 Fill in the blanks in this exercise.

1. A thesis statement is _____

    _____

    _____

2. A thesis statement has two parts: _____

    _____

    _____

3. Where should you put your thesis?_____

    _____

    _____

PRACTICE 5 Limit the following subjects that aren't narrow enough. Then add an opinion to all subjects, and make them into thesis statements.

Subject	Limited Subject	+	Opinion	=	Thesis Statement
1. Friendship	_____		_____		_____
2. Work	Managers		_____		_____
3. Winning	_____		_____		_____
4. Love	Dating		_____		_____
5. Winter	_____		_____		_____

When you write a thesis statement, keep the following guidelines in mind:

1. **Your subject should not be too broad or too narrow**. A subject or topic that is too broad would need a book to develop it. One that is too narrow leaves you nothing to say. A manageable subject is one you can write about in roughly three body paragraphs. You may find it necessary to limit your subject several times before you arrive at one that will work.

Subject:	Television
Too broad:	Prime-time TV
Still too broad:	Most popular TV shows
Good:	*NCIS*
Too narrow:	Mark Harmon

2. **State your opinion clearly**. When you state your opinion on the topic, choose your words carefully. Be direct and take a stand. Opinions such as "is interesting," "are not good," "is a problem," or "can teach us

a lot" are vague and boring. In fact, if you are specific enough about your opinion, you will be very close to a thesis statement.

Vague opinion:	*NCIS* is fun to watch.
Specific opinion:	*NCIS* teaches us about our legal system.

3. **Do not simply announce your topic.** Make an interesting statement about your topic.

Announcement:	My paper is going to be about *NCIS*.
	NCIS is the topic of this essay.
Statement:	*NCIS* is a TV show that teaches us about our legal system.

4. **Try your thesis statement (TS) as a question**. This does not mean you should actually express your thesis statement as a question in your essay. Rather, you should try thinking of your thesis statement as a question you will answer in the rest of your essay. You might want to write out your "TS question" and keep it in front of you as you draft your paper. It will help you stay focused.

Thesis statement:	The television program *NCIS* teaches us about our legal system.
TS question:	How does *NCIS* teach us about our legal system?

PRACTICE 6 Which of the following are good thesis statements? Mark B for too broad, N for too narrow, MO for missing opinion, and C for complete. Test each thesis statement by turning it into a question.

_____ 1. Schools have good education programs.

_____ 2. In America today, we face the problem of keeping our air clean.

_____ 3. Vehicles powered by natural gas will cut down on the pollution expelled by automobiles.

_____ 4. When using a computer, the user should know many things.

_____ 5. Human cloning is being studied to determine the scientific and moral consequences of the process.

_____ 6. Children in America are becoming desensitized to violence because of TV.

_____ 7. Many people do not eat meat because they cannot stand the thought of eating something that was once alive.

_____ 8. A lot of people avoid math because they have difficulty with analytical problem solving.

_____ 9. Our campus drama department will be performing *Noises Off* this spring.

_____ 10. Since the early 1980s, people have been on various health-craze diets and exercise programs.

PRACTICE 7   Complete the following thesis statements.

1. Marriage today _____.

2. _____ is my favorite class because _____.

3. Sleeping _____.

4. TV reality shows _____.

5. _____ is a role model for college students today.

Beth's Thesis Statement   Beth writes a thesis statement by stating her opinion about her subject.

Limited Subject	Opinion
I know that I learn	from many things in life.

Your Thesis Statement   Write a thesis statement here that can serve as the controlling idea for your essay.

Limited Subject	Opinion
_____	_____

Thesis Statement

_____

Writing Effectively

Writing consists of several steps that lead to a first draft. So far, you have been given a subject (learning about life) and worked with a number of prewriting techniques. You have generated ideas that you can use in your essay and have decided on a purpose and audience. In addition, you have composed a working thesis statement.

At this point, you are ready to write your essay. This chapter deals with the heart of the writing process: developing body paragraphs; organizing your essay; and writing the introduction, conclusion, and title. Once you work through this chapter, you will be more comfortable with these elements of the process and the way they function as part of the whole. Again, you will be writing alongside Beth as she goes through the writing process with you.

As you learned in the first few chapters of this text, all stages of the writing process are part of a recurring cycle that you can mold into a routine that suits your lifestyle. The more you write, the more natural this process will become for you

DEVELOPING BODY PARAGRAPHS

Now that you have written a thesis statement at the end of your introduction, you are ready to write the body paragraphs of your essay. The body paragraphs explain and support the thesis statement.

Support for Your Thesis

Which ideas will support the statement you have made in your thesis? This is the question you need to answer at this point. The supporting ideas are what make up the body of your essay. Each body paragraph covers one major idea of your thesis. The body paragraphs consist of a topic sentence and concrete details that support the topic sentence.

Student Comment:
"My teachers would always tell me to develop my paragraphs, so I used to just add a few sentences at the end of the paragraph. I know now how to make my paragraphs longer without copping out."

MyWritingLab

Understanding Development

To make sure you understand how to develop your body paragraphs, go to **MyWritingLab.com,** and choose **Developing and Organizing a Paragraph** in **The Craft of Writing** module. For this topic, read the **Overview,** watch the three **Animation** videos, and complete the **Recall, Apply,** and **Write** activities. Then check your understanding of this material by taking the **Post-test.**

PRACTICE 1 For each of the following lists, cross out any ideas that do not support the thesis statement.

1. Thesis: Children are desensitized to violence by television, video games, and comic books.

   Children don't react to the violent acts they see on TV.

   Children do not care when the heroes beat up the villains in comic books.

   Many video games cost too much.

   Children often want to be just like the sports figures they watch on TV.

   Most children learn very early in life to shoot figures in video games.

2. Thesis: Political campaigns often bring out the worst in candidates.

   Most people are either Republican or Democrat.

   Candidates try to find secrets from their opponents' pasts.

   Candidates use the media to help ruin other candidates' reputations.

   Presidential campaigns occur every four years.

   Some candidates even resort to name-calling and twisting their opponents' words.

3. Thesis: To qualify as FBI agents, applicants must meet certain requirements.

   People interested in joining the FBI as agents must have a college degree.

   FBI agents must be in great physical shape and have excellent eyesight.

   The events on 9/11 have created a great interest in the CIA.

   FBI agents work worldwide as do CIA agents.

   FBI agents must be willing to go through rigorous training and move anywhere they are assigned.

4. Thesis: Starting your own business takes a lot of planning and work.

   Prospective business owners must create a business plan in order to borrow money from a bank.

   Owning your own business is rewarding.

   People should research the current trends in the market for the type of business they plan to open.

   Sometimes business owners can get their families to work for free.

   People should determine how much money they will spend and how much money they will make so they can project possible earnings.

5. Thesis: To maintain a long-distance relationship, both people must be willing to sacrifice.

   Couples often separate when they go to different universities.

   Both parties must be sensitive to the other's needs—even at a distance.

   People have to communicate often with each other, even if it's hard to find the time.

   Both people must put extra effort into the relationship to make it work.

   My parents had a long-distance relationship.

PRACTICE 2 For each of the following thesis statements, list three supporting ideas.

1. People should always look for three qualities in an employer when searching for a job.

   _____

   _____

   _____

2. Moving away from home for the first time can be hard.

   _____

   _____

   _____

3. Animals can help people live longer.

   _____

   _____

   _____

4. Vacations can often be more strenuous than restful.

_____

_____

_____

5. Studying the right way can make a difference in a test grade.

_____

_____

_____

Essays can be different lengths and often have a varying number of ideas that support their thesis statements. The thesis statement generally determines the length of an essay and the amount of support necessary to make a point. Some statements require very little proof and might need only one body paragraph; others require much more support and might need four or more body paragraphs for a complete explanation. An essay that falls somewhere in the middle has an introduction, three body paragraphs, and a conclusion.

Beth's Supporting Ideas   Beth decided on three supporting ideas for her essay, which means she will write three body paragraphs.

Thesis Statement: I know that I learn from many things in life.

Supporting Idea 1: Taking risks

Supporting Idea 2: Watching others

Supporting Idea 3: Making mistakes

Your Supporting Ideas   Now list the support you might use for your thesis statement.

Your Thesis Statement: _____

Supporting Idea 1: _____

Supporting Idea 2: _____

Supporting Idea 3: _____

Outlining

At this stage of the writing process, many people benefit from putting their main ideas in the form of a rough or working outline. A rough outline can help you plan your essay and see the relationship of your ideas to one another. In this way, you can easily identify ideas that don't support your thesis and locate places where you need to provide more information. A rough outline can evolve and become more detailed as your paper develops.

PRACTICE 3 Fill in the following rough outlines.

1. Subject: College life

 Limited Subject: _____

 Thesis Statement: _____

  Topic Sentence: _____

  Topic Sentence: _____

  Topic Sentence: _____

2. Subject: Animal rights

 Limited Subject: _____

 Thesis Statement: _____

  Topic Sentence: _____

  Topic Sentence: _____

  Topic Sentence: _____

3. Subject: Intercollegiate sports

 Limited Subject: _____

 Thesis Statement: _____

  Topic Sentence: _____

  Topic Sentence: _____

  Topic Sentence: _____

4. Subject: Summer jobs

 Limited Subject: _____

 Thesis Statement: _____

  Topic Sentence: _____

  Topic Sentence: _____

  Topic Sentence: _____

5. Subject: The Internet

   Limited Subject: _____

   Thesis Statement: _____

      Topic Sentence: _____

      Topic Sentence: _____

      Topic Sentence: _____

Beth's Rough Outline   Here is a rough outline of Beth's ideas so far:

Thesis Statement: I know that I learn from many things in life.

   A. I learn from taking risks.

   B. I learn from watching others.

   C. I learn from making mistakes.

Your Rough Outline   Now put your ideas in outline form.

Thesis Statement: _____

   A. _____

   B. _____

   C. _____

Topic Sentences

Now you should state each of your supporting ideas in the form of a topic sentence that will be developed into a body paragraph. The decisions you made in Chapter 5 about subject, purpose, and audience will lead you to your topic sentences. Look back at your prewriting notes and think about which topics will best support your thesis statement. These will be the topics of your body paragraphs. These paragraphs will each include a topic sentence.

The topic sentence of a paragraph is its controlling idea. A typical paragraph consists of a topic sentence and details that expand on that topic sentence. A topic sentence performs two important tasks in its paragraph: (1) It supports the essay's thesis statement, and (2) it tells what the paragraph will be about. It functions best as the first or last sentence in its paragraph. Beginning or ending a paragraph with the topic sentence gives direction to the paragraph and provides a "road map" for the reader.

Like a thesis statement, a topic sentence has two parts: a topic and a statement about that topic. The topic should be limited enough to be developed in a paragraph. It should also be focused and not vague or scattered.

Topic	Limited Topic	Statement
Reading	Frequent reading	improves thinking skills.
Lotteries	Winning the lottery	will change a person's life forever.
Children	Having children	is a huge responsibility.
Hate	Hate crimes	are one of life's worst horrors.

MyWritingLab

Understanding Topic Sentences

To make sure you have a solid understanding of the fundamentals of topic sentences, go to **MyWritingLab.com,** and choose **The Topic Sentence** in **The Craft of Writing** module. For this topic, read the **Overview,** watch the **Animation** video, and complete the **Recall, Apply,** and **Write** activities. Once you complete these activities, check your mastery of topic sentences in the **Post-test.**

Student Comment:
"**Topic Sentences** was my favorite topic because it helped me learn what they should look like, and now my paragraphs and essays are stronger because of it."

PRACTICE 4 Limit the following topics. Then develop them into statements that could be topic sentences.

Topic	Limited Topic	Statement
1. Mondays	_____	_____
2. Hobbies	_____	_____
3. Theme parks	_____	_____
4. Writing	_____	_____
5. Summer	_____	_____

PRACTICE 5 Complete the following topic sentences. Make sure they are general enough to be developed into a paragraph but are not too broad.

1. Work-related injuries _____.

2. _____ is my favorite television show.

3. Sex education _____.

4. Stray dogs and cats _____.

5. _____ must be considered on my college campus.

PRACTICE 6 Write topic sentences for the following paragraphs.

1. _____

_____

_____

She watches the old ones like *Perry Mason* and can't get enough of the newer ones like CSI. But my mom really prefers the not-so-old and not-so-new mystery shows like *Matlock* and *Murder, She Wrote*. My mom will watch any of these shows for hours. My dad has a joke that she's watching all these TV shows so she can learn how to get rid of him and get away with it. I think she's just gathering information to write a book similar to these shows she loves to watch.

2. _____

_____

_____

First, you must follow the directions to install it onto your computer. Then you must read the directions to learn what you should do first with the program. It's best to read all the directions first, but most of the time people just go straight to the program and try to navigate their way through it. Once you get a handle on how to work the program, it's best just to play around and use the book only when you have questions. Mastering computer programs can be hard, but once you've done it, you can be sure you'll never forget how to use them.

3. _____

_____

_____

Because she wanted to save money for other parts of her wedding, the consultant was the first expense she cut. Everything went fine until the day of the wedding. My sister didn't get the flowers she ordered, but the ones that were delivered were OK. The cake arrived four hours late, and the reception hall wouldn't let us attach anything to the walls. And just before my sister walked into the church, she discovered that the train on her wedding dress was completely inside out. Luckily, no one but my sister and our family knew of the mishaps, but a consultant would have been worth every penny on the actual day of the wedding.

PRACTICE 7 Supply three topic sentences for each thesis statement.

1. Many people enjoy resting on Sundays.

   _____

   _____

   _____

2. Teachers should encourage all students to learn.

   _____

   _____

   _____

3. Computers enable people to function more efficiently at work, at home, and at play.

   _____

   _____

   _____

4. Planning is the key to a successful vacation.

   _____

   _____

   _____

5. The abilities to think critically, act quickly, and communicate clearly are essential in the business world.

   _____

   _____

   _____

Beth's Topic Sentences   Beth writes three topic sentences she thinks will support her thesis statement.

> **Thesis Statement:** I know that I learn from many things in life.
>> **Topic Sentence:** I have discovered that I learn a lot by taking risks.
>> **Topic Sentence:** I also benefit from watching other people.
>> **Topic Sentence:** I believe that I learn from making mistakes.

Your Topic Sentences   Develop each of the ideas you listed on page 54 into a topic sentence directly related to your thesis statement. List your thesis first.

Thesis Statement: _____

   Topic Sentence: _____

   Topic Sentence: _____

   Topic Sentence: _____

Specific Details

Now you are ready to generate the specific details that will make up the bulk of your body paragraphs. Later in this text, you will learn about different methods of developing your ideas, such as describing, comparing and contrasting, and analyzing causes and effects. For now, we are simply going to practice generating concrete supporting details and examples directly related to a specific topic. Concrete words refer to anything you can see, hear, touch, smell, or taste—such as *trees*, *boats*, *water*, *friends*, *fire alarm*, and *bread*. They make writing come alive because they help the reader picture what the writer is talking about.

PRACTICE 8 Put a check mark by the details and examples listed that support each topic sentence.

1. Many people are addicted to soap operas.

   ____ viewers get caught up in the story

   ____ people care about the characters

   ____ soap operas are often springboards for actors wanting more work

   ____ people are anxious to see what happens next

   ____ mindless but entertaining TV

   ____ viewers often strongly identify with the characters

   ____ CBS has had the number one soap opera for years

2. My parents have reversed the stereotypical roles in their marriage.

   ____ my dad decorates the house

   ____ my mom and dad both work

   ____ my sister wants to be just like our mom

   ____ my mom mows and takes care of the lawn

_____ my dad cleans the inside of the house

_____ I hope to marry someone like my mom

3. The members of every generation think they'll understand their kids' music—until they actually hear it.

_____ parents don't appreciate today's rock music

_____ parents who like rock and roll don't understand heavy metal

_____ parents become wary of musicians like Kid Rock and Marilyn Manson

_____ no parents understand new wave or punk music

_____ Dick Clark helped all kinds of musicians get established

_____ parents have a hard time letting their kids listen to rap music

_____ Elvis helped put rock and roll on the map

4. Students change their majors often throughout their academic careers.

_____ general education courses make students learn about a variety of subjects

_____ in college, students discover new interests in subjects they have never been exposed to

_____ professors bring new subjects to life for many students

_____ math is difficult for many students

_____ other students often influence a student's decision about a major

_____ the reality of the job market creates changes in majors

_____ academic performance sometimes makes students look for alternative interests

5. The best way to lose weight is through a good diet and exercise.

_____ snacking all day long can cause a person to eat more than usual

_____ people who exercise a lot need enough sleep

_____ skipping meals is counterproductive for people on diets

_____ people should exercise at least three times per week

_____ running is great exercise

_____ people should eat three sensible meals per day

_____ ESPN has many exercise shows

PRACTICE 9 For each of the following topic sentences, list five details or examples to develop them.

1. Everywhere I go, I seem to see someone I know.

   _____

   _____

   _____

   _____

   _____

2. When I was in high school, I enjoyed many different extracurricular activities.

   _____

   _____

   _____

   _____

   _____

3. People use their personal computers for many different types of business transactions.

   _____

   _____

   _____

   _____

   _____

4. Friends and family are very important parts of life.

   _____

   _____

   _____

   _____

   _____

5. People must be careful when they are swimming.

_____

_____

_____

_____

_____

Beth's Development   To come up with concrete details and examples that would support her topic sentence, Beth uses the brainstorming and focused freewriting techniques she learned in Chapter 5. This is what she wrote:

I have discovered that I learn a lot by taking risks.
   buying a used car
   quitting my new job
   leaving Aaron to come to this school
   driving way too fast
   trying new foods
   changing majors
   procrastinating in school
I also benefit from watching other people.
   moving in with roommates I don't know
   watching my friends make mistakes with their boyfriends
   looking at my parents make rules
   seeing my cousin ruin her life
   watching my brother mess up
   observing people around me get involved with drugs
   learning about other people's mistakes from my friends
I believe that I learn from making mistakes.
   cheating on the test
   believing the rumor about my best friend
   lying to my parents
   not believing my sister
   waiting too long to write a paper
   watching TV instead of studying

Here is Beth's new freewriting:

> I know I learn a lot by taking risks, watching other people, and making mistakes. I'm sure I learn in other ways too, but these are the ways that seem to give me the most information about life in general.
>
> Taking risks really helps everyone learn in life, but I think this is especially true for me. I mean, right now I'm sitting here in this class thinking about Aaron and how we want to get married someday. But I left my hometown and Aaron to come here for the nursing program. So far everything is great, but I knew it was a risk coming here. But how could I learn if I didn't?
>
> I also learn by watching other people. My parents are great role models, but it's hard to really learn from them because they are so much older. I mean, they *tell* me not to join a gang, but they're my parents. I learned more about gangs from my cousin than from my parents. Watching my cousin go through her experiences was way better than just listening to my parents. I definitely learn by watching others.
>
> And I definitely learn by making mistakes. And boy do I have tons of those. Most of my mistakes are pretty small, but I still learn from them. I think I learned the most from Mr. Turner, though, when he caught me cheating on his test. He talked to me, and that really helped. In fact, I think it's because of him that I started paying attention in class and decided to pursue nursing at this school.
>
> I will always learn about life from these sources. I guess I will always learn about life as long as I keep my eyes open, but these ways seem the most important to me right now.

Your Development   Choose at least one of the prewriting strategies you learned in Chapter 5, and use it to generate more specific details and examples for each of your topic sentences.

ORGANIZING YOUR ESSAY

You are moving along quite well in the writing process. You have determined your subject, purpose, and audience, and you have written your thesis statement. You have also written topic sentences for your body paragraphs and thought of details, examples, and facts to develop those topic sentences. You are now ready to organize your ideas. What should come first? What next?

To organize the ideas in your essay, start by considering the purpose of your essay and the way each body paragraph serves that purpose. Then, arrange your body paragraphs in a logical manner to achieve that purpose. If your essay's main purpose is informative—to describe the layout of a building, for example—you would probably arrange the details spatially. That is, you might begin with the entrance and move to the other parts of the building as if you were strolling through it. If, however, you want to persuade a reader to buy one type of car over another, you might arrange the essay so that it moves from one extreme to another—for example, from the least important feature of the car to the most important. Once you decide on the order of your paragraphs, you should then organize the details in each paragraph.

Most paragraphs and essays are organized in one of five ways:

1. From general to particular
2. From particular to general
3. Chronologically (by time)
4. Spatially (by physical order)
5. From one extreme to another

Let's look at these methods of organization one by one.

General to Particular

The most common method of organizing an essay or paragraph is from general to particular. This method begins with a general topic and becomes more specific as the essay progresses.

A paragraph organized from general to particular might look like this:

Topic Sentence
   Detail
   Detail
   Detail
   Detail

Here is an example of a paragraph organized from general to particular:

<u>When</u> I began attending college, I was very nervous because I was afraid I would not do very well in my classes. My first year, I took general education classes that reviewed a lot of the material I learned in high school. There was a lot of studying involved in these classes, <u>but</u> I was able to pass all of them. <u>Soon</u> I decided that my major would be business, so I began taking classes that dealt with business. All of the business classes were harder than the classes I had taken in general education. <u>Just when</u> I thought I would not pass

a class, I would do well on a test, <u>which</u> would raise my confidence level again. I worked very hard in every class I took and was able to pass every one. Tomorrow I am graduating with my bachelor's degree in business.

This paragraph moves from the general idea of going to college to the specific notion of taking classes, graduating, and receiving a degree. Notice that it includes such transitions as *when, but, soon, just when,* and *which.* They show the relationship among the writer's thoughts.

The skeleton of a general-to-particular essay looks like this, although the number of paragraphs and details will vary:

Introduction

    Topic sentence stating the most general point

      Detail

      Detail

      Detail

    Topic sentence stating a more specific supporting point

      Detail

      Detail

      Detail

    Topic sentence stating the most specific supporting point

      Detail

      Detail

      Detail

Conclusion

An example of an essay organized from general to particular is "The Decorated Body" on page 222. The essay begins by introducing the cultural messages connected with decorating the naked body. The author then explains what various decorations mean in different civilizations, moving to topics that become more and more specific as the essay progresses. You might want to read this selection to see how this method of organization works in a full essay.

PRACTICE 10 Turn to the essay "She" on page 154, and find two paragraphs organized from general to specific.

PRACTICE 11 Write a topic sentence for the following group of sentences. Then organize the sentences into a paragraph using general-to-particular order. Add words, phrases, or sentences as necessary to smooth out the paragraph.

Topic Sentence: _____

During these events, not only do you get to watch the athletes play their games, but you get to see former athletes announcing the action play by play.

Anytime you turn on the TV, there are at least 14 sporting events happening at one time.

You can see anything from basketball to golf to racing to fishing.

Let's face it; the likelihood of seeing a sports figure on TV is great.

And just when you think you've seen enough of the players, you are flooded with commercials that have athletes selling various products.

Particular to General

When you reverse the first method of organization, you arrange your material from particular to general. In this case, more-specific ideas start the essay or paragraph and lead up to a general statement. This type of organization is particularly effective if you suspect that your reader might not agree with the final point you are going to make. With this method, you can lead your reader to your opinion slowly and carefully.

A paragraph organized from particular to general looks like this:

Detail

Detail

Detail

Detail

Topic Sentence

Here is a paragraph with particular-to-general organization.

The water is so crystal clear that I can see every pebble settled on the bottom. A small sandy beach reaches the water's edge and makes a perfect spot to spend the afternoon. <u>Across the water</u>, I can see the mountainside covered in the greenest trees imaginable. A log cabin <u>also</u> sits among the trees halfway up the mountain, so peaceful and secluded. The puffy white clouds make the sky appear to be a brighter blue, <u>and</u> the birds seem to enjoy floating on the soft breeze. I could sit all day next to the lake in the valley and just stare at my surroundings.

This paragraph starts with specific details about the area around the lake and ends with a topic sentence. Transitions such as *across the water, also,* and *and* move readers through the paragraph.

This is how a particular-to-general essay looks, though the number of details will vary:

Introduction

  Topic sentence stating the most specific point

    Detail

    Detail

    Detail

  Topic sentence stating a less specific point

    Detail

    Detail

    Detail

  Topic sentence stating the most general point

    Detail

    Detail

    Detail

Conclusion

The essay titled "Spanglish Moves into Mainstream" on page 344 is a good example of organization from particular to general. It moves from examples of words that blend both English and Spanish to the thesis of the essay at the end—"it's the schizophrenia of trying to deal with two worlds in one." If you read this selection, you will see firsthand how this method of organization works in a complete essay.

PRACTICE 12 Turn to the essay "Why Some Kids Try Harder and Some Kids Give Up" on page 311, and find two paragraphs that demonstrate particular-to-general organization.

PRACTICE 13 Write a topic sentence for the following group of sentences. Then organize the sentences into a paragraph using particular-to-general order. Add words, phrases, or sentences as necessary to smooth out the paragraph.

Topic Sentence: _____

My mom hopes I'll order something more grown up, but I never will.

My family knew I loved pizza and always let me order one once a week.

I have always loved pepperoni, even on sandwiches and in soups.

I used to love pizza night when I lived at home.

I believe that pizza is the best food ever created.

Now when I go home, we just go to an Italian restaurant where I can order pizza.

Chronological Order

When you organize ideas chronologically, you are organizing them according to the passage of time—in other words, in the order in which they occurred. Most of the time when you tell a story or explain how to do something, you use chronological order: First this happened and then that. Or first you do this, next you do that, and so on.

A paragraph organized chronologically looks like this:

Topic Sentence
   First
   Then
   Next
   Finally

Here is an example of a paragraph organized chronologically:

> Preparing to go snowboarding for the first time can be a lot of fun. <u>First of all</u>, you must get into full gear when you arrive at the mountain. <u>Then</u>, you ride a ski lift to the top of the mountain. Once at the top, it is time to buckle your boots into the bindings on the board. The bindings must be tight, but not so tight that they are uncomfortable. <u>Next</u>, you are ready to begin your descent. On the way down the mountain, pay attention to how the board moves when pressure is applied to the toes and heels of the feet. <u>Finally</u>, you need to learn which way to lean in order to turn right and left so you can fly down the mountain. Once you have mastered the basics, you will have fun perfecting your new hobby.

This paragraph is chronological because it explains snowboarding according to a time sequence and uses transitions such as *first of all*, *then*, *next*, and *finally*.

Here is what an essay organized chronologically looks like:

Introduction
  What happened first
    Detail
    Detail
    Detail
  What happened next
    Detail
    Detail
    Detail

What happened after that
    Detail
    Detail
    Detail
Conclusion

A good example of this method of organization is the essay titled "Why Some Kids Try Harder and Some Kids Give Up" on page 311. It begins with the author describing two "mindsets" of human beings; she then follows a time sequence to explain a series of studies she conducted on these mindsets. Reading through this essay will help you understand this method of organization.

PRACTICE 14 Turn to the essay "Childhood" on page 191, and find two paragraphs that are organized chronologically.

PRACTICE 15 Write a topic sentence for the following group of sentences. Then organize the sentences into a paragraph using chronological order. Add words, phrases, or sentences as necessary to smooth out the paragraph.

Topic Sentence: _____

Spread the jelly on top of the peanut butter.

Unscrew the lids from a jar of peanut butter and a jar of jelly.

Using the knife again, remove a small amount of jelly from the jar.

Place two slices of bread on a plate.

Using the knife, remove a small amount of peanut butter from the jar.

Place the second slice of bread on top of the slice with the peanut butter and jelly on it.

First, remove a butter knife from the drawer.

Spread the peanut butter on one slice of bread with the knife.

Spatial Order

Another method of arranging details is by their relationship to each other in space. You might describe the layout of your campus from its front entrance to its back exit or the arrangement of a beautiful garden from one end to the other. Explaining a home page from top to bottom and describing a screened-in porch from inside to outside are also examples of spatial order. Beginning at one point and moving detail by detail around a specific area is the simplest way of organizing by space.

A paragraph organized spatially might look like this:

Topic Sentence
    Here
    There
    Next
    Across
    Beyond

Here is an example of a paragraph organized spatially:

It was the first football game of the season and her first football game ever as a cheerleader. Standing <u>in front of</u> the huge crowd made the butterflies in her stomach begin to flutter again. <u>In the front row</u> sat a group of her friends cheering her on. <u>Two rows behind</u> them sat her psychology professor. <u>Next to</u> her professor sat a few of her new sorority sisters. As the cheerleader looked across the aisle, she noticed a group of rowdy students screaming and cheering for their team. <u>Beyond</u> the crowd, the tall announcer's booth where all of the press people and the athletic director sat seemed to glare down at her. Any minute the music would begin to blare from that very booth, and she would begin her first half-time dance routine.

This paragraph is arranged spatially because it moves physically around the football stadium, using such words as *in front of, in the front row, two rows behind, next to,* and *beyond* as transitions.

Here is what an essay organized spatially looks like:

Introduction
    Here
        Detail
        Detail
        Detail
    There
        Detail
        Detail
        Detail
    Next
        Detail
        Detail
        Detail

Across
  Detail
  Detail
  Detail
Beyond
  Detail
  Detail
  Detail
Conclusion

An example of this method of organization is the essay titled "I Just Finished the Most Important Project of My Life" on page 158. It moves in spatial order around a mall that represents a foster child's long walk back to her mother. Reading through this essay will help you understand this method of organization.

PRACTICE 16 Turn to the essay "The Sanctuary of School" on page 188, and find two paragraphs that use spatial organization.

PRACTICE 17 Write a topic sentence for the following group of sentences. Then organize the sentences into a paragraph using spatial order. Add words, phrases, or sentences as necessary to smooth out the paragraph.

Topic Sentence: _____

The hotel's check-in desk is located on the left side of the lobby.

Two little boys are sitting quietly on the couches next to the check-in desk, waiting for their parents to finish checking in.

In the center of the lobby are four massive couches arranged in a conversational setting.

Directly across from the check-in desk is the activities counter, where people can plan their days.

Inside the front door, the guests' attention is immediately drawn to the ceiling.

Painted as a sky, the ceiling gives guests the feeling that they have never left the outdoors.

Framing the front door are two huge dolphins, each perched in the center of a water fountain.

From One Extreme to Another

Sometimes the best way to organize a paragraph is from one extreme to another: from most expensive to least expensive, from most humorous to least humorous, from least frustrating to most frustrating, and so on. Use whatever extremes make sense for your topic. You might explain how to choose a pet by elaborating on the most important qualities of an animal and then considering the least important. For example, an apartment dweller's most important consideration would be the size of the pet and its need for exercise. Least important would be watchdog qualities. To accomplish another purpose, you might reverse this order and begin with the least important quality; this method is good in persuasive writing because you end with your most important idea.

This method of organization has one distinct advantage over the other four approaches: It is the most flexible. When no other method of organization works, you can always arrange details from one extreme to another.

Here is an outline of a paragraph organized from one extreme to another:

Topic Sentence
   Most
   Next most
   Somewhat
   Least

Here is an example of a paragraph that moves from one extreme to another:

   Ever since I was old enough to join Little League teams, I have played a variety of sports. I would have to say that my <u>favorite</u> sport has always been football. Absolutely nothing can top the feeling of running for a touchdown and passing the defensive safety. My <u>next favorite</u> sport would have to be baseball. I used to love to pitch to catchers when we would work as though we were one athlete. My <u>next favorite</u> sport is basketball. As a teenager, I played guard in basketball, but eventually I got bored with the position. My <u>least favorite</u> sport is soccer. No matter how much I trained and ran before soccer season, I always got exhausted during the games—all we did was run up and down the field. Now that I'm in college, I'm grateful for the intramural teams that let me keep playing the sports I love.

This paragraph moves from most to least preferred sports and is marked by such words as *favorite, next favorite,* and *least favorite.*

Here is what an essay organized according to extremes looks like:

Introduction
   Most
      Detail
      Detail
      Detail

Next most
       Detail
       Detail
       Detail
    Somewhat
       Detail
       Detail
       Detail
    Least
       Detail
       Detail
       Detail
Conclusion

"Dating: The Soft Breakup" on page 221 is a good example of this method of organization. It begins with a discussion of ways to break up that move from most to least painful. Reading through this essay will help you understand this strategy.

PRACTICE 18 Turn to the essay "Happiness Is Catching" on page 375, and find two paragraphs that are organized from one extreme to another.

PRACTICE 19 Write a topic sentence for the following group of sentences. Then write a paragraph arranging the sentences from one extreme to another. Add words, phrases, and sentences as necessary to smooth out the paragraph. Also, label your system of classification (from most to least or from least to most).

Topic Sentence: _____

First, they have a hard time asking people for money.

Consequently, they allow debtors extra time to pay the bill.

But after a few months, the new employee has heard all the sob stories and is immune to their power.

That just makes it harder to get the money.

This may be because they believe the sob stories they hear, which probably aren't true.

Unfortunately, once the date has been extended, we all have to agree to it.

System of Classification: _____

PRACTICE 20 List the best method of development for paragraphs on the following topics.

1. How to make homemade salsa.

2. I think I am going to rearrange my dorm room to create more space.

3. What I will have for dinner tonight.

4. Today, people question the ethics of capital punishment.

5. I lift weights for an hour and run five miles every day.

PRACTICE 21 Write a topic sentence that introduces the following details in a paragraph. Then arrange the details in logical order, and write a paragraph.

Topic Sentence: _____

exercising three times a week

the advantages of aerobic exercise

exercising with a friend

the difficulty of starting an exercise routine

Beth's Organization Beth decided to organize her essay from one extreme to another—from the most important ways for her to learn to the least important. She first wants to introduce the idea of taking risks, which she believes is very important. Next, she will discuss watching others and finally learning from mistakes because she thinks she learns a lot from her own mistakes. She thinks this order might work, so she lists as many concrete details as she can under each main idea.

Here is Beth's working outline at this point:

Thesis Statement: I know that I learn from many things in life.

Taking Risks: taking risks and learning
(most important)   from them

Specific Details: finding a good nursing program; leaving
   my boyfriend back home; going to college

Watching Others: learning from watching others
(less important)

Specific Details: watching my cousin in gangs; living in
   fear; not in a gang because of her

Making Mistakes: *(least important)*	making mistakes and learning from those mistakes
Specific Details:	cheating on test; talking with Mr. Turner; learning to pay more attention in school for a better future
Concluding Thoughts:	people can learn from everything they do
Specific Details:	taking risks; watching others making mistakes

Does the method of organization Beth has chosen suit her topic? Would any other method of organization work as well?

Your Organization   What method of organization will work best for your ideas about learning? Why do you think this method will be best?

Student Comment:
"**Essay Organization** was a really hard topic for me. I exhausted it four times and really struggled, but I do feel like I now understand the difference between the various types of organization."

MyWritingLab

Understanding Organization

To see how well you remember the most common types of organization, go to **MyWritingLab.com,** and choose **Essay Organization** in the **Essay Development** module. At this point, read the **Overview,** watch the five **Animation** videos, and complete the **Recall, Apply,** and **Write** activities. Once you complete these activities, check your understanding of essay organization by taking the **Post-test.**

WRITING THE INTRODUCTION, CONCLUSION, AND TITLE

By now, you have written your thesis statement and the topic sentences for your body paragraphs. You've thought of supporting details, facts, examples, and the most effective way of organizing your thoughts. At the end of this chapter, you will write a complete first draft of your essay. But first, let's look at three important parts of your essay: the introduction, the conclusion, and the title.

You might have written some of these parts already. Some people write their introduction with their thesis; others write the introduction last. Some have an idea of how they want to conclude from the time they begin their papers; others write the conclusion last. Some struggle with a title; others write their titles as they generate their drafts. The order in which you write these three parts of an essay depends on your own personal writing process. All that matters is that your papers have a title, an introduction, several body paragraphs, and a conclusion that work together.

Introduction

The introduction to your essay—your first paragraph—should introduce your subject and stimulate your audience's interest. The introduction of an essay captures the readers' interest, gives necessary background information, and presents your thesis statement. This paragraph essentially tells readers what the essay is going to cover without going into detail or discussing specifics.

Writers generally use the introduction to lead up to their thesis statement. As a result, the sentences at the beginning of the introductory paragraph should grab your readers' attention. Some effective ways of capturing your audience's interest and giving necessary background information are to (1) furnish a vivid description; (2) tell a brief story; (3) give a revealing fact, statistic, or definition; (4) make an interesting comparison; (5) present a dramatic example; and (6) use an exciting quotation.

Also, be sure your introduction gives your readers any information they may need to follow your train of thought. One way to check that your readers have all the necessary background is to apply the five Ws and one H: *who, what, when, where, why,* and *how.* Any of this information that is important to your readers' understanding of your thesis statement should go in the introduction. You might also ask a friend to read your first draft and tell you if any background information is missing.

Beth's Introduction   Beth wrote a first draft of her introduction just to get started. She knew she would have to work with it later, but at least she was able to get some of her ideas down on paper.

> Everyone learns in different ways. Some people learn by watching, some by reading, and others by themselves. The way people learn is a part of who they are. Knowing how we learn can help us understand ourselves better. I know that I learn from many things in life.

Your Introduction   Write two different introductions for your essay. End each with your thesis statement. Use the guidelines suggested here to capture your readers' interest and, if necessary, give them background information.

Conclusion

The concluding paragraph is the final paragraph of an essay. It draws your essay to a close, giving readers a sense of closure. That is, readers feel that all the loose ends are wrapped up and the point of the essay is clear. As with introductions, there are many good techniques for writing a conclusion. You might (1) summarize the main ideas, (2) highlight the most important issue, (3) ask a question that gets readers to think about something in particular, (4) predict the future, (5) offer a solution to a problem, or (6) call readers to action. In some cases, you might want to use several of these strategies.

You should avoid two common problems in writing a conclusion. First, do not begin your conclusion with the words *in conclusion, in summary*, or *as you can see*. Your conclusion should show—not tell—that you are at the end of your essay. Second, do not introduce a new idea. The main ideas of your essay should be in your body paragraphs. The conclusion is where you finish your essay, leaving your readers with a sense of closure or completeness.

Beth's Conclusion   Here is a rough outline of what Beth wants to include in her conclusion. These are the notes she came up with at this point.

People can learn about life from just about anything.

- made me the person I am
- watching other people
- taking some risks myself
- making mistakes

Your Conclusion   Sketch out an outline or write a draft of a possible conclusion for your essay.

Title

A title is a phrase, usually no more than a few words, that gives a hint about the subject, purpose, or focus of what is to follow. For example, the main title chosen for this book, *Mosaics*, reflects a particular view of the writing process—as many bright pieces logically connected to complete a picture. In other words, that title expresses in capsule form this textbook's purpose, which is to guide writers through the process of fitting the separate pieces of their ideas into a single meaningful whole to make an essay. The title of this chapter, however, is a straightforward naming of its contents: "Writing Effectively."

Besides suggesting an essay's purpose, a good title catches an audience's attention or "hooks" readers so that they want to read more. Look at some of the essay titles in the readings in Part II. For example, "Happiness Is Catching: Why Emotions Are Contagious" attracts the readers' attention because they will probably want to find out exactly how happiness is catching. "What Are Friends For?" is a title that will naturally draw in most readers. And "Dawn's Early Light" is intriguing because it brings up so many references in American culture. Do not underline or use quotation marks around your essay titles, do not put a period at the end of your title, and be sure to capitalize your titles correctly. The first word and last word in a title are always capitalized. Capitalize all other words except articles (*a, an, the*) and short prepositions (such as *in, by, on,* or *from;* see page 500 for a more complete list of prepositions).

Beth's Title   Beth has several possible titles for her essay. She doesn't really know which one to use.

> Learning About Life
> The Way We Learn
> Everyone Can Learn

Your Title   Write three titles for your essay: (1) one that gives a hint of your subject, (2) one that gives a hint of your purpose, and (3) one that gives a hint of your focus. Make each title as catchy as you can.

MyWritingLab

Understanding the Introduction, Conclusion, and Title

To make sure you understand these special elements of an essay, go to **MyWritingLab.com,** and choose **Essay Introductions, Conclusions, and Titles** in the **Essay Development** module. For this topic, read the **Overview,** watch the four **Animation** videos, and complete the **Recall, Apply,** and **Write** activities. Then check your understanding of this topic by taking the **Post-test.**

Student Comment:
"**Essay Introductions, Conclusions, and Titles** was great because I've always had a hard time writing the first paragraph of my essays, and this topic helped me know how to make everything fit together and flow."

Beth's First Draft   In Chapters 1 through 5 and again in this chapter, you have watched Beth thinking about, planning, developing, and organizing her essay. It is now time for her to get a complete first draft down on paper. Here is Beth's first draft.

The Way We Learn

1   Everyone learns in different ways. Some people learn by watching, some by reading, and others by themselves. The way people learn is a part of who they are. Knowing how we learn can help us understand ourselves better. I know that I learn from many things in life.

2   I have discovered that I learn a lot by taking risks. Being at this college was a risk. I have a boyfriend back home, we want to get married someday. We are

hoping for a spring wedding with all of our friends and family. I left my boyfriend to come here. Coming here was a risk to our relationship. But if I am ever going to make it, I have to be willing to take risks.

3   I also benefit from watching other people. When my cousin became heavily involved with gangs, I watched my cousin live in constant fear. By watching my cousin, I made a conscious decision to be nothing like my cousin. By watching and understanding my cousin's life. I learned to live mine better.

4   I believe that I learn from making mistakes. When I was in high school, I didn't study for a major science test. So I cheated. My sister cheated once. I was so scared to do it. The teacher caught me. The teacher took the time to talk to me about the mistake I was making. This mistake made me reevaluate my education. I could have laughed off the cheating experience. I decided to slow down and learn from the experience.

5   People can learn about life from almost anything they do. They just have to be willing to do so. When I take risks, I think about what I will learn. I definitely try to learn as much as I can from watching others. When I make mistakes, I figure out why I made each mistake and how to avoid it a second time.

Your First Draft   Now write a complete first draft of your essay on learning.

MyWritingLab   **Helpful Hints**

- **Need more ideas now that you are going to write?** To generate more ideas, visit **Prewriting** in **The Craft of Writing** module of **MyWritingLab** to find out how.
- **Still struggling with your thesis statement?** Your thesis should guide the rest of your paper. **The Thesis Statement** in the **Essay Development** module of **MyWritingLab** can help you focus and refine this important sentence in your essay.

MyWritingLab™   Visit Chapter 6, "Writing Effectively," in MyWritingLab, and complete the Post-test to check your understanding of the chapter's objectives.

Revising and Editing

No matter how hard you wish it, writing does not end with your first draft. The fun of revising and editing still lies ahead of you. Revising involves the development and organization of your ideas, while editing focuses on correctness. Revising is *not* editing. **Revising** means "seeing again," and that is exactly what you should try to do when you revise your writing—see it again from as many different angles as possible. **Editing** consists of finding and correcting errors in grammar, punctuation, mechanics, and spelling. You have probably been revising and editing periodically through your entire writing process, but now is the time to perform these tasks systematically before you turn in your paper.

REVISING

More specifically, revising your writing means changing it so that it says exactly what you mean in the most effective way. Revision includes both *content* (what you are trying to say) and *form* (how you deliver your message). Having a friend or tutor read your paper before you revise it is a good idea so that you can see if you are communicating clearly.

Revising content means working with your words until they express your ideas as accurately and completely as possible. Revising form consists of working with the organization of your writing. When you revise, you should look closely at the six basic categories listed in the following checklist. This chapter will look at these revision strategies one by one.

■▌ Revising Checklist

THESIS STATEMENT

✔ Does the thesis statement contain the essay's controlling idea and an opinion about that idea?

✔ Does the thesis appear as the last sentence of the introduction?

BASIC ELEMENTS

✔ Does the title draw in the readers?

✔ Does the introduction capture the readers' attention and build up effectively to the thesis statement?

✔ Does each body paragraph deal with a single topic?

✔ Does the conclusion bring the essay to a close in an interesting way?

DEVELOPMENT

✔ Do the body paragraphs adequately support the thesis statement?

✔ Does each body paragraph have a focused topic sentence?

✔ Does each body paragraph contain *specific* details that support the topic sentence?

✔ Does each body paragraph include *enough* details to fully explain the topic sentence?

UNITY

✔ Do the essay's topic sentences relate directly to the thesis statement?

✔ Do the details in each body paragraph support the paragraph's topic sentence?

ORGANIZATION

✔ Is the essay organized logically?

✔ Is each body paragraph organized logically?

COHERENCE

✔ Are transitions used effectively so that paragraphs move smoothly and logically from one to the next?

✔ Do the sentences move smoothly and logically from one to the next?

Student Comment:
"I never fully understood revising and editing until **MyWritingLab** helped show me. Now I'm a revising and editing machine!"

| MyWritingLab | ## Understanding Revising |

To make sure you have a good sense of the revising process, go to **MyWritingLab.com,** and choose **Revising the Essay** in the **Essay Development** module. From there, read the **Overview,** watch the **Animation** videos, and complete the **Recall, Apply,** and **Write** activities. Then check your understanding of the revision process by taking the **Post-test.**

Revising Your Thesis Statement

As you learned in Chapter 5, every successful essay has a thesis that states the essay's controlling idea. It is one of the most important features of an essay because it gives direction to the entire paper. Following are some specific guidelines for making your thesis as effective as possible, beginning with questions about the thesis statement from the Revising Checklist.

THESIS STATEMENT

✔ Does the thesis statement contain the essay's controlling idea and an opinion about that idea?

✔ Does the thesis appear as the last sentence of the introduction?

As you also know from Chapter 5, a thesis statement consists of a limited subject and the writer's position on that subject. Although a thesis statement can appear anywhere in an essay, it is usually the last sentence of the introduction. Here are two examples:

Limited Subject	+ Opinion	= Thesis Statement
1. Children today	grow up too fast	Children today grow up too fast.
2. Children today	grow up too fast	Children today grow up too fast because of television, advertising, and working parents.

The first example includes the limited subject and the writer's position on that subject but also needs to introduce its topics. As the second example does, the thesis statement should introduce all the topics in its essay.

PRACTICE 1 Review the guidelines for developing a thesis statement in Chapter 5. Then write a thesis statement for each group of topic sentences listed here.

1. Thesis Statement: _____

_____

_____

Everyone needs a friend who likes to do the same things.

Everyone needs someone to share good news with.

Equally important, everyone needs a good listener during bad times.

2. Thesis Statement: _____

_____

_____

Watching a movie on the big screen of a theater makes the story and characters bigger and more interesting than life.

The sound system in a movie theater makes me feel like I'm right there in the action.

The concession stand has all sorts of candy and goodies, and I don't have to clean up my own mess afterward.

3. Thesis Statement: _____

_____

_____

Following slow drivers can cause people to experience road rage.

Tailgating can cause people to get angry.

People who weave in and out of traffic at extreme speeds make many drivers furious.

4. Thesis Statement: _____

_____

_____

Asking someone out on a first date can take a lot of courage.

Suggesting places to go or things to do is harder than it sounds.

One very embarrassing moment that would never happen on a later date always seems to happen on a first date.

5. Thesis Statement: _____

_____

_____

Signing up for a skydiving class is exciting, and all your friends think you're really cool.

Boarding the plane for your first jump is a strong dose of reality, but not quite like getting up the nerve to actually jump.

Free-falling and landing safely provide a rush that skydivers never forget.

PRACTICE 2 Write thesis statements for the following introductions.

1. _____

_____

_____

No matter how much I tell myself I am going to get up in the morning and go, I cannot seem to do it. Every night before I go to bed, I lay out my sweats and shoes and set my alarm. In the morning when the alarm rings, I push the snooze button and promise myself that I will get up in 10 minutes. This routine goes on for the next hour until I have to get up in order to make it to work on time. Once again, I have failed to get up and go to the gym, and I have deprived myself of an hour of exercise.

2. _____

_____

_____

The most important detail is to determine the number of rooms in the house. A family must consider the needs of the people living in the house and their plans for the near future. Of course, don't forget the backyard. Does the family need a fenced yard for animals or an area for the kids to play? And the family must pay attention to how well the house has been kept up. All of these items are very important details when looking for a new home.

3. _____

_____

_____

Every morning, at precisely 8:00, the couple eats breakfast at the corner café. Afterward, they go to the market for fresh fruit or vegetables and run errands. If they have no shopping to do, the couple goes home and does housework or yard work. Every afternoon at 1:00, they sit down to lunch and watch a little television. In the late afternoon, they go for a walk around the lake for a bit of exercise before preparing their dinner. After dinner, they watch the news and play a hand of cards. Soon the sun dips behind the mountain, and the couple retires for the night.

Beth's Revision   When Beth looks back at her thesis statement, she realizes it does not completely introduce what she talks about in her essay. Her thesis tells readers only that she learns about life from different things, not that she has three important ways that she learns about life.

Thesis Statement: I know that I learn from many things in life.

She decides to expand her thesis statement so that it more accurately introduces the topics that will follow in her essay:

Revised Thesis Statement: I know that I learn ~~from many things in life~~ best from taking risks, watching others, and making mistakes.

She feels this thesis statement introduces the notion of learning and the different ways she has learned.

Your Revision   With these guidelines in mind, revise your thesis statement.

Your Revised Thesis Statement: _____

Revising the Basic Elements

Now it is time to review the basic elements of your draft. These features make up the framework of an essay: the title, the introduction, the topics of the body paragraphs, and the conclusion. Your review of these elements should focus on the following questions from the Revising Checklist.

BASIC ELEMENTS

✔ Does the title draw in the readers?

✔ Does the introduction capture the readers' attention and build up effectively to the thesis statement?

✔ Does each body paragraph deal with a single topic?

✔ Does the conclusion bring the essay to a close in an interesting way?

What changes do you want to make in your title? In your introduction? In your conclusion? Do you need to split any of the body paragraphs so they deal with only one topic? These revision items ask you to make sure that all the basic elements of the essay are present and are doing the jobs they are supposed to do.

PRACTICE 3 Write an alternative title for "Between Worlds" (page 283).

PRACTICE 4 Write an alternative introduction for "How to Protect Your Identity" (page 251).

PRACTICE 5 Write an additional body paragraph for "The Sanctuary of School" (page 188).

PRACTICE 6 Write an alternative conclusion for "Childhood" (page 191).

Beth's Revision   Beth sets out to answer each of these questions one by one. Here are her responses.

✔ Does the title draw in the readers?

No. It's kind of boring.

✔ Does the introduction capture the readers' attention and build up effectively to the thesis statement?

Not really—it's too short; I could use one of the ideas introduced in Chapter 6 to make it more interesting.

✔ Does each body paragraph deal with a single topic?

Yes. I don't have to break any of them into two or more paragraphs.

✔ Does the conclusion bring the essay to a close in an interesting way?

Sort of. I guess I should look at it again and try to apply some of the material in Chapter 6 to my conclusion.

You saw Beth's first draft at the end of Chapter 6. Here is the second draft of her introduction, conclusion, and title, with her changes highlighted in bold.

Introduction

Everyone learns in different ways. Some people learn by watching, **while others learn by doing.** Some **learn** by reading, **while others learn by listening** ~~and others by themselves.~~ **Some learn best when they work independently, while others do better in groups.** The way people learn is a **major** part of who they are. Knowing how we learn can help us understand ourselves better. I know that I learn best from taking risks, watching others, and making mistakes.

Conclusion

People can learn about life from almost anything they do. They just have to be willing to do so. When I take risks, I think about what I will learn. I definitely try to learn as much as I can from watching others, **which I believe, in the case of my cousin, has already saved my life.** When I make mistakes, I figure out why I made each mistake and how to avoid it a second time. **These three ways of learning are all part of who I am today. I know I'm not finished learning yet. In fact, I don't know if I ever will be.**

Title

~~The Way We Learn~~
The Learning Curve

Your Revision Apply these questions one by one to your essay.

☐ Does the title draw in the readers?

☐ Does the introduction capture the readers' attention and build up effectively to the thesis statement?

☐ Does each body paragraph deal with a single topic?

☐ Does the conclusion bring the essay to a close in an interesting way?

Revising Your Development

An essay's development has to do with the details that support the main points. This section will guide you through the process of developing essays, starting with the questions here from the Revising Checklist.

DEVELOPMENT

✔ Do the body paragraphs adequately support the thesis statement?

✔ Does each body paragraph have a focused topic sentence?

✔ Does each body paragraph contain *specific details* that support the topic sentence?

✔ Does each body paragraph include *enough details* to fully explain the topic sentence?

When you develop an essay, you build body paragraphs one by one. These paragraphs each consist of a clearly focused topic sentence with details and evidence to support that sentence. These details should be as specific as possible, and you need to provide enough of them to prove the point you are making in each paragraph.

Specific Details An important part of developing a good essay is being able to recognize ideas that are more general (for example, *entertainment* and *exercise*) and more specific (the opening scene in *The Green Mile*). Two other essential terms to know in choosing details are *abstract* and *concrete*. Concrete words refer to items you can see, hear, touch, smell, or taste—as opposed to abstract words, which refer to ideas and concepts, such as *entertainment, frustration,* and *peacefulness*. Look at the following examples, and notice how each line becomes more detailed.

entertainment (general, abstract)

movies

classic films

Boyhood

the opening scene of *Boyhood* (specific, concrete)

Don't confuse levels of detail with examples. Compare the previous ladder with this one:

   sports
     team sports
       football
         college football
           UCLA Bruins
           Wisconsin Wolverines
           University of Texas Longhorns
           Florida State Gators

In this ladder, the four college teams are at the same level of detail. One is not more specific than another. So these last four items are just a list of examples.

As a rule, your thesis statement should be the most general statement in your essay. Your topic sentences are more specific than your thesis, and the details in your body paragraphs are the most specific items in the essay. So an outline of these elements looks like this:

   Thesis statement (general)
     Topic sentence
       Detail (specific and concrete)
       Detail (specific and concrete)
       Detail (specific and concrete)

PRACTICE 7 Underline the most specific word or phrase in each group.

1. books, library, shelves, page 42, stairs

2. computer, technology, software, power button, online help

3. backyard, swimming pool, Coppertone lotion, pool party

4. drinks, thirst, soda, Dr. Pepper, water in a frosty mug

5. pink candles on a birthday cake, dessert, dinner, sweets, chocolate candy

PRACTICE 8 Fill in each blank with a new level of concrete detail as indicated by the indentions.

1. _____

   state lottery

     _____

     _____

2. _____

     brother

     _____

     _____

3. boat

     _____

     _____

     _____

4. _____

     _____

     blue shirt with stripes

5. _____

     _____

     Thursday's newspaper

     _____

Beth's Revision   Making an essay more specific involves adding as well as rewriting words, phrases, and whole sentences. Here is one of Beth's body paragraphs with more specific details in bold type in her revision.

First Draft

I have discovered that I learn a lot by taking risks. Being at this college was a risk. I have a boyfriend back home, we want to get married someday. We are hoping for a spring wedding with all of our friends and family. I left my boyfriend to come here. Coming here was a risk to our relationship. But if I am ever going to make it, I have to be willing to take risks.

Revised with Specific Details

I have discovered that I learn a lot by taking risks. **If I didn't take risks, I think I'd never mature.** Being at this college was a risk. I have a boyfriend back home, we want to get married someday. We are hoping for a spring wedding with all of our friends

and family. I left my boyfriend to come here. Coming
here was a risk to our relationship. **Taking this risk
taught me to be responsible and trust my boyfriend
back home.** But if I am ever going to ~~make it~~ **reach
my potential,** I have to be willing to take risks.

Your Revision   Focusing on the details that are already in your essay, make
the explanations and descriptions as specific as possible.

Enough Details Not only should your details be specific and concrete, but you should furnish enough details to support each of your topic
sentences. No matter how good one detail is, it is not adequate to develop
a topic sentence. Without enough details, facts, or reasons, a paragraph can
be too short and weak to support a thesis statement. So Beth needs to add
more details to her paragraph.

PRACTICE 9 List three details that could support each of the following topic
sentences.

1. My favorite pastime is swimming.

   _____

   _____

   _____

2. Eating a balanced diet is an important part of feeling good.

   _____

   _____

   _____

3. A simple gift is often the best.

   _____

   _____

   _____

4. Working for people you like is easy.

   _____

   _____

   _____

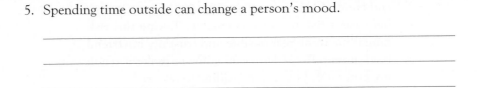

5. Spending time outside can change a person's mood.

_____

_____

_____

PRACTICE 10 Develop the following topic sentences with enough specific details.

1. Before taking a test, take a moment to relax.

2. Always discuss major decisions with someone you trust.

3. When interviewing for a job, dress appropriately.

4. My roommate is a real neat freak.

5. When reading a book, think about what you are reading.

Beth's Revision   Here is Beth's body paragraph with even more details.

Revised with More Details

I have discovered that I learn a lot by taking risks. If I didn't take risks, I think I'd never mature. Being at this college was a risk. I have a boyfriend back home, we want to get married someday. We are hoping for a spring wedding with all of our friends and family. **But I knew that this school's nursing program was better than the one in my hometown.** I left my boyfriend to come here. Coming here was a risk to our relationship. **Not coming here would have been a risk to my career.** Taking this risk taught me to be responsible and trust my boyfriend back home. **I know that I will take many risks like this throughout my life and that not all of them will work out.** But if I am ever going to reach my potential, I have to be willing to take risks.

Your Revision   Add more relevant details to your essay, remembering to make your explanations and descriptions as specific as possible.

Revising for Unity

For an essay to be unified, all of its details and topics need to be aligned. Starting with questions from the Revising Checklist, this section will help you make sure your papers have unity.

UNITY

✔ Do the essay's topic sentences relate directly to the thesis statement?

✔ Do the details in each body paragraph support the paragraph's topic sentence?

An essay is unified when its topic sentences are all related to the thesis statement and when each body paragraph discusses only one idea. Irrelevant paragraphs in essays are those that don't support the essay's thesis statement. They should be deleted or revised to fit into the essay's plan.

A paragraph's main idea is introduced in its topic sentence. All other sentences in a paragraph should expand on this idea and relate to it in some way. Information that is not about the topic sentence is irrelevant and does not belong in the paragraph.

PRACTICE 11 Cross out the topic sentences that don't support each thesis statement.

1. Thesis: Holidays are fun times in my family.

   My favorite holiday is Thanksgiving.

   July 4th always scares my dogs.

   Chanukah is a time of great celebration in my house.

   t My boyfriend doesn't understand my family.

2. Thesis: I love working with children.

   Children's games still make me laugh.

   I hate foods that are good for me. *⨉*

   I want a job that pays well.

   I have always liked babysitting.

   I have applied to work at the Children's Center on our campus.

3. Thesis: Exercise is essential for good health.

   Exercise keeps our hearts in good shape.

   Exercise is fun. *◂*

   Exercise is difficult when you are on a tight schedule. *,*

   Exercise is necessary for weight control.

   Exercise is good for us emotionally.

4. Thesis: I have learned over the years how to control my anger.

    One way is to count to 10 before I do anything.

    ⁴ I get angry easily.

    Another solution is to take a deep breath before I act.

    The solution I use most often is to take a walk.

5. Thesis: I really like to cook, but I never have the time.

    I am most creative at breakfast.

    The dish I like to make the most is a frittata.

    My class schedule keeps me busy right through dinner.

    My philosophy class is my toughest class.

    I don't like spicy foods.

PRACTICE 12 Cross out the three irrelevant sentences in the following paragraph.

I have a very bad habit of waiting until the night before an exam to begin studying, so it is very important for me to have a well-planned and productive cramming session. One time during my junior year of high school, I failed a test. I begin by putting on comfortable clothes so that when I begin to squirm and twist to try and get comfortable, I am able to move around. Next, I get a large glass of milk and several cookies to snack on. Peanut butter cookies have always been my favorite. Once I have my snack, I spread out all my books and study materials on the living room floor. I have a hardwood floor. Finally, I am ready to begin studying for the next few hours.

PRACTICE 13 Cross out the three irrelevant sentences in the following paragraph.

Most people wonder what it would be like to win the lottery and be able to spend money as they please. The odds are that even the people who buy a lottery ticket every day will never win the lottery. Winning the lottery would change most people's lives drastically. Many people say they would begin by paying all their debts. There are people in the world who buy so many items on credit that they are constantly trying to get out of debt. Other people say they would buy a new house or a new car to spoil themselves a little bit. Some people simply say they would invest the money and use it when they retire so they can live comfortably. Many elderly people are unable to continue the lifestyles they are accustomed to after retirement.

Beth's Revision   When Beth reads her paper for unity, she sees three sentences that are off topic. So she deletes them.

In Paragraph 2:   ~~We are hoping for a spring wedding with all of our friends and family.~~

In Paragraph 4:   ~~My sister cheated once. I was so scared to do it.~~

Your Revision   Read your essay carefully, and cross out any irrelevant sentences or paragraphs.

Revising Your Organization

Organization involves the order of both the paragraphs in an essay *and* the details in each paragraph. Following the guidelines in this section, beginning with the questions below from the Revising Checklist, will help you revise the organization of both the topics and details in your writing.

ORGANIZATION

✔ Is the essay organized logically?

✔ Is each body paragraph organized logically?

In Chapter 6, you learned five ways to organize your paragraphs and essays: (1) from general to particular, (2) from particular to general, (3) chronologically (by time), (4) spatially (by physical arrangement), and (5) from one extreme to another.

The organization you choose for an essay depends chiefly on your topic and overall purpose. What are you trying to accomplish? In what order should you present your evidence? Is point A the most important? If so, maybe it should be the last paragraph so you can build up to it.

After you rearrange the paragraphs in your essay, you are ready to look at the organization of the details in each paragraph. It's very likely that your essay will be organized one way (say, from least important to most important) and each of your body paragraphs will have its own method of organization. The goal for this feature of your writing is to make sure your essay and each body paragraph within your essay are organized as effectively as possible for what you are trying to accomplish.

PRACTICE 14 Put the following topics in logical order. Then label your method of organization.

1. east at the mall to the stoplight

    west at the grocery store to the flower shop

    north at the flower shop until you get to Anita's

    south at the stoplight until you hit the grocery store

Method of Organization: _____

2. sitcoms

    dramas

    documentaries

    musicals

    awards shows

Method of Organization: _____

3. community servants

    police badges

    police officers

    police office staff

    police uniforms

Method of Organization: _____

PRACTICE 15 Put the following sentences in logical order. Then identify your method of organization.

Next, I decide what I will have for dinner and begin to cook.

Then I change into comfortable clothes.

Before I completely wind down, I lay out my clothes for the next day and set my alarm clock.

This is always a good time to look at the mail or return phone calls.

While I am cooking, I listen to music or turn on the evening news.

First, I begin to relax by taking a shower.

When I return home in the evenings, I always follow the same routine.

After I eat, I do the dishes and sit down in the living room.

Finally, I watch television or read a book until I fall asleep.

Method of Organization: _____

PRACTICE 16 Put the following sentences in logical order. Then identify your method of organization.

Sweatshirts belong next to long-sleeved shirts, so they come next.

When I walk in the closet door, all of my T-shirts are hanging directly to my left in the closet.

My shoes follow the same pattern on the floor as the clothes on hangers.

Next to the T-shirts are my long-sleeved shirts.

Starting the summer clothes are the tank tops, followed by summer dresses.

Everything in my closet must be in order, or I will never be able to find anything.

All of my sweaters are stacked neatly on the shelf just above my long-sleeved sweatshirts.

Jackets, of course, go along with sweatshirts, so they are hanging next to the sweatshirts.

I have winter shoes immediately as I walk in the door, with sandals for summer toward the back of the closet.

After the jackets come the summer clothes.

Method of Organization: _____

Beth's Revision In Chapter 6, Beth decided that the best way to organize her essay was from one extreme to another (from most to least important). But now she needs to make sure that this is the most effective order for her ideas and that every paragraph is in the right place.

This is the order of the main ideas in her first draft:

Most important:	Taking risks
Next most important:	Watching others
Least important:	Making mistakes

After thinking about this order, Beth realizes that she learns more from making mistakes than from watching others. So she decides to reverse these two topics. She also remembers that she has to revise her thesis statement and her conclusion to reflect this new order.

Revised Thesis Statement: I know I learn best from taking risks, **making mistakes, and watching others.**

Revised Conclusion: People can learn about life from almost anything they do. They just have to be willing to do so. **When I take risks, I think about what I will learn. When I make mistakes, I figure out why I made each mistake and how to avoid it a second time.** I definitely try to learn as much as I can from watching others, **which I believe, in the case of my cousin, has already saved my life.** These three ways of learning are all a part of who I am today. I know I'm not finished learning yet. In fact, I don't know if I ever will be.

Also in Chapter 6, Beth organized her three body paragraphs from general to particular. At this point, she checks to see if this is the most effective order for these ideas. She thinks this order is a good choice for her body paragraphs.

Your Revision   Double-check the method of organization you chose in Chapter 6 for your essay. Do you still think this is the most effective order for what you are trying to say? Then check each body paragraph to see that the details are arranged logically.

Revising for Coherence

A paragraph or essay is coherent when it is smooth, not choppy, and when readers move logically from one thought to the next. The questions here from the Revising Checklist will be your focus in this section as you revise your writing for coherence.

COHERENCE

✔ Are transitions used effectively so that paragraphs move smoothly and logically from one to the next?

✔ Do the sentences move smoothly and logically from one to the next?

Coherent writing helps your readers see a clear relationship among your ideas. Here are four different strategies writers use to help their readers follow their train of thought from one paragraph to the next and within paragraphs: *transitions*, *repeated words*, *synonyms*, and *pronouns*.

Transitions *Transitional words and phrases* provide bridges or links between ideas and paragraphs. They show your readers how your thoughts and paragraphs are related or when you are moving to a new point. Good use of transitions makes your writing smooth rather than choppy.

Choppy:	I could have laughed off the cheating experience and the teacher. I decided to slow down and learn from the experience.
Smooth:	I could have laughed off the cheating experience and the teacher. **However**, I decided to slow down and learn from the experience.

Transitions have very specific meanings, so you should take care to make logical choices that help you communicate your exact thoughts.

Confusing:	I could have laughed off the cheating experience and the teacher. **In addition,** I decided to slow down and learn from the experience.

Here is a list of some common transitional words and phrases that will make your writing more coherent. They are classified by meaning.

Some Common Transitions

Addition:	*again, and, and then, also, besides, finally, first, further, furthermore, in addition, last, likewise, moreover, next, nor, second, third, too*
Comparison:	*in like manner, likewise, similarly*
Contrast:	*after all, and yet, at the same time, but, however, in contrast, nevertheless, on the contrary, on the other hand, otherwise, still, yet*
Emphasis:	*actually, after all, essentially, in any event, indeed, in fact, of course, to tell the truth*
Example:	*for example, for instance, in this case*
Place:	*adjacent to, beyond, here, near, nearby, opposite, there*
Purpose:	*for this purpose, to this end, with this objective*
Result:	*accordingly, as a result, consequently, hence, so, then, therefore, thus*

Summary:	as I have said, in brief, in other words, in short, in sum, on the whole, that is, to conclude, to sum up, to summarize
Time:	after a few days, afterward, at length, (at) other times, immediately, in the meantime, later, meanwhile, now, sometimes, soon, still, then

See pages 99–100 in the Handbook (Part IV) for more information on transitions.

Sometimes longer phrases provide transitions between paragraphs or main ideas. See if you can find the long transition that Beth adds to the beginning of one of the paragraphs she moved (pages 104–106). This phrase helps her readers shift gears to a new topic and makes her essay easier to follow.

PRACTICE 17 Fill in the blanks in the following paragraph with logical transitions.

> Today, an unlimited amount of information is available through the Internet. _____, some of this information may not be suitable for younger audiences. Many concerned parents asked for a way to block Internet sites they did not want their children to view. _____, a system was developed by which a parent uses a password to choose which Internet sites the household computer will and won't access. ____, children who do not know the password cannot access the blocked Internet sites. _____, parents have control over the technology in their homes and feel their children are safe when they use the Internet.

PRACTICE 18 Rewrite the following paragraph, adding at least three transitions to make it more coherent.

> In high school, I thought I had everything figured out. I never considered what I would do after graduation. I never made any plans. When I graduated, I was completely lost. I went to see a guidance counselor at the local college. I decided to go to college. I am in college and have made many plans for the future.

Repeated Words *Repeating key words* is another way of binding the ideas of an essay together and guiding readers through the details. A key word is usually a main idea in an essay. You should also know that too much repetition becomes boring.

Effective Repetition:	Coming here was a **risk** to our relationship. Not coming here would have been a **risk** to my career.

PRACTICE 19 Underline five effective repeated words or parts of words in the following paragraph.

All my life, I have gone to my grandmother's house near a lake out in farm country during the summer. This year, I'm taking my best friend from college with me. What I like most about summers at the lake is that the weather is so warm that I can swim all day long. I swim near the bridge and see the small fish swimming around the columns. Sometimes I even swim over to the docks where all of the people are loading and unloading their boats. I used to try to swim faster and faster to beat my own record. Now I just go to relax, forget about school, and think about the future.

swim / swimming

PRACTICE 20 Underline at least five effective repeated words or parts of words in the following paragraph.

For many people, reading the daily newspaper is their main source of information about the world. The front page usually gives the national news or an international political event that affects the United States. Major world events, such as an earthquake, always make front-page news. On the second page of the first section is the op-ed (opposite editorial) page, where editors and readers give their opinions on current news. The editorial and op-ed pages are among the few places in the newspaper, along with book and movie reviews, where the writing is not objective. Most newspapers have separate sections for sports, business, entertainment, classified ads, and comics. All in all, a half hour spent with the newspaper over morning coffee keeps a person up to date on world affairs and local people, places, and events.

news / newspaper

Synonyms *Synonyms* are another way to link your ideas and help you avoid ineffective repetition. Synonyms are words that have identical or similar meanings—*movie/film, feeling/emotion, fantastic/unbelievable.* They add variety and interest to your writing. A thesaurus, or book of synonyms, can help you choose synonyms for specific words. Be aware, however, that all the words in a thesaurus listing are not interchangeable. *Retreat,* for example, is listed as a synonym for *escape,* but the two words suggest two very different ways of leaving a place.

In the following example from Beth's essay, she uses *incidents* in place of one of her references to *experiences.*

Boring Repetition: She talked a lot to me about those **experiences.** By watching my cousin go through these horrible **experiences,** I made a conscious decision never to make the bad choices that my cousin made.

Synonym:	She talked a lot to me about those **experiences.** By watching my cousin go through these horrible ~~experiences~~ **incidents,** I made a conscious decision never to make the bad choices that my cousin made.

PRACTICE 21 Underline four different synonyms for *friend* in the following paragraph.

My younger brother and his friends were always starting clubs when I was young. The clubhouse and the club name were very important. The pals usually decided on a name first. I think my favorite was "The Three Amigos," even though it was not very original. Every once in a while, an acquaintance of the boys would be allowed to join the club, and the name would have to be changed. Because the boys always thought they were such sophisticated companions, they had a sign on the door that read "Associates Only—No Girls Allowed." The boys are all grown now, but I still smile every time I think about all the meetings of "The Three Amigos" that I sat outside of and listened to.

PRACTICE 22 Replace two uses of the word *actor* with two different synonyms in the following paragraph.

Being an actor seems like a glamorous career choice, but becoming famous is not easy. Many actors start out waiting on tables in restaurants, hoping to be discovered by agents dining there. Other actors go from bit part to bit part in movies and never really earn enough for a living. In the unlikely event that an actor makes it big, he or she suddenly loses all privacy. Still, there are advantages to fame, and most actors adjust quite well to the lifestyle.

Pronouns Finally, you can link your sentences with *pronouns*. Pronouns not only help you avoid needless repetition, but they also keep your writing moving at a fairly fast pace. Personal pronouns (*I, you, he, she, it, we, they*) and indefinite pronouns (*any, some, other, one*) are most commonly used as replacements for nouns.

Beth can use a pronoun to get rid of her repetition of the words *my cousin*.

Repetition:	When my cousin became heavily involved with gangs and drugs, I watched my cousin live in constant fear.
Pronoun:	When my cousin became heavily involved with gangs and drugs, I watched ~~my cousin~~ **her** live in constant fear.

For more information on pronouns, see pages 496–497 in the Handbook (Part IV).

PRACTICE 23 Underline 10 personal and indefinite pronouns in the following paragraph.

The people down the street have a very large family, which means something is always going on in their house. Sometimes when I am at their house, I cannot keep up with everything that is happening. For example, when Sandy answers the phone, she yells that it's for Ryan. Of course, Ryan has to know who it is, and the yelling continues back and forth until Ryan decides to finally pick up the phone. Sometimes when the family members are really busy, they all make dinner individually. Everyone is in the kitchen at one time trying to find something to eat while trying not to step on one another. I'm not sure I could live at the Mitchells' house, but I definitely like visiting.

PRACTICE 24 Add five pronouns where appropriate in the following paragraph.

A few days ago, Brian, Carol, Katie, and I went out to dinner. Brian, Carol, Katie, and I went to a new Italian restaurant on First Street. As soon as Brian, Carol, Katie, and I walked in the door, Brian, Carol, Katie, and I could smell the garlic, basil, and oregano in the rich tomato sauces of pizza, lasagna, and, of course, spaghetti and meatballs. Brian, Carol, Katie, and I couldn't stand it, so Brian, Carol, Katie, and I ordered immediately. The food was even better than it smelled. Before the dinner was over, Brian, Carol, Katie, and I set a date to return.

Beth's Revision When Beth checks her essay for coherence, she thinks her writing could be smoother if she uses some of these techniques. So she makes more revisions that help bind her sentences together and show the specific relationships between her ideas.

Here is Beth's essay with transitions, repeated words, synonyms, and pronouns highlighted in bold. The labels in the margins for the changes Beth made earlier are underlined.

The Learning Curve

Everyone learns in different ways. Some people learn by watching, <u>while others learn by doing</u>. Some <u>learn</u> by reading, <u>while others learn by listening</u>. <u>Some learn best when they work independently, but others do better in groups</u>. **In fact, t**~~T~~he way people learn is a major part of who they are. **So** knowing how we learn can help us understand ourselves better. I know that I learn <u>best from taking risks, making mistakes, and watching others</u>.

First, I have discovered that I learn a lot by taking risks. <u>If I didn't take risks, I think I'd never mature</u>. Being at this college was a risk. I have a boyfriend back home, we want to get married someday. <u>But I knew that this school's nursing program was better than the one in my hometown</u>, **so** I left my boyfriend to come here. Coming here was a risk to our relationship. **However, n**~~N~~ot coming here would have been a risk to my career. <u>Taking this risk taught me to be responsible and trust my boyfriend back home</u>. <u>I know that I will take many risks like this throughout my life and that not all of them will work out</u>. But if I am ever going to <u>reach my potential</u>, I have to be willing to take risks.

Also, I believe that I learn from making mistakes. **For example, w**~~W~~hen I was <u>a sophomore</u> in high school, I didn't study for a major science test. <u>I knew the test was important, but I decided to go to a party with my friends. I really needed the grade</u>, so I cheated. <u>I cut my notes into small strips of paper that I put in my desk, but</u> the teacher caught me. <u>Thank goodness ~~the teacher~~ he was a nice person</u>. ~~The teacher~~ He took the time to talk to me about the mistake I was making, <u>not only **cheating** for a grade, but **cheating** myself out of the knowledge that I could have</u>. This mistake made me reevaluate my education. ~~This mistake~~ It <u>led me into nursing by making me ~~reevaluate~~ realize what subjects I really enjoyed</u>. I could have laughed off the cheating experience and the teacher. **However,** I decided to slow down and learn from the experience.

Transition

Transition

Transition

Transition

Transition

Transition

Transition

Pronoun

Pronoun

Repetition

Pronoun

Synonym

Transition

Transition   **In addition to learning from my own actions,** I also benefit from watching other people. **For**

Transition   **instance, w~~W~~**hen my cousin became heavily involved with gangs <u>and drugs</u>, I watched ~~my cousin~~ Pronoun **her** live in constant fear. <u>She was worried that she would end up in jail, overdose on drugs, or become a "plaything" for other gang members. She worked hard to overcome that lifestyle. She talked a lot to me about those experiences.</u> By watching my cousin go through these horrible ~~experiences~~ **incidents**, I Synonym made a conscious decision <u>never to make the bad choices that</u> ~~my cousin~~ **she** made. <u>I had plenty of</u> Pronoun <u>opportunities to do so. Turning away from this life was difficult, but I did it.</u> By watching and understanding my cousin's life. I learned to live mine better.

Transition   **Essentially, p~~P~~**eople can learn about life from almost anything they do. They just have to be

Transition   willing to do so. **Now, w~~W~~**hen I take risks, I think about what I will learn. <u>When I make mistakes, I figure out why I made each mistake and how to avoid it a second time.</u> **Also,** I definitely try to Transition learn as much as I can from watching others, <u>which I believe, in the case of my cousin, has already saved my life. These three ways of learning are all part of who I am today. I know I'm not finished learning yet. In fact, I don't know if I ever will be.</u>

Transitions In addition to *however,* Beth added 12 more transitions to her essay. What are they?

_____

_____

List the meaning of five of these transitions:

1. Transition: _____   Meaning: _____

2. Transition: _____   Meaning: _____

3. Transition: _____   Meaning: _____

4. Transition: _____   Meaning: _____

5. Transition: _____   Meaning: _____

Repeated Words When Beth checked her essay for repeated key words, she saw that she referred directly to *cheating* twice in the same sentence. She decided this was an effective repetition and chose to keep it in her essay.

> He took the time to talk to me about the mistake I was making, not only **cheating** for a grade, but **cheating** myself out of the knowledge that I could have.

Synonyms When Beth looked at her essay again, she found another opportunity to use a synonym to link her ideas more clearly. Besides the addition of *incidents* for *experiences*, what other synonym does Beth use in her revision?

_____ for _____

Pronouns Finally, in addition to substituting *her* for *my cousin*, Beth found four more places to use pronouns to bind together key parts of her essay. Where are these places in her essay?

_____ for _____

_____ for _____

_____ for _____

_____ for _____

Your Revision Now it's time to make your essay more coherent.

Transitions Check the transitions in your essay. Do you use enough transitions so that your essay moves smoothly from one paragraph to the next and from one sentence to the next? Do you use your transitions logically?

Repeated Words Look at your essay to see when you might want to repeat a key word. Then revise your essay accordingly.

Synonyms Now look for places in your essay where you might add synonyms to link your sentences. Use a thesaurus (in book or electronic form) if you need help.

Pronouns Finally, check your essay for opportunities to use pronouns. Add appropriate pronouns.

Beth's Revised Essay After revising her thesis statement, her development of ideas, and the unity, organization, and coherence of her writing, Beth produced the following revised essay. All of her revisions are highlighted.

~~The Way We Learn~~
The Learning Curve

1   Everyone learns in different ways. Some people learn by watching, **while others learn by doing.** Some **learn** by reading, ~~while~~ **and others learn by listening** ~~and others by themselves~~. **Some learn best when they work independently,** ~~while~~ **but others do better in groups. In fact, t**~~T~~he way people learn is a **major** part of who they are. Knowing how we learn can help us understand ourselves better. I know that I learn ~~from many things in life~~ **best from taking risks, making mistakes, and watching others.**

2   **First,** I have discovered that I learn a lot by taking risks. **If I didn't take risks, I think I'd never mature.** Being at this college was a risk. I have a boyfriend back home, we want to get married someday. ~~We are hoping for a spring wedding with all of our friends and family.~~ **But I knew that this school's nursing program was better than the one in my hometown**~~.~~**, so** I left my boyfriend to come here. Coming here was a risk to our relationship. **However, n**~~N~~**ot coming here would have been a risk to my career. Taking this risk taught me to be responsible and trust my boyfriend back home. I know that I will take many risks like this throughout my life and that not all of them will work out.** But if I am ever going to ~~make it~~ **reach my potential,** I have to be willing to take risks.

3   **Also,** I believe that I learn from making mistakes. **For example, w**~~W~~**hen I was a sophomore** in high school, I didn't study for a major science test. **I knew the test was important, but I decided to go to a party with my friends. I really needed the grade, sS**o I cheated. ~~My sister cheated once. I was so scared to do it.~~ I cut my notes into small **strips of paper that I put in my desk, but t**~~T~~**he** teacher caught me. **Thank goodness** ~~the teacher~~ **he was a nice person.** ~~The teacher~~ **He** took the time to talk to me about the mistake I was mak-ing, **not only cheating for a grade, but cheating myself out of the knowledge that I could have.** This mistake made me reevaluate my education. ~~This mistake~~ **It** led me into nursing by making me

~~reevaluate~~ realize what subjects I really enjoyed. I could have laughed off the cheating experience **and the teacher. However,** I decided to slow down and learn from the experience.

4   **In addition to learning from my own actions,** I also benefit from watching other people. **For instance, w~~W~~**hen my cousin became heavily involved with gangs **and drugs,** I watched ~~my cousin~~ **her** live in constant fear. ~~My cousin~~ **She was worried that she would end up in jail, overdose on drugs, or become a "plaything" for other gang members. She worked hard to overcome that lifestyle. She talked a lot to me about those experiences.** By watching my cousin **go through these horrible** ~~experiences~~ **incidents,** I made a conscious decision ~~to be nothing like my cousin~~ **never to make the bad choices that** ~~my cousin~~ **she made. I had plenty of opportunities to do so. Turning away from this life was difficult, but I did it.** By watching and understanding my cousin's life. I learned to live mine better.

5   **Essentially, p~~P~~**eople can learn about life from almost anything they do. They just have to be willing to do so. **Now, w~~W~~**hen I take risks, I think about what I will learn. **When I make mistakes, I figure out why I made each mistake and how to avoid it a second time. Also,** I definitely try to learn as much as I can from watching others, **which I believe, in the case of my cousin, has already saved my life. These three ways of learning are all part of who I am today. I know I'm not finished learning yet. In fact, I don't know if I ever will be.**

Your Revised Essay   Now that you have applied all the revision strategies to your own writing, rewrite your revised essay.

EDITING

After you have revised your writing, you are ready to edit it. Editing is a two-part job. It involves (1) finding and (2) correcting errors in grammar, punctuation, mechanics, and spelling. Correct writing is as important to communicating as well-chosen words. Nothing distracts readers from what you are saying more than editing errors.

As the checklist here shows, we have divided the editing strategies into three categories: (1) sentences, (2) punctuation and mechanics, and (3) word choice and spelling. This checklist doesn't cover all the grammar and usage problems you may find in your writing, but it focuses on the main errors college students make.

⬛ Editing Checklist

SENTENCES

✔ Does each sentence have a main subject and verb?

✔ Do all subjects and verbs agree?

✔ Do all pronouns agree with their nouns?

✔ Are modifiers as close as possible to the words they modify?

PUNCTUATION AND MECHANICS

✔ Are sentences punctuated correctly?

✔ Are words capitalized properly?

WORD CHOICE AND SPELLING

✔ Are words used correctly?

✔ Are words spelled correctly?

MyWritingLab

Understanding Editing

To test your understanding of editing, go to **MyWritingLab.com,** and choose **Editing the Essay** in the **Essay Development** module. For this topic, read the **Overview,** watch the four **Animation** videos, and complete the **Recall, Apply,** and **Write** activities. Then check your mastery of the editing process by taking the **Post-test.**

Student Comment:
"I not only learned a lot from this topic, but I went back and checked out the video about Editing when I was writing my other papers—not even just for English!"

Finding Your Errors

A major part of editing is proofreading. Proofreading is reading to catch grammar, punctuation, mechanics, and spelling errors. If you do not proofread carefully, you will not catch your errors and make the final changes that will improve your writing.

There are some specific techniques for finding errors. One good method is to read your essay backward, sentence by sentence, starting with the last sentence. Taking sentences out of context lets you concentrate on individual sentences and not get caught up in reading for meaning.

Many students like to keep error logs like the one for grammar, punctuation, and mechanics in Appendix 6 and the one for spelling in Appendix 7. By the second or third paper you write, the logs will show you the types of errors you make most frequently. Then you can proofread your paper for one type of error at a time. For example, if you often write run-on sentences, you should read your paper once just to catch run-ons. Then read it again to find a second type of error and so on. The error logs can help you reduce the number of errors in your writing. By recording the correction for each error you find, you will eventually learn the corrections.

You can also use the grammar-check or spell-check features on your computer. The grammar-check will point out possible grammar errors and suggest ways to reword sentences, but it is not foolproof. You need to decide if you want to accept or reject the grammar suggestions that the computer makes. The spell-check is also not completely reliable, because it misses errors. For example, it cannot tell the difference between *there* and *their*. So you should use it cautiously.

Asking a tutor or a friend to read your writing is also a good idea. A fresh pair of eyes may see errors you have missed. When others read your writing, they might want to use the editing symbols on the inside back cover of this book to highlight your errors. You can then use the page references on the chart to guide you to the part of this textbook that explains how to correct those errors.

PRACTICE 25 Find your Editing Quotient (EQ) by taking the EQ Test in Appendix 2A. This test will help you learn what errors you have the most trouble identifying when you proofread.

PRACTICE 26 Score your EQ Test by using the answer key that follows the test in Appendix 2B. Circle the errors you missed, and chart them in Appendix 2C. Do they fall into any clear categories?

Correcting Your Errors

Whenever you find errors, you need to correct them. To guide you through this phase of the writing process, Part IV of this text provides a complete handbook of grammar and usage. As you proofread, apply each question in the Editing Checklist to your essay. If you are not sure whether you have made an error, look up the problem in Part IV. Work with your writing until you can answer yes to every question on the checklist.

PRACTICE 27 Using the Handbook in Part IV, list the page references for the 15 different types of errors you worked with in Practices 25 and 26. This will help you learn how to use the Handbook as a reference guide.

apostrophe	page _____
capitalization	page _____
comma	page _____
comma splice	page _____
confused word	page _____
dangling modifier	page _____
end punctuation	page _____
fragment	page _____
fused sentence	page _____
modifier error	page _____
pronoun	page _____
pronoun agreement	page _____
spelling	page _____
subject-verb agreement	page _____
verb form	page _____

PRACTICE 28 Turn to Appendixes 6 and 7, and start an Error Log and a Spelling Log of your own with the errors you didn't identify in Practice 25. For each error, write out the mistake and the rule from the Handbook. Then make the correction. See both appendixes for examples.

MyWritingLab

Understanding Revising and Editing

- **Not sure how to catch your reader's attention?** To get a good start on your paper, go to **Essay Introductions, Conclusions, and Titles** in the **Essay Development** module of **MyWritingLab** to find out how to grab your audience.

- **Having trouble organizing your ideas?** Get help finding a method of organization that is perfect for your paper by going to **Essay Organization** in the **Essay Development** module of **MyWritingLab.** Good organization ensures that your audience can follow your reasoning.

- **Confused about when to revise and edit?** Revising and editing are crucial parts of the writing process. To review where they fit into the writing process, see **The Writing Process** in **The Craft of Writing** module of **MyWritingLab.**

Beth's Editing   When Beth proofreads her paper for grammar, punctuation, mechanics, and spelling, she finds two errors that she looks up in Part IV and corrects. The first error is a comma splice:

Comma Splice: I have a boyfriend back home, we want to get married someday.

Beth realizes that this sentence has too many subjects and verbs without any linking words or end punctuation between them. She looks up "comma splice" on page 533 in Part IV and corrects the error by putting a coordinating conjunction (*and*) between the two clauses.

Correction: I have a boyfriend back home, **and** we want to get married someday.

Beth also finds a sentence that doesn't sound complete—it's not a sentence but a fragment:

Fragment: By watching and understanding my cousin's life.

When she looks up the problem in Part IV (page 521), she learns that a fragment is easily corrected by connecting it to another sentence.

Correction: By watching and understanding my cousin's life̶**,** I learned to live mine better.

Beth's Edited Draft   Both of these errors are corrected here in Beth's edited draft.

The Learning Curve

1   Everyone learns in different ways. Some people learn by watching, while others learn by doing. Some learn by reading, and others learn by listening. Some learn best when they work independently, but others do better in groups. In fact, the way people learn is a major part of who they are. Knowing how we learn can help us understand ourselves better. I know that I learn best from taking risks, making mistakes, and watching others.

2   First, I have discovered that I learn a lot by taking risks. If I didn't take risks, I think I'd never mature. Being at this college was a risk. **I have a boyfriend back home, and we want to get married someday.** But I knew that this school's nursing program was better than the one in my hometown, so I

left my boyfriend to come here. Coming here was a risk to our relationship. However, not coming here would have been a risk to my career. Taking this risk taught me to be responsible and trust my boyfriend back home. I know that I will take many risks like this throughout my life and that not all of them will work out. But if I am ever going to reach my potential, I have to be willing to take risks.

3   Also, I believe that I learn from making mistakes. For example, when I was a sophomore in high school, I didn't study for a major science test. I knew the test was important, but I decided to go to a party with my friends. I really needed the grade, so I cheated. I cut my notes into small strips of paper that I put in my desk, but the teacher caught me. Thank goodness he was a nice person. He took the time to talk to me about the mistake I was making, not only cheating for a grade, but cheating myself out of the knowledge that I could have. This mistake made me reevaluate my education. It led me into nursing by making me realize what subjects I really enjoyed. I could have laughed off the cheating experience and the teacher. However, I decided to slow down and learn from the experience.

4   In addition to learning from my own actions, I also benefit from watching other people. For instance, when my cousin became heavily involved with gangs and drugs, I watched her live in constant fear. She was worried that she would end up in jail, overdose on drugs, or become a "plaything" for other gang members. She worked hard to overcome that lifestyle. She talked a lot to me about those experiences. By watching my cousin go through these horrible incidents, I made a conscious decision never to make the bad choices that she made. I had plenty of opportunities to do so. Turning away from this life was difficult, but I did it. **By watching and understanding my cousin's life,, I learned to live mine better.**

5   Essentially, people can learn about life from almost anything they do. They just have to be willing to do so. Now, when I take risks, I think about what

I will learn. When I make mistakes, I figure out why I made each mistake and how to avoid it a second time. Also, I definitely try to learn as much as I can from watching others, which I believe, in the case of my cousin, has already saved my life. These three ways of learning are all part of who I am today. I know I'm not finished learning yet. In fact, I don't know if I ever will be.

Your Editing   Proofread your essay carefully to find errors, using at least two of the methods described in this chapter. Record your grammar, punctuation, and mechanics errors in the Error Log (Appendix 6) and your spelling errors in the Spelling Log (Appendix 7).

Your Edited Draft   Now write a corrected draft of your essay.

MyWritingLab™   Visit Chapter 7, "Revising and Editing," in MyWritingLab, and complete the Post-test to check your understanding of the chapter's objectives.

Writing Across the Curriculum and in the Workplace

Whether you realize it yet or not, writing will play a significant role in your life both in college and in the workplace. It is one of the few ways people have of communicating their ideas and making progress in the world. In other words, you will write for the rest of your life—to make a point, to demonstrate your knowledge of a subject, to earn a grade, to apply for a job, to get a raise. All these situations and many others require you to present your argument or state your case in writing. College is the place to perfect this ability: You will focus on your writing in your college composition class; then you will practice and refine your writing ability in the rest of your college courses.

READING, WRITING, AND THINKING IN COLLEGE AND AT WORK

Reading and writing are companion activities that engage people in the creation of thought and meaning—either as readers interpreting a text or as writers constructing one. Thinking is the link between these two processes, and critical thinking helps you raise both your reading and writing to a higher level. If you learn to apply your critical thinking skills to your reading, you will naturally be able to write critically. You must process thoughts on this higher level as you read in order to produce essays of your own on the same level. In other words, you must "import" your critical reading in order to "export" critical writing. So critical thinking is the key to success in all your communication tasks, both in college and on the job.

In all aspects of life, writing is a form of thinking. It is a way for you to express your thoughts and exchange ideas with others. Writing has two important functions in college and on the job: (1) It lets you understand someone else's ideas, and (2) it allows you to share your thinking with others, which then becomes the basis upon which people can work together and move forward. In both settings, the most important features of any communication situation are purpose and audience. Once you know these details, you can make any form of communication effective.

Both workplace and college writing focus on writing tasks with specific missions. Just as college courses require writing tasks that fulfill a certain objective, so does the workplace. Both environments ask you to adapt different types of writing to various audiences. In business, you might write letters, memos, reports, proposals, e-mails, newsletters, and brochures to accomplish specific purposes for clearly identified audiences. In like manner, you will complete academic papers and projects that include proposals, summaries, manuals, case studies, and research papers to show your professors what you know or how you would approach a specific situation.

One of the major differences between workplace writing and college writing is the expectations of those assigning the writing tasks. On the job, the emphasis is on the final product, which is generally persuasive, designed to accomplish a specific outcome for the company. In college, the emphasis is on process—using writing to learn how to think, process new information, and show someone else what you have learned. At work, you are judged and rewarded with pay for communicating your thoughts and ideas to others; in school, you are graded on your demonstration of what you have learned. In both cases, critical thinking is at the center of good performance. Once you learn how to think critically in multiple disciplines, you will become adept at adjusting your writing to different rhetorical contexts.

As you take on communication tasks in both college and work, you will learn that your mind has to make some interesting adjustments when it moves from one context to the next. To perform well in both situations, you need to recognize these shifts and learn to constantly adjust your purpose to your audience and context. But at the center of all good writing are several characteristics common to people who are successful in both arenas. They are listed here in order of importance to your performance:

- Develop a natural curiosity about the topic or task;
- Experiment with new ideas;
- See other points of view;
- Challenge your own beliefs;
- Wrestle with confusion;
- Discover relationships among ideas;
- Engage in thoughtful discussions;
- Ask meaningful questions;
- Make predictions;
- Be persistent.

These qualities define a person who wants to learn and who is willing to make adjustments in thinking from one task to the next.

PRACTICE 1 Are you conscious of any changes you make in your thinking with different tasks? What are these changes? How do they affect your performance in school or at work?

PRACTICE 2 Which of your current courses involve activities that come naturally and easily to you? Why do you think these tasks are easy for you? Which subjects are more difficult for you? Why do you think this is so?

WRITING AS A WAY OF LEARNING

First, writing is especially valuable as a means of learning—both in school and on the job. Whatever the task, if you write about it as you are reading, you will increase your chances of learning it. The reason for this is that writing helps you improve your ability to understand and process what you are reading. If you are writing about your reading, you are essentially "translating" the material into your own words so you can make sense of it.

This is an important skill at work and at school. At work, you will often have to learn new information that you might need to use in a presentation, in a report, or in some form of communication to others. Similarly, to learn new material in your classes, you should write about it in as many different ways as possible. In both settings, you are writing to yourself for the purpose of learning. The following types of writing generally produce the best results for learning new material:

- **Taking notes on your reading**
  The act of taking notes while you are reading forces you to put the reading material into your own words. In the process, you are reorganizing information, connecting ideas, restating the contents, and learning key words. These notes might take the form of personal annotations in the margins, notes on a computer or separate piece of paper, or an outline. All these activities promote a better understanding of what you are reading.

- **Writing a summary of your reading**
  Summarizing requires you to find the main ideas in the reading and then state them in your own words. Summarizing encourages you to see the relationship among these ideas and the details that support them. In order to put your reading into your own words, you first have to understand it.

- **Responding to your reading**

  Writing full sentences in response to your reading will guide you to new insights and connections that you may not have seen previously. These responses generally produce good results in reading comprehension. The most beneficial responses include personal reactions, interpretation, and analysis of the reading material. Reacting personally to a text involves bringing your own experiences to your reading; interpreting includes restating and explaining difficult portions of the material; and analyzing your reading helps you discover your point of view toward the material.

Equally important to your success at school and at work is the use of writing to communicate your ideas to others. This exchange might take place through electronic devices or on paper, but your audience for this process is important. You are no longer writing just for yourself. Your goal might be to share your ideas, communicate a specific point of view, change someone's mind on a particular issue, persuade someone to buy a product, or demonstrate what you have learned in a course. In any case, you are aware that others will be reading your writing. This "public" writing is one of the few ways for your colleagues to understand your ideas and plans and for your professors to find out what you are learning in their classes. In both areas, you might respond either by speaking or writing. At work, you need to exchange ideas to accomplish your goals. When you speak and write in your college courses, your professors learn what you know, see what is confusing you, figure out what to focus on in the next class, and ultimately teach you how to "think" in their discipline. Overall, the more writing you do, the more you will learn at work and in your classes.

PRACTICE 3 How do you think the writing tasks listed in this chapter will help your understanding of work-related material? Of different subjects in your classes? Would different activities work better in different situations?

PRACTICE 4 How could these tasks improve your writing skills? In what ways might these skills improve your performance in your classes?

DIFFERENT CONTEXTS FOR WRITING

To perform your best on any writing task, you should find out as much as you can about its purpose, audience, and specific requirements. Then dig into the topic as deeply as possible, reading the necessary material multiple times and finding sources that explain issues you don't understand. Try to see the task as an opportunity to explore ideas and enter the ongoing conversation on the topic at hand. This approach will deepen your understanding of the task as it increases your ability to think critically about the subject. In turn, these skills will place you ahead of others at work and earn you good grades in your college classes. (See Chapter 4 for an overview of the entire writing process.)

MyWritingLab

Understanding the Writing Process

This might be a good time to review the writing process so you can use it in your writing assignments across the curriculum. Go to **MyWritingLab.com,** and choose **The Writing Process** in **The Craft of Writing** module. From there, read the **Overview,** watch the two **Animation** videos, and complete the **Recall, Apply,** and **Write** activities. Then check your understanding of the process by taking the **Post-test.**

Student Comment:
"**The Writing Process** in **MyWritingLab** reminded me that the writing process has many moving parts, which I can start and stop as I develop my paper."

Academic Writing

Your professors will probably assign you several different writing tasks during a term. Each one will have a specific purpose or goal within the course. Some of the most common purposes for assigning writing from the professor's point of view are listed here:

- To help students engage as fully as possible in the course content;
- To guide students toward the important concepts in the course;
- To teach students how to think critically about the course content;
- To help students discover their own insights on specific topics;
- To let students demonstrate what they understand from readings and lectures;
- To encourage independent thinking.

During each academic term, writing assignments in courses outside of English will range from short-answer essay exams to longer research papers. No matter the assignment, writing is the primary way for you to demonstrate what you have learned in a class. But many of these writing assignments will have different requirements attached to them. They might ask you to be objective (keeping a distance from your subject) or subjective (personalizing your claims with your own experiences). They also might demand writing that is formal (with no reference to *I* or *we*) or informal (with references to *I* and *we*). Finally, some of your assignments will be research-based, which will require you to know what documentation style is used in that discipline. The main documentation styles are Modern Language

Association (MLA), used in humanities courses; American Psychological Association (APA), used in social science courses; and *Chicago Manual of Style* (CMS), used in history, business, mathematics, and science classes. (See Part III of this text for more information on research papers.)

Types of Writing Across the Curriculum Most writing assignments in college courses require synthesis, analysis, and/or research. These types of writing force you to come up with ideas and insights you didn't have before. They are intended to make you see the course content from different perspectives and help you make sense of it.

Outlined here are types of assignments you might find in courses outside of English:

Summaries
A brief statement in your own words of the writer's main point, purpose, and argument or reasoning; assigned in all disciplines;

Abstracts
A brief statement summarizing a research article or study at the beginning of the article; used in the social and natural sciences;

Reports
Informational writing, often formal and objective, like lab reports; common in the natural sciences, social sciences, and business;

Argumentative Essays or Position Papers
An essay expressing your opinions on a specific subject and providing sound evidence for those opinions; used in most subjects;

Annotated Bibliographies
A bibliography with brief summaries of each source, including how it will be used in the paper or report; assigned in all subjects;

Literature Reviews
A summary of the research on a particular topic; common in humanities, social sciences, and natural sciences;

Proposals
A paper consisting of an introduction, an explanation of the need for the project, an outline for completing the project, a proposed budget, and a timeline; often assigned in natural science and business;

Literary Analyses
A detailed study of a work or object that looks closely at each part and its relation to the whole; especially common in the humanities;

Reviews

An evaluation of a work or project with evidence to support your opinion; used in all subjects;

Letters and Memos

Forms of communication related to an organization: Letters are written to people outside an organization, memos to people inside;

Research Papers

Papers that present research on a subject, containing a thesis statement, information from sources, and original thoughts to support the thesis; assigned in all disciplines.

Your professors are constantly trying to find the best type of writing to engage you with their subject matter and promote critical thinking, reading, and writing in their disciplines. So you can actually get some insight into your professor's approach to a course through the writing assignments.

PRACTICE 5 Based on the information in this section, what do you think are the primary purposes of the writing assignments you have been given in your current courses outside of English?

PRACTICE 6 What types of writing have you been assigned in your current classes? Do you think these types of assignments are the best choices for each course? What other types of assignments in these classes would help you learn the course content?

Business Writing

In spite of the fact that much of the communication in business takes place nonverbally (through body language), writing plays a very important role in the world of work. It gives you material from someone else when you don't completely understand an issue on the job, and it gives you the opportunity to explain your own ideas to others. Effective communication is essential to progress and understanding, which, in turn, makes for a happy, healthy work environment.

As in college, most writing for work has specific purposes:

- To communicate information to other workers in the same company;
- To communicate information to those outside the company;
- To discuss problems;
- To solve problems;
- To persuade someone to do something;
- To direct someone's thinking on a specific issue.

Ultimately, good communication at work—through writing and speaking—breaks down barriers and puts people in touch with one another to realize their shared expectations and accomplish their common goals.

Types of Writing at Work   Workplace writing can be divided most easily into internal and external communication. Internal communication is meant for use within a company while external communication is for public consumption. Even more specifically, communication within a business can be upward (from employee to management), downward (from management to employee), and lateral (on the same level and on slightly different levels like assistant to supervisor).

Just as in college, most writing tasks at work also require synthesis, analysis, and/or research. However, the tasks are much more varied than the academic assignments. So at work, learning as much as you can about the context of the task, the purpose of the assignment, and the audience is extremely important for the communication to be effective. Here are some examples:

Summaries
A brief statement in your own words of the writer's main point, purpose, and argument or reasoning;

Policy Statements
A document that outlines acceptable procedures and behavior for a business;

Brochures
A folded document that introduces a company, a product, or specific services;

Letters
A piece of written communication that is generally sent from one person to another;

Newsletters
A regularly distributed publication that covers related topics that are of interest to a particular audience;

Manuals
A handbook of instructions, especially for operating a machine or learning a subject;

Product Descriptions
A structured explanation for presenting information about a specific product;

Proposals

A paper consisting of an introduction, an explanation of the need for the project, an outline for completing the project, a proposed budget, and a timeline;

Ads

An announcement of goods and/or services for sale that intends to persuade people to purchase them;

Reports

Informational writing, often formal and objective, like lab reports;

Memos

A written message in business that intends to identify and solve problems;

Pamphlets

A small, thin book that has information about a particular subject;

Logs

A list of actions that represent the history of changes in a certain aspect of a business;

Recommendations

A suggestion or proposal as to the best course of action;

Press Releases

A written or recorded communication directed at members of the news media for the purpose of announcing something newsworthy;

E-mails

Informal correspondence sent electronically from one person to another.

As you consider both academic and workplace writing, remember to go through the entire writing process as explained in Chapters 4–7, including prewriting, writing, revising, and editing. Making these stages routine as you approach any writing task will help you improve your writing and also complete the writing task in the most efficient and effective way possible.

PRACTICE 7 In what ways do you think writing on the job will help you understand the context of your job?

What types of writing have you been assigned in your current classes? In what ways do you think writing can help you understand your course content or the context of your job?

PRACTICE 8 Which types of writing provide the most natural format for you to express your ideas? Why do you think this is the case?

WHAT EVERY STUDENT SHOULD KNOW ABOUT WRITING ACROSS THE CURRICULUM

What Every Student Should Know About Writing Across the Curriculum is a free Pearson supplement that explains the value of writing in all disciplines and provides sample student papers in different subjects.

MyWritingLab™　Access this resource in Chapter 8 in MyWritingLab.

READING AND WRITING: A REVIEW

The Reading and Writing Processes

The reading process is a series of tasks that involves prereading, reading, first rereading, and second rereading.

- **Prereading:** Thinking about the title, the author, and focused questions
- **Reading:** Focusing on vocabulary, a reading strategy, the author's purpose, the author's audience
- **First Rereading:** Understanding the essay's assumptions and relationships among ideas
- **Second Rereading:** Writing questions, forming opinions, analyzing

The writing process is a series of tasks that involves prewriting, writing, revising, and editing. At any time, one activity may loop in and out of another.

- **Prewriting** consists of thinking about a topic, planning an essay, and writing a thesis statement.
  Thinking: freewriting, brainstorming, clustering, questioning, discussing
  Planning: Deciding on a subject, purpose, and audience
  Writing a thesis statement: Stating a limited subject and an opinion about that subject
- **Writing** includes developing your ideas; organizing your essay; and writing an introduction, conclusion, and title.
  Developing: Explaining ideas and adding specific details, examples, facts, and reasons

Organizing: Arranging ideas from general to particular, from particular to general, chronologically, spatially, or from one extreme to another

Writing your introduction, conclusion, and title: Writing an introduction, a conclusion, and a title that support your thesis

- **Revising** means "seeing again" and improving the aspects of an essay's organization and development.

   Thesis statement
   Basic elements
   Development
   Unity
   Organization
   Coherence

- **Editing** involves proofreading and correcting sentence, punctuation, mechanics, word choice, and spelling errors.

REVIEW PRACTICE 1 Answer the following questions.

1. What are the four main parts of the reading process?

   _____

   _____

   _____

2. What are the four main parts of the writing process?

   _____

   _____

   _____

3. What is your favorite reading strategy? Why is it your favorite?

   _____

   _____

   _____

4. What is your favorite prewriting activity? Why is it your favorite?

   _____

   _____

   _____

5. What personal rituals do you go through when you read?

_____

_____

_____

6. What personal rituals do you go through as you write?

_____

_____

_____

7. Where do you usually do your academic reading? Why do you choose this place?

_____

_____

_____

8. Where do you usually do your academic writing? Do you write your first draft on a computer? What time of day do you do your best writing?

_____

_____

_____

9. What is a thesis statement?

_____

_____

_____

10. What is the difference between topic sentences and details?

_____

_____

_____

11. What are the five main methods of organization?

_____

_____

_____

12. Do you usually ask a tutor or friend to look at your draft before you revise it? How does this procedure benefit you?

_____

_____

_____

13. What is the difference between revising and editing?

_____

_____

_____

14. What about unity is important to the writing process?

_____

_____

_____

15. What are the four strategies for making an essay coherent?

_____

_____

_____

16. In what ways can writing help you in college and at work?

_____

_____

_____

17. Draw a picture or graphic version of your own reading process. What happens first, second, third, and so on, from the time you get a reading assignment? Don't use any words in your picture.

18. Draw a picture or graphic version of your own writing process. What happens first, second, third, and so on, from the time you get a writing assignment? Don't use any words in your picture.

REVIEW PRACTICE 2 Write a thesis statement for five of the following topics. Then develop one of your thesis statements into the first draft of an essay.

1. My best friend
2. Politics

3. My best adventure

4. Animals

5. In the middle of the night

6. My family

7. My future career

8. The best car

9. Parents should never

10. Sports

REVIEW PRACTICE 3 Revise the essay you wrote for Review Practice 2, using the checklist on pages 81–82.

REVIEW PRACTICE 4 Edit the essay you wrote for Review Practice 2, using the checklist on page 109.

MyWritingLab™   Visit Chapter 8, "Writing Across the Curriculum and in the Workplace," in MyWritingLab, and complete the Post-test to check your understanding of the chapter's objectives.

Reading and Writing Effective Essays

"We do not write in order to be understood; we write in order to understand."

—CECIL DAY LEWIS

In Part I of *Mosaics,* you learned about the various phases of the reading and writing processes. You discovered that you have to work with the author of an essay to create meaning when you read and with your potential reader to produce meaning when you write. Part II of *Mosaics* focuses on nine different ways of thinking or processing information called *rhetorical modes.* In this part, you will concentrate on one mode at a time so you can understand in detail how each mode actually works. In reality, however, although an essay may emphasize one mode, several rhetorical strategies usually function together to communicate a message.

Each chapter in Part II begins with an explanation of a rhetorical strategy and then provides specific guidelines for using that strategy in reading and writing. First, the chapter features a reading selection with specific guidelines for reading critically as a prewriting strategy. Next, the chapter furnishes specific guidelines for writing a certain type of essay. Then, two writing samples demonstrate revising and editing strategies for each rhetorical mode: (1) a student essay and (2) your own essay. Students can usually see patterns in other students' writing more easily than they can in their own, so you will apply each chapter's guidelines to someone else's writing before working with your own essay in a particular mode. Finally, the chapter introduces two essays written by professional writers. The questions framing these selections will help you process the content of the essays analytically so you will be prepared to write a thoughtful essay of your own at the end of each chapter. In this section of the text, you will ultimately see how the processes of reading and writing complement each other to form a whole.

Describing

*"*When you show, you get out of the readers' way and let them come right at the experience itself.*"*

—DONALD MURRAY

Description is an essential part of your everyday life. Your friends might want to know what kind of car you just bought; your parents may ask what your new friend is like; your supervisor might need a description of the project you just finished. You constantly need to describe people, places, objects, and activities for different audiences as part of your daily routine.

In addition, you frequently use description when writing. Actually, description is a major part of writing in our personal lives, in college, and at work:

- You describe your new leather jacket on Facebook to a friend.
- You describe the damage to your car in an insurance report.
- A student describes a cell and its parts on a biology exam.
- A nurse describes the appearance of a wound in a patient report.
- A landscape contractor describes a design for a rock garden.

Description creates a picture in words to help a reader visualize something a writer has seen, heard, or done. It helps the reader understand or share a sensory experience by *showing* rather than *telling*. Description is one of our primary forms of self-expression.

At times, description is used as an end in itself. That is, you might write a description for the sole purpose of explaining how something looks, sounds, feels, tastes, or smells. For instance, you could use pure description to tell a friend about your new apartment. More often, though, description is used to help accomplish another purpose—to explain a problem, to analyze the causes and effects of an event, or to persuade your readers to change their thinking or take some specific action.

MyWritingLab | **Understanding Description**

To make sure you understand describing, go to **MyWritingLab.com,** and choose **Describing** in the **Essay Development** module. For this topic, read the **Overview,** view the **Animation** video, and complete the **Recall, Apply,** and **Write** activities. Then check your understanding of descriptive writing by taking the **Post-test.**

PREPARING TO WRITE A DESCRIPTION ESSAY

In this text, getting ready to write starts with reading. If you want to write a good description essay, you can begin by reading a good description essay and understanding how it works—in content and in structure. If you learn how to read an essay in depth, these skills will naturally transfer to your writing. But you need to be conscious of the elements of an essay so you can use these same strategies in your own writing. Reading and writing analytically in any mode are demanding skills, but they are necessary tools for succeeding in college and beyond. Like two halves of a circle, these processes complement each other and enhance your ability to perform many other tasks in life. In the next few pages, you will read an effective description essay and then answer some questions to help you discover how the essay gets its point across.

Reading a Description Essay

Writing about the dust storms of the 1930s, Margaret Bourke-White describes in the following essay the destruction they left in their path. In what ways has nature played a role in your life? What is this role? Is it positive or negative? What recent natural events have dramatically changed our entire country? What natural events have affected the world?

Using a reading strategy is an excellent way to learn how to understand all the complexities of your reading material. In other words, it helps you read critically, or analytically, which leads to analytical writing. Reading critically, or analytically, helps you understand not only *what* the essay is saying but also *how* the author is saying it. The strategy you will be applying to all the reading tasks in this chapter involves making personal connections with your reading material.

READING CRITICALLY
Making Personal Associations
with a Professional Essay

We all naturally make personal associations with our reading. However, one person's associations are usually quite different from those of someone else. Recording the associations you make with a reading selection lets you "own" the essay. It allows you to connect the author's thoughts to your own experiences. As you read the following essay, make at least five notes in the margins that relate some of your specific memories or experiences to the details in this essay. Be prepared to explain the connection between your notes and the facts in the essay.

DUST CHANGES AMERICA
by Margaret Bourke-White

Vitamin K they call it—the dust which sifts under the door sills, and stings in the eyes, and seasons every spoonful of food. The dust storms have distinct personalities, rising in formation like rolling clouds, creeping up silently like formless fog, approaching violently like a tornado. Where has it come from? It provides topics of endless speculation. Red, it is the topsoil from Oklahoma; brown, it is the fertile earth of western Kansas; the good grazing land of Texas and New Mexico sweeps by as a murky yellow haze. Or, tracing it locally, "My uncle will be along pretty soon," they say; "I just saw his farm go by." 1

The town dwellers stack their linen in trunks, stuff wet cloths along the window sills, estimate the tons of sand in the darkened air above them, paste cloth masks on their faces with adhesive tape, and try to joke about Vitamin K. But on the farms and ranches there is an attitude of despair. 2

By coincidence I was in the same parts of the country where last year I photographed the drought. As short a time as eight months ago, there was an attitude of false optimism. "Things will get better," the farmers would say. "We're not as hard hit as other states. The government will help out. This can't go on." But this year there is an atmosphere of utter hopelessness—nothing to do: no use digging out your chicken coops and pigpens after the last "duster" because the next one will be coming along soon; no use trying to keep the house clean; no use fighting off that foreclosure any longer; no use even hoping to give your cattle anything to chew on when their food crops have literally blown out of the ground. 3

It was my job to avoid dust storms, since I was commissioned by an airplane company to take photographs of their course from the air, but frequently the dust 4 storms caught up with us, and as we were grounded anyway, I started to photograph them. Thus I saw five dust-storm states from the air and from the ground.

5   In the last several years, there have been droughts and sand storms and dust-ers, but they have been localized, and always one state could borrow from another. But this year the scourge assumes tremendous proportions. Dust storms are bringing distress and death to 300,000 square miles; they are blowing over all of Kansas, all of Nebraska and Wyoming, strips of the Dakotas, about half of Colorado, sections of Iowa and Missouri, the greater part of Oklahoma, and the northern panhandle of Texas, extending into the eastern parts of New Mexico.

6   Last year, I saw farmers harvesting the Russian thistle. Never before had they thought of feeding thistles to cattle. But this prickly fodder became precious for food. This year even the Russian thistles are dying out and the still humbler soap weed be-comes as vital to the farmer as the fields of golden grain he tended in the past. Last year's thistle-fed cattle dwindled to skin and bone. This year's herds on their diet of soap weed develop roughened hides, ugly growths around the mouth, and lusterless eyes.

7   Years of the farmers' and ranchers' lives have gone into the building up of their herds. Their herds were like their families to them. When AAA [American Agricultural Association] officials spotted cows and steers for shooting during the cattle-killing days of last summer, the farmers felt as though their own children were facing the bullets. Kansas, a Republican state, has no love for the AAA. This year, winds whis-tled over land made barren by the drought and the crop-conservation program. When Wallace [Henry Agard Wallace, Secretary of Agriculture under Franklin D. Roosevelt] removed the ban on the planting of spring wheat, he was greeted by cheers. But the wheat has been blown completely out of the ground. Nothing is left but soap weed, or the expensive cotton-seed cake, and after that—bankruptcy.

8   The storm comes in a terrifying way. Yellow clouds roll. The wind blows such a gale that it is all my helper can do to hold my camera to the ground. The sand whips into my lens. I repeatedly wipe it away trying to snatch an exposure before it becomes completely coated again. The light becomes yellower, the wind colder. Soon there is no photographic light, and we hurry for shelter to the nearest farmhouse.

9   Three men and a woman are seated around a dust-caked lamp, on their faces grotesque masks of wet cloth. The children have been put to bed with towels tucked over their heads. My host greets us: "It takes grit to live in this country." They are telling stories: A bachelor harnessed the sandblast which ripped through the keyhole by holding his pots and pans in it until they were spick and span. A pilot flying over Amarillo got caught in a sand storm. His motor clogged; he took to his parachute. It took him six hours to shovel his way back to earth. And when a man from the next county was struck by a drop of water, he fainted, and it took two buckets of sand to revive him.

10   The migrations of the farmer have begun. In many of the worst-hit counties, 80 percent of the families are on relief. In the open farm country, one crop failure follows another. After perhaps three successive crop failures, the farmer can't stand it any longer. He moves in with relatives and hopes for a job in Arizona or Illinois or some neighboring state where he knows he is not needed. Perhaps he gets a job as a

cotton picker, and off he goes with his family, to be turned adrift again after a brief working period.

We passed them on the road, all their household goods piled on wagons, one   11
lucky family on a truck—lucky, because they had been able to keep their truck when the mortgage was foreclosed. All they owned in the world was packed on it; the children sat on a pile of bureaus topped with mattresses, and the sides of the truck were strapped up with bed springs. The entire family looked like a Ku Klux Klan meeting, their faces done up in masks to protect them from the whirling sand.

Near Hays, Kansas, a little boy started home from school and never arrived   12
there. The neighbors looked for him till ten at night, and all next day a band of two hundred people searched. At twilight they found him, only a quarter of a mile from home, his body nearly covered with silt. He had strangled to death. The man who got lost in his own ten-acre truck garden and wandered around choking and sniffling for eight hours before he found his house considered himself lucky to escape with his life. The police and sheriffs are kept constantly busy with calls from anxious parents whose children are lost, and the toll is mounting of people who become marooned and die in the storms.

But the real tragedy is the plight of the cattle. In a rising sand storm, cattle   13
quickly become blinded. They run around in circles until they fall and breathe so much dust that they die. Autopsies show their lungs caked with dust and mud. Farmers dread the birth of calves during a storm. The newborn animals will die within twenty-four hours.

And this same dust that coats the lungs and threatens death to cattle and men   14
alike, that ruins the stock of the storekeeper lying unsold on his shelves, that creeps into the gear shifts of automobiles, that sifts through the refrigerator into the butter, that makes housekeeping, and gradually life itself, unbearable, this swirling drifting dust is changing the agricultural map of the United States. It piles ever higher on the floors and beds of a steadily increasing number of deserted farmhouses. A half-buried plowshare, a wheat binder ruffled over with sand, the skeleton of a horse near a dirt-filled water hole are stark evidence of the meager life, the wasted savings, the years of toil that the farmer is leaving behind him.

Discovering How This Essay Works

To help you discover the elements that make this an effective description essay so you can use them in your own writing, answer the following questions in as much detail as possible.

1. What is the mood or impression that Bourke-White creates in this essay?

_____

_____

_____

2. This essay contains both facts and opinions. Find at least one fact and one opinion, and list them here.

   Fact: _____

   Opinion: _____

3. In "Dust Changes America," the author uses all five senses (seeing, hearing, touching, smelling, and tasting) to explain the sensation of dust storms. Find at least one example of each of these senses in this essay. Then circle the sense that Bourke-White relies on the most.

   Seeing: _____

   _____

   Hearing: _____

   Touching: _____

   Smelling: _____

   Tasting: _____

4. The writer works hard in this essay to use details to show her readers what she means. List three details from this essay that were especially vivid to you.

   _____

   _____

   _____

5. How does Bourke-White organize her essay? List the topics she covers; then go to pages 64–76 in Chapter 6 to help you identify her method of organization.

   _____

   _____

   _____

   _____

   _____

   _____

   Method of organization: _____

WRITING A DESCRIPTION ESSAY

Now that you have read and studied a description essay, you will be writing one of your own. This section will help you generate a rough draft that you will then revise and edit in the third section of this chapter. It will guide you through a careful reading of the writing assignment, provide several ways to generate ideas and choose a topic, and finally furnish concrete guidelines for writing an effective description essay. We encourage you to make notes and lists during this process so that you can use them when you write a draft of your own essay at the end of this section.

Reading the Prompt

The first step in writing any essay is making sure you understand the writing assignment or "prompt." The assignment attempts to "prompt" you to respond to a specific issue or question. The more thoroughly you understand the prompt, the better paper you will create. So you want to actually "interact" with the essay assignment. Applying the chapter reading strategy to your writing prompt is a good way to accomplish this goal.

READING CRITICALLY
Making Personal Associations with the Prompt

Reading
Strategy

Add your personal associations to the writing prompt below. What ideas come to mind as you read this prompt? Write as many personal notes as you can in the margins of this essay assignment. Then, underline the directions that are essential for completing this assignment. Finally, start a "conversation" with the assignment by responding to the questions at the beginning of the prompt.

Writing Prompt

What direct encounters have you had with nature? What are some of the details of these encounters? Was your general impression of these encounters positive or negative? Write an essay describing one of these encounters. Explain your experience through as many senses as possible, following the guidelines below for developing a description essay.

MyWritingLab
Complete this Writing Prompt assignment in MyWritingLab.

Thinking About the Prompt

Before you focus on a specific topic, you should generate as many ideas as you can so you have several to choose from. List some memorable experiences you have had with nature (for example, a snowstorm, a sunny day, a drought, a tornado, a sunset, a thunderstorm). Why do you remember these particular experiences? Did any of them form an impression on you that is worth writing about? Choose one of these events, and use one or more of the prewriting techniques you learned in Chapter 5 to generate as many thoughts as possible about it.

Guidelines for Writing a Description Essay

Describing is a natural process based on good observation. But some people describe items more vividly than others do. When they describe an experience, you feel as though you were there too. We can all improve our ability to describe by following a few simple guidelines. As you think about the topic you have chosen in response to the prompt above, read the following guidelines, and continue to make lists and notes that you will use when you write your draft on this prompt. After each guideline below is an explanation of how it functions in the reading selection at the beginning of this chapter so you can actually see how the element works in an essay before you apply it to your own writing.

1. **Decide on a dominant impression—the feeling or mood you want to communicate**. How do you want your readers to feel after reading your description? Good about the characters in the scene? Angry at the situation? Satisfied with the outcome? Choosing a dominant impression gives your description focus and unity. You can't possibly write down everything you observe about a person, place, incident, or object. The result would be a long, confusing—and probably boring—list. But if you first decide on a dominant impression for your description, you can then choose the details that will best communicate that impression.

In the Reading: The dominant impression Bourke-White conveys is a feeling of frustration and despair at the thought of the destruction nature can bring. This dominant impression gives her essay focus and helps her choose the details that best communicate this feeling.

In Your Writing: What dominant impression do you want to communicate in your essay? Can you put it in a sentence?

2. **Decide how much of your description should be objective (factual) and how much should be subjective (personal reaction)**. An objective description is like a dictionary definition—accurate and emotionless. Scientific and technical writing are objective. If, for example, you are describing a piece of equipment used in a chemistry experiment or the packaging needed to ship a computer, you would be objective. Subjective description, in contrast, tries to produce a specific emotional response in the reader. It focuses on feelings rather than facts and tries to activate as many senses as possible. An advertisement describing a Caribbean cruise

might be very subjective, as would a restaurant or movie review. Most descriptive writing has a combination of objective and subjective elements. The degree to which you emphasize one over the other depends on your purpose and your audience.

In the Reading: Bourke-White's essay demonstrates a good balance of objective and subjective writing. She presents the facts about the dust storms and the ways Midwesterners deal with the dust—putting linen in trunks, stuffing wet cloths in window sills, using masks on their faces, and so on. Then she mixes these facts with subjective stories about families who are suffering, a child who never makes it home from school, and cattle that are like family to their owners. This combination of objective and subjective elements makes the essay realistic and powerful at the same time.

In Your Writing: What balance of these elements will help you communicate your dominant impression most effectively? Label the items on your prewriting list either objective or subjective. Add other details to your prewriting list that will create the balance you want.

3. **Draw on your five senses to write a good description**. Although careful observation is at the heart of all good description, limiting yourself to what you see is a mistake. Effective description relies on all five senses: seeing, hearing, touching, smelling, and tasting. If you use all your senses to relay your description, your readers will be able to see, hear, touch, smell, and taste what you are describing as if they were actually there with you participating in the same experience.

In the Reading: Look again at Bourke-White's description. She draws on seeing throughout the essay but especially in paragraph 8 when she describes her attempts at taking pictures. Her description of the wind whistling over the barren land (paragraph 7) appeals to our sense of hearing. She refers to our sense of touch when she talks about the dust stinging the eyes (paragraph 1) and the cloth masks on people's faces (paragraph 2). In paragraph 13, the author talks about the cattle breathing in "so much dust that they die," which activates our sense of smell. She relies on taste when she mentions the dust seasoning the food (paragraph 1) and the cattle eating thistles (paragraph 6). Her entire essay is vivid because of all the specific sensory details she furnishes.

In Your Writing: Which senses will your essay cover? Which of your prewriting notes draw on sight, sound, touch, smell, and taste? Label the items in your notes by senses so you know what you have covered so far. Then, add more details to your notes that refer to some of the senses you haven't yet included.

4. **When you describe, try to show rather than tell your readers what you want them to know**. Your ultimate goal in writing a descriptive

essay is to give your readers an experience as close to yours as possible. Therefore, do not simply tell your readers what you saw or experienced; show them. Use your writing skills to recreate the event so your readers can see, hear, feel, smell, taste, and understand as if they were there. For example, you can tell someone you bought a "terrific new car." But if you say you bought a "beautiful, new blue Mustang with a gray interior, custom wheels, and a powerful stereo," you're *showing* your readers why you are so excited about your purchase.

In the Reading: If Bourke-White had simply stated her dominant impression (that dust storms bring frustration and despair to the Midwest) with no examples or details to support her statement, she would only be *telling* her readers how she felt. Instead, she *shows* them, which invites the readers to participate in the experience with her. Her sensory details demonstrate her main point.

In Your Writing: How can you *show* rather than just *tell* in your essay? What other details or information would show your reader exactly what your experience was like? Add these details to your prewriting list at this point.

5. **Organize your description so your readers can easily follow it**. Most descriptions are organized from general to particular (from main idea to details), from particular to general (from details to main idea), spatially (from top to bottom or left to right), or from one extreme to another (for example, from most difficult to least difficult). Because the organization of your essay often depends on your point of view, you should choose a specific perspective from which to write your description. If your description jumps around your house, referring to a picture on the wall in your bedroom, then to the refrigerator in the kitchen, and next to the quilt on your bed, your readers are likely to become confused and disoriented. They will not be able to follow you. If, however, you move from room to room in a logical way, your audience will be able to stay with you. In fact, your vision will become their vision.

In the Reading: Bourke-White organizes her essay from one extreme to another—in this case, from least to most tragic. She starts by describing the inconveniences of the dust storms on a personal level—the dirty houses, the piles of dust in the fields, the health problems. Then she moves on to the more serious issues of death on 300,000 square miles of land. The essay ends with references to farms collapsing financially, children lost in the storms, and whole families being displaced. The author leaves us at the end of her essay with a sense of loss and hopelessness that reflects the feelings of the farmers in the Midwest during a drought.

In Your Writing: Review these four patterns of organization in Chapter 6, and then look at the details and examples in your prewriting notes. List the material you have to work with so far in a few different ways. What organization pattern does each list follow? Which order will create your general impression?

Writing a Draft of Your Essay

Now is the time to collect all your personal associations, your notes, your prewriting exercises, and your lists in preparation for writing the first draft of your essay. Before you actually start writing, you might also want to review the professional essay, the writing assignment, and the chapter guidelines for writing description essays along with your notes and lists. At this point, don't think about revising or editing; just get your thoughts about the writing assignment down on paper.

MyWritingLab **Helpful Hints**

- **Need help with your dominant impression?** Creating a strong thesis statement is important in any essay because it provides a focus for your paper. If you need help creating yours, check out the video and activities in **MyWritingLab** for **Thesis Statement** in the **Essay Development** module.

REVISING AND EDITING

You are now ready to think about revising and editing. This section will take you through the guidelines for revising and editing description essays in reference to two specific writing samples: another student's essay and your own essay. Revising and editing are often much easier with someone else's writing, which is why we begin this stage with a writing sample from another student. If you can see some of the strengths and weaknesses in this essay, you might be able to locate areas for improvement in your own writing. So you will be reviewing the chapter guidelines by revising and editing another student's writing before applying the same guidelines to your own writing.

Reading a Student Description Essay

We begin by using our chapter reading strategy on a student essay. In an essay about a fond memory, a student named Abby Reed reminisces about her grandfather. Making personal associations as you read this essay will help you identify with the student writer and figure out how to improve her essay.

Reading Strategy

 READING CRITICALLY
Making Personal Associations with the Student Essay

As you read Abby's draft, write your personal associations in the margins of the essay, paying special attention to the dominant impression she creates and the senses she uses to trigger that impression.

Grandma's House

1   My grandma lives in the country, near a large, blue lake and a small, green forest. I look forward to visiting her house. I think of my grandpa when I'm there.

2   Whenever I walk into my grandma's house, I always go directly to my grandpa's favorite room—the den. I am immediately reminded of my grandpa in this room. My grandma has a soft, brown sofa and a brown leather loveseat in this small, dark room, but all I see is the old, worn chair that was my grandpa's. The chair was re-covered in an itchy tweed fabric. I used to pretend to be asleep in his chair so my grandpa would gently lift me from the coarse fabric and place me on his lap. I would lie there even though I wasn't sleeping and enjoy the warmth of his body. I remember the times I sat on his sturdy lap in that chair while he read *One Fish, Two Fish, Red Fish, Blue Fish* or *The Cat in the Hat* in his deep voice.

3   Now when I sit in his chair, I look on the mantle and see an old Air Force picture of my grandpa and three of his Air Force buddies. They are all dressed in informal flight clothes and are standing in front of a World War II airplane. Next to this picture is a single portrait of my grandpa when he was 70. This picture represents the way I still see him in my mind. His gray hair is thin, his face has light brown sun spots on it that show his years of working outdoors. His gentle, light blue eyes sparkle in a way that usually meant he was up to something mischievous. But most of all, I love looking at his smile. The right side of his mouth always turned slightly downward, but it is a smile that I would give anything to see in person just one more time.

4   I also love to play with the pipe stand that sits on the table next to my grandpa's chair. I like the worn feeling of the pipe. It once was rough with ridges but is now smooth from use. When I quietly pick up his pipe and smell the sweet tobacco that was once housed in its shell, I think of all the times I knew my grandpa were near me because of this same aroma.

5   I have wonderful memories of my grandpa. When I go to my grandma's house, I can sit in my grandpa's old chair in my grandpa's favorite room and reminisce about all the times I felt safe when my grandpa was near. I will always treasure this one tiny room, with its smells from the past and its picture of my grandpa smiling.

Revising and Editing the Student Essay

This essay is Abby's first draft, which now needs to be revised and edited. First, apply the Revising Checklist to the content of Abby's draft. When you are satisfied that her ideas are fully developed and well organized, use the Editing Checklist to correct her grammar and mechanics errors. Answer the questions, and complete the tasks in each category. Then write your suggested changes directly on Abby's draft.

Revising the Student Essay

THESIS STATEMENT

✔ Does the thesis statement contain the essay's controlling idea and an opinion about that idea?

✔ Does the thesis appear as the last sentence of the introduction?

1. Put brackets around the last sentence in Abby's introduction. Does it contain her dominant impression?

_____

2. Rewrite Abby's thesis statement if necessary so that it states her dominant impression as clearly as possible.

_____

_____

BASIC ELEMENTS

✔ Does the title draw in the readers?

✔ Does the introduction capture the readers' attention and build up effectively to the thesis statement?

✔ Does each body paragraph deal with a single topic?

✔ Does the conclusion bring the essay to a close in an interesting way?

1. Give Abby's essay an alternate title.

_____

2. Rewrite Abby's introduction so that it captures the readers' attention and builds up to the thesis statement at the end of the paragraph.

_____

_____

_____

_____

3. Does each of Abby's body paragraphs deal with only one topic?

_____

4. Rewrite Abby's conclusion using at least one suggestion from Part I.

_____

_____

_____

DEVELOPMENT

✔ Do the body paragraphs adequately support the thesis statement?

✔ Does each body paragraph have a focused topic sentence?

✔ Does each body paragraph contain *specific* details that support the topic sentence?

✔ Does each body paragraph include *enough* details to fully explain the topic sentence?

1. Write out Abby's thesis statement (revised, if necessary), and list her three topic sentences below it.

   Thesis statement: _____

   _____

   Topic 1: _____

   _____

   Topic 2: _____

   _____

   Topic 3: _____

   _____

2. Do Abby's topics adequately support her thesis statement?

_____

3. Does each body paragraph have a focused topic sentence?

_____

4. Does the essay draw on all five senses?

_____

5. Add at least one detail to Abby's essay that refers to another sense. You might get some ideas from the notes you made in the margins of Abby's essay when you read it. Label the detail you are adding.

   Sense: _____   Detail: _____

6. In what way does Abby's essay *show* rather than *tell* her readers about her memories of her grandfather?

   _____

   _____

   _____

UNITY

✔ Do the essay's topic sentences relate directly to the thesis statement?

✔ Do the details in each body paragraph support the paragraph's topic sentence?

1. Read each of Abby's topic sentences with her thesis statement (revised, if necessary) in mind. Do they go together?

   _____

2. Revise her topic sentences if necessary so they are directly related.

3. Drop or rewrite any of the sentences in her body paragraphs that are not directly related to their topic sentences.

ORGANIZATION

✔ Is the essay organized logically?

✔ Is each body paragraph organized logically?

1. Read Abby's essay again to see if all the paragraphs are arranged logically.

2. Move any paragraphs that are out of order.

3. Look closely at Abby's body paragraphs to see if all her sentences are arranged logically within paragraphs.

4. Move any sentences that are out of order.

COHERENCE

✔ Are transitions used effectively so that paragraphs move smoothly and logically from one to the next?

✔ Do the sentences move smoothly and logically from one to the next?

For a list of transitions, see pages 99–100.

1. Circle five transitions Abby uses.

2. Explain how two of these make Abby's essay easier to read.

_____

_____

   Now rewrite Abby's essay with your revisions.

Editing the Student Essay

SENTENCES

Subjects and Verbs
✔ Does each sentence have a main subject and verb?

For help with subjects and verbs, see Chapter 27.

1. Underline the subjects once and verbs twice in paragraphs 3 and 4 of your revision of Abby's essay. Remember that sentences can have more than one subject-verb set.

2. Does each of the sentences have at least one subject and verb that can stand alone?

_____

For help with fragments, see Chapter 28.

3. Did you find and correct Abby's fragment? If not, find and correct it now.

For help with run-togethers, see Chapter 29.

4. Did you find and correct Abby's run-together sentence? If not, find and correct it now.

Subject-Verb Agreement
✔ Do all subjects and verbs agree?

For help with subject-verb agreement, see Chapter 32.

1. Read aloud the subjects and verbs you underlined in your revision of Abby's essay.

2. Did you find and correct the subject and verb that do not agree? If not, find and correct them now.

Pronoun Agreement
✔ Do all pronouns agree with their nouns?

For help with pronoun agreement, see Chapter 36.

1. Find any pronouns in your revision of Abby's essay that do not agree with their nouns.

2. Correct any pronouns that do not agree with their nouns.

Modifiers
✔ Are modifiers as close as possible to the words they modify?

1. Find any modifiers in your revision of Abby's essay that are not as close as possible to the words they modify.

2. Rewrite sentences if necessary so that modifiers are as close as possible to the words they modify.

For help with modifier errors, see Chapter 39.

PUNCTUATION AND MECHANICS
Punctuation
✔ Are sentences punctuated correctly?

1. Read your revision of Abby's essay for any errors in punctuation.

2. Find the fragment and the run-together sentence you revised, and make sure they are punctuated correctly.

For help with punctuation, see Chapters 40–44.

Mechanics
✔ Are words capitalized properly?

1. Read your revision of Abby's essay for any errors in capitalization.

2. Be sure to check Abby's capitalization in the fragment and run-together sentence you revised.

For help with capitalization, see Chapter 45.

WORD CHOICE AND SPELLING
Word Choice
✔ Are words used correctly?

1. Find any words used incorrectly in your revision of Abby's essay.

2. Correct any errors you find.

For help with confused words, see Chapter 51.

Spelling
✔ Are words spelled correctly?

1. Use spell-check and a dictionary to check the spelling in your revision of Abby's essay.

2. Correct any misspelled words.

For help with spelling, see Chapter 52.

  Now rewrite Abby's essay again with your editing corrections.

Reading Your Own Description Essay

The first stage of revising your own writing is getting some distance on it. To accomplish this, you will apply the same reading strategy to your essay as you have to the other reading tasks in this chapter. Seeing your essay as a reading selection that you are trying to understand and respond to will help you revise and edit it efficiently and effectively.

Reading Strategy

READING CRITICALLY
Making Personal Associations with Your Own Essay

Just as you made personal associations with other readings in this chapter to help you understand what the author was saying, annotate your own writing with personal associations and sensory details that occur to you as you read. Then consider adding some of these notes to your essay to help your readers more clearly understand your experience as if they were there.

Revising and Editing Your Own Essay

You are now ready to revise and edit your own writing. Remember that revision involves reworking the content and organization of your essay while editing asks you to check your grammar and usage. Work first with the content, making sure your thoughts are fully developed and organized effectively before you correct your grammar and usage errors. At this stage, you should repeat these processes over and over until you feel you have a draft that says exactly what you want it to say. The checklists here will help you apply to your essay what you have learned in this chapter.

For Revising Peer Evaluation Forms, go to Appendix 4.

Revising Your Own Essay

THESIS STATEMENT

☐ Does the thesis statement contain the essay's controlling idea and an opinion about that idea?

☐ Does the thesis appear as the last sentence of the introduction?

1. What dominant impression are you trying to communicate in your essay?

2. Put brackets around the last sentence in your introduction. Does it contain your dominant impression?

_____

3. Rewrite your thesis statement if necessary so that it states your dominant impression as clearly as possible.

_____

BASIC ELEMENTS

☐ Does the title draw in the readers?

☐ Does the introduction capture the readers' attention and build up effectively to the thesis statement?

☐ Does each body paragraph deal with a single topic?

☐ Does the conclusion bring the essay to a close in an interesting way?

1. Give your essay a title if it doesn't have one.

_____

2. Does your introduction capture your readers' attention and build up to your thesis statement at the end of the paragraph?

_____

3. Does each of your body paragraphs deal with only one topic?

_____

4. Does your conclusion follow some of the suggestions offered in Part I?

_____

DEVELOPMENT

☐ Do the body paragraphs adequately support the thesis statement?

☐ Does each body paragraph have a focused topic sentence?

☐ Does each body paragraph contain _specific_ details that support the topic sentence?

☐ Does each body paragraph include _enough_ details to fully explain the topic sentence?

1. Write out your thesis statement (revised, if necessary), and list your topic sentences below it.

Thesis statement: _____

Topic 1: _____

Topic 2: _____

Topic 3: _____

2. Do your topics adequately support your thesis statement?

_____

3. Does each body paragraph have a focused topic sentence?

_____

4. Does your essay draw on all five senses?

_____

5. Record three details from your essay that represent three different senses. Label each example with the sense it refers to.

_____

Detail   **Sense**

_____   _____

_____   _____

_____   _____

6. Add at least one new detail to your essay. You might get some ideas from the margin notes you made on your essay when you reread it.

7. Does your essay *show* rather than *tell* readers what they need to know? Give three examples.

_____

_____

_____

UNITY

☐ Do the essay's topic sentences relate directly to the thesis statement?

☐ Do the details in each body paragraph support the paragraph's topic sentence?

1. Read each of your topic sentences with your thesis statement in mind. Do they go together?

_____

2. Revise your topic sentences if necessary so they are directly related.

3. Drop or rewrite any of the sentences in your body paragraphs that are not directly related to their topic sentences.

ORGANIZATION

☐ Is the essay organized logically?

☐ Is each body paragraph organized logically?

1. Read your essay again to see if all the paragraphs are arranged logically.

2. Refer to your answers to the development questions. Then identify your method of organization.

_____

3. Is the order you chose for your paragraphs the most effective approach to your topic?

_____

4. Move any paragraphs that are out of order.

5. Look closely at your body paragraphs to see if all the sentences are arranged logically within paragraphs.

6. Move any sentences that are out of order.

COHERENCE

☐ Are transitions used effectively so that paragraphs move smoothly and logically from one to the next?

☐ Do the sentences move smoothly and logically from one to the next?

1. Circle five transitions you use.

2. Explain how two of these transitions make your essay easier to read.

For a list of transitions, see pages 99–100.

_____

_____

Now rewrite your essay with your revisions.

Editing Your Own Essay

For Editing Peer Evaluation Forms, go to Appendix 6.

SENTENCES

Subjects and Verbs

☐ Does each sentence have a main subject and verb?

1. Underline the subjects once and verbs twice in a paragraph of your revised essay. Remember that sentences can have more than one subject-verb set.

For help with subjects and verbs, see Chapter 27.

2. Does each of your sentences have at least one subject and verb that can stand alone?

_____

For help with fragments, see Chapter 28.

3. Correct any fragments you have written.

For help with run-togethers, see Chapter 29.

4. Correct any run-together sentences you have written.

Subject-Verb Agreement

☐ Do all subjects and verbs agree?

For help with subject-verb agreement, see Chapter 32.

1. Read aloud the subjects and verbs you underlined in your revised essay.

2. Correct any subjects and verbs that do not agree.

Pronoun Agreement

☐ Do all pronouns agree with their nouns?

For help with pronoun agreement, see Chapter 36.

1. Find any pronouns in your revised essay that do not agree with their nouns.

2. Correct any pronouns that do not agree with their nouns.

Modifiers

☐ Are modifiers as close as possible to the words they modify?

For help with modifier errors, see Chapter 37.

1. Find any modifiers in your revised essay that are not as close as possible to the words they modify.

2. Rewrite sentences if necessary so that your modifiers are as close as possible to the words they modify.

PUNCTUATION AND MECHANICS

Punctuation

☐ Are sentences punctuated correctly?

For help with punctuation, see Chapters 40–44.

1. Read your revised essay for any errors in punctuation.

2. Make sure any fragments and run-together sentences you revised are punctuated correctly.

Mechanics

☐ Are words capitalized properly?

For help with capitalization, see Chapter 45.

1. Read your revised essay for any errors in capitalization.

2. Be sure to check your capitalization in any fragments or run-together sentences you revised.

WORD CHOICE AND SPELLING

Word Choice

☐ Are words used correctly?

For help with confused words, see Chapter 51.

1. Find any words used incorrectly in your revised essay.

2. Correct any errors you find.

For help with spelling, see Chapter 52.

Spelling

☐ Are words spelled correctly?

1. Use spell-check and a dictionary to check your spelling.

2. Correct any misspelled words.

To make a personal log of your grammar/usage errors, go to Appendix 7.

To make a personal log of your spelling errors, go to Appendix 8.

Now rewrite your essay again with your editing corrections.

More Helpful Hints

- **Want to make sure your sentences are complete?** A complete sentence has a subject and a verb. If you are missing either one, your sentence is a fragment and can become quite confusing to your reader. To see how to turn fragments into complete sentences, go to **Fragments** in the **Sentence Skills** module of **MyWritingLab**.

PRACTICING DESCRIPTION: FROM READING TO WRITING

This final section lets you practice the reading and writing skills you learned in this chapter. It includes two reading selections and several writing assignments on "your reading" and "your world." The section then offers guidance in peer evaluation and reflection, ending with suggestions about how to lead your instructor through a reading of your essay in ways that will benefit both of you.

Reading Workshop

Here are two essays that demonstrate good descriptive writing: "She" by Matthew Brooks Treacy describes a mother's love through the use of her hands, and "I Just Finished the Most Important Project of My Life" by Paul Martinez focuses on the joy and pain of foster care from the father's point of view. As you read, notice how the writers pull you into each experience through sensory details.

SHE
by Matthew Brooks Treacy

Focusing Your Attention

1. Think of a person from your childhood who had a special meaning for you as you were growing up. Who was this person? What was special about him or her?

2. In the essay you are about to read, the writer recounts the many sights, sounds, smells, textures, and tastes that he connects with his

mother. What sights, sounds, smells, textures, and tastes do you remember about a person who was influential in your childhood? Can you describe this person for someone who has never met him or her?

Expanding Your Vocabulary

The following words are important to your understanding of this essay. Highlight them throughout the essay before you begin to read. Then refer to this list as you come to these words in the essay.

futile: pointless (paragraph 1)

prostrate: face down (paragraph 1)

adamant: insistent (paragraph 1)

doctrine: set of guidelines (paragraph 2)

proverbial: well-known (paragraph 2)

omniscient: all-knowing (paragraph 2)

emu: an American ostrich (paragraph 3)

sporadic: erratic, random (paragraph 3)

aura: feeling (paragraph 4)

 Reading Strategy

READING CRITICALLY
Making Personal Associations with Your Reading

As you learned in this chapter, practice making connections with your reading by writing personal associations in the margins of this essay. Jot down anything that comes to mind. These notes will put your individual stamp on the essay with a set of memories that only you can recall. They will also help you understand the essay on an analytical level. Share your notes with one of your classmates.

SHE
by Matthew Brooks Treacy

1.   Mom says, "If you go a day without using your hands, you die." It's a principle that influences the way I do things. Nothing is ever futile. The most horrible chores ever devised by the devil in the days of man do not even leave me with a

gutted feeling anymore, though God knows they used to. Repainting a chicken shed or lying prostrate to the sun on a steel roof is never as bad as it sounds; you've used your hands, and at least *that's* worthwhile. My mother has always shingled lessons into my mind, leaving each one slightly raised for prying up later on. There was never a day when we didn't do some meaningless household task just to pass the time. She always used her hands. On top of an adamant refusal to learn the first thing about technology, manual labor just fits her. She used her hands when She shot the groundhog who had one of her zucchinis in its mouth. She used her hands when crunching rabbits under the blunt end of a hatchet for some of the best stew in the Western hemisphere. She used her hands to hang the stockings, even when my sister and I knew better than to believe in a fat guy in a red suit. In the past I have questioned her claim of devotion to me, but there were always ethics to be spaded out of the dirt she was normally covered in, sandy values scraping the back of my neck during a rough hug before bed. Loving me is something She has always done, but with a sharp manner that hides the tenderness I sometimes cry for.

My Mother is not a woman so much as she is a field of energy. Mom is a force, a kind of aura that only takes human form to be that much more intimidating. An order to cut the grass is not a request but an international doctrine, and She sits at the helm of an aircraft carrier just waiting for a rebellious child to give her reason for an atomic strike. Making us cut the grass is her method of control. There lies, somewhere beneath the tile of our kitchen, a proverbial bag of chores just waiting to be opened, like Pandora's Box. I am in constant fear that, one day, a refusal to mow will burst that bag wide open and spill hell into my life, so I do whatever I'm told. These responsibilities have become more of a tradition than a job, so I can't mind them; God forbid I break that custom. The sun bakes me like a scone on early August days, but smiles down on the Mother weeding eggplant and the neighbors selling lemonade under an oak. She works like a madwoman in the garden and still keeps an eye on whichever unlucky child has a job outside. When all is said and done, the yard has grown to the heavens, leaving me to give it the haircut of a lifetime under the omniscient eye from amongst the bean rows. It is a task that takes a lightyear, but after three hours in the field I'll gladly accept the neighbor's lemonade, no matter what's floating in it. The common image is me standing at attention and She a drill sergeant inspecting my work, looking for any surviving dandelion to give me away. I imagine She would love to find a single uncut weed to justify beating the shag out of me with the garden hose. But then, smiling a smile that would have wilted the grass anyway, She goes to get a beer and watch me finish off the front yard.

There are some unexplainable phenomena between the two of us. These things I've grown accustomed to but have never understood. It's all to do with her. No one else can really grasp just how weird our relationship is, because no one else has ever gone through another like it. The first clue that our mother–son bond was stronger than most was the day I came home to a chaotic scene and She immediately informed me, "Way to go baby, you let the emu out." That night I did homework in electrified silence, forcing down home-grown garden squash and awaiting her return. Finally the door screamed and I prepared for a verbal thrashing only to be greeted with a hug. Everything was forgotten. The homework lay strewn on the table and the snow fell as She unfolded a story that would eventually go down in family lore. It was not a story like the boring epics that college professors pride themselves on, but a *story*. It was like something told by five different people at Thanksgiving with sporadic interjections thrown in through mouthfuls of mashed potatoes and venison. There was a plot line, rising action, a climax, blood, and plenty of cursing. By the time she finished and I had chewed my lip raw, the escaped emu had been recaptured somehow by a turkey call and something resembling a German infantry tactic. I sat there in awe, swallowing repeatedly to wet my vocal cords back into coherence. "That's the most incredible thing I've ever heard," I managed to gasp, unable to get the image of my mom pulling a tackle on a bird from the Cretaceous period out of my mind. The amount of respect She lost for me that night was more than made up by my amazement and overwhelming love for this woman who brought down ostriches. Even being sentenced to double grass-cutting duty and cooking for a week didn't really sting that much. After all, I'd be using my hands.

4　　　So many times She would ruin my chances for fun. So many times I was caught when it seemed I could not be, and so many times I would be forced to dry dishes instead of climbing hay bales in the fields. Of course there will always be hay, and there will always be home. She will always be there weeping me away to college and willing me back with that same aura of power that surrounds her. Each time I will argue, but apparently dishes will never just dry themselves. And each time that I think I'm too tired to get up and turn off the dorm room TV, I will think of my mother and stumble over in the pitch black to use my hands at least one more time that day.

Thinking Critically About Content

1. Why are hands so important to the author?

2. Find at least one detail in this essay that represents each of the senses: sight, sound, smell, taste, touch.

3. What does the author mean when he says, "My mother is not a woman so much as she is a field of energy" (paragraph 2)?

Thinking Critically About Purpose and Audience

4. What dominant impression does the writer create in this description? Explain your answer in detail.

5. Do you think readers who have never met Treacy's mother can appreciate and enjoy this essay? Why or why not?

6. What details about the author's mother are most interesting to you? Why do you find them interesting?

Thinking Critically About Essays

7. If an essay is unified, all of its paragraphs are related to one central idea. Based on this explanation, is this essay unified? Explain your answer.

8. How does Treacy organize his ideas and observations in this essay? (Refer to pages 64–76 for information on organization.) Make a rough outline of the essay.

9. Where does Treacy use repetition to further this point? What words does he repeat most often? What effect does this have on the reader?

10. Describe as fully as possible the inner feelings of Treacy's mother from the information the author provides in this essay. Before you begin to write, you might want to review the writing process in Part I.

To keep track of your critical thinking progress, go to Appendix 1.

I JUST FINISHED THE MOST IMPORTANT PROJECT OF MY LIFE
by Paul Martinez

Focusing Your Attention

1. Think about the children you have or want to have some day. Can you describe your feelings toward them, whether they are part of your present or future?

2. The essay you are about to read describes the feelings of the father of a foster child who was placed back into her home after a year. From the father's perspective, their attachment was strong, and their parting, even though the child was returning to her original home, was very painful. Would you consider either adopting or caring for a foster child? What is your reasoning for your response?

Expanding Your Vocabulary

The following words are important to your understanding of this essay. Highlight them throughout the essay before you begin to read. Then refer to this list as you come to these words in the essay.

hyperbole: exaggeration (paragraph 1)

Denver Comic Con: convention in Denver for comic book authors (paragraph 5)

The Munsters: a TV series about a family of monsters (paragraph 14)

Batman'66: a TV series about the superhero Batman and Robin that started in 1966 (paragraph 14).

Reading
Strategy

READING CRITICALLY
Making Personal Associations with Your Reading

As you did with the previous essay, write any personal associations you make with this essay in the margins as you read. This process will give you some good insights into the author's approach to his topic and into his methods of developing his ideas. Write down anything at all that occurs to you. Then share your notes with one of your classmates.

I JUST FINISHED THE MOST
IMPORTANT PROJECT OF MY LIFE
by Paul Martinez

1   Ok, so I'm not that old. But I can safely say the title of this post is true. That's no hyperbole either. I've never been one to puff myself up more than I thought I deserved. This project isn't a book, it's no graphic novel, it's not the comic shop, it's none of those things. In fact this project you will never ever see.

2   About a year ago a little girl came to live with my wife Lauren and me. As a former foster child, I always promised myself I would take in a child in need before I created one. There are so many, kids out there who just need a taste of a normal life and might never get the chance if someone doesn't step forward and volunteer.

3   Well, last fall she came to us. She had been through a lot, but haven't they all? It was four days before her 8th birthday. Lauren and I were terrified. Who is this kid? What will she be like? Will we know how to handle her? You can imagine that going from zero kids to an 8 year old overnight is quite an adjustment. I think the first few days she was with us I barely slept. I checked on her constantly while she slept; she woke us up with nightmares and questions. We tried to get her to watch television to keep her busy, but the new world she was in wouldn't let her relax long enough to get lost in a television show.

4   We found out right away that there was no reason to worry because the little girl who came to live with us was the most amazing 8 year old I have ever met. And apologies go out to every other 8 year old who has ever crossed my path, but she was. Everyone said it. Every social worker, every therapist, everyone told us she was different. She was, and still is, a very smart and empathetic kid. Aware of your feelings, bright, positive, smart, she is all these things. I can honestly say she never had a dad in her life and I have never been one. The relationship was new to both of us. But she and I were as close as two people could be.

5   I traveled out of town a few times that year for several days at a time to do comic conventions. I called her when I was gone and let her know I was ok. She

made a welcome home banner for me when I traveled to Denver Comic Con. There was a time we thought we were going to adopt this kid. We thought she would be our daughter. And we always treated her like that because we never wanted her to feel different. She was scared about a lot of things and worried about the future.

At bed time was when we talked the most. We read comic books and Roald Dahl books. She told me she was scared—that she loved Lauren and me but missed her mom and brother terribly. I thought for a minute and said to her, "You have to think of it like a mall. (She loves going to the mall.) At the front of that mall your mom had to let go of your hand, but I picked it up. Lauren and I are going to walk with you all the way through that mall, and we won't let you go. On the other side, if your mom is waiting for you, then we'll let go when she takes your hand. But until then we won't let go. I promise. You're safe here."   6

She was so strong. She didn't want people to see her cry, but she cried a little that night and every once in a while when things got tough. We had court dates and visits. We had visits that got cancelled and court dates that got moved. I said, "Don't worry about that stuff, you just be a kid. At the end of this, you'll either end up with Lauren and me who love you very much and we'll bring your brother here too, or you'll end up back home with your Mom and you'll be even better than before because of all the stuff your mom is learning."   7

She never stopped loving her birth mom even when she started calling Lauren and me "Mom and Dad." And we never wanted her to stop loving her. We always supported their relationship and never missed appointments or phone calls. We always spoke highly of her mom and let her know she was doing whatever it took to get her little girl and boy back. Her brother was at a different home for reasons beyond our control.   8

So toward the end of that year, it became clear that this little amazing ball of awesomeness wasn't going to be staying with us much longer. We were told that everything was in place to have her and her brother return home. And then we were told a little while later that it was all going to happen a month sooner than we thought.   9

And so it happened. We packed up all of the things she had accumulated over the last year. Her new bike, her comic books, her army of stuffed animals she lined up on her bed every morning. We filled the car with it and met her mom at a local park. We were strong and showed her how happy we were for her mom and her. We told her how proud we were for her bravery and how good she had been in school during this hard year. We told her we would try to stay in touch. We couldn't promise we would because once she was home we had no say over that. No control. We no longer decided. I spent a year knowing what she wore to school every single day and what she ate at every meal. And now I couldn't even promise I would see her again.   10

Way back in the spring when I went to the Denver Comic Convention, it was the longest she and I had been apart since she came to us. It was about 10 days. When I saw her the day I came home, she was in a park with her mom. She spent some time hiding from me behind the swings as if she didn't know how to handle the situation. Then she slowly walked toward me and then ran the last several feet throwing her arms around my waist. She cried and wouldn't let go. At that time, in that moment, I was the most important person in the world to her, and that made   11 me feel like the most important person in the world. When she let go, she told me to never leave again for that long. I said "don't worry, I probably wouldn't."

12   The day in the park when I last saw her, we put all her things in her mom's car then put her in the passenger seat. We all said goodbye, but we worked hard to make it seem normal for her. Then I closed her car door and saw her looking at me with a confused look. She didn't understand when she would see me again or what I would be to her now. I had to turn away. I walked fast back to my car, and Lauren walked also. I couldn't look back and wave because I had already begun crying. I couldn't stop once I started. We just got in the car and left. I didn't want her to see me like that because she needed to be completely happy about going home and enjoy that reunion.

13   And so far, that has been the last time I saw her. She was going home, her family was being put back together. For her, her mom, and her brother, the system worked. They were going to be together again. For us, we were alone and our house seemed a thousand times more empty than when she first showed up.

14   There was a positive energy I can't describe while she was here, and then it was gone. She would tell me not to stay up too late drawing. She would watch *The Munsters* and *Batman'66* with me. We would draw together, read together. She and Lauren would have girl time and get their nails done. Her jokes would make me laugh at least once a day everyday. I could have written this post when she left, but I wasn't done yet. There was too much unknown. Too many question marks.

15   And then today, after I sent several emails requesting visits, I finally received a phone call. I wanted to respect their space and let them be a family again, so I never called unannounced. I just waited for contact from their side after I sent an email. I was in my new comic shop when the call came. I was in some kind of fantasy world I'd dreamed of since I was a child and I had to walk out the back door and stand by some trees at the back of the parking lot and get reminded of this last year that I was fighting hard to not think about. I got to speak to that little girl. Still my heart is confused as to why she's not here with us and why we're not a family. But I heard her voice, and it sounded so beautiful and so happy. She is happy; she's home; her family is complete again. I couldn't let her know I was feeling anything but happiness for her. I couldn't let her know how confused I was. All she ever wanted was to be back home again and now she was. The sadness, the pain, the loss. I couldn't tell her about any of that. I just told her how the dogs were doing. She told me about a boy at her new school that she had a crush on. And I said, "Well I hope he's a good boy!" And she said, "I'm not sure." That kid cracks me up.

16   I finally said goodbye. I remembered when she had phone visits with her mom and she refused to hang up first. She always waited in silence, staring at the phone until her mom hung up. I said goodbye, and then I heard her still there making a comment every few seconds. She would never hang up. So I finally had to press that little red button. I got off the phone and, while none of these emotions are over, the pain is not gone and who knows what the future will bring. At least I know Lauren and I got her to the other side of that mall and she is safely in her mom's hands again.

17   Foster care is not for everyone. Maybe it's not for you. Maybe it's not something you can handle; maybe it will hurt too much to get that close to someone and then to lose them. I can tell you first hand, it hurts like no feeling I've ever had. Foster care is

not for everyone. Of course, it's for the kids. It's to show them what a good life is. It's to teach them good habits that they can then take home and share with the rest of the family. It's to show them that no matter how tough things get and no matter how alone they feel that we live in a world where a stranger will say, "You can stay with me, and I won't let go of you again until you're safe."

I don't know what's next for any of us, and for now, I'm going to try not to worry about it.   18

Thinking Critically About Content

1. Why did Martinez and his wife decide to take in a foster child?

2. Find at least one detail in this essay for three different senses: seeing, hearing, touching, smelling, or tasting. Does Martinez draw on any one sense more than the others?

3. In paragraph 6, Martinez uses a reference to the mall to explain the process of foster care to his foster child. How does this comparison, called a simile, help the child understand what is happening? How does the author's second reference to the mall in paragraph 16 complete the image? Explain your answer in detail.

Thinking Critically About Purpose and Audience

4. What dominant impression does Martinez create in this essay?

5. Who do you think is Martinez's primary audience?

6. Explain your understanding of this essay's title.

Thinking Critically About Essays

7. Each paragraph of Martinez's essay describes a slightly different phase of his relationship with his foster daughter. Look at paragraph 11. What is its topics sentence? Do all the sentences in this paragraph relate to its topic sentence? Explain your answer.

8. If a paragraph is coherent, it is logical and easy to read. Often, well-chosen transitions help a writer achieve coherence. (Refer to pages 99–100 for a list of transitions.) Underline the words, phrases, and clauses Martinez uses as transitions in paragraph 16. How do these transitions help this paragraph read smoothly? Why do you think he uses more transitions at the beginning of the paragraph than near the end? Explain your answer.

9. Martinez ends his essay with a single-sentence paragraph. Is it effective for this essay? How does the last sentence tie the whole essay together?

To keep track of your critical thinking progress, go to Appendix 1.

10. Describe in detail what you think are the characteristics of a perfect child. Before you begin to write, you might want to review the writing process in Part I.

Writing Workshop

This final section gives you opportunities to apply what you have learned in this chapter to another writing assignment. This time, we provide very little prompting beyond a summary of the guidelines for writing a description essay. This section will let you demonstrate that you can go through the entire writing process on your own with only occasional feedback from your peers. Loop back into the chapter as necessary when you have questions so that this process becomes as automatic to you as possible before you move on to new material. Then pause at the end of the chapter to reflect briefly on what you have learned.

Guidelines for Writing a Description Essay

1. Decide on a dominant impression—the feeling or mood you want to communicate.
2. Decide how much of your description should be objective (factual) and how much should be subjective (personal reactions).
3. Draw on your five senses to write a good description.
4. When you describe, try to *show* rather than *tell* your readers what you want them to know.
5. Organize your description so that your readers can easily follow it.

Writing About Your Reading

1. In the first descriptive essay, Matthew Brooks Treacy describes his mother through the use of her hands. He draws on all five senses to describe her. Think of a person who is very important to you, a person who is part of your life now or who was part of your life in the past. Write a description of this person, drawing on as many of the senses as possible—seeing, hearing, touching, smelling, and tasting—so that your readers can know some aspects of this person as well as you do.

2. How close is your family? Write a description of your immediate or extended family that captures the closeness or distance you feel for one another.

3. What do you think are the most important features of a good description? Why are they important?

Writing About Your World

1. Place yourself in the scene above, and describe it in as much detail as possible. Imagine that you can see, hear, touch, smell, and taste everything in this picture. What are your sensations? How do you feel? Before you begin to write, decide on the dominant impression you want to convey. Then choose your details carefully.

2. Describe for your classmates a class environment that is ideal for you. What kind of classroom atmosphere makes you thrive? What should the people in your class understand about you as a student? What kind of instructor brings out the best in you? Why?

3. A national travel magazine is asking for honest descriptions (positive or negative) of places people have visited. The magazine is offering $100 to the writers of the essays chosen for publication. It welcomes both good experiences (like a place with a beautiful beach) and bad (like an absolutely awful hotel). In either case, remember to begin with the dominant impression you want to communicate.

4. Create your own description assignment (with the help of your instructor), and write a response to it.

Revising

Small Group Activity (5–10 minutes per writer) Working in groups of three or four, read your description essays to each other. Those listening should record their reactions on the Revising Peer Evaluation Forms in Appendix 4. After your group goes through this process, give your evaluation forms to the appropriate writers so that each writer has two or three peer comment sheets for revising.

Paired Activity (5 minutes per writer) Using the completed Peer Evaluation Forms, work in pairs to decide what you should revise in your essay. If time allows, rewrite some of your sentences, and have your partner look at them.

Individual Activity Rewrite your paper, using the revising feedback you received from other students.

Editing

Paired Activity (5–10 minutes per writer) Swap papers with a classmate, and use the Editing Peer Evaluation Form (Appendix 6) to identify as many grammar, punctuation, mechanics, and spelling errors as you can. If time allows, correct some of your errors, and have your partner look at them. Record your grammar, punctuation, and mechanics errors in the Error Log (Appendix 7) and your spelling errors in the Spelling Log (Appendix 8).

Individual Activity Rewrite your paper again, using the editing feedback you received from other students.

Reflecting on Your Writing   When you have completed your own essay, answer these six questions.

1. What was most difficult about this assignment?

2. What was easiest?

3. What did you learn about description by completing this assignment?

4. What do you think are the strengths of your description? Place a wavy line by the parts of your essay that you feel are very good.

5. What are the weaknesses, if any, of your paper? Place an X by the parts of your essay you would like help with. Write in the margins any questions you have.

6. What did you learn from this assignment about your own writing process—about preparing to write, about writing the first draft, about revising, and about editing?

MyWritingLab™   Visit Chapter 9, "Describing," in MyWritingLab, and complete the Post-test to check your understanding of the chapter's objectives.

Narrating

*"*I try to remember times in my life, incidents in which there was the dominating theme of cruelty or kindness or generosity or envy or happiness or glee. Then I select one.*"*

—MAYA ANGELOU

Because we are constantly telling other people about various events in our lives, we all know how to use narration. Think of how many times a day you tell someone about an event that happened to you: your accident on the way to school; the conversation you had at the bus stop yesterday; your strange experience at the restaurant last night. Narrating is an essential part of our lives. In fact, stories can teach us a lot about ourselves and the world around us.

Narration also plays an important role in our writing. Think about how many times we tell a story when we write—in our personal lives, in classes, and at work:

- You tell a friend in an e-mail about how you met the person you're now dating.
- On a history exam, a student summarizes the chain of events that led to the United States' entry into World War II.
- A student summarizes a short story in an English class.
- An emergency medical technician gives an account of her 911 calls for the day.
- A supervisor writes a report explaining an employee's accident on the job.

Narration, or storytelling, is an effective way of getting someone's attention by sharing thoughts or experiences. Like description, narration is sometimes used as an end in itself (for example, when you tell a friend a joke or the plot of a movie). But very often it's used in conjunction with explaining or persuading. You might start a term paper analyzing drug abuse, for example, with a brief story of one addict's life, or a lawyer might seek a "not guilty" verdict by telling the jury about the hardships his or her client suffered as a child. Basically, people use storytelling to help focus their readers' or listeners' attention.

| MyWritingLab | ## Understanding Narration |

To make sure you understand the concepts in the narration chapter, go to **MyWritingLab.com,** and choose **Narrating** in the **Essay Development** module. From there, read the **Overview,** watch the **Animation** video, and complete the **Recall, Apply,** and **Write** activities. Then check your understanding of narrative essays by taking the **Post-test.**

PREPARING TO WRITE A NARRATION ESSAY

As you learned in Chapter 8, the writing process starts most productively with reading a well-written essay and understanding how it works—both in content and in form. Learning how to read narration essays in depth gives you insight into the writing process in this particular rhetorical mode. Approaching narration analytically helps you raise your level of comprehension so you can function more successfully in college and in life. If you learn how to work with the author of a narration essay to understand how he or she makes meaning, your insights will transfer naturally to your writing. In the next few pages, you will read an effective narration essay and then answer some questions to help you discover how the essay makes its point.

Reading a Narration Essay

Jane Maher, who teaches college in New York City, wrote the following autobiographical essay to help her come to terms with the loss of her father. Can you think of a special event that taught you something important about life? What was the event? What did you learn?

Once again, using a reading strategy will increase your ability to understand all the complexities of your reading. In other words, it will help you read critically, or analytically, which will lead to analytical writing. If you read critically, you will achieve a high degree of understanding of *what* is being said and *how* it is being said, which will then naturally help you become a better writer. The reading strategy we will apply to all reading tasks in this chapter is called "thinking aloud."

READING CRITICALLY
Thinking Aloud as You Read a Professional Essay

Reading
Strategy

As we read and interpret an author's words, we absorb them on a literal level, add to them any implications the author suggests, think about how the ideas relate to one another, and keep the process going until the entire essay makes sense. These focused thoughts are what help us process the author's writing. On another level, however, we may stray from the essay in a variety of ways—thinking about chores we need to do, calls we forgot to return, and plans we are looking forward to on the weekend. These random ideas are only loosely related to the reading. As you might suspect, focused reading is more productive than random reading, but you can teach yourself to apply your stray ideas to a better understanding of the material. As you read this selection, stop and "think aloud" about what is on your mind throughout the text. Point out places that are confusing to you, connections you make, specific questions you have, related information you know, and personal experiences you associate with the text. In this way, you are coming to terms with what your mind actually does (both focused and randomly) as you read.

GIRL
by Jane Maher

I don't remember exactly when I began to be offended when my father called me, or other girls or women, "girl." I guess he always did it; at least I don't remember him ever not doing it. He'd often use it as a term of affection: "How's my girl today?" But just as often, he'd use it carelessly or callously, the way some men use the expression "sweetie." "Listen, girl," my father would say, "I make the rules around here."

Women, girls, were perceived by my father as less than men: less important, less intelligent, less capable, less in need of education or direction. In fact, for a long period of my life, I was so indoctrinated by my father's views, and by society's confirmation of those views, that I agreed with him.

But as I grew older, the term "girl" began to hurt me and make me angry. As my father became aware of my strong and growing aversion to the word, he'd use it even more often. "What's the matter," he'd ask. "You don't like it anymore when your old man calls you girl? You're my daughter; I'll call you whatever I want." Or he'd ask my mother, pretending I wasn't in the room, "What kind of daughter did you raise that she wants to become a man? Is she ashamed to be a girl?" The word took

1

2

3

on stronger and stronger connotations for me as I began to realize how permanently, and adversely, my father's attitudes had affected my life. I had been sent to an all-girls commercial high school. "Listen, girl," my father declared, "as long as you know typing and stenography, you'll never starve." College was not mentioned very much in our house. I was one of three daughters. If one of us had a date, my father would tell my mother to remind us "what can happen to a girl if she's not careful." When I got married, I heard my father joking with my uncle: "One down, two to go." We were objects to be dispensed with, burdens of no conceivable use to him.

4   This does not mean that he did not love us or care for us; for my entire childhood, he worked two jobs so that he could afford to send us away to the country every summer. But it was the terms upon which he loved and cared for us which were so distressing to me. Nor did I always get angry when he used the term. When my first daughter was born, he arrived at the hospital carrying a silver dollar he had saved in his collection for many years as a gift for her. "Now I've got four of you girls instead of three," he said, knowing that I knew at this special time he was only teasing and did not intend to hurt me.

5   I saw less and less of my father after I moved to Connecticut in 1980. He and my mother kept their house in Brooklyn but spent most of the winter months in Florida. Sometimes when I called on the phone, I could tell how happy he was to hear my voice. "Hey, girl, is that husband of yours taking as good care of you as I did?" But other times, over Thanksgiving dinner or while opening Christmas presents, he'd use the term as he had when I was young. "Girl, get me a little more coffee will you?" Or when I enrolled my daughter in an expensive private school: "Why spend money you don't have to, girl? She's just going to get married the way you did." I'd keep my countenance at those times; I had grown wise to my father—I wouldn't give him the satisfaction of showing my anger. That's not to say he didn't keep trying: "So now you like it when your old man calls you girl, huh? You're finally getting wise to the fact that men aren't so bad to have around when you need something."

6   And I suspected that secretly he was proud of me. Soon after I got married, I returned to college, part-time, in the evening, and graduated magna cum laude. By then, both of my daughters were in school, so I earned my master's degree from Columbia University, again part-time. It was my father who picked up my daughters from the school bus stop on the day I took my comprehensive exam. When I began to teach part-time at a local community college, my father asked my mother, again pretending I wasn't in the room, "if there was a girl around here who thought her father was going to start calling her Professor."

7   My father had always had a heart condition, exacerbated by twenty-two years as a New York City fireman, two packs of cigarettes a day, and my mother's delicious Italian cooking. When he suddenly became seriously ill, my mother got him home from Florida and into a hospital in Brooklyn in less than 24 hours. But it still wasn't soon enough. My father died before they could perform a triple bypass and before I got to say goodbye to him.

8   I had left Connecticut at nine in the morning, intending to wait out the surgery with my mother and to be with my father when he awoke. Instead, when I arrived at the hospital, one of my sisters and my mother were in a small, curtained-off section

of the intensive care unit being told by a busy, preoccupied young resident that my father had experienced very little discomfort before he died. It sounded too pat, too familiar, too convenient to me. I was overcome with the fear that my father had been alone that entire morning, that no one in that overcrowded municipal hospital had even known that he was dead until they arrived to prepare him for surgery.

They left us alone to say goodbye to him, but I was so concerned over my mother's anguish that I didn't take the time I should have to kiss him or even to touch his forehead. A nurse came in and suggested, gently, that it was time to leave. She was right, of course; another moment and my mother would have collapsed.   9

I thanked the nurse and asked her, nonchalantly, if she knew exactly when my father had died, secretly convinced that she didn't have an answer, that he had been alone all morning. "I didn't see him this morning," she replied, "but I'll get the nurse who did."   10

A young, pretty nurse appeared several minutes later. "My shift is over," she said, "but I was waiting around to see the family."   11

"Was he in pain?" my mother asked.   12

"No, not at all. He even teased me a bit. I remember his exact words. 'Go take care of the patients who need you, girl,' he said. 'I'm perfectly fine.'"   13

I wasn't exactly fine, but I have never felt more comforted in my life than when I heard that word.   14

Discovering How This Essay Works

To help you discover the elements that make this an effective narration essay so you can use them in your own writing, answer the following questions in as much detail as possible.

1. All the details in Jane Maher's essay lead to one main point. What is that point?

   _____

   _____

2. Maher answers some basic questions in her essay. Record at least two questions she answers.

   _____

   _____

3. In your opinion, which two details of Maher's are most vivid? What makes them so vivid?

   _____

   _____

4. Maher's essay becomes very exciting at times. Where are those moments in the essay? How does she build excitement?

    _____

    _____

5. How does Maher organize her essay? List her general topics; then go to pages 64–76 in Chapter 6 to identify her method of organization.

    _____

    _____

    Method of organization: _____

WRITING A NARRATION ESSAY

Now that you have read and studied a professional essay, you will be writing one of your own. This section will help you create a draft of your essay that you will then revise and edit in the next section of this chapter. It will give you guidelines for reading a writing assignment, generating ideas and choosing a specific topic, and writing an effective narration essay. To get the most out of this section, you should take notes and make lists you can draw from when you write a draft of your essay at the end of this section.

Reading the Prompt

The first step in writing any essay is making sure you understand the writing assignment or "prompt." The assignment attempts to "prompt" you to respond to a specific issue or question. The more clearly you understand the prompt, the better paper you will create. Applying the chapter reading strategy to your writing assignment is a good way to read the prompt actively rather than passively.

Reading
Strategy

READING CRITICALLY
Thinking Aloud as You Read the Prompt

As you read this prompt, stop and "think aloud" about how your mind processes these directions. Point out places that are confusing to you, connections you can make, specific questions you have, related information you know, and personal experiences you associate with the prompt.

In this way, you are hearing (and letting others hear) what your mind does (both focused and randomly) as you read. Then, underline the key words in this assignment. Finally, start a conversation with the assignment by responding to the questions at the beginning of the prompt.

Writing Prompt

What are some events in your life that have taught you important lessons? Does one event stand out in your mind? What lesson did it teach you? Choose an event that taught you something important, and write a narration essay explaining this incident and the lesson you learned. Follow the guidelines in this chapter to develop your essay.

MyWritingLab
Complete this Writing Prompt assignment in MyWritingLab.

Thinking About the Prompt

Before you choose a topic, you should generate as many thoughts and ideas as you can so you have many options to choose from. We have all learned important lessons from various events in our lives. Over time, we find that some lessons are more worthwhile than others. What events in your life have taught you something important? What specific lessons did you learn? Choose an event from your life, and use one or more of the prewriting techniques covered in Chapter 5 to generate as many ideas as possible about this event and the lesson it taught you.

Guidelines for Writing a Narration Essay

Narrating involves telling a story about an experience—one of yours or someone else's. When you write a narrative essay, you focus on a particular event and make a specific point about it. You should provide enough detail so your readers can understand as completely as possible what your experience was like. Below are some guidelines to help you make your narrative interesting. After each guideline is an explanation of how it functions in the reading selection at the beginning of this chapter so you can actually see how the element works in an essay before you apply it to your own writing.

1. **Make sure your essay has a point**. The most important feature of a narrative essay is that it makes a point. Simply recording your story step by step is a boring exercise for both writer and reader. Writing an account of your walk to class in the morning might not be particularly interesting. But the walk becomes interesting when something important or significant happens on the way. An event is significant if it helps both writer and reader understand something about themselves, about other

people, or about the world we live in. If you can complete one of the following sentences, you will produce a focused narrative:

This essay shows that . . .

This essay teaches us that . . .

In the Reading: In Jane Maher's essay, the narrator focuses on the pain she felt growing up when her father referred to her as a "girl." She thought the term was degrading until she understood, after he died, that it was really a term of endearment. Maher is able to communicate the process of growing up through her experience with this one word. Her essay teaches us that the relationship between words and emotions is complex.

In Your Writing: Now think about the essay you are going to write. What do you think its focus should be? What will be its main point? Make any notes to yourself that will remind you of your decisions here.

2. **Use the five Ws and one H to construct your story**. The five Ws and one H are the six questions—*Who? What? When? Where? Why?* and *How?*—that journalists use to make sure they cover all the basic information when they write a news story. These questions can help you come up with details and ideas for a well-developed narrative essay. You should make sure your essay answers each of these questions in detail.

In the Reading: When you look at Maher's narrative essay again, you can see that she covered the answers to all these questions:

Who was involved? Maher, her father, her mother, and the nurses
What was the central problem? Maher was offended by her father's use of the word *girl*.
When did this story take place? As Maher was growing up
Where were they? At home
Why was Maher offended? Because she thought the word *girl* was degrading to her as a person and to other females
How did the author learn from this event? She finally understood that her father's use of *girl* wasn't as offensive as she thought it was.

Because Maher covers all these basic details, the reader can appreciate her full story and understand its significance.

In Your Writing: Jot down your answers to the following questions in reference to the essay you will write.

Who? _____

What? _____

When? _____

Where? _____

Why?_____

How?_____

3. **Develop your narrative with vivid details**. Your readers will be able to imagine the events in your narrative essay if you provide specific details. In fact, the more specific your details, the more vivid your essay will become. These details should develop the ideas you generated with the six journalistic questions. At the same time, you should omit any irrelevant details that don't support your thesis statement.

In the Reading: Look again at Maher's essay. In this narrative, the author provides many specific details about the narrator: She is a girl whose father thinks girls are less important than boys; he calls her *girl*; this term starts to bother the narrator as she is growing up; she gets married and moves to Connecticut; she has two daughters; she gets her master's degree at Columbia University and starts teaching at a local community college; and her father dies of a heart attack. The amount of detail in Maher's essay helps us participate in her narrative.

In Your Writing: Look back at your prewriting notes, and see if you have enough details to make your essay interesting and lively. Add any other details that come to your mind at this point.

4. **Build excitement in your narrative with careful pacing**. To be most effective, narration should prolong the exciting parts of a story and shorten the routine facts that simply move the reader from one episode to another. If you were robbed on your way to work, for example, a good narrative describing the incident would concentrate on the traumatic event itself rather than on such boring details as what you had for breakfast or what clothes you were wearing. One writer might say, "I was robbed this morning." A better writer would draw out the exciting parts: "As I was walking to work around 7:30 this morning, a huge, angry-looking man ran up to me, thrust a gun into my stomach, and demanded my money, my new wristwatch, my credit cards, and my pants—leaving me broke and embarrassed." The details themselves tell the story.

In the Reading: Maher reveals the details in her story through some of her father's quotations that bothered her: "Listen, girl, I make the rules around here"; "Listen, girl, as long as you know typing and stenography, you'll never starve." She feels frustrated and belittled by her father, even as an adult: "Hey, girl, is that husband of yours taking as good care of you as I did?" Finally, she works through the hurtfulness when her father dies. At this point, Maher draws out the search for the nurse who could tell her if her father died alone. The pacing of her story holds our interest throughout the essay.

In Your Writing: Return to your prewriting notes, and highlight those details that you will prolong in your narrative to heighten the excitement.

Why did you choose these particular details? Do you think your readers will also find them interesting?

5. **Organize your narration so that your readers can easily follow it.** Most narrative essays follow a series of actions through time, so they are organized chronologically, or according to a time sequence. Once you choose the details you will use, you should arrange them so that your story has a clear beginning, middle, and end. If you add clear, logical transitions, such as *then*, *next*, *at this point*, and *suddenly*, you will guide your readers smoothly through your essay from one event to the next.

In the Reading: Jane Maher organizes her essay chronologically. It moves through time from her childhood to her high school days to marriage and motherhood as her father raises her, retires, and grows old. In other words, the two main characters—Maher and her father—move through normal life events. She guides her readers through her essay with such transitions as *in fact*, *as I grew older*, *when*, *sometimes*, and *soon*.

In Your Writing: Review chronological organization in Chapter 5, and then look at your prewriting list of details and examples. How should you organize the details in your story to make your point as effectively as possible? Rewrite your list of details a few different ways to help you make your decision.

Writing a Draft of Your Essay

Now is the time to collect all your "think aloud" observations, your notes, your prewriting exercises, and your lists as you prepare to write the first draft of your essay. You might also want to review the professional essay, the writing assignment, and the chapter guidelines for writing a narration essay, along with your notes and lists to get you started. At this point, don't think about revising or editing; just get your thoughts about the writing assignment down on paper.

MyWritingLab   **Helpful Hints**

- **Need help figuring out the point of your narration?** Creating a strong thesis statement is important in any essay because it provides a focus for your paper. If you need help creating yours, check out the video and activities for **Thesis Statement** in the **Essay Development** module in **MyWritingLab.**

- **Having trouble developing your ideas?** Developing your ideas with specific examples helps your readers fully understand what you want to say. For help developing your own ideas, go to **Developing** and Organizing a Paragraph in **The Craft of Writing** module in **MyWritingLab.**

- **Trying to make your point clear to the reader?** Narration essays often rely on good description of the subjects being discussed. For help with description, visit **Describing** in the **Essay Development** module of **MyWritingLab.**

REVISING AND EDITING

You are now ready to begin revising and editing your draft. This section will lead you through the guidelines for revising and editing narration essays in reference to two writing samples: another student's essay and your own essay. Revising and editing are often much easier to do with someone else's writing, which is why we begin this stage with a writing sample from another student. If you can see some of the strengths and weaknesses in this essay, you might be able to identify areas for improvement in your own writing. So you will be reviewing the chapter guidelines by revising and editing another student's writing before applying the same guidelines to your own writing.

Reading a Student Narration Essay

We will begin by using our chapter reading strategy on a student essay. In an essay about a dramatic incident, student writer Tommy Poulos tells a story that taught him an important lesson in life. Thinking aloud about the reading and about any thoughts or ideas that cross your mind as you read will help you understand the essay on your own terms so you can then figure out how to improve it.

READING CRITICALLY
Thinking Aloud as You Read the Student Essay

Reading
Strategy

As you read Tommy's essay, stop and "think aloud," saying what is on your mind as you read. Note places that are confusing to you, connections that you make, specific questions you have, related information you know, and personal experiences you associate with the ideas in the essay.

"My Brother"

1   My family and I lead a fairly quiet life. My parents go to work, and my brother and I go to school. We never make headlines with sports events or science fairs. We essentially live a normal American life out of the spotlight. It was quite a shock, then, when a lot of attention was focused on our family.

2   My brother, Wayne, was driving on a highway that is nicknamed "The Death Loop." It got its name because it's a two-lane highway that loops around the city, and many people have died because of drivers who take too many chances and cause head-on collisions. One afternoon, Wayne saw a woman's car wrecked into a guardrail with her passenger side of the car completely smashed in. The driver's side was mangled, and my brother could tell the woman inside was in trouble. Wayne didn't think twice about running up to help them. She was badly injured, but my brother knew not to move her!

3   The woman had not been wearing her seat belt. Her car was too old to have an airbag. She had obviously hit her head because she had blood gushing from a gaping wound in her forehead. She was conscious, so my brother sat with her, trying to keep her calm and awake. He kept asking her questions like if she had any children? Two other cars stopped, and my brother remembers telling one man to call 911. Wayne stayed with the woman until the paramedics arrived.

4   Wayne left the scene after giving a statement to the police. Later, he heard from the local newspapers and news stations that his heroic actions had saved the woman. In these stories, the woman's husband said he believed his wife was still alive because she had a guardian angel keeping her awake. Even the paramedics said Wayne probably kept her alive. By keeping her awake. In public, Wayne acts very humble, but in private, he is loving the attention.

5   Now my brother is the local hero. Our house used to be quiet, but since Wayne's act of heroism, it's become Grand Central Station. Everyone wants to talk to Wayne. I'm happy for him. But most of all, I'm glad Wayne realizes the importance of seat belts. He used to be macho and say seat belts were too uncomfortable to wear. Now he won't leave the driveway until everyone has buckled their seat belts. Perhaps the woman will save Wayne's life as well.

Revising and Editing the Student Essay

This essay is Tommy's first draft, which now needs to be revised and edited. First, apply the Revising Checklist to the content of Tommy's draft. When you are satisfied that his ideas are fully developed and well organized, use the Editing Checklist to correct his grammar and mechanics errors. Answer the questions, and complete the tasks in each category. Then write your suggested changes directly on Tommy's draft.

Revising the Student Essay

THESIS STATEMENT

✔ Does the thesis statement contain the essay's controlling idea and an opinion about that idea?

✔ Does the thesis appear as the last sentence of the introduction?

1. Put brackets around the last sentence in Tommy's introduction. Does it contain his main point? Does it express his opinion about that point?

_____

_____

2. Rewrite Tommy's thesis statement if necessary so that it states his main point and an opinion about that main point.

_____

_____

BASIC ELEMENTS

✔ Does the title draw in the readers?

✔ Does the introduction capture the readers' attention and build up effectively to the thesis statement?

✔ Does each body paragraph deal with a single topic?

✔ Does the conclusion bring the essay to a close in an interesting way?

1. Give Tommy's essay an alternate title. Also drop the quotation marks, since original titles should not be in quotation marks.

_____

2. Rewrite Tommy's introduction so that it captures the readers' attention and builds up to the thesis statement at the end of the paragraph.

_____

_____

_____

3. Does each of Tommy's body paragraphs deal with only one topic?

_____

4. Rewrite Tommy's conclusion using at least one suggestion from Part I.

_____

_____

_____

DEVELOPMENT

✔ Do the body paragraphs adequately support the thesis statement?

✔ Does each body paragraph have a focused topic sentence?

✔ Does each body paragraph contain *specific* details that support the topic sentence?

✔ Does each body paragraph include *enough* details to fully explain the topic sentence?

1. Write out Tommy's thesis statement (revised, if necessary), and list his three topic sentences below it.

   Thesis statement: _____

   _____

      Topic 1: _____

      _____

      Topic 2: _____

      _____

      Topic 3: _____

      _____

2. Do Tommy's topics adequately support his thesis statement?

   _____

3. Does each body paragraph have a focused topic sentence?

   _____

4. Add more specific information to two of Tommy's supporting details. You might get some ideas from the notes you made in the margins of Tommy's essay as you read aloud.

5. Add two new details to Tommy's essay that support his main idea. You might get some ideas from the margin notes you made on Tommy's essay as you read aloud.

UNITY

✔ Do the essay's topic sentences relate directly to the thesis statement?

✔ Do the details in each body paragraph support the paragraph's topic sentence?

1. Read each of Tommy's topic sentences, with his thesis statement (revised, if necessary) in mind. Do they go together?

   _____

2. Revise his topic sentences if necessary so they are directly related.

3. Drop or rewrite any of the sentences in his body paragraphs that are not directly related to their topic sentences.

ORGANIZATION

✔ Is the essay organized logically?

✔ Is each body paragraph organized logically?

1. Read Tommy's essay again to see if all the paragraphs are arranged chronologically.

2. Move any paragraphs that are out of order.

3. Look closely at Tommy's body paragraphs to see if all his sentences are arranged logically within paragraphs.

4. Move any sentences that are out of order.

COHERENCE

✔ Are transitions used effectively so that paragraphs move smoothly and logically from one to the next?

✔ Do the sentences move smoothly and logically from one to the next?

1. Circle five words or phrases Tommy repeats.

2. Explain how two of these words or phrases make Tommy's essay easier to read.

   _____

   _____

 Now rewrite Tommy's essay with your revisions.

Editing the Student Essay

SENTENCES

Subjects and Verbs

✔ Does each sentence have a main subject and verb?

For help with subjects and verbs, see Chapter 27.

1. Underline the subjects once and verbs twice in paragraph 4 of your revision of Tommy's essay. Remember that sentences can have more than one subject-verb set.

2. Does each of the sentences have at least one subject and verb that can stand alone?

For help with fragments, see Chapter 28.

3. Did you find and correct Tommy's fragment? If not, find and correct it now.

Subject-Verb Agreement

✔ Do all subjects and verbs agree?

For help with subject-verb agreement, see Chapter 32.

1. Read aloud the subjects and verbs you underlined in your revision of Tommy's essay.

2. Correct any subjects and verbs that do not agree with each other.

Pronoun Agreement

✔ Do all pronouns agree with their nouns?

For help with pronoun agreement, see Chapter 36.

1. Find any pronouns in your revision of Tommy's essay that do not agree with their nouns.

2. Did you find and correct the two pronouns that do not agree with their nouns? If not, find and correct them now.

Modifiers

✔ Are modifiers as close as possible to the words they modify?

For help with modifier errors, see Chapter 39.

1. Find any modifiers in your revision of Tommy's essay that are not as close as possible to the words they modify.

2. Rewrite sentences if necessary so that modifiers are as close as possible to the words they modify.

PUNCTUATION AND MECHANICS

Punctuation

✔ Are sentences punctuated correctly?

For help with punctuation, see Chapters 40–44.

1. Read your revision of Tommy's essay for any errors in punctuation.

2. Find the fragment you revised, and make sure it is punctuated correctly.

3. Did you find and correct Tommy's two other punctuation errors?

Mechanics

✔ Are words capitalized properly?

1. Read your revision of Tommy's essay for any errors in capitalization.

2. Be sure to check Tommy's capitalization in the fragment you revised.

For help with capitalization, see Chapter 45.

WORD CHOICE AND SPELLING

Word Choice

✔ Are words used correctly?

1. Find any words used incorrectly in your revision of Tommy's essay.

2. Correct any errors you find.

For help with confused words, see Chapter 51.

Spelling

✔ Are words used correctly?

1. Use spell-check and a dictionary to check the spelling in your revision of Tommy's essay

2. Correct any misspelled words.

 Now rewrite Tommy's essay again with your editing corrections.

For help with spelling, see Chapter 52.

Reading Your Own Narration Essay

As you return to your own writing, you should start the revision process by creating distance between you and your essay. To accomplish this, read your essay with the same reading strategy you have applied to other reading tasks in this chapter. Reading your essay as a reading selection that you need to comprehend and respond to will help you revise and edit your own work efficiently and effectively.

READING CRITICALLY
Thinking Aloud as You Read Your Own Essay

 Reading Strategy

As you begin to rework your essay, use the same technique you did in your reading. "Think aloud" as you read your own writing, saying what is on your mind as if you are the reader. Point out places that are confusing, connections you make, specific questions you have, related information you know, and personal experiences you associate with the essay. Be aware of what your mind is doing (both focused and randomly) as you read.

Revising and Editing Your Own Essay

You are now ready to revise and edit your own writing. Remember that revision involves moving ideas around and developing them as fully as you can for your readers while editing is the process of finding and correcting grammar and usage errors. When you get your ideas where you want them, then you should proofread and correct your grammar and usage errors. At this stage, you should repeat these processes until your essay achieves the purpose you set for it. The checklists here will help you apply to your essay what you have learned in this chapter.

For Revising Peer Evaluation Forms, go to Appendix 4.

Revising Your Own Essay

THESIS STATEMENT

☐ Does the thesis statement contain the essay's controlling idea and an opinion about that idea?

☐ Does the thesis appear as the last sentence of the introduction?

1. What is the main point of your essay?

   _____

2. What is your opinion about the main point?

   _____

3. Put brackets around the last sentence in your introduction. Does it contain your main point and your opinion about that point?

   _____

4. Rewrite your thesis statement if necessary so that it states your main point and your opinion.

BASIC ELEMENTS

☐ Does the title draw in the readers?

☐ Does the introduction capture the readers' attention and build up effectively to the thesis statement?

☐ Does each body paragraph deal with a single topic?

☐ Does the conclusion bring the essay to a close in an interesting way?

1. Give your essay a title if it doesn't have one.

   _____

2. Does your introduction capture your readers' attention and build up to your thesis statement at the end of the paragraph?

   _____

3. Does each of your body paragraphs deal with only one topic?

_____

4. Does your conclusion follow some of the suggestions offered in Part I?

_____

DEVELOPMENT

☐ Do the body paragraphs adequately support the thesis statement?

☐ Does each body paragraph have a focused topic sentence?

☐ Does each body paragraph contain *specific* details that support the topic sentence?

☐ Does each body paragraph include *enough* details to fully explain the topic sentence?

1. Write out your thesis statement (revised, if necessary), and list your topic sentences below it.

   Thesis statement: _____

   Topic 1: _____

   Topic 2: _____

   Topic 3: _____

2. Do your topics adequately support your thesis statement?

_____

3. Does each body paragraph have a focused topic sentence?

_____

4. Record at least one detail you use in response to each journalistic question.

   Who? _____

   What? _____

   When? _____

   Where? _____

   Why? _____

   How? _____

5. Add at least two new details to your essay that support your main idea.

UNITY

☐ Do the essay's topic sentences relate directly to the thesis statement?

☐ Do the details in each body paragraph support its topic sentence?

1. Read each of your topic sentences with your thesis statement in mind. Do they go together?

    _____

2. Revise your topic sentences if necessary so they are directly related.

3. Drop or rewrite any of the sentences in your body paragraphs that are not directly related to their topic sentences.

ORGANIZATION

☐ Is the essay organized logically?

☐ Is each body paragraph organized logically?

1. Read your essay again to see if all the paragraphs are arranged logically.

2. Refer to your answers to the development questions. Then identify your method of organization:

    _____

3. Is the order you chose for your paragraphs the most effective approach to your topic?

    _____

4. Move any paragraphs that are out of order.

5. Look closely at your body paragraphs to see if all the sentences are arranged logically within paragraphs.

6. Move any sentences that are out of order.

COHERENCE

☐ Are transitions used effectively so that paragraphs move smoothly and logically from one to the next?

☐ Do the sentences move smoothly and logically from one to the next?

1. Circle five words or phrases you repeat.

2. Explain how two of these make your essay easier to read.

    _____

    _____

 Now rewrite your essay with your revisions.

Editing Your Own Essay

For Editing Peer Evaluation Forms, go to Appendix 6.

SENTENCES

Subjects and Verbs

☐ Does each sentence have a main subject and verb?

1. Underline the subjects once and verbs twice in a paragraph of your revised essay. Remember that sentences can have more than one subject-verb set.

For help with subjects and verbs, see Chapter 27.

2. Does each of your sentences have at least one subject and verb that can stand alone?

3. Correct any fragments you have written.

4. Correct any run-together sentences you have written.

For help with fragments, see Chapter 28.

For help with run-togethers, see Chapter 29.

Subject-Verb Agreement

☐ Do all subjects and verbs agree?

1. Read aloud the subjects and verbs you underlined in your revised essay.

2. Correct any subjects and verbs that do not agree.

For help with subject-verb agreement, see Chapter 32.

Pronoun Agreement

☐ Do all pronouns agree with their nouns?

1. Find any pronouns in your revised essay that do not agree with their nouns.

For help with pronoun agreement, see Chapter 36.

2. Correct any pronouns that do not agree with their nouns.

Modifiers

☐ Are modifiers as close as possible to the words they modify?

1. Find any modifiers in your revised essay that are not as close as possible to the words they modify.

For help with modifier errors, see Chapter 37.

2. Rewrite sentences if necessary so that your modifiers are as close as possible to the words they modify.

PUNCTUATION AND MECHANICS

Punctuation

☐ Are sentences punctuated correctly?

1. Read your revised essay for any errors in punctuation.

For help with punctuation, see Chapters 40–44.

2. Make sure any fragments and run-together sentences you revised are punctuated correctly.

Mechanics

☐ Are words capitalized properly?

For help with capitalization, see Chapter 45.

1. Read your revised essay for any errors in capitalization.

2. Be sure to check your capitalization in any fragments or run-together sentences you revised.

WORD CHOICE AND SPELLING

Word Choice

☐ Are words used correctly?

For help with confused words, see Chapter 51.

1. Find any words used incorrectly in your revised essay.

2. Correct any errors you find.

Spelling

☐ Are words spelled correctly?

For help with spelling, see Chapter 52.

To make a personal log of your grammar/usage errors, go to Appendix 7.

To make a personal log of your spelling errors, go to Appendix 8.

1. Use spell-check and a dictionary to check your spelling.

2. Correct any misspelled words.

Now rewrite your essay again with your editing corrections.

MyWritingLab | **More Helpful Hints**

- **Do you need some reminders about revising?** Narration essays require a strong point of view and voice. So you need to pay special attention to point of view and voice as you revise. Go to **Revising the Essay** in the **Essay Development** module of **MyWritingLab** for some helpful guidelines.

- **Are you stuck on who did what in your narration essay?** To create a good story, you need to rely on strong verbs. Go back through your essay to make sure your verbs capture what you are trying to communicate. Go to **Subjects and Verbs** in the **Basic Grammar** module of **MyWritingLab** for some guidance and practice in creating strong verbs.

- **Do all your subjects and verbs agree?** Your subjects must agree with their verbs. This means singular subjects have singular verbs, and plural subjects have plural verbs. To double-check your essay, see **Subject-Verb Agreement** in the **Sentence Skills** module of **MyWritingLab**.

PRACTICING NARRATION: FROM READING TO WRITING

This final section gives you opportunities to practice the reading and writing skills you learned in this chapter. It includes two reading selections and several writing assignments on "your reading" and "your world." The section then guides you through effective peer evaluation and reflection exercises that teach you how to mark your essay in preparation for your instructor to read it.

Reading Workshop

Here are two essays that illustrate good narrative writing: "The Sanctuary of School," in which Lynda Barry tells a story about using her school as an escape from her home life, and "Childhood" by Alice Walker, which talks about the crops the author has planted. As you read, notice how the writers cover the journalistic questions and use vivid descriptive details to pull you into their narratives, making the main point of the essays all the more meaningful.

THE SANCTUARY OF SCHOOL
by Lynda Barry

Focusing Your Attention

1. Can you recall a time in your life when you felt particularly lonely or afraid? Write down as many facts, impressions, and memories as you can recall about that period of your life.

2. In the essay you are about to read, the writer describes a person who had a lasting impact on her. Do you think you have ever had such an important impact on someone that he or she would write an essay about you? Have you had such an impact on more than one person? Who are these people? What would they say about you in their recollections?

Expanding Your Vocabulary

The following words are important to your understanding of this essay. Start a vocabulary log of your own by recording any words you don't understand as you read. When you finish reading the essay, write down what you think the words mean. Then check your definitions in the dictionary.

sanctuary: safe place (title)

nondescript: not distinctive (paragraph 7)

monkey bars: playground equipment (paragraph 8)

breezeway: covered passage between two buildings (paragraph 13)

Reading
Strategy

READING CRITICALLY
Thinking Aloud as You Read

As you learned at the beginning of this chapter, "think aloud" as you read. Interject personal references and focused ideas into your oral reading of the essay. The clearer you make your connections, the more deeply you will understand the essay. Read the essay at least two times. Discuss with a classmate the types of ideas you had as you read (focused or random). Which one of you did more focused reading?

THE SANCTUARY OF SCHOOL
by Lynda Barry

1   I was 7 years old the first time I snuck out of the house in the dark. It was winter, and my parents had been fighting all night. They were short on money and long on relatives who kept "temporarily" moving into our house because they had nowhere else to go.

2   My brother and I were used to giving up our bedroom. We slept on the couch, something we actually liked because it put us that much closer to the light of our lives, our television.

3   At night when everyone was asleep, we lay on our pillows watching it with the sound off. We watched Steve Allen's mouth moving. We watched Johnny Carson's mouth moving. We watched movies filled with gangsters shooting machine guns into packed rooms, dying soldiers hurling a last grenade, and beautiful women crying at windows. Then the sign-off finally came, and we tried to sleep.

4   The morning I snuck out, I woke up filled with a panic about needing to get to school. The sun wasn't quite up yet, but my anxiety was so fierce that I just got dressed, walked quietly across the kitchen, and let myself out the back door.

5   It was quiet outside. Stars were still out. Nothing moved, and no one was in the street. It was as if someone had turned the sound off on the world.

6   I walked the alley, breaking thin ice over the puddles with my shoes. I didn't know why I was walking to school in the dark. I didn't think about it. All I knew was the feeling of panic, like the panic that strikes kids when they realize they are lost.

7   That feeling eased the moment I turned the corner and saw the dark outline of my school at the top of the hill. My school was made up of about 15 nondescript portable classrooms set down on a fenced concrete lot in a rundown Seattle neighborhood, but it had the most beautiful view of the Cascade Mountains. You could see them from anywhere on the playfield, and you could see them from the windows of my classroom—Room 2.

I walked over to the monkey bars and hooked my arms around the cold metal. 8
I stood for a long time just looking across Rainier Valley. The sky was beginning to
whiten, and I could hear a few birds.

In a perfect world, my absence at home would not have gone unnoticed. I would 9
have had two parents in a panic to locate me, instead of two parents in a panic to locate
an answer to the hard question of survival during a deep financial and emotional crisis.

But in an overcrowded and unhappy home, it's incredibly easy for any child to 10
slip away. The high levels of frustration, depression, and anger in my house made
my brother and me invisible. We were children with the sound turned off. And for us,
as for the steadily increasing number of neglected children in this country, the only
place where we could count on being noticed was at school.

"Hey there, young lady. Did you forget to go home last night?" It was Mr. 11
Gunderson, our janitor, whom we all loved. He was nice and he was funny and he was
old with white hair, thick glasses, and an unbelievable number of keys. I could hear
them jingling as he walked across the playfield. I felt incredibly happy to see him.

He let me push his wheeled garbage can between the different portables as he 12
unlocked each room. He let me turn on the lights and raise the window shades, and I
saw my school slowly come to life. I saw Mrs. Holman, our school secretary, walk into
the office without her orange lipstick on yet. She waved.

I saw the fifth-grade teacher, Mr. Cunningham, walking under the breezeway 13
eating a hard roll. He waved.

And I saw my teacher, Mrs. Claire LeSane, walking toward us in a red coat and call- 14
ing my name in a very happy and surprised way, and suddenly my throat got tight and my
eyes stung and I ran toward her crying. It was something that surprised both of us.

It's only thinking about it now, 28 years later, that I realize I was crying from 15
relief. I was with my teacher, and in a while I was going to sit at my desk, with my
crayons and pencils and books and classmates all around me, and for the next six
hours I was going to enjoy a thoroughly secure, warm, and stable world. It was a world
I absolutely relied on. Without it, I don't know where I would have gone that morning.

Mrs. LeSane asked me what was wrong, and when I said, "Nothing," she seem- 16
ingly left it at that. But she asked me if I would carry her purse for her, an honor
above all honors, and she asked if I wanted to come into Room 2 early and paint.

She believed in the natural healing power of painting and drawing for troubled 17
children. In the back of her room there was always a drawing table and an easel with
plenty of supplies, and sometimes during the day she would come up to you for what
seemed like no good reason and quietly ask if you wanted to go to the back table and
"make some pictures for Mrs. LeSane." We all had a chance at it—to sit apart from the
class for a while to paint, draw, and silently work out impossible problems on 11×17
sheets of newsprint.

Drawing came to mean everything to me. At the back table in Room 2, I learned 18
to build myself a life preserver that I could carry into my home....

By the time the bell rang that morning, I had finished my drawing, and Mrs. 19
LeSane pinned it up on the special bulletin board she reserved for drawings from the
back table. It was the same picture I always drew—a sun in the corner of a blue sky
over a nice house with flowers all around it.

Thinking Critically About Content

1. Notice how the writer describes herself and her brother as "children with the sound turned off" (paragraph 10) and their environment "as if someone had turned the sound off on the world" (paragraph 5). Is this an effective image? Why? What effect does it have on you? What does it tell you about Lynda Barry's childhood?

2. Why do you think the writer used warm and vivid details to describe the arrival of school employees (paragraphs 11 through 16)? How does this description affect you, compared with the description of her home life?

3. Did this essay make you compare your own childhood to Lynda Barry's?

Thinking Critically About Purpose and Audience

4. What do you think Barry's purpose is in writing this narrative essay? Explain your answer.

5. What readers do you think would most understand and appreciate this recollection?

6. In your opinion, why doesn't the writer tell us more about her parents' problems?

Thinking Critically About Essays

7. Describe in a complete sentence the writer's point of view in this essay.

8. How does Barry organize the details in this essay? Is this an effective order?

9. Explain Barry's title for this essay.

To keep track of your critical thinking progress, go to Appendix 1.

10. Explain in detail how this essay would be different if it were written by Lynda Barry's parents.

CHILDHOOD
by Alice Walker

Focusing Your Attention

1. When were you filled with wonder over some event or daily activity? What did you find exceptional about it?

2. In the essay you are about to read, the writer describes a time when she shared some details of her farming life with her daughter. Why might this exchange be important to Walker?

Expanding Your Vocabulary

The following words are important to your understanding of this essay. Start a vocabulary log of your own by recording any words you don't understand as you read. When you finish reading the essay, write down what you think the words mean. Then check your definitions in the dictionary.

harvest: produce (paragraph 2)

Finn: type of potato (paragraph 2)

Peruvian purples: type of potato (paragraph 2)

humus: organic soil (paragraph 2)

overmatured: overly ripe (paragraph 2)

chard: leafy vegetable (paragraph 3)

kale: type of cabbage (paragraph 3)

dasher: agitator for stirring (paragraph 4)

Chardonnay: type of white wine (paragraph 5)

collards: cooked greens (paragraph 5)

exemplary: exceptional (paragraph 6)

preverbal: before using words (paragraph 6)

protruding: jutting out (paragraph 7)

READING CRITICALLY
Thinking Aloud as You Read

As you did with the previous essay, "think aloud" as you read this essay by Alice Walker. This process will give you some good insights into the author's approach to her topic. Write down any new ideas that you discover. As you continue to read critically, you will deepen your understanding of this essay. Read the essay at least two times. Discuss with a classmate the types of ideas you had as you read (focused or random). Which one of you did more focused reading?

CHILDHOOD
by Alice Walker

One evening my daughter came to pick me up from the country; I had been   1
expecting her for several hours. Almost as soon as she came through the door I asked
if she knew how potatoes look before they are dug out of the ground. She wasn't sure.
Then I will show you in the morning before we head back to the city, I told her.

2   I had begun to harvest my potato crop the day before. In the spring I planted five varieties: my favorite, yellow Finn, but also Yukon gold, Peruvian purple, Irish white, and red new. Even though the summer had been chilly and there was morning shade from the large oak at the front of the garden, the potatoes came up quickly and developed into healthy plants. José, who helps me in the garden, had shoveled an extra collar of humus around each plant, and I was delighted as each of them began to bloom. It had been years since I planted potatoes. I planted them in the garden I'd previously devoted to corn because I have a schedule that often means I am far away from my garden at just the time my corn becomes ripe. Having sped home to my garden three years in a row to a plot of over-matured, tasteless corn, I decided to plant potatoes instead, thinking the worst that could happen, if I were delayed elsewhere, would be a handful of potatoes nibbled by gophers or moles.

3   I had been dreading going back to the city, where I had more things to do than I cared to think about; I sat in the swing on the deck thinking hard about what would be my last supper in the country. I had bought some green peas from the roadside stand a few miles from my house, there were chard and kale flourishing a few steps from my door, and I had brought up corn from a small hopeful planting in a lower garden. Tasting the corn, however, I discovered it had, as I'd feared, lost its sweetness and turned into starch. Then I remembered my potatoes! I grabbed a shovel, went out to the garden, and began to dig. The experience I had had digging the potatoes, before turning them into half of a delicious meal, was one I wanted my daughter to know.

4   After boiling them, I ate my newly dug potatoes, several small yellow Finns and two larger Peruvian purples, with only a dressing of butter. Organic butter with a dash of sea salt—that reminded me of the butter my mother and grandmother used to make. As I ate the mouth-watering meal, I remembered them sitting patiently beside the brown or creamy white churn, moving the dasher up and down in a steady rhythmic motion, until flecks of butter appeared at the top of the milk. These flecks grew until eventually there was enough butter to make a small mound. We owned a beautiful handcrafted butter press. It was sometimes my job to press its wooden carving of flowers into the hardening butter, making a cheerful and elegant design.

5   In the morning, just before packing the car for the ride to the city, I harvested an abundance of Chardonnay grapes, greenish-silver and refreshingly sweet; a bucket of glistening eggplant; an armful of collards and chard and kale; some dark green and snake-like cucumbers, plus a small sack of figs and half a dozen late-summer peaches. Then I took my daughter out to the neat rows of potatoes, all beginning to turn brown. Using the shovel to scrape aside the dirt, I began to reveal, very slowly and carefully, the golden and purple potatoes that rested just beneath the plants. She was enchanted. It's just like...it's just like...she said. It's just like finding gold, I offered with glee. Yes! she said, her eyes wide.

6   Though my daughter is now in her thirties, her enthusiasm reminded me of my own when I was probably no more than three. My parents, exemplary farmers and producers of fine vegetables in garden and field, had enchanted me early in just this same way. As I scraped dirt aside from another potato plant and watched as my daughter began to fill her skirt with our treasure, I was taken back to a time when

I was very young, perhaps too young even to speak. The very first memory I have is certainly pre-verbal; I was lifted up by my father or an older brother, very large and dark and shining men, and encouraged to pick red plums from a heavily bearing tree. The next is of going with my parents, in a farm wagon, to a watermelon patch that in memory seems to have been planted underneath pine trees. A farmer myself now, I realize this couldn't have been true. It is likely that to get to the watermelon patch we had to go through the pines. In any case, and perhaps this was pre-verbal as well, I remember the absolute wonder of rolling along in a creaky wooden wagon that was pulled by obedient if indifferent mules, arriving at a vast field, and being taken down and placed out of the way as my brothers and parents began to find watermelon after watermelon and bring them back, apparently, as gifts for me! In a short time the wagon was filled with large green watermelons. And there were still dozens more left to grow larger in the field! How had this happened? What miracle was this?

As soon as they finished filling the wagon, my father broke open a gigantic melon right on the spot. The "spot" being a handy boulder as broad as a table that happened to reside there, underneath the shady pines, beside the field. We were all given pieces of its delicious red and thirst-quenching heart. He then carefully, from my piece, removed all the glossy black seeds. If you eat one of these, he joked, poking at my protruding tummy, a watermelon just like this will grow inside you.   7

It will? My eyes were probably enormous. I must have looked shocked.   8

Everyone laughed.

If you put the seed into the ground, it will grow, said an older brother, who could   9
never bear to see me deceived. That's how all of these watermelons came to be here.
We planted them.

It seemed too wonderful for words. *Too incredible to be believed.* One thing
seemed as astonishing as another. That a watermelon could grow inside of me, if I   10
ate a seed, and that watermelons grew from seeds put in the ground!

When I think of my childhood at its best, it is of this magic that I think. Of   11
having a family that daily worked with nature to produce the extraordinary, and yet
they were all so casual about it and never failed to find my wonderment amusing.   12
Years later I would write poems and essays about the way growing up in the country
seemed the best of all possible worlds, regardless of the hardships that made getting by year to year, especially for a family of color in the South half a century ago,
a heroic affair.

Thinking Critically About Content

1. What characterizes Walker's country life?

2. Why did the author change her corn crop to potatoes?

3. Why was Walker dreading her return to the city?

Thinking Critically About Purpose and Audience

4. Explain your understanding of the writer's purpose in this narrative.
   What role does her daughter play in this essay?

5. Who do you think Walker's primary audience is?

6. Why does Walker marvel at the country life and the process of farming?

Thinking Critically About Essays

7. Describe Walker's point of view in this essay. Does it change throughout the piece? If so, in what ways?

8. Walker uses various details to demonstrate her wonderment throughout this essay. Which details communicate this feeling most clearly to you?

9. Walker ends her narrative with the phrase *a heroic affair*. What exactly is she referring to? Is this an effective conclusion for this narrative?

To keep track of your critical thinking progress, go to Appendix 1.

10. Tell this same story from the daughter's perspective

Writing Workshop

This final section asks you to apply what you have learned in this chapter to another writing assignment. This time, we provide very little prompting beyond a summary of the guidelines for writing a narration essay. This section will let you demonstrate that you can go through the entire writing process on your own with only occasional feedback from your peers. Loop back into the chapter as necessary when you have questions so that this process becomes as automatic to you as possible before you move on to new material. Then pause at the end of the chapter to reflect briefly on what you have learned.

Guidelines for Writing a Narration Essay

1. Make sure your essay has a point.
2. Use the five *W*s and one *H* to construct your story.
3. Develop your narrative with vivid details.
4. Build excitement in your narrative with careful pacing.
5. Organize your narration so that your readers can easily follow it.

Writing About Your Reading

1. In "The Sanctuary of School," Lynda Barry recalls the way her school and her teachers provided a sanctuary, a place where she could escape from the problems of home. Write an essay in which you recall a place, a person, or an event that made you feel safe, secure, and welcome.

2. We all deal with excitement and surprise in different ways. Explain the expressions of wonderment you have noticed. Do these expressions

vary with age? Write a narrative essay focusing on various levels of excitement you have observed.

3. What do you think are the most important features of a good story? Why are they important? What effect do they have on you?

Writing About Your World

1. Place yourself in the scene above, and write a narrative about what is happening. How did you get here? Why are you here? Where are you going from here? Be sure to decide on a main point before you begin to write.

2. Your old high school has asked you, as a graduate, to submit an essay to the newsletter recalling a job or volunteer experience you enjoyed. The editors want to inform current high school students about options for volunteer and paid work. Your purpose is to tell your story in enough interesting detail so that you convince the current high school students that the job you had is worth looking into.

3. Your college class is putting together a collection of essays that explain how classmates decided to go to their college. What happened first? When did you decide? What helped you decide? What activities or people influenced your decision the most? Tell your story in vivid detail.

4. Create your own narration assignment (with the help of your instructor) and write a response to it.

Revising

Small Group Activity (5–10 minutes per writer) Working in groups of three or four, read your narration essays to each other. Those listening should record their reactions on the Revising Peer Evaluation Forms in Appendix 4. After your group goes through this process, give your evaluation forms to the appropriate writers so that each writer has two peer comment sheets for revising.

Paired Activity (5 minutes per writer) Using the completed Peer Evaluation Forms, work in pairs to decide what you should revise in your essay. If time allows, rewrite some of your sentences, and have your partner look at them.

Individual Activity Rewrite your paper, using the revising feedback you received from other students.

Editing

Paired Activity (5–10 minutes per writer) Swap papers with a classmate, and use the Editing Peer Evaluation Form (Appendix 6) to identify as many grammar, punctuation, mechanics, and spelling errors as you can. If time allows, correct some of your errors, and have your partner look at them. Record your grammar, punctuation, and mechanics errors in the Error Log (Appendix 7) and your spelling errors in the Spelling Log (Appendix 8).

Individual Activity Rewrite your paper again, using the editing feedback you received from other students.

Reflecting on Your Writing When you have completed your own essay, answer these six questions.

1. What was most difficult about this assignment?

2. What was easiest?

3. What did you learn about narration by completing this assignment?

4. What do you think are the strengths of your narration? Place a wavy line by the parts of your essay that you feel are very good.

5. What are the weaknesses, if any, of your paper? Place an X by the parts of your essay you would like help with. Write in the margins any questions you have.

6. What did you learn from this assignment about your own writing process—about preparing to write, about writing the first draft, about revising, and about editing?

MyWritingLab™ Visit Chapter 10, "Narrating," in MyWritingLab, and complete the Post-test to check your understanding of the chapter's objectives.

Illustrating

*"*When I began to write, I found it was the best way to make sense out of my life.*"*

—JOHN CHEEVER

Giving examples to make a point is a natural part of communication. For example, if you are trying to demonstrate how much time you waste, you can cite the fact that you're on Facebook about four hours every day. Or to tell your friends how much fun you are having, you might say, "College is great because no one tells me what to do or when to go to bed. I am completely on my own." The message is in the examples you choose.

We also use examples every day to make various points in our writing. Think about the following situations that take place in our personal lives, at school, and at work.

- In a letter to your parents, you tell them how hard you are studying in college by giving them examples of your weekend study schedule.
- For a psychology course, a student gives examples of gestures, facial expressions, and posture in a paper on nonverbal communication.
- A student answers a sociology exam question by giving examples to show how children are integrated into society.
- A human resource director of a large company writes a memo on sexual harassment in the workplace, including examples of inappropriate behavior.
- The owner of a catering business writes a brochure listing examples of dinners available in different price ranges.

An example is an **illustration** of the point you want to make. Well-chosen examples, then, are the building blocks of an illustration essay.

You draw examples from your experience, your observations, and your reading. They help show—rather than tell—your readers what you mean, usually by supplying concrete details (what you see, hear, touch, smell, or taste) to support abstract ideas (such as faith, hope, understanding, and love), by providing specifics ("I like chocolate") to explain generalizations ("I like sweets"), and by giving definite references ("Turn left at the second stoplight") to clarify vague statements ("Turn left in a few blocks").

Not only do examples help make your point, but they also add interest to your writing. Would you like to read an essay stating that being a server in a restaurant is a lot harder than it looks? Or would you be more interested in reading an essay describing what it is like serving too many tables, carrying heavy trays, taking the wrong order to a table, and dealing with rude customers? The first statement *tells*, but vivid examples *show* your readers the point you want to make.

MyWritingLab

Understanding Illustration

To test your knowledge of illustrating, go to **MyWritingLab.com,** and choose **Illustrating** in the **Essay Development** module. For this topic, read the **Overview,** watch the **Animation** video, and complete the **Recall, Apply,** and **Write** activities. Then check your understanding of illustrating by taking the **Post-test.**

PREPARING TO WRITE AN ILLUSTRATION ESSAY

For our purposes in this text, beginning to write starts with reading. Reading a good illustration essay can help you write a good illustration essay if you understand how the model essay works—in content and in structure. Reading and writing are actually two halves of a whole process. For example, if you can see how a writer is accomplishing his or her purpose in your reading, you will be more likely to use that same strategy effectively in your own writing. Using these strategies critically or analytically is especially important for success in college and beyond. This section will guide you to higher levels of thinking as you learn to use illustration. In the next few pages, you will read an effective illustration essay and then answer some questions to help you discover how the essay accomplishes its purpose.

Reading an Illustration Essay

In her essay "Chantways," Lori Arviso Alvord uses examples to explain the difficulties involved in blending two cultures—Caucasian and Native American—within her profession. Are you part of an environment that makes an effort to blend more than one culture, or do you know someone who is? Which features of the cultures are similar? Which are different? Have you ever studied another culture? What did you learn?

Applying a strategy to your reading will help you achieve a deep understanding of the material. In other words, it will help you read critically or analytically. If you read critically, you will then understand your reading on this level and be able to write critically as well. Reading critically, or analytically, lets you discover not only *what* the author is saying but also *how* the author is saying it. The strategy you will apply to all reading tasks in this chapter involves dividing the essay into logical sections, or "chunks," as you read.

READING CRITICALLY
Chunking a Professional Essay

Reading Strategy

Reading an illustration essay critically means looking closely at it to discover what its purpose is and how it is structured to make its point. To understand how this essay works, circle the main idea or thesis. Then draw horizontal lines throughout the essay to separate the various topics Alvord uses to support her thesis. These lines may or may not coincide with paragraph breaks. Finally, in the margins, give each "chunk" a label or name that makes sense to you. Be prepared to explain the divisions you make.

CHANTWAYS
by Lori Arviso Alvord

In many places in the world when a person is ill, a song is sung to heal. For this to be effective, that person must let the song sink into her body and allow it to penetrate to even the cellular level of her being. In a sense, she must breathe it in.

1

A song, in physical terms, is an action made of breath and sound. It is made by the vibrations of air across a section of membranes in the throat, which are then shaped by the placement of the tongue and mouth. That is a literal description of singing, but of course there is more, much more. A song is also made from the mind, from memory, from imagination, from community, and from the heart. Like all things, a song may be seen in scientific terms or in spiritual terms. Yet neither one alone is sufficient; they need each other to truly represent the reality of the song. Singing comes from that misty place where human physiology, feeling, and spirit collide. It can even be, for some people, a holy act, a religious act, an act with great power.

2

3   Today's medical environment provides more healing options than ever for a person who becomes sick. CAT scans and MRIs picture the inside of the human body with astonishing detail; dangerous, invasive surgery has been made commonplace; and intricate operations are now performed with lasers. New drugs with capabilities formerly unimagined are being discovered every day. The Human Genome Project is mapping our DNA from prehistoric times to the present, giving us a better understanding of the evolution of genetic disorders and opening the door to the possibility of someday being able to manipulate the human genetic strand and create "better" human beings.

4   Yet another type of medicine is also being practiced on our planet. It is one that involves not only the body but the mind and the spirit; it involves not only the person but her family, her community, and her world. It involves song.

5   The notion of singing a person to wellness and health may sound strange. You may think it unusual of me, a trained physician, even to mention it. But I am not talking about a New Age or alternative treatment. I am speaking of the medicine ways of my tribe, the Navajo, where a singer is called in when someone is sick. As part of the cure, they perform a "sing" or ceremony, called a chantway. The Beauty Way, the Night Chant, the Mountain Way: different kinds of songs cure different kinds of illnesses. A Shooting Way ceremony might be used to cure an illness thought to have been caused by a snake, lightning, or arrows; a Lifeway may cure an illness caused by an accident; an Enemyway heals an illness believed to be caused by the ghosts of a non-Navajo. There even are songs for mental instability.

6   Not long ago, I learned that Navajos are not the only people on earth to recognize the power of the human voice. In places in Africa the people sing to broken bones in order to mend them. Yet the power of a song lies not in a tested, quantifiable, and clinical world, and it will not be written about in *The New England Journal of Medicine*. It will not be discussed at meetings of the American Medical Association. Many physicians, good ones, frown at the very mention of it.

7   Yet one afternoon, at the hospital where I worked as a surgeon in Gallup, New Mexico, singing was going on at the bedside of Charlie Nez. As I stood in a doorway watching the medicine man leave, I was surprised to see the elderly man who had stirred little in the preceding days, sit up straighter, and look attentive. I glanced at his chart: his heart rate was steady, and his blood pressure had stabilized. There was a new red flush of circulation in his cheeks.

8   Charlie Nez was being treated with chemotherapy, radiation, and surgery for an advanced cancer. I know this because I was one of the doctors participating in his treatment. I had performed surgery on his colon to remove a tumor.

9   But this treatment was not the entirety of the medicine he received. As I stood in the doorway listening to the song of the medicine man who stood beside him, his voice rising and falling in a familiar range of tones, I saw a minor miracle. In Charlie's eyes, for the very first time since I'd met him, was hope.

10   Any physician will tell you that unless a dying patient has hope and emotional strength, the will to live, a doctor can do little to save him. Watching that hope come back into Charlie Nez's eyes, I realized something else: it would take both medicines to help heal this patient. The only surprising thing about this realization of the two sides of medicine was that it had taken me so long to comprehend this duality, this twoness.

Discovering How This Essay Works

To help you discover the elements that make this an effective illustration essay so you can use them in your own writing, answer the following questions in as much detail as possible.

1. What main idea do you think Alvord is trying to communicate in this essay?

   _____

   _____

2. List two examples from the essay that support this main idea.

   _____

   _____

3. List two more examples from your own experience that would support Alvord's main idea.

   _____

   _____

4. In your opinion, does Alvord include enough examples to make her point? Explain your answer.

   _____

   _____

5. How is Alvord's essay arranged? List some of her examples in the order they appear; then go to pages 64–76 in Chapter 6 to identify her method of organization.

   _____

   _____

   _____

   _____

   Method of organization: _____

Writing an Illustration Essay

Now that you have studied a professional essay, you will be writing one of your own. This section will guide you through the process of writing a first draft that you will then revise and edit in the next section of this chapter. You will learn how to read a writing assignment closely and carefully, generate ideas and choose a topic, and use the chapter guidelines to write an effective illustration essay. Throughout this section, you should take notes and make lists so you can use them when you write a draft of your essay at the end of this section.

Reading the Prompt

Understanding the writing assignment or "prompt" is an important first step in the writing process itself. An assignment "prompts" you to react to a specific issue or question. The more thoroughly you understand the prompt, the better paper you will create. So you want to learn how to read the essay assignment interactively. Applying the chapter reading strategy to your writing prompt is a good way to grasp what the assignment is asking you to do.

Reading Strategy

READING CRITICALLY
Chunking the Prompt

As you read this prompt, draw horizontal lines to separate the various parts of this assignment, and use the margins to label the parts you have created. These will be very small sections because the assignment is short, but this activity will help you dissect the prompt so you understand it as thoroughly as possible. Then underline the directions that are essential for completing this assignment. Finally, start thinking about the prompt by responding to the questions within the assignment.

MyWritingLab
Complete this Writing Prompt assignment in MyWritingLab.

Writing Prompt

Do you enjoy new experiences? How do you generally react to them? Write an essay explaining your reactions to something new that you tried. Was it planned or unplanned? Did it affect you in positive ways? In negative ways? Or were the outcomes mixed? What did you learn from this experience?

Thinking About the Prompt

Before you concentrate on a single topic, you should generate as many ideas as you can so you have several ideas to choose from. When did you last try something new in your life? Was it difficult? Did you plan this new experience, or did it just happen? Do you like new experiences, or do you prefer keeping your life routine? Use one or more of the prewriting strategies you learned in Chapter 5 to recall several times you tried something new. Then think about the positive and negative aspects of trying new experiences. What value do they have in your life? What are the disadvantages of trying something new?

Guidelines for Writing an Illustration Essay

In the world of visual arts, a good illustrator is someone who makes an image or an idea come alive with the perfect drawing. The same principle applies in writing: Someone who uses illustrations, or examples, effectively can make an essay or other piece of writing come alive. Moreover, in college, most essay exam questions are based on illustration—finding the best examples to support your main point. Here are some guidelines to help you use examples effectively. As you think about the topic you have chosen in response to the prompt above, read the following guidelines, and continue to make lists and notes you will use when you write your draft. After each guideline is an explanation of how it functions in the reading selection at the beginning of this chapter so you can actually see how the element works in an essay before you apply it to your own writing.

1. **State your main point and your opinion about that point in the last sentence of your introduction.** Write a thesis statement that clearly and plainly states the main idea of your essay, and place it at the end of your introduction. This is the controlling idea of your essay and should consist of a limited subject and your opinion about that subject. You will explain this main point through the examples you furnish in the following body paragraphs.

In the Reading: In the sample essay, Alvord's introduction is two paragraphs long. She expresses her main point in the last sentence of the second paragraph: "[Singing] can even be, for some people, a holy act, a religious act, an act with great power." She introduces this idea as the focus of her essay, including her opinion ("an act with great power"), and then explains it with examples. Through her examples, the author is arguing for the treatment of mind, body, and spirit with the addition of "chantways" to traditional medical practices.

In Your Writing: Make sure the essay you write includes a thesis statement that consists of a limited subject and your opinion about that subject. Write a tentative thesis statement for your essay that captures the main point you want to make about your reactions to new experiences. Then revise it as you develop your essay.

2. **Choose examples that are relevant to your point**. In an illustration essay, examples serve as the writer's explanation. Well-chosen examples are an essay's building blocks. To help make your point, your examples must be directly related to your main idea. Irrelevant examples are distracting and cause readers to lose their train of thought. Your readers will appreciate the point you are making not because you tell them what to think but because you show them with relevant examples what you are trying to say. Keep in mind, too, that the more specific your examples are, the more likely your readers are to agree with your main idea.

Finding relevant examples is a fairly easy task. The best examples often come from your own experiences and observations. You can also draw examples from your reading—books, newspapers, and magazines. In addition, the Internet is a good place to find examples for an illustration essay.

In the Reading: Alvord's essay uses two different types of illustrations to develop her main idea. In paragraph 5, she catalogs the types of songs that Navajos call on to cure specific illnesses. Then, in paragraph 7, Alvord relates the example of Charles Nez to further her point. All her examples focus on the power of song over illness, making her essay coherent and unified.

In Your Writing: Look at the examples in your prewriting notes, and check those that support the point you want to make. Cross out those that are not related to your main idea.

3. **Choose examples your readers can identify with**. To do this, you need to know as much as possible about your audience. Once you know who your readers are, you can tailor your examples to them. In this way, your readers are most likely to follow your line of reasoning. Suppose, for instance, that you want your parents to finance an off-campus apartment for you. You are not likely to make your point by citing examples of European universities that do not provide any student housing, because this is not an idea American parents would identify with. Instead, you should furnish illustrations that address your specific situation.

In the Reading: Alvord's essay was first published in an autobiography for the general public, so she chose examples that a diverse group of people would relate to. She knew that many of these readers would have dealt with health problems and would probably identify with a discussion of cures. This singular focus keeps the attention of her readers for her entire essay and helps them see her point of view by the end of the essay.

In Your Writing: In a brief paragraph, describe the intended audience for your essay. Then look once again at your prewriting notes, and check those items that this group of people will understand best. Finally, add any other details or examples that will be especially effective with this particular group.

4. **Use a sufficient number of examples to make your point**. Nobody has a set formula for determining the perfect number of examples because that depends on the point you are trying to make. Sometimes several short examples will make your point best. Or perhaps three or four fairly detailed examples—each in its own body paragraph—work best. At other times, the most effective way to develop an essay is with a single, extended example. Usually, however, three or four examples are sufficient. If you are in doubt whether to add another example or more vivid details, you should probably do so. Most students err on the side of using too few examples or not adding enough detail to their examples.

In the Reading: For her first set of examples in paragraph 5, Alvord names six different chantways or "sings" that are used to treat patients with various illnesses or medically related problems. Later, in paragraph 7, she adds a more fully developed illustration to show how traditional medicine and nontraditional chantways can work together to promote healing and wellness. The combination of short examples followed by one extended scenario gives Alvord's essay variety and makes it interesting. Overall, she furnishes enough examples so that we understand the significance of the point she is making.

In Your Writing: Do you have enough examples in your prewriting notes to develop a good essay? If not, add some additional illustrations to your notes that will help prove your point. It is always better to provide too many rather than too few examples.

5. **Organize your examples to make your point in the clearest, strongest way**. When you have gathered enough relevant examples, you are ready to organize them into an essay. Most illustration essays are organized from general to particular (from a general statement—the thesis—to specific examples that support the general statement), from one extreme to another, or chronologically (according to a time sequence).

The examples themselves must also be organized within their paragraphs in some logical way—chronologically, spatially, or by extremes. Which example should come first? Second? Last? The simple act of arranging examples can help you and your readers make sense of an experience or idea.

In the Reading: Alvord's first set of examples that name chantways and explain how they are used in the healing process progresses from less to more serious, ending with a condition thought to involve ghosts that seems fairly difficult to treat. The author's final example is a real-life story of how chantways can work together with traditional medicine to give a cancer patient new hope. For every point Alvord makes, she provides an example. Overall, her organization is from one extreme to another.

In Your Writing: How should you organize your examples? Put your details in the order you think will most effectively accomplish your purpose. Is this the most effective method of organization to prove your main point? Move the items around until you are satisfied with their order.

Writing a Draft of Your Essay

Now is the time to collect all your chunking, your notes, your prewriting exercises, and your lists as you set out to write the first draft of your essay. In preparation for writing, you might also want to review the professional essay, the writing assignment, and the chapter guidelines, along with your notes and lists. At this point, don't think about revising or editing; just get your thoughts about the writing assignment down on paper.

Helpful Hints

- **Not sure if all your paragraphs have topic sentences?** Topic sentences are the controlling ideas of your paragraphs; in addition, each one helps support your thesis statement. If you need help with these important sentences, see **The Topic Sentence** in **The Craft of Writing** module of **MyWritingLab.**

REVISING AND EDITING

Now that you have written a first draft, you are ready to deal with revising and editing. This section will guide you through the process of revising and editing illustration essays in reference to two writing samples: another student's essay and your own essay. Revising and editing are often much easier to do with someone else's writing, which is why we begin this stage with a writing sample from another student. If you can see some of the strengths and weaknesses in another person's essay, you might be able to locate areas for improvement in your own writing. So you will be reviewing the chapter guidelines by revising and editing another student's writing before applying the same guidelines to your own writing.

Reading a Student Illustration Essay

We will begin by using our chapter reading strategy on a student essay. In the following essay, student writer Taleah Trainor uses examples to explain her relationship with Murphy's Law. Chunking this essay as you read it will help you understand the structure of the essay and figure out how to improve the content and form.

Reading
Strategy

READING CRITICALLY
Chunking the Student Essay

As you read this draft of Taleah's essay, circle the main idea or thesis. Then draw horizontal lines throughout the essay to separate the various examples Taleah uses to support her thesis. These lines may or may not coincide with paragraph breaks. Finally, write yourself notes in the margins to show how each example relates to the thesis statement. Be prepared to explain the divisions you make.

Murphy's Law

Murphy's Law: If something can go wrong, it will. I have always been familiar   1
with the concept of this law, but never from actual experience. It was not until
the summer before my first year in college that different events taught me about
Murphy's Law.

The first event was when my father informed me that on our family trip to   2
Washington, D.C. we would be using my car. Since I had made previous plans I was
not bubbling with enthusiasm. I had 14 "fun-filled" days in D.C. And to top it all
off, on the way home from D.C., my car decided to have a breakdown between two
Louisiana towns. Louisiana has a really long stretch of highway that driver's hate.
People feel like they're on it forever. Luckily, my father had AAA, our delay was short.

This particular instance had familiarized me with Murphy's Law, and for the re-   3
mainder of the summer, I began to notice it every time I turned around. At first it was
little things like catching the flu just hours before a date. After a while, it turned into
bigger hassles, like getting flat tires on the way to job interviews. I prayed my luck
would take a turn for the better rather then the worse.

Murphy showed up again on August 29, when I left my hometown to travel   4
to my new school. Having to entrust my 397-mile journey to an old AAA map, I
pictured getting sidetracked onto an out-of-the-way farm road leading me to an
uncharted town. But I did not get lost until arriving at the infamous "traffic circle"
in my new home town. Realizing my highway map was of know use in town, I franti-
cally looked around and happened to catch a glimpse of the "I ♥ Bulldogs" bumper
sticker plastered on the car in front of me. I said to myself, "Now how many cars
could have that sticker?" I convinced myself that I was in luck and that the car
in front of me was headed toward campus. I decided to follow it. After arriving in
a gruesome alley, which accurately resembled the pictures I had seen of a Third
World country, I came to the conclusion the car was not headed toward campus but
probably to the local chicken fights. Pulling in to the nearest Texaco station, directions were given to me. Three service stations later, their I was, at my new dorm on
campus. Once again, I knew that Murphy's Law had decided to play with me.

I realized Murphy's Law was becoming a permanent part of my life. If something   5
in my life could possibly go wrong, Murphy would be there to make sure of it. I had
finally come to the conclusion that Murphy, and I would be friends for life—unless,
of course, something went wrong.

Revising and Editing the Student Essay

This essay is Taleah's first draft, which now needs to be revised and
edited. First, apply the Revising Checklist to the content of Taleah's draft.
When you are satisfied that her ideas are fully developed and well organized, use the Editing Checklist to correct her grammar and mechanics errors. Answer the questions, and complete the tasks in each category. Then
write your suggested changes directly on Taleah's draft.

Revising the Student Essay

THESIS STATEMENT

✔ Does the thesis statement contain the essay's controlling idea and an opinion about that idea?

✔ Does the thesis appear as the last sentence of the introduction?

1. Put brackets around the last sentence in Taleah's introduction. Does it introduce her main point? Does it include her opinion about that point?

_____

2. Rewrite Taleah's thesis statement if necessary so that it states her main point and her opinion about that point.

_____

_____

_____

BASIC ELEMENTS

✔ Does the title draw in the readers?

✔ Does the introduction capture the readers' attention and build up effectively to the thesis statement?

✔ Does each body paragraph deal with a single topic?

✔ Does the conclusion bring the essay to a close in an interesting way?

1. Give Taleah's essay an alternate title.

_____

2. Rewrite Taleah's introduction so that it captures the readers' attention and builds up to the thesis statement at the end of the paragraph.

_____

_____

_____

3. Does each of Taleah's body paragraphs deal with only one topic?

_____

4. Rewrite Taleah's conclusion using at least one suggestion from Part I.

_____

_____

_____

DEVELOPMENT

✔ Do the body paragraphs adequately support the thesis statement?

✔ Does each body paragraph have a focused topic sentence?

✔ Does each body paragraph contain *specific* details that support the topic sentence?

✔ Does each body paragraph include *enough* details to fully explain the topic sentence?

1. Write out Taleah's thesis statement (revised, if necessary), and list her three topic sentences below it.

   Thesis statement: _____

   _____

   Topic 1: _____

   _____

   Topic 2: _____

   _____

   Topic 3: _____

   _____

2. Do Taleah's topics adequately support her thesis statement?

   _____

3. Does each body paragraph have a focused topic sentence?

   _____

4. Are Taleah's examples specific?

   _____

   Add another more specific detail to one of the examples in her essay.

5. Does she offer enough examples to make her point?

   _____

   Add at least one new example to strengthen Taleah's essay.

UNITY

✔ Do the essay's topic sentences relate directly to the thesis statement?

✔ Do the details in each body paragraph support the paragraph's topic sentence?

1. Read each of Taleah's topic sentences with her thesis statement (revised, if necessary) in mind. Do they go together?

   _____

2. Revise her topic sentences if necessary so they are directly related.

3. Drop or rewrite the two sentences in paragraph 2 that are not directly related to their topic sentence.

ORGANIZATION

✔ Is the essay organized logically?

✔ Is each body paragraph organized logically?

1. Read Taleah's essay again to see if all the paragraphs are arranged logically.

2. Move any paragraphs that are out of order.

3. Look closely at Taleah's body paragraphs to see if all her sentences are arranged logically within paragraphs.

4. Move any sentences that are out of order.

COHERENCE

✔ Are transitions used effectively so that paragraphs move smoothly and logically from one to the next?

✔ Do the sentences move smoothly and logically from one to the next?

For a list of transitions, see pages 99–100.

For a list of pronouns, see pages 496–497.

1. Circle five transitions, repetitions, synonyms, or pronouns Taleah uses.

2. Explain how two of these make Taleah's essay easier to read.

_____

_____

Now rewrite Taleah's essay with your revisions.

Editing the Student Essay

SENTENCES

Subjects and Verbs

✔ Does each sentence have a main subject and verb?

For help with subjects and verbs, see Chapter 27.

1. Underline the subjects once and verbs twice in paragraph 2 of your revision of Taleah's essay. Remember that sentences can have more than one subject-verb set.

2. Does each of the sentences have at least one subject and verb that can stand alone?

_____

3. Did you find and correct Taleah's run-together sentence? If not, find and correct it now.

For help with run-togethers, see Chapter 29.

Subject-Verb Agreement
✔ Do all subjects and verbs agree?

1. Read aloud the subjects and verbs you underlined in your revision of Taleah's essay.

For help with subject-verb agreement, see Chapter 32.

2. Correct any subjects and verbs that do not agree.

Pronoun Agreement
✔ Do all pronouns agree with their nouns?

1. Find any pronouns in your revision of Taleah's essay that do not agree with their nouns.

For help with pronoun agreement, see Chapter 36.

2. Correct any pronouns that do not agree with their nouns.

Modifiers
✔ Are modifiers as close as possible to the words they modify?

1. Find any modifiers in your revision of Taleah's essay that are not as close as possible to the words they modify.

For help with modifier errors, see Chapter 39.

2. Did you find and correct her dangling modifier? If not, find and correct it now.

PUNCTUATION AND MECHANICS

Punctuation
✔ Are sentences punctuated correctly?

1. Read your revision of Taleah's essay for any errors in punctuation.

2. Find the run-together sentence you revised, and make sure it is punctuated correctly.

For help with punctuation, see Chapters 40–44.

3. Did you find and correct Taleah's two comma errors?

Mechanics
✔ Are words capitalized properly?

1. Read your revision of Taleah's essay for any errors in capitalization.

2. Be sure to check Taleah's capitalization in the run-together sentence you revised.

For help with capitalization, see Chapter 45.

WORD CHOICE AND SPELLING

Word Choice
✔ Are words used correctly?

1. Find any words used incorrectly in your revision of Taleah's essay.

For help with confused words, see Chapter 51.

2. Did you find and correct the three confused words in Taleah's essay? If not, find and correct them now.

Spelling

✔ Are words spelled correctly?

For help with spelling, see Chapter 52.

1. Use spell-check and a dictionary to check the spelling in your revision of Taleah's essay.

2. Correct any misspelled words.

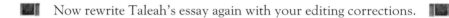

Now rewrite Taleah's essay again with your editing corrections.

Reading Your Own Illustration Essay

To revise and edit your own writing successfully, you need to create some distance between you and your essay. To accomplish this, you should first read your essay using the same reading strategy you have applied to other reading tasks in this chapter. Reading your essay as a selection you need to respond to will help you revise and edit your own work efficiently and effectively.

Reading Strategy

READING CRITICALLY
Chunking Your Own Essay

As you begin to rework your own essay, apply the same reading strategy to it that you have used throughout this chapter. Circle your thesis or main idea; then draw horizontal lines between the examples you use to support your main idea. As you label these examples in the margin, decide whether they are the best choices to prove your point. Should you change any of them? Should you explain any of them further?

Revising and Editing Your Own Essay

You are now going to revise and edit your own writing. Remember to rework your content, especially development and organization, before you correct grammar and usage errors. Revise and edit until your essay achieves the purpose you intended. The checklists here will help you apply what you learned in this chapter to your own essay.

Revising Your Own Writing

THESIS STATEMENT

☐ Does the thesis statement contain the essay's controlling idea and an opinion about that idea?

☐ Does the thesis appear as the last sentence of the introduction?

For Revising Peer Evaluation Forms, go to Appendix 4.

1. What is the main point you are trying to convey in your essay?

_____

_____

2. What is your opinion about the main point?

_____

_____

_____

3. Put brackets around the last sentence in your introduction. Does it contain your main point and your opinion about that point?

_____

_____

_____

4. Rewrite your thesis statement if necessary so that it states your main point and your opinion.

BASIC ELEMENTS

☐ Does the title draw in the readers?

☐ Does the introduction capture the readers' attention and build up effectively to the thesis statement?

☐ Does each body paragraph deal with a single topic?

☐ Does the conclusion bring the essay to a close in an interesting way?

1. Give your essay a title if it doesn't have one.

_____

2. Does your introduction capture your readers' attention and build up to your thesis statement at the end of the paragraph?

_____

3. Does each of your body paragraphs deal with only one topic?

_____

4. Does your conclusion follow some of the suggestions offered in Part I?

_____

DEVELOPMENT

☐ Do the body paragraphs adequately support the thesis statement?

☐ Does each body paragraph have a focused topic sentence?

☐ Does each body paragraph contain *specific* details that support the topic sentence?

☐ Does each body paragraph include *enough* details to fully explain the topic sentence?

1. Write out your thesis statement (revised, if necessary), and list your topic sentences below it.

    Thesis statement: _____

        Topic 1: _____

        Topic 2: _____

        Topic 3: _____

2. Do your topics adequately support your thesis statement?

_____

3. Does each body paragraph have a focused topic sentence?

_____

4. Are your examples specific?

_____

Add another more specific detail to an example in your essay.

5. Do you give enough examples to make your point?

_____

Add at least one new example to your essay.

6. Can your readers identify with your examples?

_____

UNITY

☐ Do the essay's topic sentences relate directly to the thesis statement?

☐ Do the details in each body paragraph support the paragraph's topic sentence?

1. Read each of your topic sentences with your thesis statement in mind. Do they go together?

_____

2. Revise your topic sentences if necessary so they are directly related.

3. Drop or rewrite any of the sentences in your body paragraphs that are not directly related to their topic sentences.

ORGANIZATION

☐ Is the essay organized logically?

☐ Is each body paragraph organized logically?

1. Read your essay again to see if all the paragraphs are arranged logically.

2. Refer to your answers to the development questions. Then identify your method of organization:

_____

3. Is the order you chose for your paragraphs the most effective approach to your topic?

_____

4. Move any paragraphs that are out of order.

5. Look closely at your body paragraphs to see if all the sentences are arranged logically within paragraphs.

6. Move any sentences that are out of order.

COHERENCE

☐ Are transitions used effectively so that paragraphs move smoothly and logically from one to the next?

☐ Do the sentences move smoothly and logically from one to the next?

1. Circle five transitions, repetitions, synonyms, or pronouns you use.

2. Explain how two of these make your essay easier to read.

For a list of transitions, see pages 99–100.
For a list of pronouns, see pages 496–497.

_____

_____

 Now rewrite your essay with your revisions.

Editing Your Own Writing

For Editing Peer Evaluation Forms, go to Appendix 6.

SENTENCES

Subjects and Verbs

☐ Does each sentence have a main subject and verb?

For help with subjects and verbs, see Chapter 27.

1. Underline the subjects once and verbs twice in a paragraph of your revised essay. Remember that sentences can have more than one subject-verb set.

2. Does each of your sentences have at least one subject and verb that can stand alone?

For help with fragments, see Chapter 28.
For help with run-togethers, see Chapter 29.

3. Correct any fragments you have written.

4. Correct any run-together sentences you have written.

Subject-Verb Agreement

☐ Do all subjects and verbs agree?

For help with subject-verb agreement, see Chapter 32.

1. Read aloud the subjects and verbs you underlined in your revised essay.

2. Correct any subjects and verbs that do not agree.

Pronoun Agreement

☐ Do all pronouns agree with their nouns?

For help with pronoun agreement, see Chapter 36.

1. Find any pronouns in your revised essay that do not agree with their nouns.

2. Correct any pronouns that do not agree with their nouns.

Modifiers

☐ Are modifiers as close as possible to the words they modify?

For help with modifier errors, see Chapter 39.

1. Find any modifiers in your revised essay that are not as close as possible to the words they modify.

2. Rewrite sentences if necessary so that your modifiers are as close as possible to the words they modify.

PUNCTUATION AND MECHANICS

Punctuation

☐ Are sentences punctuated correctly?

For help with punctuation, see Chapters 40–44.

1. Read your revised essay for any errors in punctuation.

2. Make sure any fragments and run-together sentences you revised are punctuated correctly.

Mechanics

☐ Are words capitalized properly?

For help with capitalization, see Chapter 45.

1. Read your revised essay for any errors in capitalization.

2. Be sure to check your capitalization in any fragments or run-together sentences you revised.

WORD CHOICE AND SPELLING

Word Choice

☐ Are words used correctly?

1. Find any words used incorrectly in your revised essay.

2. Correct any errors you find.

For help with confused words, see Chapter 51.

Spelling

☐ Are words spelled correctly?

1. Use spell-check and a dictionary to check your spelling.

2. Correct any misspelled words.

For help with spelling, see Chapter 52.

To make a personal log of your grammar/usage errors, go to Appendix 7.

Now rewrite your essay again with your editing corrections.

To make a personal log of your spelling errors, go to Appendix 8.

MyWritingLab | **More Helpful Hints**

- **Do you need some reminders about revising?** Illustrating essays require specific examples and clarity to help readers understand them. So you need to pay special attention to these features as you revise. Go to **Revising the Essay** in the **Essay Development** module of **MyWritingLab** for some helpful guidelines.

PRACTICING ILLUSTRATION: FROM READING TO WRITING

This final section allows you to practice the reading and writing skills you learned in this chapter. It includes two reading selections and several writing assignments on "your reading" and "your world." The section then leads you through peer evaluation and some reflection exercises that will help you annotate your final draft to facilitate a productive dialogue with your instructor about your paper.

Reading Workshop

Here are two essays that use examples to make their point: "Dating: The Soft Breakup" by Matt Huston gives examples from his experience to show how both dating and breaking up have changed in the digital era, and "The Decorated Body" by France Borel uses examples to talk about the importance of altering our physical appearance. As you read, notice how the writers use examples to support and advance their ideas.

DATING: THE SOFT BREAKUP
by Matt Huston

Focusing Your Attention

1. Do you find breaking up difficult? How do you handle an ex online? Do you keep in touch with your exes on social media? What is your reasoning behind this decision?

2. The essay you are about to read considers our current problems in the 21st century with breakups. He suggests that breaking up is very difficult today because of social media and poses some important questions regarding breakups. What are some different ways of handling a breakup in this electronic age?

Expanding Your Vocabulary

The following words are important to your understanding of this essay. Organize this list into two columns—words you know and words you don't know. Which of the words you don't know can you guess from their sentences?

inevitable: unavoidable (paragraph 2)

decoupled: broken up (paragraph 3)

advent: start (paragraph 4)

impeding: delaying (paragraph 5)

perpetual: continuous (paragraph 9)

undermine: weaken (paragraph 10)

vestiges: traces (paragraph 10)

dire: urgent (paragraph 11)

sever: break (paragraph 13)

ambiguity: doubt (paragraph 14)

 Reading Strategy

READING CRITICALLY
Chunking Your Reading

As you learned to do earlier, circle the main idea of the following essay, and then separate each example with horizontal lines. Label the examples in the margins. Then, share your marks with a classmate, justifying each of your decisions.

DATING: THE SOFT BREAKUP
by Matt Huston

1   Dating is a lot like science. At the very least, trial and error are an essential part of the process. And the outcome is not always the hoped-for one.

2   Breakups are in fact inevitable—you imagine a final, decisive moment when two strained sweethearts go their separate ways. They throw out the snapshots and souvenirs, mourn and mope for a while, dig into the ice cream, and sooner or later, resume the search for a suitable mate. The exes might never see each other again. Out of sight, eventually out of mind.

3   But it's 2014, and it's not so easy to erase an ex from your life. The newly decoupled might not call each other or meet up—that could be too direct—but there are other ways they stay connected. When you have 100 numbers in your cellphone and 700 friends on Facebook, links linger.

4   Deleting an ex's number or clicking "Unfriend" takes work. Worse, it can feel like salt in a wound. An ex's words and smiles may continue to float across Facebook feeds or pop up in chat windows. It's easy to keep tabs on a former partner. In ways that weren't even imagined before the advent of instant messages and status updates, broken-up partners remain, for better or worse, a part of each other's lives.

5   By impeding a definitive ending, technology has created what relationship researcher Scott Stanley dubs the "soft breakup." "There are so many easy, cheap ways to stay in contact now," says Stanley, a professor of psychology at the University of Denver. "Social media have completely transformed" the chances of persistent connection.

6   Compared with a wall of silence, a friendly text message here and an email there can take the edge off a breakup. "The soft breakup gives us a new way of saying 'I don't want to date you, but let's try to be friends,'" says Galena Rhoades, a clinical psychologist who frequently collaborates with Stanley on research. "Having the option to do a soft breakup might motivate people to get out of a relationship they know is a dead end."

7   But lingering ties come with big emotional risks. They facilitate on-again, off-again relationships even when the coupling was not ideal and needed to end.

8   Breakups are painful, and continuing connections can reinforce an impulse to turn to the ex for comfort, says Sarah Halpern-Meekin of the University of Wisconsin. Every flicker of reconnection can obscure the very sensible reasons a relationship ended.

9   At a minimum, electronic ties tempt exes to look backward. By offering a perpetual gaze into the lives of former partners, social media platforms enable exes to hang on to hope. Yet every hour spent monitoring an ex is an hour not spent searching for a better match.

10 The blurriness of breakups can undermine new relationships as well. The next partner may have a hard time tolerating any vestiges of a prior romance. "Exes may no longer be so ex," says Stanley, but jealousy is still jealousy.

11 Lingering links can also fuel anxiety in a new partner. Rhoades hears clients voice fears of being left for the ex who hovers electronically. Not every concern is so

dire, but it's worrisome enough to feel that "your partner may be sharing things that are not shared with you."

12   "We really don't like giving up options," Rhoades says, "but not giving up options makes it harder to commit to any particular option." In other words, It's harder to step into a new relationship when one foot is stuck in the past.

13   Given the drawbacks of soft breakups, wouldn't it be easier for exes to sever all ties, analog and digital? Often, prior partners are people who merit respect and whose opinions we value. We prefer to think that they view us favorably despite the unhappy ending. "If we're deleting somebody from our life, chances are the other person is doing the same, and that's uncomfortable," Rhoades says.

14   However much soft breakups blur the boundaries of romantic attachments, the new acceptance of post-breakup connection reflects a more generalized change in relationships: an increase in ambiguity at all stages of mating. Stanley points out that early in a relationship it's not uncommon for one or both individuals to wonder whether they are just hanging out or actually on a date.

15   Ambiguity can be frustrating, but it's anchored in modern fears that love will not last. It offers the illusion of emotional safety. Lack of clarity about when a relationship begins or how serious it is fosters the perception that there will be less pain when it ends, Stanley explains.

16   Ardor is harder. As a relationship unfolds, laying feelings on the line or pushing for clarity—Are we serious? Is this a long-term thing?—can seem to threaten whatever relationship exists. Romantic ambiguity is downright dangerous as relationships proceed, Stanley says. It allows one partner to make a heavy emotional investment in another who may be unwilling or unable to commit.

17   Even if social life is far more ambiguous than it used to be, "you don't have to be ambiguous in your head about what you're doing and what you want," Stanley advises. He urges the recently separated to ask themselves, "What are my bottom lines? What are the things I absolutely need in a partner, and what are the things I couldn't or shouldn't accept?"

18   Answering the questions can make it easier to let go of those who aren't for us—so we can get to know the ones who are.

Thinking Critically About Content

1. In what ways does Huston believe that dating is like science?

2. What prompted Scott Stanley to coin the term *soft breakup*? Give an example from Huston's essay of its meaning.

3. According to the researchers that Huston cites, what are two advantages and two disadvantages of soft breakups?

Thinking Critically About Purpose and Audience

4. What do you think Huston's purpose is in this essay? Explain your answer.

5. What type of audience do you think would most understand and appreciate this essay?

6. Why do you think Huston talks about the advantages of soft breakups before the disadvantages?

Thinking Critically About Essays

7. Does Huston give you enough examples to understand the complexities of soft breakups? Explain your answer.

8. What is Huston's thesis in this essay? Where is it located?

9. This essay is essentially divided into the advantages and disadvantages of soft breakups. Does each section of the essay support the author's thesis statement to make it unified? Explain your answer.

10. Explain your opinion of social media for communication today. What are its drawbacks for general communication? What are its benefits? Respond to these questions in detail.

> To keep track of your critical thinking progress, go to Appendix 1.

THE DECORATED BODY
by France Borel

Focusing Your Attention

1. In what ways have you changed your natural appearance—hair color, makeup, tattoos, piercings, and the like? Why did you make these alternations? What messages do they send to others?

2. The essay you are about to read deals with the ways we decorate our bodies. These methods vary according to someone's culture. Why do you think people in the United States change their appearance? What physical decorations are appealing to you? Which are unappealing? Why do you think you have these various reactions?

Expanding Your Vocabulary

The following words are important to your understanding of this essay. Organize this list into two columns—words you know and words you don't know. Which of the words you don't know can you guess from their sentences?

unfathomably: impossible to measure (paragraph 1)

artifice: device used to trick people (paragraph 2)

millennia: thousands of years (paragraph 3)

prevalent: widespread (paragraph 3)

aesthetically: concerned with appearances (paragraph 4)

amorous: pertaining to love (paragraph 4)

scarification: scarring of the skin (paragraph 6)

pretexts: false justifications (paragraph 8)

malleable: easily influenced (paragraph 9)

eludes: evades or escapes from (paragraph 12)

homogeneous: of the same kind (paragraph 12)

tacit: implied (paragraph 12)

adhere: stick to (paragraph 13)

 Reading Strategy

READING CRITICALLY
Chunking Your Reading

Once again, circle the thesis of the following essay, and draw horizontal lines in the essay to show the different examples the author has chosen to support his thesis. Label the examples in the margins. Then, compare your marks with those of a classmate, and justify your decisions to each other.

THE DECORATED BODY
by France Borel

"Nothing goes as deep as dress nor as far as the skin; ornaments have the dimensions of the world."

—Michel Serres, *The Five Senses*

1   Human nakedness, according to social custom, is unacceptable, unbearable, and dangerous. From the moment of birth, society takes charge, managing, dressing, forming, and deforming the child—sometimes even with a certain degree of violence. Aside from the most elementary caretaking concerns—the very diversity of which shows how subjective the motivation is—an unfathomably deep and universal tendency pushes families, clans, and tribes to rapidly modify a person's physical appearance.

2   One's genuine physical makeup, one's given anatomy, is always felt to be unacceptable. Flesh, in its raw state, seems both intolerable and threatening. In its naked state, body and skin have no possible existence. The organism is acceptable only when it is transformed, covered with signs. The body only speaks if it is dressed in artifice.

Le Vêtement incarné, les métamorphoses du corps by France Borel.

For millennia, in the four quarters of the globe, mothers have molded the shape 3
of their newborn babies' skulls to give them silhouettes conforming to prevalent criteria of beauty. In the nineteenth century, western children were tightly swaddled to
keep their limbs straight. In the so-called primitive world, children were scarred or
tattooed at a very early age in rituals which were repeated at all the most important
steps of their lives. At a very young age, children were fitted with belts, necklaces, or
bracelets; their lips, ears, or noses were pierced or stretched.

Some cultures have designed sophisticated appliances to alter physical struc- 4
ture and appearance. American Indian cradleboards crushed the skull to flatten it;
the Mangbetus of Africa wrapped knotted rope made of bark around the child's head
to elongate it into a sugar-loaf shape, which was considered to be aesthetically pleas-
ing. The feet of very young Chinese girls were bound and spliced, intentionally and
irreversibly deforming them, because this was seen to guarantee the girls' eventual
amorous and matrimonial success.[1]

Claude Lévi-Strauss said about the Caduveo of Brazil: "In order to be a man, 5
one had to be painted; whoever remained in a natural state was no different from the
beasts."[2] In Polynesia, unless a girl was tattooed, she would not find a husband. An
unornamented hand could not cook, nor dip into the communal food bowl. Pink lips
were despicable and ugly. Anyone who refused the test of the tattoo was seen to be
marginal and suspect.

Among the Tivs of Nigeria, women called attention to their legs by means of 6
elaborate scarification and the use of pearl leg bands; the best decorated calves were
known for miles around. Tribal incisions behind the ears of Chad men rendered the
skin "as smooth and stretched as that of a drum." The women would laugh at any
man lacking these incisions, and they would never accept him as a husband. Men
would subject themselves willingly to this custom, hoping for scars deep enough to
leave marks on their skulls after death.

At the beginning of the eighteenth century, Father Laurent de Lucques noted 7
that any young girl of the Congo who was not able to bear the pain of scarification and
who cried so loudly that the operation had to be stopped was considered "good for
nothing."[3] That is why, before marriage, men would check to see if the pattern traced
on the belly of their intended bride was beautiful and well-detailed.

The fact that such motivations and pretexts depend on aesthetic, erotic, hy- 8
gienic, or even medical considerations has no influence on the result, which is always
in the direction of transforming the appearance of the body. Such a transformation is
wished for, whether or not it is effective.

The body is a supple, malleable, and transformable prime material, a kind of 9
modeling clay, easily molded by social will and wish. Human skin is an ideal subject
for inscription, a surface for all sorts of marks which make it possible to differentiate
the human from the animal. The physical body offers itself willingly for tattooing or
scarring so that, visibly and recognizably, it becomes a social entity.

The absolutely naked body is considered as brutish, reduced to the level of 10
nature where no distinction is made between man and beast. The decorated body,
on the other hand, dressed (if even only in a belt), tattooed, or mutilated, publicly
exhibits humanity and membership in an established group. As Theophile Gautier

said, "The ideal disturbs even the roughest nature, and the taste for ornamentation distinguishes the intelligent being from the beast more exactly than anything else. Indeed, dogs have never dreamed of putting on earrings."

11   So, it is by their categorical refusal of nakedness that human beings are distinguished from nature. The "mark makes unremarkable"—it creates an interval between what is biologically and brutally given in the animal realm and what is won in the cultural realm. The body is tamed continuously; social custom demands, at any price—including pain, constraint, or discomfort—that wildness be abandoned.

12   Each civilization chooses—through a network of elective relationships which are difficult to determine—which areas of the body deserve transformation. These areas are as difficult to define and as shifting as those of eroticism or modesty. An individual alone eludes bodily modifications; they are the expression of a homogeneous collectivity which, at a chosen moment, comes to a tacit agreement to attack one or another part of the anatomy.

13   Whatever the choices, options, or differences may be, that which remains constant is the transformation of appearance. In spite of our contemporary western belief that the body is perfect as it is, we are constantly changing it: clothing it in musculature, suntan, or makeup; dying its head hair or pulling out its bodily hair. The seemingly most innocent gestures for taking care of the body very often hide a persistent and disguised tendency to make it adhere to the strictest of norms, reclothing it in a veil of civilization. The total nudity offered at birth does not exist in any region of the world. Man puts his stamp on man. The body is not a product of nature, but of culture.

Notes

1. Of course, there are also many different sexual mutilations, including excisions and circumcisions, which we will not go into at this time as they constitute a whole study in themselves.
2. C. Lévi-Strauss, *Tristes Tropiques* (Paris: Plon, 1955), p. 214.
3. J. Cuvelier, *Relations sur le Congo du Père Laurent de Lucques* (Brussels: Institut royal colonial belge, 1953), p. 144.

Thinking Critically About Content

1. What does Borel mean when he says, "The body only speaks if it is dressed in artifice" (paragraph 2)?

2. According to Borel, what are the primary reasons people make changes in their appearance? Do you notice any common thread in these reasons?

3. In what ways is tattooing "a social entity" (paragraph 9)?

Thinking Critically About Purpose and Audience

4. What do you think France Borel's purpose is in this essay?

5. Do you think all students would be interested in this essay? What other groups would find this essay interesting? Why?

6. Do you think this essay might change someone's opinion about body decorations? Explain your answer.

Thinking Critically About Essays

7. What is the thesis of this essay?

8. Why do you think Borel divides this essay into two parts? What is the main idea of each part? Is this an effective way to break up this essay? Explain your answer.

9. In what way does the last sentence serve as a summary for the essay?

10. Were your views on any forms of body decoration changed as a result of reading this essay? If so, in what way? Explain your answer in detail.

To keep track of your critical thinking progress, go to Appendix 1.

Writing Workshop

This final section gives you opportunities to apply what you have learned in this chapter to another writing assignment. This time, we provide very little prompting beyond a summary of the guidelines for writing an illustration essay. This section will let you demonstrate that you can go through the entire writing process on your own with only occasional feedback from your peers. Loop back into the chapter as necessary when you have questions so that this process becomes as automatic to you as possible before you move on to new material. Then pause at the end of the chapter to reflect briefly on what you have learned.

Guidelines for Writing an Illustration Essay

1. State your main point in the last sentence of your introduction.
2. Choose examples that are relevant to your point.
3. Choose examples that your readers can identify with.
4. Use a sufficient number of examples to make your point.
5. Organize your examples to make your point in the clearest, strongest way.

Writing About Your Reading

1. Contemporary American society can't make up its mind about illegal immigrants. In some cases, Americans want to allow illegal immigrants to stay in the country; in other instances, Americans say that illegal

immigrants should return to their home countries. How do you think this feud will be resolved? Give examples to explain your reasoning.

2. What are some of the differences between the generations regarding body decorations? What do you think accounts for these differences? Give examples to support your claims.

3. What do you think writers should consider first when choosing examples in an essay? How should the examples be related to the thesis statement? Why are these criteria important when working with examples?

Writing About Your World

1. Identify some common themes in the collage. Then come up with a thesis statement that explains the message of the collage. Write an essay to support your thesis statement, developed with relevant examples from the picture and from your own experience.

2. Share with your classmates your opinion on a national issue such as capital punishment, pollution regulations, required health care, or gun laws. Use examples in your body paragraphs to support your main point.

3. Why do you think Americans are interested in exercise and weight loss? What actions illustrate this attitude? Use examples or illustrations to explain your observations on the current interest in health and weight among Americans.

4. Create your own illustration assignment (with the help of your instructor), and write a response to it.

Revising

Small Group Activity (5–10 minutes per writer) Working in groups of three or four, read your illustration essays to each other. Those listening should record their reactions on the Revising Peer

Evaluation Forms in Appendix 4. After your group goes through this process, give your evaluation forms to the appropriate writers so that each writer has two or three peer comment sheets for revising.

Paired Activity (5 minutes per writer) Using the completed Peer Evaluation Forms, work in pairs to decide what you should revise in your essay. If time allows, rewrite some of your sentences, and have your partner look at them.

Individual Activity Rewrite your paper, using the revising feedback you received from other students.

Editing

Paired Activity (5–10 minutes per writer) Swap papers with a classmate, and use the Editing Peer Evaluation Form (Appendix 6) to identify as many grammar, punctuation, mechanics, and spelling errors as you can. If time allows, correct some of your errors, and have your partner look at them. Record your grammar, punctuation, and mechanics errors in the Error Log (Appendix 7) and your spelling errors in the Spelling Log (Appendix 8).

Individual Activity Rewrite your paper again, using the editing feedback you received from other students.

Reflecting on Your Writing When you have completed your own essay, answer these six questions.

1. What was most difficult about this assignment?

2. What was easiest?

3. What did you learn about illustration by completing this assignment?

4. What do you think are the strengths of your illustration? Place a wavy line by the parts of your essay that you feel are very good.

5. What are the weaknesses, if any, of your paper? Place an X by the parts of your essay you would like help with. Write in the margins any questions you have.

6. What did you learn from this assignment about your own writing process—about preparing to write, about writing the first draft, about revising, and about editing?

MyWritingLab™ Visit Chapter 11, "Illustrating," in MyWritingLab, and complete the Post-test to check your understanding of the chapter's objectives.

12

Analyzing a Process

*"*I see but one rule: to be clear.*"*

—STENDHAL

Process analysis satisfies our natural desire for basic information—how to be more assertive, how to invest in the stock market, how to eat more healthfully, or how to help your child do a better job in school.

Process analysis writing, more than other types of writing, helps you improve yourself and understand the world around you—in your immediate environment, in college, and in the workplace. Consider the following situations:

- People who are coming to visit you from out of town e-mail you for directions to your house.
- A student needs to write a paper on how to improve employee morale for a course in business management.
- A student needs to explain how to be a good listener for a midterm exam in speech communication.
- The owner of an apartment building posts a notice in the laundry room explaining how to operate the new washers and dryers.
- The manager of a shoe store has to write a memo reminding employees about the correct procedure for taking returns.

Process analysis is a form of explaining. Process analysis essays fall into one of two main types—giving directions or giving information. The first type, giving directions, tells *how to do something*, such as how to write a research paper or change the oil in your car. The second type (giving information) analyzes *how something works*, such as satellite TV or a bread machine, or *how something happened*, such as how the Soviet Union broke into separate nations. In each case, the explanation starts at the beginning and moves step by step, usually in chronological order, to the end result. Process analysis can be about something mental (how to solve a math problem) or something physical (how to pitch a tent).

Student Comment:
"I like that when I mess up on a quiz, I have the chance to retake the quiz and learn from my mistake."

MyWritingLab

Understanding Process Analysis

To make sure you understand all the important concepts connected with analyzing a process, go to **MyWritingLab.com,** and choose **Process** in the **Essay Development** module. From there, read the **Overview,** watch the two **Animation** videos, and complete the **Recall, Apply,** and **Write** activities. Then check your understanding of process analysis essays by taking the **Post-test.**

PREPARING TO WRITE A PROCESS ANALYSIS ESSAY

As you know by now, preparing to write in this text begins with reading. Reading a good process analysis essay can easily help you produce a good essay in this mode if you thoroughly understand the content and form of your reading. In fact, reading and writing are two parts of the same process. Reading process analysis essays critically involves understanding the steps of a process or the sequence of an event and then going further to evaluate the steps or sequence. Are these steps the best way to create the final product or carry out the event? Would the results have been different with another approach? Dealing with this type of inquiry in both reading and writing will raise your level of thinking in all that you do. If you learn how to approach each rhetorical mode critically, these skills will transfer to your other college work. To accomplish this, on the next few pages you will read an effective process analysis essay and then answer some questions to help you discover how the essay communicates its message.

Reading a Process Analysis Essay

In "Dare to Change Your Job and Your Life in 7 Steps," Carole Kanchier explains how to take the right risks in order to change jobs and improve your life. This essay demonstrates the first type of process analysis—how to do something. Have you ever held a job that you intensely disliked? Were you able to quit? Why or why not? Do you know what career you want to follow? What steps are you taking to prepare for it?

Applying a systematic strategy to your reading tasks will help you raise both your level of understanding and your level of thinking because it will show you how to interact with your reading. In other words, it teaches you how to read critically, which means you will understand not only *what* an essay is saying but also *how* the author is saying it. The strategy you will be applying to all reading tasks in this chapter involves graphing, or mapping, the relationships among ideas.

 Reading Strategy

READING CRITICALLY
Graphing a Professional Essay

To understand their reading material and see how it works, students often find that making drawings of its ideas and details is much more effective than outlining. Graphic organizers, or concept maps, let you literally "draw" the relationship of ideas to one another. Figuring out what framework to use for this exercise is part of the process. You can make up a drawing of your own or do a Web search for "graphic organizers" to see some different options. For the following essay, show the relationship of the ideas to one another in a graphic form that makes sense to you. Be prepared to explain your drawing.

DARE TO CHANGE YOUR JOB
AND YOUR LIFE IN 7 STEPS
by Carole Kanchier

1   Small, dark-haired, attractive, and warm, Melissa belies her 44 years. In a sharp gray suit and becoming blouse, she projects a professional yet approachable image. She is now director of training and development for a large retail outlet—and loves it.

2   "I feel good about myself," she says, "and at the end of the day, I have lots of energy left over." Melissa feels content because she believes she is doing something worthwhile. Her new position gives her life meaning and purpose. But getting there wasn't easy.

3   First a flight attendant, then a high school English teacher, then a manager in a retail store, Melissa stumbled about from what was for her one dead-end job to another. How did she finally find a meaningful, fulfilling, well-paid career? And how did she do what so many of us fail to do—dare to change?

4   A career change can take months or even years of soul-searching—10 months in Melissa's case. You need to know the steps, how to master the troublesome feelings that accompany change, where the possible dangers lie, and how to maximize your gains while minimizing your losses. While creating a life worth living isn't easy, Melissa and millions of others have shown that anything is possible.

5   In interviews and surveys with more than 30,000 people over the past 25 years, I have identified seven steps that are key to a successful career and life shift.

1. Become AWARE of Negative Feelings

Your body and mind may be sending you messages about your job satisfaction. 6
The messages may be physical—lingering colds, flu, or headaches—or verbal—"23 minutes till lunch!" or "One more day till Friday!"

Perhaps you've been working for several years in your job, and it appears to be 7
going well. You've had steady promotions, praise from superiors, and admiration from colleagues. Then one day you get a queasy feeling that something is lacking. But what? You run the film of your life in reverse but you can't figure it out. These feelings may persist for months or even years, depending on your ability to tolerate them, but, sooner or later, you have to admit you have a problem.

2. DEFINE the Problem

A good written definition of your problem can help to put you on the road 8
toward change.

First, ask yourself, "What's making me feel this way? What is it about my situa- 9
tion that is unpleasant? Does this job help me reach my goals?" If not, why?

Next, describe any barriers that may be blocking you from making a move— 10
perhaps fear of change; fear of losing a secure income, pension or other benefits; fear that the change will interfere with your relationships; or fear that you'll lose power or status.

Fear is the result of conditioning, and because it is learned, it can be unlearned. 11
Reprogram your old attitudes and beliefs with new ones by learning and practicing specific ways to overcome the fears blocking your path toward change. Think of FEAR as an acronym for "False Expectations Appear Real." Don't spend time worrying about what might happen. Focus on the now.

3. Listen to AMBIVALENCE

Milton, a rehabilitation counselor, was approached by a prospective partner to 12
start an executive recruitment agency. For weeks before making the move, he went straight to bed immediately after dinner and pulled the sheets up over his head. He tried to make light of this behavior, but he had undertaken many risks before and had never felt this way about them.

His underlying fears were prophetic. He later discovered that the hard-sell, 13
aggressive style required for executive recruiting was not for him. The difference in basic values between Milton and his partner proved such a handicap that, within five months, the two parted ways.

The decision to change can provoke mixed feelings. A certain amount of 14
ambivalence is natural. Inner emotional preparation—weighing losses as well as gains, fears as well as hopes—is a necessary prerequisite for successful risk taking.

But if the prospect of undertaking a change is so great that your stomach is 15
churning, you can't sleep, you have constant headaches, or you feel you're developing an ulcer, your body, in its wisdom, is telling you to forgo the risk.

4. PREPARE for Risk

16   The key to avoiding potential potholes is to set tentative career goals before you explore new roads. Goals force you to focus on what you really want. Years from now, as you review your life, what would you regret not having done?

17   Fantasize about the ultimate goal, your shining star. If you could do anything in the world, what would it be? Write all of your ideas or fantasies in a notebook. Include everything you want to do, be, and have. The sky is the limit. Once you know what you want, you'll be more willing to take the risks necessary to achieve it.

18   Choosing a satisfying career and lifestyle also requires a basic understanding of yourself. A variety of exercises can help. To identify your strengths, for example, list some of the successes you've had—say, substituting for your son's soccer coach. Next to each success, identify what gave you the positive feelings. Did you contribute to the team's first win of the season?

19   Also list the skills and abilities you used to bring about that success. Were you well organized and adept at working with parents? Finally, decide how your interests, needs, accomplishments, and other personal strengths add up. What pattern do they form?

20   Self-exploration is just part of the process. You also need to take a careful look at your current situation, as well as the available alternatives. Some popular reference tools, available at your local library, can help. Check out the *Occupational Handbook,* the *Dictionary of Occupational Titles,* and the *Encyclopedia of Careers and Work Issues.* The Internet also offers excellent sites for exploring general occupational fields, job descriptions, and educational opportunities.

5. NARROW Your Options

21   Successful career management hinges on finding a position that's compatible with your personal qualities and goals. Do you have the necessary intelligence and skills to do the work? Can you afford the training required for the job? Might your shortcomings—health, vision, size, or strength, for example—pose a problem?

22   To help narrow your options, draw a series of vertical and horizontal lines so that your paper is divided into squares. Across the top of the page, list the most important elements of your ideal job: income, responsibility, public image, creativity, challenge, and so on (one in each square). Down the left side of the page, list each occupational option you're considering.

23   Next, for each alternative, place a −1 in the appropriate box if that job option doesn't satisfy the criterion listed at the top of the page. If the criterion is met, but not as much as you'd like, record a 0. If the criterion is well met, record a +1. Add the points for each job option and place them in a column labeled "total" at the far right. The job with the highest score meets the greatest number of criteria that you have deemed important.

6. Take ACTION

Once you've determined your occupational goal, take steps to realize it. You'll   24
need a well-planned campaign to market yourself for the job, establish your own business, or return to school.

Stay focused on your goals, and believe you will achieve them. View failures   25
along the way as learning experiences—detours that might offer an unexpected
dividend.

7. EVALUATE the Decision

When you have worked hard at making a decision, take the time not just to en-   26
joy the outcome, but to evaluate it. Ask yourself

• Do I feel good about the move?

• What other gains did I derive from the move? What did I lose?

• What factors contributed to the success of my move?

• If I could do it all over again, what would I do differently?

• Who was most helpful in the process? Who let me down?

Evaluation is a continuous process. Assess your needs, goals, and job satisfac-   27
tion periodically to determine if your developing personality fits your position and
lifestyle. Don't wait for a crisis to clear your vision.

There really is no substitute for risk as a way to grow. Knowing you have hon-   28
estly faced the painful struggle and accepted the trade-offs, and yet proceeded in
spite of them, is extremely gratifying.

Melissa learned that the tremendous investment of energy a successful job   29
search demands is exactly what enables people to look back and say, "Win, lose, or
draw, I gave it my everything." Being able to say with satisfaction that you risked for
a dream may be the biggest prize of all.

To remain fulfilled, however, you'll need to risk again and again until you've   30
created a life in which you feel comfortable being yourself, without apology or
pretense—a life in which you can continue to have choices.

Discovering How This Essay Works

To help you discover the elements that make this an effective process
analysis essay so you can use them in your own writing, answer the following questions in as much detail as possible.

1. What should the reader be able to do by the end of this essay?

    _____

    _____

2. Who do you think Kanchier's audience is? Does she meet their needs?

   _____

   _____

3. Do you understand the process Kanchier explains? What are the seven steps of this process?

   Step 1: _____

   Step 2: _____

   Step 3: _____

   Step 4: _____

   Step 5: _____

   Step 6: _____

   Step 7: _____

   If you do not understand the process, what else do you need to know?

   _____

4. How is this essay organized? Look at the steps you listed in response to question 3; then go to pages 64–76 in Chapter 6 to help you identify the writer's method of organization.

   Method of organization: _____

5. Does the essay conclude by considering the process as a whole? Explain your answer.

   _____

   _____

   _____

WRITING A PROCESS ANALYSIS ESSAY

After working with the professional essay, you are now ready to write one of your own. This section will guide you through the process of creating a first draft that you will then revise and edit in the next section of this chapter. You will learn how to dissect a writing assignment, generate multiple ideas in response to an essay prompt, and systematically go through the guidelines for writing a process analysis essay. Throughout this process, you should write notes and make lists so you can use them when you write a draft of your essay at the end of this section.

Reading the Prompt

Before you begin to write your essay, you need to make sure you thoroughly understand your writing assignment or "prompt." A writing assignment is meant to "prompt" you to get engaged with and respond to a specific topic. The more clearly you understand the prompt, the better paper you will create. The best way to understand the details of a prompt is to learn how to truly interact with the essay assignment. Applying the chapter reading strategy to your prompt is a good way to become involved with the demands of the assignment.

READING CRITICALLY
Graphing the Prompt

Reading
Strategy

Draw your version of the following writing prompt. What tasks do you need to complete? In what order will you address them? How are these tasks related to one another? In this case, you are not graphing the ideas for your essay, but the jobs you need to complete for the assignment. You can make up a drawing of your own or do a Web search for "graphic organizers" to see some options. Then, underline the key words from this assignment in your drawing.

Writing Prompt

Think of some advice you would like to give a friend or classmate—for example, how to survive your first year of college, how to find the partner of your dreams, how to buy a used car, or how to locate good day care for your child. Then write a letter to that person with your best advice on the topic you chose. Be sure to draft a thesis that states the end result of the process and tells how many steps or stages are involved. Then, write the first draft of your essay by following the guidelines for writing a process analysis essay.

MyWritingLab
Complete this Writing Prompt assignment in MyWritingLab.

Thinking About the Prompt

As you consider this writing assignment, try to generate as many ideas as you can so you have several to choose from. Think of some topics you know a lot about and could actually advise someone on. Then choose one of them, and use one or more of the prewriting strategies you learned in Chapter 5 to generate all the ideas you can think of related to that topic. Next, organize the ideas in a way that will be clear to someone else.

Guidelines for Writing a Process Analysis Essay

Both types of process analysis call for careful step-by-step thinking, but especially the first—how to do something. If you leave out even one detail, you may confuse your reader or even endanger someone's life. If, for example, you forget to tell a patient who is coming to a doctor's office for some tests that she shouldn't eat after midnight and she has breakfast, the test results will not be accurate, and a serious medical condition might go unnoticed.

Good process analysis of the second type—how something works or how something happened—can help your reader see a product or an event in a totally new light. Without an explanation, someone looking at an assembled product or a completed event has no way of knowing how it got to the final stage. Good process analysis gives the reader a new way of "seeing" something. The following guidelines will help you write clear and complete process analysis essays. As you think about the topic you have chosen in response to the prompt above, read the following guidelines, and continue to make lists and notes that you will use when you write your draft on this prompt. After each guideline is an explanation of how it functions in the reading selection that appears at the beginning of this chapter so you can actually see how the element works in an essay before you apply it to your own writing.

1. **Express in the thesis statement what the reader should be able to do or understand by the end of the essay**. Stating the end result in the thesis statement gives your readers a road map for what follows. The thesis in a process essay should also state the number of steps or stages in the process or event. For example, someone giving directions might start by saying, "It's easy to get to the library from here with just four turns." Even if a process involves many separate steps, you should divide the list into a few manageable groups: "Most experts agree that there are four stages in overcoming an addiction." Stating the end result and the number of steps or stages in the thesis statement helps the reader follow your explanation. These statements set up the tasks.

In the Reading: Kanchier's thesis statement, which appears in paragraph 5 at the end of her introduction, tells her readers exactly what they will be able to do by the end of her article: make "a successful career and life shift." She also tells them how many steps are involved—seven. In this way, she gives a very clear road map for reading her essay.

In Your Writing: For the essay you are about to write, draft a clear thesis statement that tells the readers what they will be able to do or understand by the end of the essay, along with the number of steps or stages of the process. Make any changes in this sentence necessary to clarify your statement as you develop your essay.

2. **Know your audience**. In process analysis, more than in other types of writing, the success of your essay depends on how well you know your audience. Being familiar with your audience helps you decide how much detail to include, how many examples to add, and which terms to define.

Also keep in mind that your readers won't be able to ask you questions, so if they can't follow your explanation, they will become confused and frustrated. Whoever your audience is, clear explanations are essential.

In the Reading: Kanchier's essay was first published in *Psychology Today*, which is read mostly by educated adults. The author's audience seems to be working adults of any age who are unhappy in their jobs. Kanchier addresses them in a very businesslike way; she doesn't talk down to her audience. Knowing that being unhappy in a job is very depressing, she strives for an upbeat "you can do it" tone.

In Your Writing: Record in your prewriting notes what you know about your audience members. Who are they? What will interest them about your topic? What do they need to understand? Then, refer to these notes frequently as you write a draft of your essay.

3. **Explain the process or event clearly in the body of your essay**. By the end of a how-to essay, the reader should be able to perform the activity. By the end of a how-something-works essay, the reader should understand what is going on behind the scenes; by the end of a how-something-happened essay, the reader should understand more about a specific event.

In writing the body paragraphs of a process essay, pay special attention to transitions. Use transitions such as *first, next, then, after that*, and *finally* to guide your readers through the process from beginning to end.

In the Reading: Because Kanchier's process has seven parts, she numbers each step. This is a good idea if a process is complicated. If you are writing about a process or event with only three or four parts, you can use transitions to indicate to your readers where you are in your explanation.

In Your Writing: In preparation for your essay, list all the steps involved in your advice. Following your introduction, prepare to take your readers step by step through your message. In outlining your points, make sure you don't skip any necessary information.

4. **Organize your material logically**. Most process analysis essays are organized chronologically, or according to a time sequence. The explanation starts at one point and progresses through time to the final point. If a process or event is complicated, figure out the most logical organization for what you are explaining. For instance, playing the guitar involves pressing the strings with the fingers of one hand and strumming with the other hand. You might therefore explain each part of the process separately and then explain how the hands work together to make music.

In the Reading: Kanchier's essay is organized chronologically. The author moves from recognizing the problem to taking action and then to evaluating the action. To help readers follow along smoothly, she numbers the steps and uses transitions such as *first, next*, and *then*.

In Your Writing: Now put the items on your list in chronological order. Revise your list if any items are out of order, and add necessary information that will make your list clearer.

5. **End your essay by considering the process or event as a whole**. Don't just stop after you have explained the last step. Instead, in your conclusion, look at the process or event as a whole. There are many ways to do this. You might state why knowing about the topic is important: Understanding how to perform CPR (cardiopulmonary resuscitation) could save a life; knowing how your car runs might save you money in repair bills; uncovering the details of 9/11 might help us avoid another terrorist attack. Or you might review your introduction, summarize the stages of the process or event, call for action, or end with a fitting quotation. Whatever your method, leave your reader feeling that your essay has come to a natural close.

In the Reading: Kanchier concludes by returning to her introduction. She brings back Melissa, the person from the opening example, to emphasize the rewards of taking risks. She ends her essay by saying that a satisfying life requires taking risks again and again.

In Your Writing: How will you end your essay? Make sure you bring your reader full circle as you review your advice, restate your purpose, and bring your essay to a natural close.

Writing a Draft of Your Essay

Now is the time to collect all your graphic organizers, your notes, your prewriting exercises, and your lists as you set out to generate the first draft of your essay. Before you actually write, you might also want to review the professional essay, the writing assignment, and the chapter guidelines, along with your notes and lists. At this point, don't think about revising or editing; just get your thoughts about the writing assignment down on paper.

MyWritingLab | **Helpful Hints**

- **Having trouble developing your ideas?** Developing your ideas with specific examples helps your readers fully understand what you want to say. For help developing ideas, go to **Developing and Organizing a Paragraph** in **The Craft of Writing** module of **MyWritingLab**.

REVISING AND EDITING

Now you need to revise and edit your essay. This section will take you through the guidelines for revising and editing process analysis essays with two different writing samples: another student's essay and your own essay. Revising and editing are often much easier with someone else's writing, which is why we begin this stage with a writing sample from another student. If you can see some of the problems in this essay, you might be able to identify areas for improvement in your own writing. So you will be reviewing the chapter guidelines by revising and editing another student's writing before applying the same guidelines to your own writing.

Reading a Student Process Analysis Essay

We will begin by using our chapter reading strategy on a student essay. Student writer Emily Bliss wrote the following essay about procrastination. Mapping or drawing her ideas so they make sense will help you understand her essay and prepare you to figure out how to revise and edit it.

READING CRITICALLY
Graphing the Student Essay

Reading
Strategy

See if you can follow Emily's steps as you read her first draft by making drawings of her ideas and details. After you read the essay, show the relationship of the ideas to one another in a coherent graphic form that makes sense to you. Be prepared to explain your drawing.

You Too Can Procrastinate

My name is Emily, and I am a procrastinator. But I have discovered over the years   1
that procrastination is not all bad. Especially when I have to write. At my college,
the English instructors requires rough drafts. I have somehow mastered the art of
procrastinating but still meeting deadlines with my papers. So I have perfected a successful plan for procrastinating that I now want to share with the world.

You will know the dreaded day you have to write has arrived when you wake up   2
with a start. This day is different from the rest. You actually have to do something
about your paper today. But whatever you do, resist the temptation to sit down and
write early in the day by following two more steps. First (step 1), to avoid sitting down
to write, you can clean, take a bike ride, do the laundry, rearrange the furniture, dust
the light bulbs, and so on. But don't write. Then (step 2), when you finally think you
are ready to start writing, call a friend. Talk about anything but your paper for about
15 or 20 minutes. This final delay is what creates the tension that a real procrastinator needs to do his or her best work.

3

Whether you want to or not, you will naturally think about the assignment from the moment you get it. If you have two weeks or two months, you will spend most quiet moments haunted by your paper topic. No matter what you do, your paper topic will be bouncing around in your head giving you headaches, making you worry, wanting attention. But that's OK. Don't give in and write. Ignore it until the day before it is due.

4

At this point, your third step is to prepare your immediate environment for work. You need to get ready for serious business. Sharpen your pencils, and lay them in a row. Get out the white paper if you can't think on yellow, or get out the yellow paper if you can't think on white. Go to the kitchen for snacks. Whether or not you actually drink or eat these item's is irrelevant—as long as they are by your side. You can't be distracted if you don't have them next to you. My stomach growls really loudly when I'm hungry. Some sort of bread usually takes away the hunger pangs. Step 4 is to sit back in your chair and stare at the computer while you think long and hard about your paper. Fifth, brainstorm, list, or cluster your ideas on the colored paper of your choice. Sixth, put all your procrastination strategies aside. Its finally time to write.

5

If you follow these six simple steps, you too can become a master procrastinator. You can perform your very own procrastinating ritual and still get your first draft in on time. If you go through the same ritual every time you write. You can perfect it and get your own system for writing essays down to a science. The trick is just to make sure you start writing before you has to join Procrastinators Anonymous.

Revising and Editing the Student Essay

This essay is Emily's first draft, which now needs to be revised and edited. First, apply the Revising Checklist to the content of Emily's draft. When you are satisfied that her ideas are fully developed and well organized, use the Editing Checklist to correct her grammar and mechanics errors. Answer the questions, and complete the tasks in each category. Then write your suggested changes directly on Emily's draft.

Revising the Student Essay

THESIS STATEMENT

✔ Does the thesis statement contain the essay's controlling idea?

✔ Does the thesis appear as the last sentence of the introduction?

1. Put brackets around the last sentence in Emily's introduction. Does it state her purpose?

2. Rewrite Emily's thesis statement if necessary so that it introduces her process and states her purpose.

_____

_____

BASIC ELEMENTS

✔ Does the title draw in the readers?

✔ Does the introduction capture the readers' attention and build up effectively to the thesis statement?

✔ Does each body paragraph deal with a single topic?

✔ Does the conclusion bring the essay to a close in an interesting way?

1. Give Emily's essay an alternate title.

_____

2. Rewrite Emily's introduction so that it captures the readers' attention and builds up to the thesis statement at the end of the introduction.

_____

_____

_____

3. Does each of Emily's body paragraphs deal with only one topic?

_____

4. Rewrite Emily's conclusion using at least one suggestion from Part I.

_____

_____

_____

DEVELOPMENT

✔ Do the body paragraphs adequately support the thesis statement?

✔ Does each body paragraph have a focused topic sentence?

✔ Does each body paragraph contain _specific_ details that support the topic sentence?

✔ Does each body paragraph include _enough_ details to fully explain the topic sentence?

1. Write out Emily's thesis statement (revised, if necessary), and list her three topic sentences below it.

Thesis statement: _____

_____

Topic 1: _____

_____

Topic 2: _____

_____

Topic 3: _____

_____

2. Do Emily's topics adequately support her thesis statement?

_____

3. Do Emily's details in the essay explain the process step by step?

_____

4. Where do you need more information?

_____

5. Add at least two new details to make the steps clearer.

UNITY

✔ Do the essay's topic sentences relate directly to the thesis statement?

✔ Do the details in each body paragraph support the paragraph's topic sentence?

1. Read each of Emily's topic sentences with her thesis statement (revised, if necessary) in mind. Do they go together?

_____

2. Revise her topic sentences if necessary so they are directly related.

3. Drop or rewrite the two sentences in paragraph 4 that are not directly related to their topic sentence.

ORGANIZATION

✔ Is the essay organized logically?

✔ Is each body paragraph organized logically?

1. Read Emily's essay again to see if all the paragraphs are arranged logically. Look at your list of steps in response to question 3 after Emily's essay.

2. Reverse the two paragraphs that are out of order.

3. Look closely at Emily's body paragraphs to see if all her sentences are arranged logically within paragraphs.

4. Move any sentences that are out of order.

COHERENCE

✔ Are transitions used effectively so that paragraphs move smoothly and logically from one to the next?

✔ Do the sentences move smoothly and logically from one to the next?

1. Circle five transitions Emily uses.

2. Explain how two of these make Emily's essay easier to read.

For a list of transitions, see pages 99–100.

_____

_____

_____

 Now rewrite Emily's essay with your revisions.

Editing the Student Essay

SENTENCES

Subjects and Verbs

✔ Does each sentence have a main subject and verb?

1. Underline the subjects once and verbs twice in paragraphs 1 and 5 of your revision of Emily's essay. Remember that sentences can have more than one subject-verb set.

For help with subjects and verbs, see Chapter 27.

2. Does each of the sentences have at least one subject and verb that can stand alone?

_____

3. Did you find and correct Emily's two fragments? If not, find and correct them now.

For help with run-togethers, see Chapter 29.

Subject-Verb Agreement

✔ Do all subjects and verbs agree?

1. Read aloud the subjects and verbs you underlined in your revision of Emily's essay.

For help with subject-verb agreement, see Chapter 32.

2. Did you find and correct the two subjects and verbs that do not agree? If not, find and correct them now.

_____

Pronoun Agreement

✔ Do all pronouns agree with their nouns?

For help with pronoun agreement, see Chapter 36.

1. Find any pronouns in your revision of Emily's essay that do not agree with their nouns.

2. Correct any pronouns that do not agree with their nouns.

Modifiers

✔ Are modifiers as close as possible to the words they modify?

For help with modifier errors, see Chapter 39.

1. Find any modifiers in your revision of Emily's essay that are not as close as possible to the words they modify.

2. Rewrite sentences if necessary so that modifiers are as close as possible to the words they modify.

PUNCTUATION AND MECHANICS

Punctuation

✔ Are sentences punctuated correctly?

For help with punctuation, see Chapters 40–44.

1. Read your revision of Emily's essay for any errors in punctuation.

2. Find the two fragments you revised, and make sure they are punctuated correctly.

3. Did you find and correct Emily's two apostrophe errors? If not, find and correct them now.

Mechanics

✔ Are words capitalized properly?

For help with capitalization, see Chapter 45.

1. Read your revision of Emily's essay for any errors in capitalization.

2. Be sure to check Emily's capitalization in the fragments you revised.

WORD CHOICE AND SPELLING

Word Choice

✔ Are words used correctly?

For help with confused words, see Chapter 51.

1. Find any words used incorrectly in your revision of Emily's essay.

2. Correct any errors you find.

Spelling

✔ Are words spelled correctly?

For help with spelling, see Chapter 52.

1. Use spell-check and a dictionary to check the spelling in your revision of Emily's essay.

2. Correct any misspelled words.

Now rewrite Emily's essay again with your editing corrections.

Reading Your Own Process Analysis Essay

The most productive way to start revising and editing your own writing is to create some distance between you and your draft. To accomplish this goal, read your essay using the same reading strategy you have applied to other reading tasks in this chapter. Looking at it as a reading selection that you want to understand and respond to will help you revise and edit your draft efficiently and effectively.

READING CRITICALLY
Graphing Your Own Essay

Reading
Strategy

As you set out to revise and edit your own essay, apply the strategy you learned in this chapter for critical reading. Draw a picture of the relationship of your ideas to one another. In this way, you can check for logic and organization and make any changes you think are necessary at this time.

Revising and Editing Your Own Essay

You are now going to revise and edit your own writing. Remember that revision comes before editing and requires you to work with the content and organization of your essay while editing asks you to check your grammar and usage. The more you repeat these processes, the better draft you will write. The checklists here will help you apply to your essay what you have learned in this chapter.

Revising Your Own Essay

THESIS STATEMENT

☐ Does the thesis statement contain the essay's controlling idea and an opinion about that idea?

☐ Does the thesis appear as the last sentence of the introduction?

For Revising Peer Evaluation Forms, go to Appendix 4.

1. What is your purpose in the essay?

_____

2. Put brackets around the last sentence in your introduction. Does it state your purpose?

_____

3. Revise your thesis statement if necessary so that it states your purpose and introduces your topics.

_____

BASIC ELEMENTS

☐ Does the title draw in the readers?

☐ Does the introduction capture the readers' attention and build up effectively to the thesis statement?

☐ Does each body paragraph deal with a single topic?

☐ Does the conclusion bring the essay to a close in an interesting way?

1. Give your essay a title if it doesn't have one.

_____

2. Does your introduction capture your readers' attention and build up to your thesis statement at the end of the paragraph?

_____

3. Does each of your body paragraphs deal with only one topic?

_____

4. Does your conclusion follow some of the suggestions offered in Part I?

_____

DEVELOPMENT

☐ Do the body paragraphs adequately support the thesis statement?

☐ Does each body paragraph have a focused topic sentence?

☐ Does each body paragraph contain *specific* details that support the topic sentence?

☐ Does each body paragraph include *enough* details to fully explain the topic sentence?

1. Write out your thesis statement (revised, if necessary), and list your topic sentences below it.

Thesis statement: _____

Topic 1: _____

Topic 2: _____

Topic 3: _____

2. Do your topics adequately support your thesis statement?

_____

3. Does each body paragraph have a focused topic sentence?

_____

4. Do the details in your essay explain the process step by step?

_____

5. Where do you need more information?

_____

6. Add at least two new details to make the steps clearer.

UNITY

☐ Do the essay's topic sentences relate directly to the thesis statement?

☐ Do the details in each body paragraph support the paragraph's topic sentence?

1. Read each of your topic sentences with your thesis statement in mind. Do they go together?

_____

2. Revise your topic sentences if necessary so they are directly related.

3. Drop or rewrite any of the sentences in your body paragraphs that are not directly related to their topic sentences.

ORGANIZATION

☐ Is the essay organized logically?

☐ Is each body paragraph organized logically?

1. List the steps in your essay to make sure your process analysis is in chronological order.

2. Move any steps or paragraphs that are out of order.

_____

3. What word clues help your readers move logically through your essay?

_____

4. Look closely at your body paragraphs to see if all the sentences are arranged logically within paragraphs.

5. Move any sentences that are out of order.

COHERENCE

☐ Are transitions used effectively so that paragraphs move smoothly and logically from one to the next?

☐ Do the sentences move smoothly and logically from one to the next?

For a list of transitions, see pages 99–100.

1. Circle five transitions you use.

2. Explain how two of these make your essay easier to read.

_____

Now rewrite your essay with your revisions.

For Editing Peer Evaluation Forms, go to Appendix 6.

Editing Your Own Essay

SENTENCES

Subjects and Verbs

☐ Does each sentence have a main subject and verb?

For help with subjects and verbs, see Chapter 27.

1. Underline the subjects once and verbs twice in a paragraph of your revised essay. Remember that sentences can have more than one subject-verb set.

2. Does each of your sentences have at least one subject and verb that can stand alone?

_____

For help with fragments, see Chapter 28.

For help with run-togethers, see Chapter 29.

3. Correct any fragments you have written.

4. Correct any run-together sentences you have written.

Subject-Verb Agreement

☐ Do all subjects and verbs agree?

For help with subject-verb agreement, see Chapter 32.

1. Read aloud the subjects and verbs you underlined in your revised essay.

2. Correct any subjects and verbs that do not agree.

Pronoun Agreement

☐ Do all pronouns agree with their nouns?

For help with pronoun agreement, see Chapter 36.

1. Find any pronouns in your revised essay that do not agree with their nouns.

2. Correct any pronouns that do not agree with their nouns.

Modifiers

☐ Are modifiers as close as possible to the words they modify?

For help with modifier errors, see Chapter 39.

1. Find any modifiers in your revised essay that are not as close as possible to the words they modify.

2. Rewrite sentences if necessary so that your modifiers are as close as possible to the words they modify.

PUNCTUATION AND MECHANICS

Punctuation

☐ Are sentences punctuated correctly?

1. Read your revised essay for any errors in punctuation.

2. Make sure any fragments and run-together sentences you revised are punctuated correctly.

For help with punctuation, see Chapters 40–44.

Mechanics

☐ Are words capitalized properly?

1. Read your revised essay for any errors in capitalization.

2. Be sure to check your capitalization in any fragments or run-together sentences you revised.

For help with capitalization, see Chapter 45.

WORD CHOICE AND SPELLING

Word Choice

☐ Are words used correctly?

1. Find any words used incorrectly in your revised essay.

2. Correct any errors you find.

For help with confused words, see Chapter 51.

Spelling

☐ Are words spelled correctly?

1. Use spell-check and a dictionary to check your spelling.

2. Correct any misspelled words.

For help with spelling, see Chapter 52.

To make a personal log of your grammar/usage errors, go to Appendix 7.

To make a personal log of your spelling errors, go to Appendix 8.

Now rewrite your essay again with your editing corrections.

MyWritingLab **More Helpful Hints**

- **Forgot what to look for when you edit?** Editing helps fine-tune your paper by looking at grammar and mechanics. If you need help for what to look for when you edit your paper, check out the videos and activities in **MyWritingLab** for **Editing the Essay** in the **Essay Development** module.

PRACTICING PROCESS ANALYSIS: FROM READING TO WRITING

This final section gives you the opportunity to practice the reading and writing skills you learned in this chapter. It includes two reading selections and several writing assignments on "your reading" and "your world." The section then takes you through the routine of peer evaluation and reflection that focuses on productive ways to annotate your own essay for your instructor to read.

Reading Workshop

Here are two essays that illustrate good process analysis writing: "How to Protect Your Identity" by Brian O'Connell explains how to prevent identity theft, and "Be Cool to the Pizza Dude" by Sarah Adams describes how a life philosophy is essentially reflected in the way we treat the pizza delivery person. As you read, notice how the writers explain every step of the process carefully and completely.

HOW TO PROTECT YOUR IDENTITY
by Brian O'Connell

Focusing Your Attention

1. Think of a time when you had to explain to someone how to do something. Was it an easy or a difficult task? Did the person understand you? Was the person able to follow your directions?

2. In the process analysis essay you are about to read, the writer explains how to prevent identity theft. Have you ever told someone how to prevent something from happening? Was it useful information to those you were talking to?

Expanding Your Vocabulary

The following words are important to your understanding of this essay. As you read, circle any words you don't know beyond this list. Then break into groups, and help each other figure out the meanings of these unknown words.

cyber-means: using the Internet (paragraph 2)

breaches: security flaws (paragraph 2)

transactions: business dealings (paragraph 2)

vulnerable: open to attack (paragraph 2)

fraudulently: deceitfully (paragraph 5)

phishing: dealing with Internet theft (paragraph 7)

opt out: choose not to participate (paragraph 8)

rummage: search, dig (paragraph 8)

affidavit: a written statement (paragraph 9)

common denominator: something in common (paragraph 10)

READING CRITICALLY
Graphing Your Reading

Reading
Strategy

As you learned at the beginning of this chapter, practice drawing graphic organizers for the ideas in this essay. Exchange "pictures" with someone in your class, and write a brief statement of what your classmate's drawing communicates to you.

HOW TO PROTECT YOUR IDENTITY
by Brian O'Connell

There's an old Chinese proverb that says whoever steals an egg will steal an ox. 1
Fast forward to the 21st century, replace "egg" with a credit card number and "ox"
with your Social Security number, and you've tapped into one of the biggest threats
to the information age—identity theft.

Identity theft—the act of having your personal and financial information stolen 2
from you, often by cyber-means—is a burgeoning problem. According to an April 15,
2008, study of identity theft victims by the Poneman Institute, a Michigan-based
research group, 55 percent suffered two or more information breaches in the past
two years. According to a February 2009 report by Javelin Strategy and Research,
in 2008 the number of identity fraud victims grew 25 percent—affecting 9.9 million people. This is the first time since the report began in 2004 that the numbers
have increased. In 2007, about 8.4 million people were victims of identity theft, one
person every four seconds, which was down from more than 9 million the year before.
On Jan. 20, 2008, Heartland Payment Systems, a financial transactions company,
announced a security breach that occurred in late 2008 that left tens of millions
of credit cards vulnerable to cyber-fraud. Heartland doesn't know yet how many

accounts were breached, but it handles payment processing for 250,000 customers, 40 percent of which are restaurants. Heartland processes over 100 million transactions each month, according to company chief financial officer Robert Baldwin.

3   The good news is that taking action to stem ID theft is both easy and doable. CreditCards.com asked some leading information security experts what steps to take to secure your personal identity and here is what they had to say:

4   1. **Be aware**: First, how do you know your identity has been breached? Bruce Cornelius, chief marketing officer at Canoga Park, California-based CreditReport.com, says you'll know when you start getting letters and phone calls saying your application for credit has been approved or rejected, or you notice that your credit card statement has charges you never approved. Another red flag is getting phone calls from collection agencies saying you owe money.

5   2. **Act fast**: The key is to get out in front of the problem as soon as possible—before heavier damage can be done. "Oftentimes thieves will use your credit card data to commit non-financial identity theft crimes which become much larger problems," says Justin Yurek, president of Denver-based IDWatchdog.com. "As thieves begin to truly clone your identity, they can move from buying items in your name to committing crimes in your name, or obtaining employment benefits in your name, or obtaining medical services in your name. Unlike a thief fraudulently purchasing products in your name, there is no easy reversal for these crimes, and the consequences to the victim are much more severe."

6   3. **Prevention defense**: ID theft specialists say that the real key in stopping identity breaches is in prevention. "To prevent identity theft, cardholders need to guard their cards and keep secret any identifying information about their accounts," says Scott Crawford, CEO of DebtGoal.com. "This includes shredding account statements and keeping account and personal information secret. Look through your statement carefully to identify transactions that you didn't initiate, and take advantage of alerts that your credit institution offers. Many allow you to get alerts for abnormal transactions that can warn you of potential fraud on your account."

7   4. **Check URLs**: Always check a Web site's URL and security certificate before entering in your personal information. "With phishing schemes becoming increasingly sophisticated, it is important to ensure that you are doing business with the person you think you are and not an imposter," says Yurek. "Also, never send your personal information, such as a Social Security number or credit card number, in a non-secure format, such as an e-mail."

8   5. **Play it close to the vest**: Always keep your personal information as private as possible, and take concrete steps to eliminate your "financial footprint." "Don't give out your Social Security number unless it is absolutely necessary," says Scott Stevenson, founder and CEO of Eliminate ID Theft. "If you do not

want credit offers to come to you, contact the three credit reporting agencies and 'opt out' of these offers. They should remove your name for two years from mailing and telemarketing lists. Don't carry your Social Security card, passport, or birth certificate in your wallet or purse, and only carry the credit cards that you need." Stevenson also advocates checking the "inquiry" section of your credit report to see if there are unsolicited creditors reviewing your credit that you haven't done business with. Be careful about your mail habits too. "Don't mail bills or any documents like tax forms from your personal mailbox. Take them directly to the post office or pay them online. Thieves will rummage through your mailbox and take your valuable information."

6. **Contact the authorities**: If you've been the victim of an identity theft crime, contact the police as soon as possible. CreditReport.com's Cornelius also advises to close all accounts you didn't open and ones that were taken over. "Also use the Federal Trade Commission's identity theft affidavit from the FTC Web site, to file a complaint that can be used to investigate identity theft," adds Cornelius. "Then file a report with your local police department and in the community where the identity theft occurred. Get copies of this police report to help you prove to credit card companies and banks that your identity was stolen."   9

One common denominator among all ID theft experts? Get ahead of the problem before it gets ahead of you. That way, both your egg and your ox are well protected.   10

Thinking Critically About Content

1. How does O'Connell explain the "egg" and the "ox" (paragraph 1) in the 21st century?

2. What is one example the author cites to demonstrate the current magnitude of identity theft?

3. What are the six steps to O'Connell's plan for preventing identity theft?

Thinking Critically About Purpose and Audience

4. What is O'Connell's purpose in this essay?

5. Who do you think would benefit from the information in this essay? Explain your answer.

6. Which piece of O'Connell's advice do you find most useful for your lifestyle?

Thinking Critically About Essays

7. Describe in a complete sentence the author's point of view in his last paragraph.

8. How does O'Connell organize his essay? Write a rough outline to show his method of organization.

9. Choose a paragraph from his essay, and explain how it is developed.

To keep track of your critical thinking progress, go to Appendix 1.

10. Explain in detail why identity theft is such an enormous problem in the information age.

BE COOL TO THE PIZZA DUDE
by Sarah Adams

Focusing Your Attention

1. Do you have any general philosophies about the way you choose to live?

2. In the essay you are about to read, the writer explains that the way people treat the pizza delivery person says a great deal about their values. Can you think of something that captures one of your philosophies about life? What is it, and what does it represent?

Expanding Your Vocabulary

The following words are important to your understanding of this essay. As you read, circle any words you don't know beyond this list. Then break into groups, and help each other figure out the meanings of these unknown words.

digits: fingers (paragraph 2)

harried: busy (paragraph 2)

beacon: guiding light (paragraph 2)

empathy: understanding (paragraph 3)

bestow: give (paragraph 6)

Reading Strategy

READING CRITICALLY
Graphing Your Reading

As you did with the previous essay, draw a graphic organizer for the ideas in the following essay. Make the drawing so accurate that someone could look at it and understand the basic concepts in the essay. Compare your drawing with someone else's in your class, and write a brief statement about the reading from your classmate's graphic organizer.

BE COOL TO THE PIZZA DUDE
by Sarah Adams

If I have one operating philosophy about life, it is this: "Be cool to the pizza delivery dude; it's good luck." Four principles guide the pizza dude philosophy.   1

Principle 1: Coolness to the pizza delivery dude is a practice in humility and for-giveness. I let him cut me off in traffic, let him safely hit the exit ramp from the left lane, let him forget to use his blinker without extending any of my digits out the win-dow or towards my horn because there should be one moment in my harried life when a car may encroach or cut off or pass and I let it go. Sometimes when I have become so certain of my ownership of my lane, daring anyone to challenge me, the pizza dude speeds by me in his rusted Chevette. His pizza light atop his car glowing like a beacon reminds me to check myself as I flow through the world. After all, the dude is delivering pizza to young and old, families and singletons, gays and straights, blacks, whites and browns, rich and poor, vegetarians and meat lovers alike. As he journeys, I give safe passage, practice restraint, show courtesy, and contain my anger.   2

Principle 2: Coolness to the pizza delivery dude is a practice in empathy. Let's face it: We've all taken jobs just to have a job because some money is better than none. I've held an assortment of these jobs and was grateful for the paycheck that meant I didn't have to share my Cheerios with my cats. In the big pizza wheel of life, sometimes you're the hot bubbly cheese and sometimes you're the burnt crust. It's good to remember the fickle spinning of that wheel.   3

Principle 3: Coolness to the pizza delivery dude is a practice in honor, and it reminds me to honor honest work. Let me tell you something about these dudes: They never took over a company and, as CEO, artificially inflated the value of the stock and cashed out their own shares, bringing the company to the brink of bankruptcy, resulting in 20,000 people losing their jobs while the CEO builds a home the size of a luxury hotel. Rather, the dudes sleep the sleep of the just.   4

Principle 4: Coolness to the pizza delivery dude is a practice in equality. My measurement as a human being, my worth, is the pride I take in performing my job—any job—and the respect with which I treat others. I am the equal of the world not because of the car I drive, the size of the TV I own, the weight I can bench press, or the calculus equations I can solve. I am the equal to all I meet because of the kind-ness in my heart. And it all starts here—with the pizza delivery dude.   5

Tip him well, friends and brethren, for that which you bestow freely and will-ingly will bring you all the happy luck that a grateful universe knows how to return.   6

Thinking Critically About Content

1. What does the pizza dude represent for Adams and the general public?

2. What are the four principles that make up Adams's "pizza dude philosophy"? What is important about these principles?

3. Why does Adams insist that we treat the "pizza dude" with respect? What will this treatment bring us in return?

Thinking Critically About Purpose and Audience

4. What do you think the purpose of this essay is?

5. How do you think a general audience would respond to Adams's four principles?

6. Why does Adams compare the pizza light on the pizza dude's car to "a beacon"? What does a beacon represent for Adams's purpose?

Thinking Critically About Essays

7. Describe in a complete sentence the writer's tone.

8. Why do you think Adams uses an employee at a pizza restaurant to prove her point?

9. What do you think is Adams's rationale for organizing her four principles as she did? Is this an effective order for her message? Explain your answer.

To keep track of your critical thinking progress, go to Appendix 1.

10. How would you rewrite the essay from the perspective of the pizza employee? What four guidelines might he or she suggest for treating customers well? Be sure to note the benefit of this treatment in your statement.

Writing Workshop

This final section offers you opportunities to apply what you have learned in this chapter to another writing assignment. This time, we provide very little prompting beyond a summary of the guidelines for writing a process analysis essay. This section will let you demonstrate that you can go through the entire writing process on your own with only occasional feedback from your peers. Loop back into the chapter as necessary when you have questions so that this process becomes as automatic to you as possible before you move on to new material. Then pause at the end of the chapter to reflect briefly on what you have learned.

 Guidelines for Writing a Process Analysis Essay

1. State in the thesis statement what the reader should be able to do or understand by the end of the essay.
2. Know your audience.
3. Explain the process clearly in the body of your essay.
4. Organize your material logically.
5. End your essay by considering the process as a whole.

Writing About Your Reading

1. In the first essay, O'Connell talks about how we need to "get ahead of the problem before it gets ahead of you." Are you aware of a need for this timing in other aspects of your life? How can thoughtful timing get you what you want? Explain a process that involved getting something you wanted by timing your words and/or actions with care.

2. Think of something in your experience that represents an important life lesson, like the pizza dude does for Adams. Then write an essay similar to Adams' article, explaining how this symbol works.

3. Which type of process analysis do you find most interesting—the how-to essays or the background explanations? Explain your answer.

Writing About Your World

1. Place yourself in a scene similar to the one here, and write a process analysis essay explaining something that you find as interesting as this person finds this activity. Be sure to cover all steps or stages of the process you are discussing.

2. Choose an appliance or a piece of equipment that you understand well, and write a process analysis essay explaining how it works. Don't identify the item in your essay. Then see if the class members can guess what device you are talking about.

3. Research the history of your college or university, and write an essay explaining its background to prospective students. Be sure to give a focus to your study and decide on a purpose before you begin writing.

4. Write your own process analysis assignment (with the help of your instructor), and write a response to it.

Revising

Small Group Activity (5–10 minutes per writer) In groups of three or four, read your process analysis essays to each other. Those listening should record their reactions on a copy of the Revising Peer Evaluation Forms in Appendix 4. After your group goes through this process, give your evaluation forms to the appropriate writers so that each writer has two or three peer comment sheets for revising.

Paired Activity (5 minutes per writer) Using the completed Peer Evaluation Forms, work in pairs to decide what you should revise in your essay. If time allows, rewrite some of your sentences, and have your partner look at them.

Individual Activity Rewrite your paper, using the revising feedback you received from other students.

Editing

Paired Activity (5–10 minutes per writer) Swap papers with a classmate, and use the Editing Peer Evaluation Form (Appendix 6) to identify as many grammar, punctuation, mechanics, and spelling errors as you can. If time allows, correct some of your errors, and have your partner look at them. Record your grammar, punctuation, and mechanics errors in the Error Log (Appendix 7) and your spelling errors in the Spelling Log (Appendix 8).

Individual Activity Rewrite your paper again, using the editing feedback you received from other students.

Reflecting on Your Writing   When you have completed your own essay, answer these six questions.

1. What was most difficult about this assignment?

2. What was easiest?

3. What did you learn about process analysis by completing this assignment?

4. What do you think are the strengths of your process analysis? Place a wavy line by the parts of your essay that you feel are very good.

5. What are the weaknesses, if any, of your paper? Place an X by the parts of your essay you would like help with. Write in the margins any questions you have.

6. What did you learn from this assignment about your own writing process—about preparing to write, about writing the first draft, about revising, and about editing?

MyWritingLab™ Visit Chapter 12, "Analyzing a Process," in MyWritingLab, and complete the Post-test to check your understanding of the chapter's objectives.

Comparing and Contrasting

"The difference between the right word and the almost-right word is really a large matter—'tis the difference between the lightning-bug and the lightning."

—MARK TWAIN

Comparison and contrast are at the heart of our democratic society. Our competitive natures encourage us to compare our lives to those of others so we can try to better ourselves. Even if we simply attempt to improve on our "personal best," comparison and contrast keep us striving for more. In school, we learn about different writers, different cultures, different musical instruments, and different political platforms by comparing them to one another. And every day we make decisions based on comparisons of one sort or another—which clothes we should wear, which person we should date, which apartment we should rent, which job we should take. Comparisons help us establish a frame of reference and figure out where we fit into the larger world around us.

On another level, comparison and contrast are also part of our writing. They play an important role in our personal lives, in our college courses, and in the workplace, as in the following situations:

- Someone looking for a new car does comparison shopping on the Internet.
- A student doing a report in a nursing course compares and contrasts traditional and alternative approaches to medical care.
- For an exam in anthropology, a student compares and contrasts two different Native American cultures.
- An insurance agent prepares a report for a client that compares and contrasts several different insurance policies.
- A travel agent compares and contrasts two travel packages for a client.

259

Comparison and contrast help us understand one subject by putting it next to another. When we *compare*, we look for similarities, and when we *contrast*, we look for differences. Nearly always, however, comparison and contrast are part of the same process. For this reason, we often use the word *compare* to refer to both techniques.

MyWritingLab

Understanding Comparison/Contrast

To check your understanding of comparison and contrast, go to **MyWritingLab.com,** and choose **Compare and Contrast** in the **Essay Development** module. From there, read the **Overview,** watch the **Animation** video, and complete the **Recall, Apply,** and **Write** activities. Then check your understanding of comparison and contrast by taking the **Post-test.**

PREPARING TO WRITE A COMPARISON/CONTRAST ESSAY

Once again, preparing to write in this text starts with reading. Reading a good comparison/contrast essay can lead to writing a good essay in that rhetorical mode if you actually see how the content and form of the essay function. Looking closely at how a comparison/contrast essay works will improve your reading comprehension and transfer over time to your writing. Like two halves of a circle, the reading and writing processes function together and, as you learn how they operate, will serve you well in your college courses and in life. To accomplish this, you will read an effective comparison on the next few pages and then answer some questions to help you learn how the essay achieves its purpose.

Reading a Comparison/Contrast Essay

In his essay "The Revolutionary Effect of the Paperback Book," Clive Thompson compares and contrasts the introduction of the e-reader to that of Pocket Books in 1939. Do you read books digitally? In traditional book form? Or both? Do you read differently in these two mediums?

Reading with the aid of a specific strategy is a productive way to learn how to read critically. Reading critically means you understand the content on a high level and have the potential to write on that level as well. Reading critically, or analytically, will help you understand not only *what* the essay is saying but also *how* the author is saying it. The strategy you will apply to all reading tasks in this chapter focuses on peer teaching.

READING CRITICALLY
Peer Teaching a Professional Essay

 Reading
Strategy

Teaching something to your peers is an excellent way to check your understanding of a concept or skill. To practice this technique, the class must first divide the following essay into four parts of four paragraphs each. The class members should then get into four groups and choose one of the sections. After identifying the main ideas, the details, and their relationship to one another, each group should teach its section to the rest of the class. This strategy is called "peer teaching."

THE REVOLUTIONARY EFFECT
OF THE PAPERBACK BOOK
by Clive Thompson

1   The iPhone became the world's best-selling smartphone partly because Steve Jobs was obsessed with the ergonomics of everyday life. If you want people to carry a computer, it had to hit the "sweet spot" where it was big enough to display "detailed, legible graphics, but small enough to fit comfortably in the hand and pocket."

2   Seventy-five years ago, another American innovator had the same epiphany: Robert Fair de Graff realized he could change the way people read by making books radically smaller. Back then, it was surprisingly hard for ordinary Americans to get good novels and nonfiction. The country only had about 500 bookstores, all clustered in the biggest 12 cities, and hardcovers cost $2.50 (about $40 in today's currency).

3   De Graff revolutionized that market when he got backing from Simon & Schuster to launch Pocket Books in May 1939. A petite 4 by 6 inches and priced at a mere 25 cents, the Pocket Book changed everything about who could read and where. Suddenly people read all the time, much as we now peek at e-mail and Twitter on our phones. And by working with the often gangster-riddled magazine-distribution industry, De Graff sold books where they had never been available before—grocery stores, drugstores, and airport terminals. Within two years, he'd sold 17 million. "They literally couldn't keep up with demand," says historian Kenneth C. Davis, who documented De Graff's triumph in his book *Two-Bit Culture*. "They tapped into a huge reservoir of Americans who nobody realized wanted to read."

4   Other publishers rushed into the business. And, like all forms of new media, pocket-sized books panicked the elites. Sure, some books were quality literature, but the biggest sellers were mysteries, westerns, thinly veiled smut—a potential "flood of trash" that threatened to "debase further the popular taste," as the social critic Harvey Swados worried. But the tumult also gave birth to new and distinctly

5   American literary genres, from Mickey Spillane's gritty detective stories to Ray Bradbury's cerebral science fiction.

The financial success of the paperback became its cultural downfall. Media conglomerates bought the upstart pocket-book firms and began hiking prices and chasing after quick-money best-sellers, including jokey fare like *101 Uses for a Dead Cat*. And while paperbacks remain commonplace, they're no longer dizzingly cheaper than hardcovers.

6   Instead, there's a new reading format that's shifting the terrain. Mini-tablets and e-readers not only fit in your pocket but they allow your entire library to fit in your pocket. And, as with De Graff's invention, e-readers are producing new forms, prices, and publishers.

7   The upshot, says Mike Shatzkin—CEO of the Idea Logical Company, a consultancy for publishers—is that "more reading is taking place," as we tuck it into ever more stray moments. But he also worries that as e-book consumers shift more to multifunctional tablets, reading might take a back seat to other portable entertainment: more "Angry Birds," less Jennifer Egan. Still, whatever the outcome, the true revolution in portable publishing began not with e-books but with De Graff, whose paperback made reading into an activity that travels everywhere.

Discovering How This Essay Works

To help you recognize the elements that make this an effective comparison/contrast essay so you can use them in your own writing, answer the following questions in as much detail as possible.

1. What do you think Thompson's main point is in this essay?

    _____

    _____

    _____

2. What exactly is Thompson comparing or contrasting?

    _____

    _____

3. Which of Thompson's examples prove to you that e-books will make different demands on both our reading and writing?

    _____

    _____

4. What subtopics or "points" does the author compare?

    _____

    _____

5. Does Thompson discuss all the subtopics for one subject (reading) and then all the subtopics for the other subject (writing) subject by subject? Or does he discuss both subjects for each subtopic point by point?

_____

_____

WRITING A COMPARISON/CONTRAST ESSAY

Now that you have read and studied the professional essay, you are ready to write one of your own. This section will guide you through the process of generating a draft that you will then revise and edit in the third section of this chapter. You will learn how to read the writing assignment carefully, generate ideas and choose a topic, and finally follow the guidelines for writing an effective comparison/contrast essay. Throughout this section, you should keep records of your thoughts and ideas so you can use them when you write a draft of your essay at the end of this section.

Reading the Prompt

Getting ready to write means first understanding the writing assignment or "prompt." Any assignment given to you will try to "prompt" you to respond to a specific issue or question. The more thoroughly you understand the prompt, the better paper you will create. So you want to learn how to interact with the essay assignment to make sure you understand all its complexities. Applying the chapter reading strategy to your writing assignment is a good way to accomplish this goal.

 READING CRITICALLY
Peer Teaching the Prompt

 Reading
Strategy

Divide the writing assignment that follows into four small parts. Divide the class into four groups. Then each group should brainstorm and discuss the different ways to interpret and respond to its section of the prompt. After this discussion, a spokesperson from each group should summarize the group's discussion for the entire class. Everyone will benefit from understanding the various perspectives they now have on the details of this assignment and their relationship to one another. Write notes in the margins of the assignment as each group presents its findings.

MyWritingLab
Complete this Writing Prompt
assignment in MyWritingLab.

Writing Prompt

Write an essay comparing and contrasting two methods of escape and relaxation. How are they alike? How are they different? Decide what point you want to make before you start writing. Form a clear thesis statement, and follow the guidelines below for writing a comparison/contrast essay.

Thinking About the Prompt

Before you focus on a specific topic, you should generate as many ideas as you can so you have several to choose from for your essay. Think of several ways you might escape or relieve stress. What do you like about these methods of relaxation? Use one or more of the prewriting strategies you learned in Chapter 5 to generate ideas about these forms of escape. Why do they work for you?

Guidelines for Writing a Comparison/Contrast Essay

To write a comparison/contrast essay, consider two items that have something in common, such as cats and dogs (both are family pets) or cars and motorcycles (both are means of transportation). (A discussion of cats and motorcycles, for example, would not be very interesting or useful because the two do not have any common features.) This is the basic rule underlying the following guidelines for writing a good comparison/contrast essay. As you think about the topic you have chosen in response to the prompt above, read the following guidelines, and continue to make lists and notes you will use when you write your draft. After each guideline is an explanation of how it functions in the reading selection at the beginning of this chapter so you can actually see how the element works in an essay before you apply it to your own writing.

1. **Decide what point you want to make with your comparison, and include it in your thesis statement**. A comparison/contrast essay is usually written for one of two purposes: to examine the subjects separately or to show the superiority of one over the other. This purpose should be made clear in your thesis statement.

In the Reading: In the sample essay, Thompson's point, or thesis, is that "the Pocket Book changed everything about who could read and where" (paragraph 3). He compares the revolutionary innovation of reading pocket books to current reading on electronic devices.

In Your Writing: What point do you want to make about relaxation and escape with your comparison? Jot down some notes about your main point, which will guide your selection of topics to compare.

2. **Choose items to compare and contrast that will make your point most effectively**. Usually, the subjects you plan to compare and contrast

have many similarities and differences. Your task, then, is to look over the ideas you generated in prewriting and choose the best points for making your comparison clearly and strongly.

In the Reading: In his essay, Thompson compares his subjects—pocket books and e-readers—on four points:

Point 1: Degree of innovation
Point 2: Size
Point 3: New forms, prices, and publishers
Point 4: Amount of reading among consumers

In Your Writing: Now look at your prewriting notes, and select the relaxation methods you are going to compare. Are the items you intend to compare from the same category?

3. **Use as many specific details and examples as possible to expand your comparison**. The most common way of developing a comparison/contrast essay is to use description and example. Generate as many details and examples as you can for each of your subjects. Try to think of both obvious and not-so-obvious points of comparison.

In the Reading: In "The Revolutionary Effect of the Paperback Book," Thompson relies heavily on examples to make his point. Here are some of the details he furnishes: seventy-five years ago, Robert de Graff, 500 bookstores, $2.50 for hardcovers, May 1939, 4 by 6 inches, price of 25 cents, 17 million books sold, Kenneth C. Davis's *Two-Bit Culture*, Harvey Swados, Mickey Spillane, Ray Bradbury, and *101 Uses of a Dead Cat*.

In Your Writing: Look at your prewriting notes once again, and add as many examples as possible to the relaxation methods you have chosen to compare. Then, go back through your notes, and add some vivid details to them. Make the details as numerous and as specific as you can so you will produce an interesting, informative essay.

4. **Develop your comparison in a balanced way**. Having selected the points on which you will compare your two subjects, you are ready to develop the comparison in your body paragraphs. You should make sure, however, that your treatment of each subject is balanced. This means that, first, you must cover the same topics for each subject. In other words, you should give equal coverage to both subjects, no matter what your conclusion is. In addition, you ought to spend the same amount of time on each point. If you describe one of your subjects in detail, be sure to also describe the other. In like manner, you should provide a similar number of examples for both subjects. In this way, your readers will feel that you have been fair to both subjects and that you are not presenting a biased discussion favoring one subject over the other.

In the Reading: Thompson spends more time describing the revolution of pocket books than the introduction of e-readers because he is trying to prove that mobile reading started in 1939 rather than in the present. But he covers all four main topics for both subjects.

In Your Writing: Return to your prewriting lists and notes. Is your list balanced, with the same number of details for each method of relaxation in your comparison? Should any other items be on your list? Should any topics be deleted? Work on your list until you feel it is focused and complete.

5. **Organize your essay subject by subject or point by point—or combine the two approaches**. When you are ready to write, you have three choices for organizing a comparison/contrast essay: (1) subject by subject (AAA, BBB), (2) point by point (AB, AB, AB), or (3) a combination of the two.

In the subject arrangement, you say everything you have to say about the first subject, A, before you move on to talk about the second subject, B. In a point-by-point arrangement, both subjects are compared on point 1; then both are compared on point 2; and so on through all the points.

To choose which method of organization would be most effective, just use your common sense. If the subjects themselves are the most interesting part of your essay, use the subject pattern. But if you want single characteristics to stand out, use the point-by-point approach.

In the Reading: Thompson's essay is arranged subject by subject. Here is what his essay's organization looks like:

Subject A: The pocket-sized book
  Point 1: Degree of innovation
  Point 2: Size
  Point 3: New forms, prices, and publishers
  Point 4: Amount of reading among consumers

Subject B: E-readers
  Point 1: Degree of innovation
  Point 2: Size
  Point 3: New forms, prices, and publishers
  Point 4: Amount of reading among consumers

In Your Writing: How do you plan to organize your essay? Will your comparison be organized by general subjects, specific points, or a combination of the two? Which is the most effective order for what you are trying to accomplish? Revise your list one more time, if necessary, so that its organization supports your purpose.

Writing a Draft of Your Essay

Now is the time to collect all your peer teaching notes, your prewriting exercises, and your lists as you prepare to generate the first draft of your essay. For this task, you might also want to review the professional essay, the writing assignment, and the chapter guidelines for writing comparison/contrast essays, along with your notes and lists. At this point, don't think about revising or editing; just get your thoughts about the writing assignment down on paper.

MyWritingLab **Helpful Hints**

- **Have you forgotten the elements of the writing process?** You can review **The Writing Process** in **The Craft of Writing** module of **MyWritingLab.** This topic provides an overview of the process and explains how it can help you create a coherent essay.

REVISING AND EDITING

You are now ready to begin revising and editing your essay. This section will lead you through the guidelines for revising and editing comparison/contrast essays with two specific writing samples: another student's essay and your own essay. The processes of revising and editing are often much easier with someone else's writing, which is why we begin this stage with a writing sample from another student. If you can uncover some of the problems in this essay, you might more easily be able to see areas for improvement in your own writing. So you will be reviewing the chapter guidelines by revising and editing another student's writing before applying the same guidelines to your own writing.

Reading a Student Comparison/Contrast Essay

We will begin by using our chapter reading strategy on a student's comparison/contrast essay. The essay, "The Truth About Cats and Dogs," was written by a student named Maria Castillo. Planning what you will pass on to your classmates as you read this essay will help you focus your attention and prepare you to look for ways to improve this essay.

Reading
Strategy

READING CRITICALLY
Peer Teaching the Student Essay

Read Maria's essay, focusing on her purpose. Then, think about how you will present her main point to your class in a creative way. Think of an approach to this task that no one else will pursue. You might also present your peer teaching ideas to each other in groups and then prepare a group presentation for the class. Take notes on the highlights of these presentations by your classmates. This strategy makes sure that you understand the content of an essay well enough to present it to others. Write some notes to yourself in the margins before you discuss the essay as a class.

The Truth About Cats and Dogs

1   The majority of people in the world will say that dogs are man's best friends and that cats were put on this earth to aggravate dogs. Some people are closet cat lovers, meaning he or she is afraid to tell family and friends that they actually like cats. Others will proudly state, "I hate cats, except for yours." People who resist cats do so because they believe they are; aloof, self-centered, and dull. People prefer dogs because they are friendly, protective, and playful. However, cats exhibit these same qualities and deserve the same respect as dogs.

2   Dogs have always been considered to be friendly, but cats can also fit this description. Dogs stay by their owners' sides and live to make their masters happy. They are the first to greet their family at the front door, they want nothing more than to be praised by their owners. Yet cats are much the same way. They, too, will be at the front door when their family gets home and are always excited to see them. They usually sit near their owners just to be by their sides. And despite what some people believe, a cat does come when they're called. Birds do not sit with their owners unless they are trained. Cats are very friendly to their owners.

3   As much as dogs love to play, so do cats. Most dogs love to play with chew toys, searching for the hidden-squeaker treasure. They often parade around with their "kill" until their masters notice their triumph. Some owners will awaken to find that their dogs have strewn all their toys all over the house. Dogs love the toys they know are theirs. However, so do cats. Cats will make a toy out of anything that will slide across a tile floor, whether it's a hair clip, a milk jug ring, a toy mouse, or a spool of thread. They can amuse themselves for hours. If the toy-of-the-day gets trapped under the refrigerator, cats will whine and wait for their owner to get the toy. Cats just love to play.

4   Even though dogs are great defenders, cats have been known to protect the family as well. Dogs bark or growl whenever they want to alert their owners to possible danger. They stand at the door and wait for their owners to check for danger. If they see their owner being attacked, they will attack the enemy. Most people think cats

would just stand by and watch, but this simply isn't true. Cats also alert their owners of danger by growling or standing to stiff attention. They, too, stand near the door waiting for their owner to react. Cats have been known to bite people who harm their loved ones. Cats can be excellent watch animals.

    Dogs and cats are a lot alike. People say cats are very different from dogs, but this is   5
not the case. The truth is, most people love to hate cats. It's now an old American pastime. But it's time for all cat lovers to unite and prove that it can be a cat-eat-cat world too.

Revising and Editing the Student Essay

This essay is Maria's first draft, which now needs to be revised and edited. First, apply the Revising Checklist to the content of Maria's draft. When you are satisfied that her ideas are fully developed and well organized, use the Editing Checklist to correct her grammar and mechanics errors. Answer the questions, and complete the tasks in each category. Then write your suggested changes directly on Maria's draft.

Revising the Student Essay

THESIS STATEMENT

✔ Does the thesis statement contain the essay's controlling idea?

✔ Does the thesis appear as the last sentence of the introduction?

1. Put brackets around the last sentence in Maria's introduction. Does it contain her main point?

_____

2. Rewrite Maria's thesis statement if necessary so that it states her main point and introduces her topics.

_____

_____

_____

BASIC ELEMENTS

✔ Does the title draw in the readers?

✔ Does the introduction capture the readers' attention and build up effectively to the thesis statement?

✔ Does each body paragraph deal with a single topic?

✔ Does the conclusion bring the essay to a close in an interesting way?

1. Give Maria's essay an alternate title.

   _____

2. Rewrite Maria's introduction so that it captures readers' attention and builds up to the thesis statement at the end of the paragraph.

   _____

   _____

   _____

3. Does each of Maria's body paragraphs deal with only one topic?

   _____

4. Rewrite Maria's conclusion using at least one suggestion from Part I.

   _____

   _____

   _____

DEVELOPMENT

✔ Do the body paragraphs adequately support the thesis statement?

✔ Does each body paragraph have a focused topic sentence?

✔ Does each body paragraph contain *specific* details that support the topic sentence?

✔ Does each body paragraph include *enough* details to fully explain the topic sentence?

1. Write out Maria's thesis statement (revised, if necessary), and list her three topic sentences below it.

   Thesis statement: _____

   _____

   _____

   Topic 1: _____

   _____

   Topic 2: _____

   _____

   Topic 3: _____

   _____

2. Do Maria's topic sentences adequately support her thesis statement?

_____

3. Does each body paragraph have a focused topic sentence?

_____

4. Do Maria's details adequately characterize both cats and dogs?

_____

5. Where do you need more information?

_____

6. Make two of Maria's details more specific.

7. Add at least two new details to make her comparison clearer.

UNITY

✔ Do the essay's topic sentences relate directly to the thesis statement?

✔ Do the details in each body paragraph support the paragraph's topic sentence?

1. Read each of Maria's topic sentences with her thesis statement (revised, if necessary) in mind. Do they go together?

2. Revise her topic sentences if necessary so they are directly related.

3. Drop or rewrite the sentence in paragraph 2 that is not directly related to its topic sentence.

ORGANIZATION

✔ Is the essay organized logically?

✔ Is each body paragraph organized logically?

1. Read Maria's essay again to see if all the paragraphs are arranged logically.

2. Reverse the two paragraphs that are out of order.

3. Look closely at Maria's body paragraphs to see if all her sentences are arranged logically within paragraphs.

4. Move any sentences that are out of order.

COHERENCE

✔ Are transitions used effectively so that paragraphs move smoothly and logically from one to the next?

✔ Do the sentences move smoothly and logically from one to the next?

1. Add two transitions to Maria's essay.

For a list of transitions, see pages 99–100.

2. Circle five synonyms Maria uses.

3. Explain how two of these synonyms make Maria's essay easier to read.

_____

_____

_____

 Now rewrite Maria's essay with your revisions.

Editing the Student Essay

SENTENCES

Subjects and Verbs
✔ Does each sentence have a main subject and verb?

For help with subjects and verbs, see Chapter 27.

1. Underline Maria's subjects once and verbs twice in paragraph 2 of your revision of Maria's essay. Remember that sentences can have more than one subject-verb set.

2. Does each of Maria's sentences have at least one subject and verb that can stand alone?

_____

For help with run-togethers, see Chapter 29.

3. Did you find and correct Maria's run-together sentence? If not, find and correct it now.

Subject-Verb Agreement
✔ Do all subjects and verbs agree?

For help with subject-verb agreement, see Chapter 32.

1. Read aloud the subjects and verbs you underlined in your revision of Maria's essay.

2. Correct any subjects and verbs that do not agree.

Pronoun Agreement
✔ Do all pronouns agree with their nouns?

For help with pronoun agreement, see Chapter 36.

1. Find any pronouns in your revision of Maria's essay that do not agree with their nouns.

2. Did you find and correct the two pronouns that do not agree with their nouns?

Modifiers

✔ Are modifiers as close as possible to the words they modify?

1. Find any modifiers in your revision of Maria's essay that are not as close as possible to the words they modify.

2. Rewrite sentences if necessary so modifiers are as close as possible to the words they modify.

For help with modifier errors, see Chapter 39.

PUNCTUATION AND MECHANICS

Punctuation

✔ Are sentences punctuated correctly?

1. Read your revision of Maria's essay for any errors in punctuation.

2. Find the run-together sentence you revised, and make sure it is punctuated correctly.

3. Did you find and correct Maria's semicolon error? If not, find and correct it now.

For help with punctuation, see Chapters 40–44.

Mechanics

✔ Are words capitalized properly?

1. Read your revision of Maria's essay for any errors in capitalization.

2. Be sure to check Maria's capitalization in the run-together sentence you revised.

For help with capitalization, see Chapter 45.

WORD CHOICE AND SPELLING

Word Choice

✔ Are words used correctly?

1. Find any words used incorrectly in your revision of Maria's essay.

2. Correct any errors you find.

For help with confused words, see Chapter 51.

Spelling

✔ Are words spelled correctly?

1. Use spell-check and a dictionary to check the spelling in your revision of Maria's essay.

2. Correct any misspelled words

For help with spelling, see Chapter 52.

Now rewrite Maria's essay again with your editing corrections.

Reading Your Own Comparison/Contrast Essay

The first stage of revising your own writing is creating some distance between you and your draft. To accomplish this, apply the same reading strategy to your own writing that you have been using throughout this chapter. Treating your essay as a reading selection that you are trying to understand and respond to will help you revise and edit your own work efficiently and effectively.

Reading Strategy

READING CRITICALLY
Peer Teaching Your Own Essay

Once you have a draft, apply the chapter reading technique to your own writing. Divide yourselves into groups of three or four, swap essays, and then "teach" someone else's essay to the group. Summarize the writer's main point, and then briefly explain the details and their relationship to the essay's main idea. Point out gaps and problems as you move from person to person.

Revising and Editing Your Own Essay

You are now ready to revise and edit your own writing. Remember that revision involves reworking the development and organization of your essay, while editing asks you to check your grammar and usage. Continue to revise and edit until your essay fulfills its intended purpose. Work first with the essay's content and then with the grammar and usage. The checklists here will help you apply to your essay what you have learned in this chapter.

Revising Your Own Essay

For Revising Peer Evaluation Forms, go to Appendix 4.

THESIS STATEMENT

☐ Does the thesis statement contain the essay's controlling idea and an opinion about that idea?

☐ Does the thesis appear as the last sentence of the introduction?

1. What main point are you trying to make in your essay?

_____

2. Put brackets around the last sentence in your introduction. Does it contain your main point?

_____

3. Rewrite your thesis statement if necessary so that it states your main point and introduces your topics.

BASIC ELEMENTS

☐ Does the title draw in the readers?

☐ Does the introduction capture the readers' attention and build up effectively to the thesis statement?

☐ Does each body paragraph deal with a single topic?

☐ Does the conclusion bring the essay to a close in an interesting way?

1. Give your essay a title if it doesn't have one.

   _____

2. Does your introduction capture your readers' attention and build up to your thesis statement at the end of the paragraph?

   _____

3. Does each of your body paragraphs deal with only one topic?

   _____

4. Does your conclusion follow some of the suggestions offered in Part I?

   _____

DEVELOPMENT

☐ Do the body paragraphs adequately support the thesis statement?

☐ Does each body paragraph have a focused topic sentence?

☐ Does each body paragraph contain *specific* details that support the topic sentence?

☐ Does each body paragraph include *enough* details to fully explain the topic sentence?

1. Write out your thesis statement (revised, if necessary), and list your topic sentences below it.

   Thesis statement: _____

        Topic 1: _____

        Topic 2: _____

        Topic 3: _____

2. Do your topics adequately support your thesis statement?

   _____

3. Does each body paragraph have a focused topic sentence?

   _____

4. Do you cover the same characteristics of both topics?

   _____

5. Where do your readers need more information?

   _____

6. Make two of your details more specific.

7. Add at least two new details to make your comparison clearer.

UNITY

☐ Do the essay's topic sentences relate directly to the thesis statement?

☐ Do the details in each body paragraph support the paragraph's topic sentence?

1. Read each of your topic sentences with your thesis statement in mind. Do they go together?

   _____

2. Revise your topic sentences if necessary so they are directly related.

3. Drop or rewrite any of the sentences in your body paragraphs that are not directly related to their topic sentences.

ORGANIZATION

☐ Is the essay organized logically?

☐ Is each body paragraph organized logically?

1. Read your essay again to see if all the paragraphs are arranged logically.

2. How is your essay organized: subject by subject, point by point, or a combination of the two?

   _____

3. Is the order you chose for your paragraphs the most effective approach to your subject?

   _____

4. Move any paragraphs that are out of order.

5. Look closely at your body paragraphs to see if all the sentences are arranged logically within paragraphs.

6. Move any sentences that are out of order.

COHERENCE

☐ Are transitions used effectively so that paragraphs move smoothly and logically from one to the next?

☐ Do the sentences move smoothly and logically from one to the next?

1. Add two transitions to your essay.

2. Circle five synonyms you use.

For the list of transitions, see pages 99–100.

3. Explain how two of these make your essay easier to read.

_____

_____

_____

Now rewrite your essay with your revisions.

Editing Your Own Essay

For Editing Peer Evaluation Forms, go to Appendix 6.

SENTENCES

Subjects and Verbs

☐ Does each sentence have a main subject and verb?

1. Underline the subjects once and verbs twice in a paragraph of your revised essay. Remember that sentences can have more than one subject-verb set.

For help with subjects and verbs, see Chapter 27.

2. Does each of your sentences have at least one subject and verb that can stand alone?

3. Correct any fragments you have written.

4. Correct any run-together sentences you have written.

For help with fragments, see Chapter 28.
For help with run-togethers, see Chapter 29.

Subject-Verb Agreement

☐ Do all subjects and verbs agree?

1. Read aloud the subjects and verbs you underlined in your revised essay.

2. Correct any subjects and verbs that do not agree.

For help with subject-verb agreement, see Chapter 32.

Pronoun Agreement

☐ Do all pronouns agree with their nouns?

1. Find any pronouns in your revised essay that do not agree with their nouns.

For help with pronoun agreement, see Chapter 36.

2. Correct any pronouns that do not agree with their nouns.

Modifiers

☐ Are modifiers as close as possible to the words they modify?

1. Find any modifiers in your revised essay that are not as close as possible to the words they modify.

For help with modifier errors, see Chapter 39.

2. Rewrite sentences if necessary so that your modifiers are as close as possible to the words they modify.

PUNCTUATION AND MECHANICS

Punctuation

☐ Are sentences punctuated correctly?

For help with punctuation, see Chapters 40–44.

1. Read your revised essay for any errors in punctuation.

2. Make sure any fragments and run-together sentences you revised are punctuated correctly.

Mechanics

☐ Are words capitalized properly?

For help with capitalization, see Chapter 45.

1. Read your revised essay for any errors in capitalization.

2. Be sure to check your capitalization in any fragments or run-together sentences you revised.

WORD CHOICE AND SPELLING

Word Choice

☐ Are words used correctly?

For help with confused words, see Chapter 51.

1. Find any words used incorrectly in your revised essay.

2. Correct any errors you find.

Spelling

☐ Are words spelled correctly?

For help with spelling, see Chapter 52.

To make a personal log of your grammar/usage errors, go to Appendix 7.

1. Use spell-check and a dictionary to check your spelling.

2. Correct any misspelled words.

To make a personal log of your spelling errors, go to Appendix 8.

Now rewrite your essay again with your editing corrections.

MyWritingLab **More Helpful Hints**

- **Do you need some reminders about revising?** Comparison/contrast essays require well-developed paragraphs and good paragraph unity. So you need to pay special attention to development and unity as you revise. Go to **Revising the Essay** in the **Essay Development** module of **MyWritingLab** to get some help with these features of the revising process.

PRACTICING COMPARISON AND CONTRAST: FROM READING TO WRITING

This final section lets you practice the reading and writing skills you learned in this chapter. It includes two reading selections and several writing assignments on "your reading" and "your world." The section then takes you through a peer evaluation activity and a reflection exercise that teach you how to annotate your paper in ways that will benefit both you and your instructor.

Reading Workshop

Here are two essays that illustrate good comparison/contrast writing: "American Space, Chinese Place" by Yi-Fu Tuan compares the concept of space in two different cultures, and "Between Worlds" by Tony Cohan compares and contrasts a writer's life in two separate locations. As you read, notice how the writers make their points through thoughtful, detailed comparisons and contrasts.

AMERICAN SPACE, CHINESE PLACE
by Yi-Fu Tuan

Focusing Your Attention

1. Are you aware of how most Americans respond to space in our culture? Do you generally like open spaces or closed spaces?

2. The essay you are about to read compares the American concept of space with that of the Chinese. Do you know any culture that thinks differently than we do about space? What are the differences? The similarities? What is the source of these differences and similarities?

Expanding Your Vocabulary

The following words are important to your understanding of this essay. Start a vocabulary log of your own by recording any words you don't understand as you read. When you finish reading the essay, write down what you think the words mean. Then check your definitions in the dictionary.

> **exurbia:** prosperous areas beyond the suburbs (paragraph 1)
>
> **vistas:** pleasant views (paragraph 1)
>
> **ambiance:** the atmosphere of a place (paragraph 2)
>
> **terrestrial:** relating to the earth (paragraph 2)
>
> **wanderlust:** a strong desire to travel (paragraph 3)
>
> **pecuniary:** relating to money (paragraph 3)

nostalgia: sentimental longing for the past (paragraph 4)

beckons: encourages someone to approach (paragraph 5)

Reading
Strategy

READING CRITICALLY
Peer Teaching Your Reading

As you learned at the beginning of this chapter, practice peer teaching by dividing the following essay into logical pieces and teaching
it to each other. This time, get into five small groups (one for each
paragraph), and study your paragraph as deeply as you can in the time
allowed. Then teach it to the rest of the class.

place = location
+ space.
+ Society

AMERICAN SPACE, CHINESE PLACE
by Yi-Fu Tuan

1   Americans have a sense of space, not of place. Go to an American home in
exurbia, and almost the first thing you do is drift toward the picture window. How
curious that the first compliment you pay your host inside his house is to say how
lovely it is outside his house! He is pleased that you should admire his vistas. The
distant horizon is not merely a line separating earth from sky, it is a symbol of the
future. The American is not rooted in his place, however lovely: his eyes are drawn
by the expanding space to a point on the horizon, which is his future. By contrast,
consider the traditional Chinese home. Blank walls enclose it.

2   Step behind the spirit wall and you are in a courtyard with perhaps a miniature
garden around the corner. Once inside the private compound, you are wrapped in an
ambiance of calm beauty, an ordered world of...buildings, pavement, rock, and deco-
rative vegetation. But you have no distant view: nowhere does space open out before
you. Raw nature in such a home is experienced only as weather, and the only open
space is the sky above. The Chinese is rooted in his place. When he has to leave, it is
not for the promised land on the terrestrial horizon, but for another world altogether
along the vertical, religious axis of his imagination.

3   The Chinese tie to place is deeply felt. Wanderlust is an alien sentiment. The
Taoist classic Tao Te Ching captures the ideal of rootedness in place with these
words: "Though there may be another country in the neighborhood so close that
they are within sight of each other and the crowing of cocks and barking of dogs
in one place can be heard in the other, yet there is no traffic between them; and
throughout their lives the two peoples have nothing to do with each other." In
theory if not in practice, farmers have ranked high in Chinese society. The reason
is not only that they are engaged in the "root" industry of producing food but that,

unlike pecuniary merchants, they are tied to the land and do not abandon their country when it is in danger.

Nostalgia is a recurrent theme in Chinese poetry. An American reader of translated Chinese poems will be taken aback—even put off—by the frequency as well as the sentimentality of the lament for home. To understand the strength of this sentiment, we need to know that the Chinese desire for stability and rootedness in place is prompted by the constant threat of war, exile, and the natural disasters of flood and drought.

Forcible removal makes the Chinese keenly aware of their loss. By contrast, Americans move, for the most part, voluntarily. Their nostalgia for home town is really longing for childhood to which they cannot return: in the meantime the future beckons and the future is "out there" in open space. When we criticize American rootlessness we tend to forget that it is a result of ideals we admire, namely, social mobility and optimism about the future. When we admire Chinese rootedness, we forget that the word "place" means both location in space and position in society: to be tied to place is also to be bound to one's station in life, with little hope of betterment. Space symbolizes hope, place, achievement, and stability.

Thinking Critically About Content

1. What are the main differences between American homes and Chinese homes? Where is the focus in both of these settings?

2. What is "exurbia" (paragraph 1)?

3. In what ways are the Chinese rooted in their places?

Thinking Critically About Purpose and Audience

4. Why do you think Tuan wrote this essay?

5. Who do you think is his main audience?

6. How could space symbolize "hope, place, achievement, and stability" (paragraph 5)? How are all these notions related?

Thinking Critically About Essays

7. What is Tuan's thesis statement? How does he lead up to this thesis?

8. Explain how the topic sentence works in paragraph 5. Does it supply the controlling idea for the entire paragraph?

9. This is one of the shortest essays in this collection. Does Tuan get his point across effectively in this essay, or does he need more paragraphs? Explain your answer.

10. Do you agree or disagree with his general conclusions about the Chinese and American concepts of space? Write a detailed response to some of Tuan's observations.

To keep track of your critical thinking progress, go to Appendix 1.

BETWEEN WORLDS
by Tony Cohan

Focusing Your Attention

1. Do you ever feel like you live in two or more different worlds? What are they?

2. In the essay you are about to read, the author compares and contrasts the "worlds" of San Miguel de Allende in Mexico and Los Angeles from a writer's point of view. What similarities and differences do you imagine that Cohan discovered?

Expanding Your Vocabulary

The following words are important to your understanding of this essay. Start a vocabulary log of your own by recording any words you don't understand as you read. When you finish reading the essay, write down what you think the words mean. Then check your definitions in the dictionary.

entwine: weave (paragraph 1)

revelatory: revealing (paragraph 1)

mired: buried (paragraph 1)

recession: decline (paragraph 1)

unkempt: messy, untidy (paragraph 4)

la frontera: border (paragraph 5)

calibrations: adjustments (paragraph 6)

referent: point of reference (paragraph 7)

jargon: specialized language (paragraph 7)

deciphering: figuring out (paragraph 7)

corrido: run (paragraph 8)

Proustian: emotional (paragraph 8)

feigned: pretend (paragraph 9)

reticent: uncommunicative, silent (paragraph 9)

xenophobic: afraid of strangers or foreigners (paragraph 9)

primordial: primitive (paragraph 9)

brujos: wizards (paragraph 9)

audibility: hearing (paragraph 10)

near-monastic: almost monk-like (paragraph 13)

muster: create (paragraph 13)

sabor: flavor (paragraph 13)

ambiente: atmosphere (paragraph 13)

celebratory: festive (paragraph 14)

norteño bands: bands from northern Mexico (paragraph 14)

patina: shine (paragraph 14)

conditional: tentative (paragraph 14)

corrugated: with parallel ridges (paragraph 17)

lumpen detritus: accumulated debris (paragraph 17)

READING CRITICALLY
Peer Teaching Your Reading

Reading
Strategy

As you did with the previous reading, teach the following essay to each other in class. This time, divide into two large groups and then break those groups in half (one for California and one for Mexico). So each large group will study both cultures in this essay. After separate discussions in your groups, you will present your findings to the rest of the class. With two groups working on each culture, this is an excellent way to make sure you understand all the details in a complex essay.

BETWEEN WORLDS
by Tony Cohan

Our fourth year in Mexico. We live between worlds these days, frequent flyers. 1
The Mexican cycles of seasons and holidays entwine us deeper in town and country.
Friends come and go, fall in love, split up; babies are born. Our life in San Miguel de
Allende remains the intimate sum of our days—sensual, revelatory, engaged. Mexico,
still mired in post-earthquake recession, muddles through somehow. New friends
emerge: Arnaud, a Haitian poet in exile who has awakened me to Caribbean culture;
a Chilean painter and his wife; a Mexican professor.

Our world widens southward. The sprawling lands below the Rio Grande, a mere 2
blip on CNN or ABC, remain to us norteamericanos, after all these centuries, the New
World. Often after a flight from California we remain in Mexico City to explore, see
new friends, venture out into other regions—Oaxaca, Guerrero, Yucatán, Chiapas—
before returning to San Miguel, the heart's abode.

Still we feel unsettled at times, uneasily poised between cultures: losing a foot- 3
hold in the old country, still on tourist visas in the new one. Masako's art bursts with
imagery found here. Slowly Mexico takes root in my work, too: yet the language I hear

and speak every day is not the one I write in. Gore Vidal, in an introduction to Paul Bowles's collected short stories, touches on the problem: "Great American writers are supposed not only to live in the greatest country in the world...but to write about that greatest of all human themes: the American Experience." A novelist friend I work with in PEN, the international writers group, says only half jokingly, "Careful you don't become a *desaparecido,* a disappeared person, yourself."

4   Sometimes I do fear liking Mexico too much, getting lost in it. One day I saw a scraggly, unkempt gringo on the Mexico City metro around my age with bad teeth and a bad haircut, tangled in another land, beyond return. He reminded me of Russians I'd seen in China, poor and disheveled, hunched atop bundles in train stations—the ones who'd stayed on too long.

5   On plane trips back to California, I gaze down at the Sea of Cortez: tidal blue stripes graduating from pale agate to turquoise to aquamarine. Salty inlets and rust basins, green algal meadows. Violet badlands etched with tiny straight-line roads, barren as Mars. We cross *la frontera,* that invisible, charged border, and belly down over L.A.'s carpet of light. From the back of a taxi running up the 405, the city spreads away before us, a bobbing, firefly-infested lake.

6   We stay on friends' couches, house-sit, sublet. We see people necessary to the work we do, thumbing our Rolodexes, trying to make the days count. Observing age's effects upon our parents, we make careful calibrations between desire and duty. Sometimes we talk of buying another place in L.A. just to have an anchor in the home country, but we can't summon the interest. We hurry through our tasks so we can leave all the sooner.

7   Old friends are busy climbing up, clinging to, falling off career ladders. The conversation is the same one we checked out on six months earlier, different only in detail, with television and movies the referent, not live experience or books. I'm losing the jargon, the codes, the names of things. In conversations I blank on celebrities' names, hip expressions. Car alarms go off like crazy toys. Helicopters throb overhead, spotlighting evil. The nightly news imbues pedestrian acts with hysterical urgency. Few people walk for pleasure. There's little time to talk, and seldom of important things. It's easier to get some tasks done, as long as you don't need another human: I spend hours deciphering new telephone message menus, wading through oceans of calling options, waiting on hold. Arnaud, my Haitian poet friend in San Miguel, refers to revisiting his beloved Haiti as *the exile of return.*

8   Mexico in memory can be flat, flavorless, a postcard—like trying to remember sex or a good meal. It lives in the senses, not the mind, collapsing all abstractions into the brimming moment. Yet hearing a *corrido* on the radio or Spanish spoken in an L.A. market can unleash a near-overwhelming, Proustian effect, bringing tears. Now I understand better the mariachis' howling laments of memory and loss.

9   In California we don't talk much about Mexico. We've grown tired of the blank stares, the feigned interest, the allusions to Tijuana and the border towns, the beaches of Cabo or Cancún. Now I know why Mina and Paul used to be so reticent. In glossy, xenophobic, dollar-grubbing late-eighties U.S.A., Mexico is buzzless: a torpid blank somewhere south. Mexico, grail to generations of artists, site of primordial revelation— Mayan temples, *brujos,* muralists, hallucinatory mushrooms—has fallen off the map.

This whorled, ornate neighbor civilization, secretly and essentially entwined with ours, is invisible, its people among us silent, nameless wraiths who clip lawns and clear tables.

In a West Hollywood eatery, we sit with friends, poking at endive salad, designer pizza. A plate glass window offers a view of the foothills behind the Strip. A Sade tape teases the threshold of lyric audibility. Noticing the nine-dollar taco on the menu, we glance at each other.

"Yes, but what do you *do* there?" one friend asks.

How to describe a trip to the Tuesday market? A four-hour dinner with Carlos, Elenita, Arnaud, and Colette in our patio by the Quebrada bridge? Waking up to the bells' sweet clangor? Hurrying along the cobbles in the rain, ducking under archways? How to describe Friday lunches at El Caribe or checking out Thomas More's *Utopia* at the little bilingual library and actually reading it through? It's as if we have a secret life, in a secret place.

I used to like L.A.: the cool speed, the indifference to history, the near-monastic life of house, car, house. It freed the mind to run along some ever widening horizon line. Flatness, the absence of affect: not a bad place for a writer. There's no world out there so you invent one. I can't muster that appreciation any longer. I want taste, smell, *sabor, ambiente.* I want the human shape to my days.

In another sense, though, Mexico has redeemed L.A. to me. I've discovered a buried city there—a Latino L.A., warm and celebratory, where Spanish traces an invisible heart line deeper than place. In the course of my days, I may encounter a man or woman hailing from Guanajuato or Jalisco or Oaxaca, and matters of truth and fullness of heart may pass between us, and much laughter: riches invisible to most of my other friends. I can trace Los Lobos riffs back to *norteño* bands that come through our part of Mexico: Los Tigres del Norte, Los Bukis. California street names and foods reveal their origins. Suddenly the century-old Anglo patina looks flimsy, conditional.

Sometimes I get energy off the displacement, the dislocation, the back-and-forth. Each country seems the antidote to the other's ills. "In Rio, dreaming of New England/In New England, dreaming of Rio," the poet Elizabeth Bishop wrote.

Sometimes it feels like the two countries, through me, dream each other.

Invariably our L.A. trips end with a visit to the storage bin in Glendale. We introduce the seven-digit code, pass through the security gates, inch down aisles of identical metal containers and cinder-block structures. We remove the lock, raise the corrugated door, and consider the lumpen detritus of our former life.

We shut the door, lock it, drive off.

Finally, our lists checked off, we head back to Mexico. At journey's end, the Flecha Amarilla bus pulls into the dusty turnaround at the foot of San Miguel. We step out into darkness, as on that first night four years ago. The street dogs, the boys who want a coin to help with the baggage, the waiting taxi driver—those shades that so alarmed us then—appear to us now as town greeters, familiars. Wending up unlit streets once mysterious but intimate now from walking them, we make small talk with the taxi driver. "*Sí,*" he says. "*Un poco frío.*" A little chilly. At Calle Quebrada we drag our bags down the dark stairwell, brush past a pair of young lovers. We open the door. The dusky smell of the last mesquite fire we'd built hits us. Our luggage slumps to the stone floor, our hands unclench. We're back.

Thinking Critically About Content

1. What do you think is Cohan's main point in this essay?
2. Why does Cohan call San Miguel "the heart's abode" (paragraph 2)?
3. In what ways is Cohan "poised between cultures" (paragraph 3)?

Thinking Critically About Purpose and Audience

4. Why do you think Cohan wrote this essay?
5. Who would be most interested in this essay?
6. How does this essay make you feel about your hometown?

Thinking Critically About Essays

7. Name four points of comparison and four points of contrast in this essay.
8. How are most of the paragraphs in this essay organized? Use one paragraph to explain your answer.
9. Is Cohan's title effective? Explain your answer.

To keep track of your critical thinking progress, go to Appendix 1.

10. Write a short fable about a similarity or difference between two cities you know.

Writing Workshop

This final section provides opportunities for you to apply what you have learned in this chapter to another writing assignment. This time, we furnish very little prompting beyond a summary of the guidelines for writing a comparison/contrast essay. This section will let you demonstrate that you can go through the entire writing process on your own with only occasional feedback from your peers. Loop back into the chapter as necessary when you have questions so that this process becomes as automatic to you as possible before you move on to new material. Then pause at the end of the chapter to reflect briefly on what you have learned.

Guidelines for Writing a Comparison/Contrast Essay

1. Decide what point you want to make with your comparison, and state it in your thesis statement.
2. Choose items to compare and contrast that will make your point most effectively.
3. Use as many specific details and examples as possible to expand your comparison.
4. Develop your comparison in a balanced way.
5. Organize your essay subject by subject or point by point—or combine the two approaches.

Writing About Your Reading

1. In the first essay, Yi-Fu Tuan talks about the changes he sees in two countries' concepts of space. But even in a single culture, we often think in different ways about space. Some people like to be physically close to others, some touch people while they talk, and others keep their distance at all times. Compare and contrast your personal notion of space with that of another person. What is the same between you two? What is different?

2. Expand the fable you wrote in response to question 10 after Tony Cohan's essay by adding more characters and more points.

3. What process do you have to go through to come up with an interesting comparison or contrast? How is it different from the process you go through for other rhetorical modes?

Writing About Your World

1. Compare and contrast the two buildings in the picture here. Which details in both buildings are different? Which are the same? What is the overall message you get from these two buildings? Look at both the obvious and the not so obvious.

2. Choose a job advertised in your local newspaper's classified section, and write a cover letter to the employer comparing yourself to your probable competition. What are your best qualifications compared to others who might be applying for this job? What are your weaknesses in comparison to them? Why would you be the best candidate for the job?

3. Discuss the similarities and differences between two cities that you know well. How are they the same? How are they different? What do you

think accounts for these similarities and differences? When you write your essay, consider whether a subject-by-subject or a point-by-point organization would be more effective.

4. Create your own comparison/contrast assignment (with the help of your instructor), and write a response to it.

Revising

Small Group Activity (5–10 minutes per writer) Working in groups of three or four, read your comparison/contrast essays to each other. Those listening should record their reactions on the Revising Peer Evaluation Forms in Appendix 4. After your group goes through this process, give your evaluation forms to the appropriate writers so that each writer has two or three peer comment sheets for revising.

Paired Activity (5 minutes per writer) Using the completed Peer Evaluation Forms, work in pairs to decide what you should revise in your essay. If time allows, rewrite some of your sentences, and have your partner look at them.

Individual Activity Rewrite your paper, using the revising feedback you received from other students.

Editing

Paired Activity (5–10 minutes per writer) Swap papers with a classmate, and use the Editing Peer Evaluation Form (Appendix 6) to identify as many grammar, punctuation, mechanics, and spelling errors as you can.† If time allows, correct some of your errors, and have your partner look at them. Record your grammar, punctuation, and mechanics errors in the Error Log (Appendix 7) and your spelling errors in the Spelling Log (Appendix 8).

Individual Activity Rewrite your paper again, using the editing feedback you received from other students.

Reflecting on Your Writing   When you have completed your own essay, answer these six questions.

1. What was most difficult about this assignment?

2. What was easiest?

3. What did you learn about comparison and contrast by completing this assignment?

4. What do you think are the strengths of your comparison/contrast essay? Place a wavy line by the parts of your essay that you feel are very good.

5. What are the weaknesses, if any, of your paper? Place an X by the parts of your essay you would like help with. Write in the margins any questions you have.

6. What did you learn from this assignment about your own writing process—about preparing to write, about writing the first draft, about revising, and about editing?

MyWritingLab™ Visit Chapter 13, "Comparing and Contrasting," in MyWritingLab, and complete the Post-test to check your understanding of the chapter's objectives.

14

Dividing and Classifying

"Words are the copies of your ideas."

—HUGH BLAIR

Division and classification ensure that we have a certain amount of order in our lives. In fact, we constantly use these two processes to navigate through each day. Thanks to division and classification, you know where to find the milk in the grocery store and information on the brain in your anatomy textbook. Also, considering your likes and dislikes, you use division and classification to choose a major and a career. These ways of processing information are such a natural part of everyday life that we often don't even know we are using them.

In addition, we regularly use division and classification when we write. Actually, division and classification are a vital part of our written communication every day—in our personal lives, in college courses, and in the workplace:

- You divide your expenses into categories to create a budget.
- A student classifies the presentations in her communications class by level of difficulty.
- For a science course, a student writes a report on types of hazardous materials.
- A banker prepares a flier about the types of savings accounts available.
- The manager of a music store suggests to the corporate office a new system for arranging CDs.

Like comparison and contrast, division and classification are really two parts of the same process. **Division** is sorting—dividing something into its basic parts, such as a home into rooms. Division moves from a single, large category (home) to many smaller subcategories (kitchen, bath, living room, and so forth). **Classification,** grouping items together, moves in the opposite direction, from many subgroups to a single, large category. For example, pieces of furniture in the den, bedroom, and kitchen can all be classified as furniture. Division and classification help us organize information so we can make sense of our complex world. Dividing large categories into smaller ones (division) and grouping many items into larger categories (classification) both help us sort through information we need on a daily basis.

MyWritingLab

Understanding Division/Classification

To make sure you have a good understanding of what you just learned about dividing and classifying, go to **MyWritingLab.com,** and choose **Division and Classification** in the **Essay Development** module. From there, read the **Overview,** watch the **Animation** video, and complete the **Recall, Apply,** and **Write** activities. Then check your understanding of division and classification by taking the **Post-test.**

PREPARING TO WRITE A DIVISION/ CLASSIFICATION ESSAY

For best results, you should start your writing process by reading. Understanding how a good division/classification essay works—in content and form—will teach you how to write a good division/classification essay. Learning how to read division/classification essays analytically will help you become a better writer. As you see how an essay is constructed and how a thesis is developed in this mode, you will be able to apply what you discover to your own writing. Therefore, on the next few pages, you will read an effective division/classification essay and then answer some questions that will help you discover how the essay works.

Reading a Division/Classification Essay

Here is a sample division/classification essay by Pattison Counseling and Meditation Center called "Know Your Stress." It divides and classifies types of emotional stress and stress triggers. What causes stress for you? Why is understanding stress important?

Applying a reading strategy to this essay will teach you how to understand and respond to your reading analytically. In other words, it will help you read critically, which in turn will show you how to write critically. Reading critically, or analytically, will lead you to understanding not only *what* the essay is saying but also *how* the author is saying it. The strategy you will be applying to all the reading tasks in this chapter is summarizing.

Reading
Strategy

READING CRITICALLY
Summarizing a Professional Essay

As you read more difficult essays, the ability to summarize is essential. A summary features the main ideas of a selection in a coherent paragraph. First, identify the main ideas in your reading; then fold them into a paragraph with logical transitions so your sentences flow from one to another. After you write a summary of the following selection, draft three questions for discussion from your summary.

KNOW YOUR STRESS
by Pattison Counseling and Meditation Center

1   Stress can be a challenge to explain, for it means different things to different people. For example, cooking can be a huge stress to some but enjoyable for others. While there is no definitive agreement over what the specific definition of stress should be, the most common definition is "physical, mental or emotional strain or tension." Another popular definition is "a condition or feeling experienced when a person perceives that external demands exceed the personal and social resources the individual is able to mobilize." In other words, you feel unable to deal with the demands being made on you, and this is causing a negative response within you.

2   First, let's tackle the types of negative emotional stress that may be plaguing you. Then we will offer some ways in which you can reduce and manage your stress.

Three Types of Emotional Stress

3   Stress management can be complicated and confusing because there are different types of stress, each with its own characteristics, symptoms, duration, and treatment approaches:

4   **Acute Stress** – Acute stress is the most common form of stress and is short-lived. It can be beneficial and create motivation, like cramming for an exam or finishing

Livestrong.com

a report under a deadline. Acute stress is also thrilling and exciting in small doses, but too much is exhausting. Take water skiing, for example. Starting out, it is fun and exhilarating. After two hours or more, it becomes tiring and mentally draining. Prolonged acute stress can cause anger or irritability, anxiety, and depression in the short term but does not carry the extensive damage that prolonged stress carries over the long-term.

Episodic Acute Stress – This type of stress emerges in people who live dis-   5 ordered and chaotic lives – those who suffer acute stress frequently. Always running late but never on time or if something can go wrong, it does, are the hallmarks of people suffering from episodic acute stress. You have seen the type: over-aroused, short-tempered, irritable, tense, and anxious from having too many irons in the fire and making too many self-inflicted demands. Sufferers of episodic acute stress generally have either Type A personalities or are worry warts – their lifestyles and personalities are so ingrained with this behavior that they often see nothing wrong with the way they live. Such lifestyles can lead to persistent tension headaches, migraines, hypertension, and heart disease.

Chronic Stress – Chronic stress is the long-term, debilitating stress often seen   6 in individuals suffering from unending poverty, dysfunctional families, despised careers, life in war zones, or unhappy marriages with no way out. Some chronic stresses can stem from traumatic childhood experiences that have created a belief system that causes the stress sufferer to view the world as a threatening place. The person with chronic stress usually sees no end to their miserable situation and gives up searching for solutions. Chronic stress can lead to suicide, violence, heart attacks, stroke, and cancer.

Identify Your Stress Triggers

Once you have identified your level of stress, the next step is to learn what trig-   7 gers your stress response. A good way to identify your sources of stress is to make a list of situations, concerns, or challenges that elevate your stress levels. Here are some areas to consider:

External Stressors – major life changes like marriage or the death of a loved one;   8 your environment – noisy, too little light, dangerous neighborhood; unpredictable events – discovering your pay has been cut unexpectedly or uninvited houseguests arriving out of the blue; workplace – endless emails, impossible workload, urgent deadlines; social – meeting new people, going out on a blind date.

Internal Stressors – fears like fear of public speaking or fear of failure; lack of   9 control – not being able to control outcomes in life like medical test results; childhood beliefs – a belief system carried over from childhood trauma like not living up to expectations or inadequacy.

When you have spent a few minutes listing some or your stress triggers, you are   10 ready to begin the journey towards reducing and managing your stress.

Discovering How This Essay Works

To help you discover the elements that make this an effective division/classification essay so you can use them in your own writing, answer the following questions in as much detail as possible.

1. What do you think the author's general purpose is in this essay?

   _____

   _____

2. What are the types of stress the author discusses in this essay?

   _____

   _____

3. Explain each of these categories in your own words.

   _____

   _____

   _____

4. How does the author organize these categories? Go to pages 64–76 in Chapter 6 if you need help with this question.

   _____

5. A transition is a word or phrase that builds a bridge to the next sentence. List two transitions from this essay.

   _____

   _____

   _____

WRITING A DIVISION/CLASSIFICATION ESSAY

Now that you have read and studied the model essay, you will be writing one of your own. This section will help you generate a draft that you will then revise and edit in the third section of this chapter. It will guide you through a careful reading of the writing assignment, give you several ways to generate ideas and choose a topic, and finally furnish you with concrete guidelines for writing an effective division/classification essay. We encourage you to write notes and make lists throughout this process so you can use them when you write a draft of your essay at the end of this section.

Reading the Prompt

The first step in writing an essay, once again, is making sure you understand the writing assignment or "prompt." The assignment is what "prompts" you to respond to a specific issue or question. The more you understand about the prompt, the better paper you will create. So you want to learn how to read the essay assignment interactively. Applying the chapter reading strategy to the prompt is a good way to understand the most intricate details of the writing assignment.

READING CRITICALLY
Summarizing the Prompt

Reading
Strategy

Put the following writing assignment in your own words. What are the main tasks of this prompt? How are they related to one another? Write out your understanding of the prompt; then exchange papers with two other classmates so you can read other versions of the assignment. Finally, revise your statement to include what you learned from the statements you read.

Writing Prompt

Write an essay explaining some of your pet peeves. How did these pet peeves start? Why do you have them? After you have generated an extensive list of your pet peeves, divide your list into distinct categories, organize your categories, and write your essay by following the guidelines for writing a division/classification paper.

MyWritingLab
Complete this Writing Prompt assignment in MyWritingLab.

Thinking About the Prompt

Before you write your essay, generate as many pet peeves as you can so you have a good list to work with. Everyone has pet peeves. What are yours? How did you develop these pet peeves? Do your pet peeves fall into any particular categories? Use one or more of the prewriting strategies you learned in Chapter 5 to explore this topic.

Guidelines for Writing a Division/Classification Essay

To write a division/classification essay, keep in mind that the same items can be divided and classified in many different ways. Your friends probably don't all arrange their closets the way you do, and no two kitchens are organized exactly alike. The United States can be divided many different ways—into 50 states, 4 regions (Northeast, Midwest, South, and Pacific), and 6 time zones (Eastern, Central, Mountain, Pacific, Alaska, and Hawaii). Similarly, in writing you can divide and classify a topic in many different ways. Whatever your method of dividing or classifying, use the following guidelines to help you write an effective division/classification essay. As you think about the topic you have chosen in response to the prompt above, read the following guidelines, and continue to make lists and notes that you will use when you write your draft. After each guideline is an explanation of how it functions in the reading selection at the beginning of this chapter so you can actually see how the element works in an essay before you apply it to your own writing.

1. **Decide on your purpose for writing, and make it part of your thesis statement.** Dividing and classifying in themselves are not particularly interesting. But they are very useful techniques if you are trying to make a specific point. That point, or purpose, should be clearly stated in your thesis or in your first paragraph. Look at these two examples:

A. There are three main types of dangerous drivers on the road today.

B. Being aware of the three main types of dangerous drivers on the road today could save your life.

Both thesis statements name a category—dangerous drivers—but only thesis statement B gives the reader a good reason to keep reading: Knowing the three types could save your life.

In the Reading: In our sample essay, the authors use division and classification to explain types of stress and types of stress triggers. The authors suggest at the end of the essay that understanding stress is necessary for managing our stress.

In Your Writing: In response to the prompt, what will be the purpose of your essay? Draft a tentative thesis statement that clearly expresses your purpose. You will then revise your thesis as you develop your essay.

2. **Divide your topic into categories that don't overlap.** Because most subjects can be classified in different ways, your next task in writing a division/classification essay is to decide on what basis you will divide your subject into categories. First, gather information to come up with a list of all the possible topics. Second, determine how you will put these topics into categories. Next, make sure some of your topics don't fit in two categories. Your categories should be separate enough so that your topics fall into one category only. Also, don't add a category at the last minute to accommodate a topic. Keep adjusting your categories until they work with your thesis.

In the Reading: In the sample essay, the authors divide stress into three categories: (1) acute stress; (2) episodic acute stress, and, (3) chronic stress. They might have tried to divide this topic in other ways, such as mental and physical stress; positive and negative stress; or a combination of these categories. But none of these options would be effective. The first two groupings are too general to supply the detailed information that the Counseling and Meditation Center gives us. The third set of categories would force the authors to place some topics into two separate categories, which would be confusing. The Center's more specific categories are very effective in communicating their message.

In Your Writing: Look at your prewriting notes, and determine the categories you will create. Do you have enough examples in each category? Generate as many new pet peeves as possible, along with details to explain them. Make sure your categories and/or lists of examples support your purpose.

3. **Clearly explain each category.** With division, you are trying to show what differences break the items into separate groups or types. With classification, you let the similarities in the items help you set up categories that make sense. In either case, you need to explain each category fully and provide enough details to help your readers see your subject in a new way. To do this, use vivid description and carefully chosen examples. Comparison and contrast (Chapter 13) are also useful techniques because when you classify items, you are looking at how they are alike (comparison) and how they are different (contrast).

In the Reading: The authors use comparison and contrast to place their ideas into categories. Then they clarify each category by providing more detailed information about each one. As a result, they explain each of their categories fully and clearly.

In Your Writing: How will you explain each of your categories? What other rhetorical modes could you use in your essay to support and expand on your division/classification? Make some additional notes to yourself on these questions before you write a draft of your essay.

4. **Organize your categories logically.** Your method of organization should make sense and be easy for readers to follow. Most often, this means organizing from one extreme to another. For example, you might organize your types from most obvious to least obvious. Or you might move from least important to most important, from least humorous to most humorous, from largest to smallest—or the other way around. In every case, though, try to end with the category that is most memorable.

In the Reading: Our sample essay is arranged from one extreme to another—from least to most debilitating. The categories move from serious to more serious in nature, and each is more difficult to manage.

In Your Writing: How will you organize your essay? Which type of pet peeves will you talk about first? Which will be second and third? Think through your method of organization before you write a draft of your essay.

5. **Use transitions to move your readers through your essay.** Transitions will help your readers move from one category to another so they can easily follow your train of thought. They will also keep your essay from sounding choppy or boring.

In the Reading: Because the authors give their categories headings, they don't need to use transitions to move from one category to another. But they do use transitions within their paragraphs. Here are some effective transitions from the essay: "after" (paragraph 5); "but" (paragraph 5); "but" (paragraph 6); "once" (paragraph 7); and "when" (paragraph 10). These words serve as traffic signals that guide the readers through this essay.

In Your Writing: After you write a draft of your essay, take the time to read it slowly, looking specifically for ideas that should be linked with transitions for the readers.

Writing a Draft of Your Essay

Now is the time to collect all your personal associations, your notes, your prewriting exercises, and your lists as you begin the first draft of your essay. You also might want to review the professional essay, the writing assignment, and the chapter guidelines for writing division/classification essays, along with your notes and lists, to help you create your draft. At this point, don't think about revising or editing; just get your thoughts about the writing assignment down on paper.

MyWritingLab   **Helpful Hints**

- **Trying to make your point clear to the reader?** Division and classification essays often rely on good description of the subjects discussed. For help with description, visit **Describing** in the **Essay Development** module of **MyWritingLab.**

REVISING AND EDITING

You are now ready to revise and edit your writing. This section will take you through the guidelines for revising and editing division/classification essays with two specific writing samples: another student's essay and your own essay. The processes of revising and editing are often much easier with someone else's writing, which is why we begin this stage with a writing sample from another student. If you can see some of the problems in this essay, you might be able to locate areas for improvement in your own writing. So you will be reviewing the chapter guidelines by revising and editing another student's writing before applying the same guidelines to your own writing.

Reading a Student Division/Classification Essay

We will begin by using our chapter reading strategy on the following essay. Student writer Sergio Mendola uses division and classification in an essay about neighbors called "Won't You Be My Neighbor?" In it, he divides and classifies neighbors into specific categories to prove a point. Summarizing the essay will help you find the writer's main point and understand his reasoning so you can then figure out how to improve his paper.

READING CRITICALLY
Summarizing the Student Essay

Reading Strategy

On your first reading of Sergio's essay, underline his main point. During your second reading, note in the margins the ideas that support his main idea. Then write a summary in a coherent paragraph of your own words with logical transitions so your sentences flow from one another. Finally, draft three questions for discussion that come from your summary.

Won't You Be My Neighbor?

1   Neighborhoods can be strange places. Every one is different, but they are all made up of the same ingredient—neighbors. In today's world, though, most people don't know there neighbors. It's not like the '50s. When people knew what their neighbors were doing. But in every neighborhood today, you can find at least one Mystery Neighbor, one Perfect Cleaver Family, and one Good Neighbor Family.

2   The first type of neighbor everyone has is the Perfect Cleaver Family. This family has the perfect parents and the perfect children. They are the June and Ward Cleavers of today. They have 2.5 perfect children. Although these children get in their share of minor trouble, the children never repeat the same mistake after the parents express their disappointment. And then, to avoid future disappointments, the children always keep their parents' values in mind before making decisions. Eddie Haskell left a lot to be desired. I don't know what his values are. The Cleaver-type children later become heart surgeons or police chiefs in order to help the world around them. These neighbors are the role models for everyone else.

3   Then there is the Mystery Neighbor. The Mystery Neighbor remains aloof, and the only way the other neighbors know someone lives at the Mystery House is because the newspaper disappears sometime during the day and the lawn somehow gets mowed every week. Every once in a while, a car will sit in the driveway, but no one knows for sure if the car belongs to the people who own the house. Neighborhood children make up stories about the Mystery Neighbor, which are based on nothing and compete with the best urban legends. The Mystery Neighbor is usually a workaholic or a traveling salesperson, but this doesn't stop the neighbors from wondering.

4   The best type of neighbor in any neighborhood is the Good Neighbor Family. Made up of very reliable people. This family is always reaching out to other neighbors. Whenever something goes wrong, someone from the Good Neighbor Family is the first person at the doorstep to lend a helping hand. These neighbors will water the plants and feed the animals for people on vacation who always want to help others. They create the kinds of friendships that continue even when one family moves away. Sometimes the parents might try to "fix up" their boy and girl children so that the families relationship can be legally cemented for life. The Good Neighbor Family is one that everyone hopes to encounter at least once in a lifetime.

5   This mixture of neighbors makes up a very good neighborhood. It creates a neighborhood that functions smoothly and thoughtfully. And even though people don't no their neighbors like they used to 50 years ago, they will probably find at least three different types of neighbors if they look hard enough: the Perfect Cleaver Family, the Mystery Neighbor, and the Good Neighbor Family. It would be sad to be missing any one of them.

Revising and Editing the Student Essay

This essay is Sergio's first draft, which now needs to be revised and edited. First, apply the Revising Checklist to the content of Sergio's draft. When you are satisfied that his ideas are fully developed and well organized, use the Editing Checklist to correct his grammar and mechanics errors. Answer the questions, and complete the tasks in each category. Then write your suggested changes directly on Sergio's draft.

Revising the Student Essay

THESIS STATEMENT

✔ Does the thesis statement contain the essay's controlling idea?

✔ Does the thesis appear as the last sentence of the introduction?

1. Put brackets around the last sentence in Sergio's introduction. Does it introduce his purpose?

2. Rewrite Sergio's thesis statement if necessary so that it states his purpose and introduces his topics.

_____

BASIC ELEMENTS

✔ Does the title draw in the readers?

✔ Does the introduction capture the readers' attention and build up effectively to the thesis statement?

✔ Does each body paragraph deal with a single topic?

✔ Does the conclusion bring the essay to a close in an interesting way?

1. Give Sergio's essay an alternate title.

_____

2. Rewrite Sergio's introduction so that it captures the readers' attention and builds up to the thesis statement at the end of the paragraph.

_____

_____

_____

3. Does each of Sergio's body paragraphs deal with only one topic?

_____

4. Rewrite Sergio's conclusion using at least one suggestion from Part I.

_____

_____

_____

DEVELOPMENT

✔ Do the body paragraphs adequately support the thesis statement?

✔ Does each body paragraph have a focused topic sentence?

✔ Does each body paragraph contain _specific_ details that support the topic sentence?

✔ Does each body paragraph include _enough_ details to fully explain the topic sentence?

1. Write out Sergio's thesis statement (revised, if necessary), and list his three topic sentences below it.

Thesis statement: _____

_____

Topic 1: _____

_____

Topic 2: _____

_____

Topic 3: _____

_____

2. Do Sergio's topics adequately support his thesis statement?

_____

3. Does each body paragraph have a focused topic sentence?

_____

4. Do Sergio's details adequately explain his categories?

_____

5. Where do you need more information?

_____

6. Make two of Sergio's details more specific.

7. Add two new details to make his essay clearer.

UNITY

✔ Do the essay's topic sentences relate directly to the thesis statement?

✔ Do the details in each body paragraph support the paragraph's topic sentence?

1. Read each of Sergio's topic sentences with his thesis statement (revised, if necessary) in mind. Do they go together?

_____

2. Revise his topic sentences if necessary so they are directly related.

3. Drop or rewrite the two sentences in paragraph 2 that are not directly related to their topic sentences.

ORGANIZATION

✔ Is the essay organized logically?

✔ Is each body paragraph organized logically?

1. Read Sergio's essay again to see if all the paragraphs are arranged logically.

2. Reverse the two paragraphs that are out of order.

3. Look closely at Sergio's body paragraphs to see if all his sentences are arranged logically within paragraphs.

4. Move any sentences that are out of order.

COHERENCE

✔ Are transitions used effectively so that paragraphs move smoothly and logically from one to the next?

✔ Do the sentences move smoothly and logically from one to the next?

1. Add two transitions to Sergio's essay.

2. Circle five transitions, repetitions, synonyms, or pronouns Sergio uses.

3. Explain how two of these make Sergio's essay easier to read.

For a list of transitions, see pages 99–100.

For a list of pronouns, see pages 496–497.

_____

_____

_____

 Now rewrite Sergio's essay with your revisions.

Editing the Student Essay

SENTENCES

Subjects and Verbs

✔ Does each sentence have a main subject and verb?

1. Underline the subjects once and verbs twice in paragraphs 1 and 4 of your revision of Sergio's essay. Remember that sentences can have more than one subject-verb set.

For help with subjects and verbs, see Chapter 27.

2. Does each of the sentences have at least one subject and verb that can stand alone?

_____

3. Did you find and correct Sergio's two fragments? If not, find and correct them now.

For help with fragments, see Chapter 28.

Subject-Verb Agreement

✔ Do all subjects and verbs agree?

1. Read aloud the subjects and verbs you underlined in your revision of Sergio's essay.

For help with subject-verb agreement, see Chapter 32.

2. Correct any subjects and verbs that do not agree.

Pronoun Agreement

✔ Do all pronouns agree with their nouns?

For help with pronoun agreement, see Chapter 36.

1. Find any pronouns in your revision of Sergio's essay that do not agree with their nouns.

2. Correct any pronouns that do not agree with their nouns.

Modifiers

✔ Are modifiers as close as possible to the words they modify?

For help with modifier errors, see Chapter 39.

1. Find any modifiers in your revision of Sergio's essay that are not as close as possible to the words they modify.

2. Did you find and correct Sergio's modifier error? If not, find and correct it now.

PUNCTUATION AND MECHANICS

Punctuation

✔ Are sentences punctuated correctly?

For help with punctuation, see Chapters 40–44.

1. Read your revision of Sergio's essay for any errors in punctuation.

2. Find the two fragments you revised, and make sure they are punctuated correctly.

3. Did you find and correct the missing apostrophe in Sergio's essay?

Mechanics

✔ Are words capitalized properly?

For help with capitalization, see Chapter 45.

1. Read your revision of Sergio's essay for any errors in capitalization.

2. Be sure to check Sergio's capitalization in the fragments you revised.

WORD CHOICE AND SPELLING

Word Choice

✔ Are words used correctly?

For help with confused words, see Chapter 51.

1. Find any words used incorrectly in your revision of Sergio's essay.

2. Did you find and correct his three confused words? If not, find and correct them now.

Spelling

✔ Are words spelled correctly?

For help with spelling, see Chapter 52.

1. Use spell-check and a dictionary to check the spelling in your revision of Sergio's essay.

2. Correct any misspelled words.

 Now rewrite Sergio's essay again with your editing corrections.

Reading Your Own Division/Classification Essay

The first stage of revising and editing your own writing is creating some distance between you and your essay. To accomplish this, you will apply to your essay the same reading strategy you have been practicing throughout this chapter. Treating your essay as a reading selection that you are trying to understand and respond to will help you revise and edit your own work efficiently and effectively.

READING CRITICALLY
Summarizing Your Own Essay

Reading Strategy

Now write a summary of your own essay. See if your thesis and main ideas are clear and easy to identify. Make sure the connections between the ideas in your summary are logical and understandable. Are these connections also clear in your essay? Change any elements of your essay that will make your main ideas clearer and more logical to your readers.

Revising and Editing Your Own Essay

Now you are ready to revise and edit your own essay. Remember that revision involves reworking the content and organization of your essay while editing asks you to check your grammar and usage. At this stage, you should repeat these processes until you feel you have a draft that says exactly what you want it to say. The checklists here will help you apply to your essay what you have learned in this chapter.

Revising Your Own Essay

For Revising Peer Evaluation Forms, go to Appendix 4.

THESIS STATEMENT

☐ Does the thesis statement contain the essay's controlling idea and an opinion about that idea?

☐ Does the thesis appear as the last sentence of the introduction?

1. What is the purpose or general message you want to send to your readers?

2. Put brackets around the last sentence in your introduction. Does it explain your purpose?

_____

3. Rewrite your thesis statement if necessary so that it states your purpose and introduces your topics.

_____

BASIC ELEMENTS

☐ Does the title draw in the readers?

☐ Does the introduction capture the readers' attention and build up effectively to the thesis statement?

☐ Does each body paragraph deal with a single topic?

☐ Does the conclusion bring the essay to a close in an interesting way?

1. Give your essay a title if it doesn't have one.

_____

2. Does your introduction capture your readers' attention and build up to your thesis statement at the end of the paragraph?

_____

3. Does each of your body paragraphs deal with only one topic?

_____

4. Does your conclusion follow some of the suggestions offered in Part I?

_____

DEVELOPMENT

☐ Do the body paragraphs adequately support the thesis statement?

☐ Does each body paragraph have a focused topic sentence?

☐ Does each body paragraph contain *specific* details that support the topic sentence?

☐ Does each body paragraph include *enough* details to fully explain the topic sentence?

1. Write out your thesis statement (revised, if necessary), and list your topic sentences below it.

    Thesis statement: _____

       Topic 1: _____

       Topic 2: _____

       Topic 3: _____

2. Do your topics adequately support your thesis statement?

_____

3. Does each body paragraph have a focused topic sentence?

_____

4. Do your details adequately explain your categories?

_____

5. Where do you need more information?

_____

6. Make two of your details more specific.

7. Add at least two new details to make your essay clearer.

UNITY

☐ Do the essay's topic sentences relate directly to the thesis statement?

☐ Do the details in each body paragraph support the paragraph's topic sentence?

1. Read each of your topic sentences with your thesis statement in mind. Do they go together?

_____

2. Revise your topic sentences if necessary so they are directly related.

3. Drop or rewrite any of the sentences in your body paragraphs that are not directly related to their topic sentences.

ORGANIZATION

☐ Is the essay organized logically?

☐ Is each body paragraph organized logically?

1. Read your essay again to see if all the paragraphs are arranged logically.

2. Refer to your answers to the development questions. Then identify your method of organization:

_____

3. Is the order you chose for your paragraphs the most effective approach to your topic?

_____

4. Move any paragraphs that are out of order.

5. Look closely at your body paragraphs to see if all the sentences are arranged logically within paragraphs.

6. Move any sentences that are out of order.

COHERENCE

☐ Are transitions used effectively so that paragraphs move smoothly and logically from one to the next?

☐ Do the sentences move smoothly and logically from one to the next?

For a list of transitions, see pages 99–100.
For a list of pronouns, see pages 496–497.

1. Add two transitions to your essay.

2. Circle five transitions, repetitions, synonyms, or pronouns you use.

3. Explain how two of them make your paragraphs easier to read.

_____

_____

 Now rewrite your essay with your revisions.

For Editing Peer Evaluation Forms, go to Appendix 6.

Editing Your Own Essay

SENTENCES

Subjects and Verbs

☐ Does each sentence have a main subject and verb?

For help with subjects and verbs, see Chapter 27.

1. Underline the subjects once and verbs twice in a paragraph of your revised essay. Remember that sentences can have more than one subject-verb set.

2. Does each of your sentences have at least one subject and verb that can stand alone?

_____

For help with fragments, see Chapter 28.
For help with run-togethers, see Chapter 29.

3. Correct any fragments you have written.

4. Correct any run-together sentences you have written.

Subject-Verb Agreement

☐ Do all subjects and verbs agree?

For help with subject-verb agreement, see Chapter 32.

1. Read aloud the subjects and verbs you underlined in your revised essay.

2. Correct any subjects and verbs that do not agree.

Pronoun Agreement

☐ Do all pronouns agree with their nouns?

1. Find any pronouns in your revised essay that do not agree with their nouns.

2. Correct any pronouns that do not agree with their nouns.

For help with pronoun agreement, see Chapter 36.

Modifiers

☐ Are modifiers as close as possible to the words they modify?

1. Find any modifiers in your revised essay that are not as close as possible to the words they modify.

2. Rewrite sentences if necessary so that your modifiers are as close as possible to the words they modify.

For help with modifier errors, see Chapter 39.

PUNCTUATION AND MECHANICS

Punctuation

☐ Are sentences punctuated correctly?

1. Read your revised essay for any errors in punctuation.

2. Make sure any fragments and run-together sentences you revised are punctuated correctly.

For help with punctuation, see Chapters 40–44.

Mechanics

☐ Are words capitalized properly?

1. Read your revised essay for any errors in capitalization.

2. Be sure to check your capitalization in any fragments or run-together sentences you revised.

For help with capitalization, see Chapter 45.

WORD CHOICE AND SPELLING

Word Choice

☐ Are words used correctly?

1. Find any words used incorrectly in your revised essay.

2. Correct any errors you find.

For help with confused words, see Chapter 51.
For help with spelling, see Chapter 52.

Spelling

☐ Are words spelled correctly?

1. Use spell-check and a dictionary to check your spelling.

2. Correct any misspelled words.

To make a personal log of your grammar/usage errors, go to Appendix 7.

Now rewrite your essay again with your editing corrections.

To make a personal log of your spelling errors, go to Appendix 8.

MyWritingLab | **More Helpful Hints**

• **Are you looking for a way to make your essay more interesting to read?** See **Varying Sentence Structure** in the **Usage and Style** module of **MyWritingLab.** By changing the order of the items in your sentences, you can keep your readers interested and communicate your ideas more effectively.

PRACTICING DIVISION/CLASSIFICATION: FROM READING TO WRITING

This final section lets you practice the reading and writing skills you learned in this chapter. It includes two reading selections and several writing assignments on "your reading" and "your world." The section then guides you through peer evaluation and reflection, ending with suggestions about how to lead your instructor through a reading of your essay in ways that will benefit both of you.

Reading Workshop

Here are two essays that illustrate good division and classification writing: "Why Some Kids Try Harder and Some Kids Give Up" by Tracy Cutchlow classifies different types of intelligence, while "What Are Friends For?" by Marion Winik discusses different types of friends. As you read, notice how the authors' categories support the points they are making.

WHY SOME KIDS TRY HARDER AND SOME KIDS GIVE UP
by Tracy Cutchlow

Focusing Your Attention

1. What do you believe makes people intelligent? How do some get smarter, growing in intelligence, and others stay the same? What makes the difference in these two groups?

2. In the essay you are about to read, the writer divides and classifies the development of intelligence. Do you feel you are naturally smart? Do you have to work at your studies? Do you enjoy learning and working at it? Where do you think you got your drive to improve yourself?

Expanding Your Vocabulary

The following words are important to your understanding of this essay. Organize this list into two columns—words you know and words you don't know. Which of the words you don't know can you guess from their sentences?

mindset: belief system, mental habits (paragraph 3)

cultivated: developed (paragraph 5)

conjugation: verb form (paragraph 17)

READING CRITICALLY
Summarizing Your Reading

 Reading Strategy

As you learned at the beginning of this chapter, practice your summary skills on the following essay. Then work with someone in the class, and write a single paragraph that represents both of your summaries.

WHY SOME KIDS TRY HARDER AND SOME KIDS GIVE UP
by Tracy Cutchlow

My toddler struggled to buckle the straps on her high chair. "Almost," she muttered as she tried again and again. "Almost," I agreed, trying not to hover. When she got it, I exclaimed, "You did it! It was hard, but you kept trying, and you did it. I'm so proud of you." 1

The way I praised her effort took a little effort on my part. If I hadn't known better, I might have just said, "Clever girl!" (Or even "Here, let me help you with that.") What's so bad about that? Read on. 2

Stanford researcher Carol Dweck has been studying motivation and perseverance since the 1960s. And she found that children fall into one of two categories: 3

- Those with a fixed mindset, who believe their successes are a result of their innate talent or smarts

- Those with a growth mindset, who believe their successes are a result of their hard work

Fixed mindset: "If you have to work hard, you don't have ability." Kids with a fixed mindset believe that you are stuck with however much intelligence you're born with. They would agree with this statement: "If you have to work hard, you don't have ability. If you have ability, things come naturally to you." When they fail, these kids feel trapped. They start thinking they must not be as talented or smart as everyone's been telling them. They avoid challenges, fearful that they won't look smart. 4

5 **Growth mindset: "The more you challenge yourself, the smarter you become."** Kids with a growth mindset believe that intelligence can be cultivated: the more learning you do, the smarter you become. These kids understand that even geniuses must work hard. When they suffer a setback, they believe they can improve by putting in more time and effort. They value learning over looking smart. They persevere through difficult tasks.

6 What creates these beliefs in our kids? The type of praise we give them—even starting at age 1.

The research

7 In one study, Dweck gathered up fifth graders, randomly divided them in two groups, and had them work on problems from an IQ test. She then praised the first group for their intelligence: "Wow, that's a really good score. You must be smart at this."

8 She praised the second group for their effort: "Wow, that's a really good score. You must have tried really hard."

9 She continued to test the kids, including presenting them with a choice between a harder or easier task.

10 Kids praised for their effort tended to take the challenging task, knowing they could learn more. They were more likely to continue feeling motivated to learn and to retain their confidence as problems got harder.

11 Kids praised for their intelligence requested the easier task, knowing there was a higher chance of success. They lost their confidence as problems got harder, and they were much more likely to inflate their test scores when recounting them.

12 Later, Dweck and her colleagues took the study out of the lab and into the home. Every four months for two years, Stanford and University of Chicago researchers visited fifty-three families and recorded them for ninety minutes as they went about their usual routines. The children were 14 months old at the start of the study.

13 Researchers then calculated how often parents used each type of praise: praising effort; praising character traits; and "other praise" that has a neutral effect, like "Good!" and "Wow!"

14 They waited five years.

15 Then the researchers surveyed the children, now 7 to 8 years old, on their attitudes toward challenges and learning. Children with a growth mindset tended to be more interested in challenges. Which kids had a growth mindset? Those who had heard more process praise as toddlers.

16 I give more examples of ways to praise effort in my book, *Zero to Five: 70 Essential Parenting Tips Based on Science.*

Can you unfix a fixed mindset?

17 I got an email from an inner-city high school teacher. "Is it too late to learn algebra, or third-person singular conjugation, or rocket science if you didn't [develop a growth mindset] when you were 4 years old?" she asked.

18 Dweck had the same question. So she took middle-schoolers and college students who had fixed mindsets. She found that the students were able to improve

their grades when they were taught that the brain is like a muscle: intelligence is not fixed.

It's not too late—not for your kids and not for you. Salman Khan of Khan Academy is on a mission to let you know it. He created an inspiring video, based on Dweck's work, titled "You Can Learn Anything."   19

The message: The brain is like a muscle. The more you use it, the stronger it gets. The way you exercise your brain is by embracing challenges, practicing skills, learning new things. As Khan puts it, "the brain grows most by getting questions wrong, not right."   20

Which is why, when my toddler was trying to snap her own buckle, I needed to encourage her to take on the challenge by saying, "Almost!" and "Try again" instead of "Here, let me do that for you."   21

Pass it on

Sharing is caring, as they say. "If society as a whole begins to embrace the struggle of learning, there is no end to what that could mean for global human potential," Khan writes. So pass it on!   22

Thinking Critically About Content

1. Cutchlow divides and classifies the ways we develop intelligence into two different categories. What are these categories?

2. What are the main differences in these categories? What characterizes the people in each category?

3. What does Khan mean when he says, "The brain grows most by getting questions wrong, not right" (paragraph 20)?

Thinking Critically About Purpose and Audience

4. What do you think Cutchlow's purpose is in this essay?

5. What makes this purpose both personal and academic?

6. Who do you think is Cutchlow's main audience?

Thinking Critically About Essays

7. Explain how the topic sentence works in paragraph 12. Does it supply the controlling idea for the entire paragraph?

8. Choose a paragraph from this essay, and explain whether it is unified. Be as specific as possible.

9. Do you think the author's title is effective? Why or why not?

10. What role does intelligence play in your life? Divide and classify its role in your life over the years.

To keep track of your critical thinking progress, go to Appendix 1.

WHAT ARE FRIENDS FOR?
by Marion Winik

Focusing Your Attention

1. Who do you rely on to talk out your problems? To confide in? To tell secrets to? How do these people fit into your life? How do you fit into theirs?

2. In the essay you are about to read, the author divides and classifies the types of friends people generally have. What do you think these types are?

Expanding Your Vocabulary

The following words are important to your understanding of this essay. Organize this list into two columns—words you know and words you don't know. Which of the words you don't know can you guess from their sentences?

half-slip: undergarment worn by women (paragraph 1)

innumerable: too many to count (paragraph 2)

Aquarena Springs: a theme park in San Marcos, Texas, that is now a preservation and education center (paragraph 2)

infallible: unfailing (paragraph 6)

indispensable: absolutely necessary (paragraph 8)

wistful: nostalgic (paragraph 10)

ill-conceived: poorly planned (paragraph 10)

inopportune: inconvenient (paragraph 11)

tonic: boost (paragraph 14)

 Reading
Strategy

 ## READING CRITICALLY
Summarizing Your Reading

Once again, write a summary of the following essay, and exchange it with another person in your class. Then combine your two summaries into one summary that accurately represents the main ideas in this essay.

WHAT ARE FRIENDS FOR?
by Marion Winik

I was thinking about how everybody can't be everything to each other, but some people can be something to each other, thank God, from the ones whose shoulders you cry on to the ones whose half-slips you borrow to the nameless ones you chat with in the grocery line.

Buddies, for example, are the workhorses of the friendship world, the people out there on the front lines, defending you from loneliness and boredom. They call you up, they listen to your complaints, they celebrate your successes and curse your misfortunes, and you do the same for them in return. They hold out through innumerable crises before concluding that the person you're dating is no good, and even then understand if you ignore their good counsel. They accompany you to a movie with subtitles or to see the diving pig at Aquarena Springs. They feed your cat when you are out of town and pick you up from the airport when you get back. They come over to help you decide what to wear on a date. Even if it is with that creep.

What about family members? Most of them are people you just got stuck with, and though you love them, you may not have very much in common. But there is that rare exception, the Relative Friend. It is your cousin, your brother, maybe even your aunt. The two of you share the same views of the other family members. Meg never should have divorced Martin. He was the best thing that ever happened to her. You can confirm each other's memories of things that happened a long time ago. Don't you remember when Uncle Hank and Daddy had that awful fight in the middle of Thanksgiving dinner? Grandma always hated Grandpa's stamp collection; she probably left the windows open during the hurricane on purpose.

While so many family relationships are tinged with guilt and obligation, a relationship with a Relative Friend is relatively worry-free. You don't even have to hide your vices from this delightful person. When you slip out Aunt Joan's back door for a cigarette, she is already there.

Then there is that special guy at work. Like all the other people at the job site, at first he's just part of the scenery. But gradually he starts to stand out from the crowd. Your friendship is cemented by jokes about co-workers and thoughtful favors around the office. Did you see Ryan's hair? Want half my bagel? Soon you know the names of his turtles, what he did last Friday night, exactly which model CD player he wants for his birthday. His handwriting is as familiar to you as your own.

Though you invite each other to parties, you somehow don't quite fit into each other's outside lives. For this reason, the friendship may not survive a job change. Company gossip, once an infallible source of entertainment, soon awkwardly accentuates the distance between you. But wait. Like School Friends, Work Friends share certain memories which acquire a nostalgic glow after about a decade.

A Faraway Friend is someone you grew up with or went to school with or lived in the same town as until one of you moved away. Without a Faraway Friend, you would never get any mail addressed in handwriting. A Faraway Friend calls late at night, invites you to her wedding, always says she is coming to visit but rarely shows up. An actual visit from a Faraway Friend is a cause for celebration and binges of all kinds. Cigarettes, Chips Ahoy, bottles of tequila.

8   Faraway Friends go through phases of intense communication, then may be out of touch for many months. Either way, the connection is always there. A conversation with your Faraway Friend always helps to put your life in perspective: When you feel you've hit a dead end, come to a confusing fork in the road, or gotten lost in some crackerbox subdivision of your life, the advice of the Faraway Friend—who has the big picture, who is so well acquainted with the route that brought you to this place—is indispensable.

9   Another useful function of the Faraway Friend is to help you remember things from a long time ago, like the name of your seventh-grade history teacher, what was in that really good stir-fry, or exactly what happened that night on the boat with the guys from Florida.

10   Ah, the Former Friend. A sad thing. At best a wistful memory, at worst a dangerous enemy who is in possession of many of your deepest secrets. But what was it that drove you apart? A misunderstanding, a betrayed confidence, an unrepaid loan, an ill-conceived flirtation. A poor choice of spouse can do in a friendship just like that. Going into business together can be a serious mistake. Time, money, distance, cult religions: all noted friendship killers. You quit doing drugs, you're not such good friends with your dealer anymore.

11   And lest we forget, there are the Friends You Love to Hate. They call at inopportune times. They say stupid things. They butt in, they boss you around, they embarrass you in public. They invite themselves over. They take advantage. You've done the best you can, but they need professional help. On top of all this, they love you to death and are convinced they're your best friend on the planet.

12   So why do you continue to be involved with these people? Why do you tolerate them? On the contrary, the real question is, What would you do without them? Without Friends You Love to Hate, there would be nothing to talk about with your other friends. Their problems and their irritating stunts provide a reliable source of conversation for everyone they know. What's more, Friends You Love to Hate make you feel good about yourself, since you are obviously in so much better shape than they are. No matter what these people do, you will never get rid of them. As much as they need you, you need them too.

13   At the other end of the spectrum are Hero Friends. These people are better than the rest of us; that's all there is to it. Their career is something you wanted to be when you grew up—painter, forest ranger, tireless doer of good. They have beautiful homes filled with special handmade things presented to them by villagers in the remote areas they have visited in their extensive travels. Yet they are modest. They never gossip. They are always helping others, especially those who have suffered a death in the family or an illness. You would think people like this would just make you sick, but somehow they don't.

14   A New Friend is a tonic unlike any other. Say you meet her at a party. In your bowling league. At a Japanese conversation class, perhaps. Wherever, whenever, there's that spark of recognition. The first time you talk, you can't believe how much you have in common. Suddenly, your life story is interesting again, your insights fresh, your opinion valued. Your various shortcomings are as yet completely invisible.

15   It's almost like falling in love.

Thinking Critically About Content

1. How many types of friends does Winik introduce? What are they?

2. On what basis does Winik create these categories?

3. In what ways is a new friend "a tonic" (paragraph 14)?

Thinking Critically About Purpose and Audience

4. Why do you think Winik wrote this essay?

5. Who would be most interested in this essay?

6. How does this essay make you feel about the role of friends in your life?

Thinking Critically About Essays

7. How does Winik organize her essay? Why do you think she puts her categories in this order?

8. How does the author develop each category? Use one paragraph to explain your answer.

9. Explain Winik's title.

10. Write a detailed description of one of your friends. Why is this person a friend of yours?

To keep track of your critical thinking progress, go to Appendix 1.

Writing Workshop

This final section provides opportunities for you to apply what you have learned in this chapter to another writing assignment. This time, we furnish very little prompting beyond a summary of the guidelines for writing a division/classification essay. This section will let you demonstrate that you can go through the entire writing process on your own with only occasional feedback from your peers. Loop back into the chapter as necessary when you have questions so that this process becomes as automatic to you as possible before you move on to new material. Then pause at the end of the chapter to reflect briefly on what you have learned.

 Guidelines for Writing a Division/Classification Essay

1. Decide on your purpose for writing, and make it part of your thesis statement.
2. Divide your topic into categories that don't overlap.
3. Clearly explain each category.
4. Organize your categories logically.
5. Use transitions to move your readers through your essay.

Writing About Your Reading

1. In the first essay, Cutchlow uses Carol Dweck's classification of two different mindsets to explain our mental activity. Develop a classification system that explains the differences in people's physical activity, and write an essay discussing your categories and their significance.

2. Divide and classify your friends into meaningful categories, and write an essay explaining your classification system.

3. What process do you have to go through to come up with an interesting comparison or contrast? How is it different from the process you go through for other rhetorical modes?

Writing About Your World

1. Looking at the picture here, think of the types of activities college students do in their spare time. Classify these activities into a few categories, and explain their advantages and disadvantages.

2. What are some rituals in your own life? Do these rituals serve a purpose in your life? Use division and classification to explain three rituals that you follow.

3. We all dream about trips we'd like to take. Sometimes we get to take one of these trips. Others have to remain dreams. What are your ideal trips? Discuss the types of trips you would like to take. What categories do they fall into? Why do you dream about these types of travel?

4. Create your own division/classification assignment (with the help of your instructor), and write a response to it.

Revising

Small Group Activity (5–10 minutes per writer) Working in groups of three or four, read your division/classification essays to each other. Those listening should record their reactions on the

Revising Peer Evaluation Forms in Appendix 4. After your group goes through this process, give your evaluation forms to the appropriate writers so that each writer has two or three peer comment sheets for revising.

Paired Activity (5 minutes per writer) Using the completed Peer Evaluation Forms, work in pairs to decide what you should revise in your essay. If time allows, rewrite some of your sentences and have your partner look at them.

Individual Activity Rewrite your paper, using the revising feedback you received from other students.

Editing

Paired Activity (5–10 minutes per writer) Swap papers with a classmate, and use the Editing Peer Evaluation Form (Appendix 6) to identify as many grammar, punctuation, mechanics, and spelling errors as you can. If time allows, correct some of your errors and have your partner look at them. Record your grammar, punctuation, and mechanics errors in the Error Log (Appendix 7) and your spelling errors in the Spelling Log (Appendix 8).

Individual Activity Rewrite your paper again, using the editing feedback you received from other students.

Reflecting on Your Writing   When you have completed your own essay, answer these six questions.

1. What was most difficult about this assignment?

2. What was easiest?

3. What did you learn about division and classification by completing this assignment?

4. What do you think are the strengths of your division/classification essay? Place a wavy line by the parts of your essay that you feel are very good.

5. What are the weaknesses, if any, of your paper? Place an X by the parts of your essay you would like help with. Write in the margins any questions you have.

6. What did you learn from this assignment about your own writing process—about preparing to write, about writing the first draft, about revising, and about editing?

MyWritingLab™   Visit Chapter 14, "Dividing and Classifying," in MyWritingLab, and complete the Post-test to check your understanding of the chapter's objectives.

CHAPTER 15

Defining

*"*Writers, most of all, need to define their tasks...their themes, their objectives.*"*

—HENRY SEIDAL CANBY

All communication depends on our understanding of a common set of definitions. If we did not work from shared definitions, we would not be able to carry on coherent conversations, write clear letters and reports, or understand any form of media.

It's no surprise, then, that we regularly use definitions in writing—in our personal lives, in college courses, and in the workplace:

- You e-mail a friend to define your responsibilities at your new job.
- A student has to define melody, harmony, and rhythm on a music appreciation quiz.
- For a criminal justice course, a student begins a report with definitions of criminal law and civil law.
- A financial planner prepares a summary sheet defining the basic financial terms a client needs to know.
- The manager of a sporting goods shop writes a classified ad for an opening on the staff.

Definition is the process of explaining what a word, an object, or an idea is. A good definition focuses on what is special about a word or an idea and what sets it apart from similar words or concepts. Definitions help us understand basic concrete terms (*cell phone, large fries, midterm exams*), discuss important events in our lives (*baseball game, graduation, dentist appointment*), and grasp complex ideas (*friendship, courage, success*). Definitions are the building blocks that help us make sure both writer and reader (or speaker and listener) are working from the same basic understanding of terms and ideas.

Definitions vary greatly. They can be as short as one word (a *hog* is a motorcycle) or as long as an essay or even a book. Words or ideas that require such extended definitions are usually abstract, complex, and controversial. Think, for example, how difficult it might be to define an abstract idea like *equality* compared to concrete words such as *dog* or *cat*.

MyWritingLab | **Understanding Definition**

To see how well you understand definition essays, go to **MyWritingLab. com,** and choose **Definition** in the **Essay Development** module. From there, read the **Overview,** watch the **Animation** video, and complete the **Recall, Apply,** and **Write** activities. Then check your understanding of definition by taking the **Post-test.**

PREPARING TO WRITE A DEFINITION ESSAY

As in previous chapters, preparing to write begins with reading. To learn how to write a good definition essay, you need to read a good definition essay and understand how it is put together—logically and structurally. Reading definition essays in depth will help you write effective definition essays. You will find that the two processes of reading and writing work together to help you process information on a very high level. So after you read the following essay, you will be asked some questions that will help you discover how the essay communicates its message.

Reading a Definition Essay

In the following essay, Lars Eighner writes an extended definition of the fine art of "Dumpster diving," or rummaging through Dumpsters, the large trash containers designed to be raised and emptied into garbage trucks. Have you ever witnessed someone Dumpster diving? Have you yourself ever found something in the trash that you took home? What causes people to live out of Dumpsters? How would you survive if you lost your home?

Using a reading strategy is an effective way to learn how to read analytically. Understanding your reading analytically will lead to analytical writing. Reading critically, or analytically, will help you understand not only *what* the essay is saying but also *how* the author is saying it. The strategy you will apply to all reading tasks in this chapter involves reacting critically to your reading material.

Reading
Strategy

READING CRITICALLY
Reacting Critically to a Professional Essay

Forming your own opinions and coming up with meaningful ideas in response to your reading are very important parts of the reading process. As you read the following essay, record your notes on a separate piece of paper. First, draw a vertical line down the center of your paper. Then, as you read, write the author's main ideas on the left and your reactions to those ideas on the right side of the paper. Be prepared to explain the connection between your notes and the material in the essay.

DUMPSTER DIVING
by Lars Eighner

1   I began Dumpster diving about a year before I became homeless. I prefer the term *scavenging*. I have heard people, evidently meaning to be polite, use the word *foraging,* but I prefer to reserve that word for gathering nuts and berries and such, which I also do, according to the season and opportunity.

2   I like the frankness of the word *scavenging*. I live from the refuse of others. I am a scavenger. I think it a sound and honorable niche, although if I could I would naturally prefer to live the comfortable consumer life, perhaps—and only perhaps—as a slightly less wasteful consumer owing to what I have learned as a scavenger.

3   Except for jeans, all my clothes come from Dumpsters. Boom boxes, candles, bedding, toilet paper, medicine, books, a typewriter, a virgin male love doll, coins sometimes amounting to many dollars—all came from Dumpsters. And, yes, I eat from Dumpsters, too.

4   There is a predictable series of stages that a person goes through in learning to scavenge. At first the new scavenger is filled with disgust and self-loathing. He is ashamed of being seen.

5   This stage passes with experience. The scavenger finds a pair of running shoes that fit and look and smell brand-new. He finds a pocket calculator in perfect working order. He finds pristine ice cream, still frozen, more than he can eat or keep. He begins to understand: People do throw away perfectly good stuff, a lot of perfectly good stuff.

6   At this stage he may become lost and never recover. All the Dumpster divers I have known come to the point of trying to acquire everything they touch. Why not take it, they reason; it is all free. This is, of course, hopeless, and most divers come to realize that they must restrict themselves to items of relatively immediate utility.

The finding of objects is becoming something of an urban art. Even respectable, employed people will sometimes find something tempting sticking out of a Dumpster or standing beside one. Quite a number of people, not all of them of the bohemian type, are willing to brag that they found this or that piece in the trash. 7

But eating from Dumpsters is the thing that separates the dilettanti from the professionals. Eating safely involves three principles: using the senses and common sense to evaluate the condition of the found materials; knowing the Dumpsters of a given area and checking them regularly; and seeking always to answer the question Why was this discarded? 8

Yet perfectly good food can be found in Dumpsters. Canned goods, for example, turn up fairly often in the Dumpsters I frequent. I also have few qualms about dry foods such as crackers, cookies, cereal, chips, and pasta if they are free of visible contaminants and still dry and crisp. Raw fruits and vegetables with intact skins seem perfectly safe to me, excluding, of course, the obviously rotten. Many are discarded for minor imperfections that can be pared away. 9

A typical discard is a half jar of peanut butter—though non-organic peanut butter does not require refrigeration and is unlikely to spoil in any reasonable time. One of my favorite finds is yogurt—often discarded, still sealed, when the expiration date has passed—because it will keep for several days, even in warm weather. 10

No matter how careful I am, I still get dysentery at least once a month, oftener in warm weather. I do not want to paint too romantic a picture. Dumpster diving has serious drawbacks as a way of life. 11

I find from the experience of scavenging two rather deep lessons. The first is to take what I can use and let the rest go. I have come to think that there is no value in the abstract. A thing I cannot use or make useful, perhaps by trading, has no value, however fine or rare it may be. 12

The second lesson is the transience of material being. I do not suppose that ideas are immortal, but certainly they are longer-lived than material objects. 13

The things I find in Dumpsters, the love letters and rag dolls of so many lives, remind me of this lesson. Now I hardly pick up a thing without envisioning the time I will cast it away. This, I think, is a healthy state of mind. Almost everything I have now has already been cast out at least once, proving that what I own is valueless to someone. 14

I find that my desire to grab for the gaudy bauble has been largely sated. I think this is an attitude I share with the very wealthy—we both know there is plenty more where whatever we have came from. Between us are the rat-race millions who have confounded their selves with the objects they grasp and who nightly scavenge the cable channels for they know not what. 15

I am sorry for them. 16

Discovering How This Essay Works

To help you recognize the elements that make this an effective definition essay so you can use them in your own writing, answer the following questions in as much detail as possible.

1. What does this essay define?

   _____

2. How does the author explain his definition: (1) by making comparisons or finding synonyms, (2) by stating what the term is not, or (3) by putting the term into a category for us to understand?

   _____

3. What three specific examples from the essay helped you understand what Dumpster diving is?

   _____

   _____

   _____

4. What other rhetorical modes that you have already studied (describing, narrating, illustrating, etc.) does Eighner use to develop his definition?

   _____

   _____

5. How does Eighner organize the examples in his essay? See pages 64–76 in Chapter 6 if you need help with this question.

   _____

WRITING A DEFINITION ESSAY

Now that you have read and studied the model essay, you will be writing one of your own. This section will help you generate a draft that you will then revise and edit in the third section of this chapter. It will teach you how to read a writing assignment carefully, how to generate ideas and choose a topic, and finally how to write a draft of the essay by following the chapter guidelines. We encourage you to take notes and make lists throughout this process so you can use them when you write a draft of your essay at the end of this section.

Reading the Prompt

When you set out to write any essay, you first need to understand the writing assignment or "prompt." An essay assignment attempts to "prompt" you to react and respond to a specific issue or question. The more clearly you understand the prompt, the better essay you will create. So you want to learn how to interact with the essay assignment as thoroughly as possible. Applying the chapter reading strategy to your writing assignment is a good way to read your assignment actively rather than passively.

READING CRITICALLY
Reacting Critically to the Prompt

Reading
Strategy

After you read the following prompt, draw a vertical line down the center of a sheet of paper. Record the tasks of the assignment on the left and your ideas about those tasks on the right. Write as many notes as you can about each task. Then, underline in the left column the key words for completing this assignment.

Writing Prompt

Everyone has a clear idea of what a sense of security is. What does this term mean to you? Write an essay defining security. Use the following guidelines to help you develop a draft.

MyWritingLab
Complete this Writing Prompt assignment in MyWritingLab.

Thinking About the Prompt

Before you focus on a specific topic, you should generate as many ideas as you can so you have several to choose from. What do you think of when you hear the word *security?* What associations do you make with this word? What examples does it bring to mind? Use one or more of the prewriting strategies you learned in Chapter 5 to generate ideas for writing an extended definition of this term.

Guidelines for Writing a Definition Essay

Clear definitions give writers and readers a mutual starting point on the road to successful communication. Sometimes a short summary and an example are all that's needed. But in the case of abstract and complex words or ideas, a writer may use several approaches to a definition. Use the following guidelines to help you write an extended definition essay. As you think about the topic you have chosen in response to the prompt above, read the following guidelines, and continue to make lists and notes that you will use when you write your draft. After each guideline is an explanation of how it functions in the reading selection at the beginning of this chapter so you can actually see how each element works in an essay before you apply it to your own writing.

1. **Choose your word or idea carefully, and give a working definition of it in your thesis statement.** First, choose a word or idea that can be defined and explained from several angles, or you will end up with a short, lifeless essay. At the same time, give your readers a working definition right

at the start. Put that brief, basic definition in your thesis statement so readers have a mental hook on which to hang the definitions and explanations in the rest of your essay. Also include the purpose of your essay in your thesis statement.

In the Reading: At the start of his essay, Eighner defines *Dumpster diving* as "scavenging," explaining, "I live from the refuse of others." This simple, direct definition—furnished at the beginning—guides readers through the rest of the essay.

In Your Writing: In the essay you are going to write, what will be your purpose? Write yourself some notes that might develop into a clear thesis statement. Draft a tentative thesis if you are ready to do so.

2. **Decide how you want to define your term: by synonym, by negation, or by category.** These are the three common ways to develop a definition.

- When you define by using a *synonym*, you furnish readers with a similar word or a short explanation with synonyms.

In the Reading: Eighner uses a synonym right at the beginning of his essay. *Dumpster diving* is an informal term that is used by city people to refer to taking garbage out of trash bins. Apartment houses and office buildings often use Dumpsters to hold garbage until it is taken to the dump. Because *Dumpster* is not a term that everyone knows and because the meaning of the expression *Dumpster diving* is not immediately obvious, Eighner provides the synonym *scavenging*, which most people will understand.

- When you define a word by *negation*, you say what the term is not. That is, you define a term by contrasting it with something else.

In the Reading: Eighner uses definition by negation twice in his essay. First, he states that "scavenging" is not "foraging," meaning that it is not gathering nuts and berries. He also says that life as a scavenger is not a comfortable consumer life. The rest of his essay explains his life as a scavenger.

- Defining a term by *category* is a more formal type of definition, as in a dictionary. Defining by category has two parts: the class or general category the word belongs to and the way the word is different from other words in that group. For example, *heart* might be defined as "the organ that pumps blood through the body." The general category is *organ*, and it is different from other organs (brain, lungs, stomach, liver, and so on) because it pumps blood.

In the Reading: Eighner doesn't use this type of definition directly. He does, however, suggest that scavenging falls into the category of *lifestyle* in paragraph 2 when he compares his life as a scavenger to the life of a consumer.

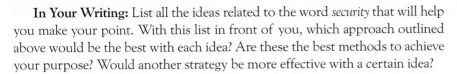

In Your Writing: List all the ideas related to the word *security* that will help you make your point. With this list in front of you, which approach outlined above would be the best with each idea? Are these the best methods to achieve your purpose? Would another strategy be more effective with a certain idea?

3. **Develop your definition with examples.** Nearly every definition can be improved by adding examples. Well-chosen examples show your definition in action. Definitions can be *objective* (strictly factual, as in a dictionary definition) or *subjective* (combined with personal opinions). A definition essay is usually more subjective than objective because you are providing your personal opinions about a word or concept. You are explaining to your readers your own meaning, which is what makes your essay interesting. If your readers wanted an objective definition, they could go to a dictionary.

In the Reading: Eighner uses examples throughout his essay to expand on his definition. Paragraph 3 consists entirely of examples of items he has found in Dumpsters. Later he gives examples of the kinds of food he finds, including canned goods, cookies and crackers, raw fruits and vegetables, peanut butter, and yogurt. These examples help Eighner strike a balance in his definition between objective (factual) and subjective (personal) references. From these and Eighner's other examples, we get a very clear idea of how a person can live by Dumpster diving.

In Your Writing: Do you have enough examples on your prewriting list for your definition essay? Take some time to brainstorm and record a few more details that come to mind. Think of your topic from as many different perspectives as possible.

4. **Use other rhetorical strategies—such as description, comparison, or process analysis—to support your definition.** When you write a definition essay, you should look at your word or idea in many different ways. The other techniques you have learned for developing body paragraphs can help you expand your definition even further. Perhaps a description, a short narrative, or a comparison will make your definition come alive.

In the Reading: In addition to examples, Eighner uses process analysis, classification, and cause and effect to expand his definition. He uses one type of process analysis (how something happens) to explain the four stages that new Dumpster divers go through. His three rules for eating safely are also process analysis (how to do something). He draws on classification to name the types of foods he finds and then gives examples of each category. At the end of his essay, he uses cause and effect when he explains that Dumpster diving (the cause) has taught him two lessons (the effects): that only items you can use are valuable and that material objects don't last.

In Your Writing: Now that you have a well-developed list of ideas and examples, think about the rhetorical strategies that will best support your specific ideas. Where could you use description? Narration? Comparison/

Contrast? Make some notes on your prewriting list about the rhetorical modes that will be most effective in your definition.

5. **Organize your essay in a logical way.** Because a definition essay can be developed through several strategies and techniques, there is no set pattern of organization. So you need to figure out the most logical way to explain your word or idea. You might move from particular to general or from general to particular. Or you might arrange your ideas from one extreme to the other, such as from most important to least important, least dramatic to most dramatic, or most familiar to least familiar. In some cases, you might organize your definition chronologically or spatially. Or you might organize part of your essay one way and the rest another way. What's important is that you move in some logical way from one point to another so your readers can follow your train of thought.

In the Reading: Eighner organizes his essay chronologically. He says he started Dumpster diving about a year before he became homeless. Now he is homeless and lives by Dumpster diving. He defines the term in two ways (synonym and negation) and gives examples of the items he finds. Then he switches to a general-to-particular organization in paragraphs 7–11, explaining how someone learns to dive in general and then how to dive for food in particular. The last five paragraphs conclude the essay.

In Your Writing: How will you organize the details in your essay? What order would be most effective to get your main point across to your readers? Choose a method of organization from those listed in this guideline.

Writing a Draft of Your Essay

Now is the time to collect all your reactions, your notes, your prewriting exercises, and your lists as you start the process of writing your essay. You also might want to review the professional essay, the writing assignment, and the chapter guidelines for writing definition essays, along with your notes and lists, to help you write a draft of your essay. At this point, don't think about revising or editing; just get your thoughts about the writing assignment down on paper.

MyWritingLab **Helpful Hints**

- **Are you struggling with creating an interesting title?** A good title can jumpstart your essay. The title of an essay grabs the readers' attention so they can understand your message clearly. If you need help with this feature, go to **Essay Introductions, Conclusions, and Titles** in the **Essay Development** module of **MyWritingLab.**

REVISING AND EDITING OPTIONS

You are now ready to begin revising and editing. This section will take you through the guidelines for revising and editing definition essays with two specific writing samples: another student's essay and your own essay. The processes of revising and editing are often much easier with someone else's writing, which is why we begin this stage with a writing sample from another student. If you can see some of the problems in this essay, you might be able to find areas for improvement in your own writing. So you will be reviewing the chapter guidelines by revising and editing another student's writing before applying the same guidelines to your own writing.

Reading a Student Definition Essay

We will begin by using our chapter reading strategy on this essay. In the following essay, "True Friends," student writer Francine Feinstein defines *friendship*. Listing your reactions across from the author's main points as you read this essay will help you understand the logic behind it so you can revise and edit her writing in preparation for revising and editing your own writing.

READING CRITICALLY
Reacting Critically to the Student Essay

Reading Strategy

As you read Francine's essay, record your notes on a separate piece of paper. First, draw a vertical line down the center of a sheet of paper. Then, write Francine's main ideas on the left and your reactions to those ideas on the right side of the page. Be prepared to explain the connection between your notes and the material in the essay.

True Friends

Many people throw the term "friend" around loosely. They think they have friends at work, friends at school, and friends from the Internet. But is all these people really friends? The word "friend" seems to be used today to refer to anyone from long-term to short-term relationships. However, a true friend is someone who will always be there in times of need, who will always be the best company, and who will always listen and give advice. 1

Without any questions asked, a good friend will always be there in times of need. No matter how bad a problem is, a true friend will be the person who sits up nights 2 and take days off work just to sit with a friend. If someone is in trouble with a difficult paper a friend will help brainstorm to figure out the problem. If someone is sick, a friend will be the first one at the door with chicken soup and will baby-sit the kids until the sick person feel better. I hate the feeling of being sick. If someone is stranded across town with a broken-down car, a friend will drop everything to make a rescue and drive the person wherever he or she needs to go. Not everyone has a friend like this a true friend will always be the first one there, no matter what.

3   Most of all, a true friend is also someone who will listen and give reliable advice. Some people will listen to problems and then give the advice that they think will work best for them, but that advice isn't necessarily best for their friend. Other people will listen but then interject personal stories that relate to the problem but don't solve it. But a true friend listens to a problem and gives suggestions to help a friend figure out the best solution for himself or herself. In other words, a true friend knows how to listen and help a person solve problems.

4   In addition, a friend is someone who is always great company, because friends have so much in common with each other. Imagine working out together, grabbing a sandwich, and then spending the evening just talking—about life, about good times, about bad times, about classes at school. Right now my classes are really hard. At the end of the day, friends might rent their favorite DVD and make some fresh popcorn. Sometimes they even seem to be on the same biological clock, getting tired and waking up at the same time. Friends can always be themselves around each other.

5   The word "friend" may be misused in the English language, but at least we can agree on what true friends are. True friends are hard to find. But once you find them, they will always be there, listen to you and be the best people to spend time with. No wonder true friends are so rare!

Revising and Editing the Student Essay

This essay is Francine's first draft, which now needs to be revised and edited. First, apply the Revising Checklist to the content of Francine's draft. When you are satisfied that her ideas are fully developed and well organized, use the Editing Checklist to correct her grammar and mechanics errors. Answer the questions, and complete the tasks in each category. Then write your suggested changes directly on Francine's draft.

Revising the Student Essay

THESIS STATEMENT

✔ Does the thesis statement contain the essay's controlling idea?

✔ Does the thesis appear as the last sentence of the introduction?

1. Put brackets around the last sentence in Francine's introduction. Does it state her purpose?

    _____

    _____

2. Rewrite Francine's thesis statement if necessary so that it states her purpose and introduces her topics.

    _____

BASIC ELEMENTS

✔ Does the title draw in the readers?

✔ Does the introduction capture the readers' attention and build up effectively to the thesis statement?

✔ Does each body paragraph deal with a single topic?

✔ Does the conclusion bring the essay to a close in an interesting way?

1. Give the writer's essay an alternate title.

    _____

2. Rewrite Francine's introduction so that it captures the readers' attention and builds up to the thesis statement at the end of the paragraph.

    _____

    _____

    _____

3. Does each of Francine's body paragraphs deal with only one topic?

    _____

4. Rewrite Francine's conclusion using at least one suggestion from Part I.

    _____

    _____

    _____

DEVELOPMENT

✔ Do the body paragraphs adequately support the thesis statement?

✔ Does each body paragraph have a focused topic sentence?

✔ Does each body paragraph contain *specific* details that support the topic sentence?

✔ Does each body paragraph include *enough* details to fully explain the topic sentence?

1. Write out Francine's thesis statement (revised, if necessary), and list her three topic sentences below it.

   Thesis statement: _____

   _____

   _____

   Topic 1: _____

   _____

   Topic 2: _____

   _____

   Topic 3: _____

   _____

2. Do Francine's topic sentences adequately support her thesis statement?

   _____

3. Does each body paragraph have a focused topic sentence?

   _____

4. Do the examples in the essay help define *friend?*

   _____

5. Where do you need more information?

   _____

6. Make two of Francine's details more specific.

7. Add at least two new details to make her essay clearer.

UNITY

✔ Do the essay's topic sentences relate directly to the thesis statement?

✔ Do the details in each body paragraph support the paragraph's topic sentence?

1. Read each of Francine's topic sentences with her thesis statement in mind. Do they go together?

   _____

2. Revise her topic sentences if necessary so they are directly related.

3. Drop or rewrite the sentences in paragraph 2 and in paragraph 4 that are not directly related to their topic sentence.

ORGANIZATION

✔ Is the essay organized logically?

✔ Is each body paragraph organized logically?

1. Read Francine's essay again to see if all the paragraphs are arranged logically.

2. Reverse the two paragraphs that are out of order.

3. Look closely at Francine's body paragraphs to see if all her sentences are arranged logically within paragraphs.

4. Move any sentences that are out of order.

COHERENCE

✔ Are transitions used effectively so that paragraphs move smoothly and logically from one to the next?

✔ Do the sentences move smoothly and logically from one to the next?

1. Add two transitions to Francine's essay.

2. Circle five transitions Francine uses.

For a list of transitions, see pages 99–100.

3. Explain how two of these make Francine's essay easier to read.

_____

_____

 Now rewrite Francine's essay with your revisions.

Editing the Student Essay

SENTENCES

Subjects and Verbs

✔ Does each sentence have a main subject and verb?

1. Underline the subjects once and verbs twice in paragraphs 1 and 2 of your revision of Francine's essay. Remember that sentences can have more than one subject-verb set.

For help with subjects and verbs, see Chapter 27.

2. Does each of the sentences have at least one subject and verb that can stand alone?

For help with run-togethers, see Chapter 29.

3. Did you find and correct Francine's run-together sentence? If not, find and correct it now.

Subject-Verb Agreement
✔ Do all subjects and verbs agree?

For help with subject-verb agreement, see Chapter 32.

1. Read aloud the subjects and verbs you underlined in your revision of Francine's essay.

2. Did you find and correct the three subjects and verbs that do not agree?

Pronoun Agreement
✔ Do all pronouns agree with their nouns?

For help with pronoun agreement, see Chapter 36.

1. Find any pronouns in your revision of Francine's essay that do not agree with their nouns.

2. Correct any pronouns that do not agree with their nouns.

Modifiers
✔ Are modifiers as close as possible to the words they modify?

For help with modifier errors, see Chapter 39.

1. Find any modifiers in your revision of Francine's essay that are not as close as possible to the words they modify.

2. Rewrite sentences if necessary so that modifiers are as close as possible to the words they modify.

PUNCTUATION AND MECHANICS

Punctuation
✔ Are sentences punctuated correctly?

For help with punctuation, see Chapters 40–44.

1. Read your revision of Francine's essay for any errors in punctuation.

2. Find the run-together sentence you revised, and make sure it is punctuated correctly.

3. Did you find and correct the two comma errors in Francine's essay?

Mechanics
✔ Are words capitalized properly?

For help with capitalization, see Chapter 45.

1. Read your revision of Francine's essay for any errors in capitalization.

2. Be sure to check Francine's capitalization in the run-together sentence you revised.

WORD CHOICE AND SPELLING

Word Choice

✔ Are words used correctly?

1. Find any words used incorrectly in your revision of Francine's essay .

   For help with confused words, see Chapter 51.

2. Correct any errors you find.

Spelling

✔ Are words spelled correctly?

1. Use spell-check and a dictionary to check the spelling in your revision of Francine's essay.

   For help with spelling, see Chapter 52.

2. Correct any misspelled words.

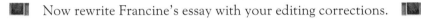

 Now rewrite Francine's essay with your editing corrections.

Reading Your Own Definition Essay

The first stage of revising your own writing is creating some distance between you and your essay. To accomplish this, you will be reading your essay with the same reading strategy you have applied to other reading tasks in this chapter. Reading your essay as a reading selection that you are trying to understand and respond to will help you revise and edit your own work efficiently and effectively.

READING CRITICALLY
Reacting Critically to Your Own Essay

Reading Strategy

As you begin to rework your essay, use the same technique you have practiced throughout the chapter. Just as you identified the author's ideas and recorded your reactions to them to help you understand what the essay was saying, record the ideas from your own writing on the left side of a piece of paper and your reactions to them on the right. Expand your essay with any new ideas that surface from this exercise.

Revising and Editing Your Own Essay

You are now ready to revise and edit your own writing. Remember that revision involves reworking the content and organization of your essay while editing asks you to check your grammar and usage. Work first with the content, making sure your thoughts are fully developed and organized effectively before you turn to your grammar and usage errors. Repeating these processes again and again will ensure that you are producing the best draft possible. The checklists here will help you apply to your essay what you have learned in this chapter.

For Revising Peer Evaluation Forms, go to Appendix 4.

Revising Your Own Essay

THESIS STATEMENT

☐ Does the thesis statement contain the essay's controlling idea?

☐ Does the thesis appear as the last sentence of the introduction?

1. What are you defining?

   _____

2. What is the purpose of your definition essay?

   _____

3. Put brackets around the last sentence in your introduction. Does it state your purpose?

   _____

4. Rewrite your thesis statement if necessary so that it states your purpose and introduces your topics.

BASIC ELEMENTS

☐ Does the title draw in the readers?

☐ Does the introduction capture the readers' attention and build up effectively to the thesis statement?

☐ Does each body paragraph deal with a single topic?

☐ Does the conclusion bring the essay to a close in an interesting way?

1. Give your essay a title if it doesn't have one.

   _____

2. Does your introduction capture your readers' attention and build up to your thesis statement at the end of the paragraph?

   _____

3. Does each of your body paragraphs deal with only one topic?

   _____

4. Does your conclusion follow some of the suggestions offered in Part I?

   _____

DEVELOPMENT

☐ Do the body paragraphs adequately support the thesis statement?

☐ Does each body paragraph have a focused topic sentence?

☐ Does each body paragraph contain *specific* details that support the topic sentence?

☐ Does each body paragraph include *enough* details to fully explain the topic sentence?

1. Write out your thesis statement (revised, if necessary), and list your topic sentences below it.

    Thesis statement: _____

        Topic 1: _____

        Topic 2: _____

        Topic 3: _____

2. Do your topics adequately support your thesis statement?

    _____

3. Does each body paragraph have a focused topic sentence?

    _____

4. Do the examples in the essay help develop your definition?

    _____

5. Where do you need more information?

    _____

6. Make two of your details more specific.

7. Add at least two new details to make your definition clearer.

UNITY

☐ Do the essay's topic sentences relate directly to the thesis statement?

☐ Do the details in each body paragraph support the paragraph's topic sentence?

1. Read each of your topic sentences with your thesis statement in mind. Do they go together?

    _____

2. Revise your topic sentences if necessary so they are directly related.

3. Drop or rewrite any of the sentences in your body paragraphs that are not directly related to their topic sentences.

ORGANIZATION

☐ Is the essay organized logically?

☐ Is each body paragraph organized logically?

1. Read your essay again to see if all the paragraphs are arranged logically.

2. Refer to your answers to the development questions. Then identify your method of organization:

_____

3. Is the order you chose for your paragraphs the most effective approach to your topic?

_____

4. Move any paragraphs that are out of order.

5. Look closely at your body paragraphs to see if all the sentences are arranged logically within paragraphs.

6. Move any sentences that are out of order.

COHERENCE

☐ Are transitions used effectively so that paragraphs move smoothly and logically from one to the next?

☐ Do the sentences move smoothly and logically from one to the next?

For a list of transitions, see pages 99–100.

1. Add two transitions to your essay.

2. Circle five transitions you use.

3. Explain how two of them make your essay easier to read.

_____

_____

Now rewrite your essay with your revisions.

For Editing Peer Evaluation Forms, go to Appendix 6.

Editing Your Own Essay

SENTENCES

Subjects and Verbs

☐ Does each sentence have a main subject and verb?

For help with subjects and verbs, see Chapter 27.

1. Underline the subjects once and verbs twice in a paragraph of your revised essay. Remember that sentences can have more than one subject-verb set.

2. Does each of your sentences have at least one subject and verb that can stand alone?

_____

3. Correct any fragments you have written.

4. Correct any run-together sentences you have written.

For help with fragments, see Chapter 28.
For help with run-togethers, see Chapter 29.

Subject-Verb Agreement

☐ Do all subjects and verbs agree?

1. Read aloud the subjects and verbs you underlined in your revised essay.

2. Correct any subjects and verbs that do not agree.

For help with subject-verb agreement, see Chapter 32.

Pronoun Agreement

☐ Do all pronouns agree with their nouns?

1. Find any pronouns in your revised essay that do not agree with their nouns.

2. Correct any pronouns that do not agree with their nouns.

For help with pronoun agreement, see Chapter 36.

Modifiers

☐ Are modifiers as close as possible to the words they modify?

1. Find any modifiers in your revised essay that are not as close as possible to the words they modify.

2. Rewrite sentences if necessary so that your modifiers are as close as possible to the words they modify.

For help with modifier errors, see Chapter 39.

PUNCTUATION AND MECHANICS

Punctuation

☐ Are sentences punctuated correctly?

1. Read your revised essay for any errors in punctuation.

2. Make sure any fragments and run-together sentences you revised are punctuated correctly.

For help with punctuation, see Chapters 40–44.

Mechanics

☐ Are words capitalized properly?

1. Read your revised essay for any errors in capitalization.

2. Be sure to check your capitalization in any fragments or run-together sentences you revised.

For help with capitalization, see Chapter 45.

WORD CHOICE AND SPELLING

Word Choice

☐ Are words used correctly?

For help with confused words, see Chapter 51.

1. Find any words used incorrectly in your revised essay.

2. Correct any errors you find.

Spelling

☐ Are words spelled correctly?

For help with spelling, see Chapter 52.

To make a personal log of your grammar/usage errors, go to Appendix 7.

1. Use spell-check and a dictionary to check your spelling.

2. Correct any misspelled words.

To make a personal log of your spelling errors, go to Appendix 8.

Now rewrite your essay again with your editing corrections.

MyWritingLab **More Helpful Hints**

- **Do your explanations need some rewriting?** One of the most important features of a definition essay is the words and phrases that explain other words and phrases. These groups of words need to be as close to each other as possible. To learn more about these guidelines, visit **Misplaced or Dangling Modifiers** in the **Sentence Skills** module of **MyWritingLab.**

PRACTICING DEFINITION: FROM READING TO WRITING

This final section provides practice with the reading and writing skills you learned in this chapter. It includes two reading selections and several writing assignments on "your reading" and "your world." The section then gives you guidance with peer evaluation and a reflection exercise that shows you how to annotate your essay for your instructor in ways that will benefit both of you.

Reading Workshop

Here are two good definition essays: "What is Parkour?" by the World Freerunning Parkour Federation defines parkour as an evolving sport, and "Spanglish Moves into Mainstream" by Daniel Hernandez explains how and why English and Spanish words and phrases are combined in many American communities on a daily basis. As you read, notice how the writers make their points through well-chosen examples and details.

WHAT IS PARKOUR?
by the World Freerunning Parkour Federation

Focusing Your Attention

1. Have you ever had trouble defining a new idea, activity, or object? How would you start a definition of an activity that has not been defined before?

2. The essay you are about to read uses examples to explain this fairly new activity. Do you think we have room for another sport in our world? Explain your reasoning.

Expanding Your Vocabulary

The following words are important to your understanding of this essay. Highlight them throughout the essay before you begin to read. Then refer to this list as you come across these words in the essay.

phenomenon: a unique experience (paragraph 1)

tic-tac: a movement involving pushing off a wall (paragraph 2)

kong vault: the act of moving over an object and gaining distance (paragraph 2)

gap jump: a jump that makes a body airborne (paragraph 2)

morphing: changing (paragraph 3)

READING CRITICALLY
Reacting Critically to Your Reading

 Reading Strategy

As you have throughout this chapter, practice generating your reactions to your reading by recording the author's ideas on the left side of a piece of paper and your own reactions on the right. These notes will also help you understand the essay on an analytical level. Share your notes with someone else in the class.

WHAT IS PARKOUR?
by The World Freerunning Parkour Federation

The word comes from the French "parcours," which literally means, "the   1
way through" or "the path." What we now all know as "Parkour" with a "k" had

its origins in a training program for French Special Forces known as "Parcours du combatant," or "The Path of the Warrior." It was David Belle, a French dude, son of a Parcours Warrior and the "inventor" of Parkour, who changed the "c" to a "k" and, along with his comrades, the Yamakazi, began the worldwide movement you are now officially a part of and which also includes the phenomenon known as Freerunning. (Confused yet? Don't give up! You're almost there!)

2   According to the strictest definition, Parkour is the act of moving from point "a" to point "b" using the obstacles in your path to increase your efficiency. Sounds like a fun game, right? A basic repertoire of moves developed over the years, like the "tic-tac," the "kong vault," and the "gap jump," make Parkour immediately recognizable to most people who see it, even if they don't know what it's called!

3   But a funny thing happened on the way to Point B. The cool, super-creative moves that the Yamakazi came up with started morphing, and since there was no one chasing them (most of the time), their efficiency got less and less important to some of the Yamakazi, who decided they wanted to start throwing flips and just generally expressing themselves through movement. The leader of that splinter group was named Sebastian Foucan, the guy from the beginning of *Casino Royale*. David Belle decided he wanted to stick with efficiency, so he and Sebastian went their separate ways, and "two" sports started developing along separate but parallel paths.

4   For a long time, people argued about which was which (and which was better!), but while they were busy doing that, a bunch of new guys (and some girls) came along and started training, together or separately, picking up the skills they saw on YouTube, coming up with their own that played to their unique strengths and interests, and then sharing them through their own videos. Some liked to time themselves, some were just out to express themselves. Some did it in urban environments, some in the forest. Some thought it should never be competitive or commercialized in any way. Some were anxious to compete because that was in their nature. And what do all these busy people call what they do? In the end, most of them decided it was all just movement, and more importantly, it was all just play.

5   So what do we here at the WFPF believe Parkour (and Freerunning) to be? I will tell you what we know, and that is that Parkour, fundamentally, is a philosophy and a way a life. It's a way of looking at any environment and believing in your heart that there is no obstacle in life that cannot be overcome. Everyone is a unique individual, so no two people will come up with the exact same solution, but there is a "way through" for us all.

6   Little kids all learn to walk at their own pace and in their own way; they don't start by jumping off rooftops, and no matter how many times they fall, they never give up. The basic fact never changes. We just need to pick ourselves up and start to play with whatever is challenging us right now and to hold to the motto that to Know Obstacles is to Know Freedom!

Thinking Critically About Content

1. What is the main idea of this essay?

2. What does The World Freerunning Parkour Federation mean when they say, "Everyone is a unique individual, so no two people

will come up with the exact same solution, but there is a 'way through' for us all" (paragraph 5)?

3. Think of a synonym for "Freedom" in paragraph 6. What is The World Freerunning Parkour Federation implying about freedom in this paragraph?

Thinking Critically About Purpose and Audience

4. What do you think The World Freerunning Parkour Federation's purpose is in this essay?

5. Who do you think is their primary audience?

6. What would The World Freerunning Parkour Federation's audience say parkour and life have in common?

Thinking Critically About Essays

7. How does The World Freerunning Parkour Federation use examples in this definition essay?

8. What would The World Freerunning Parkour Federation say is his actual definition of *parkour*?

9. Is the writers' informal approach to the subject effective? Explain your answer.

10. Write a paragraph defining *obstacles* from the athlete's point of view.

To keep track of your critical thinking progress, go to Appendix 1.

SPANGLISH MOVES INTO MAINSTREAM
by Daniel Hernandez

Focusing Your Attention

1. Have you ever made up words? What were the sources of these creations?

2. The essay you are about to read discusses the various ways we have combined English and Spanish in the United States over the years. Do you live in an area that draws from more than one language? What signs of multiple languages do you see in your immediate environment?

Expanding Your Vocabulary

The following words are important to your understanding of this essay. Highlight them throughout the essay before you begin to read. Then refer to this list as you get to these words in the essay.

carne asada: grilled marinated beef (paragraph 1)

vernacular: ordinary language (paragraph 3)

abominable: horrible (paragraph 3)

prevalence: popularity (paragraph 4)

authenticity: a sense of realism (paragraph 4)

bastion: fortress (paragraph 6)

legitimate: valid (paragraph 7)

demographic: characteristics of a population (paragraph 8)

recedes: disappears (paragraph 8)

replenishing: replacing (paragraph 9)

 Reading
Strategy

READING CRITICALLY
Reacting Critically to Your Reading

Once again, practice generating your reactions to your reading by recording the author's ideas on the left side of a piece of paper and your own reactions on the right. This activity will help you understand this essay at a deeper level than reading without annotating it. Share your notes with someone in the class.

SPANGLISH MOVES INTO MAINSTREAM
by Daniel Hernandez

1   On a muggy Sunday afternoon at the Duenas, mariachi music jumped from a boombox on the concrete in the driveway. The roasted smells of "carne asada" lingered over a folding picnic table, like the easy banter between cousins.

"Le robaron la troca con everything. Los tires, los rines," a visiting cousin said.
Translation: "They robbed the truck with everything. The tires, the rims."
"Quieres watermelon?" offered Francisco Duenas, a 26-year-old housing counselor, holding a jug filled with sweet water and watermelon bits.
"Tal vez tiene some of the little tierrita at the bottom."
Translation: "Want watermelon? It might have some of the little dirt at the bottom."

2   When the Duenas family gathers for weekend barbecues, there are no pauses between jokes and gossip, spoken in English and Spanish. They've been mixing the languages effortlessly, sometimes clumsily, for years, so much so that the back-and-forth is not even noticed.

Spanglish, the fluid vernacular that crosses between English and Spanish, has been a staple in Hispanic life in California since English-speaking settlers arrived in the 19th century. For much of that time, it has been dismissed and derided by language purists—"neither good, nor bad, but abominable," as Mexican writer Octavio Paz famously put it.   3

The criticism has done little to reduce the prevalence of Spanglish, which today is a bigger part of bilingual life than ever. Now, it's rapidly moving from Hispanic neighborhoods into the mainstream. Spanglish is showing up in television and films, as writers use it to bring authenticity to their scripts and get racy language past network executives.   4

Marketers use it to sell everything from bank accounts to soft drinks. Hallmark now sells Spanglish greeting cards. McDonald's is rolling out Spanglish TV spots that will air on both Spanish- and English-language networks.   5

In academia, once a bastion of anti-Spanglish sentiment, the vernacular is studied in courses with names like "Spanish Phonetics" and "Crossing Borders." Amherst College professor Ilan Stavans published a Spanglish dictionary with hundreds of entries—from "gaseteria" (which means "gas station") to "chaqueta" (for "jacket," instead of the Spanish word "saco"). Stavans said new Spanglish words are created all the time, altering traditional notions of language purity that remained strong a generation ago.   6

Growing up, "I was told in school that you shouldn't mix the languages," said Stavans, whose college plans to hold the first Conference of Spanglish in April. "There used to be this approach that if you use a broken tongue, you have a broken tongue. It's not about broken tongues; it's about different tongues, and they are legitimate. I think you're going to see a lot more of that."   7

The rise of Spanglish says a lot about the demographic shifts in California and other states with large Hispanic populations. Migration movements are traditionally accompanied by the mixing of the native language with the newly acquired one. Within a generation or two, the old-country tongue—whether Polish, Chinese, or Italian—usually recedes.   8

But unlike immigrants from Europe and Asia, Hispanics are separated from their cultural homeland, not by vast oceans, but by the border with Mexico and the 90 miles between Cuba and the Florida Keys. The Hispanic immigrant population is constantly replenishing itself. Meanwhile, Spanish-language media, such as industry giants Telemundo and Univision, continue to grow, meaning the immigrants' original language remains a force in the community.   9

Today, Spanglish is especially popular among young urban Hispanics who are US-born—people like Francisco Duenas, who was raised in South Gate, California, lives near downtown Los Angeles, and works in an office in South Los Angeles. Spanglish, he said, allows him to bridge two cultures: the largely Spanish-speaking world of his parents and the English-language world of work and friends. "I think this Spanglish, it's a way of saying, 'Look, I can do both,'" Duenas said. "And I think here in Los Angeles particularmente, it's not necessary to speak just Spanish or English. No puedes describir la vida aqui (you can't describe life here) without speaking both."   10

11   As Spanglish spreads, academics and marketers are finding that it's much more complicated than simply forming sentences with both Spanish and English words. The most basic part of Spanglish is "code-switching," in which someone inserts or substitutes words from one language into another. For instance, Spanglish might sound like "Vamos a la store para comprar milk." ("Let's go to the store to buy milk.")

12   A more complicated form of Spanglish involves making up words, essentially switching languages within a word itself. It can happen when a word or phrase is translated literally, like "perro caliente" for "hot dog." In other instances, Spanglish is created when an English word is Hispanicized, such as "troca" or "troque" for "truck."

13   Just where the sudden popularity of code-switching will end is a matter of debate. Jim Boulet, Jr., executive director of English First, a lobbying group opposed to bilingual education and which has railed against Spanglish, thinks the boom is a fleeting trend. He and other critics see Spanglish as a form of slang, not a new language. "There's always been some form of that," he said. "At one point it was Yiddish, then the black urban slang, and now Spanglish is the new 'in' thing."

14   But while academics try to break down Spanglish to understand how it is used, others say it's a code so spontaneous that it's impossible to fully unravel. It's "a state of mind," said San Diego cartoonist Lalo Alcaraz, whose nationally syndicated strip "La Cucaracha" includes code-switching. "It's the schizophrenia of trying to deal with two worlds in one."

15   First-generation Hispanics roughly between the ages of 14 and 28 represent the fastest-growing youth demographic, according to the US Census Bureau.

Thinking Critically About Content

1. Write a definition of *Spanglish* in your own words.

2. What are the origins of Spanglish?

3. What is "code-switching"?

Thinking Critically About Purpose and Audience

4. Why do you think Hernandez wrote this essay?

5. Who do you think is his primary audience?

6. What do you suspect the primary audience for this essay thinks of Spanglish and its use in society today?

Thinking Critically About Essays

7. In your opinion, is the scene in the first paragraph effective? Explain your answer.

8. Give some examples from your own experience of words and/ or phrases from different languages. Are these examples common where you live?

9. What rhetorical modes does Hernandez use to develop his definition? Give one example of each.

10. Choose one paragraph, and write an analysis of its mood and tone.

To keep track of your critical thinking progress, go to Appendix 1.

Writing Workshop

This final section offers opportunities for you to apply what you have learned in this chapter to another writing assignment. This time, we provide very little prompting beyond a summary of the guidelines for writing a definition essay. This section will let you demonstrate that you can go through the entire writing process on your own with only occasional feedback from your peers. Loop back into the chapter as necessary when you have questions so that this process becomes as automatic to you as possible before you move on to new material. Then pause at the end of the chapter to reflect briefly on what you have learned.

Guidelines for Writing a Definition Essay

1. Choose your word or idea carefully, and give a working definition of it in your thesis statement.
2. Decide how you want to define your term: by synonym, by negation, or by category.
3. Develop your definition with examples.
4. Use other rhetorical strategies, such as description, comparison, or process analysis, to support your definition.
5. Organize your essay in a logical way.

Writing About Your Reading

1. In the first essay, Isaac Asimov defines *intelligence*. Write your own definition of another state of mind, such as *joy*, *fear*, *loneliness*, or *stress*.

2. Using Hernandez's method of development through example, define for your class a made-up word of your own.

3. Now that you have studied different approaches to the process of definition, what makes a definition effective or useful for you? Apply what you have studied about definition to your answer.

Writing About Your World

1. What does education mean to you? Define *education* as portrayed in this picture.

2. The concept of *family* has undergone a number of changes over the past few years. How would you define this term in our current society?

3. Define one of the following abstract terms: *fear, love, inferiority, wonder, pride, self-control, discipline, anger, freedom, violence, assertiveness, courtesy, kindness.*

4. Create your own definition assignment (with the help of your instructor), and write a response to it.

Revising

Small Group Activity (5–10 minutes per writer) Working in groups of three or four, read your definition essays to each other. The listeners should record their reactions on the Revising Peer Evaluation Forms in Appendix 4. After your group goes through this process, give your evaluation forms to the appropriate writers so that each writer has two or three peer comment sheets for revising.

Paired Activity (5 minutes per writer) Using the completed Peer Evaluation Forms, work in pairs to decide what you should revise in your essay. If time allows, rewrite some of your sentences, and have your partner look at them.

Individual Activity Rewrite your paper, using the revising feedback you received from other students.

Editing

Paired Activity (5–10 minutes per writer) Swap papers with a classmate, and use the Editing Peer Evaluation Form (Appendix 6) to identify as many grammar, punctuation, mechanics, and spelling errors as you can. If time allows, correct some of your errors, and have your partner look at them. Record your grammar, punctuation, and mechanics errors in the Error Log (Appendix 7) and your spelling errors in the Spelling Log (Appendix 8).

Individual Activity Rewrite your paper again, using the editing feedback you received from other students.

Reflecting on Your Writing   When you have completed your own essay, answer these six questions.

1. What was most difficult about this assignment?

2. What was easiest?

3. What did you learn about definition by completing this assignment?

4. What do you think are the strengths of your definition essay? Place a wavy line by the parts of your essay that you feel are very good.

5. What are the weaknesses, if any, of your paper? Place an X by the parts of your essay you would like help with. Write in the margins any questions you have.

6. What did you learn from this assignment about your own writing process—about preparing to write, about writing the first draft, about revising, and about editing?

MyWritingLab™   Visit Chapter 15, "Defining," in MyWritingLab, and complete the Post-test to check your understanding of the chapter's objectives.

CHAPTER 16

Analyzing Causes and Effects

*"*The act of writing is one of the most powerful problem-solving tools humans have at their disposal.*"*

—TOBY FULWILER

We are born with a natural curiosity. Wanting to know why things happen is one of our earliest, most basic instincts: Daddy, why is the sky blue? Closely related to this desire to understand *why* is our interest in *what* will happen as a result of some particular action: If I stay outside much longer, will I get a bad sunburn? In fact, thinking about causes and effects is not only part of human nature but also an advanced mental process and the basis for most decisions we make in life. When faced with a decision, we naturally consider it from different perspectives. If we choose option A, what will happen? What if we choose B—or C? In other words, we look at the possible results—the effects—of the choices and then make up our minds.

Analyzing causes and effects is also an essential part of our writing lives. We use cause-and-effect writing in our personal lives, in college, and in the marketplace:

- A volunteer for a mayor's campaign designs a poster explaining how a vote for this candidate will benefit the city.
- In a paper for a psychology course, a student discusses the causes of schizophrenia.
- A student explains on a history exam the effects of the Civil Rights Act of 1964.
- A sales representative writes a report to her manager explaining why she didn't meet her sales projections.
- The owner of a florist shop writes a letter of complaint to one of his suppliers about the negative effect of late deliveries on sales.

Analyzing **causes and effects** requires the ability to look for connections between two or more items or events and to analyze the reasons for those connections. As the name implies, this writing strategy is composed of two parts: cause and effect. To understand **causes,** we look in the past for reasons that something happened. To discover **effects,** we look to the future for possible results of an action. In other words, we break a situation into parts so we can look at the relationships between its parts and then reach conclusions that are logical and useful.

MyWritingLab	## Understanding Cause and Effect

To enhance your understanding of causes and effects, go to **MyWritingLab.com,** and choose **Cause and Effect** in the **Essay Development** module. For this topic, read the **Overview,** watch the **Animation** video, and complete the **Recall, Apply,** and **Write** activities. After that, check your understanding of cause and effect by taking the **Post-test.**

PREPARING TO WRITE A CAUSE/EFFECT ESSAY

In this book, preparing to write starts with reading. Learning how to read cause/effect essays analytically will benefit your writing. Understanding how a reading selection actually works (in both form and content) will show you how to develop your own writing assignments. So, in the next few pages, you will read an effective cause/effect essay and then answer some questions to help you discover for yourself how the essay communicates its message.

Reading a Cause/Effect Essay

In "Why Do Schools Flunk Biology?" LynNell Hancock makes the point that education in the United States is stuck in the nineteenth century. She deals with both the causes and the effects of students' ability to learn. What do you think of our educational system at the high school level? What do you think of the high school you attended?

Using a reading strategy is an effective way to learn how to read analytically. If you read analytically, you will more likely be able to write analytically. Reading critically, or analytically, will help you understand not only *what* the essay is saying but also *how* the author is saying it. The strategy you will apply to all the reading tasks in this chapter involves making connections among ideas in your reading material.

Reading Strategy

READING CRITICALLY
Making Connections in a Professional Essay

Distinguishing causes from effects is an important part of understanding a cause/effect essay. After the first reading of a cause/effect essay, divide a sheet of paper into two parts with a vertical line. Then, as you read the essay for a second time, record the causes in the left column and the results on the right. Draw lines from each cause to its related effect (if applicable). Be prepared to explain the connection between your lists and the details in the essay.

WHY DO SCHOOLS FLUNK BIOLOGY?
by LynNell Hancock

1   Biology is a staple at most American high schools. Yet when it comes to the biology of the students themselves—how their brains develop and retain knowledge—school officials would rather not pay attention to the lessons. Can first graders handle French? What time should school start? Should music be cut? Biologists have some important evidence to offer. Not only are they ignored, but their findings are often turned upside down.

2   Force of habit rules the hallways and classrooms. Neither brain science nor education research has been able to free the majority of America's schools from their nineteenth-century roots. If more administrators were tuned in to brain research, scientists argue, not only would schedules change, but subjects such as foreign language and geometry would be offered to much younger children. Music and gym would be daily requirements. Lectures, worksheets, and rote memorization would be replaced by hands-on materials, drama, and project work. And teachers would pay greater attention to children's emotional connections to subjects. "We do more education research than anyone else in the world," says Frank Vellutino, a professor of educational psychology at State University of New York at Albany, "and we ignore more as well."

3   Plato once said that music "is a more potent instrument than any other for education." Now scientists know why. Music, they believe, trains the brain for higher forms of thinking. Researchers at the University of California, Irvine, studied the power of music by observing two groups of preschoolers. One group took piano lessons and sang daily in chorus. The other did not. After eight months the musical 3-year-olds were expert puzzlemasters, scoring 80 percent higher than their playmates did in spatial intelligence—the ability to visualize the world accurately.

4   This skill later translates into complex math and engineering skills. "Early music training can enhance a child's ability to reason," says Irvine physicist Gordon

Shaw. Yet music education is often the first "frill" to be cut when school budgets shrink. Schools on average have only one music teacher for every 500 children, according to the National Commission on Music Education.

Then there's gym—another expendable hour by most school standards. Only 36 percent of school children today are required to participate in daily physical education. Yet researchers now know that exercise is good not only for the heart. It also juices up the brain, feeding it nutrients in the form of glucose and increasing nerve connections—all of which make it easier for kids of all ages to learn. Neuroscientist William Greenough confirmed this by watching rats at his University of Illinois at Urbana–Champaign lab. One group did nothing. A second exercised on an automatic treadmill. A third was set loose in a Barnum & Bailey obstacle course requiring the rats to perform acrobatic feats. These "supersmart" rats grew "an enormous amount of gray matter" compared with their sedentary partners, says Greenough. Of course, children don't ordinarily run such gauntlets; still, Greenough believes, the results are significant. Numerous studies, he says, show that children who exercise regularly do better in school.

The implication for schools goes beyond simple exercise. Children also need to be more physically active in the classroom, not sitting quietly in their seats memorizing subtraction tables. Knowledge is retained longer if children connect not only aurally but emotionally and physically to the material, says University of Oregon education professor Robert Sylwester in A Celebration of Neurons.

Good teachers know that lecturing on the American Revolution is far less effective than acting out a battle. Angles and dimensions are better understood if children chuck their work sheets and build a complex model to scale. The smell of the glue enters memory through one sensory system, the touch of the wood blocks another, the sight of the finished model still another. The brain then creates a multidimensional mental model of the experience—one easier to retrieve. "Explaining a smell," says Sylwester, "is not as good as actually smelling it."

Scientists argue that children are capable of far more at younger ages than schools generally realize. People obviously continue learning their whole lives, but the optimum "windows of opportunity for learning" last until about the age of 10 or 12, says Harry Chugani of Wayne State University's Children's Hospital of Michigan. Chugani determined this by measuring the brain's consumption of its chief energy source, glucose. (The more glucose it uses, the more active the brain.) Children's brains, he observes, gobble up glucose at twice the adult rate from the age of 4 to puberty. So young brains are as primed as they'll ever be to process new information. Complex subjects such as trigonometry or foreign language shouldn't wait for puberty to be introduced. In fact, Chugani says, it's far easier for an elementary-school child to hear and process a second language—and even speak it without an accent. Yet most U.S. districts wait until junior high to introduce Spanish or French—after the "windows" are closed.

Reform could begin at the beginning. Many sleep researchers now believe that most teens' biological clocks are set later than those of their fellow humans. But high school starts at 7:30 a.m., usually to accommodate bus schedules. The result can be wasted class time for whole groups of kids. Making matters worse, many kids have trouble readjusting their natural sleep rhythm. Dr. Richard Allen of Johns Hopkins University found that teens went to sleep at the same time whether they had to be at school by 7:30 a.m. or 9:30 a.m. The later-to-rise teens not only get more sleep, he says; they also get better grades. The obvious solution would be to start school later when kids hit puberty. But at school, there's what's obvious, and then there's tradition.

10   Why is this body of research rarely used in most American classrooms? Not many administrators or school-board members know it exists, says Linda Darling-Hammond, professor of education at Columbia University's Teachers College. In most states, neither teachers nor administrators are required to know much about how children learn in order to be certified. What's worse, she says, decisions to cut music or gym are often made by noneducators, whose concerns are more often monetary than educational. "Our school system was invented in the late 1800s, and little has changed," she says. "Can you imagine if the medical profession ran this way?"

Discovering How This Essay Works

To help you recognize the elements that make this an effective cause/effect essay so you can use them in your own writing, answer the following questions in as much detail as possible.

1. What is Hancock analyzing in this essay?

   _____

   _____

2. List two details or examples from this essay that support the essay's main point.

   _____

   _____

3. List two cause/effect relationships that Hancock explains.

   _____

   _____

4. Do you feel Hancock gets to the real problems connected with why our educational system is lagging behind the times? Explain your answer.

   _____

   _____

   _____

5. How does Hancock organize the topics in her essay? Go to pages 64–76 in Chapter 6 to help you identify her method of organization.

   _____

WRITING A CAUSE/EFFECT ESSAY

Now that you have read and studied the model essay, you will be writing one of your own. This section will help you generate a draft that you will then revise and edit in the third section of this chapter. It will guide you here through a careful reading of the writing assignment, give you several ways to generate ideas and choose a topic, and finally furnish you with concrete guidelines for writing an effective cause/effect essay. We encourage you to write notes and lists throughout this process so you can use them when you write a draft of your essay at the end of this section.

Reading the Prompt

Writing any essay starts with making sure you understand the writing assignment or "prompt." An assignment attempts to "prompt" you to respond to a specific issue or question. The more completely you understand the prompt, the better paper you will create. So you want to learn how to read the essay assignment actively rather than passively. Applying the chapter reading strategy to your prompt is a good way to achieve this level of interaction.

READING CRITICALLY
Making Connections in the Prompt

 Reading Strategy

What are the tasks you need to perform in the writing prompt? Put a vertical line down the center of a blank sheet of paper, and list the assignment tasks on the left and what you need to do to complete those tasks on the right. Then write as many personal notes as you can in the margins of your lists. Finally, underline the key words for completing this assignment.

Writing Prompt

Write an essay analyzing one change you think is especially necessary in our high school educational system. What caused the current problem as you see it? Why is this change necessary? What will be the results of this change? Write your analysis, following the guidelines for writing a cause/effect essay.

MyWritingLab
Complete this Writing Prompt assignment in MyWritingLab.

Thinking About the Prompt

Before you focus on a specific topic, you should generate as many ideas as you can so you have several to choose from. What can be improved in our educational system at the high school level? What do you want to change? What would be the possible results of these changes? What do you want to keep the same? Use one or more of the prewriting techniques you learned in Chapter 5 to generate ideas on this subject.

Guidelines for Writing a Cause/Effect Essay

When you write a cause/effect essay, your purpose is to give your readers some insight into the causes and effects of an event or a situation. Cause/effect writing is based on your ability to analyze. Good cause/effect essays follow a few simple guidelines. As you think about the topic you have chosen in response to the prompt above, read the following guidelines, and continue to make lists and notes that you will use when you write your draft on this prompt. After each guideline is an explanation of how it functions in the reading selection at the beginning of this chapter so you can actually see how the element works in an essay before you apply it to your own writing.

1. **Write a thesis statement that explains what you are analyzing.** Cause/effect thinking requires you to look for connections between two or more situations. That is, you want to discover what caused an incident (causes) or what its results (effects) might be. Your essay can focus on the causes, the effects, or some combination of the two.

In the Reading: In her essay, Hancock puts her thesis statement at the end of her first paragraph: "Not only are they [biologists] ignored, but their findings are often turned upside down." She goes on to say that if school administrators paid attention to research (the cause), we would see many changes (the effects), which she names. The rest of the essay examines each effect in detail.

In Your Writing: As you think about our educational system, what will you analyze in your essay? Write a rough draft of your thesis statement. Does this sentence say what you are going to analyze?

2. **Choose facts, details, and reasons to support your thesis statement.** Cause/effect essays are usually written to prove a specific point. As a result, your body paragraphs should consist mainly of facts, details, and reasons—not opinions. Your reader should be able to check what you are saying, and any opinions you include should be based on clear evidence.

In the Reading: Because Hancock sets out to prove that American education ignores research, she must name specific research studies that help prove her point. She breaks her subject into five areas: music, gym, teaching methods, curriculum (subjects studied), and school hours. She then cites evidence in each area. For example, in the area of music, she describes research at the University of California, Irvine; for gym, she discusses rat studies from the University of Illinois; for curriculum, she describes research done at Wayne State University's Children's Hospital.

Hancock also quotes many experts, such as Frank Vellutino, a professor of educational psychology at State University of New York at Albany (paragraph 2), and gives statistics from the National Commission on Music Education (paragraph 4). A reader could check every one of Hancock's research studies, quotations, statistics, and observations. By providing facts and reasons rather than opinions in her body paragraphs, Hancock proves her point—that American education is not paying attention to current research about learning.

In Your Writing: Use one of the prewriting techniques outlined in Chapter 5 to generate facts, details, and reasons on the topic you have chosen. Develop your notes as fully as possible so you can write a well-developed essay.

3. **Do not mistake coincidence for cause or effect.** If you get up every morning at 5:30 a.m., just before the sun rises, you cannot conclude that the sun rises *because* you get up. The relationship between these two events is coincidence. Confusing coincidence with cause and effect is faulty reasoning—reasoning that is not logical. To avoid errors in reasoning, you can look deeper into the issues connected with your subject. The more you search for real causes and effects, the less likely you will be misled by coincidence.

In the Reading: Hancock does not seem to mistake coincidence for cause or effect in any part of her essay. If, however, she had said that ignoring research on how teens learn has resulted in fewer students studying foreign languages today compared with 40 years ago, her reasoning would be faulty. She has no evidence to prove that the research about how students learn and the decline in students taking foreign languages in high school are related. It's only a coincidence that the research has been ignored and that fewer students study foreign languages today.

In Your Writing: Annotate your prewriting notes with comments about causes and effects that are related. Make sure you are not basing any of your reasoning on coincidence.

4. **Search for the real causes and effects connected with your subject.** Just as you wouldn't stop reading halfway through a good murder mystery, you shouldn't stop too early in your analysis of causes and effects. Keep digging. The first reasons or results you uncover are often not the real reasons or results. Suppose a character in a mystery novel dies by slipping in the shower. A good detective would try to find out what caused the fall and would learn that someone administered a drug overdose that caused the victim to fall in the shower. In other words, you are looking for the most basic cause or effect.

In the Reading: Through a large amount of evidence, Hancock shows us that she has searched hard to discover the real causes and effects of why American education is lagging behind the times. She names two causes—administrators ignore research and noneducators make decisions about education—and then explains the effects of ignoring research in five areas of education.

In Your Writing: Do your prewriting notes include the *real* causes and effects for your topic? If you explore any of the items in your notes, would you discover deeper reasons for your conclusions about our educational system? Dig even further into this subject by making a list of causes and results related to your deductions so far.

5. **Organize your essay so your readers can easily follow your analysis.** Though it may be difficult to think through the causes and effects of a situation, organizing this type of essay is usually straightforward. Your thesis statement tells what you are going to analyze. Then your body paragraphs discuss the main causes or effects in a specific order—in chronological order, from one extreme to another, from general to particular, or from particular to general. You might, for example, use chronological order to show how one effect led to another and then to a third. Or you might move from the most important cause or effect to the least important. Your goal in a cause/effect essay is to get your readers to agree with you and see a certain issue or situation the same way you do. To accomplish this purpose, your readers need to be able to follow what you are saying.

In the Reading: Hancock discusses five effects of ignoring research on how students learn, moving from particular to general. First, she deals with the two subjects school boards often cut for budgetary reasons—music and gym. From these specific classes, she moves to more general concerns—teaching methods and curriculum. Finally, she discusses high school hours, the most general topic of all. In other words, she organizes her essay from specific to general, moving from specific classes to the general logistics of the school day.

In Your Writing: How will you organize your essay: general to specific, specific to general, chronological, or from one extreme to another? (See Chapter 6 for explanations of these.) Is the method of organization you've chosen the best option for achieving your purpose? How will you arrange the details in your paragraphs? Reorganize your prewriting to fit your methods of organization so you are ready to write your essay.

Writing a Draft of Your Essay

Now is the time to collect all your reactions, your notes, your prewriting exercises, and your lists as you set out to write the first draft of your essay. In addition, you might want to review the professional essay, the writing assignment, and the chapter guidelines for writing cause/effect essays, along with your notes and lists, to help you get started. At this point, don't think about revising or editing; just get your thoughts about the writing assignment down on paper.

Helpful Hints

- **Does your essay have a specific point?** Cause/effect essays require you to have a focus for your discussion. If you are having trouble finding a purpose or focus, go to **Thesis Statement** in the **Essay Development** module of **MyWritingLab** for help.

REVISING AND EDITING

You are now ready to think about revising and editing. This section will take you through the guidelines for revising and editing cause/effect essays with two specific writing samples: another student's essay and your own essay. The processes of revising and editing are often much easier with someone else's writing, which is why we begin this stage with a writing sample from another student. If you can locate some of the problems in this essay, you might be able to identify areas for improvement in your own writing. So you will be reviewing the chapter guidelines by revising and editing another student's writing before applying the same guidelines to your own writing.

Reading a Student Cause/Effect Essay

We will begin by using our chapter reading strategy on this essay. In his essay "The Budget Crisis," student writer Jefferson Wright explores the problems of budget cuts at his college. Making connections between causes and effects as you read this essay will help you understand Jefferson's reasoning and get ready to revise and edit his essay in preparation for revising and editing your own writing.

READING CRITICALLY
Making Connections in the Student Essay

Reading
Strategy

As you read Jefferson's essay, see if you can find the points in his draft that deal with causes. When does he focus on effects? After a first reading of the essay, divide a sheet of paper into two parts with a vertical line. As you read the essay for a second time, record the causes in the left column and the results on the right. Draw lines from each cause to its related effect (if applicable). Try to find the deepest level of cause and effect that Jefferson discusses. Be prepared to explain the connection between your lists and the details in the essay.

The Budget Crisis

1   The local college has a budget crisis. Now, when a staff person quits their job or retires, no one is hired to replace that person. This wouldn't be of great concern to most students, except now the lack of money is starting to affect the campus grounds. The college no longer has the money to replace some of the maintenance and facilities crew, which means the campus grounds, classrooms, and offices are no longer well maintained.

2   A campus that used to be beautiful has turned into a wasteland because of the neglect in keeping up its grounds. The small maintenance crew simply cannot handle the workload necessary to maintain the campus. The flower beds in front of the buildings have not been weeded, so now it has more weeds than flowers. Trash that is thrown around the campus has not been picked up. Around every doorway are cigarette butts ground into the concrete. People shouldn't smoke anyway. It's not a great habit. There are old newspapers and candy wrappers caught on grass that has not been mowed in over two weeks, making the grounds look like the aftermath of a concert. Trash cans are overflowing with garbage and have colonies of flies circling them. The outside of the campus just looks unkempt and uncared for.

3   However, the campus grounds are not all that is ugly. The classroom buildings are also neglected. Everything inside is as messy as outside. The floors that used to shine are now covered with a sticky gray film. There are spills on the floors by all the soft drink machines. The bulletin boards are never cleaned off, so people just put new flyers over three or four layers of old flyers. On warm days, a strange smell overwhelms the classrooms, which the students have named "the biohazard." Restrooms are in desperate need of attention. And would probably fail any government check. The campus is really disgusting.

4   But the students aren't the only people suffering; the teachers are feeling the effects also. Their offices have ants crawling from various cracks in the walls. The dust in their offices is two inches thick. Spiders have woven cobwebs high in the windows and corners of the offices. Making both teachers and students wonder exactly where the insects hide during the day. Many light bulbs are broken near the offices, and the fluorescent bulbs flicker as if it is dancing to an unheard rhythm. The offices are as bad as the rest of the campus.

5   The condition of the campus can hardly be blamed on the maintenance crew. They are constantly working and trying to keep up with the workload. The problem lies in the fact that by the time they finish one job, two or more weeks pass by before they can get back to that job. There just isn't enough money to hire the necessary personnel to cover the demands of the job. The college should put money into hiring more maintenance personnel before students transfer to other colleges because of the condition of this one. Why can't the college just spend the necessary money to make the campus beautiful again.

Revising and Editing the Student Essay

This essay is Jefferson's first draft, which now needs to be revised and edited. First, apply the Revising Checklist to the content of Jefferson's draft. When you are satisfied that his ideas are fully developed and well organized, use the Editing Checklist to correct his grammar and mechanics errors. Answer the questions, and complete the tasks in each category. Then write your suggested changes directly on Jefferson's draft.

Revising the Student Essay

THESIS STATEMENT

✔ Does the thesis statement contain the essay's controlling idea?

✔ Does the thesis appear as the last sentence of the introduction?

1. Put brackets around the last sentence in Jefferson's introduction. What does it say he is analyzing?

   _____

2. Rewrite Jefferson's thesis statement if necessary so that it states his purpose and introduces all his topics.

   _____

   _____

BASIC ELEMENTS

✔ Does the title draw in the readers?

✔ Does the introduction capture the readers' attention and build up effectively to the thesis statement?

✔ Does each body paragraph deal with a single topic?

✔ Does the conclusion bring the essay to a close in an interesting way?

1. Give Jefferson's essay an alternate title.

   _____

   _____

2. Rewrite Jefferson's introduction so that it captures the readers' attention and builds up to the thesis statement at the end of the paragraph.

   _____

   _____

3. Does each of Jefferson's body paragraphs deal with only one topic?

_____

4. Rewrite Jefferson's conclusion using at least one suggestion from Part I.

_____

_____

DEVELOPMENT

✔ Do the body paragraphs adequately support the thesis statement?

✔ Does each body paragraph have a focused topic sentence?

✔ Does each body paragraph contain *specific* details that support the topic sentence?

✔ Does each body paragraph include *enough* details to fully explain the topic sentence?

1. Write out Jefferson's thesis statement (revised, if necessary), and list his topic sentences below it.

Thesis statement: _____

_____

_____

Topic 1: _____

_____

Topic 2: _____

_____

Topic 3: _____

_____

2. Do the topics adequately develop the essay's thesis statement?

_____

3. Does each body paragraph have a focused topic sentence?

_____

4. Does Jefferson get to the *real* causes and effects in his essay?

_____

5. Where do you need more information?

_____

6. Make two of Jefferson's details more specific.

7. Add at least two new details to make his essay clearer.

UNITY

✔ Do the essay's topic sentences relate directly to the thesis statement?

✔ Do the details in each body paragraph support the paragraph's topic sentence?

1. Read each of Jefferson's topic sentences with his thesis statement. Do they go together?

   _____

2. Revise his topic sentences if necessary so they are directly related.

3. Drop or rewrite the two sentences in paragraph 2 that are not directly related to their topic sentence.

ORGANIZATION

✔ Is the essay organized logically?

✔ Is each body paragraph organized logically?

1. Read Jefferson's essay again to see if all the paragraphs are arranged logically.

2. Move any paragraphs that are out of order.

3. Do you think his method of organization is the most effective one for his purpose? Explain your answer.

   _____

   _____

4. Look closely at Jefferson's body paragraphs to see if his sentences are arranged logically within paragraphs.

5. Move the sentence in paragraph 2 that is out of order.

COHERENCE

✔ Are transitions used effectively so that paragraphs move smoothly and logically from one to the next?

✔ Do the sentences move smoothly and logically from one to the next?

1. Add two transitions to Jefferson's essay.

2. Circle five pronouns Jefferson uses.

3. Explain how two of these make Jefferson's essay easier to read.

For a list of transitions, see pages 99–100.
For a list of pronouns, see pages 496–497.

   _____

   _____

 Now rewrite Jefferson's essay with your revisions.

Editing the Student Essay

SENTENCES

Subjects and Verbs

✔ Does each sentence have a main subject and verb?

For help with subjects and verbs, see Chapter 27.

1. Underline the subjects once and verbs twice in paragraphs 3 and 4 of your revision of Jefferson's essay. Remember that sentences can have more than one subject-verb set.

2. Does each of the sentences have at least one subject and verb that can stand alone?

For help with fragments, see Chapter 28.

3. Did you find and correct Jefferson's two fragments? If not, find and correct them now.

Subject-Verb Agreement

✔ Do all subjects and verbs agree?

For help with subject-verb agreement, see Chapter 32.

1. Read aloud the subjects and verbs you underlined in your revision of Jefferson's essay.

2. Correct any subjects and verbs that do not agree.

Pronoun Agreement

✔ Do all pronouns agree with their nouns?

For help with pronoun agreement, see Chapter 36.

1. Find any pronouns in your revision of Jefferson's essay that do not agree with their nouns.

2. Did you find and correct the three pronoun agreement errors in Jefferson's essay? If not, find and correct them now.

Modifiers

✔ Are modifiers as close as possible to the words they modify?

For help with modifier errors, see Chapter 39.

1. Find any modifiers in your revision of Jefferson's essay that are not as close as possible to the words they modify.

2. Rewrite sentences if necessary so that modifiers are as close as possible to the words they modify.

PUNCTUATION AND MECHANICS

Punctuation

✔ Are sentences punctuated correctly?

1. Read your revision of Jefferson's essay for any errors in punctuation.

2. Find the two fragments you revised, and make sure they are punctuated correctly.

3. Did you find and correct Jefferson's two errors in end punctuation? If not, find and correct them now.

For help with punctuation, see Chapters 40–44.

Mechanics
✔ Are words capitalized properly?

For help with capitalization, see Chapter 45.

1. Read your revision of Jefferson's essay for any errors in capitalization.

2. Be sure to check Jefferson's capitalization in the fragments you revised.

WORD CHOICE AND SPELLING

Word Choice
✔ Are words used correctly?

1. Find any words used incorrectly in your revision of Jefferson's essay.

For help with confused words, see Chapter 51.

2. Correct any errors you find.

Spelling
✔ Are words spelled correctly?

1. Use spell-check and a dictionary to check the spelling in your revision of Jefferson's essay.

For help with spelling, see Chapter 52.

2. Correct any misspelled words.

Now rewrite Sergio's essay again with your editing corrections.

Reading Your Own Cause/Effect Essay

The first phase of revising your own writing is creating some distance between you and your essay. To accomplish this, you will apply the same reading strategy to your own writing that you have used on other reading tasks in this chapter. Reading your essay as a reading selection you are trying to understand and respond to will help you revise and edit your own work efficiently and effectively.

Reading
Strategy

READING CRITICALLY
Making Connections in Your Own Essay

As you begin to rework your essay, use the same technique on it that you have been practicing throughout the chapter. List in two columns the causes and effects that you discuss in your essay. Then, draw lines from causes to related effects, making sure the relationship between these items is clear. Revise any connections on your lists that are unclear.

Revising and Editing Your Own Essay

You are now ready to revise and edit your own writing. Remember that revision involves reworking the content and organization of your essay while editing asks you to check your grammar and usage. Work first with the content, making sure your thoughts are fully developed and organized effectively before you correct your grammar and usage errors. The more times you repeat these processes, the better your draft will be. The checklists here will help you apply to your essay what you have learned in this chapter.

Revising Your Own Essay

For Revising Peer Evaluation Forms, go to Appendix 4.

THESIS STATEMENT

☐ Does the thesis statement contain the essay's controlling idea?

☐ Does the thesis appear as the last sentence of the introduction?

1. What are you analyzing?

   _____

2. Put brackets around the last sentence in your introduction. What do you say you are analyzing in this sentence?

   _____

3. Rewrite your thesis statement if necessary so that it states your purpose and introduces your topics.

BASIC ELEMENTS

☐ Does the title draw in the readers?

☐ Does the introduction capture the readers' attention and build up effectively to the thesis statement?

☐ Does each body paragraph deal with a single topic?

☐ Does the conclusion bring the essay to a close in an interesting way?

1. Give your essay a title if it doesn't have one.

    _____

2. Does your introduction capture your readers' attention and build up to your thesis statement at the end of the paragraph?

    _____

3. Does each of your body paragraphs deal with only one topic?

    _____

4. Does your conclusion follow some of the suggestions offered in Part I?

    _____

DEVELOPMENT

☐ Do the body paragraphs adequately support the thesis statement?

☐ Does each body paragraph have a focused topic sentence?

☐ Does each body paragraph contain s*pecific* details that support the topic sentence?

☐ Does each body paragraph include *enough* details to fully explain the topic sentence?

1. Write out your thesis statement (revised, if necessary), and list your topic sentences below it.

    Thesis statement: _____

    Topic 1: _____

    Topic 2: _____

    Topic 3: _____

2. Do your topics adequately support your thesis statement?

    _____

3. Does each body paragraph have a focused topic sentence?

    _____

4. Do you get to the *real* causes and effects in your essay?

    _____

5. Where do you need more information?

    _____

6. Make two of your details more specific.

7. Add at least two new details to make your cause/effect clearer.

UNITY

☐ Do the essay's topic sentences relate directly to the thesis statement?

☐ Do the details in each body paragraph support the paragraph's topic sentence?

1. Read each of your topic sentences with your thesis statement in mind. Do they go together?

_____

2. Revise your topic sentences if necessary so they are directly related.

3. Drop or rewrite any of the sentences in your body paragraphs that are not directly related to their topic sentences.

ORGANIZATION

☐ Is the essay organized logically?

☐ Is each body paragraph organized logically?

1. Read your essay again to see if all the paragraphs are arranged logically.

2. Refer to your answers to the development questions. Then identify your method of organization:

_____

3. Move any paragraphs that are out of order.

4. Look closely at your body paragraphs to see if all the sentences are arranged logically within paragraphs.

5. Move any sentences that are out of order.

COHERENCE

☐ Are transitions used effectively so that paragraphs move smoothly and logically from one to the next?

☐ Do the sentences move smoothly and logically from one to the next?

For a list of transitions, see pages 99–100.
For a list of pronouns, see pages 496–497.

1. Add two transitions to your essay.

2. Circle five pronouns you use.

3. Explain how two of these make your essay easier to read.

_____

_____

 Now rewrite your essay with your revisions.

Editing Your Own Essay

For Editing Peer Evaluation Forms, go to Appendix 6.

SENTENCES

Subjects and Verbs

☐ Does each sentence have a main subject and verb?

For help with subjects and verbs, see Chapter 27.

1. Underline the subjects once and verbs twice in a paragraph of your revised essay. Remember that sentences can have more than one subject-verb set.

2. Does each of your sentences have at least one subject and verb that can stand alone?

For help with fragments, see Chapter 28.

3. Correct any fragments you have written.

For help with run-togethers, see Chapter 29.

4. Correct any run-together sentences you have written.

Subject-Verb Agreement

☐ Do all subjects and verbs agree?

1. Read aloud the subjects and verbs you underlined in your revised essay.

2. Correct any subjects and verbs that do not agree.

For help with subject-verb agreement, see Chapter 32.

Pronoun Agreement

☐ Do all pronouns agree with their nouns?

1. Find any pronouns in your revised essay that do not agree with their nouns.

2. Correct any pronouns that do not agree with their nouns.

For help with pronoun agreement, see Chapter 36.

Modifiers

☐ Are modifiers as close as possible to the words they modify?

1. Find any modifiers in your revised essay that are not as close as possible to the words they modify.

For help with modifier errors, see Chapter 39.

2. Rewrite sentences if necessary so that your modifiers are as close as possible to the words they modify.

PUNCTUATION AND MECHANICS

Punctuation

☐ Are sentences punctuated correctly?

1. Read your revised essay for any errors in punctuation.

For help with punctuation, see Chapters 40–44.

2. Make sure any fragments and run-together sentences you revised are punctuated correctly.

Mechanics

☐ Are words capitalized properly?

For help with capitalization, see Chapter 45.

1. Read your revised essay for any errors in capitalization.

2. Be sure to check your capitalization in any fragments or run-together sentences you revised.

WORD CHOICE AND SPELLING

Word Choice

☐ Are words used correctly?

For help with confused words, see Chapter 51.

1. Find any words used incorrectly in your revised essay.

2. Correct any errors you find.

Spelling

☐ Are words spelled correctly?

For help with spelling, see Chapter 52.

To make a personal log of your grammar/usage errors, go to Appendix 7.

1. Use spell-check and a dictionary to check your spelling.

2. Correct any misspelled words.

To make a personal log of your spelling errors, go to Appendix 8.

Now rewrite your essay again with your editing corrections.

MyWritingLab **More Helpful Hints**

- **Do you know the difference between active and passive voice?**
  Using active voice can help you include more details and create a clear picture of a cause/effect relationship. To learn more about how to use active voice, go to **Consistent Verb Tense and Voice** in the **Sentence Skills** module of **MyWritingLab**.

PRACTICING CAUSE/EFFECT: FROM READING TO WRITING

This final section allows you to practice the reading and writing skills you learned in this chapter. It includes two reading selections and several writing assignments on "your reading" and "your world." The section then guides you through peer evaluation and a reflection exercise with suggestions for annotating your final draft in ways that will benefit both your instructor and you.

Reading Workshop

The two essays in this chapter show cause and effect at work: The first essay, "Does Thinking Fast Mean You're Thinking Smarter?" by Maria Konnio, explores the connection between fast reactions and smartness. The second essay, "Happiness Is Catching: Why Emotions Are Contagious" by Stacey Colino, analyzes the role of moods in our daily lives. As you read, notice how the writers make their points through thoughtful, detailed reasoning.

DOES THINKING FAST MEAN YOU'RE THINKING SMARTER?
by Maria Konnikova

Focusing Your Attention

1. What do you believe thinking fast might have to do with smartness? How quickly do your smartest friends process information?

2. The essay you are about to read summarizes some interesting research on the relationship of the speed at which we think to the level of our intelligence. Do you generally process information quickly or slowly? Is this your natural speed?

Expanding Your Vocabulary

The following words are important to your understanding of this essay. As you read, circle any words you don't know beyond this list. Then break into groups, and help each other figure out the meanings of these unknown words.

anthropometric: body measurement (paragraph 1)

psychometrics: the process of measuring mental capacities (paragraph 2)

eugenics: selective breeding (paragraph 2)

proxy: substitute (paragraph 2)

correlation: relationship (paragraph 3)

anesthetics: pain killers (paragraph 3)

inconclusive: questionable, not decisive (paragraph 4)

trajectory: path (paragraph 6)

protocol: procedure (paragraph 6)

variability: ability to change (paragraph 6)

deceptive: misleading (paragraph 8)

Reading
Strategy

READING CRITICALLY
Making Connections in Your Reading

As you've learned throughout this chapter, practice recognizing causes and effects by listing them from the following essay. Put them in two columns on a separate sheet of paper. These lists will help you understand the essay on an analytical level. Compare your notes with those of a classmate.

DOES THINKING FAST MEAN YOU'RE THINKING SMARTER?
by Maria Konnikova

1   In 1884, at his specially built Anthropometric Laboratory in London, Sir Francis Galton charged visitors three pence to undergo simple tests to measure their height, weight, keenness of sight and "swiftness of blow with fist." The laboratory, later moved to the South Kensington Museum, proved immensely popular—"its door was thronged by applicants waiting patiently for their turn," Galton said—ultimately collecting data on some 17,000 individuals.

2   One measure that deeply interested Galton, who is recognized as "the father of psychometrics" for his efforts to quantify people's mental abilities (and scorned as the founder of the eugenics movement because of his theories about inheritance), was speed. He believed that reaction time was one proxy for human intelligence. With a pendulum-based apparatus for timing a subject's response to the sight of a disc of paper or the sound of a hammer, Galton collected reaction speeds averaging around 185 milliseconds, split seconds that would become notorious in the social sciences.

3   For decades other researchers pursued Galton's basic idea—speed equals smarts. While many recent tests have found no consistent relationship, some have demonstrated a weak but unmistakable correlation between short reaction times and high scores on intelligence tests. If there is a logic to the link, it's that the faster nerve signals travel from your eyes to the brain and to the circuits that trigger your motor neurons, anesthetics.

4   Psychologist Michael Woodley of Umea University in Sweden and his colleagues had enough confidence in the link, in fact, to use more than a century of data on reaction times to compare our intellect with that of the Victorians. Their findings call into question our cherished belief that our fast-paced lives are a sign of our productivity, as well as our mental fitness. When the researchers reviewed reaction times from 14 studies conducted between the 1880s and 2004 (including Galton's largely inconclusive data set), they found a troubling decline that, they

calculated, would correspond to a loss of an average of 1.16 IQ points a decade. Doing the math, that makes us mentally inferior to our Victorian predecessors by about 13 IQ points.

The Victorian era was "marked by an explosion of creative genius," Woodley and   5
his colleagues write. There was, after all, the first world's fair, the rise of railways, anesthetics and tennis. While environmental factors can surely boost specific skills (some researchers thank better education and nutrition for increases in IQ over the last few decades), Woodley appears to argue, from the biological perspective, our genes are making us dumber.

Critics, however, aren't as quick to agree on our apparent downward mental   6
trajectory. Whether or not we're dumbing down, they argue, resurrecting old data from independent studies with different protocols is not the best way to find out. Reaction times are known to vary depending on how much a study emphasizes accuracy, whether participants practice in advance and the nature of the test signal itself. Some researchers now think that other measures of reaction times are more telling. They look at the variability in response time rather than the average, or they add decision making, so you react to a flash of light only if it is, say, red.

As a society, we certainly equate speed with smarts. Think fast. Are you quick-   7
witted? A quick study? A whiz kid? Even Merriam-Webster bluntly informs us that slowness is "the quality of lacking intelligence or quickness of mind." But we also recognize something counterintuitive about accepting full-stop that people who react faster are smarter. That's why, even though athletic training improves reaction time, we wouldn't scout for the next Einstein at a basketball game. Intelligence probably has a lot to do with making fast connections, but it surely has just as much to do with making the right connections.

Even the perception of speed can be deceptive. When things come easily or   8
quickly, when we don't have to struggle, we tend to feel smarter, a concept termed fluency. In one study, Adam Alter and fellow psychologists at New York University asked volunteers to answer a series of questions typed in either a crisp, clear font (a fluent experience) or a slightly blurred, harder to read version (a disfluent one). The people who had to work harder ended up processing the text more deeply and responding to the questions more accurately.

We tell athletes to think fast. But when we want a well-reasoned decision, we   9
say think long and hard, which isn't all that different from think slow.

Thinking Critically About Content

1. What is Konnikova analyzing in this essay?

2. The author is very forthright about the causes and effects that have to do with the speed of our thinking. From this author's perspective, what is the most fundamental cause and the ultimate effect?

3. How can speed be deceptive in studies of smartness?

Thinking Critically About Purpose and Audience

4. What do you think Konnikova's purpose is in this essay?

5. Who do you think is her primary audience?

6. Explain the essay's title.

Thinking Critically About Essays

7. Konnikova opens her essay with some background on the researcher Sir Francis Galton. Do you think this is an effective beginning for this essay? Explain your answer.

8. Paragraph 6 gives us a hint that our intelligence may not be as clearly connected with speed as we initially thought. How does the writer organize her details in this paragraph?

9. What is the topic sentence of paragraph 8? Do all the sentences in that paragraph support this topic sentence? Explain your answer.

To keep track of your critical thinking progress, go to Appendix 1.

10. Write a paragraph about your speed as a student in different subjects. Does your processing time vary with different courses and topics? What patterns can you see from your answer?

HAPPINESS IS CATCHING: WHY EMOTIONS ARE CONTAGIOUS
by Stacey Colino

Focusing Your Attention

1. Are you easily influenced by other people's moods? How do you know this?

2. In the essay you are about to read, Stacey Colino explains how we "catch" the feelings of others. Think of someone who generally makes you happy and someone who usually makes you sad. What is the difference between these two people? How do they each approach life? How do they each relate to you?

Expanding Your Vocabulary

The following words are important to your understanding of this essay. As you read, circle any words you don't know beyond this list. Then break into groups, and help each other figure out the meanings of these unknown words.

elation: joy, happiness (paragraph 1)

euphoria: extreme happiness (paragraph 1)

inoculate against: become immune to, resist (paragraph 1)

milliseconds: thousandths of a second (paragraph 2)

synchronize: coordinate (paragraph 2)

extroverts: outgoing people (paragraph 4)

engulfed: completely surrounded, overwhelmed (paragraph 5)

introverts: shy, quiet people (paragraph 5)

susceptible to: easily influenced by (paragraph 8)

mimicry: copying (paragraph 9)

READING CRITICALLY
Making Connections in Your Reading

Reading
Strategy

As you did with the previous essay, list the causes and effects in the following essay on a separate sheet of paper. Then draw lines from specific causes to the related effects. This process will give you some good insights into the author's approach to her topic and her methods of developing her ideas. Compare your notes with those of one of your classmates.

HAPPINESS IS CATCHING:
WHY EMOTIONS ARE CONTAGIOUS
by Stacey Colino

Researchers have found that emotions, both good and bad, are nearly as contagious as colds and flus. You can catch elation, euphoria, sadness, and more from friends, family, colleagues, even strangers. And once you understand how to protect yourself, you can inoculate yourself against the bad.

Mood "infection" happens in milliseconds, says Elaine Hatfield, Ph.D., a professor of psychology at the University of Hawaii in Honolulu and coauthor of *Emotional Contagion* (Cambridge University Press, 1994). And it stems from a primitive instinct: During conversation, we naturally tend to mimic and synchronize our facial expressions, movements, and speech rhythms to match the other person's. "Through this, we come to feel what the person is feeling," explains Dr. Hatfield. In other words, it puts us in touch with their feelings and affects our behavior.

Not surprisingly, spouses are especially likely to catch each other's moods, but so are parents, children, and good friends. In fact, a recent study at the University of Texas Medical Branch at Galveston found that depression was highly contagious among college roommates. "The same thing can occur with a spouse or co-worker, where one person is moderately depressed," says study author Thomas E. Joiner Jr., Ph.D., assistant professor of psychiatry and behavioral sciences.

1

2

3

people in your cycle. in your life

4   Dr. Hatfield's research shows that extroverts and emotionally expressive people tend to transmit their feelings more powerfully. There's also a breed of people who, consciously or not, may want or need you to feel what they feel; they're the ones who live by the adage "misery loves company." They manipulate other people's moods—perhaps without even realizing it—to gain the upper hand or to feel better about themselves. "They express emotion to get a response—perhaps attention or sympathy," says Ross Buck, Ph.D., professor of communication sciences and psychology at the University of Connecticut.

5   On the other hand, some personality types are more likely to be engulfed by others' moods. Introverts are vulnerable because they're easily aroused. So are highly sensitive individuals who react physically to emotionally charged situations—their hearts flutter before giving a speech, for example.

6   If anyone knows how quickly moods spread, it's Ginny Graves, 33, a San Francisco writer. Last year, when she was pregnant with her first child, her mood took a nosedive every time she saw a particular friend.

7   "Basically nothing good was going on in her life—she didn't like her job, and she was obsessed with her weight," recalls Ginny. "I tried to bolster her up, but whenever I talked to her, I'd feel tense and tired." Afterward, Ginny was left with a case of the moody blues that lingered a day or so.

8   Indeed, there's some evidence that women may be particularly susceptible to catching moods, perhaps because we're better able to read other people's emotions and body language, according to psychologist Judith Hall, Ph.D., professor of psychology at Northeastern University in Boston.

9   Since women perceive facial expressions so readily, we may be more likely to mimic them—and wind up sharing the feeling. Just how mimicry leads to catching a mood is not known, notes John T. Cacioppo, Ph.D., professor of psychology at Ohio State University and coauthor of *Emotional Contagion*. One theory holds that when you frown or smile, the muscular movements in your face alter blood flow to the brain, which in turn affects mood; another theory maintains that the sensations associated with specific facial expressions trigger emotional memories—and hence the feelings—linked with those particular expressions.

10   With any luck, we catch the happy moods—infectious laughter at a dinner party or a colleague's enthusiasm for a project, for instance. Some psychologists suspect, however, that negative emotions—especially depression and anxiety—may be the most infectious of all. "For women, stress and depression are like emotional germs—they jump from one person to the next," notes Ellen McGrath, Ph.D., a psychologist in Laguna Beach, California, and author of *When Feeling Bad Is Good* (Bantam, 1994).

11   Being susceptible to other people's moods does make for a rich emotional life. But let's face it: When you catch a happy mood, you don't want to change it. Downbeat emotions are harder to deal with. And who wants her life to be ruled by other people's bad moods?

12   Fortunately, there are ways to protect yourself from unpleasant emotions, while letting yourself catch the good ones. For starters, pay attention to how you feel around different people, suggests Dr. McGrath. Then label your emotions—noting, for

example, whether you feel optimistic around your best friend or gloomy after seeing your aunt. Then ask yourself if you're feeling what you do because you actually feel that way or because you've caught a mood from the other person. Just recognizing that an emotion belongs to someone else, not you, can be enough to short-circuit its transmission.

Once you know how people affect you, you can be more selective about whom 13
you spend time with. Instead of going on an all-day outing with family members who bring you down, for instance, try spending shorter periods of time with them. Another solution is to give yourself a time-out: It could be as simple as a restroom break during an intense dinner.

Putting up emotional barriers is not the answer, though. If the channels are 14
open, both positive and negative influences flow in. Shutting out the bad precludes you from catching joyful moods, too. Instead, it's better to monitor the floodgates— and to come to your own rescue when you feel yourself catching other people's negativity. And if you get swept up in another person's excitement, sit back and enjoy the ride.

Thinking Critically About Content

1. What is Colino analyzing in this essay? How does her title help focus her analysis?

2. Name two causes and two effects of people's moods.

3. How does Colino suggest that you can protect yourself from unpleasant emotions?

Thinking Critically About Purpose and Audience

4. Why do you think Colino wrote this essay?

5. Considering that this essay was originally published in the magazine *Family Circle*, who do you think Colino's intended audience is? Explain your answer.

6. Are you susceptible to other people's moods? Why or why not?

Thinking Critically About Essays

7. The author of this essay quotes many authorities in the field of psychology. Are these quotations convincing to you? Explain your answer.

8. Which of Colino's paragraphs deal primarily with causes? With effects? Do you think this is a good balance? Explain your answer.

9. Find five transitions in Colino's essay that work well, and explain why they are effective.

[handwritten annotations in right margin: "(result) Effect." and "Happiness is the result of many factors, such as social, emotional, and behavior factors."]

To keep track of your critical thinking progress, go to Appendix 1.

10. Discuss the emotional climate in the place where you live. Are you able to separate your emotions from those of the people you live with? Are you affected by the emotions of roommates, friends, family? How might you manage emotional swings after reading this essay?

Writing Workshop

This final section provides opportunities for you to apply what you have learned in this chapter to another writing assignment. This time, we furnish very little prompting beyond a summary of the guidelines for writing a cause/effect essay. This section will let you demonstrate that you can go through the entire writing process on your own with only occasional feedback from your peers. Loop back into the chapter as necessary when you have questions so that this process becomes as automatic to you as possible before you move on to new material. Then pause at the end of the chapter to reflect briefly on what you have learned.

Guidelines for Writing a Cause/Effect Essay

1. Write a thesis statement that explains what you are analyzing.
2. Choose facts, details, and reasons to support your thesis statement.
3. Do not mistake coincidence for cause or effect.
4. Search for the real causes and effects connected with your subject.
5. Organize your essay so that your readers can easily follow your analysis.

Writing About Your Reading

1. Are you currently dealing with any personal dilemmas? What are they? Does one bother you more than the others? Write an essay analyzing the causes and effects of this particular dilemma.

2. In "Happiness Is Catching," Stacey Colino talks about how contagious moods are. Do you think you might have been responsible for putting someone in a good or bad mood? What were the circumstances? How did someone "catch" your mood? Write an essay analyzing the causes and effects of the situation.

3. How would looking closely at causes and effects help you live a better life? How would the process of discovering causes and effects help you think through your decisions and problems more logically? Explain your answer.

Writing About Your World

1. Explain how the scene above got started. What caused this reaction? Why did it happen? What were the results of the actions pictured here? Write an essay focusing on either the causes or the effects of this scene.

2. We all deal with change differently, but it is generally difficult to accept change in our lives. Think of a significant change in your life, and write about its causes and effects. What was the incident? What were the circumstances connected with the incident?

3. Write an essay that analyzes a current social problem—homelessness, drugs, environmental concerns—including the reasons for its existence.

4. Create your own cause/effect assignment (with the help of your instructor), and write a response to it.

Revising

Small Group Activity (5–10 minutes per writer) Working in groups of three or four, read your cause/effect essays to each other. Those listening should record their reactions on the Revising Peer Evaluation Forms in Appendix 4. After your group goes through this process, give your evaluation forms to the appropriate writers so that each writer has two or three peer comment sheets for revising.

Paired Activity (5 minutes per writer) Using the completed Peer Evaluation Forms, work in pairs to decide what you should revise in your essay. If time allows, rewrite some of your sentences, and have your partner look at them.

Individual Activity Rewrite your paper using the revising feedback you received from other students.

Editing

Paired Activity (5–10 minutes per writer) Swap papers with a classmate, and use the Editing Peer Evaluation Form (Appendix 6) to identify as many grammar, punctuation, mechanics, and spelling errors as you can. If time allows, correct some of your errors, and have your partner look at them. Record your grammar, punctuation, and mechanics errors in the Error Log (Appendix 7) and your spelling errors in the Spelling Log (Appendix 8).

Individual Activity Rewrite your paper again using the editing feedback you received from other students.

Reflecting on Your Writing   When you have completed your own essay, answer these six questions.

1. What was most difficult about this assignment?

2. What was easiest?

3. What did you learn about cause and effect by completing this assignment?

4. What do you think are the strengths of your cause/effect essay? Place a wavy line by the parts of your essay that you feel are very good.

5. What are the weaknesses, if any, of your paper? Place an X by the parts of your essay you would like help with. Write in the margins any questions you have.

6. What did you learn from this assignment about your own writing process—about preparing to write, about writing the first draft, about revising, and about editing?

MyWritingLab™   Visit Chapter 16, "Analyzing Causes and Effects," in MyWritingLab, and complete the Post-test to check your understanding of the chapter's objectives.

Arguing

*"*Those who do not know their opponent's arguments do not completely understand their own.*"*

Counterargument.

—DAVID BENDER

Argument may be our most important form of communication because it helps us get what we want in life. The main reason people argue is to persuade someone of something. When you want to get a certain job, sell your car, or borrow some money, you need to present your request clearly and convincingly. On the flip side, others try to persuade you to do things all the time: Politicians make speeches trying to persuade you to vote for them; your friends try to persuade you to go to a movie when you know you should study for an exam; TV commercials, magazine ads, and billboards everywhere try to persuade you to buy this cereal or that car.

As you might suspect, your ability to argue in writing is also important in life. In fact, writing arguments is fundamental to your success on a personal level, in college courses, and in the workplace:

- The chairperson for your college reunion sends a letter with clear reasons why everyone should attend this year.

- In a freshman composition course, a student writes an essay arguing for same-sex marriage.

- In a sociology class, a student writes a paper claiming that laws against hate crimes need to be stronger.

- A sales representative writes a letter arguing that customers should order supplies from him rather than from his competitor.

- A restaurant owner writes an advertisement to persuade people to eat at her restaurant.

The purpose of **arguing** is to persuade someone to take a certain action or to think or feel a specific way. You can use either logical arguments (based on facts and reasoning) or emotional arguments (based on vivid description and details) to achieve your purpose.

Some of the most important laws affecting people's lives in the United States are the result of arguments made to the Supreme Court. Lawyers argue such issues as gun control, abortion, immigrants' rights, and drunk driving. If, for instance, lawmakers are trying to get stricter jail sentences for drunk driving, they might rely heavily on facts and statistics (logical evidence). But then they might add an emotional element by describing the mangled bike, the bloodstained clothes, and the grief in the faces of the parents of a 12-year-old girl killed by a drunk driver as she rode her bike home from school. Such an appeal to feelings would create a much stronger argument than statistics alone.

The better you are at arguing—in both thinking and writing—the more you will get what you want out of life (and out of college). Arguing effectively means getting the pay raise you hope for, the refund you deserve, and the grades you've worked hard for. Argumentation is a powerful tool.

MyWritingLab　Understanding Argument

To test your knowledge of argument, go to **MyWritingLab.com,** and choose **Argument** in the **Essay Development** module. For this topic, read the **Overview,** watch the **Animation** video, and complete the **Recall, Apply,** and **Write** activities. Then check your understanding of argumentative essays by taking the **Post-test.**

PREPARING TO WRITE AN ARGUMENT ESSAY

As in previous chapters, preparing to write begins with reading. Writing good arguments will result from reading good arguments if you understand in detail how the essay works—in content and in structure. But you need to be conscious of the many elements that function together to make an argument essay successful. As a result, in the next few pages, you will read an effective argument essay and then answer some questions to help you discover how the author develops his essay.

Reading an Argument Essay

The following argument, "Jim Crow Policing" by Bob Herbert, tries to persuade its readers that law-enforcement agents should not take action based on race alone. It uses a combination of logic and emotion to achieve its purpose. Have you ever been stopped by the police because of your appearance? If you have, what was your reaction? If you haven't, how do you think you would react?

Using a reading strategy is an effective way to learn how to read analytically. Understanding your reading analytically will lead to analytical writing. Reading critically, or analytically, will help you understand not only *what* the essay is saying but also *how* the author is saying it. The strategy you will apply to all the reading tasks in this chapter involves recognizing facts and opinions in your reading material.

READING CRITICALLY
Recognizing Facts and Opinions
in a Professional Essay

Reading
Strategy

Reading an argument critically calls for very high-level skills. You need to understand your reading on a literal level, know the difference between opinions and facts, and come up with your own thoughts on the topic by challenging the author's ideas. As you read the following essay for the first time, highlight facts in one color and the author's opinions in another color. Then, put an X by any facts or opinions that you do not agree with or that you want to question in some way. Be prepared to explain any marks you make on the essay.

JIM CROW POLICING   Cobout discrimination)
by Bob Herbert

The New York City Police Department needs to be restrained. The nonstop humiliation of young black and Hispanic New Yorkers, including children, by police officers who feel no obligation to treat them fairly or with any respect at all is an abomination. That many of the officers engaged in the mistreatment are black or Latino themselves is shameful.

Statistics will be out shortly about the total number of people who were stopped and frisked by the police in 2009. We already have the data for the first three-quarters of the year, and they are staggering. During that period, more than 450,000 people were stopped by the cops, an increase of 13 percent over the same period in 2008.

The respect. cn

1

2

were non-white

3   An overwhelming 84 percent of the stops in the first three-quarters of 2009 were of black or Hispanic New Yorkers. It is incredible how few of the stops yielded any law-enforcement benefit. Contraband, which usually means drugs, was found in only 1.6 percent of the stops of black New Yorkers. For Hispanics, it was just 1.5 percent. For whites, who are stopped far less frequently, contraband was found 2.2 percent of the time.

showing facts,

4   The percentages of stops that yielded weapons were even smaller. Weapons were found on just 1.1 percent of the blacks stopped, 1.4 percent of the Hispanics, and 1.7 percent of the whites. Only about 6 percent of stops result in an arrest for any reason.

statistics,

5   Rather than a legitimate crime-fighting tool, these stops are a despicable, racially oriented tool of harassment. And the police are using it at the increasingly enthusiastic direction of Mayor Michael Bloomberg and Police Commissioner Ray Kelly. There were more than a half-million stops in New York City in 2008, and when the final tally is in, we'll find that the number only increased in 2009.

6   Not everyone who is stopped is frisked. When broken down by ethnic group, the percentages do not at first seem so wildly disproportionate. Some 59.4 percent of all Hispanics who were stopped were also frisked, as were 56.6 percent of blacks and 46 percent of whites. But keep in mind, whites composed fewer than 16 percent of the people stopped in the first place.

7   These encounters with the police are degrading and often frightening, and the real number of people harassed is undoubtedly higher than the numbers reported by the police. Often the cops will stop, frisk, and sometimes taunt people who are at their mercy, and then move on—without finding anything, making an arrest, or recording the encounter as they are supposed to.

8   Even the official reasons given by the police for the stops are laughably bogus. People are stopped for allegedly making "furtive movements," for wearing clothes "commonly used in a crime," and, of course, for the "suspicious bulge." My wallet, my notebook, and my cell phone would all apply.

9   The police say they also stop people for wearing "inappropriate attire for the season." I saw a guy on the Upper West Side wearing shorts and sandals a couple weeks ago. That was certainly unusual attire for the middle of January, but it didn't cross my mind that he should be accosted by the police.

10   The Center for Constitutional Rights has filed a class-action lawsuit against the city and the Police Department over the stops. Several plaintiffs detailed how their ordinary daily lives were interrupted by cops bent on harassment for no good reason. Lalit Carson was stopped while on a lunch break from his job as a teaching assistant at a charter school in the Bronx. Deon Dennis was stopped and searched while standing outside the apartment building in which he lives in Harlem. The police arrested him, allegedly because of an outstanding warrant. He was held for several hours, then released. There was no outstanding warrant.

emotion argument

11   There are endless instances of this kind of madness. People going about their daily business, bothering no one, are menaced out of the blue by the police, forced to spread themselves face down in the street or plaster themselves against a wall or bend over the hood of a car to be searched. People who object to the harassment are often threatened with arrest for disorderly conduct.

emotion (facts)

The Police Department insists that these stops of innocent people—which are un-constitutional, by the way—help fight crime. And they insist that the policy is not rac-ist. Paul Browne, the chief spokesman for Commissioner Kelly, described the stops as "life-saving." And he has said repeatedly that the racial makeup of the people stopped and frisked is proportionally similar to the racial makeup of people committing crimes.

That is an amazingly specious argument. The fact that a certain percentage of criminals may be black or Hispanic is no reason for the police to harass individuals from those groups when there is no indication whatsoever that they have done anything wrong.

It's time to put an end to Jim Crow policing in New York City.

[handwritten margin notes: 12 ← people said on the other side ; 13 specious argument ; 14 (or mean overall is wrong)]

Discovering How This Essay Works

To help you recognize the elements that make this an effective argu-ment essay so you can use them in your own writing, answer the following questions in as much detail as possible.

1A. What is Herbert's main point?

_____

_____

_____

B. Is it debatable? (Does it have more than one side?)

_____

2. Whom do you think Herbert is addressing in this essay?

_____

3. What evidence does the author use to support his main idea? List below one example of each type of evidence in his essay.

Facts: _____

Statistics: _____

Statements from authorities: _____

Examples and personal stories: _____

4. When does Herbert anticipate an opposing point of view?

_____

_____

5. Where does Herbert find some common ground with his readers?

_____

6. What would you label Herbert's tone or mood?

_____

7. How does Herbert organize the topics in his essay: general to particular, particular to general, or from one extreme to another? (Go to pages 64–76 if you want help with this question.)

_____

WRITING AN ARGUMENT ESSAY

Now that you have read and studied an argument essay, you will be writing one of your own. This section will help you generate a draft that you will then revise and edit. It will guide you through a careful reading of the writing assignment, give you several ways to generate ideas and choose a topic, and finally furnish you with concrete guidelines for writing an effective argument essay. We encourage you to write notes and lists throughout this process so you can use them when you write a draft of your essay at the end of this section.

Reading the Prompt

As you know by now, writing an effective essay always starts with understanding the writing assignment or "prompt." An essay assignment "prompts" you to respond to a specific issue or question. The better you understand the prompt, the better paper you will create. So you want to learn how to read the essay assignment actively rather than passively. Applying the chapter reading strategy to your writing assignment is a good way to achieve this level of interaction.

 Reading Strategy

READING CRITICALLY
Recognizing Facts and Opinions in the Prompt

As you read the following prompt for the first time, highlight directions in one color and clues about the content in another color. Then, put an X by any parts of the assignment you want to question in some way. Be prepared to explain any marks you make on the assignment. Next, as you read the assignment again, write on a separate piece of paper some possible topics on the left and your opinions about those topics on the right. Finally, review all the key directions in the assignment so you address all aspects of the prompt.

Writing Prompt

Choose a controversial issue on your campus or in the news that interests you. Write an essay that presents your opinion on this issue. Follow the guidelines for writing an argument essay. As you write your draft, be sure you support your opinions with reasons. If something in print inspired this assignment, attach it to your essay before you turn it in.

Thinking About the Prompt

Consult your campus or local newspaper for ideas on this assignment, and choose an issue that interests you. Then, use one or more of the prewriting techniques you learned in Chapter 5 to generate ideas on the topic. What is the exact issue? Why is it important? Why do so many people care about it? How do you think the issue should be resolved?

Guidelines for Writing an Argument Essay

When you write an argument essay, choose a subject that matters to you. If you have strong feelings, you will find it much easier to gather evidence and convince your readers of your point of view. Keep in mind, however, that your readers might feel just as strongly about the opposite side of the issue. The following guidelines will help you write a good argument essay. As you think about the topic you have chosen in response to the prompt above, read the following guidelines and continue to make lists and notes you will use when you write your draft on this prompt. After each guideline is an explanation of how it functions in the reading selection at the beginning of this chapter so you can actually see how the element works in an essay before you apply it to your own writing.

1. **State your opinion on your topic in your thesis statement.** To write a thesis statement for an argument essay, you must take a stand for or against an action or an idea. In other words, your thesis statement should be debatable—that is, it should be a statement that can be argued or challenged and will not be met with agreement by everyone who reads it. Your thesis statement should introduce your subject and state your opinion about that subject.

In the Reading: Bob Herbert's thesis is in his first paragraph: "The New York City Police Department needs to be restrained." This is a debatable thesis. Some other statements on the topic of law enforcement would not be good thesis statements.

Not debatable: Law-enforcement authorities in the United States often rely on profiling in their jobs.

Not debatable: Some law-enforcement agencies have strict rules regarding ethnic profiling.

Herbert sets up his essay with some facts and statistics about the practice in New York of stopping and frisking blacks and Hispanics. This background information supports his thesis statement.

In Your Writing: Consider the essay you will be writing on a controversial issue. What will you include in your thesis statement? Jot down your subject and your opinion about that subject.

2. **Find out as much as you can about your audience before you write.** Knowing your readers' background and feelings on your topic will help you choose the best supporting evidence and examples. Suppose you want to convince people in two different age groups to quit smoking. You might tell the group of teenagers that cigarettes make their breath rancid, their teeth yellow, and their clothes smell bad. But with a group of adults, you might discuss the alarming statistics on lung and heart disease associated with long-term smoking.

In the Reading: Herbert's essay was first published in *The New York Times,* which addresses a fairly educated audience. The original readers probably agreed with him on this issue. So he chooses his support as if he is talking to people who agree with him.

In Your Writing: What do you know about the people who will be reading your essay on a controversial issue? Can you find out any more about them? Are the details listed in your prewriting exercise geared toward this audience? Revise your list so it relates directly to the audience you have identified.

3. **Choose evidence that supports your thesis statement.** Evidence is probably the most important factor in writing an argument essay. Without solid evidence, your essay is nothing more than opinion; with it, your essay can be powerful and persuasive. If you supply convincing evidence, your readers will not only understand your position but perhaps agree with it.

Evidence can consist of facts, statistics, statements from authorities, and examples or personal stories. Examples and personal stories can be based on your own observations, experiences, and reading, but your opinions are not evidence. You can also develop your ideas with the writing strategies you learned in Chapters 9 through 16. Comparison/contrast, definition, and cause/effect can be particularly useful in building an argument. Use any combination of evidence and writing strategies that will help support your thesis statement.

In the Reading: In his essay, Herbert uses several different types of evidence. Here are some examples:

Facts

Not everyone who is stopped is frisked. (paragraph 6)

Often the cops will stop, frisk, and sometimes taunt people who are at their mercy, and then move on—without finding anything, making an arrest, or recording the encounter as they are supposed to. (paragraph 7)

The Center for Constitutional Rights has filed a class-action lawsuit against the city and the Police Department over the stops. (paragraph 10)

People who object to the harassment are often threatened with arrest for disorderly conduct. (paragraph 11)

Statistics

[M]ore than 450,000 people were stopped by the cops....(paragraph 2)

An overwhelming 84 percent of the stops in the first three-quarters of 2009 were of black or Hispanic New Yorkers. (paragraph 2)

Contraband...was found in only 1.6 percent of the stops of black New Yorkers. (paragraph 2)

For Hispanics, it [contraband] was just 1.5 percent. (paragraph 2)

For whites,...contraband was found 2.2 percent of the time. (paragraph 2)

Weapons were found on just 1.1 percent of the blacks stopped, 1.4 percent of the Hispanics, and 1.7 percent of the whites. (paragraph 4)

Only about 6 percent of stops result in an arrest for any reason. (paragraph 4)

Some 59.4 percent of all Hispanics who were stopped were also frisked, as were 56.6 percent of blacks and 46 percent of whites. (paragraph 6)

[W]hites composed fewer than 16 percent of the people stopped in the first place. (paragraph 6)

Statements from Authorities

Paul Browne, the chief spokesman for Commissioner Kelly, described the stops as "life-saving." (paragraph 12)

Examples and Personal Stories

Lalit Carson was stopped while on a lunch break from his job as a teaching assistant at a charter school in the Bronx. (paragraph 10)

Deon Dennis was stopped and searched while standing outside the apartment building in which he lives in Harlem. (paragraph 10)

In Your Writing: What types of evidence will you use in your essay to support your thesis? Chart your evidence, and decide if you need to add any more information. Should this new information be a different type of evidence? Expand your list of evidence with enough details to make your argument convincing to your audience.

4. **Anticipate opposing points of view.** In addition to stating and supporting your position, anticipating and responding to opposing views are

important. Presenting only your side of the argument leaves half the story untold—the opposition's half. If you admit that there are opposing arguments and answer them, you are more likely to move your readers in your direction.

In the Reading: In paragraph 12, Herbert acknowledges that the police department believes that the act of stopping innocent people helps fight crime, but in the same sentence the author points out that this practice is unconstitutional. Also in paragraph 12, Herbert quotes Paul Browne as saying these stops are "life-saving," which Herbert leaves uncontested so the readers will make up their own minds on this issue, based on the other information Herbert has provided in his essay. Finally, Herbert cites Commissioner Kelly's comment that the races of the people stopped represent the racial makeup of the criminals in New York City and then points out the flaws in this argument in paragraph 13.

In Your Writing: How will those opposed to your position react to your argument? What do you suspect they will disagree with? Why will they disagree with those points? What can you include to counter their opposing viewpoints?

5. **Find some common ground.** Pointing out common ground between you and your opponent is also an effective strategy. *Common ground* refers to points of agreement between two opposing positions. For example, one person might be in favor of gun control and another strongly opposed. But they might find common ground—agreement—in the need to keep guns out of teenagers' hands. Locating some common ground is possible in almost every situation. When you state in your essay that you agree with your opponent on certain points, your reader sees you as a fair person.

In the Reading: Most of his readers would agree with Herbert that stopping people too often and for little reason becomes harassment at some point. He mentions this three times in his essay (paragraphs 5, 10, and 11), each time in a slightly different context to help people realize this potential feature of the police stops.

In Your Writing: What do you think most of your readers (even your opponents) will agree with? Why will they agree with those points? What details can you include to build on this common ground?

6. **Maintain a reasonable tone.** Just as you probably wouldn't win an argument by shouting or making nasty or sarcastic comments, don't expect your readers to respond well to such tactics. Keep the "voice" of your essay calm and sensible. Your readers will be much more open to what you have to say if they think you are a reasonable person.

In the Reading: Herbert maintains a reasonable tone throughout his essay. Even when he quotes some unbelievable statistics, as in paragraphs 2 and 3, or uses an occasional harsh word (*abomination* in paragraph 1 or *despicable* in paragraph 5), he keeps his voice under control and therefore earns the respect of his readers.

In Your Writing: As you write your first draft, make sure you maintain a reasonable, calm voice. State your position clearly, and support your points with well-chosen evidence.

7. **Organize your essay so it presents your position as effectively as possible.** By the end of your essay, you want your audience to agree with you. So you want to organize your essay in such a way that your readers can easily follow it. The number of paragraphs may vary, depending on the nature of your assignment, but the following outline shows the order in which the features of an argument essay are most effective:

Outline

Introduction
    Background information
    Introduction of subject
    Statement of your opinion
Body Paragraphs
    Common ground
    Lots of evidence (logical and emotional)
    Opposing point of view
    Response to opposing point of view
Conclusion
    Restatement of your position
    Call for action or agreement

The arrangement of your evidence in an argument essay depends to a great extent on your readers' opinions. Most arguments will be organized from general to particular, from particular to general, or from one extreme to another. When you know that your readers already agree with you, arranging your details from general to particular or from most to least important is usually most effective. With this order, you are building on your readers' agreement and loyalty as you explain your thinking on the subject.

If you suspect your audience does not agree with you, reverse the organization of your evidence and arrange it from particular to general or from least to most important. In this way, you can take your readers step by step through your reasoning in an attempt to get them to agree with you.

In the Reading: Bob Herbert's essay presents his reasoning from general to particular, assuming most of the readers of *The New York Times* will agree with him. Here is a skeleton outline of his essay.

Introduction: Paragraph 1

Statement of opinion—"The New York City Police Department needs to be restrained."

Background information—approach of New York Police Department
Introduction of subject—mistreatment of blacks and Hispanics

Body Paragraphs: Paragraphs 2–13

Common ground

Lots of evidence (logical and emotional)

Paragraphs 2–4: Logical statistics

Paragraph 5: Emotional outcry followed by another statistic (a half-million stops in New York City in 2008)

Paragraph 6: Fact (Not everyone is frisked), followed by more statistics about frisking

Paragraph 7: Opinion (these stops are degrading and frightening), fact (cops sometimes stop people to taunt them)

Opposing point of view

Paragraph 8 and 9: Reasons for stopping people countered by author

More evidence

Paragraphs 10 and 11: Examples of stopping by police as harassment

Opposing point of view

Paragraph 12: Stops fight crime; stops are not racist; stops are "life-saving"; races of people stopped represent racial proportion of criminals

Response to opposing point of view

Paragraph 12: Stops of innocent people are unconstitutional

Paragraph 13: Race with no other evidence is not reason for police to harass people

Conclusion: Paragraph 14

Restatement of your position

Paragraph 14: Restatement of first sentence of essay with more specific references

Call for action or agreement

Paragraph 14: Put an end to Jim Crow policing in New York City

In Your Writing: How will you organize your essay—from general to particular, from particular to general, or from one extreme to another? Is this the most effective order for what you are trying to say to your particular audience? Would another method of organization be more effective? Rearrange the details in your prewriting notes until you are sure they are in the best order for what you are trying to accomplish.

Writing a Draft of Your Essay

Now is the time to collect your notes, your prewriting exercises, and your lists as you begin to generate the first draft of your essay. In addition, you might want to review the professional essay, the writing assignment, and the chapter guidelines for writing argument essays, along with your notes and lists, to help you get started. At this point, don't think about revising or editing; just get your thoughts about the writing assignment down on paper.

MyWritingLab | **Helpful Hints**

- **Have you drawn on all aspects of the writing process in creating your draft?** All the steps in the writing process are important. The activities on **The Writing Process** in **The Craft of Writing** module of **MyWritingLab** can help you learn how to write effective papers.

REVISING AND EDITING

You are now ready to begin revising and editing. This section will take you through the guidelines for revising and editing argument essays with two specific writing samples: another student's essay and your own essay. Revising and editing are often much easier with someone else's writing, which is why we begin this stage with a writing sample from another student. If you can recognize some of the problems in this essay, you might be able to recognize areas for improvement in your own writing. So you will be reviewing the chapter guidelines by revising and editing another student's writing before applying the same guidelines to your own writing.

Reading a Student Argument Essay

We will begin by using our chapter reading strategy on a student essay. In her essay "Online vs. Traditional Classes," student writer Cyndi Pourgerami argues that traditional classes have more advantages for learning than online courses. Separating facts from opinions will help you follow Cyndi's argument and figure out how to improve her essay.

Reading
Strategy

READING CRITICALLY
Recognizing Facts and Opinions in the Student Essay

As you read Cyndi's essay, record your notes on a separate piece of paper. First, draw a vertical line down the center of the paper. Then, as you read, write Cyndi's main ideas on the left and your reactions to those ideas on the right side of the page. Be prepared to explain the connection between your notes and the material in the essay.

logic and reasoning
↓

Online vs. Traditional Classes

1   The face of the college classroom has evolved over the years, but not more so than in the 21st century. With the invention of the Internet, the prevalence of personal computers, and the overwhelming use of cell phones, many would argue that brick-and-mortar classrooms are becoming obsolete due to the technologies available in this day and age. Although the need for multiple learning options for all types of students is important, traditional classes in a classroom with an instructor are more conducive to learning than online courses.

logic

2   On most campuses, part of the college experience involves meeting new people and networking in person with students and professors. Although not impossible to do in an online course. It is much easier to meet and talk with people in a classroom setting. According to a study conducted by Zhang, Zhao, and Zhao regarding students and communication, "A number of students reported that although [online courses] are interesting and effective, they would still prefer to go to traditional classrooms if they had a choice, since e-learning environments cannot create the real life on a campus." Because most online discussion forums focus on class material, there are fewer opportunities to get to know classmates or talk with them about ideas other then class material. This applies to student-teacher relationships as well. A student who needs a letter of recommendation is more likely to receive that letter based on what the instructor knows about him or her from class, this knowledge of a student's character is much harder to assess in an online course because professors rarely, if ever, know or see their students in these classes.

reasoning

3   In addition to preventing social interaction outside of class, online courses also detract from meaningful, in-class interaction. Many educators would argue that much of the learning that transpires in a class happens in discussions focused on the course content. Students have the opportunity to hear from and question their professors, they also get to add thoughts and/or arguments that help create a better, more in-depth understanding of a topic or concept. Online classes hinder this type of discussion because the normal back-and-forth conversation between instructors and their students is not usually as large a part of an online class as it is of a traditional class. Although some online courses incorporate message boards and encourage dialogue among students, more often than not

these posts are done because they are required, Not because of intellectually stimulating conversation. In addition to students interacting in a more constricted manner, the instructor cannot act as a moderator who guides or structures the conversation because most online classes do not happen in real time. Students and teachers reply at their convenience (the whole purpose of an online course), which usually transforms student-to-student learning into simple snippets of thought posted for credit. This exchange of ideas in an online setting is not usually equivalent to that which occurs in a physical classroom; therefore, the maximum potential for learning is not as great in an online class.

Students who need an online course to help them save time in their everyday lives don't necessarily understand that online courses require students to have different skills and abilities to succeed. When taking an online class for the first time, learning how to navigate through unfamiliar online territory, which can put students behind at the start of the course, is important. In addition, depending on a student's level of digital literacy, he/she may find e-courses more difficult than traditional courses due to the unavoidable glitches that occur with any technology. Weather its a bad Internet connection or a computer crash, students may wind up regretting that they enrolled in an online course to save time if they aren't as computer savvy as they need to be.

Another deterrent to learning in online courses is the possibility of additional unexpected costs. Students who are not familiar with computers or who don't have a computer at home are at a significant disadvantage. Many would argue that students who don't own a computer would not enroll in an online course, but they fail to realize that many students will enroll in any section of a course that is available, regardless of whether it's online or not. Those who do not own a computer must either commute to a library or to the home of a family member or friend to access their class, spending extra time and money they probably don't have. Otherwise, they must purchase a computer, which is a substantial cost in addition to tuition. All these costs offset any potential savings an online course may have initially offered a student. Students may also have to upgrade to a high-speed Internet connection or purchase software to participate in an online course.

Although online classes do offer benefits for non-traditional students, these types of courses can actually be detrimental to learning. Online classes can discourage healthy social networking outside of class and, therefore, reduce the support students get from their peers. In addition, learning may be threatened by online courses because students are unable to interact with their professors in person and because they aren't getting meaningful, immediate feedback on the coarse content in real time. Finally, unexpected costs and additional time required for online classes may overshadow any advantages these classes might potentially offer for learning. As a result, traditional, in-person classes continue to offer students the best opportunity to master their course material and succeed in college.

Revising and Editing the Student Essay

This essay is Cyndi's first draft, which now needs to be revised and edited. First, apply the Revising Checklist to the content of Cyndi's draft. When you are satisfied that her ideas are fully developed and well organized, use the Editing Checklist to correct her grammar and mechanics errors. Answer the questions, and complete the tasks in each category. Then write your suggested changes directly on Cyndi's draft.

Revising the Student Essay

THESIS STATEMENT

✔ Does the thesis statement contain the essay's controlling idea?

✔ Does the thesis appear as the last sentence of the introduction?

1. Put brackets around the last sentence in Cyndi's introduction. Does it contain her opinion?

_____

Is it debatable?

_____

2. Rewrite Cyndi's thesis statement if necessary so that it states her opinion and is debatable.

_____

BASIC ELEMENTS

✔ Does the title draw in the readers?

✔ Does the introduction capture the readers' attention and build up effectively to the thesis statement?

✔ Does each body paragraph deal with a single topic?

✔ Does the conclusion bring the essay to a close in an interesting way?

1. Give Cyndi's essay an alternate title.

_____

2. Rewrite Cyndi's introduction so that it captures the readers' attention in another way and builds up to the thesis statement at the end of the paragraph.

_____

_____

_____

3. Does each of Cyndi's body paragraphs deal with only one topic?

_____

4. Rewrite Cyndi's conclusion using at least one suggestion from Part I.

_____

_____

_____

DEVELOPMENT

✔ Do the body paragraphs adequately support the thesis statement?

✔ Does each body paragraph have a focused topic sentence?

✔ Does each body paragraph contain *specific* details that support the topic sentence?

✔ Does each body paragraph include *enough* details to fully explain the topic sentence?

1. Write out Cyndi's thesis statement (revised, if necessary), and list her topic sentences below it.

Thesis statement: _____

_____

_____

Topic 1: _____

_____

Topic 2: _____

_____

Topic 3: _____

_____

Topic 4: _____

_____

2. Do Cyndi's topics adequately support her thesis statement?

_____

3. Does each body paragraph have a focused topic sentence?

_____

4. Does her evidence support her topic sentences?

_____

5. What type of evidence does Cyndi provide in each body paragraph?

Paragraph 2: _____

Paragraph 3: _____

Paragraph 4: _____

Paragraph 5: _____

What type of evidence does she use the most? _____

6. Is this a good choice for what she is trying to argue? Why or why not?

_____

7. Where do you need more information?

_____

UNITY

✔ Do the essay's topic sentences relate directly to the thesis statement?

✔ Do the details in each body paragraph support the paragraph's topic sentence?

1. Read each of Cyndi's topic sentences with her thesis statement in mind. Do they go together?

_____

2. Revise her topic sentences if necessary so they are directly related.

3. Drop or rewrite any sentences in her body paragraphs that are not directly related to their topic sentences.

ORGANIZATION

✔ Is the essay organized logically?

✔ Is each body paragraph organized logically?

1. Outline Cyndi's essay to see if all her ideas are arranged logically.

_____

_____

_____

_____

_____

_____

2. Do you think her method of organization is the most effective one for her purpose? Explain your answer.

_____

_____

3. Move any paragraphs that are out of order.

4. Look closely at Cyndi's body paragraphs to see if all her sentences are arranged logically within paragraphs.

5. Move any sentences that are out of order.

COHERENCE

✔ Are transitions used effectively so that paragraphs move smoothly and logically from one to the next?

✔ Do the sentences move smoothly and logically from one to the next?

1. Add two transitions to Cyndi's essay.

2. Circle five transitions, repetitions, synonyms, or pronouns Cyndi uses.

3. Explain how two of these make Cyndi's essay easier to read.

For a list of transitions, see pages 99–100.
For a list of pronouns, see pages 496–497.

_____

_____

_____

_____

 Now rewrite Cyndi's essay with your revisions.

Editing the Student Essay

SENTENCES

Subjects and Verbs

✔ Does each sentence have a main subject and verb?

1. Underline the subjects once and verbs twice in paragraphs 2 and 3 of your revision of Cyndi's essay. Remember that sentences can have more than one subject-verb set.

For help with subjects and verbs, see Chapter 27.

2. Does each of the sentences have at least one subject and verb that can stand alone?

_____

3. Did you find and correct Cyndi's two fragments and two run-together sentences? If not, find and correct them now.

For help with fragments and run-togethers, see Chapters 28 and 29.

Subject-Verb Agreement

✔ Do all subjects and verbs agree?

For help with subject-verb agreement, see Chapter 32.

1. Read aloud the subjects and verbs you underlined in your revision of Cyndi's essay.

2. Correct any subjects and verbs that do not agree.

Pronoun Agreement
✔ Do all pronouns agree with their nouns?

For help with pronoun agreement, see Chapter 36.

1. Find any pronouns in your revision of Cyndi's essay that do not agree with their nouns.

2. Correct any pronouns that do not agree with their nouns.

Modifiers
✔ Are modifiers as close as possible to the words they modify?

For help with modifier errors, see Chapter 39.

1. Find any modifiers in your revision of Cyndi's essay that are not as close as possible to the words they modify.

2. Did you find and correct Cyndi's one modifier error? If not, find and correct it now.

PUNCTUATION AND MECHANICS

Punctuation
✔ Are sentences punctuated correctly?

For help with punctuation, see Chapters 40–44.

1. Read your revision of Cyndi's essay for any errors in punctuation.

2. Find the two fragments and two run-together sentences you revised, and make sure they are punctuated correctly.

Mechanics
✔ Are words capitalized properly?

For help with capitalization, see Chapter 45.

1. Read your revision of Cyndi's essay for any errors in capitalization.

2. Be sure to check Cyndi's capitalization in the fragments and run-together sentences you revised.

WORD CHOICE AND SPELLING

Word Choice
✔ Are words used correctly?

For help with confused words, see Chapter 51.

1. Find any words used incorrectly in your revision of Cyndi's essay.

2. Did you find and correct the four words Cyndi uses incorrectly? If not, find and correct them now.

Spelling
✔ Are words spelled correctly?

1. Use spell-check and a dictionary to check the spelling in your revision of Cyndi's essay.

2. Correct any misspelled words.

 Now rewrite Cyndi's essay again with your editing corrections.

For help with spelling, see Chapter 52.

Reading Your Own Argument Essay

The first stage of revising your own writing is creating some distance between you and your essay. To accomplish this, you will read your essay with the same reading strategy you have applied to other reading tasks in this chapter. Reading your essay as a reading selection that you are trying to understand and respond to will help you revise and edit your own work efficiently and effectively.

READING CRITICALLY
Recognizing Facts and Opinions in Your Own Essay

Reading
Strategy

As you begin to rework your essay, apply the same technique to your writing that you have been practicing throughout this chapter. Highlight your own opinions and facts in two different colors to demonstrate that you see the difference between the two. Then make sure you support each of your main ideas with enough details to make your point.

Revising and Editing Your Own Essay

You are now ready to revise and edit your own writing. Remember that revision involves reworking the development and organization of your essay while editing asks you to check your grammar and usage. Work first with the content, making sure your thoughts are fully developed and organized effectively before you consider your grammar and usage errors. Repeating the revising and editing processes several times will ensure that you have written the best paper possible. The checklists here will help you apply what you have learned in this chapter to your essay.

Revising Your Own Essay

For Revising Peer Evaluation Forms, go to Appendix 4.

THESIS STATEMENT

☐ Does the thesis statement contain the essay's controlling idea?

☐ Does the thesis appear as the last sentence of the introduction?

1. What is the subject of your essay?

   _____

2. Put brackets around the last sentence in your introduction. Does it contain your opinion?

   _____

   Is it debatable?

   _____

3. Rewrite your thesis statement if necessary so that it states your opinion and is debatable.

BASIC ELEMENTS

☐ Does the title draw in the readers?

☐ Does the introduction capture the readers' attention and build up effectively to the thesis statement?

☐ Does each body paragraph deal with a single topic?

☐ Does the conclusion bring the essay to a close in an interesting way?

1. Give your essay a title if it doesn't have one.

   _____

2. Does your introduction capture your readers' attention and build up to your thesis statement at the end of the paragraph?

   _____

3. Does each of your body paragraphs deal with only one topic?

   _____

4. Does your conclusion follow some of the suggestions offered in Part I?

   _____

DEVELOPMENT

☐ Do the body paragraphs adequately support the thesis statement?

☐ Does each body paragraph have a focused topic sentence?

☐ Does each body paragraph contain *specific* details that support the topic sentence?

☐ Does each body paragraph include *enough* details to fully explain the topic sentence?

1. Write out your thesis statement (revised, if necessary), and list your topic sentences below it.

Thesis statement: _____

    Topic 1: _____

    Topic 2: _____

    Topic 3: _____

    Topic 4: _____

    Topic 5: _____

2. Do your topics adequately support your thesis statement?

_____

3. Does each body paragraph have a focused topic sentence?

_____

4. Does your evidence support your topic sentences? List and label at least one type of evidence you use for each of your topics.

    Topic 1: Evidence: _____

        Type: _____

    Topic 2: Evidence: _____

        Type: _____

    Topic 3: Evidence: _____

        Type: _____

    Topic 4: Evidence: _____

        Type: _____

    Topic 5: Evidence: _____

        Type: _____

What type of evidence do you use the most?

_____

Is this a good choice for what you are trying to argue?

_____

5. Where do you need more information?

_____

UNITY

☐ Do the essay's topic sentences relate directly to the thesis statement?

☐ Do the details in each body paragraph support the paragraph's topic sentence?

1. Read each of your topic sentences with your thesis statement in mind. Do they go together?

_____

2. Revise your topic sentences if necessary so they are directly related.

3. Drop or rewrite any of the sentences in your body paragraphs that are not directly related to their topic sentences.

ORGANIZATION

☐ Is the essay organized logically?

☐ Is each body paragraph organized logically?

1. Outline your essay to see if all the paragraphs are arranged logically.

2. Do you think your method of organization is the most effective one for your purpose? Explain your answer.

3. Move any paragraphs that are out of order.

4. Look closely at your body paragraphs to see if all the sentences are arranged logically within paragraphs.

5. Move any sentences or ideas that are out of order.

COHERENCE

☐ Are transitions used effectively so that paragraphs move smoothly and logically from one to the next?

☐ Do the sentences move smoothly and logically from one to the next?

For a list of pronouns, see pages 99–100.
For a list of transitions, see pages 496–497.

1. Add two transitions to your essay.

2. Circle five transitions, repetitions, synonyms, or pronouns you use.

3. Explain how two of these make your essay easier to read.

_____

_____

Now rewrite your essay with your revisions.

For Editing Peer Evaluation Forms, go to Appendix 6.

Editing Your Own Essay

SENTENCES

Subjects and Verbs

☐ Does each sentence have a main subject and verb?

1. Underline the subjects once and verbs twice in a paragraph of your revised essay. Remember that sentences can have more than one subject-verb set.

2. Does each of your sentences have at least one subject and verb that can stand alone?

For help with subjects and verbs, see Chapter 27.

---

3. Correct any fragments you have written.

4. Correct any run-together sentences you have written.

For help with fragments, see Chapter 28.
For help with run-togethers, see Chapter 29.

Subject-Verb Agreement
☐ Do all subjects and verbs agree?

1. Read aloud the subjects and verbs you underlined in your revised essay.

2. Correct any subjects and verbs that do not agree.

For help with subject-verb agreement, see Chapter 32.

Pronoun Agreement
☐ Do all pronouns agree with their nouns?

1. Find any pronouns in your revised essay that do not agree with their nouns.

2. Correct any pronouns that do not agree with their nouns.

For help with pronoun agreement, see Chapter 36.

Modifiers
☐ Are modifiers as close as possible to the words they modify?

1. Find any modifiers in your revised essay that are not as close as possible to the words they modify.

2. Rewrite sentences if necessary so that your modifiers are as close as possible to the words they modify.

For help with modifier errors, see Chapter 39.

PUNCTUATION AND MECHANICS

Punctuation
☐ Are sentences punctuated correctly?

1. Read your revised essay for any errors in punctuation.

2. Make sure any fragments and run-together sentences you revised are punctuated correctly.

For help with punctuation, see Chapters 40–44.

Mechanics
☐ Are words capitalized properly?

1. Read your revised essay for any errors in capitalization.

2. Be sure to check your capitalization in any fragments or run-together sentences you revised.

For help with capitalization, see Chapter 45.

WORD CHOICE AND SPELLING

Word Choice

☐ Are words used correctly?

For help with confused words, see Chapter 51.

1. Find any words used incorrectly in your revised essay.

2. Correct any errors you find.

Spelling

☐ Are words spelled correctly?

For help with spelling, see Chapter 52.

1. Use spell-check and a dictionary to check your spelling.

To make a personal log of your grammar/usage errors, go to Appendix 7.

2. Correct any misspelled words.

To make a personal log of your spelling errors, go to Appendix 8.

Now rewrite your essay again with your editing corrections.

MyWritingLab **More Helpful Hints**

- **Do you use borrowed information in your essay?** Incorporating statistics and quotes from experts into your essay can help you persuade your reader, but misusing quotation marks can damage your credibility. To make sure you are using these marks properly, watch the video on **Quotation Marks** in the **Punctuation, Mechanics, and Spelling** module of **MyWritingLab.**

PRACTICING ARGUMENT: FROM READING TO WRITING

This final section offers practice in the reading and writing skills you learned in this chapter. It includes two reading selections and several writing assignments on "your reading" and "your world." The section then offers guidance in peer evaluation and reflection, ending with suggestions about how to annotate your essay for your instructor in ways that will benefit both of you.

Reading Workshop

Here are three examples of good argument essays: "Wrong Call for Regulating Sexting" by Warner Todd Huston, which tries to persuade readers that we must take action at home to stop the "crass" attitudes of our teens, and two essays on lowering the drinking age—"Time to Lower the Drinking Age" by Mary Kate Cary and "The Perils of Lower Drinking Age" by Steve Chapman. As you read, notice how the writers make their claims through thoughtful, detailed reasoning.

WRONG CALL FOR REGULATING SEXTING
by Warner Todd Huston

Focusing Your Attention

1. At what age or in what situation do you think children understand the dangers of the Internet?

2. In the essay you are about to read, the writer discusses the dangers connected with sending to others nude or revealing pictures electronically. What do you think some of these issues are?

Expanding Your Vocabulary

The following words are important to your understanding of this essay. To help you add them to your vocabulary, write out a synonym and an example from your own experience for each new word.

circumspect: discrete (paragraph 2)

salacious: sexy (paragraph 2)

surged: moved quickly (paragraph 2)

epithets: labels (paragraph 3)

ribbing: teasing (paragraph 3)

sexting: to send sexy pictures through text messaging (paragraph 4)

low-born: unimportant (paragraph 4)

intrusive: interfering (paragraph 4)

agitating: making a fuss (paragraph 6)

onus: responsibility (paragraph 6)

crass: ridiculous (paragraph 9)

raunchy: sexually inappropriate (paragraph 10)

non-chalant: relaxed (paragraph 10)

precipitated: caused (paragraph 10)

instilled: taught (paragraph 10)

propriety: respectability (paragraph 10)

taunting: teasing (paragraph 11)

promulgated: spread (paragraph 13)

epidemic: outbreak (paragraph 16)

coarsening: to make rude (paragraph 17)

Reading
Strategy

READING CRITICALLY
Recognizing Facts and Opinions in Your Reading

As you have practiced throughout this chapter, separate the facts and opinions in the following essay by highlighting them in two different colors. Then put an X by any points that you disagree with or want to challenge. These notes will give you insights into the topic and guide you to a deeper level of understanding. Compare your notes with someone else's in the class.

WRONG CALL FOR
REGULATING SEXTING
by Warner Todd Huston

1   No one wants to see a beautiful 18-year-old girl commit suicide. No one wants to make any worse the pain that surviving family members feel. No one wants to make light of the situation that causes a child or young person to choose suicide either. But high emotion makes for bad laws, and this is no exception.

2   Last year, Jessica Logan imagined that she was sending a nude cell-phone photo of herself only to her new boyfriend. But he was not as circumspect as she might have hoped, passing the salacious picture to his friends and they to theirs, until it surged through some seven Cincinnati high schools.

example

3   It wasn't long before Jessica was the butt of jokes and the target of epithets like "slut" and "porn queen." The ribbing shook her so hard that she hanged herself in her bedroom last July.

4   And now, parents Albert and Cynthia Logan want new laws passed to somehow stop "sexting" of nude or half nude photos from one teen's cell-phone to another. Unfortunately, such laws are just a bad idea. They will do nothing to stop the low-born practice, while only piling more strangling regulations on the business community as well as giving government and police officials even more intrusive powers into our individual lives.

5   There is nothing wrong with trying to convince kids that emailing nude photos of themselves is not a good idea, of course, and the Logans are undertaking that effort.

But the there-ought-to-be-a-law mentality is not effective here, as it isn't in most cases on such emotional issues.

Absurdly, the Logans are agitating to place more onus on schools for stopping this new age problem of "cyberbullying" and "sexting."

"Schools need to understand our kids are targeting each other and technology is being used as a weapon," said [Internet safety expert] Aftab. "None of them (the schools) know what to do. Many of them...think it's not their problem. They want to close their eyes and put fingers in their ears, saying it's a home issue."

Sorry, parents, but if your children are sending nude cell-phone photos of themselves to each other, the solution is not to force schools to get involved. The solution is to take away the darn cell-phone!

Sadly, what we have here is not a lack of laws, but a crass culture. A national study by the National Campaign to Prevent Teen and Unplanned Pregnancy revealed that one in five teen girls or 22 percent say they have electronically sent or posted nude or semi-nude images online of themselves.

Salacious attitudes are instilled in kids by raunchy entertainment, coarse advertising, and the non-chalant attitude of parents to these influences. It needs to be pointed out that this sad suicide was precipitated in the first place by the girl sending the nude photo to a boyfriend she only had been dating for two months. Sadly, this young girl was not instilled with an attitude of propriety in her behavior. Just as sadly, she is not alone. Too many of our children never seem to be told what behavior is unacceptable in our country today.

There is a reason, though, that this poor child was so hard hit by the taunting she was confronted with. We lack a sense of shame in our culture, and when it hits it is like a ton of bricks that many don't quite understand. Young Jessica suddenly found herself with a bad reputation, deserved or no, because of her own actions. "I watched her get kicked out of maybe three or four pa`rties over the summer just for having 'a reputation,'" said Steven Arnett, a friend of hers who graduated last year from Moeller High School.

This is a sad, sad object lesson for other kids imagining there are no consequences for sending salacious photos of themselves all across the Internet. There ARE consequences to your actions. This must be learned by our youth, but it is a lesson that is missing from society today.

Unfortunately, just the wrong sort of lesson is being promulgated by teachers, lawmakers, and these parents with this incident. "It is a form of bullying, and that is something we cannot tolerate. The difficulty is stopping it.... That's why we stress with our kids that the moment you push 'send,' the damage is done," said Sycamore Superintendent Adrienne James. All the onus put on "the bullying" and none put on the person that sent the nude photo to begin with is simply not a complete lesson. The better lesson is to focus equally on both the sender and the bullies, not just the bullies. The wrap up is typical of the wrong-headed emphasis we too often place on the situations that confront us in our modern society.

Albert and Cynthia Logan have gone public with Jessie's story, hoping to change vague state laws that don't hold anyone accountable for sexting. They also want to warn kids about what can happen when nude cell-phone photos are shared.

15   "We want a bill passed," Cynthia Logan said.

16   "It's a national epidemic. Nobody is doing anything—no schools, no police officers, no adults, no attorneys, no one."

17   It isn't the laws that are the problem. It's the overindulgence of kids' "self-esteem," a complete lack of moral instruction, a coarsening of our society, and a corresponding assumption by too many parents that everyone else should be responsible for their own children's behavior.

18   Again, it is horrendous that this beautiful young woman took her own life over this embarrassment. But it is the lack of imagining that actions have consequences, that embarrassment is a result, that reputations can be destroyed with casual actions little thought out, that all too often is a lesson learned too late.

19   It isn't only the Logans' fault. There is little doubt that they loved their daughter. But this incident is indicative of some major errors in our society that need to be fixed. If they aren't, these heart-wrenching incidents will grow until the total breakdown of society is complete, and no "law" will stop it.

Thinking Critically About Content

1. What does Huston see as the relationship between kids' attitudes today and "raunchy entertainment" (paragraph 10)?

2. Why does the author think a law for controlling sexting is "wrongheaded" (paragraph 13)?

3. What does the author mean by the statement "What we have here is not a lack of laws, but a crass culture" (paragraph 9)?

Thinking Critically About Purpose and Audience

4. What do you think Huston's purpose is in this essay?

5. Who do you think would be most interested in this essay?

6. What effect do you think this essay would have on parents?

Thinking Critically About Essays

7. Describe in a complete sentence the writer's argument.

8. Why do you think Huston cites statistics about sexting (paragraph 9) to support his argument?

9. Do you think the story about Jessica Logan is an effective way to start this essay? Explain your answer.

10. This essay argues against the Logans' solution to the growing sexting problem but doesn't offer any concrete alternatives. Write a paragraph with some clear, realistic suggestions for solving this new problem in our society.

To keep track of your critical thinking progress, go to Appendix 1.

ARGUING A POSITION

Focusing Your Attention

1. If you were asked to take a position for or against a topic of great importance to you or to society, what are some of the topics you would consider?

2. In the two essays that you will be reading, one writer claims that reducing the legal drinking age will have a positive effect on our drinking problems in this country. The other writer claims that lowering the drinking age is irresponsible and will lead to even more problems. Before you read these essays, try to predict some of the arguments each author will make.

READING CRITICALLY
Recognizing Facts and Opinions in Your Reading

Reading
Strategy

Once again, highlight the facts and opinions in both of the following essays, put an X by ideas you disagree with, and form your own opinions about the issue of America's drinking age. Be prepared to defend your thoughts with details from the essays and examples from your own experience.

TIME TO LOWER THE DRINKING AGE
by Mary Kate Cary

Expanding Your Vocabulary

The following words are important to your understanding of this essay. To help you add them to your vocabulary, write out a synonym and an example from your own experience for each new word.

mandated: required (paragraph 3)

comply: obey (paragraph 3)

opioids: substances containing opium (paragraph 6)

tranquilizers: sleeping pills (paragraph 6)

impaired: weakened (paragraph 8)

exemplified: demonstrated (paragraph 8)

hazing: torturing connected with fraternities (paragraph 8)

inclusion: being included (paragraph 8)

astronomically: extremely (paragraph 9)

hyperbole: exaggeration (paragraph 10)

TIME TO LOWER THE DRINKING AGE
by Mary Kate Cary

1   I was telling my college-age daughter recently that back in the olden days when I went to college, you could fill a red Solo cup with beer at a fraternity party and sip it all night long. No one knew if it was your first beer or your 10th. There was no need for "pregaming"—binge drinking in private apartments or dorms before heading out in public. And unlike today, college kids didn't tend to use fake IDs as much.

2   That's because when I was an undergrad, the drinking age was 18. Fraternities had kegs out in the open on university property, and student gatherings on campus often included beer. I remember university police regularly strolling through the fraternity parties, making sure everything was under control. That tended to keep a lid on things.

3   Then, 30 years ago this summer, President Ronald Reagan signed into law the Federal Uniform Drinking Age Act of 1984, which mandated that all states adopt 21 as the legal drinking age over the next five years. States that did not comply faced a cut in their federal highway funds; by 1988, all 50 states had moved the minimum drinking age to 21.

4   The well-intentioned leaders of Mothers Against Drunk Driving were able to convince politicians that a vote against the bill was a vote in favor of drunken driving, and they succeeded in gaining unanimous passage in both the House and the Senate. According to the MADD website, the National Highway Traffic Safety Administration estimates that the law has saved about 900 lives a year.

5   Drunken driving deaths have decreased over the last three decades in large part because we now throw the book at drunken drivers in this country: All 50 states currently define a driver's having a blood-alcohol concentration of 0.08 or higher as a crime; 42 states suspend drivers' licenses on the first offense. Every state also now has some type of ignition interlock law, requiring devices to be installed in the vehicles of convicted drunken drivers that prevent a vehicle from starting if the driver breathes into the device and produces a breath-alcohol level above a preset limit. Thanks to MADD, drunken driving isn't the problem it used to be.

6   The Centers for Disease Control and Prevention reports that in 2010 drug overdoses caused more deaths than motor vehicle crashes among people 25 to 64 years old. The CDC estimates that from 1999 to 2010 drug overdose death rates jumped 102 percent. While first-time use of illegal street drugs such as heroin by young people increased from 90,000 users in 2006 to 156,000 in 2012, it's abuse of prescription drugs that has really skyrocketed. One recent report cited by the Department of Justice says that between 1993 and 2005, the proportion of college students abusing opioids like Vicodin and OxyContin jumped 343 percent and 450 percent for tranquilizers like Xanax and Valium.

Prescription drug use among young people at colleges is, along with binge drinking, part of the epidemic of pregaming. The CDC reported that alcohol is responsible for more than 4,300 deaths annually among underage youth. The CDC also found that young people between the ages of 12 and 20 drink 11 percent of all the alcohol consumed in the U.S., and more than 90 percent of this alcohol is consumed during binge drinking.   7

Here's the problem with both binge drinking and drug abuse: When you're that impaired, you do things you wouldn't normally do. In an April speech, Dartmouth College's president listed the outrages he now witnesses regularly: "From sexual assaults on campus ... to a culture where dangerous drinking has become the rule and not the exception ... to a general disregard for human dignity as exemplified by hazing, parties with racist and sexist undertones, disgusting and sometimes threatening insults hurled on the Internet ... to a social scene that is too often at odds with the practices of inclusion that students are right to expect on a college campus in 2014." I doubt that list is unique to just one Ivy League school.   8

President Obama recently announced the creation of the White House Task Force to Protect Students from Sexual Assault, after stating that "1 in 5 women on college campuses has been sexually assaulted during their time there." (If that were true, as one critic pointed out, the crime rates on college campuses would be astronomically higher than America's most violent cities.)   9

Despite the hyperbole from the White House, we can all agree that sexual assault as a result of alcohol and drug abuse is a very serious problem on America's college campuses. But forming a task force in Washington probably won't help. Allowing states to lower the legal drinking age would. The U.S. is one of only seven nations in the entire world with a drinking age of 21. Most Western democracies allow their citizens to fight in wars, vote in elections, and drink alcohol at age 18—as do even China and North Korea.   10

I'd rather see my kids sipping beer out of a red Solo cup at a well-patrolled fraternity party than drinking shots and popping a Vicodin in someone's basement off campus. Lowering the drinking age will help slow the need for pregaming and bring the college fake ID business to a dead stop. It can't help but reduce the binge drinking, drug overdoses, and sexual assaults.   11

Thirty years ago, drunken driving was the problem. Now that is less true. Let's take a lesson from MADD and make a vote against lowering the drinking age to 18 a vote for drug overdoses and sexual assaults against young women. Times have changed.   12

THE PERILS OF A LOWER DRINKING AGE
by Steve Chapman

Expanding Your Vocabulary

The following words are important to your understanding of this essay. To help you add them to your vocabulary, write out a synonym and an example from your own experience for each new word.

clandestine: secret (paragraph 2)

enforcement: implementation (paragraph 8)

immortality: never dying (paragraph 11)

franchise: agreement (paragraph 13)

disruptive: distracting (paragraph 7)

hyperactive: overactive (paragraph 7)

detrimental: dangerous (paragraph 8)

condoning: supporting (paragraph 9)

THE PERILS OF A LOWER DRINKING AGE
by Steve Chapman

1 Life is full of surprises, and some 100 college presidents think they have stumbled on one. They think there is too much problem drinking on campus—no surprise there—and suggest we might solve the problem by changing the drinking age. They don't propose to raise it to 25. They want to lower it to 18.

2 The group behind the petition they signed, Choose Responsibility, says the current drinking age is a failure. It has "not resulted in significant constructive behavioral change among our students," the statement says, and in fact has spawned "a culture of dangerous, clandestine 'binge-drinking'—often conducted off-campus."

3 It's true that in the old days, there was no college culture of clandestine, off-campus binge drinking. It was out in the open, right on the quad. Another difference back then: There was more of it.

4 At the risk of stating the obvious, that's at least partly because in most states, the drinking age was under 21. Youngsters could buy booze legally, so they did what you would expect. They drank more and got drunk more.

5 It's bizarre to blame the higher age for today's staggering undergraduates. According to Monitoring the Future, an ongoing research project at the University of Michigan, binge drinking has not risen since 1988, when 21 became the minimum drinking age throughout the country. Among college students and other college-age Americans, the rate is lower today than it was then, and the decline has been even bigger among high-school students.

6 It's true the progress stalled around 1996. But how can that be blamed on the higher drinking age? By then, it had been the national norm for nearly a decade.

7 In spite of the law, plenty of 18-to-20-year-olds somehow manage to get wasted on a regular basis. But a law can be helpful without being airtight. This one has curbed not only the use of alcohol among young people but its dangerous abuse.

8 Since 1988, according to the National Highway Traffic Safety Administration, drunk-driving deaths have dropped in all age groups. That's due in part to stricter enforcement and changing public attitudes about drinking and driving.

9 But they dropped most among those younger than 21. In that group, the number of alcohol-related fatalities has been cut nearly in half—even as the number of non-alcohol-related traffic deaths has been stable.

This is not a coincidence. When states lowered their drinking age in the 1970s, they got more drunk-driving deaths among teenagers than similar states that stayed at 21. A 1983 study in the Journal of Legal Studies concluded that any state that "raises its drinking age can expect the nighttime fatal crashes of drivers of the affected age groups to drop by about 28 percent." 10

There are other arguments for lowering the age. Maybe the most popular is that if you're old enough to join the Army and die for your country, you're old enough to buy a beer. But there is a good reason to avoid such blind consistency. Among the qualities that make 18-year-olds such good soldiers are their fearlessness and sense of immortality—traits that do not mix well with alcohol. 11

Besides, we don't have a single age threshold for adulthood. We give driver's licenses to 16-year-olds, but a 20-year-old Marine returning from Iraq will find he may not buy a handgun or gamble in a casino. 12

Why permit 18-year-olds to vote but not drink? Because they have not shown a disproportionate tendency to abuse the franchise, to the peril of innocent bystanders. 13

Another reason is that extending the vote to 18-year-olds doesn't let even younger people gain illicit access to the polls. But if high-school seniors could legally patronize a liquor store, sophomores would find it much easier to get party fuel. Raising the drinking age to 21 reduced alcohol-related traffic fatalities not only among 18-year-olds, who lost the right to drink, but 16-year-olds, who never had it. 14

It's not hard to make a logical case for allowing 18-year-olds to buy alcohol, but only if you disregard the practical effects of letting them do something that many of them are not mature enough to handle. In this debate, the ultimate wisdom comes from Supreme Court Justice Oliver Wendell Holmes, who reminded us that sometimes a page of history is worth a volume of logic. 15

Thinking Critically About Content

1. Make a list of the reasons, evidence, and statistics each writer uses to convince the reader of his or her position.

2. Explain how both writers use various laws about drinking to argue different positions.

3. Which essay contains the most convincing evidence in your opinion? Why is it so convincing to you?

Thinking Critically About Purpose and Audience

4. What do you think the writers' purposes are in these essays?

5. How does each author use the arguments they oppose to bolster their own opinion? In other words, how does each argue against the opposition?

6. If you changed your mind as a result of reading one of these essays, what in the essay caused the change?

Thinking Critically About Essays

7. State each writer's point of view in a single sentence.

8. How do both writers organize their essays? Make a rough outline of each essay to demonstrate your answer.

9. Which points do the two writers agree on? Which points do they disagree on? Explain your answer.

10. Write your own argument about the relationship between a specific alcohol-related problem and the legal drinking age.

Writing Workshop

This final section provides opportunities for you to apply what you have learned in this chapter to another writing assignment. This time, we furnish very little prompting beyond a summary of the guidelines for writing an argument essay. This section will let you demonstrate that you can go through the entire writing process on your own with only occasional feedback from your peers. Loop back into the chapter as necessary when you have questions so that this process becomes as automatic to you as possible before you move on to new material. Then pause at the end of the chapter to reflect briefly on what you have learned.

Guidelines for Writing an Argument Essay

1. State your opinion on your topic in your thesis statement.
2. Find out as much as you can about your audience before you write.
3. Choose evidence that supports your thesis statement.
4. Anticipate opposing points of view.
5. Find some common ground.
6. Maintain a reasonable tone.
7. Organize your essay so that it presents your position as effectively as possible.

Writing About Your Reading

1. In "Wrong Call for Regulating Sexting," Huston tries to convince his readers that sexting is the result of a moral breakdown in our culture. Argue for or against Huston's stand on this issue. What do you think are the main causes of this new epidemic?

2. The pro and con essays in the chapter deal mainly with the drinking age as it relates to college drinking. Think of another strategy for fighting irresponsible drinking, and attempt to convince a group in authority to try your solution to the problem. Gather as much evidence as you can before you begin to write.

3. How can being able to develop good arguments and persuade people of your point of view help you in life? How might this ability give you the edge over other people in the job market?

Writing About Your World

1. Explain what the photographer had in mind in creating this pictorial statement about littering. How does it appeal to its viewers? Write an essay explaining what the ad communicates.

To keep track of your critical thinking progress, go to Appendix 1.

2. Argue for or against a controversial political issue. Take a firm stand, and develop an essay supporting your position. You might want to look at the headlines in the newspaper to get some ideas for this assignment.

3. Write a letter to a potential employer for the job of your dreams, arguing that you are the best candidate for the job. Try to convince the employer not only that you are the perfect person for the job but also that you can take the position in new directions. Follow the format for a well-developed argument essay.

4. Create your own argument essay assignment (with the help of your instructor), and write a response to it.

Revising

Small Group Activity (5–10 minutes per writer) Working in groups of three or four, read your argument essays to each other. Those listening should record their reactions on the Revising Peer Evaluation Forms in Appendix 4. After your group goes through this process, give your evaluation forms to the appropriate writers so that each writer has two or three peer comment sheets for revising.

Paired Activity (5 minutes per writer) Using the completed Peer Evaluation Forms, work in pairs to decide what you should revise in your essay. If time allows, rewrite some of your sentences, and have your partner look at them.

Individual Activity Rewrite your paper, using the revising feedback you received from other students.

Editing

Paired Activity (5–10 minutes per writer) Swap papers with a classmate, and use the Editing Peer Evaluation Form (Appendix 6) to identify as many grammar, punctuation, mechanics, and spelling errors as you can. If time allows, correct some of your errors, and have your partner look at them. Record your grammar, punctuation, and mechanics errors in the Error Log (Appendix 7) and your spelling errors in the Spelling Log (Appendix 8).

Individual Activity Rewrite your paper again, using the editing feedback you received from other students.

Reflecting on Your Writing   When you have completed your own essay, answer these six questions.

1. What was most difficult about this assignment?

2. What was easiest?

3. What did you learn about arguing by completing this assignment?

4. What do you think are the strengths of your argument? Place a wavy line by the parts of your essay that you feel are very good.

5. What are the weaknesses, if any, of your paper? Place an X by the parts of your essay you would like help with. Write in the margins any questions you have.

6. What did you learn from this assignment about your own writing process—about preparing to write, about writing the first draft, about revising, and about editing?

MyWritingLab™   Visit Chapter 17, "Arguing," in MyWritingLab, and complete the Post-test to check your understanding of the chapter's objectives.

The Research Paper

"In order to understand complex issues and situations and events, we need to analyze them from multiple perspectives; every position or every viewpoint ought to have reasons to support it; and the quality of the conclusion is dependent on the quality of the reasoning that went before it."

—John Chaffee

Part III discusses the research paper, also called *term paper* and *documented essay*, from assignment to final draft. It explains not only what this type of essay is but also how to write one, step by step. It provides you with a student model of a research paper and then guides you through the process of writing one on a topic of your own.

18

Recognizing a Research Paper

The content of a research paper is based mainly on facts, statistics, and the opinions of others. The main difference between a research paper and other essays is that writers use information from other reading material when writing a research paper. In other words, writers consult books, periodicals, and the Internet to find facts, statistics, and other data to support their main points.

Just as you develop the body of most essays with common knowledge or personal experience, you should develop a documented essay with trustworthy evidence from sources. To begin choosing appropriate sources, you must have a good sense of your thesis statement. Then, set out to find research that will back up your thesis. This support, or evidence, is the foundation of a research paper and should be carefully integrated with your original ideas.

In a research paper, the title provides a clue about the subject of the essay. The introduction gives some background for understanding the topic and then states the purpose of the paper in a thesis statement. Body paragraphs provide evidence to back up the thesis statement, and the conclusion wraps up the essay by referring to the thesis statement and bringing the paper to a close.

Student Comment:
"I never really knew what a research paper was until now. I read the chapters in the book and then watched the video in **MyWritingLab** on my own."

| MyWritingLab | **Understanding the Research Paper** |

To make sure that you fully understand what a research paper entails, go to **MyWritingLab.com,** and choose **Research Process** in the **Research** module. From there, read the **Overview,** and watch the video called **Animation: Recognizing a Research Paper** to learn about the main features of this type of writing.

The following essay by student writer Mary Minor is a good example of a research paper. She solidly proves her thesis statement by using books and articles from many different sources as evidence in her supporting paragraphs. As you read the first paragraph of this draft of her essay, notice her thesis statement. Then, in each supporting paragraph that follows the introductory paragraph, be aware of how this student develops her essay and supports her thesis statement with material from other sources.

Children as Robots

Catchy title

When children are infants, they are measured by certain "norms" to see if they are progressing through developmental stages at the rate of other infants their age. The norms are never clear cut, and they leave room for individual differences. When a child hits the age of two or enters day care, "norms" become very important. More than in any other time in history, the 1990s brought about a change in norms that left parents confused. Now, in the twenty-first century, the "terrible twos" and "trying threes" no longer seem to be the best descriptions of toddlerhood. Today, children who are too terrible at the age of two or too trying at the age of three are diagnosed with either Attention Deficit Disorder (ADD) or Attention Deficit Hyperactivity Disorder (ADHD). According to the Director of Neuropsychology at Children's Hospital of Atlanta, "Research shows a 700 percent increase in medication being used to treat ADHD since the 1990s alone" (Burns), and children continue to be diagnosed at an alarming rate. Children are often misdiagnosed with ADD or ADHD and suffer unnecessarily when medicated for a disorder they may not have.

1

Interesting comparison

Direct quotation

Thesis statement

In-text citation (MLA)

Page and paragraph numbers no longer necessary for online sources except for electronic versions of articles in print

The American Psychological Association now classifies this phenomenon as one disease with subcategories and has only recently adjusted its stance on ADHD to be categorized as a neurodevelopmental disorder (American 11). The *Diagnostic and Statistical Manual of Medical Disorders* (DSM-5) defines ADHD as a disorder characterized by "impairing levels of inattention, disorganization, and/or hyperactivity-impulsivity" (American 32). DSM-5 also defines "inattention and disorganization," as well as "hyperactivity-impulsivity." Inattention and disorganization "entail inability to stay on task, seeming not to listen, and losing materials, at levels that are inconsistent with age or developmental level," while hyperactivity-impulsivity "entails overactivity, fidgeting, inability to stay seated, intruding into other people's activities, and inability to wait—symptoms that are

2

excessive for age or developmental level" (American 32). What's more, the disease ADD has become the most common childhood mental heath disorder (CDC) in the United States today, afflicting "over 4 percent of all adults and 11 percent of U.S. children" (Saul 1; Arnold et al. 2). L. Alan Sroufe, Professor Emeritus of psychology at the University of Minnesota's Institute of Child Development, claims that drugs are too often used to solve conflicts with children: "We should be asking why we rely so heavily on these drugs." He argues that "the large-scale medication of children feeds into a societal view that all of life's problems can be solved with a pill" (Sroufe "Problems" 1). Given the fact that children are identified as having this disease based on what a person may consider "normal" behavior, the fact that nobody can agree on what "normal" means is unfortunate for the children being diagnosed. As a result, specialists need to be careful when recommending treatments for what could be everyday behavior.

3   Many children today who do not fit the "norm" of adult expectations may be diagnosed with ADD. Labeling a child's behavior based on a set of "norms" is ludicrous since these qualities cannot accurately be measured, let alone defined. The National Center for Learning Disabilities (*NCLD.org*) states that there can be some confusion in the diagnosis and treatment of children with learning disabilities, ADD, and ADHD: "Both LD and ADHD are the result of neurobiological disorders.... There is no foolproof way to test for either of them." Even though we have a definition of this disorder, nobody really knows for sure what the exact cause is or how the symptoms should be treated. Sroufe feels that parents should be aware that "studies tell us nothing about whether the observed anomalies were present at birth or whether they resulted from trauma, chronic stress or other early-childhood experiences" (Sroufe "Problems" 1). In an article in *The New England Journal of Medicine*, Dr. Marsha Rappley contends that the diagnosis is controversial because of the "subjective nature" of the test, leading many professionals to believe that ADD and ADHD are "overdiagnosed and overtreated" (171). If our leading professionals in the field can't decide on a reliable and accurate diagnostic test, we surely can't expect that they can identify a case of ADHD.

4   Another shocking theory, presented by Richard Saul, head of the Diagnostic and Developmental Center, states that the disease ADHD as understood by today's culture does not exist. In his book *ADHD Does Not Exist: The Truth About Attention Deficit and Hyperactivity Disorder*, Saul argues that "attention

Margin annotations:

Quotation used to define problem

Statistic

Source introduced before quotation; no citation necessary

Transition from definition to further problems

Transition sentence to new topic

Only page number needed since author already introduced

deficit and hyperactivity are primarily symptoms of other conditions" (xvii). ADHD is unique in the fact that as an "illness," it is defined more by its symptoms than its cause. In fact, there are over twenty medical conditions that can account for the symptoms of ADHD, including vision and hearing problems, absence seizures, or other mental disorders (Saul 2). Children would benefit and live far more productive and happy lives if they were correctly diagnosed and treated for the true underlying condition. Yet numerous children are diagnosed with ADHD and are medicated because of it.

Considering the dubious nature of the disease, there are as many speculations about the cause of ADD and ADHD as there are experts. Unfortunately, the ones lost in the confusion are the children, and this is due to the fact that Ritalin, the most widely used method of treatment for this disorder, appears to work so well that few additional medical tests are done. Insurance companies and teachers often encourage parents to see drugs as the answer; Sroufe counters, "Drugs get everyone—politicians, scientists, teachers and parents—off the hook. Everyone except the children, that is" (Sroufe "Problems" 1). While Ritalin seems to work for many children, Dr. Rappley is concerned about its side effects. Studies show that short-term use of Ritalin can cause appetite suppression, stomachaches, headaches, and slowing down of growth (Rappley 168, 179). Unfortunately, evidence remains unclear on the effectiveness of medicating children diagnosed with ADHD.

Unfortunately, teachers are often the first to be involved in diagnosing a child, and they often see, according to Sroufe, "improved behavior in almost every short-term study" (Sroufe "Problems" 1). Parents are often pressured into placing their children on drugs with the hope that those children will receive better grades and play better with other children. However, this pressure may be unwarranted. Sroufe points out that "stimulants generally have the same effects for all children and adults. They enhance the ability to concentrate, especially when tasks are not inherently interesting or when one is fatigued or bored, but they don't improve broader learning abilities" (Sroufe "Ritalin" 1). The reason that stimulants like Ritalin and Adderall work so well is the same reason that adults return again and again to coffee and other caffeinated beverages during their work. Any child or adult would experience a change in behavior when subjected to stimulants, regardless of whether they suffer from ADHD or not. Teachers may see a more agreeable child, but Ritalin and other stimulants cannot make children more creative, better problem solvers, or faster learners.

Transition sentence to next paragraph about Ritalin

5

Citation after paraphrase

6

7   Prescribing the regular use of stimulants to young children may increase their likelihood of abusing the drug or other illicit drugs in the future. Children prescribed stimulants like Ritalin and Adderall "develop a tolerance to the drug, and thus its efficacy disappears" after prolonged use (Sroufe "Ritalin" 1). Because of this, Ritalin may become the new gateway drug. Professors of Psychology at the University of Albany, Bianca Jardin, Alison Looby, and Mitch Earleywine have conducted and published a study of Ritalin and Adderall abuse among college students diagnosed with ADHD. Their findings "suggest that approximately 56% of youths aged 4 to 17 receive [Ritalin or Adderall] for treatment of their ADHD" (373). As they begin college, these students face a higher risk of abusing or forming a dependence on these drugs. The shocking results of the study conducted by Jardin, Looby, and Earlywine concluded that of 42 students already using prescription Ritalin or Adderall, "forty-five percent of participants reported misusing their medication" (375). Many students are able to access Ritalin and Adderall for recreational or non-medical use; how much easier must it be for students already prescribed these drugs by their doctors? The negative consequences of abusing such stimulants include "suicidal and homicidal ideation, seizure, and various cardiac complications, such as hypertension, hypotension, tachycardia, palpitations, and dysrhythmias" (373). If students begin using Ritalin in elementary school, they will likely develop a very high tolerance to the drug by the time they reach college, creating a cascading effect of dependence, abuse, and the subsequence dangers to their health and safety. Furthermore, "those who misuse are more likely to report using alcohol, nicotine, marijuana, ecstasy, and cocaine" (374). The implications of this study for today's college students are frightening, and the findings should caution parents against turning to stimulants for their children.

8   When doctors quote the Hippocratic Oath, they say, "I will apply dietetic measures for the benefit of the sick according to my ability and judgment; I will keep them from harm and injustice" ("Hippocratic Oath" 239). Sworn to dietetically treat their patients, doctors should remember this oath before prescribing drugs for a disease that nobody can prove exists. Certainly, there must be more holistic or alternative methods of diagnosing and treating children with apparent behavioral issues. Perhaps doctors should turn to therapies that rely on non-pharmacological practices and only turn to drugs as a last resort, especially when the lives of children are at stake.

Credible opinion used to support argument

Statistic

Opposite argument addressed

Opposite argument refuted

Page number included for online article also in print

Facts used to show other possible reasons for hyperactivity in children

Conclusion   Perhaps these "diseases" are nothing more than a belief   9
system in an ever-increasing conformist society. Every effort
should be made to find the cause of the real medical problems
underlying ADD and ADHD before we even think about giving our children drugs. A doctor who doesn't order medical
tests for a child with symptoms of ADD is negligent to say
the least, and the failure of a doctor to discuss alternatives
to drug therapy with parents when diagnosing ADHD is more
than inexcusable; it is unforgivable. More patients would seek   Reference
alternative treatments like behavior therapy if they knew their   to thesis
child was diagnosed on the basis of nothing more than a list of   statement
symptoms that cannot be defined or measured. After all, most
parents do not want their child placed on long-term stimulant
Call to   drugs. It is time to say good-bye to conformist American class-
action   rooms and diagnoses. Perhaps some people don't fit the norm   Concluding
because they have personalities.   statement

Alphabetical
order

Works Cited

Double-   American Psychiatric Association. *The Diagnostic and*   Book
spaced with   *Statistical Manual of Medical Disorders.* Arlington, VA: "Print"
no extra   APA, 2013. Print.   and "Web"
spaces   Arnold, L. Eugene, et al. "Effect of Treatment Modality on   required
between   Long-Term Outcomes in Attention-Deficit/Hyperactivity   in MLA
entries   Disorder: A Systematic Review." *PLOS ONE* 10.2 (2015):   citations
1–19. *ASP.* Web. 11 Apr. 2015.

Online   Burns, Thomas G. "ADHD Over-Diagnosed?" *The Atlanta*   Web
source   *Journal-Constitution.* Cox Media Group, 17 Mar. 2009.   address
Web. 8 Dec. 2015.   omitted
CDC. "Children's Mental Health—New Report." *Centers for*   unless
Disease Control and Prevention. 21 May 2013. Web. 11   reader
Apr. 2015.   probably
All lines   "Confusion over ADD, AD/HD, and Learning Disabilities."   can't
after   *National Center for Learning Disabilities.* National Center   locate
the first   for Learning Disabilities, Inc., 6 Mar. 2009. Web. 9 Dec.   source
indented   2015.   without it

Journal   "Hippocratic Oath." *World Book Encyclopedia.* Vol. 9. 2010   Encyclopedia
article   ed. Print.
General-   Jardin, Bianca, Alison Looby, and Mitch Earleywine.
circulation   "Characteristics of College Students With Attention-Deficit
publication   Hyperactivity Disorder Symptoms Who Misuse Their
Medications." *Journal of American College Health* 59.5
(2011): 373–377. *ASP.* Web. 11 Apr. 2015.

Rappley, Marsha. "Attention Deficit Hyperactivity Disorder."
The New England Journal of Medicine 352.2 (2005):
165–173. Print.

Saul, Richard. *ADHD Does Not Exist: The Truth About
Attention Deficit and Hyperactivity Disorder.* New York:
Harper Collins, 2014. Print.

Sroufe, L. Alan. "Problems in Diagnosing and Treating ADD/
ADHD." Editorial. *New York Times* 29 Jan. 2012: SR1.
Web. 10 May 2015.

—. "Ritalin Gone Wrong." *New York Times* 28 Jan. 2012.
Web. 11 Apr. 2015.

Page number included for online article also in print

PRACTICE 1 Before continuing, choose one of the following topics for your own writing in the rest of Part III:

Police brutality	Government spending	Date rape
Alzheimer's disease	Steroids	Child abuse
Herbal medicine	Pollution	Alcohol and crime
Assisted suicide	Drug treatment programs	Bilingual education
Nursing homes	Cloning	Censorship

MyWritingLab™ Visit Chapter 18, "Recognizing a Research Paper," in MyWritingLab, and complete the Post-test to check your understanding of the chapter's objectives.

19

Avoiding Plagiarism

Plagiarism is using someone else's words or ideas as if they were your own. Because it is dishonest, plagiarism is a serious offense in college and beyond. When you work with sources, you must give credit to the authors who wrote them. In other words, if you quote, paraphrase, or summarize from another source, you must provide your reader with information about that source, such as the author's name, the title of the book or essay, and the year it was written. Whenever you use other people's words or ideas without giving them credit, you are plagiarizing.

If you don't cite your sources properly, readers will think certain words and ideas are yours when they actually came from someone else. When you steal material in this way in college, you may be dismissed from school. When you commit the same offense in the professional world, you can get fired or end up in court. So make sure you understand what plagiarism is as you move through this chapter.

MyWritingLab

Understanding Plagiarism

Understanding what plagiarism is and how to avoid it are very important when you are using sources. To find out more about plagiarism, go to **MyWritingLab.com,** and choose **Research Process** in the **Research** module. From there, watch the video called **Animation: Avoiding Plagiarism** as many times as necessary in order to master the basic concepts of this serious offense.

Student Comment:
"Plagiarism was a mystery to me until this chapter."

COMMON KNOWLEDGE

If you are referring to information such as historical events, dates of presidents' terms, and known facts (like the effects of ultraviolet rays or smoking), you do not have to cite a source. This material is called *common knowledge* because it can be found in a number of different sources. You can use this information freely because you are not borrowing anyone's original words or ideas.

ORIGINAL IDEAS

If you want to use someone's specific words or ideas, you must give that person credit by recording where you found this information. This process is called *citing* or *documenting* your sources, and it involves noting in your paper where you found the idea. Because research papers are developed around sources that support your position, citations are an essential ingredient in any term paper.

As you saw in Mary Minor's paper in Chapter 18, every source is acknowledged at least twice: (1) in the paper directly after a quotation or idea and (2) at the end of the paper in a list. The first type of citation is known as an in-text citation, and the second type is a list of sources cited in the paper. These two types of documentation work together for the readers. At the note-taking stage, you should make sure you have all the information on your sources that you will need later to acknowledge them in proper form in your paper. Having to track down missing details when you prepare your list of works cited is frustrating and time-consuming.

PRACTICE 1 Identify the following information as either common knowledge (CK) or original (O).

1. _____ In a typical day, for humans to drink the equivalent of what the glassy-winged sharpshooter insect drinks, humans would have to drink 4,000 gallons of liquid, half the amount in a standard swimming pool.

2. _____ William Shakespeare was born and died on the same day, April 23—52 years apart.

3. _____ Abraham Lincoln was shot in Ford's Theatre by John Wilkes Booth.

4. _____ A human cannot survive more than three days without water.

5. _____ The Paleozoic era produced the first shellfish and corals in the Cambrian period, the first fish in the Ordovician period, and the first land plants in the Silurian period.

6. _____ Denzel Washington has won two Oscars, one for his supporting role in *Glory* and one for the starring role in *Training Day*.

7. _____ Aerobic respiration consists of oxygen plus organic matter that produces carbon dioxide, water, and energy.

8. _____ The success of *American Idol* caused many other talent shows to be produced.

9. _____ A recession is a good time to train yourself for a new job.

10. _____ AIDS is a disease that can be contracted by having unprotected sex.

USING AND SYNTHESIZING SOURCES

When writers use more than one source in an essay, they are *synthesizing* their sources. In other words, they are taking pieces of information from different sources and weaving them into their own argument. If you've written any type of paper using more than one source, you were synthesizing material.

As you write a research paper, your own argument establishes the order of your ideas. Then your sources provide evidence or proof for your argument. Look at how Mary Minor uses sources. Here is a paragraph from her first draft:

> (1) Many children today who do not fit the "norm" of adult expectations may be diagnosed with ADD. (2) Labeling a child's behavior based on a set of "norms" is ludicrous since these qualities cannot accurately be measured, let alone defined. (3) The National Center for Learning Disabilities (*NCLD.org*) states that there can be some confusion in the diagnosis and treatment of children with learning disabilities, ADD, and ADHD: "Both LD and ADHD are the result of neurobiological disorders....There is no foolproof way to test for either of them." (4) Sroufe feels that parents should be aware that "studies tell us nothing about whether the observed anomalies were present at birth or whether they resulted from trauma, chronic stress or other early-childhood experiences" (Sroufe "Problems" 1). (5) In an article in *The New England Journal of Medicine*, Dr. Marsha Rappley contends that the diagnosis is controversial because of the "subjective nature" of the test, leading many professionals to believe that ADD and ADHD are "overdiagnosed and overtreated" (171).

As Mary was revising this paragraph, she realized she was forcing the reader to make connections between her sources and her argument because she was not providing explanations that made those connections. So she revised her paragraph, connecting her sources to her own ideas and making her argument clearer. Mary's additions are in bold type.

> (1) Many children today who do not fit the "norm" of adult expectations may be diagnosed with ADD. (2) Labeling a child's behavior based on a set of "norms" is ludicrous since these qualities

cannot accurately be measured, let alone defined. (3) The National Center for Learning Disabilities states that there can be some confusion in the diagnosis and treatment of children with learning disabilities, ADD, and ADHD: "Both LD and ADHD are the result of neurobiological disorders.... There is no foolproof way to test for either of them." **(4) Even though we have a definition of this disorder, nobody really knows for sure the exact cause or how the symptoms should be treated.** (5) Sroufe feels that parents should be aware that "studies tell us nothing about whether the observed anomalies were present at birth or whether they resulted from trauma, chronic stress or other early-childhood experiences" (SR1). (6) In an article in *The New England Journal of Medicine*, Dr. Marsha Rappley contends that the diagnosis is controversial because of the "subjective nature" of the test, leading many professionals to believe that ADD and ADHD are "overdiagnosed and overtreated" (171). **(7) If our leading professionals in the field can't decide on a reliable and accurate diagnostic test, we surely can't expect that they can identify a case of ADHD.**

By adding the fourth sentence, "Even though we have a definition of this disorder, nobody really knows for sure the exact cause or how the symptoms should be treated," Mary explains in her own voice the significance of the previous quotation and tells her readers what she wants them to think about after they read it. Similarly, the sentence Mary adds to the end of this paragraph also furthers her argument by clarifying the quotation before it: "If our leading professionals in the field can't decide on a reliable and accurate diagnostic test, we surely can't expect that they can identify a case of ADHD." This sentence, which also acts as the paragraph's concluding sentence, shows readers that the professionals are arguing among themselves about the disease, so we should be suspicious of any diagnosis of it. Notice also how this last sentence provides a transition into Mary's discussion about the scarcity of reliable tests for ADHD.

To better understand how Mary's paragraph works as a combination of her ideas and her sources, look at the following breakdown of her paragraph:

(1) **Mary's** topic sentence

(2) **Mary's** explanation of her topic sentence, extending the idea of norms

(3) **Quotation** from Source A, *National Center for Learning Disabilities Web site*, which provides information about ADD

(4) **Mary's** statement about Source A, elaborating on the issue

(5) **Quotation** from Source B, L. Alan Sroufe, who shows us we really don't know much about ADD

(6) **Paraphrase/quotation** from Source C, Marsha Rappley, who explains the controversy surrounding ADD

(7) **Mary's** statement that pulls sources together and emphasizes the problem with definitions of ADHD

This skeleton outline of Mary's paragraph should help you see how she balances her opinions/observations and her sources so they work as one unit that supports her main argument. If you get stuck while writing your own paragraphs, referring back to this outline might help you see where to add information.

Before you get to this stage, however, you must think about what information you want to use from your sources and how you might present that information. Once you have a tentative thesis statement, you can start working directly with your evidence.

DIRECT QUOTATION, PARAPHRASE, AND SUMMARY

Now that you see how to incorporate sources into your argument, you need to decide whether you will quote, paraphrase, or summarize them. This section explains these three options to you. We will begin with an original source and show you how to take and acknowledge material from this source in different ways. The following quotation is from "Does Thinking Fast Mean You're Thinking Smarter?" by Maria Konnikova. It was published on the *Smithsonian Magazine's* Web site, Smithsonian.com, in April 2014. There are 9 paragraphs in this essay; the following excerpt is paragraph 7. (The complete essay appears in Chapter 16 of this text.)

Original Source

As a society, we certainly equate speed with smarts. Think fast. Are you quick-witted? A quick study? A whiz kid? Even Merriam-Webster bluntly informs us that slowness is "the quality of lacking intelligence or quickness of mind." But we also recognize something counterintuitive about accepting full-stop that people who react faster are smarter. That's why, even though athletic training improves reaction time, we wouldn't scout for the next Einstein at a basketball game. Intelligence probably has a lot to do with making fast connections, but it surely has just as much to do with making the right connections.

Direct Quotation

If you use a direct quotation from another source, you must put the exact material you want to use in quotation marks:

Maria Konnikova, in her essay "Does Thinking Fast Mean You're Thinking Smarter?," offers her view on intelligence: "Intelligence probably has a lot to do with making fast connections, but it surely has just as much to do with making the right connections" (par. 7).

Direct Quotation with Some Words Omitted

If you want to leave something out of the quotation, use three dots (with spaces before and after each dot). Omitting words like this is known as *ellipsis*.

> Maria Konnikova, in her essay "Does Thinking Fast Mean You're Thinking Smarter?," reveals her thoughts on intelligence: "As a society, we certainly equate speed with smarts, . . . but it surely has just as much to do with making the right connections" (par. 7).

Paraphrase

When you paraphrase, you are restating the main ideas of a quotation **in your own words.** *Paraphrase* literally means "similar phrasing," so it is usually about the same length as the original. Paraphrasing is one of the most difficult skills to master in college, but one trick you can use is to read the material, put it aside, and write a sentence or two from memory. Then compare what you wrote with the original to make sure they are similar but not exactly the same. If you look at the source while you are trying to paraphrase it, you might inadvertently take a word or phrase from the original, which would make, you guilty of plagiarism.

Even though this information is in your own words, you still need to let your readers know where you found it. A paraphrase of our original source might look like this:

> Maria Konnikova, in her essay "Does Thinking Fast Mean You're Thinking Smarter?," explains that although our society tends to believe that people who are able to think fast are more intelligent than those who process information more slowly, intelligence isn't just about quick thinking. The ability to make smart connections is just as important as fast thinking when it comes to a person's level of intelligence (par. 7).

Summary

To summarize, state the author's main idea in your own words. A summary is much briefer than the original or a paraphrase. As with a paraphrase, you need to furnish the details of your original source. Here is a summary of our original source:

> Maria Konnikova, in her essay "Does Thinking Fast Mean You're Thinking Smarter?," contends that being able to make connections is just as important as being able to think fast when it comes to a person's level of intelligence (par. 7).

TAKING NOTES ON SOURCES

As you consider using your sources as direct quotations, paraphrases, and summaries, you will need to keep careful track of them. For the list of sources at the end of your paper, you should provide your reader with several items of information for each source you use. The best time to start keeping track of this information is when you are taking notes.

When you take notes, notecards are an excellent tool because you can move them around as your paper takes shape. Put only one idea on a notecard. Taking notes this way will save you a lot of time in the future because you won't be scrambling around looking for the information on the source you just quoted. Taking notes electronically is another option, either on a computer or with apps of flashcards or notecards. Whatever your choice, if you cannot find the original source for information you used in your paper and therefore cannot tell your reader where you found the quotation, then you cannot use the material.

As you read your sources, you should decide whether you might want to directly quote, paraphrase, or summarize the material. A general rule to follow is that you never want to have more than 10 percent of your source material appear in your paper as direct quotes, which means 90 percent of the information from sources you use in your essay should be paraphrased or summarized. A good method for determining whether or not you should use a direct quotation is to ask yourself if the phrasing is the best possible way to relay the information. If you can't communicate the original any better than the original, then you should use a direct quotation. In most cases, however, try to put your research into your own words. Only occasionally should you use the author's exact words in your paper. These guidelines are especially important to keep in mind as you are reading and taking notes on your sources.

To avoid plagiarism when taking notes and writing your paper, record all the information you will need later to cite your sources.

For a book:

- Book title
- Author or authors
- Editor or editors (if applicable)
- City where published
- Publisher
- Year of publication
- Medium of publication
- Access date

For an article:

- Article title
- Author or authors
- Title of the magazine or journal
- Date of issue (for a magazine)
- Year and volume number (for a journal)
- Pages on which the article appeared
- Medium of publication
- Access date

If you put all this information on one card for each of your sources, you can record just the author's last name on all other cards from that same source. If you are using more than one book or article by the same author, add the source's date to the card. For both books and articles, you should also record the page where you found the information. That way you can easily find it again or cite it in your paper.

The format in which this information should be presented will depend on the field of study. A good handbook will help you with the formats of the various documentation styles, which include Modern Language Association (MLA) style for the humanities, American Psychological Association (APA) style for the social sciences, and Chicago Manual style (CMS) for mathematics and science. Make sure you understand which documentation style your instructor wants you to use, because they are all slightly different from each other.

In this book, we are using the Modern Language Association style of citation. The Monnikova essay in the MLA format would look like this:

> Konnikova, Maria. "Does Thinking Faster Mean You're Thinking Smarter?" Smithsonian.com, April 2014. Web. 4 Dec. 2015.

PRACTICE 2 Quote from, paraphrase, and summarize the following original sources. Document the source correctly in each case by looking up the MLA documentation style in a handbook.

1. The following paragraph is from "Wrong Call for Regulating Sexting" by Warner Todd Huston and was originally published in *Publius' Forum: The Podcast* on March 25, 2009, accessed on May 30, 2015. The URL is http://www.publiusforum.com/2009/03/25/teen-suicide-brings-wrong-call-for-regulation/. (The complete essay appears in Chapter 17 of this text.)

> Unfortunately, just the wrong sort of lesson is being promulgated by teachers, lawmakers, and these parents with this incident. "It is a form of bullying, and that is something we cannot tolerate. The difficulty is stopping it.... That's why we stress with our

kids that the moment you push 'send,' the damage is done," said Sycamore Superintendent Adrienne James. All the onus put on "the bullying" and none put on the person that sent the nude photo to begin with is simply not a complete lesson. The better lesson is to focus equally on both the sender and the bullies, not just the bullies. The wrap up is typical of the wrong-headed emphasis we too often place on the situations that confront us in our modern society.

Quotation: _____

_____

_____

Paraphrase: _____

_____

_____

Summary: _____

_____

_____

Works Cited Citation: _____

_____

_____

2. The following paragraph is from "Childhood" by Alice Walker. It originally appeared in *Dream Me Home Safely: Writers on Growing Up in America*, a collection of narrative essays edited by Susan Richards Shreve and published in 2003. The quoted paragraph appears on page 203. (The complete essay appears in Chapter 10 of this text.)

> In the morning, just before packing the car for the ride to the city, I harvested an abundance of Chardonnay grapes, greenish-silver and refreshingly sweet; a bucket of glistening eggplant; an armful of collards and chard and kale; some dark green and snake-like cucumbers, plus a small sack of figs and half a dozen late-summer peaches. Then I took my daughter out to the neat rows of potatoes, all beginning to turn brown. Using the shovel to scrape aside the dirt, I began to reveal, very slowly and carefully, the golden and purple potatoes that rested just beneath the plants. She was enchanted. It's just like…it's just like…she said. It's just like finding gold, I offered with glee. Yes! she said, her eyes wide.

Quotation: _____

_____

_____

Paraphrase: _____

_____

_____

Summary: _____

_____

_____

Works Cited Citation: _____

_____

_____

_____

3. The following paragraph is from "How to Protect Your Identity" by Brian O'Connell. It was originally published on the CreditCards.com Web site on February 10, 2009, and it was accessed June 5, 2015. The URL is http://www.creditcards.com/credit-card-news/six-ways-to-protect-ID-in-a-data-breach-1282.php. (The complete essay appears in Chapter 12 of this text.)

> **2. Act fast:** The key is to get out in front of the problem as soon as possible—before heavier damage can be done. "Oftentimes thieves will use your credit card data to commit nonfinancial identity theft crimes which become much larger problems," says Justin Yurek, president of Denver-based IDWatchdog.com. "As thieves begin to truly clone your identity, they can move from buying items in your name to committing crimes in your name, or obtaining employment benefits in your name, or obtaining medical services in your name. Unlike a thief fraudulently purchasing products in your name, there is no easy reversal for these crimes, and the consequences to the victim are much more severe."

Quotation: _____

_____

_____

Paraphrase: _____

_____

_____

Summary: _____

_____

_____

Works Cited Citation: _____

_____

_____

4. The following paragraph is from "Dating: The Soft Break-Up" by Matt Huston. It was originally published on September 2, 2014, and found on June 7, 2015, on *Psychology Today's* Web site at https://www. psychologytoday.com/articles/201410/dating-the-soft-breakup. There were 18 paragraphs in this essay; the following excerpt is paragraph 14.

> However much soft breakups blur the boundaries of romantic attachments, the new acceptance of post-breakup connection reflects a more generalized change in relationships: an increase in ambiguity at all stages of mating. Stanley points out that early in a relationship it's not uncommon for one or both individuals to wonder whether they are just hanging out or actually on a date (Huston, par. 14).

Quotation: _____

_____

_____

Paraphrase: _____

_____

_____

Summary: _____

_____

_____

Works Cited Citation: _____

_____

_____

5. The following paragraph is from the essay "What Are Friends For?" by Marion Winik. It was originally published on pages 85–89 in a book titled *Telling: Confessions, Concessions, and Other Flashes of Light*, which was published by Villard Books in New York City in 1994. The quoted paragraph appeared on page 89. (The complete essay appears in Chapter 14 of this text.)

> At the other end of the spectrum are Hero Friends. These people are better than the rest of us; that's all there is to it. Their career is something you wanted to be when you grew up—painter, forest ranger, tireless doer of good. They have beautiful homes filled with special handmade things presented to them by villagers in the remote areas they have visited in their extensive travels. Yet they are modest. They never gossip. They are always helping others, especially those who have suffered a death in the family or an illness. You would think people like this would just make you sick, but somehow they don't.

Quotation: _____

_____

_____

Paraphrase: _____

_____

_____

Summary: _____

_____

_____

Works Cited Citation: _____

_____

_____

_____

MyWritingLab™   Visit Chapter 19, "Avoiding Plagiarism," in MyWritingLab, and complete the Post-test to check your understanding of the chapter's objectives.

Finding Sources

No matter what you are studying in college, you should know how to find sources using the library through a computer. You can access an enormous amount of information that will help you generate paper topics, teach you new information, challenge your thinking, support your opinions, and make you smile. In today's electronic world, learning how to use the resources available through the library's services is a basic survival skill.

MyWritingLab	**Understanding Sources**

Finding sources for your paper can be difficult if you don't know where to look. To learn how to locate helpful sources, go to **MyWritingLab. com,** and choose **Research Process** in the **Research** module. From there, watch the video called **Animation: Finding Sources,** and return to this video throughout Part III when you have questions about finding sources.

Student Comment:
"The **Finding Sources** video explains the research process from yet another angle. It was very helpful to me personally."

CREDIBILITY OF SOURCES

When you are looking for information to use in your documented essays, you must be careful about what you choose. Your sources must be **R**elevant, **R**eliable, and **R**ecent. This "three **R**s" approach to finding sources will help you locate convincing evidence to support your arguments.

Here are some questions that will help you evaluate your sources:

The 3Rs: Relevant, Reliable, Recent

Relevant

- Does the source focus on your subject?
- Does the source deal in depth with the topic?

Reliable

- What is the origin of the source?
- Is the author an expert in the field?
- Is the author biased?
- Does the source represent all sides of an issue?
- Are the author's claims well supported?

Recent

- Is the source current enough for your subject and your purpose?

Our student writer found sources that did a thorough job of supporting her thesis statement. Information from articles in the books, journals, and magazines she cited speaks to the average citizen. Even though these are not highly technical scientific sources, the evidence in them fulfills our "3R" criteria: **R**elevant, **R**eliable, and **R**ecent.

Because anyone can put material on the Internet, you need to make sure you are not using biased or unreliable information in your academic papers. To use Web sites intelligently, follow these four guidelines.

1. **Check the end of a Web URL address.** It will most likely be either .edu, .gov, .org, or .com. The first two are reputable resources, but you must be careful of .org ("organization") and .com ("commercial") sources because anyone can host these sites. For example, www.whitehouse.com is not a site for the President's home, as you might suspect. On the other hand, .edu, which stands for "education," and .gov, which refers to "government," are generally reliable. Any site, however, has the potential for bias, and you should consider the material carefully.

2. **Pay attention to the argument a site makes.** Who is the author, and what is his or her purpose for entering information on the site? If you log on to a Martin Luther King Jr. site and are inundated with racial slurs, chances are you've found a site that was created by a faction of the Ku Klux Klan or a similar group. So if the information does not fit the site or if the author has an obvious agenda, avoid the site.

3. **Make sure the site is providing facts and not just opinions.** For academic purposes, facts and statistics are generally more useful than opinions. If you are looking for a site that deals with gun control, you'll want to avoid a site that tells you story after story about innocent children dying or praises American liberty but fails to give you any specific information. Instead, you'll want to find a site that gives you examples that can be verified and supported with statistics.

4. **Check that the site furnishes information about the other side of the argument.** If a site provides you with details only about its own

viewpoint, you should wonder why it is omitting information. If you find a site on prayer in school and only see opinions about the reasons prayer should not be allowed in schools, you should be curious about why the site doesn't present the argument on the other side. Will facts about the other side make you change your mind? The best sites provide both sides of an argument so the source can, in turn, show why one side is more valid than the other. If you find a Web site that does not offer balanced information, consider it biased, and avoid it.

These four guidelines will help you determine whether or not you should use information you find on the Web. But if you want to be certain the information you are using will be acceptable to your instructor, you should rely principally on academic sources, such as published literature in the library databases, for the bulk of your research. There are, however, a number of "open source" academic Web sites where you can access articles that have been *peer reviewed* or *refereed*. This means the authors send their essays to the editors of a publication, who send the essays anonymously to readers for review. If the readers accept the pieces for publication, they consider the essays to be well researched and worth reading. If you can, you should use only these sources. Please note, however, that you still need to evaluate your peer-reviewed sources to make sure their arguments are sound.

CONSULTING ACADEMIC DATABASES

The best places to begin searching for sources are academic databases. You should have access to these services from home through your library's home page or from a computer in your library. You may need a reference librarian to help you find these for the first time.

Academic Databases

Academic databases can direct you to an incredible number of books and journals on a wide range of subjects. The following are some examples of academic databases and their primary uses.

Academic Database	Primary Use
Biological and Agriculture Index	Agriculture and Biology
Business Full Text	Business and Finance
Education Full Text	Education
General Science Full Text	Astronomy, Biology, Botany, Chemistry, Geology, Genetics, Mathematics, Medicine, Nutrition, Oceanography, Physics, Physiology, and Zoology

Humanities Full Text	Archeaology, Art, Communications, Dance, Film, Folklore, Gender Studies, History, Journalism, Linguistics, Music, Performing Arts, Philosophy, Religion, and Theology
OmniFile Full Text Mega	Multidisciplinary database that includes indexing, abstracts, and full text from the Wilson Education, General Science, Humanities, Readers' Guide, Social Sciences, and Business databases. It also includes the full-text articles from the Wilson Applied Science and Technology, Art, Biological and Agricultural, Legal, and Library Literature and Information Science databases.
Readers' Guide Full Text	Indexing and abstracting of the most popular general-interest periodicals published in the United States and Canada
Social Sciences Full Text	Addiction Studies, Anthropology, Community Health, Criminal Justice, Economics, Environmental Studies, Ethics, Family Studies, Gender Studies, Geography, Gerontology, International Relations, Law, Minority Studies, Public Administration, Political Science, Psychiatry, Psychology, Public Welfare, Social Work, Sociology, and Urban Studies
ABI Inform	News and business
Dow Jones	News and business
EBSCOhost	Many subject areas
Expanded Academic ASAP	General information in several disciplines
HRAF	Ethnographies
Lexis-Nexis	News, business, and law
WilsonWeb	Popular magazines and newspapers, Social Science, Humanities, Business, General Science, and Education journals
Academic Press's IDEAL	Articles published by academic publishers

American Chemical Society's Web Editions	American Chemical Society's 26 scientific journals
American Mathematical Journals	American Mathematical Society's proceedings and transactions
JSTOR	Back issues of core journals in the Humanities, Social Sciences, and Sciences
Project Muse	Humanities, Social Sciences, and Math

Using Boolean Connectors or Operators

The Boolean connectors or operators used in a search are *AND, OR,* and *NOT*. By using these words, you can limit the search and find information directly related to your topic. Most databases no longer require that you type in the Boolean operators manually. They provide multiple search boxes, normally separated by a default *AND*. You would type each term (for example, *children* in the first box and *attention deficit disorder* in the second). Then, you should separate your terms with the Boolean connector *AND* (for example, *children AND attention deficit disorder*). This asks the computer to find all the records in which these two terms are combined. If you put *OR* between the keywords (*children OR attention deficit disorder*), you are separating the words and asking the computer to find articles and books for either one of them. If you add *NOT* (*children NOT adults*), you limit the search by excluding certain terms from the search.

Accessing Sources

Once you type your topic into the search function of a database, the computer will display the number of articles and books it has found in a "results list." Following are some examples of articles found on the topic of *children AND attention deficit disorder* in online databases.

From OMNI Full Text Mega

Entry 3 of 5477

Title: Adaptive Multimodal Treatment for Children with Attention-Deficit/Hyperactivity Disorder: An 18 Month Follow-Up

Journal Name: *Child Psychology and Human Development*

Source: *Child Psychology and Human Development*, v. 46, no. 1 (Feb 2015), p. 44–56

Publication Year: 2015

ISSN: 0009398X

Language of Document: English

Date Entered:

Database: OmniFile Full Text Mega

Accession Number: 100399239

Persistent URL: http://web.a.ebscohost.com/ehost/detail/
detail?vid=14&sid=db8115e2-f477-46da-a6e7-be4f5acc75d5%40se
ssionmgr4003&hid=4212&bdata=JnNpdGU9ZWhvc3QtbGl2ZQ
%3d%3d#db=ofm&AN=100399239

From EBSCOhost

Entry 18 of 13,930

Title: Attention deficit/hyperactivity disorder and medication with stimulants in young children: A DTI study

Authors: de Luis-Garcia, Rodrigo

Cabus-Pinol, Gemma

Imaz-Roncero, Carlos

Argibay-Quinones, Daniel

Barrio-Arranz, Gonzalo

Aja-Fernandez, Santiago

Alberola-Lopez, Carlos

Source: *Progress in Neuro-Psychopharmacology & Biological Psychiatry*, March 2015, Vol. 57 (March 2015), pp. 176-184

Document Type: Article

Subject Terms:

* ATTENTION-deficit hyperactivity disorder
* METHYLPHENIDATE
* ROBUST control
* WHITE matter (Nerve tissue)
* PYRAMIDAL tract
* CHILDREN– Health

Geographic Terms:

Abstract:

The relationship between **attention deficit/hyperactivity disorder** (ADHD) and white matter connectivity has not been well established yet, specially for **children** under 10 years of age. In addition, the effects of treatment on brain structure have not been sufficiently explored from a Diffusion Tensor Imaging (**DTI**) perspective. In this **study**, the influence of treatment with methylphenidate in the white matter of **children** with ADHD was investigated using two different and complementary **DTI** analysis methods: Tract-Based Spatial Statistics (TBSS) and a robust tractography selection method. No significant differences were found in Fractional Anisotropy (FA) between medicated, drug-naïve patients and healthy controls, but a reduced Mean Diffusivity (MD) was found in ADHD patients under treatment with respect to both healthy controls and drug-naïve ADHD patients. Also, correlations were found between MD increases and performance indicators of ADHD. These findings may help elucidate the nature of white matter alterations in ADHD, their relationship with symptoms and the effects of treatment with psychostimulants. [ABSTRACT FROM AUTHOR]

Author Affiliations:

[1]Laboratorio de Procesado de Imagen (LPI), Universidad de Valladolid, Spain

[2]Hospital Clínico Universitario, Valladolid, Spain

[3]ISSN: 0278-5846

[4]Accession Number: 99898448

[5]Persistent link to this record (Permalink):

http://web.b.ebscohost.com/ehost/detail/
detail?vid=3&sid=36353138-51d2-41dc-913d-85aa2ff6ac3c#40sessi
onmgr111&hid=115&bdata=JnNpdGU9ZWhvc3QtbGl2ZQ%3d
%3d%db=a9h&AN=99898448

Database: Academic Search Premier

From JSTOR

Response Inhibition in Preschoolers at Familial Risk for Attention Deficit Hyperactivity Disorder: A Behavioral and Electrophysiological Stop-Signal Study

Author(s): Andrea Berger, Uri Alyagon, Hadas Hadaya, Naama Atzaba-Poria, and Judith G. Auerbach

Source: Child Development, Vol. 84, No. 5 (Sept./Oct. 2013), p. 1616-1632

Published by: Wiley on behalf of the Society for Research in Child Development

Stable URL: http://www.jstor.org/stable/10.2307/24029472?Search
=yes&resultItemClick=true&&searchUri=%2Faction%2FdoAdv
ancedResults%3Ff6%3Dall%26amp%3Bgroup%3Dnone%26amp
%3Bc3%3DAND%26amp%3Bq4%3D%26amp%3Bwc%3Don%
26amp%3Bq1%3D%26amp%3Bq6%3D%26amp%3Bq5%3D%2
6amp%3Bc5%3DAND%26amp%3Bed%3D%26amp%3Bf3%3D
all%26amp%3Bf1%3Dall%26amp%3Bf0%3Dall%26amp%3Bisb
n%3D%26amp%3Bf5%3Dall%26amp%3Bsd%3D%26amp%3Bc
6%3DAND%26amp%3Bacc%3Don%26amp%3Bq3%3D%26am
p%3Bc4%3DAND%26amp%3Bq2%3D%26amp%3Bla%3D%2
6amp%3Bpt%3D%26amp%3Bc2%3DAND%26amp%3Bf2%3D
all%26amp%3Bf4%3Dall%26amp%3Bq0%3Dchildren%2BAND
%2Battention%2Bdeficit%2Bdisorder%26amp%3Bc1%3DAND
%26amp%3Bso%3Drel%26amp%3Bsi%3D76

Notice that these examples contain all of the information you need for citing those works in the text and at the end of your paper. So make sure you keep lists like this when you print them so that you can cite your sources correctly.

PRACTICE 1 For each of the following topics, find a book and two articles from different academic databases. Record the title, author, and database where you found each one.

Example: Topic: children *and* attention deficit disorder

Academic Database: Omni Full Text Mega

Title: "Adaptive Multimodal Treatment for Children with Attention-Deficit/Hyperactivity Disorder: An 18 Month Follow-Up"

Author: Döpfner M., Ise E., Wolff Metternich-Kaizman, T., Schürmann, S., Rademacher C., Breuer D.

Academic Database: Academic Search Premier in EBSCOhost

Title: "Attention deficit/hyperactivity disorder and medication with stimulants in young children: A DTI study"

Author: de Luis-García, R., Cabús-Piñol, G., Imaz-Roncero, C., Argibay-Quiñones, D., Barrio-Arranz, G., Aja-Fernández, S., Alberola-López, C.

Academic Database: JSTOR

Title: "Response Inhibition in Preschoolers at Familial Risk for Attention Deficit Hyperactivity Disorder: A Behavioral and Electrophysiological Stop-Signal Study"

Author: Berger, A., Alyagon, U., Hadaya, H., Atzaba-Poria, N., Auerbach, J.G.

1. Topic: Drug testing in college sports

Book ⎰ Academic Database: _____

Title: _____

Author: _____

Article 1 ⎰ Academic Database: _____

Title: _____

Author: _____

Article 2 ⎰ Academic Database: _____

Title: _____

Author: _____

2. Topic: Affirmative action and the workforce

Book ⎰ Academic Database: _____

Title: _____

Author: _____

Article 1 ⎰ Academic Database: _____

Title: _____

Author: _____

Article 2 ⎰ Academic Database: _____

Title: _____

Author: _____

3. Topic: Prison pampering

Book ⎰ Academic Database: _____

Title: _____

Author: _____

Article 1 ⎰ Academic Database: _____

Title: _____

Author: _____

Article 2 ⎰ Academic Database: _____

Title: _____

Author: _____

4. Topic: Women in combat

Book

  Academic Database: _____

  Title: _____

  Author: _____

Article 1

  Academic Database: _____

  Title: _____

  Author: _____

Article 2

  Academic Database: _____

  Title: _____

  Author: _____

5. Topic: Using animals for testing

Book

  Academic Database: _____

  Title: _____

  Author: _____

Article 1

  Academic Database: _____

  Title: _____

  Author: _____

Article 2

  Academic Database: _____

  Title: _____

  Author: _____

SEARCHING FOR WEB SITES

To find a Web site related to your topic, go to the Internet through whichever browser you have (for example, Firefox or Internet Explorer). When you access a search engine such as Google or Yahoo, it will search millions of Web sites. Using the advanced search options will allow you to narrow or expand your search. Here are some variations our student writer explored while conducting her research:

Topic	Other Possible Topics
Children and Attention Deficit Disorder	ADD and kids
	Behavioral disorders in kids
	ADD and ADHD in children

Symptoms of ADD

Adolescents and ADD

Treatments of behavioral disorders

When the search is complete, your search engine will list the different Web sites in the order of most to least probable relevance to you. It will also briefly describe each Web site. After the description, you will most often find the Web site address. The following are three "hits" or Web sites from www.google.com for the topic *children* and *attention deficit disorder*.

1. *CHADD—Children and Adults with Attention Deficit Disorders*

   Children and Adults with Attention-Deficit/Hyperactivity Disorder (CHADD) is a national nonprofit, tax-exempt organization providing education, advocacy, and support for individuals with AD/HD.

   www.chadd.org

2. *ADD/ADHD in Children: Helpguide.org*

   This Web site describes signs and symptoms of attention deficit disorder with and without hyperactivity and provides resources for parents of children with ADD/ADHD.

   www.helpguide.org

3. *NIMH National Institute of Mental Health—Attention Deficit Hyperactivity Disorder*

   This government-sponsored Web site provides facts about attention deficit/hyperactivity disorder among other mental illnesses.

   www.nimh.nih.gov/health/publications/attention-deficit-hyperactivity-disorder/index.shtml?rf=71264

PRACTICE 2 For each of the following topics, find a different Web page through a different search engine, and list the Web page title, the explanation, and the Web address.

Example: Topic: Children and attention deficit disorder

   Search engine: google.com

   Web page title: "CHADD—Children and Adults with Attention Deficit Disorders"

   Explanation: Children and Adults with Attention-Deficit/Hyperactivity Disorder (CHADD) is a national nonprofit, tax-exempt organization providing education, advocacy, and support for individuals with AD/HD.

   Web address: www.chadd.org

1. Topic: Bilingual education in California

   Search engine: _____

   Web page title: _____

   Explanation: _____

   _____

   _____

   Web address: _____

2. Topic: Benefits of privatizing the U.S. space program

   Search engine: _____

   Web page title: _____

   Explanation: _____

   _____

   _____

   Web address: _____

3. Topic: Legalizing marijuana

   Search engine: _____

   Web page title: _____

   Explanation: _____

   _____

   _____

   Web address: _____

4. Topic: Homeopathic medicine

   Search engine: _____

   Web page title: _____

   Explanation: _____

   _____

   _____

   Web address: _____

5. Topic: Women's soccer

   Search engine: _____

Web page title: _____

Explanation: _____

_____

_____

Web address: _____

USING THE LIBRARY

Once you have compiled a list of books and journals from academic databases or from Web sites, you should use your library to check out books or copy journal articles that are not available online. Usually, academic publishers make their current publications available online, but older articles may need to be located in the library's periodical collection and copied.

First, access your library's online catalog to see if your library has the book. If you have difficulty locating a book using the catalog, ask a librarian for help. You might also inquire whether this information is available online. You can search for authors and subjects through your library's catalog in much the same way you would search online databases. But because you have already done the preliminary research, all you have to do is search for the books and journals you need. Find the "title" section of the catalog, and type in the title of the book or journal you need.

If you are searching for a chapter or an essay contained in a book, be sure to type in the main book title. For example, if you searched for "I Just Wanna Be Average" (by Mike Rose), your library computer will tell you that the library does not carry it. You must type in the title of the book it came from, *Lives on the Boundary*, to find the essay. Once you have located the titles of your books or journals in the library's catalog, you should write down the call numbers so you can find the sources in your library. Then it's just a matter of finding the book itself in the stacks. If you need help, don't hesitate to ask a librarian.

PRACTICE 3 Find five books from research you have done or are currently doing. Then, using the "title" portion of your library's catalog, locate the call numbers.

Example: Title: *Youth Culture: Identity in a Postmodern World*

Call number: HV 1431 Y684 1998

1. Title: _____

   Call number: _____

2. Title: _____

    Call number: _____

3. Title: _____

    Call number: _____

4. Title: _____

    Call number: _____

5. Title: _____

    Call number: _____

MyWritingLab™ Visit Chapter 20, "Finding Sources," in MyWritingLab, and complete the Post-test to check your understanding of the chapter's objectives.

Writing a Research Paper

A research paper is really just an essay with supporting material that comes from other sources. This type of writing assignment has all the elements of a typical essay. The following chart compares a standard essay and a research paper.

Standard Essay		Research Paper
Introduction with thesis statement	⟷	Introduction with thesis statement
Body paragraphs with facts and personal experience to support thesis statement	⟷	Body paragraphs with documented evidence to support thesis statement
Concluding paragraph	⟷	Concluding paragraph

Keep this outline in mind as you read how to construct a good research paper in this chapter.

MyWritingLab	**Understanding How to Write Research Papers**

Before you go any further, go to **MyWritingLab.com,** and choose **Research Process** in the **Research** module. From there, watch the video called **Animation: How to Write a Research Paper.** Try to get a sense of the entire process before we move ahead with detailed instruction.

Student Comment:
"The video on **How to Write a Research Paper** gave me the concrete details I needed to learn how to develop a research paper."

Studying some clear guidelines is the best way to continue the process of learning how to write good term papers.

CHOOSE A SUBJECT

1. **Choose a subject.** You might be choosing a subject from infinite possibilities or working with an assigned topic. Doing some general reading online or in the library is often necessary to get you started. As you consider various topics, you should ask one very important question before you begin planning your essay: Will you be able to find enough information to back up your thesis statement? To make sure you are able to find enough material to use as good evidence in the body paragraphs of your essay, you must take some time to choose a subject, narrow that subject, and then write a working thesis statement. You will prove this thesis statement with the information you find when you search for sources on your topic. If you were writing a research paper on pursuing a degree in college, for example, your initial prewriting for the thesis statement might look like this:

General Subject:	College and university degrees
More Specific:	Bachelor's degree
More Specific:	Bachelor's degree in English

This limited subject would be perfect for a research paper. You could search for books, catalogs, and periodicals on what it takes to earn a bachelor's degree in English from various colleges and universities. While you are looking, you could be thinking about how to narrow your subject even further.

In the Student Paper: Mary Minor (in Chapter 18) might have started with a general topic like "childhood disorders," limited it to "childhood behavioral disorders," and finally settled on "ADD and ADHD as childhood behavioral disorders."

PRACTICE 1 Choose a topic from the list on page 426. Why did you choose this topic?

PRACTICE 2 Limit this topic so that you can write a paper about five pages long.

WRITE A THESIS STATEMENT

2. **Write a good, clear thesis statement about your subject.** Just as a thesis statement is the controlling idea of an essay, a thesis statement also provides the controlling idea for your argument in a research paper. This statement will guide the writing of your entire paper. Your assignments throughout college will usually be broad topics. To compose a good

research paper, you need to narrow a broad topic to an idea you can prove within a limited number of pages. A working thesis statement will provide the direction for your essay, and the evidence you collect in your research is what proves the thesis statement.

A good way to start your first draft is to read some general sources on your topic. This reading will help you discover the range of your subject and will guide you toward a thesis. Before you start writing the first draft of your paper, make sure you write a sentence that clearly states your topic and your position on that topic. This is your working thesis statement and will be the controlling idea for your entire paper. Your thesis may change several times before your essay is finished, but making this statement and taking a position is a necessary first step. It will help you move from the broad subject of your assignment to your own perspective on the topic, which will focus your essay and save you time in your search for good resources to back up your thesis statement.

Just as in a standard essay, the thesis statement in your research paper is a contract between you and your readers. The thesis statement tells your readers what the main idea of your essay will be and sets guidelines for the paragraphs in the body of your essay. If you don't deliver what your thesis statement promises, your readers will be disappointed. The thesis statement is usually the last sentence in the introduction. It outlines your purpose and position on the essay's general topic and gives your readers an idea of the type of resources you will use to develop your essay.

In the Student Paper: Mary Minor's controlling idea or thesis statement appears at the end of her first paragraph:

> Children are often misdiagnosed with ADD or ADHD and suffer unnecessarily when medicated for a disorder they may not have.

Her entire essay is about children who are too readily diagnosed with ADD or ADHD simply because they do not fall into society's "norm" for children's behavior. The paragraphs following this thesis statement supply evidence that proves her claim is true.

PRACTICE 3 List your thoughts and opinions on the topic you chose in Practice 1.

PRACTICE 4 Put your topic and your position on that topic into a working thesis statement.

FIND SOURCES TO SUPPORT YOUR THESIS

3. **Find sources that are relevant, reliable, and recent to support your thesis statement.** The thesis statement of a research paper is really only the beginning of the process. To convince your readers that what you

say in your essay is worth reading, you must support your thesis statement with evidence. The evidence of a term paper lies in the sources you use to back up your thesis statement. The sources must be relevant, reliable, and recent. This "three Rs" approach to supporting evidence in a research paper will help you write a solid essay with convincing evidence.

In the Student Paper: Mary Minor's thesis statement suggests that young children are being too readily diagnosed with ADD and ADHD. To convince her readers that her thesis is correct, she uses a book, scientific journals, an encyclopedia, online journal articles, and general-circulation magazines as sources of evidence. Here is a breakdown of how she uses her sources.

- **Books:** *The Diagnostic and Statistical Manual of Medical Disorders* and *ADHD Does Not Exist: The Truth About Attention Deficit and Hyperactivity Disorder*

  These sources provide well-researched information from an expert's point of view. Mary uses these sources strategically throughout her paper to help define the scope of her study.

- **Scientific journals:** *Journal of American College Health*, *The New England Journal of Medicine*

  These sources supply the reader with specific evidence put forth by experts in the field of ADD and ADHD research and diagnosis. Mary uses this information to prove that her thesis statement is true.

- **Encyclopedia:** *World Book Encyclopedia*

  Mary uses this source to provide the reader with an understandable definition of the Hippocratic Oath. This definition plays an important role in Mary's stance on her topic. However, you should not rely too heavily on encyclopedias and dictionaries in academic papers.

- **Web sites:** *Centers for Disease Control and Prevention*, *National Center for Learning Disabilities*

  The information on this site confirms the confusion experts face when diagnosing ADD and ADHD cases.

- **General-circulation publications (print and online)**: *PLOS ONE*, *The Atlanta Journal-Constitution*, *The New York Times*

  These sources supply information readily available at a newsstand yet highly informative and applicable to Mary's topic. Information from articles in these magazines speaks to the average citizen. Even though these are not scientific journals, the evidence in them is extremely useful because it was intended to make specialized information understandable to the general reader.

Mary Minor uses sources in her essay that do a thorough job of supporting her thesis statement. Information from articles in these books, journals, and magazines speaks to the average citizen. Even though they are not highly technical scientific sources, the evidence in them is relevant, reliable, and recent.

PRACTICE 5 Review Chapter 20 to make sure you understand the options available to you for finding sources to use in your essay.

PRACTICE 6 Find five sources that provide information about the limited topic you chose. Make sure they are relevant, reliable, and recent.

TAKE NOTES ON YOUR SOURCES

4. **Take notes to avoid plagiarism.** Now is the time to read your sources and take careful notes—putting the ideas in your own words or putting the writer's words in quotation marks if you record the exact words. You should also note the page numbers of all information you record. If you don't take notes carefully, you will never be able to trace information you want to use in your paper to its original source. Also, trying to put someone's ideas into your own words at the note-taking stage is a very good skill that will help you as you write.

Taking notes on notecards (electronic or paper) allows you to move your cards around and put ideas into different paragraphs. When you rearrange cards, you can work with them until you think the order will support what you are trying to prove. This notecard method actually saves time in the long run.

In the Student Paper: Mary Minor had to read and take notes on all the sources she found. She first made a set of bibliography cards with a notecard for every source she found. For the books, she put book title, author or editor, city where published, publisher, year of publication, medium of publication, and the access date on each card; for the articles, she recorded article title, author, title of the magazine or journal, date of issue or volume and issue numbers, page numbers, medium of publication, and the access date on each card. Then she began to read her sources. She wrote only one idea or quotation on a notecard, and she remembered to record on each notecard the author's name and the page number on which she found the information. She also made sure, as she took notes, to restate information in her own words or else put the author's exact words in quotation marks.

PRACTICE 7 Review Chapter 19 to make sure you understand what plagiarism is and how to avoid it.

PRACTICE 8 Read and take notes on your sources using notecards. Make sure each of your cards has a source and page number on it.

MAKE A WORKING OUTLINE

5. **Make a working outline of your ideas.** To do this, you just need to start rearranging the notecards you have made. Start by putting all your notecards on the computer screen or on your desk into small stacks of related ideas. Which ideas might work well together? Which should you put in the introduction? Which do you want to save for your conclusion? When you get all your notecards in stacks, label each group of cards according to its topic. These labels will then become the topics of your paper. You are now ready to start a working outline.

A good way to begin an outline is to write your tentative thesis statement at the top of a page and then list under that thesis the topics you have created. These topics should be arranged in some logical order that will help you prove your main point. Each topic should also directly support your thesis statement. Leave room in your outline to add subtopics and details throughout the paper. This outline then becomes a guide for your writing. It will change and grow with every paragraph that you add to your paper.

In the Student Paper: Mary started developing her paper by putting related notecards into stacks. Next, she labeled her stacks of notecards and then organized these topics in different ways until they started making sense to her. Her list of topics, with her thesis statement at the top, became her working outline. She eventually turned these topics into topic sentences for her body paragraphs. The stack of cards for each topic became the content of her body paragraphs.

PRACTICE 9 Divide your notecards (on paper or on the computer) into topics that logically support your thesis statement. Then label each stack of cards.

PRACTICE 10 Start a working outline of your paper by listing your thesis statement and your supporting topics.

WRITE YOUR INTRODUCTION

6. **Construct an introduction that leads to your thesis statement.** The introduction to a research paper is your chance to make a great first impression. Just like a firm handshake and a warm smile at a job interview, an essay's introduction should capture your readers' interest, set the tone for your essay, and state your specific purpose. Introductions often function like funnels. They typically begin with general information and then narrow the focus to your position on a particular issue. Regardless of your method, your introduction should "hook" your readers by grabbing their attention and letting them know what you are going to try to prove in your essay.

To lead up to the thesis statement, your introductory paragraph should stimulate your readers' interest. Some effective ways of capturing your audience's attention and giving necessary background information are (1) to use a quotation; (2) to tell a story that relates to your topic; (3) to provide a revealing fact, statistic, or definition; (4) to offer an interesting comparison; or (5) to ask an intriguing question. Be sure your introduction gives readers all the information they will need to follow your logic through the rest of your paper.

In the Student Paper: Mary's introduction starts out with a hypothetical situation that parents face as their children may or may not develop "normally." The paragraph then discusses parents' confusion with their children's behavior and introduces ADD and ADHD. The last sentence of the first paragraph contains Mary's thesis statement and ends the introduction.

PRACTICE 11 Make a rough outline of your ideas for a possible introduction to your research paper.

PRACTICE 12 Write a rough draft of your introduction, ending with your thesis statement.

DEVELOP YOUR SUPPORTING PARAGRAPHS

7. **Develop as many supporting paragraphs, or body paragraphs, as you think are necessary to explain your thesis statement.** Following the introductory paragraph, a research paper includes several body paragraphs that support and explain the essay's thesis statement. Each body paragraph covers a topic directly related to the thesis statement.

Supporting paragraphs, or body paragraphs, usually include a topic sentence—which is a general statement of the paragraph's contents—and examples or details that support the topic sentence. (See Chapter 6 for methods to use when you develop and organize paragraphs.)

To write your supporting paragraphs, you should first organize your notecards within each of your stacks. Next, add these details to your working outline. Then write your supporting paragraphs by following your working outline and your notecards. Make adjustments in your outline as you write so you can keep track of your ideas and make sure you are developing them in a logical fashion. The body of the paper and your outline should change and develop together with each sentence you write.

After you write your body paragraphs, look at your thesis statement again to make sure it introduces what you say in the rest of your paper. Your thesis statement should refer to all of your topics, even if only indirectly, in the order you discuss them. It should also prepare your readers for the conclusions you are going to draw.

In the Student Paper: Mary's paper contains eight body paragraphs, each making a separate point that is directly related to her thesis:

Paragraph	Point
2	ADD and ADHD are defined as "a short attention span" and are the most commonly diagnosed childhood diseases.
3	Diagnosing children who do not fit a "norm" is ludicrous, especially since there is no accurate definition or diagnosis of ADD or ADHD.
4	ADHD is not actually a disease itself; it is a set of symptoms.
5	There are as many theories about the causes of ADD and ADHD as there are experts, so we are only treating the symptoms of these disorders.
6	Teachers, parents, and students get caught up in the diagnosis.
7	Over time, patients often abuse Ritalin and Adderall.
8	Drugs for ADD and ADHD should be a last resort.

Like the foundation of a solid building, these paragraphs provide support for the position Mary takes in her thesis statement. The stronger the supporting paragraphs are, the stronger the paper will be.

In addition to strong topic sentences, you should also use concluding sentences in your body paragraphs to help reinforce your thesis statement or build a transition to the next paragraph. Concluding sentences bring a paragraph to a close just like a conclusion brings an essay to a close, and well-crafted concluding sentences also focus your readers on the highlights of your argument.

PRACTICE 13 Organize the notecards within each of your stacks so they make sense. Add these details to your working outline.

PRACTICE 14 Write a rough draft of your body paragraphs. Remember that you will be revising and editing this draft a little later, so just concentrate on getting your ideas written up in a logical way. Revise your thesis statement, if necessary, to introduce all your body paragraphs.

USE YOUR SOURCES AS EVIDENCE

8. **Use your sources as evidence for your argument.** Although your argument will evolve as you read your sources, you should decide on your general position before you begin to take notes. Be sure to find appropriate sources that help you develop your argument. The best way to do this is to tell your readers the significance of the direct quotations, paraphrases, or summaries that you use.

In the Student Paper: Look, for example, at one of the paragraphs in Mary's paper:

> Considering the dubious nature of the disease, there are as many speculations about the cause of ADD and ADHD as there are experts. Unfortunately, the ones lost in the confusion are the children, and this is due to the fact that Ritalin, the most widely used method of treatment for this disorder, appears to work so well that few additional medical tests are done. Insurance companies and teachers often encourage parents to see drugs as the answer; Sroufe counters, "Drugs get everyone—politicians, scientists, teachers and parents—off the hook. Everyone except the children, that is" (Sroufe "Problems" 1). While Ritalin seems to work for many children, Dr. Rappley is concerned about its side effects. Studies show that short-term use of Ritalin can cause appetite suppression, stomachaches, headaches, and slowing down of growth (Rappley 168, 179). Unfortunately, evidence remains unclear on the effectiveness of medicating children diagnosed with ADHD.

Notice how Mary does not stop with her sources' remarks. Instead, she includes a point about the significance of what each source says. She reminds her readers that she is arguing against drugging young children unnecessarily.

If you simply provide a series of quotations and let them argue for you, you are not demonstrating your understanding of the quotations or showing how they fit into your argument. Make sure to use the quotations as support for your argument and not let them serve as the argument itself.

PRACTICE 15 Consider the different ways your sources will support your own argument. Then organize them in a manner that best helps you prove your main point.

PRACTICE 16 Include your sources as evidence to support your argument in your body paragraphs. Be careful not to choose sources haphazardly to include in your body paragraphs. You need to have a reason for using each of your sources.

WRITE YOUR CONCLUSION

9. **Write a concluding paragraph.** The concluding paragraph is the final paragraph of an essay. In its most basic form, it should summarize the main points of the essay and remind readers of the thesis statement.

The best conclusions expand on these two basic requirements and bring the essay to a close with one of these creative strategies: (1) Ask a question that provokes thought on the part of the readers, (2) predict the future, (3) offer a solution to a problem, or (4) call the readers to action. Each of these options sends a specific message and creates a slightly different effect at the end of the paper. The most important responsibility of the last paragraph is to bring the essay to an effective close. It is the last information that readers see before they form their own opinions or take action.

In the Student Paper: Mary's conclusion offers a solution to the problem raised in the second sentence of the paragraph:

> Every effort should be made to find the cause of the real medical problems underlying ADD and ADHD before we even think about giving our children drugs.

Toward the end of her conclusion, she calls the reader to action:

> It is time to say good-bye to conformist American classrooms and diagnoses.

She ends by reflecting on her thesis in one last, short line:

> Perhaps some people don't fit the norm because they have personalities.

Her concluding paragraph refocuses the reader's attention on the problem, offers a solution, and then calls the readers to action.

PRACTICE 17 Make a rough outline of your ideas for a possible conclusion to your research paper. Choose a strategy that will effectively bring your paper to a close.

PRACTICE 18 Write a rough draft of your conclusion, reminding your readers of your thesis statement.

ADD A CREATIVE TITLE

10. **Add a creative title.** Your title is what readers see first in any paper. A title is a phrase, usually no more than a few words, placed at the beginning of your essay that suggests or sums up the subject, purpose, or focus of the essay. Some titles are very imaginative, drawing on different sources for their meaning. Others are straightforward, like the title of

this chapter: "Writing a Research Paper." Besides suggesting an essay's purpose, a good title catches an audience's attention.

In the Student Paper: Mary Minor's title, "Children as Robots," will catch most readers' attention because referring to children as "robots" is intriguing, and readers will want to find out just how and why this might occur. That's exactly what a title should do—make your readers want to read your paper.

PRACTICE 19 Jot down some catchy titles for your paper.

PRACTICE 20 Choose a title for your paper.

CHECK YOUR DOCUMENTATION FORMAT

11. **Check your sources and documentation format within your paper (in-text citations) and at the end (Works Cited/References page).** Finding and using good, solid sources for evidence in a research paper are essential, and equally important is the acknowledgment of those sources. If you use a source and do not cite it correctly or forget to cite it, you are guilty of plagiarism, which can lead to a failing grade on the paper. So you need to learn when to cite a source (Chapter 19), what documentation style to use—MLA, APA, or other appropriate format (Chapter 22), and how to cite sources (Chapter 22). You should check with your instructor to find out which format you should use in a particular course.

The two types of citations support each other: (a) The *in-text citation* indicates the source of a quotation or idea right after it appears in the essay; (b) then, at the end, a list of all the sources cited in the paper must appear on the *Works Cited* or *References* page. Many textbooks demonstrate the various forms of documentation, so you should look up the format that your instructor wants you to use. Then keep this text handy when you write papers with sources.

In the Student Paper: Mary uses the MLA format for her paper, which she wrote for an English class. Usually, English instructors ask their students to use MLA. Mary includes a variety of sources in her paper, which we can use to illustrate the two types of citations. Listed here are some sample in-text citations, with the corresponding entries at the end of Mary's paper.

Book—name of author, title of book, city of publication, publisher, date of publication, medium of publication

In-Text Citation: (Saul 2)

Works Cited: Saul, Richard. *ADHD Does Not Exist: The Truth About Attention Deficit and Hyperactivity Disorder*. New York: Harper Collins, 2014. Print.

Note: The addition of the publication's medium (print or web) is a new feature of MLA citations in Works Cited.

Journal—name of author, title of article, name of journal, volume number, year, page number, medium of publication

> **In-Text Citation:** (171)
>
> **Works Cited:** Rappley, Marsha. "Attention Deficit Hyperactivity Disorder." *The New England Journal of Medicine* 352.2 (2005): 165–173. Print.

Note: Because Mary introduced Rappley in her paper before the in-text citation, she only needs to provide a page number and not the author's name in the citation.

Encyclopedia—name of author, title of article, name of encyclopedia, volume number, year, medium of publication

> **In-Text Citation:** ("Hippocratic Oath" 239)
>
> **Works Cited:** "Hippocratic Oath." *World Book Encyclopedia*. Vol. 9. 2010 ed. Print.

Note: If the author is not given, begin with the title of the article.

Online Database—name of author, title of article, name of original source, volume, medium of publication, and access date

> **In-Text Citation:** (Sroufe "Problems" 1)
>
> **Works Cited:** Sroufe, L. Alan. "Problems in Diagnosing and Treating ADD/ADHD." Editorial. *The New York Times* 29 Jan. 2012: SR1. Web. 10 May 2012.

Note: Mary knows that page and paragraph numbers are no longer required in MLA citations for online sources unless the source is also in print format. Because she found this article electronically in print format, the page numbers are included in these citations.

Web site—name of author, title of article, name of Web site, name of publisher, publication date, medium of publication, and access date

> **In-Text Citation:** No in-text citation is necessary for the reference to the *NCLD Web site* in paragraph 3 of Mary's paper.

Note: Because Mary has already introduced the Web site name (*National Center for Learning Disabilities*) and because there is no author for this Web site, no parenthetical in-text citation is necessary.

Works Cited: "Confusion over ADD, AD/HD, and Learning Disabilities." *National Center for Learning Disabilities.* National Center for Learning Disabilities, Inc., 6 Mar. 2009. Web. 9 Dec. 2009.

Note: Because page and paragraph numbers are no longer required in MLA citations for online sources unless the source is also in print format, Mary did not include them in either the in-text citation or the Works Cited because this article is not also in print format.

These examples from Mary's essay are just a few of the various types of sources you will probably use in your term papers. Every source is cited in a slightly different way, depending on the type of source and the documentation style. Not even the best writers know the correct format for every source they use. So when you have chosen your sources and determined that they are relevant, reliable, and recent (the three *R*s), your last step is to consult an appropriate, current manual or Web site to make sure you cite each source correctly.

PRACTICE 21 Make sure the material from every source in your essay has an in-text citation. Then create a list of sources at the end of your paper in an approved documentation format (see Chapter 22).

PRACTICE 22 Check the format of your in-text citations and your list of works cited by consulting a current handbook.

MyWritingLab™ Visit Chapter 21, "Writing a Research Paper," in MyWritingLab, and complete the Post-test to check your understanding of the chapter's objectives.

22

Documenting Sources

As you have already learned in this part of the text, you must document each source you use in your research paper with two types of citations that support each other: an in-text citation and an end-of-paper citation. Both kinds of citations are important, and both follow very strict guidelines based on the documentation style you use.

INTRODUCING YOUR SOURCES

Once you evaluate your sources and figure out which ones will help establish your argument, you then need to learn how to seamlessly integrate them into your paper. In other words, you need to introduce them effectively while showing readers they are credible and offer valuable evidence to back up your argument. Integrating your sources into your argument will help your readers understand the kind of information you are using. You also must show them you are using credible sources and evidence based on fact.

When you use a source for the first time, always (1) introduce the author(s), using the full name(s); (2) give the title of the source (use quotes for works inside larger works and italics for books); and (3) quote or paraphrase the information you need to build your argument. Here are some examples of effective ways to introduce L. Alan Sroufe's argument in paragraph 2 of Mary Minor's paper:

1. L. Alan Sroufe, Professor Emeritus of psychology at the University of Minnesota's Institute of Child Development, claims that drugs are too often used to solve conflicts with children.

2. Drugs, claims L. Alan Sroufe, Professor Emeritus of psychology at the University of Minnesota's Institute of Child Development, are too often used to solve conflicts with children.

3. According to L. Alan Sroufe, Professor Emeritus of psychology at the University of Minnesota's Institute of Child Development, drugs are too often used to solve conflicts with children.

4. Drugs are too often used to solve conflicts with children, claims L. Alan Sroufe, Professor Emeritus of psychology at the University of Minnesota's Institute of Child Development.

5. Professor Emeritus of psychology at the University of Minnesota's Institute of Child Development L. Alan Sroufe claims that drugs are too often used to solve conflicts with children.

6. L. Alan Sroufe claims, as Professor Emeritus of psychology at the University of Minnesota's Institute of Child Development, that drugs are too often used to solve conflicts with children.

These model sentences are only a few options for introducing Sroufe's ideas; you can probably think of many more. Notice how all of these examples use his title so that readers understand he is an authority on his subject. Also, note that the verbs in these examples each express a slightly different meaning. Finally, you should refer to the author by last name only—"according to Sroufe"—each subsequent time you use the source and mention the author.

DOCUMENTATION FORMAT

As you document your sources, you should know that documentation styles vary from discipline to discipline. Ask your instructor about the particular documentation style he or she wants you to follow. Three of the major documentation styles are Modern Language Association (MLA), used in humanities courses; American Psychological Association (APA), used in social science courses; and *Chicago Manual of Style* (CMS), used in history, mathematics, and science classes. Even though documentation styles vary somewhat from one field to another, the basic concept behind documentation is the same in all disciplines: You must give proper credit to other writers by acknowledging the sources of the summaries, paraphrases, and quotations you use to support the ideas in your documented essay. Remember that you have two goals in any citation: (1) to acknowledge the author and (2) to help the readers locate the material. Once you grasp this basic concept, you will have no trouble avoiding plagiarism.

Because you may have to write different papers using all of these documentation styles, you should have a basic understanding of their differences.

In-Text Citations

The major difference among in-text citations for MLA, APA, and CMS is that MLA and APA use parenthetical references while CMS uses a footnote/endnote system. Look at the differences in the following sentences:

MLA: In an article in *The New England Journal of Medicine*, Dr. Marsha Rappley contends that the diagnosis is controversial because of the "subjective nature" of the test, leading many professionals to believe that ADD and ADHD are "overdiagnosed and overtreated" (171).

APA: In an article in *The New England Journal of Medicine*, Dr. Marsha Rappley (2005) contends that the diagnosis is controversial because of the "subjective nature" of the test, leading many professionals to believe that ADD and ADHD are "overdiagnosed and overtreated" (p. 171).

CMS: In an article in *The New England Journal of Medicine*, Dr. Marsha Rappley contends that the diagnosis is controversial because of the "subjective nature" of the test, leading many professionals to believe that ADD and ADHD are "overdiagnosed and overtreated" (171).[1]

Notice that the format in these examples varies slightly. MLA and APA both furnish the page number for the source, but APA cites the page number with a "p." and MLA without a "p." APA also includes the year the article was written. For CMS, a reader would find the publication information (including the page number of the source) in a footnote/endnote.

On the other hand, certain in-text features are similar in all three documentation styles:

- You should include citation information directly after every quotation.
- You should include citation information after you have finished paraphrasing a source. (This could extend to more than one sentence.)
- Punctuation follows the parenthetical citation, not the quotation.
- Longer quotes are indented in block form and do not require quotation marks. (MLA block indents = 1" [2 tabs]; APA block indents = 1/2" [1 tab])
- Blocked quotes are double spaced in the same size font as the paper.

End-of-Paper Citations

One of the most obvious differences among MLA, APA, and CMS is how they list their sources at the end of the paper: MLA includes a "Works Cited" page, APA lists "References," and CMS has a "Bibliography." Some general differences exist among these three lists of sources. Works Cited and References pages list only those sources cited in the paper. These sources are listed alphabetically. Your in-text citations will work with your reference page in that the in-text citations tell the readers the name and page number of the source you are using, and the Works Cited/References pages provide readers with the full bibliographic information.

A Bibliography lists every source you looked at while researching your paper. Documentation styles that include a Bibliography use a separate page for notes to show which of the sources in the Bibliography you actually cited in your paper. Pages for notes use a numbering system that corresponds to a number in the body of the paper. Writers using a Bibliography have the advantage of showing their readers all the sources they read for the paper, even if they took no material directly from a source.

Regardless of which documentation style you use, the source lists at the end of the paper are all formatted the same:

- The title is centered, and the title is in regular font. In other words, the title is not bolded, underlined, put in quotation marks, or italicized (unless you include another title in your own title).
- The page numbers are continuous from the body of the paper.
- The entries are all double-spaced.
- The entries all use a hanging indent (which can be accessed on a computer either through the "Paragraph" feature under "Format" or by manipulating the hourglass on the ruler bar). *Note:* Some documentation styles prefer paragraph indenting.
- The entries are all alphabetized. *Note:* If you have a source written by more than one author, do not rearrange authors' names in a single entry so they appear alphabetically. Leave the order as it appears in your source.

Regardless of the documentation style, the in-text citations, end-of-paper sources, and footnotes/endnotes (if applicable) all work together to help readers know all the bibliographic information about the source you are using.

MLA Versus APA

Because MLA and APA are the most popular documentation styles, you should know the major differences between the two. The logic behind both documentation styles is very similar, but subtle differences exist in each format.

In-Text Citations

MLA	APA
• Authors' full names are used.	• Author's last name and first initial are used.
• Dates don't necessarily have to be mentioned.	• Dates must follow the author's name either in the sentence or in parentheses following the sentence.
• A parenthetical citation includes author's last name and a page number: (Turner 49).	• A parenthetical citation includes author's last name, date, and a page number: (Turner, 2005, p. 49).

Works Cited/References Page Notice the differences in the following citations. MLA and APA both require the same information, but just in a different order and with different capitalization.

MLA:

Rappley, Marsha. "Attention Deficit Hyperactivity Disorder." *The New England Journal of Medicine* 352.2 (2005): 165–173. Print.

APA:

Rappley, Marsha. (2005). Attention Deficit Hyperactivity Disorder. *The New England Journal of Medicine, 352*(2), 165–173.

For more on the differences between MLA and APA (as well as the other documentation styles), consult a research handbook.

USING A HANDBOOK

In order to learn how to cite sources properly, you need to know how to navigate a research handbook. Handbooks provide information on both in-text and end-of-paper citations. After writing a few research papers, you'll become quite adept at introducing your sources and using in-text citations, but you will never remember how to cite one kind of source from another. Therefore, knowing how to navigate a handbook is important to documenting your sources properly. Once you understand the logic of citing, you should be able to use the handbook quite easily.

Look at the following source from Mary's Works Cited:

Jardin, Bianca, Alison Looby, and Mitch Earleywine. "Characteristics of College Students With Attention-Deficit Hyperactivity Disorder Symptoms Who Misuse Their Medications." *Journal of American College Health* 59.5 (2011): 373–377. ASP. Web. 11 Apr. 2015.

In order to put this entry together, you need to look at two different source examples: (1) How to Cite Two or More Authors and (2) How to Cite an Article in a Scholarly Journal. If this source were found online, you would also need to include retrieval date, or the date you found the article. Sometimes, you'll need to look at three or four different source examples in order to piece together one entry on your Works Cited list or other reference page; you can't expect to find an example for every source you have. So when you use a handbook and cannot figure out how to cite a source, chances are the answer is there somewhere; you just have to find it and piece together a citation using the logic of other entries. Once you understand how to use the documentation styles sections of a handbook, you'll always be able to figure out how to properly cite sources.

If you have difficulty understanding the logic of your handbook or cannot figure out how to cite a specific source, you might want to consider a trip to your campus's tutoring center where a tutor could show you how it works. And, of course, you can always ask your instructor.

MyWritingLab™ Visit Chapter 22, "Documenting Sources," in MyWritingLab, and complete the Post-test to check your understanding of the chapter's objectives.

Revising and Editing a Research Paper

In this chapter, you will revise and edit a new student term paper and then revise and edit your own paper. The checklists for this process are provided within the chapter, which guides you through this procedure step by step.

REVISING AND EDITING A STUDENT'S RESEARCH PAPER

Here is the first draft of an essay written by Max Felter, a student. It demonstrates the guidelines for writing a successful essay with sources that you have learned in Chapters 18 through 22.

Love in the Workplace

1   Love happens—sometimes very unexpectedly—in all types of situations. Considering how much time most people spend at work, the workplace is one of the most common origins of romantic relationships. Finding common interests with someone is fairly easy when both people work together. Of course, problems can result from intra-office romances, which some employers may try to avoid by making specific policies against dating co-workers. In my opinion, however, office dating can work.

2   In some circumstances, workers get to know each other so well that a love connection is a natural outcome. In his blog entitled "The Joys and Pains of Workplace Dating: When Do Office Romances Become a Problem?," Dr. Steve Albrecht, an authority in the areas of business and psychology, notes that "because folks spend so much time at work, in close proximity to each other, and travel and meet for lunch or

drinks alone or in groups, attractions develop." Over time, "The chemistry of adults working together means sometimes the heart wants what the heart wants, thereby overwhelming the reasoning brain" (Albrecht). In these situations, coworkers may begin to date even if they are acting against their company's policy on dating.

Dating in the workplace is more common than people may realize. In "The   3
State of the Office Romance, 2015," Susan Adams of *Forbes* magazine cites two surveys that demonstrate the prevalence of dating among co-workers. Together, the surveys show that 37 to 51 percent of employees have dated someone they work with (Adams 1). Even the low end of this range shows that romantic relationships are common at work.

From these surveys, Adams also discovered that couples whose relationships   4
start at work are just as successful as those who meet elsewhere. In fact, 30 percent of workplace romances result in marriage (Adams 1). Based on the assumption that marriage is a sign of a successful relationship, workplace dating seems even more fruitful than the alternatives, such as meeting at a bar. In "Together, at Home and at Work," Bruce Feiler lists a number of long-lasting, high-profile couples who have strong working relationships. The list includes politicians such as the Clintons and the Obamas as well as entertainers such as actress Frances McDormand and her director/husband Joel Coen (Feiler 1). These examples of happy marriages between coworkers demonstrate that love and work can coexist.

Workplace romances is nothing new. According to an expert in couples' psy-   5
chology whom Feiler consulted, "Couples working together was the norm for most of human history, from family farms to mom-and-pop shops" (1). Such arrange-ments were very common in the passed. However, according to a 20-year university study that Feiler cites, couples jointly run less than two percent of modern family-owned businesses (1). The notion that couples should not be working together is relatively new.

Nonetheless, workplace dating creates very real challenges today. Since many   6
people bring their stress from work home with them. Work issues often put a strain on relationships. For couples who are coworkers, this problem works both ways (Feiler 2), conflicts at home can be reflected at work in the same way that problems at work can come home. Similar situations can arise even if a couple does not live together. In theory, one bad date with a coworker could result in months—or even years—of trouble on the job.

Without a doubt, workplace dating can have a negative impact on any work   7
enviernment. Labor and management journalist Rick Bell examines these problems in an editorial entitled "Workplace Romance? We Can Work It Out." He claims that office dating is easy to romanticize: "It starts with birds merrily chirping outside the window, shoeless footsies under the conference table, and goo-goo eyes above it" (Bell 50). However, not all workplace romances have happy endings. Some workplace relationships lead to a "division of loyalties ...,[a] dissolution of friend-ships," or even "accusations of stalking outside of work" (Bell 50). With sexual harassment as such a hot-button issue, employers may feel the need to protect themselves from the possible fallout from failed intra-office relationships by estab-lishing policies against them.

8   Even if nothing as dramatic as stalking occurs in response to a failed workplace romance, other negative consequences may occur. In a report entitled "Why Are You Dating Him? Contemporary Motives for Workplace Romances," communication researchers Renee L. Cowan and Sean M. Moran explore some of those consequences. From their research, Cowan and Moran conclude that love at work, whether it fails or not, can weaken lines of effective communication and cause a decline in productivity (15). In one survey, roughly one-fourth of the respondents admitted to feelings of discomfort in the workplace as a result of dating a coworker (Adams 2). These are problems that business managers naturally want to resolve and avoid altogether. Some organizations even go so far as to have those in work relationships sign so-called "love contracts" that protect the business from any resulting legal complications (Albrecht). From the perspective of most employers, the personal relationships of their employees are not worth the risk of having a less profitable financial quarter.

9   However, from the perspective of coworkers in love, the bottom line has nothing to do with money. In "The Debate over the Prohibition of Romance in the Workplace," C. Boyd argues that workers have the moral right to date one another. Statistics show that for each report of sexual harassment that is averted by anti-dating regulations, over 700 healthy relationships are blocked (Boyd 333). Therefore, from a utilitarian perspective, to ban dating in the workplace does more harm than good. As Boyd states, "The main consequence of a universal ban on workplace romance" results in "the denial of [the] right of freedom of association" (333). In other words, preventing employees from dating in the workplace may be considered a breach of constitutional rights. For that reason, workforce managers should not be allowed to stop their employees from dating; they should take action only in cases where a particular romance has had a negative effect on workplace productivity.

10   Love is not something that can be micromanaged. If the workers themselves cannot control who they fall in love with, managers have little hope of regulating it. The fact that some of society's most sucessful individuals have found love at work and that such partnerships have been a staple of society for a very long time demonstrates that workplace dating does not always cause problems. As the experts explain, more often than not, romantic and business partnerships can co-exist in long-term harmony, and everyone should have the right to find love wherever it may be.

Works Cited

Adams, Susan. "The State of the Office Romance, 2015." *Forbes.com. Forbes.* 13 February 2015. Web. 13 February 2015.

Albrecht, Steve. "The Joys and Pains of Workplace Dating: When Do Office Romances Become a Problem?" *psychologytoday.com. Psychology Today.* 31 January 2014. Web. 17 February 2015.

Bell, Rick. "Workplace Romance? We Can Work It Out." *Workforce* 94.2 (2015): 50. *Academic Search Premier.* Web. 13 February 2015.

Boyd, C. "The Debate over the Prohibition of Romance in the Workplace." *Journal of Business Ethics* 97.2 (2010): 325-338. *OmniFile Full Text Mega.* Web. 18 February 2015.

Cowan, Renee L. and Sean M. Horan. "Why Are You Dating Him? Contemporary Motives for Workplace Romances." *Qualitative Research Reports in Communication* 15.1 (2014): 9–16. *Academic Search Premier.* Web. 13 February 2015.

Feiler, Bruce. "Together, at Home and at Work." *nytimes.com. New York Times.* 15 November 2013. Web. 15 February 2015.

Max's first draft now needs to be revised and edited. First, apply the following Revising Checklist to the content of Max's draft. When you are satisfied that his ideas are fully developed and well organized, use the Editing Checklist to correct his grammatical and mechanics errors. Answer the questions, and complete the tasks in each category. Then write your suggested changes directly on Max's draft.

Revising the Student Research Paper

THESIS STATEMENT

✔ Does the thesis statement contain the essay's controlling idea and an opinion about that idea?

✔ Does the thesis appear as the last sentence of the introduction?

1. What is the main idea in Max's research paper?

_____

2. Put brackets around Max's thesis statement. Does it introduce his main point?

_____

3. Rewrite it to introduce all the topics in his essay.

_____

_____

BASIC ELEMENTS

✔ Does the title draw in the readers?

✔ Does the introduction capture the readers' attention and build up effectively to the thesis statement?

✔ Does each body paragraph deal with a single topic?

✔ Does the conclusion bring the essay to a close in an interesting way?

1. Give Max's essay an alternate title.

_____

2. Rewrite Max's introduction so that it captures the readers' attention in a different way and builds up to the thesis statement at the end of the paragraph.

_____

_____

_____

_____

3. Does each body paragraph in Max's essay deal with only one topic?

_____

4. Rewrite Max's conclusion with a twist of your own.

_____

_____

_____

_____

DEVELOPMENT

✔ Do the body paragraphs adequately support the thesis statement?

✔ Does each body paragraph have a focused topic sentence?

✔ Does each body paragraph contain *specific* details that support the topic sentence?

✔ Does each body paragraph include *enough* details to fully explain the topic sentence?

✔ Are the sources relevant, reliable, and recent?

✔ Are references given for original sources to avoid plagiarism?

✔ Is the documentation format correct—in the paper and at the end?

1. Do Max's topic sentences support his thesis statement? Write out your revision of Max's thesis statement, and list his six topic sentences.

Thesis: _____

_____

_____

Topics: _____

_____

_____

_____

_____

_____

_____

_____

_____

_____

_____

_____

_____

_____

_____

_____

_____

2. Does your revised thesis statement accurately introduce Max's topic sentences?

_____

3. Are Max's examples specific?

_____

Add an even more specific detail to one of his paragraphs.

4. Does he offer enough examples or details in each paragraph?

_____

5. Are Max's sources relevant, reliable, and recent?

For help, see Chapter 20.

_____

6. Does he give references for all original sources in his paper?

For help, see Chapter 22.

_____

7. Is the documentation format correct in his paper?

For help, see Chapter 22.

_____

8. Is the format of his Works Cited page correct?

For help, see Chapter 22.

_____

UNITY

✔ Do the essay's topic sentences relate directly to the thesis statement?

✔ Do the details in each body paragraph support the paragraph's topic sentence?

1. Read each of Max's topic sentences with his thesis statement in mind. Do they go together?

_____

2. Revise any topic sentences that are not directly related to his thesis.

3. Read each of Max's paragraphs with its topic sentence in mind. Drop or rewrite any sentences that are not directly related to the paragraph's topic sentences.

ORGANIZATION

✔ Is the essay organized logically?

✔ Is each body paragraph organized logically?

1. Review your list of Max's topics in item 1 under "Development," and decide if it is organized logically.

2. What is his method of organization?

_____

3. Read Max's paper again to see if all his sentences are arranged logically.

4. Move any sentences that are out of order.

COHERENCE

✔ Are transitions used effectively so that paragraphs move smoothly and logically from one to the next?

✔ Do the sentences move smoothly and logically from one to the next?

For a list of transitions, see pages 99–100.

1. Circle five transitions that Max uses.

2. Explain how three of these transitions make Max's paper easier to read.

_____

_____

 Now rewrite Max's essay with your revisions.

Editing the Student Research Paper

SENTENCES

Subjects and Verbs

✔ Does each sentence have a main subject and verb?

1. Underline the subjects once and verbs twice in paragraph 6 of Max's essay. Remember that sentences can have more than one subject-verb set.

   For help with subjects and verbs, see Chapter 27.

2. Does each sentence have at least one subject and verb that can stand alone?

3. Did you find and correct Max's fragment in paragraph 6? If not, find and correct it now.

   For help with fragments, see Chapter 28.

4. Did you find and correct Max's run-together sentence in paragraph 6? If not, find and correct it now.

   For help with run-togethers, see Chapter 29.

Subject-Verb Agreement

✔ Do all subjects and verbs agree?

1. Read aloud the subjects and verbs in paragraph 5 of Max's revised essay.

   For help with subject-verb agreement, see Chapter 32.

2. Correct any subjects and verbs that do not agree.

3. Now read aloud the subjects and verbs in the rest of his revised essay.

4. Correct any subjects and verbs that do not agree.

Pronoun Agreement

✔ Do all pronouns agree with their nouns?

1. Find any pronouns in your revision of Max's essay that do not agree with their nouns.

   For help with pronoun agreement, see Chapter 36.

2. Correct any pronouns that do not agree with their nouns.

Modifier Errors

✔ Are modifiers as close as possible to the words they modify?

1. Find any modifiers in your revision of Max's essay that are not as close as possible to the words they modify.

   For help with modifier errors, see Chapter 39.

2. Rewrite sentences if necessary so that modifiers are as close as possible to the words they modify.

PUNCTUATION AND MECHANICS

Punctuation

✔ Are sentences punctuated correctly?

For help with punctuation, see Chapters 40–44.

1. Read your revision of Max's essay for any errors in punctuation.

2. Make sure any fragments and run-together sentences you revised are punctuated correctly.

Mechanics
✔ Are words capitalized properly?

For help with capitalization, see Chapter 45.

1. Read your revisions of Max's essay for any errors in capitalization.

2. Be sure to check the capitalization in the fragments and run-together sentences you revised.

WORD CHOICE AND SPELLING

Confused Words
✔ Are words used correctly?

For help with confused words, see Chapter 51.

1. Find any words used incorrectly in your revision of Max's essay.

2. Did you find and correct the confused word?

Spelling
✔ Are words spelled correctly?

For help with spelling, see Chapter 52.

1. Use spell-check and a dictionary to check the spelling in your revision of Max's essay.

2. Did you find and correct his two misspelled words?

     Now rewrite Max's paper again with your editing corrections.

For Research Paper Peer Evaluation Forms, go to Appendix 5.

REVISING AND EDITING YOUR OWN RESEARCH PAPER

Now revise and edit the essay you wrote in Chapter 21. The following questions will help you apply the Revising and Editing Checklists to your own writing.

MyWritingLab | **Reviewing Revising**

Need a brush-up on revising? Go to **Revising Your Essay** in the **Essay Development** module of **MyWritingLab** to review all the ways to revise a paper before you begin to work here with your own research paper.

Revising Your Own Research Paper

THESIS STATEMENT

☐ Does the thesis statement contain the essay's controlling idea?

☐ Does the thesis appear as the last sentence of the introduction?

1. What is the main idea of your research paper?

   _____

2. Put brackets around your thesis statement. Does it introduce your main idea?

   _____

3. How can you change it to introduce all the topics in your paper?

   _____

   _____

BASIC ELEMENTS

☐ Does the title draw in the readers?

☐ Does the introduction capture the readers' attention and build up effectively to the thesis statement?

☐ Does each body paragraph deal with a single topic?

☐ Does the conclusion bring the essay to a close in an interesting way?

1. Give your essay an alternative title.

   _____

2. Does your introduction capture the readers' attention and build up to the thesis statement at the end of the paragraph?

   _____

3. Does each of your body paragraphs deal with only one topic?

   _____

4. Does your conclusion bring the essay to a close in an interesting way?

   _____

DEVELOPMENT

☐ Do the body paragraphs adequately support the thesis statement?

☐ Does each body paragraph have a focused topic sentence?

☐ Does each body paragraph contain *specific* details that support the topic sentence?

☐ Does each body paragraph include *enough* details to fully explain the topic sentence?

☐ Are the sources relevant, reliable, and recent?

☐ Are references given for original sources to avoid plagiarism?

☐ Is the documentation format correct—in the paper and at the end?

1. Do your topics support your thesis statement? List your revised thesis statement and your topics.

    Thesis: _____

      Topics: _____

              _____

              _____

2. Are your examples specific? Add another more specific detail to at least one of your paragraphs.

3. Do you furnish enough examples or details in each paragraph? Add at least one new example or detail to one of your paragraphs.

For help, see Chapter 20.   4. Check your sources to make sure they are relevant, reliable, and recent. Find new sources if necessary.

For help, see Chapter 22.   5. Do you give references for all original sources in your paper to avoid plagiarism?

For help, see Chapter 22.   6. Is the documentation format correct in your paper?

For help, see Chapter 22.   7. Is the format of your Works Cited page correct?

UNITY

☐ Do the essay's topic sentences relate directly to the thesis statement?

☐ Do the details in each body paragraph support the paragraph's topic sentence?

1. Read each of your topic sentences with your thesis statement in mind. Do they go together?

    _____

2. Revise your topic sentences so they are directly related.

3. Read each of your paragraphs with its topic sentence in mind.

4. Drop or rewrite any sentences in your body paragraphs that are not directly related to their topic sentences.

ORGANIZATION

☐ Is the essay organized logically?

☐ Is each body paragraph organized logically?

1. Review the list of your topics in item 1 under "Development," and decide if your topics are organized logically.

2. What is your method of organization?

   _____

   _____

3. Do you think your method of organization is the most effective one for your purpose? Explain your answer.

   _____

   _____

4. Read your essay again to see if all your sentences are arranged logically.

5. Move any sentences that are out of order.

COHERENCE

☐ Are transitions used effectively so that paragraphs move smoothly and logically from one to the next?

☐ Do the sentences move smoothly and logically from one to the next?

1. Circle five transitions, repetitions, synonyms, or pronouns you use.

2. Explain how two of these make your essay easier to read.

For a list of transitions, see pages 99–100.
For a list of pronouns, see pages 496–497.

Now rewrite your paper with your revisions.

Editing Your Own Research Paper

For Editing Peer Evaluation Forms, go to Appendix 6.

MyWritingLab **Reviewing Editing**

Forgot what editing is all about? Editing helps you fine-tune your paper so your grammar and mechanics help you say exactly what you mean. If you need help with what to look for when you edit your paper, check out **Editing the Essay** in the **Essay Development** module of **MyWritingLab.**

SENTENCES

Subjects and Verbs

☐ Does each sentence have a main subject and verb?

1. In a paragraph of your choice, underline your subjects once and verbs twice. Remember that sentences can have more than one subject-verb set.

For help with subjects and verbs, see Chapter 27.

For help with fragments, see Chapter 28.

2. Does each sentence have at least one subject and verb that can stand alone?

_____

For help with run-togethers, see Chapter 29.

3. Correct any fragments you have written.

4. Correct any run-together sentences you have written.

Subject-Verb Agreement

☐ Do all subjects and verbs agree?

For help with subject-verb agreement, see Chapter 32.

1. Read aloud the subjects and verbs you underlined in your revised essay.

2. Correct any subjects and verbs that do not agree.

Pronoun Agreement

☐ Do all pronouns agree with their nouns?

For help with pronoun agreement, see Chapter 36.

1. Find any pronouns in your revised essay that do not agree with their nouns.

2. Correct any pronouns that do not agree with their nouns.

Modifiers

☐ Are modifiers as close as possible to the words they modify?

For help with modifier errors, see Chapter 39.

1. Find any modifiers in your revised essay that are not as close as possible to the words they modify.

2. Rewrite sentences if necessary so that your modifiers are as close as possible to the words they modify.

PUNCTUATION AND MECHANICS

Punctuation

☐ Are sentences punctuated correctly?

For help with punctuation, see Chapters 40–44.

1. Read your revised essay for any errors in punctuation.

2. Make sure any fragments and run-together sentences you revised are punctuated correctly.

Mechanics

☐ Are words capitalized properly?

For help with capitalization, see Chapter 45.

1. Read your revised essay for any errors in capitalization.

2. Be sure to check your capitalization if you revised any fragments or run-together sentences.

WORD CHOICE AND SPELLING

Word Choice

☐ Are words used correctly?

1. Find any words used incorrectly in your revised essay.

2. Correct any errors you find.

For help with confused words, see Chapter 51.

Spelling

☐ Are words spelled correctly?

1. Use spell-check and a dictionary to check your spelling.

2. Correct any misspelled words.

For help with spelling, see Chapter 52.

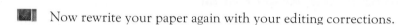

Now rewrite your paper again with your editing corrections.

MyWritingLab™ Visit Chapter 23, "Revising and Editing a Research Paper," in MyWritingLab, and complete the Post-test to check your understanding of the chapter's objectives.

24

Writing Workshop

WRITING A RESEARCH PAPER

This chapter will serve as a review of Part III as it also gives you some guided practice in writing research papers. First, it provides a summary of the guidelines for writing a term paper and then furnishes you with some new research topics. The rest of the chapter is devoted to the processes of revising and editing.

Guidelines for Writing a Research Paper

1. Choose a subject.
2. Write a good, clear thesis statement about your subject.
3. Find sources that are relevant, reliable, and recent to support your thesis statement.
4. Take notes to avoid plagiarism.
5. Make a working outline of your ideas.
6. Construct an introduction that leads to your thesis statement.
7. Develop as many supporting paragraphs, or body paragraphs, as you think are necessary to explain your thesis statement.
8. Use your sources as evidence for your argument.
9. Write a concluding paragraph.
10. Add a creative title.
11. Check your sources and documentation format within your paper (in-text citations) and at the end (Works Cited/References page).

Your Topics

1. Research the changes in the antidrug ads over the past five years. How have they changed? Are they more or less effective now? Write an essay explaining these changes.

2. Research a controversial political issue of your choice. Then take a firm stand on the issue, and develop an essay supporting your position. You might want to look at headlines in the newspaper to get some ideas for this assignment.

3. Research a special trip you want to take. Get all the information you need. Then write a letter to a close friend, inviting him or her to join you.

4. Create your own assignment (with the help of your instructor), and write a response to it.

REVISING WORKSHOP

Small Group Activity (5–10 minutes per writer) In groups of three or four, read your research papers to each other. The listeners should record their reactions on a copy of the Research Paper Peer Evaluation Form in Appendix 5. After your group goes through this process, give your evaluation forms to the appropriate writers so that each writer has two or three peer comment sheets for revising.

Paired Activity (5 minutes per writer) Using the completed Peer Evaluation Forms, work in pairs to decide what you should revise in your essay. If time allows, rewrite some of your sentences, and have your partner check them.

Individual Activity Rewrite your paper, using the revising feedback you received from other students.

EDITING WORKSHOP

Paired Activity (5–10 minutes per writer) Swap papers with a classmate, and use the Editing Peer Evaluation Form (Appendix 6) to identify as many grammar, punctuation, mechanics, and spelling errors as you can. Mark the errors on the student paper with the correction symbols on the inside back cover. If time allows, correct some of your errors, and have your partner check them.

Individual Activity Rewrite your paper again, using the editing feedback you received from other students. Record your grammar errors in the Error Log (Appendix 7) and your spelling errors in the Spelling Log (Appendix 8).

MyWritingLab

Pearson Tutor Services

Want another set of eyes on your essay? Pearson Tutor Services allows you to submit papers on any subject and have personalized feedback within 48 hours from someone who is highly qualified in that subject. In **MyWritingLab,** click **Pearson Tutor Services** for more information on this extremely beneficial service.

REFLECTING ON YOUR WRITING

When you have completed your own essay, answer these six questions:

1. What was most difficult about this assignment?

2. What was easiest?

3. What did you learn about research papers by completing this assignment?

4. What do you think are the strengths of your paper? Place a wavy line in the margin by the parts of your essay you feel are very good.

5. What are the weaknesses, if any, of your paper? Place an X in the margin by the parts of your essay you would like help with. Write in the margins any questions you have.

6. What did you learn from this assignment about your own writing process—about preparing to write, about writing the first draft, about revising, and about editing?

MyWritingLab™ Visit Chapter 24, "Writing Workshop," in MyWritingLab, and complete the Post-test to check your understanding of the chapter's objectives.

The Handbook

This part of *Mosaics* provides you with a complete handbook for editing your writing. You can use it as a reference tool as you write or as a source of instruction and practice in areas where you need work. This handbook consists of nine units:

The chapters in each unit start with a **self-test** to help you identify your strengths and weaknesses in that area. Then the chapters teach specific sentence skills and provide exercises so you can practice what you have learned. You will really know this material when you can use it in your own writing. As a result, each chapter ends with an exercise that asks you to **write your own sentences** and then work with another student to **edit each other's writing.**

The **Editing Symbols** on the inside back cover are marks you can use to highlight errors in your papers. In addition, the Error Log (Appendix 6) and Spelling Log (Appendix 7) will help you tailor the instruction to your own needs and keep track of your progress.

The Basics

This handbook uses very little terminology. But sometimes talking about language and the way it works is difficult without a shared understanding of certain basic grammar terms. For this reason, your instructor may ask you to study parts of this unit to review basic grammar—parts of speech, phrases, and clauses. You might also use this unit for reference.

This section has two chapters:

Chapter 25: Parts of Speech
Chapter 26: Phrases and Clauses

25

Parts of Speech

In the following paragraph, label the parts of speech listed here:

4 verbs (v)	2 adverbs (adv)
4 nouns (n)	2 prepositions (prep)
2 pronouns (pro)	2 conjunctions (conj)
2 adjectives (adj)	2 interjections (int)

Professional basketball is definitely this nation's best spectator sport. The talented players move around the court so quickly that the audience never has a chance to become bored. Boy, I'll never forget that Saturday night last February when my favorite uncle took me to see the Spurs game against the Trailblazers. It was an important home game for San Antonio, so the arena was packed. The Spurs were behind throughout most of the game, but they pulled through and won with a three-pointer in the last few seconds. Wow! I have never seen so many people on their feet, screaming at the top of their lungs.

(Answers are in Appendix 3.)

Every sentence is made up of a variety of words that play different roles. Each word, like each part of a coordinated outfit, serves a distinct function. These functions fall into eight categories:

1. Verbs

2. Nouns

3. Pronouns

4. Adjectives

5. Adverbs

6. Prepositions

7. Conjunctions

8. Interjections

Some words, such as *is*, can function in only one way—in this case, as a verb. Other words, however, can serve as different parts of speech depending on how they are used in a sentence. For example, look at the different ways the word *show* can be used:

Verb: The artists **show** their work at a gallery.
(*Show* is a verb here, telling what the artists do.)

Noun: The **show** will start in 10 minutes.
(*Show* functions as a noun here, telling what will start in 10 minutes.)

Adjective: The little boy loves to sing **show** tunes.
(*Show* is an adjective here, modifying, or explaining, the noun *tunes*.)

MyWritingLab	**Understanding Parts of Speech**

To learn more about parts of speech, go to **MyWritingLab.com,** and choose **Parts of Speech, Phrases, and Clauses** in the **Basic Grammar** module. From there, watch the video called **Animation: Parts of Speech, Phrases, and Clauses.** Then, return to this chapter, which will go into more detail about parts of speech and give you opportunities to practice using them. Finally, you will apply your understanding of parts of speech to your own writing.

Student Comment:
"After being out of school for over 20 years, I forgot a lot about writing—especially grammar. The Parts of Speech topic helped me brush up on what I had forgotten."

Verbs

The **verb** is the most important word in a sentence because every other word depends on it in some way. Verbs tell what's going on in a sentence.

There are three types of verbs: action, linking, and helping. An **action verb** tells what someone or something is doing. A **linking verb** tells what someone or something is, feels, or looks like. Sometimes an action or linking verb has **helping verbs**—words that add information, such as when an action is taking place. A **complete verb** consists of an action or linking verb and any helping verbs.

Action: The girl **wandered** too far from the campsite.

Action: Luca **ran** to the bus stop.

Linking: He **looks** very tired.

Linking: It **was** a real surprise to see you.

Helping: My aunt and uncle **will be** arriving tomorrow.

Helping: My grandmother **has** been very ill lately.

Complete Verb: My aunt and uncle **will be arriving** tomorrow.

Complete Verb: My grandmother **has been** very ill lately.

PRACTICE 1: Recall/Identify In each of the following sentences, underline the complete verbs. Some sentences have more than one verb.

1. I read *Moby Dick* for my literature class.

2. The best place for inexpensive fast food is Taco Bell.

3. You seem tired.

4. I wonder if Chad is going to be attending.

5. The teenager climbed to the top of the mountain before he stopped for lunch.

PRACTICE 2: Apply Fill in each blank in the following paragraph with a verb.

   This year my sister (1) _____ to get married. She and her fiancé (2) _____ in Dallas, Texas, so I had to buy a plane ticket from Los Angeles. First, I tried the computer and (3) _____ all of the Web sites that people talk about, but I couldn't find any good deals. Finally, I (4) _____ a travel agent and asked her to tell me what my best options were. The best deal she (5) _____ was $280 round-trip, so I charged it to a credit card. I guess my sister is worth it.

PRACTICE 3: Write Your Own Write a sentence of your own for each of the following verbs.

1. was sitting _____

2. handled _____

3. seems _____

4. had been taking _____

5. buy _____

Nouns

People often think of **nouns** as "naming words" because they iden-tify—or name—people (*student, Susan, mom, server*), places (*city, ocean, Thomasville*), or things (*bush, airplane, chair, shirt*). Nouns also name ideas (*liberty, justice*), qualities (*bravery, patience*), emotions (*sadness, happiness*), and actions (*challenge, compromise*). A **common noun** names something general (*singer, hill, water, theater*). A **proper noun** names something spe-cific (*Nicole Kidman, Angel Falls, Coke, McDonald's*).

Hint: To test whether a word is a noun, try putting *a, an,* or *the* in front of it:

> **Nouns:**   a squirrel, an orange, the hope
> **NOT Nouns:**   a funny, an over, the eat

This test does not work with proper nouns:

> **NOT**   a Natalie, the New York

PRACTICE 4: Recall/Identify Underline all the nouns in the following sentences.

1. The Golden Gate Bridge is a popular tourist attraction in San Francisco.

2. Collectors will spend much money on limited-edition coins.

3. My son is wearing my favorite shirt.

4. In October, we are planning a trip to Seattle.

5. *Top Chef* was voted the most popular TV cooking show.

PRACTICE 5: Apply Fill in each blank in the following paragraph with a noun that will make each sentence complete.

Last May, I joined a volunteer organization called (1)_____. Within a month, the secretary left, and I was nominated to take his place. I had to put all of the (2)_____ about the organization and its members into my computer and then create a mail merge. With this database, I was able to make labels and (3)_____ very easily. My first assignment was to create a form letter and send it to all of the (4)_____ who promised to send money to the group. I finally saw the (5)_____ of all the grammar lessons I had in my English classes, and I learned that writing good letters is harder than I thought.

PRACTICE 6: Write Your Own Write a sentence of your own for each of the following nouns.

1. pastor _____

2. Sea World _____

3. strength _____

4. audience _____

5. actions _____

Pronouns

Pronouns can do anything nouns can do. In fact, **pronouns** can take the place of nouns. Without pronouns, you would find yourself repeating nouns and producing boring sentences. Compare the following sentences, for example:

> **George** drove **George's** car very fast to **George's** house because **George** had to get home early.

> **George** drove **his** car very fast to **his** house because **he** had to get home early.

There are many different types of pronouns, but you need to focus only on the following four types for now.

Most Common Pronouns

Personal (refer to people or things)

Singular:	First person:	*I, me, my, mine*
	Second person:	*you, your, yours*
	Third person:	*he, she, it, him, her, hers, his, its*
Plural:	First person:	*we, us, our, ours*
	Second person:	*you, your, yours*
	Third person:	*they, them, their, theirs*

Demonstrative (point out someone or something)

Singular:	*this, that*
Plural:	*these, those*

Relative (introduce a dependent clause)

who, whom, whose, which, that

Indefinite (refer to someone or something general, not specific)

Singular: *another, anybody, anyone, anything, each, either,*
                           everybody, everyone, everything, little, much,
                           neither, nobody, none, no one, nothing, one,
                           other, somebody, someone, something

Plural: *both, few, many, others, several*

Either Singular or Plural: *all, any, more, most, some*

Hint: When any of these words are used with nouns, they are pronouns
used as adjectives.

Adjective: He can have **some candy.**

Pronoun: He can have **some.**

Adjective: The baby wants **that toy.**

Pronoun: The baby wants **that.**

PRACTICE 7: Recall/Identify Underline all the pronouns in the following
sentences. Don't underline words that look like pronouns but are really
adjectives.

1. Some of the wedding guests were vegetarians.

2. Those are the biggest shoes I have ever seen.

3. Somebody had better admit to this.

4. After his car was stolen, everything else seemed to go wrong for
   him too.

5. Does anyone else need anything while I'm up?

PRACTICE 8: Apply In the following paragraph, replace the nouns in parentheses with pronouns.

    Mike first tried rollerblading when (1) _____ (Mike)
was 19. It was pretty funny to watch (2) _____ (Mike) buy
the shin guards and wrist guards, put (3) _____ (the shin
guards and wrist guards) on, and then roll down the sidewalk out
of control. (4) _____ (Mike's) two best friends, Carl and
Luis, wanted to learn also, but when they saw the hard time Mike
was having, (5) _____ (Carl and Luis) were too afraid.

PRACTICE 9: Write Your Own Write a sentence of your own for each of the following pronouns.

1. anyone _____

2. these _____

3. who _____

4. many _____

5. our _____

Adjectives

Adjectives modify—or describe—nouns or pronouns. Adjectives generally make sentences clear and vivid.

> **Without Adjectives:** She brought an umbrella, a towel, and an iPod to the beach.
>
> **With Adjectives:** She brought a **bright orange** umbrella, a **striped blue** towel, and a **new** iPod to the beach.

PRACTICE 10: Recall/Identify Underline all the adjectives in the following sentences.

1. His long black goatee was formed into two sharp points.

2. The talented musicians gave a two-hour concert for an excited audience.

3. James Patterson's latest novel, *14th Deadly Sin*, is about a successful detective and the dangerous risks she has to take to survive.

4. Getting a good parking place is sometimes impossible.

5. Matthew signed his name using a smooth ballpoint pen.

PRACTICE 11: Apply Fill in each blank in the following paragraph with an adjective.

My girlfriend and I went to a (1) _____ baseball game at the Anaheim Stadium last weekend. The Angels were playing the Texas Rangers, and the Rangers were much more (2) _____. This year, the Rangers have (3) _____ infielders, and their batters are pretty (4) _____ also. Overall, the teams were unequally matched, and it was (5) _____ that one of them was going to lose pretty badly.

PRACTICE 12: Write Your Own Write a sentence of your own for each of the following adjectives.

1. gorgeous _____

2. dark _____

3. tempting _____

4. thrifty _____

5. sixth _____

Adverbs

Adverbs modify—or describe—adjectives, verbs, and other adverbs. They do *not* modify nouns. Adverbs also answer the following questions:

How?	thoughtfully, kindly, briefly, quietly
When?	soon, tomorrow, late, now
Where?	inside, somewhere, everywhere, there
How often?	daily, always, annually, rarely
To what extent?	generally, specifically, exactly, very

Hint: Notice that adverbs often end in *-ly*. That might help you recognize them.

PRACTICE 13: Recall/Identify Underline all the adverbs in the following sentences.

1. He almost passed Stephanie when he was running aimlessly down the hall.

2. That was the very last time George Clooney was on television.

3. It was quite disappointing to lose after nearly six months of training.

4. Are you absolutely sure you remembered to set the alarm?

5. I try to buy groceries weekly so we are never missing the basic necessities.

PRACTICE 14: Apply Fill in each blank in the following paragraph with an adverb.

When Shanika (1) _____ lost her job at the grocery store, she felt desperate. She (2) _____ began calling her friends and relatives, asking if they knew of any job openings. (3) _____ for Shanika, her Aunt Betsy owned a hair salon that needed a receptionist. Shanika didn't know anything about beauty parlors, but she (4) _____ agreed to work there because she needed the money. After only three weeks, Shanika became very interested in the salon, and she (5) _____ decided to take classes at a local beauty college and earn a license in cosmetology.

PRACTICE 15: Write Your Own Write a sentence of your own for each of the following adverbs.

1. sometimes _____

2. hardly _____

3. gently _____

4. too _____

5. tomorrow _____

Prepositions

Prepositions indicate relationships among the ideas in a sentence. Something is *at, in, by, next to, behind, around, near,* or *under* something else. A preposition is always followed by a noun or a pronoun called the **object of the preposition.** Together, they form a **prepositional phrase.**

Preposition	+	Object	=	Prepositional Phrase
Near	+	the beach	=	near the beach
For	+	the party	=	for the party

Here is a list of some common prepositions.

Common Prepositions

about	beside	into	since
above	between	like	through
across	beyond	near	throughout
after	by	next to	to
against	despite	of	toward
among	down	off	under
around	during	on	until
as	except	on top of	up
at	for	out	upon
before	from	out of	up to
behind	in	outside	with
below	in front of	over	within
beneath	inside	past	without

Hint: *To* + a verb (as in *to go, to come, to feel*) is not a prepositional phrase. It is a verb phrase, which we will deal with later in this chapter.

PRACTICE 16: Recall/Identify Underline all the prepositions in the following sentences.

1. When I stepped off the bus, I looked down the street and saw an old man in a white hat.

2. The cabin is over the big hill, past the creek, and up a winding dirt path.

3. If you go to Maui, stay in Kaanapali at a resort hotel beside the ocean.

4. The paper in my printer is jammed, so the light on the top won't stop blinking.

5. After the party, I found confetti in my hair, on the carpet, behind the sofa, and in all four corners of the room.

PRACTICE 17: Apply Fill in each blank in the following paragraph with a preposition.

I was so surprised when I saw Carlos walking (1) _____ campus toward me. The last time we talked was eight months ago, when he was still living (2) _____ Kendra. He decided to take some time (3) _____ work to finish his degree, and he was hoping to have it completed (4) _____ the next year. I was very proud (5) _____ him for setting these priorities.

PRACTICE 18: Write Your Own Write a sentence of your own for each of the following prepositions.

1. with _____

2. beside _____

3. on top of _____

4. until _____

5. against _____

Conjunctions

Conjunctions connect groups of words. Without conjunctions, most of our writing would be choppy and boring. The two types of conjunctions are easy to remember because their names state their purpose: *Coordinating conjunctions* link equal ideas, and *subordinating conjunctions* make one idea subordinate to—or dependent on—another.

Coordinating conjunctions connect parts of a sentence of equal importance or weight. These parts can be **independent clauses,** a group of words with a subject and verb that can stand alone as a sentence. (See page 509.)

There are only seven coordinating conjunctions:

Coordinating Conjunctions

and	*but*	*or*	*nor*	*for*	*so*	*yet*

Coordinating: Johanna **and** Melvin arrived late.

Coordinating: My sister wanted to go shopping **and** I jogging.

Coordinating: The teacher was very demanding, **but** I learned a lot from him.

Subordinating conjunctions join two ideas by making one dependent on the other. The idea introduced by the subordinating conjunction becomes a **dependent clause,** a group of words with a subject and a verb that cannot stand alone as a sentence. (See page 509.) The other part of the sentence is an independent clause.

Here are some common subordinating conjunctions.

Common Subordinating Conjunctions

after	*because*	*since*	*until*
although	*before*	*so*	*when*
as	*even if*	*so that*	*whenever*
as if	*even though*	*than*	*where*
as long as	*how*	*that*	*wherever*
as soon as	*if*	*though*	*whether*
as though	*in order that*	*unless*	*while*

                                   Dependent Clause

Subordinating: I won't leave **until** he comes home.

                                   Dependent Clause

Subordinating: **Unless** you study more, you won't be accepted to college.

PRACTICE 19: Recall/Identify Underline all the conjunctions in the following sentences.

1. My best personality trait is my sense of humor, but people also say I'm a good listener.

2. The homecoming game was a lot of fun, yet I didn't see anyone I knew.

3. While the other people were touring the city, Thomas stayed in the hotel room and took a nap.

4. Carmen will be in our study group as long as we meet at her house.

5. Shane volunteered to take us to the airport even though his car seats only four people.

PRACTICE 20: Apply Fill in each blank in the following paragraph with a conjunction.

Babysitting is definitely not an easy job, (1) _____ it is a fast way to make money. One couple I babysit for has two children, and (2) _____ one of them is a perfect angel, the other one is constantly getting into trouble. Michael is the troublemaker, (3) _____ he is six years old. (4) _____ I arrive at his house, he runs to his room and begins pulling everything off of his bookshelves. Of course, I clean everything up (5) _____ his parents get home, so they never see how messy the house gets when they leave.

PRACTICE 21: Write Your Own Write a sentence of your own for each of the following conjunctions.

1. or _____

2. even if _____

3. whether _____

4. yet _____

5. since _____

Interjections

Interjections are words that express strong emotion, surprise, or disappointment. An interjection is usually followed by an exclamation point or a comma.

Interjection: **Whoa!** You're going too fast.
Interjection: **Ouch,** that hurt!

Other common interjections include *aha, alas, great, hallelujah, neat, oh, oops, ouch, well, whoa, yeah,* and *yippee.*

PRACTICE 22: Recall/Identify Underline all the interjections in the following sentences.

1. My goodness! This wind is going to blow down my fence!

2. I just won the lottery! Hallelujah!

3. Boy, I'm beat. I can't walk another step.

4. We just got a new car! Cool!

5. Good grief! Am I the only one working today?

PRACTICE 23: Apply Fill in each blank in the following paragraph with an interjection.

    (1) _____ , I thought that was the easiest test this professor has ever given. (2) _____ ! I was really worried about this test. (3) _____ , it's over! I spent two weeks solid studying for this test. For the last two nights, I've slept only four hours. (4) _____ , am I ever tired. But at least the test is behind me, (5) _____ !

PRACTICE 24: Write Your Own Write a sentence of your own for each of the following interjections.

1. help _____

2. mercy _____

3. wow _____

4. yippee _____

5. ouch _____

CHAPTER REVIEW

REVIEW PRACTICE 1: Recall/Identify Use the following abbreviations to label the underlined words in these sentences.

v	Verb	adv	Adverb
n	Noun	prep	Preposition
pro	Pronoun	conj	Conjunction
adj	Adjective	int	Interjection

1. <u>Wow</u>, that <u>man</u> looks just like my uncle Bob.

2. Tiffany <u>is going</u> shopping at the new mall on <u>Harbor Boulevard</u> <u>tomorrow</u>.

3. Frank is <u>truly</u> my best friend, <u>but</u> sometimes he can't keep a <u>secret</u>.

4. <u>Whenever</u> Lindsay feels sad, she <u>drives</u> into the mountains and looks at the <u>stars</u>.

5. The most popular music <u>artist of</u> the 1960s was <u>definitely</u> Elvis Presley.

6. <u>Gee</u>, are you sure <u>we</u> had to read the <u>entire</u> novel before class <u>today</u>?

7. Ryan wants to take piano <u>lessons</u> so he can <u>compose</u> music for the poetry <u>he</u> has written.

8. Mikella took her dog to the vet <u>and</u> found out <u>it</u> has a <u>lung</u> infection.

9. Though I didn't <u>want</u> to accept the job, I felt pressured <u>by</u> my mother.

10. This morning was <u>dark</u> and cloudy, <u>so</u> I stayed <u>in</u> bed until noon.

REVIEW PRACTICE 2: Apply Fill in each blank in the following paragraph with an appropriate word as indicated.

   The most foolish purchase I ever made was a new (1)_____ (noun) for my computer. When I went to the (2) _____ (adjective) store, the salesman (3) _____ (verb) that I needed this item. I asked him what the part would do (4) _____ (preposition) my computer, and he promised it would make a big difference in the way the computer operated. (5) _____ (interjection), did I believe him! I knew my computer was pretty old, (6) _____ (conjunction) I really didn't want to spend a lot of money on it. Still, I (7) _____ (adverb) bought the part and took (8) _____ (pronoun) home to try it out. After I (9) _____ (verb), I turned on the computer, and it began to heat up. Suddenly, smoke began coming (10) _____ (preposition) the hard drive, and I realized the computer had just crashed.

REVIEW PRACTICE 3: Write Your Own Write your own paragraph about your favorite pet. What did you name it? What kind of animal was it?

MyWritingLab™   Complete this "Write Your Own" exercise for Chapter 25 in the MyWritingLab "Activities: Your Textbook" module.

REVIEW PRACTICE 4: Editing Through Collaboration Exchange paragraphs from Review Practice 3 with a classmate, and do the following:

1. Circle any words that are used incorrectly.

2. Underline any words that don't make sense.

Then return the paragraph to its writer, and use the information in this chapter to edit your own paragraph. Record your errors on the Error Log in Appendix 7.

MyWritingLab™   Visit Chapter 25, "Parts of Speech," in MyWritingLab, and complete the Post-test to check your understanding of the chapter's objectives.

Phrases and Clauses

Underline the phrases and put the clauses in brackets in the following sentences.

- Using the computer, I got most of the research done for my report.
- To be totally confident, I checked for spelling and grammar errors twice.
- Susan lives in the gray house at the end of Maple Avenue behind the bank.
- Magdalena will be a great attorney because she argues so well.
- You don't understand the math concept, so I will keep going over it with you.

(Answers are in Appendix 3.)

Understanding the difference between phrases and clauses is the first step toward writing correct, effective sentences. This chapter will give you that information that you can then use in your own writing.

MyWritingLab

Understanding Phrases and Clauses

To learn more about phrases and clauses, go to **MyWritingLab.com**, and choose **Parts of Speech, Phrases, and Clauses** in the **Basic Grammar** module. For this topic, watch the video called **Animation: Parts of Speech, Phrases, and Clauses.** Then, return to this chapter, which will go into more detail about phrases and clauses and give you opportunities to practice using them. Finally, you will apply your understanding of phrases and clauses to your own writing.

Student Comment:
"From a combination of MyWritingLab and *Mosaics,* I now understand that seeing the difference between phrases and clauses is essential for writing correct sentences."

PHRASES

A **phrase** is a group of words that function together as a unit. Phrases cannot stand alone, however, because they are missing a subject, a verb, or both.

Phrases: the silver moon, a boneless fish

Phrases: threw out the trash, navigated the river, floated to the top

Phrases: after piano lessons, in the crowded boat, by the beach

Phrases: jumping into the water, to be smart

Notice that all these groups of words are missing a subject, a verb, or both.

PRACTICE 1: Recall/Identify Underline 10 phrases in the following sentences.

1. Walking to the store, I did see two small boys riding bicycles.

2. My favorite hobbies have to be mountain biking and snow skiing.

3. If you want something for a snack, look in the cabinet above the refrigerator.

4. The grocery store clerk scanned the items and pointed to the total at the bottom of the register tape.

5. I was buying a few antiques at the little store in downtown McKinley.

PRACTICE 2: Apply Fill in each blank in the following paragraph with a phrase.

Marci, my roommate, drove (1) _____ this weekend because she wanted to visit her relatives there. She also mentioned that there is an outlet mall in the city, where she plans to (2) _____ for some (3) _____. She said the drive is only about two hours, and she listens to the radio (4)_____. I think her relatives are in the food industry, so maybe she'll come home (5) _____.

PRACTICE 3: Write Your Own Write a sentence of your own for each of the following phrases.

1. the brave contestant _____

2. hoping to be chosen _____

3. on the blackboard _____

4. to make a point _____

5. encouraged by the reward money _____

CLAUSES

Like phrases, **clauses** are groups of words. But unlike phrases, a clause always contains a subject and a verb. There are two types of clauses: *independent* and *dependent*.

An **independent clause** contains a subject and a verb and can stand alone and make sense by itself. Every complete sentence must have at least one independent clause.

Independent Clause: The doctor held the baby very gently.

Now look at the following group of words. It is a clause because it contains a subject and a verb. But it is a **dependent clause** because it is introduced by a word that makes it dependent, *because*.

Dependent Clause: **Because** the doctor held the baby very gently.

This clause cannot stand alone. It must be connected to an independent clause to make sense. Here is one way to complete the dependent clause and form a complete sentence.

Dependent   **Independent**
Because the doctor held the baby very gently, the baby stopped crying.

Hint: Subordinating conjunctions (such as *since, although, because, while*) and relative pronouns (*who, whom, whose, which, that*) make clauses dependent. (For more information on subordinating conjunctions, see page 502, and on relative pronouns, see page 496.)

PRACTICE 4: Recall/Identify Each of the following sentences is made up of two clauses. Circle the coordinating or subordinating conjunctions and relative pronouns. Then label each clause either independent (Ind) or dependent (Dep).

1. As soon as Vanessa arrived, she began telling the others what to do.

2. When the car approached, the driver turned off the headlights.

3. We wanted to know that you arrived safely.

4. Tomas can turn in his paper late, but he will not receive full credit.

5. Mr. Johnson was the teacher who influenced my life the most.

PRACTICE 5: Apply Add an independent or dependent clause that will complete each sentence and make sense.

Steven, (1) who _____, takes his textbooks to the beach to study. He says that (2) whenever _____, the sound of the ocean relaxes him. Of course, he also enjoys the view. One night he stayed out (3) until _____, and his parents were afraid that something awful had happened to him. I'm sure he just lost track of time, (4) unless _____. He is definitely a "beach bum" (5) because _____.

PRACTICE 6: Write Your Own Write five independent clauses. Then add at least one dependent clause to each independent clause.

CHAPTER REVIEW

REVIEW PRACTICE 1: Recall/Identify Underline the phrases, and put the clauses in brackets in each of the following sentences.

1. He wants to go to the store before registering for classes.

2. When you arrive, I'll tell you the best answer.

3. Why do you think he was late?

4. While they laughed, Laura and I cried.

5. Tad wanted to date Samantha, but she is dating Reggie.

6. When you get back from your errands, I want to talk to you.

7. After dress rehearsal, the cast felt very good about their opening the next day.

8. I was amazed to discover that skydiving is lots of fun.

9. I can't cash my check until you put money in the bank.

10. When you leave the party, I will be waiting for you.

REVIEW PRACTICE 2: Apply Fill in each blank in the following paragraph with an appropriate phrase or clause, as indicated.

I can't remember when I had so much fun. The weather was perfect; the rides _____ (phrase) were exciting; and I spent all day with my _____ (phrase). _____ (clause), I will definitely owe you some money. I can't believe I ran out of money so early _____ (phrase). After we count our money at the next picnic area, _____ (clause). When we make that decision, we can then set _____ (phrase).

REVIEW PRACTICE 3: Write Your Own Write your own paragraph about your favorite sport—whether as a spectator or a participant. Why do you like this sport? What do you get out of it?

> **MyWritingLab™** Complete this "Write Your Own" exercise for Chapter 26 in the MyWritingLab "Activities: Your Textbook" module.

REVIEW PRACTICE 4: Editing Through Collaboration Exchange paragraphs from Review Practice 3 with a classmate, and do the following:

1. Underline any phrases that do not read smoothly.

2. Put an X in the margin where you find a dependent clause that is not connected to an independent clause.

Then return the paragraph to its writer, and use the information in this chapter to edit your own paragraph. Record your errors on the Error Log in Appendix 7.

> **MyWritingLab™** Visit Chapter 26, "Phrases and Clauses," in MyWritingLab, and complete the Post-test to check your understanding of the chapter's objectives.

Sentences

Writing complete, correct sentences is one of the most difficult tasks for college writers. It involves understanding the transition from oral to written English. As a student, you must make decisions about sentences that you don't deal with when you speak, such as what makes up a sentence and how to punctuate it. What is important, however, is that you address these issues. This unit will help you start making the transfer from oral to written English.

To help you start editing your writing, we will focus on the following sentence elements:

Subjects and Verbs

Underline the subjects once and the verbs twice in the following sentences.

- You are my best friend.
- Hang up your clothes.
- They really wanted to be here tonight.
- He made a sandwich and put it in a brown paper bag.
- Susie and Tom went to the dance.

(Answers are in Appendix 3.)

A sentence has a message to communicate, but for that message to be meaningful, the sentence must have a subject and a verb. The subject is the topic of the sentence—what the sentence is about. The verb is the sentence's motor. It moves the message forward to its destination. Without these two parts, a sentence is not complete.

MyWritingLab

Understanding Subjects and Verbs

To find out more about this topic, go to **MyWritingLab.com,** and choose **Subjects and Verbs** in the **Basic Grammar** module. Then, watch the video called **Animation: Subjects and Verbs.** Next, return to this chapter, which will go into more detail about these elements and give you opportunities to practice them. Finally, you will apply your understanding of subjects and verbs to your own writing.

Student Comment:
"This program lets me go back and look at a topic again if I feel like I didn't get it. With lectures, there's no rewind button."

SUBJECTS

To be complete, every sentence must have a subject. The **subject** tells whom or what the sentence is about.

Subject
↓
He   always came home on time.

Action **movies**   appeal to teenagers.

Compound Subjects

When two or more separate words tell what the sentence is about, the sentence has a **compound subject.**

Compound Subject: **Painting** and **sewing** are my hobbies.
Compound Subject: **My brother** and **I** live with my grandmother.

Hint: Note that *and* is not part of the compound subject.

Unstated Subjects

Sometimes a subject does not actually appear in a sentence but is understood. This occurs in commands and requests. The understood subject is always *you*, meaning either someone specific or anyone in general.

Command: Get up now, or you'll be late.
                                       s
Unstated Subject: **(You)** get up now, or you'll be late.

Request: Write me an e-mail soon, please.
                                       s
Unstated Subject: **(You)** write me an e-mail soon, please.

Subjects and Prepositional Phrases

The subject of a sentence cannot be part of a prepositional phrase. A **prepositional phrase** is a group of words that begins with a **preposition,** a word like *in, on, under, after,* or *from.* Here are some examples of prepositional phrases:

in the yard	**next to** it	**before** supper
on the plane	**behind** the chair	**instead of** me
under the rug	**around** the circle	**across** the road
after school	**into** the boat	**for** the family
from the White House	**during** the storm	**at** college

(See page 500 for a more complete list of prepositions.)

If you are looking for the subject of a sentence, first cross out all the prepositional phrases. Then figure out what the sentence is about.

~~During the game,~~ the coaches and the players had a fight ~~with the other team.~~

The new store ~~around the corner~~ sells designer jeans.

Some ~~of our luggage~~ was lost ~~on the trip.~~

PRACTICE 1: Recall/Identify Cross out the prepositional phrases in each of the following sentences, and then underline the subjects.

1. The golfer stood quietly in front of the ball.

2. Marty and Mike gave a presentation at the big convention.

3. Two of the graduates had perfect grade point averages.

4. Before I go to the store, I need to check my account balance.

5. Get the mayonnaise out of the refrigerator.

PRACTICE 2: Apply Fill in each blank in the following sentences with a subject without using a person's name.

1. _____ was voted the best restaurant in this area.

2. Walking to class, _____ thought seriously about changing his major.

3. Sometimes, _____ is a great bargain.

4. _____ and _____ are two very positive personality traits.

5. _____ was late to work again.

PRACTICE 3: Write Your Own Write five sentences of your own, and underline the subjects.

VERBS

To be complete, a sentence must have a verb as well as a subject. A **verb** tells what the subject is doing or what is happening.

Verb
↓

He   always **came** home on time.

Action movies   **appeal** to teenagers.

Action Verbs

An **action verb** tells what a subject is doing. Some examples of action verbs are *skip*, *ski*, *stare*, *flip*, *breathe*, *remember*, *restate*, *sigh*, *cry*, *decrease*, *write*, and *pant*.

Action: The children **laughed** at the clown.

Action: The car **crashed** into the tree.

Linking Verbs

A **linking verb** connects the subject to other words in the sentence that say something about it. Linking verbs are also called **state-of-being verbs** because they do not show action. Rather, they say that something "is" a particular way. The most common linking verb is *be* (*am*, *are*, *is*, *was*, *were*).

Linking: The horses **are** in the stable.

Linking: I **am** unhappy with the results.

Other common linking verbs are *remain*, *act*, *look*, *grow*, and *seem*.

Linking: Darnell **remains** enthusiastic about school.

Linking: I **act** happy even when I'm not.

Linking: The yard **looks** neglected.

Linking: She **grew** fonder of her aunt.

Linking: Lupe **seems** happy with her new house.

Some words, like *smell* and *taste*, can be either action verbs or linking verbs.

Action: I **smell** smoke.
Linking: This house **smells** like flowers.

Action: She **tasted** the soup.
Linking: It **tasted** too salty.

Compound Verbs

Just as a verb can have more than one subject, some subjects can have more than one verb. These are called **compound verbs.**

Compound: She **cooks** and **cleans** every day.

Compound: He **runs** and **swims** twice a week in the summer.

Hint: A sentence can have both a compound subject and a compound verb.

   s   s   v   v

Joe and **Mitchell jumped** into the boat and **started** the motor.

Helping Verbs

Often the **main verb** (the action verb or linking verb) in a sentence needs help to convey its meaning. **Helping verbs** add information, such as when an action took place. The **complete verb** consists of a main verb and all its helping verbs.

Complete Verb: The children <u>**will**</u> return tomorrow.

Complete Verb: It <u>**might**</u> rain this weekend.

Complete Verb: We <u>**should have**</u> gone to the concert.

Complete Verb: My uncle <u>**has**</u> given me money for Christmas.

Complete Verb: My sister <u>**will be**</u> coming for my wedding.

Complete Verb: You <u>**should**</u> not go home with him.

Hint: Note that *not* isn't part of the helping verb. Similarly, *never, always, only, just,* and *still* are never part of the verb.

Complete Verb: I <u>**have**</u> always **liked** history classes.

The most common helping verbs are

    be, am, is, are, was, were
    have, has, had
    do, did

Other common helping verbs are

    may, might
    can, could
    will, would
    should, used to, ought to

PRACTICE 4: Recall/Identify Underline the complete verbs in each of the following sentences.

1. The students seemed tired in class Monday morning.

2. One of my professors is a popular public speaker.

3. High school students must read *The Scarlet Letter*.

4. Timothy will go to the championships.

5. Get out of the rain.

PRACTICE 5: Apply Fill in each blank in the following sentences with a verb. Avoid using *is*, *are*, *was*, and *were* except as helping verbs.

1. Chad _____ extreme pain after falling from the ladder and landing on his back.

2. The specialist _____ her client about the different options.

3. Both the parents and the teachers _____ about the need for more meetings.

4. My ill child _____ throughout the night.

5. Red stickers on the price tags _____ the sale items.

PRACTICE 6: Write Your Own Write five sentences of your own, and underline all the verbs in each.

CHAPTER REVIEW

REVIEW PRACTICE 1: Recall/Identify Underline the subjects once and the verbs twice in each of the following sentences. Cross out the prepositional phrases first.

1. The horses in the corral are being trained for racing.

2. Matilda received a scholarship for her biology research.

3. Salespeople can earn thousands of dollars in commissions every year.

4. Each month, my office pays us for overtime.

5. The bikes and the helmets are on sale right now.

6. I am going to the grocery store for dinner.

7. Tonya's computer crashed the other day, and she used mine for her homework.

8. Grandma will not join us for dinner.

9. Joe and Christine are building a new house.

10. The baby played with the blocks and stacked them on top of each other.

REVIEW PRACTICE 2: Apply Fill in the missing subjects or verbs in each of the following sentences.

1. Tonight's dinner _____ like leftovers.

2. _____ can't remember where we said we would meet.

3. Taking that midterm _____ my hardest challenge last week.

4. The catcher and the pitcher _____ with the referee.

5. If you want to go with us, you _____ to come along.

6. When Tiffany left this morning, _____ didn't know when she would be back.

7. _____ wear lab coats to set them apart from students.

8. Yesterday I _____ an old box of letters from my friends in high school.

9. (You) _____ your room before we leave.

10. _____ was the best entertainment of the evening.

REVIEW PRACTICE 3: Write Your Own Write a paragraph about a major decision you made within the past three years. How has it affected your life? What did you learn from the process?

MyWritingLab™ Complete this "Write Your Own" exercise for Chapter 27 in the MyWritingLab "Activities: Your Textbook" module.

REVIEW PRACTICE 4: Editing Through Collaboration Exchange paragraphs from Review Practice 3 with another student, and do the following:

1. Underline the subjects once.

2. Underline the verbs twice.

Then return the paragraph to its writer, and edit any sentences in your own paragraph that do not have both a subject and a verb. Record your errors on the Error Log in Appendix 7.

MyWritingLab™ Visit Chapter 27, "Subjects and Verbs," in MyWritingLab, and complete the Post-test to check your understanding of the chapter's objectives.

Fragments

Put an X by the sentences that are fragments.

- _____ I wanted to go to the gym yesterday.
- _____ Whose tie doesn't match his suit.
- _____ Giving up his seat for an elderly woman.
- _____ Paul asked for the most popular menu item.
- _____ While the captain was away from the cockpit.

(Answers are in Appendix 3.)

One of the most common errors in college writing is the fragment. A fragment is a piece of a sentence punctuated as a complete sentence. But it does not express a complete thought. Once you learn how to identify fragments, you can avoid them in your writing.

ABOUT FRAGMENTS

A complete sentence must have both a subject and a verb. If one or both are missing or if the subject and verb are introduced by a dependent word, you have only part of a sentence, a **fragment.** Even if it begins with a capital letter and ends with a period, it cannot stand alone and must be corrected in your writing. The five most common types of fragments are explained in this chapter.

Type 1: Afterthought Fragments
He goes to school during the day. **And works at night.**

Type 2: *-ing* Fragments
Finding no one at the house. Kenny walked back home.

Type 3: *to* **Fragments**
The school started a tutoring program. **To help improve SAT scores.**

Type 4: Dependent-Clause Fragments
Because I decided to go back to school. My boss fired me.

Type 5: Relative-Clause Fragments
Last summer I visited Rome. **Which is a beautiful city.**

MyWritingLab   **Understanding Fragments**

To help you understand this sentence error, go to **MyWritingLab. com,** and choose **Fragments** in the **Sentence Skills** module. From there, watch the video called **Animation: Fragments.** Then, return to this chapter, which will go into more detail about these errors and give you opportunities to practice correcting them. Finally, you will apply your understanding of fragments to your own writing.

IDENTIFYING AND CORRECTING FRAGMENTS

Once you have identified a fragment, you have two options for correcting it. The rest of this chapter discusses the five types of fragments and the corrections for each type.

Correction 1:   *Connect the fragment to the sentence before or after it.*

Correction 2:   *Make the fragment into an independent clause:*
                     (a) either add the missing subject and/or verb, or
                     (b) drop the subordinating word before the fragment.

Type 1: Afterthought Fragments

Afterthought fragments occur when you add an idea to a sentence but don't punctuate it correctly.

Fragment: He goes to school during the day. **And works at night.**

The phrase *And works at night* is punctuated and capitalized as a complete sentence. Because this group of words lacks a subject, however, it is a fragment.

Correction 1:   *Connect the fragment to the sentence before or after it.*
Example: He goes to school during the day **and** works at night.

Correction 2: *Make the fragment into an independent clause.*

Example: He goes to school during the day. **He** works at night.

The first correction connects the fragment to the sentence before it. The second correction makes the fragment an independent clause with its own subject and verb.

PRACTICE 1A: Recall/Identify Underline the afterthought fragments in each of the following sentences.

1. The men on the opposing team were very strong. Everyone was scared to play them. Especially me.

2. Mark peered into the window of his locked car and saw his keys. Stuck in the ignition.

3. I am thinking about buying a really special car next year. For example, a Chevy Tahoe.

4. Carlene turned in her paper on time and knew she would get a good grade. Because she really liked her topic.

5. "Keeping up with the Joneses" is an expression. That my mother uses a lot.

PRACTICE 1B: Correct Correct the fragments in Practice 1A by rewriting each sentence.

PRACTICE 2: Apply Correct the following afterthought fragments using both correction 1 and correction 2. Rewrite any corrected sentences that you think could be smoother.

1. The child drew in a coloring book. With brand-new crayons.

2. I am going to buy some new books to read. For example, the *Hunger Games* series.

3. Jennifer usually drives very fast. Sometimes running stop signs.

4. My friends are going to the beach. In Santa Barbara for the weekend.

5. He walked over to my desk very slowly. And smiled in a playful way.

PRACTICE 3: Write Your Own Write five afterthought fragments of your own, and correct them.

Type 2: *-ing* Fragments

Words that end in *-ing* are forms of verbs that cannot be the main verbs in their sentences. For an *-ing* word to function as a verb, it must have a helping verb with it (*be*, *do*, or *have*; see page 517).

Fragment: **Finding no one at the house.** Kenny went back home.

Finding is not a verb in this sentence because it has no helping verb. Also, this group of words is a fragment because it has no subject.

Correction 1:   *Connect the fragment to the sentence before or after it.*
Example: **Finding no one at the house,** Kenny went back home.

Correction 2:   *Make the fragment into an independent clause.*
Example: **He found no one at the house.** Kenny went back home.

Hint: When you connect an *-ing* fragment to a sentence, you should usually insert a comma between the two sentence parts, whether the *-ing* part comes at the beginning or the end of the sentence.

Kenny walked back home, **finding no one at the house.**

Finding no one at the house, Kenny walked back home.

PRACTICE 4A: Recall/Identify Underline the *-ing* fragments in each of the following sentences.

1. Driving to the store. I thought about all the things I needed to buy.

2. The baseball player dropped the ball. Tripping over his shoelace while running to make the catch.

3. Mr. Holland was the best music teacher I ever had. Treating everyone with respect.

4. I plan to read at least one book each month. Challenging my brother to do the same.

5. Wanting to leave her parents' house. Marissa got married when she was 18 years old.

PRACTICE 4B: Correct Correct the fragments in Practice 4A by rewriting each sentence.

PRACTICE 5: Apply Correct each of the following *-ing* fragments using both methods. Remember to insert a comma in most cases when using correction 1.

1. Making the best grade in the class. Carlos was excited to tell his parents about it.

2. I think I'll get an A on the exam. Studying as hard as I did.

3. Looking back at my senior year in high school. I can't believe I dated that guy.

4. Wondering whether he left his car windows down. Shawn saw the rain begin to fall.

5. Jamar was glad he survived the accident. Seeing the damage to his car.

PRACTICE 6: Write Your Own Write five -*ing* fragments of your own, and correct them.

Type 3: to Fragments

When *to* is added to a verb (*to see, to hop, to skip, to jump*), the combination cannot be a main verb in its sentence. As a result, this group of words is often involved in a fragment.

Fragment: The school started a tutoring program. **To improve SAT scores.**

Because *to* + a verb cannot function as the main verb of its sentence, *to improve SAT scores* is a fragment as it is punctuated here.

Correction 1:   *Connect the fragment to the sentence before or after it.*
Example: The school started a tutoring program **to improve SAT scores.**

Correction 2:   *Make the fragment into an independent clause.*
Example: The school started a tutoring program. **It wanted to improve SAT scores.**

Hint: A *to* fragment can also occur at the beginning of a sentence. In this case, insert a comma between the two sentence parts when correcting the fragment.

To improve SAT scores, the school started a tutoring program.

PRACTICE 7A: Recall/Identify Underline the *to* fragments in each of the following sentences.

1. To make the crowd more excited. The rodeo clown came out and chased the bull around the arena.

2. To grow perfect roses. You should attend free classes at Home Depot.

3. The baby screamed loudly. To tell his parents he was hungry.

4. We stopped eating fried foods and sweets. To lose weight before summer.

5. To improve their chances of getting to the World Series. The Los Angeles Dodgers made sure Clayton Kershaw was ready for the game.

PRACTICE 7B: Correct Correct the fragments in Practice 7A by rewriting each sentence.

PRACTICE 8: Apply Correct the following *to* fragments using both correction 1 and correction 2. Try putting the fragment at the beginning of the sentence instead of always at the end. Remember to insert a comma when you add the *to* fragment to the beginning of a sentence.

1. Avoid driving faster than the posted speed limit. To get the best gas mileage.

2. He wanted to buy a new suit. To impress his boss.

3. Suzanne told Warren that she had a boyfriend. To avoid hurting his feelings.

4. The bank is closed on Labor Day. To give the employees time with their families.

5. I put the names and addresses in a mail merge. To make it easier to print labels.

PRACTICE 9: Write Your Own Write five *to* fragments of your own, and correct them.

Type 4: Dependent-Clause Fragments

A group of words that begins with a **subordinating conjunction** (see the list that follows) is called a **dependent clause** and cannot stand alone. Even though it has a subject and a verb, it is a fragment because it depends on an independent clause to complete its meaning. An **independent clause** is a group of words with a subject and a verb that can stand alone. (See pages 509–510 for help with clauses.)

Here is a list of some commonly used subordinating conjunctions that create dependent clauses.

Subordinating Conjunctions

after	because	since	until
although	before	so	when
as	even if	so that	whenever

as if	even though	than	where
as long as	how	that	wherever
as soon as	if	though	whether
as though	in order that	unless	while

Fragment: <u>Because</u> I decided to go back to school. My boss fired me.

This sentence has a subject and a verb, but it is introduced by a subordinating conjunction, *because*. As a result, this sentence is a dependent clause and cannot stand alone.

Correction 1:   *Connect the fragment to the sentence before or after it.*
Example: **Because I decided to go back to school,** my boss fired me.

Correction 2:   *Make the fragment into an independent clause.*
Example: ~~Because~~ I decided to go back to school. My boss fired me.

Hint: If the dependent clause comes first, put a comma between the two parts of the sentence. If the dependent clause comes second, the comma is not necessary.

Because I decided to go back to school, my boss fired me.

My boss fired me **because I decided to go back to school.**

PRACTICE 10A: Recall/Identify Underline the dependent-clause fragments in each of the following sentences.

1. I love to eat sushi. Although it's sometimes very expensive.

2. It is good to know some trivia. So that you can participate in lots of conversations.

3. After the child finished riding on it. The rocking horse stood in the corner.

4. I will have Thanksgiving dinner at my house again. As long as my parents get along with my in-laws.

5. Before she goes to work in the morning. Margaret takes her children to school.

PRACTICE 10B: Correct Correct the fragments in Practice 10A by rewriting each sentence.

PRACTICE 11: Apply Correct the following dependent-clause fragments using both correction 1 and correction 2. When you use correction 1, remember to add a comma if the dependent clause comes first.

1. Manny takes his basketball with him. Wherever he goes.

2. While I'm out of town. My mother will take care of my house.

3. The power bill is higher this month. Though we didn't run the air conditioner very often.

4. When she got home from work. Jamie made green beans for dinner.

5. Russ always watches TV for an hour. After he finishes studying.

PRACTICE 12: Write Your Own Write five dependent-clause fragments of your own, and correct them.

Type 5: Relative-Clause Fragments

A **relative clause** is a dependent clause that begins with a relative pronoun: *who, whom, whose, which,* or *that.* When a relative clause is punctuated as a sentence, the result is a fragment.

> **Fragment:** Last summer I visited Rome. **Which is a beautiful city.**

Which is a beautiful city is a clause fragment that begins with the relative pronoun *which.* This word automatically makes the words that follow it a dependent clause called a relative clause, so they cannot stand alone as a sentence.

Correction 1: *Connect the fragment to the sentence before or after it.*
Example: Last summer I visited Rome, **which is a beautiful city.**

Correction 2: *Make the fragment into an independent clause.*
Example: Last summer I visited Rome. **It is a beautiful city.**

PRACTICE 13A: Recall/Identify Underline the relative-clause fragments in the following sentences.

1. I made an appointment with the doctor. Whom my cousin recommended.

2. The dog ate the vegetables. That the child threw on the ground.

3. The station got a new captain. Who transferred from another department.

4. At the car wash, I talked to the man. Whose nametag said "Sylvester."

5. Karen got a job at the bakery. Which makes fresh donuts every morning.

PRACTICE 13B: Correct Correct the fragments in Practice 13A by rewriting each sentence.

PRACTICE 14: Apply Correct the following relative-clause fragments using both correction 1 and correction 2.

1. Paul studied for the midterm with Charlotte. Who scored the highest on the first exam.

2. My girlfriend works at the bank. That is located on the corner of F Street and Market Avenue.

3. I put more memory in my computer. Which cost me about $70.

4. My boss is the man with the goatee. Whose ties are usually very colorful.

5. Penny shops only at grocery stores. That offer coupons.

PRACTICE 15: Write Your Own Write five relative-clause fragments of your own, and correct them.

CHAPTER REVIEW

REVIEW PRACTICE 1: Recall/Identify Underline the fragments in the following paragraph.

Buying an old home can be a good experience. If the house is inspected thoroughly before any papers are signed. Thinking we were getting an incredible deal. We rushed into buying a 30-year-old house in an established neighborhood. The house had lots of personality and big living rooms. To make it perfect for entertaining. Unfortunately, there were several problems with the house that we didn't see right away. For example, plumbing problems. Faulty wiring. Not enough insulation. We put thousands of dollars into repairs. Before we could even invite our friends over for dinner. Even though the house wasn't expensive to buy. It became very expensive for us to maintain. Eventually, we had to sell it. To keep from losing more money. The man who bought it was a contractor. Who could do most of the repairs himself. Which is a big advantage that we didn't have.

REVIEW PRACTICE 2: Apply Correct all the fragments you underlined in Review Practice 1 by rewriting the paragraph.

REVIEW PRACTICE 3: Write Your Own Write a paragraph about your dream vacation. Where would you go? How long would you stay? Who would go with you, or would you go alone?

MyWritingLab™ | Complete this "Write Your Own" exercise for Chapter 28 in the MyWritingLab "Activities: Your Textbook" module.

REVIEW PRACTICE 4: Editing Through Collaboration Exchange paragraphs from Review Practice 3 with another student, and do the following:

1. Put brackets around any fragments that you find.

2. Identify the types of fragments that you find.

Then return the paper to its writer, and use the information in this chapter to correct any fragments in your own paragraph. Record your errors on the Error Log in Appendix 7.

MyWritingLab™ | Visit Chapter 28, "Fragments," in MyWritingLab, and complete the Post-test to check your understanding of the chapter's objectives.

29

Fused Sentences and Comma Splices

Mark any incorrect sentences here with a slash between the independent clauses that are not joined properly.

- The rainstorm washed out my garden, I had just planted spring bulbs.
- When we cleaned the house, we found the TV remote control it was between the sofa cushions.
- People in authority are often criticized and seldom thanked.
- The kids didn't find all of the Easter eggs during the hunt, when we finally found them, they were rotten.
- You should ask Aubri to cut your hair she's been cutting mine for four years.

(Answers are in Appendix 3.)

When we cram two separate statements into a single sentence without correct punctuation, we create *fused sentences* and *comma splices*. These run-together sentences generally distort our message and cause problems for our readers. In this chapter, you will learn how to identify and avoid these errors in your writing.

IDENTIFYING FUSED SENTENCES AND COMMA SPLICES

Whereas a fragment is a piece of a sentence, **fused sentences** and **comma splices** are made up of two sentences written as one. In both cases, the first sentence runs into the next without the proper punctuation between the two.

Fused Sentence: The bus stopped we got off.

Comma Splice: The bus stopped, we got off.

Both of these sentences incorrectly join two independent clauses. The difference between them is one comma.

MyWritingLab

Understanding Fused Sentences and Comma Splices

Student Comment:
"The videos are great! I finally get comma splices!"

To learn more about these sentence errors, go to **MyWritingLab. com,** and choose **Run-Ons** in the **Sentence Skills** module. For this topic, watch the video called **Animation: Run-Ons.** Then, return to this chapter, which will go into more detail about these errors and give you opportunities to practice correcting them. Finally, you will apply your understanding of fused sentences and comma splices to your own writing.

A **fused sentence** is two sentences "fused" or jammed together without any punctuation. Look at these examples:

Fused Sentence: Rosa's favorite subject is math she always does very well on her math tests.

This example consists of two independent clauses with no punctuation between them:

1. Rosa's favorite subject is math.
2. She always does very well on her math tests.

Fused Sentence: My grandfather likes to cook his own meals he doesn't want anyone to do it for him.

This example also consists of two independent clauses with no punctuation between them:

1. My grandfather likes to cook his own meals.
2. He doesn't want anyone to do it for him.

Like a fused sentence, a **comma splice** incorrectly joins two independent clauses. However, a comma splice puts a comma between the two independent clauses. The only difference between a fused sentence and a comma splice is the comma. Look at the following examples:

Comma Splice: Rosa's favorite subject is math, she always does very well on her math tests.

Comma Splice: My grandfather likes to cook his own meals, he doesn't want anyone to do it for him.

Both of these sentences consist of two independent clauses. But a comma is not the proper punctuation to separate these two clauses.

PRACTICE 1: Recall/Identify Put a slash between the independent clauses that are not joined correctly.

1. Paul plays hockey every Thursday he usually gets home after dark.

2. My mom always tucked me into bed at night, that's what I remember most about her.

3. Toni borrowed my pencil yesterday then she lost it.

4. My boyfriend made my favorite cake for my birthday, I had to eat the whole thing.

5. The child needed a bone marrow transplant, we raised $10,000 last night for her cause.

PRACTICE 2: Recall/Identify For each incorrect sentence in the following paragraph, put a slash between the independent clauses that are not joined properly.

The fitness craze is sweeping across America, it seems like everyone has a gym membership. The best-selling food items have "light," "lite," or "fat free" on the packaging, and people are watching their cholesterol and counting calories. Only the thinnest models are shown in food advertisements they symbolize good health, responsible eating habits, and overall physical attractiveness. Ironically, thin people are even used in ads for unhealthy food items, like candy and soft drinks, this sends a very confusing message to the consumer. The stereotypes are not fair not everyone can have the "perfect" body seen in the ads. Some people are just born with bigger body shapes, and there is nothing wrong or unattractive about that. These people should learn to eat healthy foods, they should not try to be unnaturally thin.

PRACTICE 3: Write Your Own Write five fused sentences. Then write the same sentences as comma splices.

CORRECTING FUSED SENTENCES AND COMMA SPLICES

You have four different options for correcting your fused sentences and comma splices.

1. *Separate the two sentences with a period, and capitalize the next word.*

2. *Separate the two sentences with a comma, and add a coordinating conjunction (and, but, for, nor, or, so, or yet).*

3. *Change one of the sentences into a dependent clause with a subordinating conjunction (such as if, because, since, after, or when) or a relative pronoun (who, whom, whose, which, or that).*

4. *Separate the two sentences with a semicolon.*

Correction 1: Use a Period

Separate the two sentences with a period, and capitalize the next word.

Rosa's favorite subject is math. **She** always does very well on her math tests.

My grandfather likes to cook his own meals. **He** doesn't want anyone to do it for him.

PRACTICE 4: Apply Correct all the sentences in Practice 1 using correction 1.

PRACTICE 5: Apply Correct the paragraph in Practice 2 using correction 1.

PRACTICE 6: Write Your Own Correct the sentences you wrote in Practice 3 using correction 1.

Correction 2: Use a Coordinating Conjunction

Separate the two sentences with a comma, and add a coordinating conjunction (and, but, for, nor, or, so, or yet).

Rosa's favorite subject is math, **so** she always does very well on her math tests.

My grandfather likes to cook his own meals, **and** he doesn't want anyone to do it for him.

PRACTICE 7: Apply Correct all the sentences in Practice 1 using correction 2.

PRACTICE 8: Apply Correct the paragraph in Practice 2 using correction 2.

PRACTICE 9: Write Your Own Correct the sentences you wrote in Practice 3 using correction 2.

Correction 3: Create a Dependent Clause

Change one of the sentences into a dependent clause with a subordinating conjunction (such as if, because, since, after, *or* when) *or a relative pronoun (*who, whom, whose, which, *or* that).

Rosa's favorite subject is math **because** she always does very well on her math tests.

Because my grandfather likes to cook his own meals, he doesn't want anyone to do it for him.

For a list of subordinating conjunctions, see page 502.

Hint: If you put the dependent clause at the beginning of the sentence, add a comma between the two sentence parts.

Because she always does very well on her math tests, Rosa's favorite subject is math.

PRACTICE 10: Apply Correct all the sentences in Practice 1 using correction 3.

PRACTICE 11: Apply Correct the paragraph in Practice 2 using correction 3.

PRACTICE 12: Write Your Own Correct the sentences you wrote in Practice 3 using correction 3.

Correction 4: Use a Semicolon

Separate the two sentences with a semicolon.

Rosa's favorite subject is math; she always does very well on her math tests.

My grandfather likes to cook his own meals; he doesn't want anyone to do it for him.

You can also use a **transition,** a word or an expression that indicates how the two parts of the sentence are related, with a semicolon. A transition often makes the sentence smoother. It is preceded by a semicolon and followed by a comma.

Rosa's favorite subject is math; **as a result,** she always does very well on her math tests.

My grandfather likes to cook his own meals; **therefore,** he doesn't want anyone to do it for him.

Here are some transitions commonly used with semicolons:

Transitions Used with a Semicolon Before and a Comma After

also	for instance	in fact	of course
consequently	furthermore	instead	otherwise
finally	however	meanwhile	similarly
for example	in contrast	nevertheless	therefore

PRACTICE 13: Apply Correct all the sentences in Practice 1 using correction 4.

PRACTICE 14: Apply Correct the paragraph in Practice 2 using correction 4.

PRACTICE 15: Write Your Own Correct the sentences you wrote in Practice 3 using correction 4.

CHAPTER REVIEW

REVIEW PRACTICE 1: Recall/Identify Label each of the following sentences as fused (F), comma splice (CS), or correct (C).

1. _____ My sister woke up late this morning, she made us late for school.

2. _____ River rafting can be dangerous you need an experienced guide.

3. _____ When I dyed my hair black, I didn't know it might turn my scalp black too, it did.

4. _____ People who compete in triathlons are excellent athletes because the events are very difficult.

5. _____ Mike made an ice sculpture in his art class it was a penguin with a fish in its mouth.

6. _____ Terry needed to mow his lawn, the grass was very high, and the neighbors were complaining.

7. _____ I drove my car without engine oil, and the repairs were incredibly expensive.

8. _____ The big earthquake was on the front page of the newspaper many homes and businesses were destroyed.

9. _____ We had the perfect beach vacation planned, but then it rained the whole time we were so disappointed.

10. _____ If you stay out in the sun very long, you should use sunblock, skin cancer is a horrible disease.

REVIEW PRACTICE 2: Apply Correct the fused sentences and comma splices in Review Practice 1.

REVIEW PRACTICE 3: Write Your Own Write a paragraph about your favorite season of the year. Why do you enjoy it? What do you do during this time of year?

MyWritingLab™ Complete this "Write Your Own" exercise for Chapter 29 in the MyWritingLab "Activities: Your Textbook" module.

REVIEW PRACTICE 4: Editing Through Collaboration Exchange paragraphs from Review Practice 3 with another student, and do the following:

1. Put brackets around any sentences that have more than one independent clause.

2. Circle the words that connect these clauses.

Then return the paper to its writer, and use the information in this chapter to correct any run-together sentences in your own paragraph. Record your errors on the Error Log in Appendix 7.

MyWritingLab™ Visit Chapter 29, "Fused Sentences and Comma Splices," in MyWritingLab, and complete the Post-test to check your understanding of the chapter's objectives.

Verbs

Verbs can do just about anything we ask them to do. Because they have so many forms, they can play lots of different roles in a sentence: The bells *ring* on the hour; voices *rang* through the air; we could hear the clock *ringing* miles away. As you can see from these examples, even small changes, like a single letter, mean something; as a result, verbs make communication more interesting and accurate. But using verbs correctly takes concentration and effort on your part.

In this unit, we will discuss the following aspects of verbs and verb use:

Chapter 30: Regular and Irregular Verbs
Chapter 31: Verb Tense
Chapter 32: Subject-Verb Agreement
Chapter 33: More on Verbs

Regular and Irregular Verbs

Underline the complete verbs in each of the following sentences. Then mark an X if the form of any of the verbs is incorrect.

- _____ The pipe has bursted.
- _____ Sim reacted to the scene calmly.
- _____ I bought my car at an auction.
- _____ We had hid in the basement.
- _____ Sorry, I eated all the cookies.

(Answers are in Appendix 3.)

All verbs are either regular or irregular. **Regular verbs** form the past tense and past participle by adding *-d* or *-ed* to the present tense. If a verb does not form its past tense and past participle this way, it is called an **irregular verb.**

Student Comment:
"As a non-English speaker, **MyWritingLab** helps me remember grammar rules."

MyWritingLab **Understanding Regular and Irregular Verbs**

To improve your understanding of verbs, go to **MyWritingLab.com,** and choose **Regular and Irregular Verbs** in the **Basic Grammar** module. From there, watch the video called **Animation: Regular and Irregular Verbs.** Then, return to this chapter, which will go into more detail about verbs and give you opportunities to practice them. Finally, you will apply your understanding of regular and irregular verbs to your own writing.

REGULAR VERBS

Here are the principal parts (present, past, and past participle forms) of some regular verbs. They are **regular verbs** because their past tense and past participle end in *-d* or *-ed*. The past participle is the verb form often used with helping verbs like *have, has,* or *had.*

Some Regular Verbs

PRESENT TENSE	PAST TENSE	PAST PARTICIPLE (USED WITH HELPING VERBS LIKE *HAVE, HAS, HAD*)
talk	*talked*	*talked*
sigh	*sighed*	*sighed*
drag	*dragged*	*dragged*
enter	*entered*	*entered*
consider	*considered*	*considered*

The different forms of a verb tell when something happened—in the *present* (I *talk*) or in the *past* (I *talked*, I *have talked*, I *had talked*).

PRACTICE 1: Recall/Identify Put an X to the left of the incorrect verb forms in the following chart.

Present Tense	Past Tense	Past Participle
1. _____ clap	_____ clapped	_____ clapped
2. _____ help	_____ helpt	_____ helped
3. _____ watched	_____ watched	_____ watched
4. _____ gaze	_____ gazed	_____ gazd
5. _____ reclined	_____ reclined	_____ reclined

PRACTICE 2: Apply Write the correct forms of the following regular verbs.

	Present Tense	Past Tense	Past Participle
1. smoke	_____	_____	_____
2. create	_____	_____	_____
3. paste	_____	_____	_____

4. buzz   _____   _____   _____

5. pick   _____   _____   _____

PRACTICE 3: Write Your Own Write five sentences using at least five of the verb forms from Practice 2

IRREGULAR VERBS

Irregular verbs do not form their past tense and past participle with -d or -ed. That is why they are irregular. Some follow certain patterns (_spring, sprang, sprung; ring, rang, rung; drink, drank, drunk; sink, sank, sunk_). But the only sure way to know the forms of an irregular verb is to spend time learning them. As you write, you can check a dictionary or the following list.

Irregular Verbs

PRESENT	PAST	PAST PARTICIPLE (USED WITH HELPING VERBS LIKE _HAVE, HAS, HAD_)
am	was	been
are	were	been
be	was	been
bear	bore	borne, born
beat	beat	beaten
begin	began	begun
bend	bent	bent
bid	bid	bid
bind	bound	bound
bite	bit	bitten
blow	blew	blown
break	broke	broken
bring	brought (not brang)	brought (not brung)
build	built	built
burst	burst (not bursted)	burst
buy	bought	bought
choose	chose	chosen

come	came	come
cost	cost (not costed)	cost
cut	cut	cut
deal	dealt	dealt
do	did (not done)	done
draw	drew	drawn
drink	drank	drunk
drive	drove	driven
eat	ate	eaten
fall	fell	fallen
feed	fed	fed
feel	felt	felt
fight	fought	fought
find	found	found
flee	fled	fled
fly	flew	flown
forget	forgot	forgotten
forgive	forgave	forgiven
freeze	froze	frozen
get	got	got, gotten
go	went	gone
grow	grew	grown
hang[1] (a picture)	hung	hung
has	had	had
have	had	had
hear	heard	heard
hide	hid	hidden
hurt	hurt (not hurted)	hurt
is	was	been
know	knew	known
lay	laid	laid
lead	led	led
leave	left	left

(continued)

lend	lent	lent
lie[2]	lay	lain
lose	lost	lost
meet	met	met
pay	paid	paid
prove	proved	proved, proven
put	put	put
read [rēēd]	read [rĕd]	read [rĕd]
ride	rode	ridden
ring	rang	rung
rise	rose	risen
run	ran	run
say	said	said
see	saw (not seen)	seen
set	set	set
shake	shook	shaken
shine[3] (a light)	shone	shone
shrink	shrank	shrunk
sing	sang	sung
sink	sank	sunk
sit	sat	sat
sleep	slept	slept
speak	spoke	spoken
spend	spent	spent
spread	spread	spread
spring	sprang (not sprung)	sprung
stand	stood	stood
steal	stole	stolen
stick	stuck	stuck
stink	stank (not stunk)	stunk
strike	struck	struck, stricken
strive	strove	striven, strived

swear	*swore*	*sworn*
sweep	*swept*	*swept*
swell	*swelled*	*swelled, swollen*
swim	*swam*	*swum*
swing	*swung*	*swung*
take	*took*	*taken*
teach	*taught*	*taught*
tear	*tore*	*torn*
tell	*told*	*told*
think	*thought*	*thought*
throw	*threw*	*thrown*
understand	*understood*	*understood*
wake	*woke*	*woken*
wear	*wore*	*worn*
weave	*wove*	*woven*
win	*won*	*won*
wring	*wrung*	*wrung*
write	*wrote*	*written*

1. *Hang* meaning "execute by hanging" is regular: *hang, hanged, hanged*.
2. *Lie* meaning "tell a lie" is regular: *lie, lied, lied*.
3. *Shine* meaning "brighten by polishing" is regular: *shine, shined, shined*.

PRACTICE 4: Recall/Identify Put an X to the left of the incorrect verb forms in the following chart.

Present Tense	Past Tense	Past Participle Tense
1. _____ bear	_____ beared	_____ borne
2. _____ shrink	_____ shrank	_____ shrank
3. _____ swing	_____ swung	_____ swang
4. _____ deal	_____ dealed	_____ dealt
5. _____ chose	_____ chose	_____ chosen

PRACTICE 5: Apply Write the correct forms of the following irregular verbs.

	Present Tense	Past Tense	Past Participle
1. am	_____	_____	_____
2. write	_____	_____	_____
3. sweep	_____	_____	_____
4. fall	_____	_____	_____
5. swell	_____	_____	_____

PRACTICE 6: Write Your Own Write five sentences using at least five of the verb forms from the chart in Practice 5.

USING *LIE/LAY* AND *SIT/SET* CORRECTLY

Two pairs of verbs are often used incorrectly—*lie/lay* and *sit/set*.

Lie/Lay

	Present Tense	Past Tense	Past Participle
lie (recline or lie down)	*lie*	*lay*	*(have, has, had) lain*
lay (put or place down)	*lay*	*laid*	*(have, has, had) laid*

The verb *lay* always takes an object. You must lay something down:

Lay down *what?*
Lay down *your books.*

Sit/Set

	Present Tense	Past Tense	Past Participle
sit (get into a seated position)	*sit*	*sat*	*(have, has, had) sat*
set (put or place down)	*set*	*set*	*(have, has, had) set*

Like the verb *lay*, the verb *set* must always have an object. You must set something down:

> Set *what?*
> Set *the presents* over here.

PRACTICE 7: Recall/Identify Underline the correct verb in the following sentences.

1. After I (sat, set) down, I felt much better.

2. All day I have (lain, laid) in my room watching TV.

3. He has (lay, laid) the blanket down for our picnic.

4. We had to (sat, set) our watches to exactly the same time.

5. (Lie, Lay) the pieces of the puzzle out on the table, please.

PRACTICE 8: Apply Fill in each blank in the following sentences with the correct form of *lie/lay* or *sit/set*.

1. Suzy has _____ in the bathtub for so long that her skin has wrinkled.

2. I could have _____ in the moonlight looking at the stars all night.

3. The cook _____ out all the ingredients.

4. Please _____ those heavy boxes down before you strain your back.

5. I think I will go and _____ down for a while.

PRACTICE 9: Write Your Own Write five sentences using variations of *lie/lay* or *sit/set*.

CHAPTER REVIEW

REVIEW PRACTICE 1: Recall/Identify Write out the past tense and past participle of each verb listed here, and then identify the verb as either regular or irregular.

Present Tense	Past Tense	Past Participle	Type of Verb
1. brush	_____	_____	_____
2. fix	_____	_____	_____
3. wear	_____	_____	_____
4. buy	_____	_____	_____
5. suffer	_____	_____	_____
6. have	_____	_____	_____
7. type	_____	_____	_____
8. feel	_____	_____	_____
9. touch	_____	_____	_____
10. teach	_____	_____	_____

REVIEW PRACTICE 2: Apply Fill in each blank in the following sentences with a regular or irregular verb that makes sense.

1. Yesterday, I _____ at my computer and tried to write my essay.

2. Tilda _____ over to my house last night.

3. I always smile and _____ my hand to the people on the Mardi Gras floats.

4. Geraldo has _____ his drink all over the waitress.

5. Carlos and Tom have _____ class again.

6. You should never _____ an infant; doing so can cause brain damage and death.

7. The groom smiled at his bride and _____ the ring on her third finger.

8. The plumbing in the house has _____ a leak.

9. Mary Ann _____ the picture in her bedroom.

10. All cozy in my bed, I _____ right through the earthquake.

REVIEW PRACTICE 3: Write Your Own Write a paragraph explaining the most important parts of your daily routine. Be sure to explain why each activity is important.

> MyWritingLab™ Complete this "Write Your Own" exercise for Chapter 30 in the MyWritingLab "Activities: Your Textbook" module.

REVIEW PRACTICE 4: Editing Through Collaboration Exchange paragraphs from Review Practice 3 with another student, and do the following:

1. Circle any verb forms that are not correct.

2. Suggest a correction for these incorrect forms.

Then return the paper to its writer, and use the information in this chapter to correct the verb forms in your own paragraph. Record your errors on the Error Log in Appendix 7.

> MyWritingLab™ Visit Chapter 30, "Regular and Irregular Verbs," in MyWritingLab, and complete the Post-test to check your understanding of the chapter's objectives.

31

Verb Tense

TEST YOURSELF

Underline the complete verbs in each sentence. Then mark an X if the form of any of the verbs is incorrect.

- _____ Jean always laugh when I tell that joke.
- _____ Mark jumped over the hurdle and crossed the finish line.
- _____ I had spoke to the sales clerk about a discount.
- _____ Students ain't allowed to bring food and drink into the computer lab.
- _____ My two cats be playing in the sunshine.

(Answers are in Appendix 3.)

When we hear the word *verb*, we often think of action. We also know that action occurs in time. We are naturally interested in whether something happened today or yesterday or if it will happen at some time in the future. The time of an action is indicated by the **tense** of a verb, specifically in the ending of a verb or in a helping word. This chapter discusses the most common errors in using verb tense.

Student Comment:
"I got to watch the **Verb Tense** video three times. In a lecture, I'd only get to hear it once."

| MyWritingLab | **Understanding Verb Tense** |

To find out more about this subject, go to **MyWritingLab.com,** and choose **Tense** in the **Basic Grammar** module. From there, watch the video called **Animation: Tense.** Then, return to this chapter, which will go into more detail about tense and give you opportunities to practice it. Finally, you will apply your understanding of verb tense to your own writing.

PRESENT TENSE

One of the most common errors in college writing is reversing the present-tense endings—adding an *-s* where none is needed and omitting the *-s* where it is required. This error causes problems in subject-verb agreement. Make sure you understand this mistake, and then proofread carefully to avoid it in your writing.

Present Tense

Singular		Plural	
INCORRECT	CORRECT	INCORRECT	CORRECT
NOT *I walks*	*I walk*	***NOT*** *we walks*	*we walk*
NOT *you walks*	*you walk*	***NOT*** *you walks*	*you walk*
NOT *he, she, it walk*	*he, she, it walks*	***NOT*** *they walks*	*they walk*

You also need to be able to spot these same errors in sentences.

Incorrect	**Correct**
That car run me off the road.	**That car ran** me off the road.
My mother hate my boyfriend.	**My mother hates** my boyfriend.
You speaks too fast.	**You speak** too fast.
They trims the trees once a year.	**They trim** the trees once a year.

PRACTICE 1A: Recall/Identify Underline the present-tense errors in each of the following sentences.

1. I loves to sit in a cool theater on a hot summer day.

2. You babbles too much.

3. My baby sister play well with her cousin.

4. We seems to be lost.

5. Next week, they plans on going to the party after the show.

PRACTICE 1B: Correct Correct the present-tense errors in Practice 1A by rewriting each sentence.

PRACTICE 2: Apply Fill in each blank in the following paragraph with the correct present-tense verbs.

My brother always (1) _____ me to help him with his paper route. Usually I don't mind because he (2) _____ me money and we (3) _____ to work together. It's strange, too, because I actually (4) _____ rolling up the papers. But lately my brother has been sleeping late while I do all the work. So I told him I was going on strike until I got either more money or more help. Do you know what he did? He fired me! Can you (5) _____ that?

PRACTICE 3: Write Your Own Write a sentence of your own for each of the following present-tense verbs.

1. relieve _____

2. feels _____

3. skates _____

4. asks _____

5. skip _____

PAST TENSE

Just as we know that a verb is in the present tense by its ending, we can tell that a verb is in the past tense by its ending. Regular verbs form the past tense by adding *-d* or *-ed*. But some writers forget the ending when they are writing in the past tense. Understanding this problem and then proofreading carefully will help you catch this error.

Past Tense

Singular		Plural	
INCORRECT	CORRECT	INCORRECT	CORRECT
NOT I walk	I walked	*NOT* we walk	we walked
NOT you walk	you walked	*NOT* you walk	you walked
NOT he, she, it walk	he, she, it walked	*NOT* they walk	they walked

You also need to be able to spot these same errors in sentences.

Incorrect	**Correct**
She run fast.	**She ran** fast.
He see the game.	**He saw** the game.
The girl study hard.	**The girl studied** hard.
Yes, **we learn** a lot.	Yes, **we learned** a lot.

PRACTICE 4A: Recall/Identify Underline the past-tense errors in the following sentences.

1. When we were in high school, we talk on the phone for hours.

2. The radio station play the song over and over again.

3. Yesterday you edit your work.

4. She close all the windows when she left.

5. I just realize that I have already done these exercises.

PRACTICE 4B: Correct Correct the past-tense errors in Practice 4A by rewriting each sentence.

PRACTICE 5: Apply Fill in each blank in the following paragraph with the correct past-tense verb.

Yesterday, it was so hot that several of my friends (1) _____ to go to the beach. They (2) _____ a lunch, put on their swimsuits, and (3) _____ into the car. Sadly, I had a cold, so I (4) _____ home. Boy, am I glad I did! My friends were stuck in traffic for two hours with no air conditioning. This is the one time I (5) _____ my lucky stars for a cold.

PRACTICE 6: Write Your Own Write a sentence of your own for each of the following past-tense verbs.

1. rained _____

2. fixed _____

3. sipped _____

4. lifted _____

5. visited _____

USING HELPING WORDS WITH PAST PARTICIPLES

Helping words are used with the past participle form, *not* with the past-tense form. It is incorrect to use a helping verb (such as *is, was, were, have, has,* or *had*) with the past tense. Make sure you understand how to use helping words with past participles, and then proofread your written work to avoid making these errors.

Incorrect	Correct
They **have went.**	They **have gone.**
She **has decide** to get married.	She **has decided** to get married.
I **have ate** breakfast already.	I **have eaten** breakfast already.
We **had took** the test early.	We **had taken** the test early.

PRACTICE 7A: Recall/Identify Underline the incorrect helping words and past participles in each of the following sentences.

1. I have sang that song in French.

2. Kendra and Misty have hid all the Easter eggs.

3. The plane has flew over the ocean.

4. We have did all the necessary repairs to the fence.

5. She has forget the phone number.

PRACTICE 7B: Correct Correct the helping verb and past participle errors in Practice 7A by rewriting each sentence.

PRACTICE 8: Apply Fill in each blank in the following paragraph with helping verbs and past participles that make sense.

It all started in elementary school. I was a new student and didn't know a single person. For two weeks, I (1) _____ my lunch alone. No one had even talked to me. Even though I didn't show it, my classmates' neglect (2) _____ my feelings. My little heart (3) _____. But one day, a wonderful boy named John happened to notice me. I (4) _____ my lunch, so he decided to share his with me. From that day forward, we (5) _____ the best of friends.

PRACTICE 9: Write Your Own Write a sentence of your own for each of the following helping words and past participles.

1. have drunk _____

2. has seen _____

3. had woven _____

4. has risen _____

5. have hidden _____

USING *-ING* VERBS CORRECTLY

Verbs ending in *-ing* describe action that is going on or that was going on for a while. To be a complete verb, an *-ing* verb is always used with a helping verb. Two common errors occur with *-ing* verbs:

1. Using *be* or *been* instead of the correct helping verb
2. Using no helping verb at all

Learn the correct forms, and proofread carefully to catch these errors.

Incorrect	**Correct**
The car **be going** too fast.	The car **is going** too fast.
	The car **was going** too fast.
The car **been going** too fast.	The car **has been going** too fast.
	The car **had been going** too fast.
We **watching** a movie.	We **are watching** a movie.
	We **have been watching** a movie.
	We **were watching** a movie.
	We **had been watching** a movie.

PRACTICE 10A: Recall/Identify Underline the incorrect helping verbs and *-ing* forms in each of the following sentences.

1. The cat be chasing the dog!

2. The patient been waiting for the doctor for over an hour.

3. That building be leaning to the side for over 20 years.

4. I feeling sick because I ate an entire pizza by myself.

5. We be driving down Sunset Boulevard.

PRACTICE 10B: Correct Correct the verb form errors in Practice 10A by re-writing each sentence.

PRACTICE 11: Apply Fill in each blank in the following paragraph with the correct helping verb and *-ing* form.

      I (1) _____ one of the best days of my life. It started while I (2) _____ my clothes and found $20 in my pocket. Then on my way to work, I was pulled over by a police officer. While he (3) _____ out the ticket, I made him laugh so hard that he tore it up and let me go with a warning. But the best part of my day happened while I was at work. I (4) _____ to the radio when I heard my name announced. I had just won a trip to Hawaii! I (5) _____ up and down and screaming. My boss was so happy for me that he gave me the rest of the day off.

PRACTICE 12: Write Your Own Write a sentence of your own for each of the following verbs.

1. is wishing _____

2. has been writing _____

3. were laying _____

4. was driving _____

5. had been sailing _____

PROBLEMS WITH *BE*

The verb *be* can cause problems in both the present tense and the past tense. The following chart demonstrates these problems. Learn how to use these forms correctly, and then always proofread your written work carefully to avoid these errors.

The Verb *be*

Present Tense

Singular		Plural	
INCORRECT	CORRECT	INCORRECT	CORRECT
NOT I *be/ain't*	I *am/am not*	*NOT* we *be/ain't*	we *are/are not*
NOT you *be/ain't*	you *are/are not*	*NOT* you *be/ain't*	you *are/are not*
NOT he, she, it	he, she, it	*NOT* they *be/ain't*	they *are/are not*
be/ain't	*is/is not*		

Past Tense

Singular		Plural	
INCORRECT	CORRECT	INCORRECT	CORRECT
NOT I *were*	I *was*	*NOT* we *was*	we *were*
NOT you *was*	you *were*	*NOT* you *was*	you *were*
NOT he, she, it *were*	he, she, it *was*	*NOT* they *was*	they *were*

PRACTICE 13A: Recall/Identify Underline the incorrect forms of *be* in each of the following sentences.

1. I ain't going to travel by plane.

2. You is going to have to study for this exam.

3. He be the person you need to talk to about enrollment.

4. You was supposed to take your clothes off before you ironed them.

5. They was not having any fun.

PRACTICE 13B: Correct Correct the incorrect forms of *be* in Practice 13A by rewriting each sentence.

PRACTICE 14: Apply Fill in each blank in the following paragraph with the correct form of *be*.

    Crystal (1) _____ an adventurous person. She (2) _____ willing to try just about anything, and she usually talks me into going along with her. We have jumped out of a plane, off a bridge, and off a mountain—with a parachute or a bungee cord, of course. But when she decided we should have our belly buttons pierced, I panicked. Now, I (3) _____ not a coward, but I knew this little adventure (4) _____ going to hurt. Danger I like, but pain—well, that's a different story. This (5) _____ one adventure I had to say no to.

PRACTICE 15: Write Your Own Write a sentence of your own for each of the following verbs.

1. am not _____

2. is _____

3. was _____

4. are _____

5. were _____

PROBLEMS WITH *DO*

    Another verb that causes sentence problems in the present and past tenses is *do*. The following chart shows these problems. Learn the correct forms, and proofread to avoid errors.

The Verb *do*

Present Tense

Singular		Plural	
INCORRECT	CORRECT	INCORRECT	CORRECT
NOT I *does*	I *do*	*NOT* we *does*	we *do*
NOT you *does*	you *do*	*NOT* you *does*	you *do*
NOT he, she, it *do*	he, she, it *does*	*NOT* they *does*	they *do*

Past Tense

Singular		Plural	
INCORRECT	CORRECT	INCORRECT	CORRECT
NOT I *done*	I *did*	*NOT* we *done*	we *did*
NOT you *done*	you *did*	*NOT* you *done*	you *did*
NOT he, she, it *done*	he, she, it *did*	*NOT* they *done*	they *did*

PRACTICE 16A: Recall/Identify Underline the incorrect forms of *do* in each of the following sentences.

1. We always does the prewriting exercises before organizing our essays.

2. She done it again.

3. You does a good job even when you don't have to.

4. Yes, that computer certainly do need a new modem.

5. Henry, you done let the cat out!

PRACTICE 16B: Correct Correct the incorrect forms of *do* in Practice 16A by rewriting each sentence.

PRACTICE 17: Apply Fill in each blank in the following paragraph with the correct form of *do*.

I (1) _____ believe it was love at first sight. She had the prettiest brown eyes and the silkiest blonde hair I had ever seen. My friends warned me that she wasn't right for me, but they (2) _____ n't understand—we were made for each other.

Now, I admit that she (3) _____ slobber a bit and her hair (4) _____ shed in the summer, but she's always happy to see me and doesn't mind my stupid mistakes. Adopting Porsche, my golden retriever, was the best thing I ever (5) _____ .

PRACTICE 18: Write Your Own Write a sentence of your own for each of the following verbs.

1. do _____

2. does _____

3. did _____

4. does _____

5. do _____

PROBLEMS WITH *HAVE*

Along with *be* and *do*, the verb *have* causes sentence problems in the present and past tenses. The following chart demonstrates these problems. Learn the correct forms, and proofread to avoid errors with *have*.

The Verb *have*

Present Tense

Singular		Plural	
INCORRECT	CORRECT	INCORRECT	CORRECT
NOT I *has*	I *have*	*NOT* we *has*	we *have*
NOT you *has*	you *have*	*NOT* you *has*	you *have*
NOT he, she, it *have*	he, she, it *has*	*NOT* they *has*	they *have*

Past Tense

Singular		Plural	
INCORRECT	CORRECT	INCORRECT	CORRECT
NOT I *has*	I *had*	*NOT* we *has*	we *had*
NOT you *have*	you *had*	*NOT* you *has*	you *had*
NOT he, she, it *have*	he, she, it *had*	*NOT* they *has*	they *had*

PRACTICE 19A: Recall/Identify Underline the incorrect forms of *have* in each of the following sentences.

1. We has already taken up too much space.

2. Yesterday, I has money in my account; today I has none.

3. If George is late, then he have to come in through the back entrance.

4. You has a great deal of courage when dealing with angry customers.

5. Sabine and Jackie has taken the rest of the afternoon off.

PRACTICE 19B: Correct Correct the incorrect forms of *have* in Practice 19A by rewriting each sentence.

PRACTICE 20: Apply Fill in each blank in the following paragraph with the correct form of *have*.

    "I (1) _____ a secret," said my little brother Bubba, "but you (2) _____ to promise not to tell." Now Bubba (3) _____ the most wonderful imagination, and I knew to expect the unexpected because we (4) _____ shared many secrets in the past. So I said, "OK, what is it?" He leaned closer, cupped his hand to my ear, and whispered, "Babies don't really come from the stork." "No!" I exclaimed, pretending to be shocked. "Where do they come from?" I asked. "Why, they come from eggs," he proudly said. I (5) _____ the hardest time keeping a straight face.

PRACTICE 21: Write Your Own Write a sentence of your own for each of the following verbs.

1. have _____

2. has _____

3. had _____

4. has _____

5. have _____

CHAPTER REVIEW

REVIEW PRACTICE 1: Recall/Identify Underline the incorrect verb forms in the following sentences. Check problem areas carefully: Is an *-s* needed, or is there an unnecessary *-s* ending? Do all past-tense regular verbs end in *-d* or

-ed? Is the past participle used with helping words? Is the correct helping verb used with *-ing* verbs? Are the forms of *be, do,* and *have* correct?

1. Janet and Henry likes to go for long drives in the mountains.

2. Our high school band has strove to be the best in the nation.

3. I be sorry for your troubles.

4. I enjoys a hot cup of coffee while I work.

5. You done a wise thing when you signed up for classes early.

6. The birds be flying south for the winter.

7. I have wove the tapestry threads back together.

8. That fat cat been sleeping in the sun all day.

9. Those two girls think they has all the answers.

10. Last Christmas, we bake most of our gifts.

REVIEW PRACTICE 2: Apply Correct the errors in Review Practice 1 by rewriting each sentence.

REVIEW PRACTICE 3: Write Your Own Write a short paragraph describing your favorite pet. Be careful to use all verbs in the correct tense. Check in particular for errors with *be, do,* and *have.*

MyWritingLab™   Complete this "Write Your Own" exercise for Chapter 31 in the MyWritingLab "Activities: Your Textbook" module.

REVIEW PRACTICE 4: Editing Through Collaboration Exchange paragraphs from Review Practice 3 with another student, and do the following:

1. Underline any incorrect tenses.

2. Circle any incorrect verb forms.

Then return the paper to its writer, and use the information in this chapter to correct any verb errors in your own paragraph. Record your errors on the Error Log in Appendix 7.

MyWritingLab™   Visit Chapter 31, "Verb Tense," in MyWritingLab, and complete the Post-test to check your understanding of the chapter's objectives.

32

Subject-Verb Agreement

Underline the subjects once and the complete verbs twice in the following sentences. Put an X by the sentence if its subject and verb do not agree.

- _____ Neither the shorts nor the shirt fit me.
- _____ Chips and dip is my favorite snack.
- _____ There were a large storm last night.
- _____ Some of the soil, along with the fertilizer, are for the orchard.
- _____ Cotton and silk are more comfortable than wool.

(Answers are in Appendix 3.)

Almost every day, we come across situations that require us to reach an agreement with someone. For example, you and a friend might have to agree on which movie to see, or you and your manager might have to agree on how many hours you'll work in the coming week. Whatever the issue, agreement is essential in most aspects of life—including writing. In this chapter, you will learn how to resolve conflicts in your sentences by making sure your subjects and verbs agree.

Student Comment:
"If your writing is weak, you should try doing the **MyWritingLab** exercises while you read the chapters in *Mosaics*. It will help you become a better writer."

MyWritingLab | **Understanding Subject-Verb Agreement**

To expand your understanding of this subject, go to **MyWritingLab. com**, and choose **Subject-Verb Agreement** in the **Sentence Skills** module. Then, watch the video called **Animation: Subject-Verb Agreement.** Next, return to this chapter, which will go into more detail about this topic and give you opportunities to practice it. Finally, you will apply your understanding of subject-verb agreement to your own writing.

SUBJECT-VERB AGREEMENT

Subject-verb agreement simply means that singular subjects must be paired with singular verbs and plural subjects with plural verbs. Look at this example:

Singular: **She works** in Baltimore.

The subject *she* is singular because it refers to only one person. The verb *works* is singular and matches the singular subject. Here is the same sentence in plural form:

Plural: **They work** in Baltimore.

The subject *they* is plural, referring to more than one person, and the verb *work* is also plural.

PRACTICE 1: Recall/Identify Underline the verb that agrees with its subject in each of the following sentences.

1. In her free time, Cassie (be, is) a volunteer nurse.

2. The girls usually (store, stores) their gear in the lockers.

3. Rocky, my 80-pound dog, (eat, eats) more food in a day than I do.

4. I (do, does) all of my reading for my classes at least one week ahead of time.

5. You (has, have) something green in your hair.

PRACTICE 2: Apply Fill in each blank in the following sentences with a present-tense verb that agrees with its subject.

1. Every evening, Michael _____ by the fire.

2. They _____ many questions.

3. Neil _____ everything chocolate.

4. We rarely _____ down that path, for it is always dark and eerie.

5. He _____ to only classical music.

PRACTICE 3: Write Your Own Write five sentences of your own, and underline the subjects and verbs. Make sure that your subjects and verbs agree.

WORDS SEPARATING SUBJECTS AND VERBS

With sentences as simple and direct as *She works in Baltimore*, checking that the subject and verb agree is easy. But problems can arise when words come between the subject and the verb. Often the words between the subject and verb are prepositional phrases. If you follow the advice given in Chapter 27, you will be able to find the subject and verb: *Cross out all the prepositional phrases in a sentence. The subject and verb will be among the words that are left.* Here are some examples:

$$\overset{s}{}\qquad\qquad\overset{v}{}$$

Prepositional Phrases: The **notebook** ~~for history class~~ **is** ~~in my backpack~~.

When you cross out the prepositional phrases, you can see that the singular subject, *notebook*, and the singular verb, *is*, agree.

$$\overset{s}{}\qquad\qquad\overset{v}{}$$

Prepositional Phrases: The **roses** ~~in my garden~~ **bloom** ~~in April~~.

When you cross out the prepositional phrases, you can see that the plural subject, *roses*, and the plural verb, *bloom*, agree.

PRACTICE 4: Recall/Identify Underline the subject once and the verb twice in each of the following sentences. Cross out the prepositional phrases first. Put an X to the left of any sentence in which the subject and verb do not agree.

1. _____ Cindy, unlike many people today, do so much for others.

2. _____ That man in the red pants think a lot about his social life.

3. _____ Frog legs, in spite of popular opinion, tastes like frog legs.

4. _____ The flowers in the garden smell nice.

5. _____ The economy in America seem to be getting stronger.

PRACTICE 5: Apply Fill in each blank in the following sentences with a present-tense verb that agrees with its subject.

1. My little brother, despite being told otherwise, still _____ in Santa Claus.

2. The train for San Francisco _____ in the station at 7:45 p.m.

3. MTV, like several other channels, _____ to air more reality shows.

4. The boxes in the hallway _____ in the moving van.

5. The wind during a thunderstorm always _____ me.

PRACTICE 6: Write Your Own Write five sentences of your own with at least one prepositional phrase in each, and underline the subjects and verbs. Make sure your subjects and verbs agree.

MORE THAN ONE SUBJECT

Sometimes a subject consists of more than one person, place, thing, or idea. These subjects are called **compound** (as discussed in Chapter 27). Follow these three rules when matching a verb to a compound subject:

1. When compound subjects are joined by *and*, use a plural verb.

   Plural: Thursday and Friday were hot days.

   The singular words *Thursday and Friday* together make a plural subject. Therefore, the plural verb *were* is needed.

2. When the subject appears to have more than one part but the parts refer to a single unit, use a singular verb.

   Singular: Macaroni and cheese is Eli's favorite food.

   Macaroni is one item and *cheese* is one item, but Eli does not eat one without the other, so they form a single unit. Because they are a single unit, they require a singular verb—*is*.

3. When compound subjects are joined by *or* or *nor*, make the verb agree with the subject closest to it.

   Singular: Neither hot dogs nor chicken was on the menu.

   The part of the compound subject closest to the verb is *chicken*, which is singular. Therefore, the verb must be singular—*was*.

   Plural: Neither chicken nor hot dogs were on the menu.

   This time, the part of the compound subject closest to the verb is *hot dogs*, which is plural. Therefore, the verb must be plural—*were*.

PRACTICE 7: Recall/Identify Underline the verb that agrees with its subject in each of the following sentences. Cross out the prepositional phrases first.

1. You and I (was, were) going the wrong way down a one-way street.

2. Chicken and dumplings (taste, tastes) better with a little salt and pepper.

3. Either the mosquitoes or the wind (cause, causes) my skin problems.

4. Celery and peanut butter (is, are) my favorite snack.

5. Neither the professor nor the students (knows, know) the answer to this question.

PRACTICE 8: Apply Fill in each blank in the following sentences with a present-tense verb that agrees with its subject. Avoid *is* and *are*. Cross out the prepositional phrases first.

1. Either lilies or tulips _____ well in the spring.

2. Pie and ice cream _____ the best dessert.

3. The ants and flies in the house _____ me.

4. The train and the passengers _____ sometime this evening.

5. Neither the entrees nor the dessert _____ appetizing tonight.

PRACTICE 9: Write Your Own Write a sentence of your own for each of the following compound subjects. Make sure your subjects and verbs agree.

1. either the handouts or the manuscript _____

2. brooms and brushes _____

3. neither the nurses nor the doctor _____

4. ham and cheese _____

5. the horse and her foal _____

VERBS BEFORE SUBJECTS

When the subject follows its verb, the subject may be hard to find, which makes the process of agreeing subjects and verbs difficult. Subjects come after verbs in two particular situations: when the sentence begins with *here* or *there* and when a question begins with *Who*, *What*, *Where*, *When*, *Why*, or *How*. Here are some examples:

Verb Before Subject: Here **are** the **decorations** ~~for the party~~.

Verb Before Subject: There **is iced tea** ~~in the refrigerator~~.

In sentences that begin with *here* or *there*, the verb always comes before the subject. Don't forget to cross out prepositional phrases to help you identify the subject. One of the words that's left will be the subject, and then you can check that the verb agrees with it.

               v   s

Split Verb: Who **is** that attractive **man** ~~in the blue suit?~~

               v   s   v

Split Verb: Where **are** the valuable **paintings kept**?

               v   s   v

Split Verb: When **are you flying** ~~to Rome?~~

In questions that begin with *Who, What, When, Where, Why,* and *How,* the verb comes before the subject, as in the first example, or is split by the subject, as in the last two examples.

PRACTICE 10: Recall/Identify Underline the subject once and the verb twice in each of the following sentences. Cross out the prepositional phrases first.

1. Here lies the cause of the problem despite the evidence.
2. Who is the leader of your group?
3. How do you feel after your recent operation?
4. Where in the world are my keys?
5. There on the table are your books.

PRACTICE 11: Apply Fill in each blank in the following sentences with a verb that agrees with its subject. Cross out the prepositional phrases first.

1. Where _____ the rest of the apricot pie?
2. Over the hill, there _____ a great swimming hole.
3. Why _____ their dirty clothes on the bathroom floor?
4. How many times _____ your sister asked you to fix that hair dryer?
5. What _____ this mess in the front yard?

PRACTICE 12: Write Your Own Write a sentence of your own for each of the following words and phrases. Make sure your subjects and verbs agree.

1. there may be _____
2. what has been _____
3. how did he _____
4. when is _____
5. here is _____

COLLECTIVE NOUNS

Collective nouns name a group of people or things. Examples include such nouns as *army, audience, band, class, committee, crew, crowd, family, flock, gang, jury, majority, minority, orchestra, senate, team,* and *troop*. Collective nouns can be singular or plural. They are singular when they refer to a group as a single unit. They are plural when they refer to the individual actions or feelings of the group members.

s   v

Singular: The string **quartet performs** three times a year.

Quartet refers to the entire unit or group. Therefore, it requires the singular verb *performs*.

s   v

Plural: The string **quartet get** their new instruments on Monday.

Here *quartet* refers to the individual members, who will each get a new instrument, so the plural verb *get* is used.

PRACTICE 13: Recall/Identify Underline the correct verb in each of the following sentences. Cross out the prepositional phrases first.

1. The audience (listen, listens) intently to the guest speaker.

2. The majority (have, has) voted at different polling booths.

3. The orchestra (play, plays) different selections, depending on the concert.

4. Our high school cheerleading squad (is, are) all going to different colleges.

5. The litter of puppies (get, gets) a bath today.

PRACTICE 14: Apply Fill in each blank in the following sentences with a present-tense verb that agrees with its subject. Cross out the prepositional phrases first.

1. A flock of geese always _____ south for the winter.

2. The crew _____ trouble making sure everyone has a good time.

3. The school orchestra _____ this competition every year.

4. The army _____ students who have degrees as officers.

5. The senate _____ according to individual beliefs.

PRACTICE 15: Write Your Own Write a sentence of your own using each of the following words as a plural subject. Make sure your subjects and verbs agree.

1. committee _____

2. gang _____

3. class _____

4. minority _____

5. group _____

INDEFINITE PRONOUNS

Indefinite pronouns do not refer to anyone or anything specific. Some indefinite pronouns are always singular, and some are always plural. A few can be either singular or plural, depending on the other words in the sentence. When an indefinite pronoun is the subject of a sentence, the verb must agree with the pronoun. Here is a list of indefinite pronouns:

Indefinite Pronouns

ALWAYS SINGULAR		ALWAYS PLURAL	EITHER SINGULAR OR PLURAL
another	*neither*	*both*	*all*
anybody	*nobody*	*few*	*any*
anyone	*none*	*many*	*more*
anything	*no one*	*others*	*most*
each	*nothing*	*several*	*some*
either	*one*		
everybody	*other*		
everyone	*somebody*		
everything	*someone*		
little	*something*		
much			

                   s   v

Singular: **No one** ever **changes** at work.

                  s   v

           Everybody refuses to work harder.

> **Plural:**   Many **take** long lunches and **go** home early.
>
> s   v   v
>
> **Others stay** late but **are** tired and unmotivated.

The pronouns that can be either singular or plural are singular when they refer to singular words and plural when they refer to plural words.

> **Singular:**   **Some** of Abby's *day* **was** hectic.

Some is singular because it refers to *day*, which is singular. The singular verb *was* agrees with the singular subject *some*.

> **Plural:**   **Some** of Abby's *co-workers* **were** late.

Some is plural because it refers to *co-workers*, which is plural. The plural verb *were* agrees with the plural subject *some*.

PRACTICE 16: Recall/Identify   Underline the verb that agrees with its subject in each of the following sentences. Cross out the prepositional phrases first.

1. All of my money (is, are) gone.

2. Both of the pools (was, were) treated with chlorine.

3. No one (do, does) more work than she.

4. Something (fly, flies) into my window every night and (buzz, buzzes) around my head.

5. Most of Omar's friends (seem, seems) friendly.

PRACTICE 17: Apply   Fill in each blank in the following sentences with a present-tense verb that agrees with its subject. Cross out the prepositional phrases first.

1. Most of the people _____ to work in the mornings.

2. No one really _____ if he will accept the job.

3. Both _____ the consequences of their actions.

4. None of the fake contestants _____ it was a joke.

5. Somebody _____ moving my things off my desk.

PRACTICE 18: Write Your Own Write a sentence of your own using each of the following words as a subject, combined with one of the following verbs: *is, are, was, were.* Make sure your subjects and verbs agree.

1. anything _____

2. others _____

3. some _____

4. any _____

5. several _____

CHAPTER REVIEW

REVIEW PRACTICE 1A: Recall/Identify Underline the subject once and the verb twice in each of the following sentences. Cross out the prepositional phrases first. Then put an X to the left of each sentence in which the subject and verb do not agree. Correct the subjects and verbs that don't agree by rewriting the incorrect sentences.

1. _____ There sit the man who will be the next president of the United States.

2. _____ The moon and the stars in the evening sky shines brightly.

3. _____ The team usually practice off the track every Tuesday.

4. _____ Some of the fish in that tank appear to be sick.

5. _____ Doctor, how is the patient in room 204?

6. _____ Something very sharp keep punching me in the back.

7. _____ Sour cream and onion are my favorite type of dip.

8. _____ Here are the recipe from my grandmother.

9. _____ Neither the chairs nor the table match the décor in this room.

10. _____ My gang of artistic friends finds the new trends exciting.

REVIEW PRACTICE 1B: Correct Correct verbs that don't agree with their subjects in Review Practice 1A by rewriting the correct sentences.

REVIEW PRACTICE 2: Apply Fill in each blank in the following sentences with a present-tense verb that agrees with its subject.

1. My gang _____ late for the show.

2. Neither wind nor rain nor snow _____ us from going outside.

3. Here _____ where Eugene's great-grandmother built her first house.

4. Several of the guests _____ the secret code to the room back stage.

5. None of the water _____ safe for drinking.

6. Where _____ the tourists go for information about hotels?

7. Nothing _____ to be wrong with the car.

8. The track team _____ 5 miles every day, regardless of the weather.

9. Steven's mother and father _____ planning a vacation to Paris.

10. There in that apartment building ____ my former high school principal.

REVIEW PRACTICE 3: Write Your Own Write a paragraph explaining why you did or did not join a committee, team, or other group. Make sure that your subjects and verbs agree.

MyWritingLab™   Complete this "Write Your Own" exercise for Chapter 32 in the MyWritingLab "Activities: Your Textbook" module.

REVIEW PRACTICE 4: Editing Through Collaboration Exchange paragraphs from Review Practice 3 with another student, and do the following.

1. Underline the subject once in each sentence.

2. Underline the verbs twice.

3. Put an X by any verbs that do not agree with their subjects.

Then return the paper to its writer, and use the information in this chapter to correct any subject-verb agreement errors in your own paragraph. Record your errors on the Error Log in Appendix 7.

MyWritingLab™   Visit Chapter 32, "Subject-Verb Agreement," in MyWritingLab, and complete the Post-test to check your understanding of the chapter's objectives.

More on Verbs

Label each sentence I if the verb tenses are inconsistent or P if the sentence uses the passive voice.

- _____ George raced across the field and catches the ball.
- _____ The old record was broken by Justin.
- _____ That painting was done by a famous artist.
- _____ In the future, we may live on Mars, and we have produced our food in greenhouses.
- _____ First, the baker prepares the dough, and then she will cut out the cookies.

(Answers are in Appendix 3.)

Verbs communicate the action and time of each sentence. So it is important that you use **verb tense** consistently. Also, you should strive to write in the **active,** not the passive, **voice.** This chapter provides help with both of these sentence skills.

MyWritingLab

Understanding More on Verbs

To learn more about verbs, go to **MyWritingLab.com,** and choose **Consistent Verb Tense and Active Voice** in the **Sentence Skills** module. From there, watch the **Animation** video called **Animation: Active and Passive Voice.** Then, return to this chapter, which will go into more detail on verbs and give you opportunities to practice them. Finally, you will apply your understanding of verbs to your own writing.

Student Comment:
"This video on Verb Tense and Active Voice helped me understand verbs better because they were fresh in my mind when I went back to write my papers. No more verb errors for me!"

CONSISTENT VERB TENSE

Verb tense refers to the time an action takes place—in the present, the past, or the future. The verb tenses in a sentence should be consistent. That is, if you start out using one tense, you should not switch tenses unless absolutely necessary. Switching tenses can be confusing. Here are some examples:

	Present	Present
NOT	When the sun **sinks** into the bay and the moon **rises**	

                                                                       Past
from behind the trees, the pelicans **flew** away to the south.

	Present	Present
Correct:	When the sun **sinks** into the bay and the moon **rises**	

                                                           Present
from behind the trees, the pelicans **fly** away to the south.

_____

	Past	Present
NOT	They **skidded** off the road yesterday when the rain **is** heavy.	

	Past
Correct:	They **skidded** off the road yesterday when the rain

Past
was heavy.

_____

                                        Future
NOT   My brother **will receive** his degree in June, and then

                        Present
he **moves** to Boston.

                                        Future
Correct: My brother **will receive** his degree in June, and then

                        Future
he **will move** to Boston.

PRACTICE 1A: Recall/Identify In the following sentences, write C if the verb tense is consistent or I if it is inconsistent.

1. _____ Scott walked to the store and buy some milk.

2. _____ Last evening, Charles waited at the park for his friends, but they never make it.

3. _____ According to the instructor, we will need to bring a change of clothes, and we have to get all of our medical records updated.

4. _____ They grilled fresh fish over the fire and sleep under the stars.

5. _____ The salesclerk was rude to me, yet I thanked her anyway.

PRACTICE 1B: Correct Correct the verb tense errors in Practice 1A by re-writing the inconsistent sentences.

PRACTICE 2: Apply Fill in each blank in the following sentences with consistent verbs.

1. During Kendra's vacation, she _____ along the beach and _____ souvenirs for her friends and family.

2. Out of the box _____ the cat, and then he _____ under the table.

3. Oh, no, I _____ to bring the decorations for the prom, and I _____ the invitations sitting on my kitchen counter.

4. Actors and singers generally _____ a lot of media coverage and _____ featured on many special television shows.

5. Madonna's music and videos _____ many people, but her loyal fans _____ her.

PRACTICE 3: Write Your Own Write five sentences of your own with at least two verbs in each. Make sure your tenses are consistent.

USING THE ACTIVE VOICE

In the **active voice,** the subject performs the action. In the **passive voice,** the subject receives the action. Compare the following two examples:

Passive Voice: The mayor **was accused** of stealing **by the police.**

Active Voice: **The police accused** the mayor of stealing.

The active voice adds energy to your writing. Here is another example. Notice the difference between active and passive.

Passive Voice: **A cake was baked** for Tim's birthday **by my grandmother.**

Active Voice: **My grandmother baked a cake** for Tim's birthday.

PRACTICE 4A: Recall/Identify Write A if the sentence is in the active voice and P if it is in the passive voice.

1. _____ The astronauts landed on the moon and planted a flag.

2. _____ Flowers are being sent to the funeral home.

3. _____ Jordan hit the ball over the fence into the neighbor's yard.

4. _____ The experimental medicines were shipped to the laboratory for further testing.

5. _____ People who heckle the politicians will be escorted from the building.

PRACTICE 4B: Correct Rewrite the passive sentences in Practice 4A in the active voice.

PRACTICE 5: Apply Complete the following sentences in the active voice.

1. Many boxes of clothes _____

2. A can of hairspray _____

3. A plate of food _____

4. The boy's hat _____

5. The trip _____

PRACTICE 6: Write Your Own Write five sentences in the passive voice. Then rewrite them in the active voice.

CHAPTER REVIEW

REVIEW PRACTICE 1: Recall/Identify Label each sentence I if the verb tenses are inconsistent, P if the sentence is in the passive voice, or C if the sentence is correct. Then revise the inconsistent and passive sentences by rewriting them.

1. _____ You should pick up the trash in the yard.

2. _____ The yacht keeps listing to the left and will need to be fixed before anyone can board her.

3. _____ The ornaments sitting above the fireplace were given to my grandmother by famous people and were some of her favorite belongings.

4. _____ Tomorrow, you and I will go to the lake and fished for trout.

5. _____ I drank the Sprite and eat all the cookies.

6. _____ Ken wished he had remembered his girlfriend's birthday and prays that she will forgive him.

7. _____ The wad of gum was placed under the desk by a naughty boy.

8. _____ The piano is played by Jeannie, and the songs are sung by Mark.

9. _____ Your purchases will be sent to you later this week.

10. _____ Caring individuals think of others before themselves and perform unselfish acts.

REVIEW PRACTICE 2: Apply Fill in each blank with consistent, active verbs.

1. Mike _____ the house on time but _____ stuck in traffic.

2. I _____ the hot coffee too quickly and _____ my tongue.

3. The pebble in my shoe _____ my foot, so I _____ down.

4. The bird _____ out the window and _____ south.

5. Clare still _____ in the Easter Bunny, but then she _____ only 3 years old.

REVIEW PRACTICE 3: Write Your Own Write a paragraph about a recent, difficult decision you have made. Be sure to give the reasons for your decision. Keep your tenses consistent, and use the active voice.

> **MyWritingLab™** Complete this "Write Your Own" exercise for Chapter 33 in the MyWritingLab "Activities: Your Textbook" module.

REVIEW PRACTICE 4: Editing Through Collaboration Exchange paragraphs from Review Practice 3 with another student, and do the following:

1. Circle all verbs that are not consistent in tense.

2. Underline any verbs in the passive voice.

Then return the paper to its writer, and use the information in this chapter to correct any verb consistency or voice errors in your own paragraph. Record your errors on the Error Log in Appendix 7.

> **MyWritingLab™** Visit Chapter 33, "More on Verbs," in MyWritingLab, and complete the Post-test to check your understanding of the chapter's objectives.

Pronouns

Pronouns generally go almost unnoticed in writing and speaking, even though these words can do anything nouns can do. In fact, much like your inborn sense of balance, pronouns work in sentences to make your writing precise and coherent. Without pronouns, writers and speakers would find themselves repeating nouns over and over, producing unnatural, boring sentences. For example, notice how awkward the following paragraph is without pronouns:

> Robert wrote a rough draft of Robert's essay last night. Then Robert asked Robert's girlfriend to read over Robert's essay with Robert. After Robert's girlfriend helped Robert find errors, Robert made corrections. Then Robert set aside the essay for a day before Robert took the essay out and began revising again.

When we let pronouns take over and do their jobs, we produce a much more fluent paragraph:

> Robert wrote a rough draft of his essay last night. Then he asked his girlfriend to read over his essay with him. After she helped Robert find errors, he made corrections. Then he set aside the essay for a day before he took it out and began revising again.

Problems with pronouns occur when the words pronouns refer to aren't clear or when pronouns and their antecedents—the words they refer to—are too far apart. In this unit, we will deal with the following aspects of pronouns:

Chapter 34: Pronoun Problems
Chapter 35: Pronoun Reference and Point of View
Chapter 36: Pronoun Agreement

Pronoun Problems

Correct the pronoun errors in the following sentences.

- The ball was their's to begin with.
- Tom told Valerie and I the most exciting story.
- James can type a lot faster than me.
- Those there running shoes are Kim's.
- Me and Julio are going to the movies tonight.

(Answers are in Appendix 3.)

Pronouns are words that take the place of nouns. They help us avoid repeating nouns. In this chapter, we'll discuss five types of pronoun problems: (1) using the wrong pronoun as a subject, (2) using the wrong pronoun as an object, (3) using an apostrophe with a possessive pronoun, (4) misusing pronouns in comparisons, and (5) misusing demonstrative pronouns.

MyWritingLab

Understanding Pronoun Problems

To help you understand this topic, go to **MyWritingLab.com,** and choose **Pronoun Case** in the **Sentence Skills** module. For this topic, watch the video called **Animation: Pronoun Case.** Then, return to this chapter, which will go into more detail about pronouns and give you opportunities to practice them. Finally, you will apply your understanding of pronoun case to your own writing.

Student Comment:
"With **MyWritingLab**, I can try the exercises as many times as possible and not feel stupid."

PRONOUNS AS SUBJECTS

Single pronouns as subjects usually don't cause problems.

Subject Pronoun: **I** attended the opera with my aunt and uncle.
Subject Pronoun: **They** relocated to New York.

You wouldn't say "*Me* attended the game" or "*Them* went to Los Angeles." But an error often occurs when a sentence has a compound subject and one or more of the subjects is a pronoun.

NOT The boys and us competed all the time.
Correct: The boys and **we** competed all the time.

NOT Her and me decided to go to Paris.
Correct: **She and I** decided to go to Paris.

To test whether you have used the correct form of the pronoun in a compound subject, try each subject alone.

Subject Pronoun? The boys and us competed for the trophy.
Test: The boys competed for the trophy. **YES**
Test: Us competed for the trophy. **NO**
Test: We competed for the trophy. **YES**
Correction: The boys and we competed for the trophy.

Here is a list of subject pronouns:

Subject Pronouns

SINGULAR	PLURAL
I	*we*
you	*you*
he, she, it	*they*

PRACTICE 1: Recall/Identify Underline the pronouns used as subjects in each of the following sentences.

1. Diane and he will be gone for at least a week.

2. He is going to have to work faster if he wants to meet the deadline.

3. "I really don't want to go," he said.

4. We cannot use the elevator because it is not working.

5. She and I have been best friends since I can remember.

PRACTICE 2: Apply Fill in each blank in the following paragraph with a subject pronoun.

At first, my friends had me convinced that (1) _____ should go on the annual deep-sea fishing trip. (2) _____ spoke on and on about how much fun the last trip was. But before long, Brian admitted that (3) _____ got sick once the boat was out at sea. Then Misty explained how the captain of the boat cut off the heads of the fish and gutted them. (4) _____ found the whole process exciting. (5) _____ can just imagine my reaction! I don't think I'll be joining my friends on their fishing trip.

PRACTICE 3: Write Your Own Write a sentence of your own for each of the following subject pronouns.

1. they _____

2. you _____

3. he _____

4. it _____

5. I _____

PRONOUNS AS OBJECTS

One of the most frequent pronoun errors is using a subject pronoun when the sentence calls for an object pronoun. The sentence may require an object after a verb, showing that someone or something receives the action of the verb. Or an object of a preposition may be called for (see page 500 for a list of prepositions).

NOT   She gave **Kenisha and I** some money.
Correct: She gave **Kenisha and me** some money.

NOT   The secret is between **you and I.**
Correct: The secret is between **you and me.**

Like the subject pronoun error, the object pronoun error usually occurs with compound objects. Also like the subject pronoun error, you can test whether you are using the correct pronoun by using each object separately.

Object Pronoun? She gave **Kenisha and I** some money.

Test: She gave **Kenisha** some money. **YES**

Test: She gave **I** some money. **NO**

Test: She gave **me** some money. **YES**

Correction: She gave **Kenisha and me** some money.

Here is a list of object pronouns:

Object Pronouns

SINGULAR	PLURAL
me	us
you	you
him, her, it	them

PRACTICE 4: Recall/Identify Underline the correct object pronoun in each of the following sentences.

1. Natalie's grandmother raised (her, she) since she was 5.

2. The wonderful neighbors welcomed (we, us) to the community with a cake.

3. Corrina accidentally sprayed my sister and (I, me) with the hose.

4. All are going on the trip except for you and (him, he).

5. For (her, she), I will sit through this awful movie.

PRACTICE 5: Apply Fill in each blank in the following sentences with an object pronoun.

1. Between the two of _____, we should be able to fix the problem.

2. He asked you and _____ to the same dance.

3. Unlike _____, I am going to take emergency gear on this hiking trip.

4. According to you and _____, the test will take one hour.

5. The priest took _____ on a tour of the temple.

PRACTICE 6: Write Your Own Write a sentence of your own for each of the following object pronouns.

1. us _____

2. him _____

3. me _____

4. them _____

5. her _____

POSSESSIVE PRONOUNS

Possessive pronouns show ownership (my *house*, her *baseball*, our *family*). (See pages 496–497 for a list of pronouns.) An apostrophe is used with nouns to show ownership (Jack's *dog*, the farmer's *tractor*, the people's *opinions*). But an apostrophe is never used with possessive pronouns.

Possessive Pronouns

SINGULAR	PLURAL
my, mine	*our, ours*
your, yours	*your, yours*
his, her, hers	*their, theirs*

NOT	That house is **their's.**
Correct:	That house is **theirs.**
NOT	The book on the table is **your's.**
Correct:	The book on the table is **yours.**
NOT	The dog chased **it's** tail.
Correct:	The dog chased **its** tail.

PRACTICE 7: Recall/Identify Underline the correct possessive pronoun in each of the following sentences.

1. The computer needs its monitor fixed.

2. Both of my aunts live in New Mexico.

3. That piece of cake on the counter is hers.

4. The children left their toys in the driveway.

5. Hey! That was his.

PRACTICE 8: Apply Fill in each blank in the following sentences with a possessive pronoun.

1. These books aren't _____ , so they must be _____ .

2. _____ dogs bothered the neighbors so much that we had to move.

3. The filming crew left _____ equipment on the set.

4. Look at John's dog carrying _____ bowl in his mouth.

5. The copy machine won't work because _____ ink cartridge is empty.

PRACTICE 9: Write Your Own Write a sentence of your own for each of the following possessive pronouns.

1. mine _____

2. theirs _____

3. his _____

4. its _____

5. our _____

PRONOUNS IN COMPARISONS

Sometimes pronoun problems occur in comparisons with *than* or *as*. An object pronoun may be mistakenly used instead of a subject pronoun. To find out if you are using the right pronoun, finish the sentence as shown here.

NOT   She can analyze poems better than **me.**
Correct: She can analyze poems better than **I** [can analyze poems].

NOT   Lilly is not as good a piano player as **him.**
Correct: Lilly is not as good a piano player as **he** [is].

Hint: Sometimes an object pronoun is required in a *than* or *as* comparison. But errors rarely occur in this case because the subject pronoun sounds so unnatural.

NOT   Kay dislikes him more than she dislikes **I.**
Correct: Kay dislikes him more than she dislikes **me.**

PRACTICE 10: Recall/Identify Underline the correct pronoun in each of the following comparisons.

1. Mark is much neater than (I, me).

2. Cindy, the head majorette at our high school, can twirl a baton as well as (we, us).

3. Simone is not as talented an artist as (him, he).

4. Those other puppies are much fatter than (they, them).

5. Carlos is just as happy as (she, her).

PRACTICE 11: Apply Fill in each blank in the following sentences with an appropriate pronoun for comparison.

1. After he appeared in *Star Wars*, Harrison Ford became a bigger star than _____ .

2. Joey can throw a ball as far as _____ .

3. My friends managed to stay longer in the haunted house than _____ did.

4. He makes you just as mad as he makes _____ .

5. Julia, whose parents are well-known artists, is a more talented painter than _____ .

PRACTICE 12: Write Your Own Write a sentence of your own using each of the following pronouns in *than* or *as* comparisons.

1. I _____

2. she _____

3. they _____

4. we _____

5. he _____

DEMONSTRATIVE PRONOUNS

There are four demonstrative pronouns: *this*, *that*, *these*, and *those*. **Demonstrative pronouns** point to specific people or objects. Use *this* and *these* to refer to items nearby and *that* and *those* to refer to items farther away. Look at the following examples.

Demonstrative (near):	**This** is my room.
Demonstrative (near):	**These** are yesterday's notes.
Demonstrative (farther):	**That** is the town hall.
Demonstrative (farther):	**Those** are the cheerleaders for the other team.

Sometimes demonstrative pronouns are not used correctly.

NOT	**Correct**
this here, that there	this, that
these here, these ones	these
them, those there, those ones	those

NOT	**Them** are the clothes she bought.
Correct:	**Those** are the clothes she bought.

NOT	I'd like to have **these here** books.
Correct:	I'd like to have **these** books.

NOT	I found **those ones** in the attic.
Correct:	I found **those** in the attic.

NOT	**Those there** are the ones I like.
Correct:	**Those** are the ones I like.

When demonstrative pronouns are used with nouns, they become adjectives.

Pronoun:	**That** is mine.
Adjective:	**That computer** is mine.

Pronoun:	**Those** are actions you may regret.
Adjective:	You may regret **those actions.**

The problems that occur with demonstrative pronouns can also occur when these pronouns act as adjectives.

NOT	Please give me **that there** paper.
Correct:	Please give me **that** paper.

PRACTICE 13A: Recall/Identify Underline the demonstrative pronoun errors in each of the following sentences.

1. The babies usually play with those there toys.

2. This here test is just too difficult.

3. I believe that there pair of shoes will do nicely for this outfit.

4. These ones should be brought in out of the rain.

5. I can carry this here if you'll take this here.

PRACTICE 13B: Correct Correct the demonstrative pronoun errors in Practice 13A by rewriting the incorrect sentences.

PRACTICE 14: Apply Fill in each blank in the following sentences with a logical demonstrative pronoun.

1. _____ are the skates he wanted.

2. Would you like _____ curtains for your house?

3. _____ Corvette belongs to my uncle.

4. She baked _____ cookies herself.

5. I want _____ for my bathroom.

PRACTICE 15: Write Your Own Write four sentences of your own, one using each demonstrative pronoun. Be sure you don't use these pronouns as adjectives in your sentences.

CHAPTER REVIEW

REVIEW PRACTICE 1: Recall/Identify Underline the pronoun errors in each of the following sentences.

1. The football team and us went out for pizza after the game.

2. I think the fish is trying to tell you its' tank needs to be cleaned.

3. That secret was supposed to remain between you and I.

4. My brother at age four was as big as him at age six.

5. These here tarts are the best I've ever tasted.

6. Due to the power outage, him and me had dinner by candlelight.

7. I do believe you are stronger than him.

8. Hers' money is already spent even though she started out with $100.

9. One of my high school teachers taught she and me how to fly a plane.

10. I know that those there headphones belong to me.

REVIEW PRACTICE 2: Apply Correct the pronoun errors in Review Practice 1 by rewriting the incorrect sentences.

REVIEW PRACTICE 3: Write Your Own Write a short paragraph about your most treasured object. Why is it one of your favorite possessions?

MyWritingLab™　Complete this "Write Your Own" exercise for Chapter 34 in the MyWritingLab "Activities: Your Textbook" module.

REVIEW PRACTICE 4: Editing Through Collaboration Exchange paragraphs from Review Practice 3 with another student, and do the following:

1. Circle all pronouns.

2. Check that all the subject and object pronouns are used correctly. Also check that possessive pronouns, pronouns used in comparisons, and demonstrative pronouns are used correctly. Put an X through any that are not in the correct form.

Then return the paper to its writer, and use the information in this chapter to correct the pronoun errors in your own paragraph. Record your errors on the Error Log in Appendix 7.

MyWritingLab™　Visit Chapter 34, "Pronoun Problems," in MyWritingLab, and complete the Post-test to check your understanding of the chapter's objectives.

Pronoun Reference and Point of View

Underline the pronouns in these sentences. Then put an X over any pronouns that are confusing or unclear.

- It says to schedule your own appointments.
- Millie and Tanya were going to Las Vegas, but her car broke.
- I created a backup plan because you should always be prepared for the unexpected.
- You know they are covering up evidence of alien beings.
- Jimmy forgot questions 1 and 10, but he remembered it the next day.

(Answers are in Appendix 3.)

Anytime you use a pronoun, it must clearly refer to a specific word. The word it refers to is called its **antecedent.** Two kinds of problems occur with pronoun references: The antecedent may be unclear, or the antecedent may be missing. You should also be careful to stick to the same point of view in your writing. If, for example, you start out talking about *I*, you should not shift to *you* in the middle of the sentence.

MyWritingLab	**Understanding Pronoun Reference and Point of View**

To learn more about these pronoun features, go to **MyWritingLab. com,** and choose **Pronoun Reference and Point of View** in the **Sentence Skills** module. Next, watch the video called **Animation:**

Student Comment:
"MyWritingLab along with *Mosaics* and help from my instructor really provided me with the ability to be a better writer."

Pronoun Reference and Point of View. Then, return to this chapter, which will go into more detail about these topics and give you opportunities to practice them. Finally, you will apply your understanding of pronoun reference and point of view to your own writing.

PRONOUN REFERENCE

Sometimes a sentence is confusing because the reader can't tell what a pronoun is referring to. The confusion may occur because the pronoun's antecedent is unclear or is completely missing.

Unclear Antecedents

In the following examples, the word each pronoun is referring to is unclear.

Unclear: A bucket and an oar lay in the boat. As Rachel reached for **it,** the boat moved.

(Was Rachel reaching for *the bucket* or *the oar?* Only Rachel knows for sure.)

Clear: A bucket and an oar lay in the boat. As Rachel reached for **the bucket,** the boat moved.

Clear: A bucket and an oar lay in the boat. As Rachel reached for **the oar,** the boat moved.

Unclear: Michael told Oliver that **he** should change jobs.

(Does *he* refer to *Michael* or *Oliver?* Only the writer knows.)

Clear: Michael told Oliver that **Oliver** should change jobs.

Clear: Talking with Oliver, **Michael** said that **Michael himself** should change jobs.

How can you be sure that every pronoun you use has a clear antecedent? First, you can proofread carefully. Probably an even better test, though, is to ask a friend to read what you have written and tell you if your meaning is clear or not.

Missing Antecedents

Every pronoun should have a clear antecedent—the word it refers to. But what happens when there is no antecedent at all? The writer's message is not communicated. Two words in particular should alert you to the possibility of missing antecedents: *it* and *they.*

The following sentences have missing antecedents:

Missing Antecedent:	In a recent political poll, **it** shows that most people consider their votes unimportant.
	(What does *it* refer to? It has no antecedent.)
Clear:	A **recent political poll** shows that most people consider their votes unimportant.
Missing Antecedent:	**They** say that a fool and his money are soon parted.
	(Who is *they?*)
Clear:	**An old saying** states that a fool and his money are soon parted.

PRACTICE 1A: Recall/Identify Underline the pronouns in each of the following sentences. Then put an X next to any sentences with missing or unclear antecedents.

1. _____ According to recent surveys, it says that more people are getting a college education.

2. _____ My red pen should be in my purse, but I can't find it.

3. _____ The sitting room must have its baseboards cleaned.

4. _____ Talking with Kesha and Mindy, I learned that she is moving to Texas!

5. _____ They say you can catch more flies with honey than with vinegar.

PRACTICE 1B: Correct Correct the sentences with pronoun errors in Practice 1A by rewriting them.

PRACTICE 2: Apply Correct the unclear or missing pronoun references in the following sentences by rewriting them. Pronouns that should be corrected are underlined.

1. <u>It</u> says that we are all required to be at the meeting.

2. <u>They</u> always told me to treat people the way I want to be treated.

3. According to Sue and Hanna, <u>she</u> has been accepted into Yale.

4. We have chocolate and vanilla ice cream, but <u>it</u> tastes better.

5. <u>It</u> indicates that we should have turned left at the first light.

PRACTICE 3: Write Your Own Write five sentences of your own using pronouns with clear antecedents.

SHIFTING POINT OF VIEW

Point of view refers to whether a statement is made in the first person, the second person, or the third person. Each person—or point of view— requires different pronouns. The following chart lists the pronouns for each point of view.

Point of View

First Person:	*I, we*
Second Person:	*you, you*
Third Person:	*he, she, it, they*

If you begin writing from one point of view, you should stay in that point of view. Do not shift to another point of view. For example, if you start out writing *I*, you should continue with *I* and not shift to *you*. Shifting point of view is a very common error in college writing.

Shift: If **a person** doesn't study, **you** will not do well in school.

Correct: If **a person** doesn't study, **he or she** will not do well in school.

Shift: **I** changed jobs because **you** have more opportunities here.

Correct: **I** changed jobs because **I** have more opportunities here.

PRACTICE 4A: Recall/Identify Underline the pronouns that shift in point of view in the following sentences.

1. If you don't eat a good diet, they may find their health suffering.

2. One can always find unique merchandise at the more exclusive stores, but you have to be willing to pay the price.

3. I hinted that I didn't want to take part in the play, but you never knew if you got the message across.

4. I see a couple of concerts a year because everyone needs a little culture in his or her life.

5. I've already started writing my research paper because you should never wait until the last minute.

PRACTICE 4B: Correct Correct the point-of-view errors in Practice 4A by rewriting the incorrect sentences.

PRACTICE 5: Apply Complete the following sentences with pronouns that stay in the same point of view.

1. I decided to pack lightly and carry my luggage on board the airplane, so ____ know my luggage will arrive when I do.

2. I should taste these dishes because ____ never know if I'm going to like them until I try them.

3. A person is expected to follow the rules of the road; otherwise, _____ may cause an accident.

4. I always wear a smile on my face because ____ never know who might be around.

5. One should pay attention; then ____ might not feel so confused.

PRACTICE 6: Write Your Own Write a sentence of your own for each of the following pronouns. Be sure the pronouns have clear antecedents and do not shift point of view.

1. they _____

2. you _____

3. I _____

4. it _____

5. we _____

CHAPTER REVIEW

REVIEW PRACTICE 1: Recall/Identify Label the following sentences U if the antecedent is unclear, M if the antecedent is missing, or S if the sentence shifts point of view. Then correct the pronoun errors by rewriting the incorrect sentences.

1. ____ If one forgets the answer, then you should look it up.

2. ____ They say you should never accept rides from strangers.

3. ____ Janie bought milk, bread, cheese, and lettuce at the grocery store, but she left it in the car.

4. ____ A person should always look both ways before crossing the street; otherwise, you might get hit by a car.

5. ____ Stacy and Myra have already left for the show, but she forgot her wallet.

6. ____ It explains that the majority of the citizens are in favor of the proposed freeway.

7. ____ I asked my friends about my decision because you always value your friends' advice.

8. ____ It pointed out that "every cloud has a silver lining."

9. ____ Steven told Jason that he was going to be late.

10. ____ I ordered two pairs of jeans, a pair of shorts, and a pair of shoes from a catalog. I received it one week later.

REVIEW PRACTICE 2: Apply Correct the pronoun errors in the following sentences by rewriting each incorrect sentence.

1. I am going to purchase the most expensive champagne I can find, for you know that will impress the guests.

2. According to this announcement, it says we need to arrive no later than 2:00 p.m.

3. Jake and Dean will probably get into good colleges, even though he has a higher GPA.

4. A person should manage time wisely because you only have 24 hours in a day.

5. They are always carrying on about how bad the humidity is in the South.

6. Before Carla and Trisha left town, she bought a new swimsuit.

7. We were gossiping about Jarrett and Jeremy when he walked right by us.

8. One should study for the test if you want to pass it.

9. I had my hands full with a squirming puppy and a hissing cat until I decided to set him down.

10. You know what they say: "Never go to bed with a wet head."

REVIEW PRACTICE 3: Write Your Own Write a paragraph about a new experience you have had. Include at least six different pronouns.

 Complete this "Write Your Own" exercise for Chapter 35 in the MyWritingLab "Activities: Your Textbook" module.

REVIEW PRACTICE 4: Editing Through Collaboration Exchange paragraphs from Review Practice 3 with another student, and do the following.

1. Underline all pronouns.

2. Draw arrows to the words they modify.

3. Put an X through any pronouns that do not refer to a clear antecedent or that shift point of view.

Then return the paper to its writer, and use the information in this chapter to correct any pronoun reference and point-of-view errors in your own paragraph. Record your errors on the Error Log in Appendix 7.

 Visit Chapter 35, "Pronoun Reference and Point of View," in MyWritingLab, and complete the Post-test to check your understanding of the chapter's objectives.

36

Pronoun Agreement

Underline the pronouns in each sentence, and draw an arrow to their antecedents. Put an X over any pronouns that do not agree with their antecedents.

- Somebody left his lights on in his car.
- A judge must put aside her bias.
- Each of the children needs their permission slip signed.
- None of the fans could keep their voices quiet.
- A motorcyclist must take care of her gear.

(Answers are in Appendix 3.)

As you learned in Chapter 27, subjects and verbs must agree for clear communication. If the subject is singular, the verb must be singular; if the subject is plural, the verb must be plural. The same holds true for pronouns and the words they refer to—their *antecedents*. They must agree in number—both singular or both plural. Usually, **pronoun agreement** is not a problem, as these sentences show:

Singular: Dr. Gomez told **his** patient to stop smoking.

Plural: Carlos and Gina took **their** children to Disney World.

Student Comment:
"Instructors always talked about pronouns agreeing with one another, and I always thought they just meant pronouns are friendly with one another. Now, I know that it's about the relationship between the pronouns and what they refer to."

MyWritingLab

Understanding Pronoun Agreement

For more information about this topic, go to **MyWritingLab.com**, and choose **Pronoun-Antecedent Agreement** in the **Sentence Skills** module. From there, watch the video called **Animation: Pronoun Agreement.** Then, return to this chapter, which will go into more detail about pronoun agreement and give you opportunities to practice it. Finally, you will apply your understanding of pronoun agreement to your own writing.

INDEFINITE PRONOUNS

Pronoun agreement may become a problem with indefinite pronouns. Indefinite pronouns that are always singular give writers the most trouble.

NOT	**One** of the students finished **their** test early.
	(How many students finished early? Only one, so use a singular pronoun.)
Correct:	**One** of the students finished **her** test early.
Correct:	**One** of the students finished **his** test early.
NOT	**Somebody** just drove **their** new car into a ditch.
	(How many people just drove a car into a ditch? One person, so use a singular pronoun.)
Correct:	**Somebody** just drove **her** new car into a ditch.
Correct:	**Somebody** just drove **his** new car into a ditch.

Here is a list of indefinite pronouns that are always singular:

Singular Indefinite Pronouns

another	*everybody*	*neither*	*one*
anybody	*everyone*	*nobody*	*other*
anyone	*everything*	*none*	*somebody*
anything	*little*	*no one*	*someone*
each	*much*	*nothing*	*something*
either			

Hint: A few indefinite pronouns can be either singular or plural, depending on their meaning in the sentence. These pronouns are *any, all, more, most,* and *some.*

Singular:	**Some** of the money was left over, so we gave **it** to charity.
Plural:	**Some** of the donations were left over, so we gave **them** to charity.

In the first sentence, *money* is singular, so the singular pronoun *it* is used. In the second sentence, *donations* is plural, so the plural pronoun *them* is used.

PRACTICE 1: Recall/Identify Underline the correct pronoun from the choices in parentheses, and be prepared to explain your choices.

1. All of the infants had (his or her, their) footprints and handprints recorded at the hospital.

2. None of the cars needs (its, their) tires changed.

3. Anyone can get (his or her, their) high school diploma.

4. Before anybody can join the club, (he or she, they) must fill out an enrollment form.

5. The farmers and the farmworkers need (his or her, their) work hours shortened.

PRACTICE 2: Apply Fill in each blank in the following sentences with a pronoun that agrees with its antecedent.

1. Fabiola and Fabian asked _____ questions at the same time.

2. Everyone should listen more closely to _____ teacher.

3. Matt lost _____ backpack at the park.

4. Someone who could do a thing like that should have _____ head examined.

5. Something in the car leaked all _____ fluids onto the driveway.

PRACTICE 3: Write Your Own Write a sentence of your own for each of the following pronouns.

1. none _____

2. other _____

3. no one _____

4. everything _____

5. someone _____

AVOIDING SEXISM

In the first section of this chapter, you learned that you should use singular pronouns to refer to singular indefinite pronouns. For example, the indefinite pronoun *someone* requires a singular pronoun—*his* or *her* (not the plural *their*). But what if you don't know whether the person referred to is male or female? Then you have a choice: (1) You can say *he or she* or *his or her*; (2) you can make the sentence plural; or (3) you can rewrite the sentence to avoid the problem. You should not ignore half the population by referring to all humans as a single gender.

NOT	If **anyone** wants to go, **he** is welcome to do so.
Correct:	If **anyone** wants to go, **he or she** is welcome to do so.
Correct:	**People** who want to go are welcome to do so.

NOT	**Everyone** remembered to bring **his** lunch.
Correct:	**Everyone** remembered to bring **his or her** lunch.
Correct:	**All** the students remembered to bring **their** lunch.

Sexism in writing can also occur in ways other than with indefinite pronouns. We often assume doctors, lawyers, and bank presidents are men and nurses, schoolteachers, and secretaries are women. But that is not very accurate.

NOT	Ask a **fireman** if **he** thinks the wiring is safe.
	(Why automatically assume the person fighting fires is a male instead of a female?)
Correct:	Ask a **firefighter** if **he or she** thinks the wiring is safe.

NOT	The **mailman** delivered my neighbor's mail to my house by mistake.
	(Because both men and women deliver mail, the more correct term is *mail carrier*.)
Correct:	The **mail carrier** delivered my neighbor's mail to my house by mistake.

NOT	An **assistant** cannot reveal **her** boss's confidential business.
	(Why leave the men who are assistants out of this sentence?)
Correct:	An **assistant** cannot reveal **his or her** boss's confidential business.
Correct:	**Assistants** cannot reveal **their** bosses' confidential business.

PRACTICE 4A: Recall/Identify Underline the sexist references in the following sentences.

1. The chairperson should keep his board informed of new developments.

2. A nurse gives her time and patience freely.

3. Each person is responsible for makeup work if he misses an assignment.

4. Everybody must cook food if she plans to eat.

5. A good sailor knows his knots.

PRACTICE 4B: Correct Correct the sexist pronouns in Practice 4A by rewriting the incorrect sentences.

PRACTICE 5: Apply Fill in each blank in the following sentences with an appropriate pronoun.

1. A technician might become frustrated with _____ job.

2. A hairdresser who attracts celebrity customers can name _____ price.

3. An accountant needs help with _____ accounts.

4. Somebody wrote _____ phone number on the bathroom wall.

5. Sometimes a child forgets _____ lunch.

PRACTICE 6: Write Your Own Write a sentence of your own for each of the following antecedents. Include at least one pronoun in each sentence.

1. doctor _____

2. politician _____

3. police officer _____

4. spokesperson _____

5. FBI agent _____

CHAPTER REVIEW

REVIEW PRACTICE 1: Recall/Identify Underline and correct the pronoun errors in the following sentences.

1. Anyone who wants <u>their</u> book signed should stand in this line.

2. A good assistant keeps <u>her</u> dictionary within easy reach.

3. A surfer can lose <u>his</u> wave.

4. Only one of the contestants turned in <u>their</u> enrollment form on time.

5. The politician who cares about <u>his</u> people will win the election.

6. Each of the photographers has <u>their</u> own camera.

7. Everyone needs <u>their</u> funny bone tickled every now and then.

8. A tattoo artist should always clean <u>her</u> equipment before each new client.

9. A teacher should always ask <u>her</u> students if they understand the assignment.

10. Someone that messy should clean <u>their</u> room more often.

REVIEW PRACTICE 2: Apply Fill in each blank in the following sentences with an appropriate pronoun.

1. Neither of the criminals wanted _____ picture taken.

2. A racecar driver depends on _____ car and skill to win the race.

3. A housecleaner brings _____ own supplies.

4. Each of the boys can do _____ own work.

5. None of the students wanted to disappoint _____ teacher.

6. At the reunion, everyone talked to _____ friends.

7. Another person left _____ homework behind.

8. Somebody needs to water _____ lawn.

9. Everyone should be nice to _____ neighbors.

10. Nobody should park _____ car in a no-parking zone.

REVIEW PRACTICE 3: Write Your Own Write a paragraph describing your favorite type of music. Why is it your favorite?

MyWritingLab™ Complete this "Write Your Own" exercise for Chapter 36 in the MyWritingLab "Activities: Your Textbook" module.

REVIEW PRACTICE 4: Editing Through Collaboration Exchange paragraphs from Review Practice 3 with another student, and do the following:

1. Underline any pronouns.

2. Circle any pronouns that do not agree with the words they refer to.

Then return the paper to its writer, and use the information in this chapter to correct any pronoun agreement errors in your own paragraph. Record your errors on the Error Log in Appendix 7.

MyWritingLab™ Visit Chapter 36, "Pronoun Agreement," in MyWritingLab, and complete the Post-test to check your understanding of the chapter's objectives.

Modifiers

Words that modify—usually called adjectives and adverbs—add details to sentences, either describing, limiting, or identifying so that sentences become more vivid and interesting. They work like accessories in our everyday lives. Without jewelry, scarves, ties, and cuff links, we are still dressed. But accessories give a little extra flair to our wardrobe. Without modifiers, writing would be bland, boring, and lifeless. However, to use adjectives and adverbs correctly, you must learn about their different forms and functions.

In the chapters in this unit, you will learn about adjectives, adverbs, and various problems with the placement of these words in sentences:

Chapter 37: Adjectives
Chapter 38: Adverbs
Chapter 39: Modifier Errors

Adjectives

Underline the adjectives in the following sentences. Then put an X over the adjectives that are used incorrectly.

- The kites were very colorful.
- She has the worstest hair color that I have ever seen.
- We were more busier this week than last week.
- He is the oldest of the two brothers.
- The Ford Mustang is more better than the Nissan Sentra.

(Answers are in Appendix 3.)

Adjectives are modifiers. They help us communicate more clearly (I have a *green* car; I want a *red* one) and vividly (the movie was *funny* and *romantic*). Without adjectives, our language would be drab and boring.

MyWritingLab **Understanding Adjectives**

To understand more about this part of speech, go to **MyWritingLab.com,** and choose **Adjectives and Adverbs** in the **Basic Grammar** module. From there, watch the video called **Animation: Adjectives.** Then, return to this chapter, which will go into more detail about adjectives and give you opportunities to practice using them. Finally, you will apply your understanding of these modifiers to your own writing.

USING ADJECTIVES

Adjectives are words that modify—or describe—nouns or pronouns. Adjectives often tell how something or someone looks: *dark, light, tall, short, large, small*. Most adjectives come before the words they modify, but with linking verbs (such as *is, are, look, become,* and *feel*), adjectives follow the words they modify.

Adjectives Before a Noun:	We felt the **cold, icy** snow.
Adjectives After a Linking Verb:	The snow was **cold** and **icy**.

PRACTICE 1: Recall/Identify In the following sentences, underline the adjectives, and circle the words they modify.

1. Michael left a shiny red apple on the wooden desk on Monday morning.

2. Mrs. Johnson gave the two-year-old boy a piece of hard candy.

3. Our family doctor wants us to come in for our annual checkups.

4. I read a great book by John Grisham last week.

5. Grandma's beautiful garden is a quiet place for me to read, draw, or take a quick nap.

PRACTICE 2: Apply Fill in each blank in the following sentences with logical adjectives.

During my (1) _____ year of high school, I asked the head cheerleader to go to the prom with me. I was (2) _____ when she agreed to be my date, and I really wanted to impress her. I rented an expensive tuxedo, bought a (3) _____ corsage for her to wear on her wrist, and made sure to pick her up on time. The (4) _____ price was worth it because when we arrived at the dance, all of my buddies patted me on the back and said, "You two look (5) _____ together!"

PRACTICE 3: Write Your Own Write a sentence of your own for each of the following adjectives.

1. curious _____

2. durable _____

3. thirteen _____

4. helpful _____

5. short-tempered _____

COMPARING WITH ADJECTIVES

Most adjectives have three forms: a **basic** form, a **comparative** form (used to compare two items or indicate a greater degree), and a **superlative** form (used to compare three or more items or indicate the greatest degree).

For positive comparisons, adjectives form the comparative and superlative in two different ways.

1. For one-syllable adjectives and some two-syllable adjectives, use *-er* to compare two items and *-est* to compare three or more items.

Basic	Comparative (used to compare two items)	Superlative (used to compare three or more items)
bold	bolder	boldest
warm	warmer	warmest
numb	number	numbest
wise	wiser	wisest

2. For some two-syllable adjectives and all longer adjectives, use *more* to compare two items and *most* to compare three or more items.

Basic	Comparative (used to compare two items)	Superlative (used to compare three or more items)
friendly	more friendly	most friendly
peaceful	more peaceful	most peaceful
wonderful	more wonderful	most wonderful
appropriate	more appropriate	most appropriate

For negative comparisons, use *less* to compare two items and *least* to compare three or more items.

Basic	Comparative (used to compare two items)	Superlative (used to compare three or more items)
loud	less loud	least loud
funny	less funny	least funny
popular	less popular	least popular

Hint: Some adjectives are not usually compared. For example, one person cannot be *more dead* than another. Here are some more examples.

broken	*final*	*square*
empty	*impossible*	*supreme*
equal	*singular*	*unanimous*

PRACTICE 4: Recall/Identify Underline the adjectives, and note whether they are basic (B), comparative (C), or superlative (S).

1. __S__ The most logical decision would be to appoint Sam to the position.

2. __B__ Today the students showed how dedicated they can be.

3. __C/B__ Mita was happier about the engagement than her father was.

4. __S__ The strongest students always score the highest on the exam.

5. __C__ The food Nora and Richard ate on vacation was less healthy than what they eat at home.

PRACTICE 5: Apply Fill in each blank in the following paragraph with the correct comparative or superlative form of the adjective in parentheses.

    One summer afternoon, I was hiking high in the mountains when the sky above me grew suddenly (1) __darker__ (dark) than I have ever seen it. It looked like rain was going to fall soon, and I happened to be in an (2) __the most unsheltered__ (unsheltered) place on the mountain. I looked around to find the (3) __most suitable__ (suitable) tree to sit under, but there weren't any that would protect me. Even the (4) __thickest__ (thick) tree was very puny and wouldn't keep the rain off of my head. Quickly, I realized I had no option but to run (5) __faster__ (fast) than the rain to find shelter farther down the hill.

PRACTICE 6: Write Your Own Write a sentence of your own for each of the following adjectives.

1. a superlative form of *pretty* _____

2. the basic form of *sensible* _____

3. a comparative form of *talented* _____

4. a superlative form of *disgusting* _____

5. a comparative form of *tall* _____

COMMON ADJECTIVE ERRORS

Two types of problems occur with adjectives used in comparisons.

1. Instead of using one method for forming the comparative or superlative, both are used. That is, both *-er* and *more* or *less* are used to compare two items or both *-est* and *most* or *least* are used to compare three or more items.

    NOT　　My youngest son is **more taller** than his brothers.

    Correct:　My youngest son is **taller** than his brothers.

    NOT　　This is the **most happiest** day of my life.

    Correct:　This is the **happiest** day of my life.

2. The second type of error occurs when the comparative or superlative is used with the wrong number of items. The comparative form should be used for two items and the superlative for three or more items.

    NOT　　Marina is the **smartest** of the two sisters.

    Correct:　Marina is the **smarter** of the two sisters.

    NOT　　History is the **harder** of my three classes this semester.

    Correct:　History is the **hardest** of my three classes this semester.

PRACTICE 7A: Recall/Identify Underline the adjectives in the following sentences that are used incorrectly in comparisons. Mark sentences that are correct C.

1. _____ The most rudest customers are usually the ones who are trying to get something for free.

2. _____ Bob and Chad are both good-looking, but Bob is smartest.

3. _____ This class would be more fun if we could meet outside sometimes.

4. _____ The most rainiest day of the year was April 15.

5. _____ The bigger house in town is at 1859 Pine Street.

PRACTICE 7B: Correct Correct the adjective errors in Practice 7A by rewriting the incorrect sentences.

PRACTICE 8: Apply Choose the correct adjective forms in the following paragraph to complete the sentences.

Giving the dog a bath is the (1) _____ (more difficult, most difficult) chore in our house, and somehow it always seems to be my job. My sister Stephanie and I share most of the chores, but I am definitely (2) _____ (more responsible, most responsible) than she is. Usually, I do my chores without complaining, but bathing the dog is just unfair. We have an Australian sheepdog, and he is the (3) _____ (clumsiest, most clumsiest) thing alive. He seems to find every puddle of mud and sticky stuff to step in, and it quickly gets all over his fur. Unfortunately, though, he has a great dislike for baths, so the struggle to wash him is (4) _____ (trickiest, trickier) than it should be. And Stephanie is no help at all. While I'm fighting to hose him down, she just stands back and laughs at me, which makes me even (5) _____ (madder, more madder).

PRACTICE 9: Write Your Own Write a sentence of your own for each of the following adjectives.

1. strongest _____

2. more truthful _____

3. most gracious _____

4. larger _____

5. most frightening _____

USING GOOD AND BAD CORRECTLY

The adjectives *good* and *bad* are irregular. They do not form the comparative and superlative like most other adjectives. Here are the correct forms for these two irregular adjectives:

Basic	Comparative (used to compare two items)	Superlative (used to compare three or more items)
good	better	best
bad	worse	worst

Problems occur with *good* and *bad* when writers don't know how to form their comparative and superlative forms.

NOT	more better, more worse, worser, most best, most worst, bestest, worstest
Correct:	better, worse, best, worst

These errors appear in sentences in the following ways:

NOT	That is the **worstest** food I've ever tasted.
Correct:	That is the **worst** food I've ever tasted.

NOT	Air pollution is getting **more worse** every year.
Correct:	Air pollution is getting **worse** every year.

PRACTICE 10A: Recall/Identify In the following sentences, underline the forms of *good* and *bad* used correctly, and circle the forms of *good* and *bad* used incorrectly.

1. Both options are good, but getting a raise is more better than getting time off from work.

2. Giving that presentation in my psychology class was the worstest experience of my college career.

3. Giving your time to a charity is more good than just giving your money.

4. Sean wanted to go to Princeton, but his grades were worse than he thought.

5. Doing the laundry is more worse than getting a root canal.

PRACTICE 10B: Correct Correct the errors with *good* and *bad* in Practice 10A by rewriting the incorrect sentences.

PRACTICE 11: Apply Using the correct forms of *good* and *bad*, complete the following paragraph.

The (1) _____ day of my life was July 8, 2001. I remember it (2) _____ than any other. I had just bought a brand new convertible and was taking it to the beach for a couple of days of fun in the sun. Fortunately, my (3) _____ friend, Tara, was with me, because just 20 miles outside town, the engine of my dream car overheated! What was (4) _____ was that neither of us had a cell phone and the closest gas station was more than a mile away. We finally found a phone and called another friend, and then we waited and waited for a tow truck. After spending more than $3,000 in repairs, I found that my dream car had become my (5) _____ nightmare.

PRACTICE 12: Write Your Own Write a sentence of your own for each of the following forms of *good* and *bad*.

1. best _____

2. bad _____

3. worse _____

4. better _____

5. worst _____

CHAPTER REVIEW

REVIEW PRACTICE 1: Recall/Identify Label the following adjectives basic (B), comparative (C), superlative (S), or not able to be compared (X).

1. __C__ sillier

2. __S__ most ridiculous

3. __B__ dead

4. _____ tempting

5. _____ more stubborn

6. _____ meatiest

7. _____ most appealing

8. _____ broken

9. _____ tired

10. _____ lovelier

REVIEW PRACTICE 2: Apply Supply the comparative and superlative forms (both positive and negative) for each of the following adjectives.

Basic	Comparative	Superlative
1. welcome	more welcome	most welcome
2. justifiable	more / less —	most / least —
3. scary	scarier / less scary	scariest / least scary

4. kind _____ kinder _____ _____ kindest / least _____

5. mystical more/ less _____ mystical _____ _____ least / most mystical _____

6. strong _____ stronger / less stronger _____ _____ strongest / least strong _____

7. foolish more/ less _____ foolisher _____ most / least _____ foolishest _____

8. confusing less/ more _____ confusing _____ _____ most / least _____

9. extraordinary _____ more/ less _____ _____ most / least _____

10. loving _____ more/ less _____ _____ most / least _____

REVIEW PRACTICE 3: Write Your Own Write a paragraph describing the first pet you ever owned. What kind of animal was it? What did it look like? How did it act? What did you name it, and why did you choose that name?

MyWritingLab™   Complete this "Write Your Own" exercise for Chapter 37 in the MyWritingLab "Activities: Your Textbook" module.

REVIEW PRACTICE 4: Editing Through Collaboration Exchange paragraphs from Review Practice 3 with another student, and do the following:

1. Underline all the adjectives.

2. Circle those that are not in the correct form.

Then return the paper to its writer, and use the information in this chapter to correct any adjective errors in your own paragraph. Record your errors on the Error Log in Appendix 7.

MyWritingLab™   Visit Chapter 37, "Adjectives," in MyWritingLab, and complete the Post-test to check your understanding of the chapter's objectives.

Adverbs

Underline the adverbs in the following sentences. Then put an X over the adverbs that are used incorrectly.

- The pants fit me too loose, so I returned them to the store.
- Tori wasn't never so happy as after she won the lottery.
- When Madeline returned from Paris, she said she had a real good time.
- We happily made more ice cream when our first supply ran out.
- I wanted so bad to win the race, but I couldn't catch up.

(Answers are in Appendix 3.)

Like adjectives, adverbs help us communicate more clearly (she talked *slowly*) and more vividly (he sang *beautifully*). Adverbs make sentences more interesting.

MyWritingLab

Understanding Adverbs

To learn more about these modifiers, go to **MyWritingLab.com,** and choose **Adjectives and Adverbs** in the **Basic Grammar** module. From there, watch the video called **Animation: Adverbs.** Then, return to this chapter, which will go into more detail about adverbs and give you opportunities to practice using them. Finally, you will apply your understanding of this part of speech to your own writing.

Student Comment:
"Anytime you're having difficulty with an essay, refer back to **MyWritingLab** and review whatever it is you're having trouble with because it really does help."

USING ADVERBS

Adverbs modify verbs, adjectives, and other adverbs. They answer the questions *How? When? Where? How often?* and *To what extent?* Look at the following examples.

How?	My grandfather walked **slowly** up the stairs.
When?	Classes **always** begin after Labor Day.
Where?	Music lessons are held **here.**
How often?	I shop at Kmart **regularly.**
To what extent?	The airport is **extremely** busy during the holidays.

Some words are always adverbs, including *here, there, not, never, now, again, almost, often,* and *well.*

Other adverbs are formed by adding *-ly* to an adjective:

Adjective	**Adverb**
dim	*dimly*
soft	*softly*
careless	*carelessly*

Hint: Not all words ending in *-ly* are adverbs. Some—such as *friendly, early, lonely, chilly,* and *lively*—are adjectives.

PRACTICE 1: Recall/Identify In the following sentences, underline the adverbs, and circle the words they modify.

1. We drove quickly to Los Angeles so we wouldn't miss the concert.

2. I never saw that girl again.

3. Dirk suddenly changed his mind and agreed to host the party.

4. Stephen successfully completed the nursing program.

5. When the children became impatient during the drive, we continuously told them, "We're almost there."

PRACTICE 2: Apply Fill in each blank in the following sentences with an adverb that makes sense.

Sam's mom (1) _____ drove him to the airport, where he caught a plane to Houston, Texas. He was going to visit his grandparents (2) _____. Sam was only 10 years old, but he had

(3) _____ flown alone before. When the plane landed in Houston, Sam (4) _____ grabbed his carry-on luggage and (5) _____ ran to meet "Papa" and "Nonny."

PRACTICE 3: Write Your Own Write a sentence of your own for each of the following adverbs.

1. now _____

2. briskly _____

3. innocently _____

4. lazily _____

5. often _____

COMPARING WITH ADVERBS

Like adjectives, most adverbs have three forms: a **basic** form, a **comparative** form (used to compare two items), and a **superlative** form (used to compare three or more items). For positive comparisons, adverbs form the comparative and superlative forms in two different ways:

1. For one-syllable adverbs, use *-er* to compare two items and *-est* to compare three or more items.

Basic	Comparative (used to compare two items)	Superlative (used to compare three or more items)
soon	*sooner*	*soonest*
fast	*faster*	*fastest*

2. For adverbs of two or more syllables, use *more* to compare two items and *most* to compare three or more items.

Basic	Comparative (used to compare two items)	Superlative (used to compare three or more items)
strangely	*more strangely*	*most strangely*
carefully	*more carefully*	*most carefully*
happily	*more happily*	*most happily*

For negative comparisons, adverbs, like adjectives, use *less* to compare two items and *least* to compare three or more items.

	Comparative (used to compare two items)	Superlative (used to compare three or more items)
Basic		
close	*less close*	*least close*
quickly	*less quickly*	*least quickly*
creatively	*less creatively*	*least creatively*

Hint: Like adjectives, certain adverbs are not usually compared. Something cannot last *more eternally* or work *more invisibly*. The following adverbs cannot logically be compared.

endlessly	*eternally*	*infinitely*
equally	*impossibly*	*invisibly*

PRACTICE 4: Recall/Identify Underline the adverbs, and note whether they are basic (B), comparative (C), or superlative (S).

1. _____ When Jack joined the gym, he began to lose weight more quickly.

2. _____ The sun shone more brightly after the rain stopped.

3. _____ Valencia is the most rapidly growing city in southern California.

4. _____ People enroll less often in the morning classes than the afternoon classes.

5. _____ Priscilla rudely interrupted her mother and walked out of the room.

PRACTICE 5: Apply Fill in each blank in the following paragraph with the correct comparative or superlative form of the adverb in parentheses.

At one time, *Highlights* was the (1) _____ (widely) read children's magazine. It had (2) _____ (simply) written stories for the younger readers and (3) _____ (intellectually) challenging games for the older kids than any other magazine. Because of the wide variety of material in each issue, *Highlights* was the (4) _____ (highly) acclaimed publication for American youth. Now, though, *Highlights* has lots of competition, and big publishers are creating magazines for young readers (5) _____ (often) than they used to.

PRACTICE 6: Write Your Own Write a sentence of your own for each of the following adverbs.

1. a superlative form of *readily* _____

2. a comparative form of *eagerly* _____

3. the basic form of *unhappily* _____

4. a superlative form of *angrily* _____

5. a comparative form of *honestly* _____

ADJECTIVE OR ADVERB?

One of the most common errors with modifiers is using an adjective when an adverb is called for. Keep in mind that adjectives modify nouns and pronouns, whereas adverbs modify verbs, adjectives, and other adverbs. Adverbs *do not* modify nouns or pronouns. Here are some examples.

NOT   She spoke too **slow.** [adjective]
Correct: She spoke too **slowly.** [adverb]

NOT   We were **real** sorry about the accident. [adjective]
Correct: We were **really** sorry about the accident. [adverb]

PRACTICE 7A: Recall/Identify Underline the adverbs in the following sentences. Write C next to the sentences that are correct.

1. _____ Adam Sandler's character snored loud in *Little Nicky.*

2. _____ I rocked the baby gently to put her to sleep.

3. _____ Mr. Simpson talked too quick, and I didn't understand the assignment.

4. _____ Before we left the zoo, we checked the map careful to make sure we'd seen everything.

5. _____ Cook the beans slow so they don't burn.

PRACTICE 7B: Correct Correct the adverb errors in Practice 7A by rewriting the incorrect sentences.

PRACTICE 8: Apply Choose the correct adverb to complete the sentences in the following paragraph.

Zack and I went to Six Flags Magic Mountain last weekend and had a (1) _____ (real, really) good time. When we pulled into the parking lot, we could hear the roller coasters zooming (2) _____ (loudly, loud) overhead, and we could smell the yummy junk food. After we got through the gates, we ran (3) _____ (quick, quickly) to the line for the ride Shockwave. The line moved along (4) _____ (smoothly, smooth), and we were on the ride within 20 minutes. When Shockwave was over, we (5)_____ (glad, gladly) got in line to ride it again.

PRACTICE 9: Write Your Own Write a sentence of your own for each of the following adverbs.

1. specifically _____

2. tightly _____

3. greatly _____

4. sadly _____

5. coldly _____

DOUBLE NEGATIVES

Another problem involving adverbs is the **double negative**—using two negative words in one clause. Examples of negative words include *no, not, never, none, nothing, neither, nowhere, nobody, barely,* and *hardly*. A double negative creates the opposite meaning of what is intended.

NOT   She **never** had **no** time to rest.

The actual meaning of these double negatives is "She did have time to rest."

Correct: She had **no** time to rest.

NOT   My brother does **not** give me **nothing.**

The actual meaning of these double negatives is "My brother does give me something."

Correct: My brother does **not** give me **anything.**

Double negatives often occur with contractions.

NOT   There **aren't hardly** any apples left.

The actual meaning of these double negatives is "There are plenty of apples left."

Correct: There are **hardly** any apples left.

Using two negatives is confusing and grammatically wrong. Be on the lookout for negative words, and use only one per clause.

PRACTICE 10A: Recall/Identify Mark each of the following sentences either correct (C) or incorrect (X).

1. _____ He didn't never study, but he always passed the tests.

2. _____ Tabitha wasn't hardly four years old when her mother passed away.

3. _____ Nobody showed up for none of the practices last week.

4. _____ Hawkins doesn't really know what he wants to do.

5. _____ I wouldn't go nowhere with him.

PRACTICE 10B: Correct Correct the double negatives in Practice 10A by rewriting the incorrect sentences.

PRACTICE 11: Apply Choose the correct negative modifiers to complete the following paragraph.

     Last summer, I went to the beach and (1) _____ (was hardly, wasn't hardly) prepared for the sunshiny weather. I didn't buy (2) _____ (any, no) sunscreen before I left because I had a decent tan already. To my surprise, I started to burn after only three hours on the beach, and there (3) _____ (wasn't nothing, wasn't anything) I could do about it. I thought the burning feeling wouldn't (4) _____ (ever, never) go away. And no matter what lotions and ointments I put on, I couldn't get (5) _____ (no, any) relief. Next time, I'll remember to bring some sunscreen.

PRACTICE 12: Write Your Own Write a sentence of your own for each of the following negative words.

1. never _____

2. not _____

3. barely _____

4. nobody _____

5. nowhere _____

USING *GOOD/WELL* AND *BAD/BADLY* CORRECTLY

    The pairs *good/well* and *bad/badly* are so frequently misused that they deserve special attention. *Good* is an adjective; *well* is an adverb or adjective.

Use *good* with a noun (n) or after a linking verb (lv).

Adjective: Juan is a **good** boy.

Adjective: She looks **good.**

Use *well* for someone's health or after an action verb (av).

Adjective: He is **well** again. [health]

Adverb: The baby sleeps **well** at night.

Bad is an adjective; *badly* is an adverb.
Use *bad* with a noun (n) or after a linking verb (lv). Always use *bad* after *feel* if you're talking about emotions.

Adjective: He seems like a **bad** person.

Adjective: I feel **bad** that I got a ticket.

Use *badly* with an adjective (adj) or after an action verb (av).

Adverb: The house was **badly** burned.

Adverb: He swims **badly.**

PRACTICE 13A: Recall/Identify Label each of the following sentences either correct (C) or incorrect (X).

1. __X__ I want to do good in this job so my boss will like me.   *well*

2. __X__ My favorite team is playing bad this week.   *badly*

3. __C__ Vilma sings well and is pursuing a career in opera.

4. __C__ Rachel said she felt bad about Mr. Brown's accident.

5. __X__ I wanted so bad to go diving, but I couldn't.   *badly*

PRACTICE 13B: Correct Correct the adverb errors in Practice 13A by rewriting the incorrect sentences.

PRACTICE 14:   Apply Choose the correct modifiers to complete the following paragraph.

When Scott was in high school, there was only one thing he could do really (1) _____ (good, well). He struggled with academics, he played most sports very (2) _____ (bad, bad-ly), and he was never popular with the girls. But his one strength was music. From the moment he picked up his first guitar, he was always (3) _____ (good, well) at creating songs. Fortunately, his natural talent earned him several (4) _____ (good, well) scholarship offers from big-name universities. Unfortunately, his (5) _____ (bad, badly) study habits in high school made college more difficult for him, but he survived.

PRACTICE 15: Write Your Own Write a sentence of your own for each of the following modifiers.

1. well _____

2. badly _____

3. good _____

4. bad _____

5. well _____

CHAPTER REVIEW

REVIEW PRACTICE 1: Recall/Identify Underline the correct word in each of the following sentences.

1. Tia and Sue Ann studied together for the midterm, but Tia took notes (more, most) thoroughly.

2. We don't have (no, any) money for rent this month.

3. His speech seemed to go on (endlessly, more endlessly, most endlessly).

4. Of all the teachers at this school, Mrs. Thompson speaks the (more clearly, most clearly).

5. Jose drives (more fast, faster) than I do.

6. During the baseball game, I struck out (less, least) often than Jack did.

7. She plays the flute very (good, well) and is in the orchestra.

8. My senior year in high school, I was voted (less, least) likely to drop out of college.

9. He hurt his knee so (bad, badly) it required medical attention.

10. The children were (real, really) tired after spending the day at the lake.

REVIEW PRACTICE 2:   Apply Fill in each blank in the following paragraph with an adverb that makes sense. Try not to use any adverb more than once.

   Working as a food server can be very challenging. I take my job (1) _____ than the other servers, so I can (2) _____ count on coming home with better tips. But sometimes there are customers I just can't please, no matter how (3) _____ I want to. Also, there are the minor problems that happen (4) _____, like the kitchen running out of chicken or the bartender forgetting to make the drinks for my table. Because I'm determined to do my job (5) _____, though, my customers like me and keep coming back.

REVIEW PRACTICE 3:   Write Your Own If you could prepare anything you wanted for dinner tonight, what would you make? Write a paragraph about this meal. How would you prepare it? How would you serve it? How many courses would it consist of?

MyWritingLab™   Complete this "Write Your Own" exercise for Chapter 38 in the MyWritingLab "Activities: Your Textbook" module.

REVIEW PRACTICE 4:   Editing Through Collaboration Exchange paragraphs from Review Practice 3 with another student, and do the following:

1. Underline all the adverbs.

2. Circle those that are not in the correct form.

3. Put an X above any double negatives.

Then return the paper to its writer, and use the information in this chapter to correct any adverb errors in your own paragraph. Record your errors on the Error Log in Appendix 7.

MyWritingLab™   Visit Chapter 38, "Adverbs," in MyWritingLab, and complete the Post-test to check your understanding of the chapter's objectives.

Modifier Errors

Underline the modifier problem in each sentence.

- After studying together, his grades really improved.
- Before doing the laundry, the car needed to be washed.
- To get a good job, the interview must go well.
- The professor told the class he was retiring before he dismissed them.
- I wrote a letter to the newspaper that complained about rising power bills.

(Answers are in Appendix 3.)

As you know, a modifier describes another word or group of words. Sometimes, however, a modifier is too far from the words it refers to (*misplaced modifier*), or the word it refers to is missing altogether (*dangling modifier*). As a result, the sentence is confusing.

| MyWritingLab | **Understanding Modifier Errors** |

To expand your understanding of modifier errors, go to **MyWritingLab. com,** and choose **Misplaced or Dangling Modifiers** in the **Sentence Skills** module. From there, watch the video called **Animation: Misplaced or Dangling Modifiers.** Then, return to this chapter, which will go into more detail about these errors and give you opportunities to practice correcting them. Finally, you will apply your understanding of modifier errors to your own writing.

Student Comment:
"When I had trouble with a question in **MyWritingLab,** I opened up my *Mosaics* book to that chapter and looked for help. Between that and the videos, I mastered **Modifier Errors** in one try!"

MISPLACED MODIFIERS

A modifier should be placed as close as possible to the word or words it modifies, but this does not always happen. A **misplaced modifier** is too far from the word or words it refers to, making the meaning of the sentence unclear. Look at these examples.

NOT   The instructor explained why plagiarism is wrong **on Friday.**

(Is plagiarism wrong only on Friday? Probably not. So the modifier *on Friday* needs to be moved closer to the word it actually modifies.)

Correct: The instructor explained **on Friday** why plagiarism is wrong.

NOT   In most states, it is illegal to carry liquor in a car **that has been opened.**

(It is the liquor, not the car, that must not have been opened. So the modifier *that has been opened* needs to be moved closer to the word it modifies.)

Correct: In most states, it is illegal to carry liquor **that has been opened** in a car.

Certain modifiers that limit meaning are often misplaced, causing problems. Look at how meaning changes by moving the limiting word *only* in the following sentences:

Only Aunt Emily says that Lilly was a bad cook.
(Aunt Emily says this, but no one else does.)

Aunt Emily **only** says that Lilly was a bad cook.
(Aunt Emily says this, but she doesn't really mean it.)

Aunt Emily says **only** that Lilly was a bad cook.
(Aunt Emily says this but nothing more.)

Aunt Emily says that **only** Lilly was a bad cook.
(Lilly—and no one else—was a bad cook.)

Aunt Emily says that Lilly **only** was a bad cook.
(Aunt Emily says that there were some who were good cooks and that Lilly was the only bad one.)

Aunt Emily says that Lilly was **only** a bad cook.
(Lilly was a bad cook, but she wasn't bad at other things.)

Aunt Emily says that Lilly was a bad cook **only.**
(Lilly was a bad cook, but she wasn't bad at other things.)

Here is a list of common limiting words:

almost	*hardly*	*merely*	*only*
even	*just*	*nearly*	*scarcely*

PRACTICE 1A: Recall/Identify Underline the misplaced modifiers in the following sentences.

1. Tina told Tom that to win the lottery she had a great chance.

2. The car leaked all its oil by the time I called a mechanic in the driveway.

3. Brittany went to the mall with Jim wearing her favorite hat.

4. I sold Luigi my old watch after I bought an expensive new one for $10.

5. We made a pie in the kitchen with lots of blueberries.

PRACTICE 1B: Correct Correct the misplaced modifiers in Practice 1A by rewriting the incorrect sentences.

PRACTICE 2: Apply Fill in each blank in the following paragraph with a modifier that makes sense. Include at least two phrases.

Several years ago, Roger owned a (1) _____ farm in Kentucky where he grew corn and wheat. He also had (2) _____ orchards of apples that he (3) _____ harvested every September. His children had (4) _____ the farm. Shortly before Roger died, he trained his children (5) _____ the family business.

PRACTICE 3: Write Your Own Write a sentence of your own for each of the following modifiers.

1. before summer _____

2. since the company hired him _____

3. while driving to the store _____

4. after she bought the car _____

5. though no one was there _____

DANGLING MODIFIERS

Modifiers are "dangling" when they have nothing to refer to in a sentence. **Dangling modifiers** (starting with an *-ing* word or with *to*) often appear at the beginning of a sentence. Here is an example.

NOT   **Reaching the top of the hill**, the view was beautiful.

A modifier usually modifies the words closest to it. So the phrase *Reaching the top of the hill* modifies *view*. But it's not the view that reaches the top of the hill. In fact, there is no logical word in the sentence that the phrase modifies. It is left dangling. You can correct a dangling modifier in one of two ways—by inserting the missing word that is referred to or by rewriting the sentence.

Correct: **Reaching the top of the hill**, we saw a beautiful view.
Correct: **When we reached the top of the hill**, the view we saw was beautiful.

NOT   **To get into the movie**, an ID must be presented.
Correct: **To get into the movie**, you must present an ID.
Correct: You must present an ID **to get into the movie.**

NOT   The garage was empty **after moving the tools.**
Correct: **After moving the tools**, we had an empty garage.
Correct: The garage was empty **after we moved the tools.**

PRACTICE 4A: Recall/Identify Underline the dangling modifiers in the following sentences.

1. To get a good deal, time must be spent comparing prices.

2. Screaming for help, the chair fell over with the little boy in it.

3. As an only daughter with four brothers, there was never enough food in the house.

4. To get a driver's license, two tests must be passed.

5. Giving the dog a bath, the bathroom floor became flooded.

PRACTICE 4B: Correct Correct the dangling modifiers in Practice 4A by rewriting the incorrect sentences.

PRACTICE 5: Apply Fill in each blank in the following paragraph with a modifier that makes sense. Include at least two phrases.

(1) _____ professional baseball teams begin spring training. The coaches plan on (2) _____ weight lifting and lots of
running. Hundreds of (3) _____ athletes begin training each
season, but within days, many get cut from the major league teams.
These men usually get placed on (4) _____ teams. They hope
to play well throughout the season and (5) _____ move up.

PRACTICE 6: Write Your Own Write a sentence of your own for each of the
following phrases.

1. warm and bright _____

2. shaking my hand _____

3. to understand the opposite sex _____

4. getting a chance to see the ocean _____

5. to win an argument _____

CHAPTER REVIEW

REVIEW PRACTICE 1: Recall/Identify Underline the modifier errors in the following sentences.

1. Turning in my essay late, my computer crashed.

2. I am flying to Atlanta on Friday and returning Monday to attend a
    wedding.

3. To make a perfect chocolate dessert, the oven temperature must be
    carefully watched.

4. I put away my clothes and then called some friends in the closet.

5. Throwing the ball across the room, the lamp fell over and broke.

6. Jennifer complained that she forgot to send out invitations in an angry
    voice.

7. I found a pressed flower in my Shakespeare textbook from my
    wedding.

8. Driving to the movie theater, teenagers kept stepping out into the
    street in front of us.

9. Maria has a picture of her cousins at the beach in her locker.

10. To please your parents, good grades should be earned on every report card.

REVIEW PRACTICE 2: Apply Rewrite the sentences in Review Practice 1 so the phrases you underlined are as close as possible to the words they modify.

REVIEW PRACTICE 3: Write Your Own Write a paragraph about your greatest accomplishment. What did you do? How hard did you work for it? What was your reward?

MyWritingLab™   Complete this "Write Your Own" exercise for Chapter 39 in the MyWritingLab "Activities: Your Textbook" module.

REVIEW PRACTICE 4: Editing Through Collaboration Exchange paragraphs from Review Practice 3 with another student, and do the following:

1. Underline any misplaced modifiers.

2. Put brackets around any dangling modifiers.

Then return the paper to its writer, and use the information in this chapter to correct any modifier problems in your own paragraph. Record your errors on the Error Log in Appendix 7.

MyWritingLab™   Visit Chapter 39, "Modifier Errors," in MyWritingLab, and complete the Post-test to check your understanding of the chapter's objectives.

Punctuation

Can you imagine streets and highways without stoplights or traffic signs? Driving would become a life-or-death adventure as motorists made risky trips with no signals to guide or protect them. Good writers, like conscientious drivers, prefer to leave little to chance. They observe the rules of punctuation to ensure that the readers arrive at their intended meaning. Without punctuation, sentences would run together, ideas would be unclear, and words would be misread. Writers need to use markers—like periods, commas, and dashes—to help them communicate as efficiently and effectively as possible.

Look at the difference punctuation makes in the meaning of the following letter.

Dear John:

I want a man who knows what love is all about. You are generous, kind, thoughtful. People who are not like you admit to being useless and inferior. You have ruined me for other men. I yearn for you. I have no feelings whatsoever when we're apart. I can be forever happy—will you let me be yours?   Susan

Dear John,

I want a man who knows what love is. All about you are generous, kind, thoughtful people, who are not like you. Admit to being useless and inferior. You have ruined me. For other men, I yearn. For you, I have no feelings whatsoever. When we're apart, I can be forever happy. Will you let me be?   Yours, Susan

This unit will help you write the love letter you actually want to write—with the punctuation that gets your message across. It will also provide you with guidelines for using the following punctuation:

End Punctuation

Add the appropriate end punctuation to the following sentences.

- How are we going to get there
- That's amazing
- Get me a Pepsi, please
- This will never happen to me
- Can you make your own dinner tonight

(Answers are in Appendix 3.)

End punctuation signals the end of a sentence in three ways: The **period** ends a statement, the **question mark** signals a question, and the **exclamation point** marks an exclamation.

MyWritingLab

Understanding End Punctuation

To improve your understanding of these forms of punctuation, go to **MyWritingLab.com,** and choose **Final Punctuation** in the **Punctuation, Mechanics, and Spelling** module. For this topic, watch the video called **Animation: Final Punctuation.** Then, return to this chapter, which will go into more detail about these punctuation marks and give you opportunities to practice them. Finally, you will apply your understanding of end punctuation to your own writing.

Student Comment:
"**MyWritingLab** gives explanations when the answers are wrong AND when they are right."

PERIOD

Periods are used in sentences, abbreviations, and numbers.

1. A period is used with statements, mild commands, and indirect questions.

Statement:	The boy rode to school on the bus.
Command:	Ride the bus to school today.
Indirect Question:	I asked him why he rode the bus to school today.

2. A period is also used with abbreviations and numbers.

Abbreviations:	Mr. Johnson lives at 9 Kings Rd., next door to Dr. Tina López.
Numbers:	$16.95 4.5 $876.98 0.066

PRACTICE 1: Recall/Identify In the following sentences, circle the periods used incorrectly, and add those that are missing.

1. Walt is buying the house on the corner of Sonora Ave and Eureka St

2. I bought a new computer monitor for $210.0.0.

3. Mr. Bernard just married Ms Walters

4. Tara's dentist is named Dr Jones, and his office is on 4th. St

5. Bring your child to the library at Jackson Drive. and Lovejoy Pl..

PRACTICE 2: Apply Add periods to the following paragraph where they are needed.

Jane Seymour is a very talented actress who stars in a TV series called *Dr Quinn, Medicine Woman* Ms Seymour also raised twin boys and wrote a book about her experience mothering twins Her husband, Mr Frank Walters, was very supportive of her acting and writing activities He helped with the children and has even offered inspiring quotes for her book The book, published by St Martin's Press, sold for $20 50 in 2000

PRACTICE 3: Write Your Own Write a sentence of your own for each of the following descriptions.

1. a statement about cooking

2. a statement including a dollar amount

3. a statement including an address with an abbreviated street name

4. an indirect question about a psychology midterm

5. a command to do a household chore

QUESTION MARK

The question mark is used after a direct question.

Question Mark: Do you have homework to do?

Question Mark: "Can you get your homework done on time?"
her mother asked.

PRACTICE 4: Recall/Identify In the following sentences, circle the question marks used incorrectly, and add those that are needed.

1. Did you buy that jacket only last week.

2. I wonder when the party starts?

3. Stephanie said, "Are you wearing my watch?"

4. Tina asked Whit how he was feeling?

5. This is my biggest concern: How are we going to protect the rain forests.

PRACTICE 5: Apply Add question marks to the following paragraph where they are needed.

What are the three most important things to remember about writing. First, choose topics you are interested in. Why should you write about something that bores you. Second, remember that writing is a process. Should you ever turn in your first draft. No way. Writing gets better and better the more drafts you write. Third, give yourself plenty of time for editing and revision. Don't you think it's better that you catch the errors before your instructor does. Writing will be less of a chore if you remember these things and apply them to each assignment.

PRACTICE 6: Write Your Own Write a sentence of your own for each of the following descriptions.

1. a direct question about driving _____

2. an indirect question about your favorite sport _____

3. a direct question about a family member _____

4. an indirect question about the next major holiday _____

5. a direct question about lunch _____

EXCLAMATION POINT

The exclamation point indicates strong feeling. If it is used too often, it is not as effective as it could be. You shouldn't use more than one exclamation point at a time.

Exclamation Point:　Never!

Exclamation Point:　You don't mean it!

Exclamation Point:　Give me my homework or I'll scream!

Exclamation Point:　"You scared me to death!" she said.

PRACTICE 7: Recall/Identify Circle the exclamation marks used incorrectly, and add those that are needed.

1. That's outrageous.

2. I can't believe it.

3. He said! "Great job, Julian"

4. You can't mean that?

5. "Don't hurt my baby," yelled the mother.

PRACTICE 8: Apply Add exclamation points to the following paragraph where appropriate.

Paintball is my favorite pastime, and I play every weekend. It's so much fun. Last Saturday, Steve and Jay were on one team, and Tim and I were on another. Within an hour, Tim and I cornered Jay and took him out. "Pop.Pop." But suddenly, Steve came around a tree and pointed his paintball gun right at Tim.

"Duck," I yelled.

Tim quickly hit the ground, but it was too late. "Pop. Pop."

"Yeah," Steve yelled as he hit Tim right in the chest with paintballs.

But I was even quicker. "Pop." One shot and Steve had red paint right in the middle of his stomach.

"Last remaining survivor again," I screamed in delight.

PRACTICE 9: Write Your Own Write five sentences of your own using exclamation points correctly.

CHAPTER REVIEW

REVIEW PRACTICE 1: Recall/Identify For each sentence, add the correct end punctuation.

1. Do you have any tattoos

2. Stop lying to me

3. Are you sure you can help me

4. No! Not yet

5. Is there a problem with this software

6. Sometimes I think I'll never graduate

7. My cousin wants to know if we're going to leave soon

8. Take the keys to my car

9. That's impossible

10. You should study tomorrow while you're off work

REVIEW PRACTICE 2: Apply Turn sentences 1–5 into questions and sentences 6–10 into exclamations.

1. The plumber came today.

2. The Jets are going to win the Super Bowl.

3. Delores made the afghan.

4. You are going to be my date.

5. The baby hasn't been fed yet.

6. Don't forget to do the dishes.

7. We have ten minutes to get on the plane.

8. Are you serious?

9. I don't want to tell you.

10. This is a great day.

REVIEW PRACTICE 3: Write Your Own Write a paragraph about an emotional experience or event in your life. Was it exciting, happy, sad, disappointing, frustrating, or challenging? What happened? Who was involved? Include all three types of end punctuation—period, question mark, and exclamation point.

MyWritingLab™ Complete this "Write Your Own" exercise for Chapter 40 in the MyWritingLab "Activities: Your Textbook" module.

REVIEW PRACTICE 4: Editing Through Collaboration Exchange paragraphs from Review Practice 3 with another student, and do the following:

1. Circle any errors in end punctuation.

2. Suggest the correct punctuation above your circle.

Then return the paragraph to its writer, and use the information in this chapter to correct any end punctuation errors in your own paragraph. Record your errors on the Error Log in Appendix 7.

MyWritingLab™ Visit Chapter 40, "End Punctuation," in MyWritingLab, and complete the Post-test to check your understanding of the chapter's objectives.

Commas

Add commas to the following sentences.

- We drove to the beach and we had a picnic.
- Before I eat breakfast I take a multivitamin.
- "This is my favorite restaurant" said Matt.
- Email though makes corresponding easy and fast.
- They were married on February 14 2004 in Las Vegas Nevada.

(Answers are in Appendix 3.)

The **comma** is the most frequently used punctuation mark, but it is also the most often misused. Commas make sentences easier to read by separating the parts of sentences. Following the rules in this chapter will help you write clear sentences that are easy to read.

MyWritingLab | **Understanding Commas**

To find out more about commas, go to **MyWritingLab.com,** and choose **Commas** in the **Punctuation, Mechanics, and Spelling** module. From there, watch the video called **Animation: Commas.** Then, return to this chapter, which will go into more detail about this punctuation mark and give you opportunities to practice using it. Finally, you will apply your understanding of commas to your own writing.

Student Comment:
"I used to put commas just anywhere in a sentence, and now, thanks to **MyWritingLab** and *Mosaics*, I use them correctly AND I know the reason why they're there."

COMMAS WITH ITEMS IN A SERIES

Use commas to separate items in a series. You should place commas between all items in a series.

Series: The house had three bedrooms, two baths, and a pool.

Series: She caught the fish, cleaned it, and then cooked it.

Series: William can have a new car if his grades improve, if he gets a job, and if he does his chores at home.

Sometimes this rule applies to a series of adjectives in front of a noun, but sometimes it does not. Look at these two examples.

Adjectives with Commas: The **foggy, cold** weather is finally over.

Adjectives Without Commas: The **loose bottom** knob fell off my TV.

Both of these examples are correct. So how do you know whether or not to use commas? You can use one of two tests. One test is to insert the word *and* between the adjectives. If the sentence makes sense, use a comma. Another test is to switch the order of the adjectives. If the sentence still reads clearly, use a comma between the two words.

Test 1:   The **foggy and cold** weather is finally over. **OK, so use a comma**
Test 2:   The **cold, foggy** weather is finally over. **OK, so use a comma**

Test 1:   The **loose and bottom** knob fell off my TV. **Not OK, so no comma**
Test 2:   The **bottom loose** knob fell off my TV. **Not OK, so no comma**

PRACTICE 1: Recall/Identify In the following sentences, circle the commas that are used incorrectly, and add those that are missing.

1. In my free time, I like to read sew, and make jelly.

2. My girlfriend is very good, at tennis, volleyball, and golf.

3. The best things, about gardening are the relaxation, the sense of accomplishment, and the feeling of being one with nature.

4. To play professional basketball, one must practice regularly, play competitively and get a big break.

5. The sofa the ottoman and the computer desk, are going to be donated to Goodwill.

PRACTICE 2: Apply Add the missing commas to the following paragraph.

We are flying to Dallas this weekend to attend a friend's wedding. Before we leave, I need to do the laundry pay the bills and arrange for a house sitter. My husband's childhood friend is the one getting married, so he also hopes to see some of his other friends there— especially Gene Brad and Dwayne. During the past two months, we bought airline tickets arranged for a rental car and reserved a hotel room. Now all we have to do is make it to the airport on time! I'm also trying to decide whether to wear navy pink or gray, and my husband is getting his best suit altered. Though it has required lots of time energy and money, we are really looking forward to this trip.

PRACTICE 3: Write Your Own Write a sentence of your own for each of the following sets of items.

1. three things to do at the mall _____

2. three sports you like to play _____

3. three items on a to-do list _____

4. three popular magazines _____

5. three of your favorite snack foods _____

COMMAS WITH INTRODUCTORY WORDS

Use a comma to set off an introductory word, phrase, or clause from the rest of its sentence. If you are unsure whether to add a comma, try reading the sentence with your reader in mind. If you want your reader to pause after the introductory word or phrase, you should insert a comma.

Introductory Word:	**No,** it didn't rain.
Introductory Word:	**Really,** the weather wasn't as bad as we thought it would be.
Introductory Phrase:	**On the whole,** this is a great town to live in.
Introductory Phrase:	**To prove this to my relatives,** I took them for a tour of the town.
Introductory Clause:	**As the doors opened,** the light poured in.
Introductory Clause:	**When the movie was over,** everyone was silent.

PRACTICE 4: Recall/Identify In the following sentences, circle the commas that are used incorrectly, and add those that are missing.

1. Three years, ago we lived in Boise.

2. As the fire continued, to burn the firefighters feared it would get out of control.

3. Sure, I can take you to the store.

4. After spilling the water the little boy began to cry.

5. The next time you go, to Macy's can you pick up a gift certificate for me?

PRACTICE 5: Apply Add the missing commas to the following paragraph.

When Terina was seven years old we took her to Disneyland. Because she was tall enough to ride all of the rides she really enjoyed herself. First we had to take pictures with Mickey and Minnie. Of course we couldn't miss them! Next we got in line for Space Mountain, which turned out to be Terina's favorite ride. By the end of the day we had ridden Space Mountain five times.

PRACTICE 6: Write Your Own Write a sentence of your own for each of the following introductory words, phrases, or clauses.

1. well _____

2. when we thought it was almost over _____

3. yes _____

4. as the mail carrier arrived _____

5. wanting to win the lottery _____

COMMAS WITH INDEPENDENT CLAUSES

Use a comma before *and, but, for, nor, or, so,* and *yet* when they join two independent clauses. Remember that an independent clause must have both a subject and a verb.

Independent Clauses:	The boy flew to London, **and** he took a boat to France.
Independent Clauses:	He enjoyed the flight, **but** he liked the boat ride more.

Hint: Do not use a comma when a single subject has two verbs.

      s   v   **no comma** v

                      ↓

The **boy flew** to London and **left** for France the next day.

Adding a comma when none is needed is one of the most common errors in college writing assignments. Only if the second verb has its own subject should you add a comma.

      s   v   **comma**   s   v

                      ↓

The **boy flew** to London, and **he left** for France the next day.

PRACTICE 7: Recall/Identify In the following sentences, underline the subjects once and the coordinating conjunctions twice. Then circle any commas that are used incorrectly, and add those that are missing.

1. My computer crashed, so I lost my whole research paper.

1. The car looks great, and drives even better.

2. Going to the mountains was a good idea and we had a very nice time.

3. The cat will curl up on the sofa, or the rug by the fireplace.

4. My cousin wants to get married but I think she's too young.

PRACTICE 8: Apply Add the missing commas to the following paragraph.

      For my last birthday, my grandmother gave me $100 so I wanted to spend it on clothes. I went to the mall and I found three outfits that were perfect. I couldn't decide on just one but I didn't have enough money for them all. I needed the dressy outfit more yet the casual outfit was a great bargain. Finally, I settled on one suit but I'm saving money to go back and get the others. I'll go back within a month or maybe I'll just wait until after my next birthday.

PRACTICE 9: Write Your Own Write a sentence of your own using each of the following coordinating conjunctions to separate two independent clauses.

1. or _____

2. and _____

3. so _____

4. but _____

5. yet _____

COMMAS WITH INTERRUPTERS

Use a comma before and after a word or phrase that interrupts the flow of a sentence. Most words that interrupt a sentence are not necessary for understanding the main point of a sentence. Setting them off makes it easier to recognize the main point.

Word: My next-door neighbor, **Carlos,** is from Portugal.

Word: I didn't hear the phone ring, **however,** because I was in the shower.

Phrase: My history textbook, *Ancient Rome,* is on the desk.

Phrase: One of the most popular vacation spots, **according to recent surveys,** is Disneyland.

Phrase: Mr. Colby, **president of the school board,** has been elected mayor.

A very common type of interrupter is a clause that begins with *who, whose, which, when,* or *where* and is not necessary for understanding the main point of the sentence:

Clause: The new mall, **which is downtown,** has three restaurants.

Because the information "which is downtown" is not necessary for understanding the main idea of the sentence, it is set off with commas.

Clause: Carol Roth, **who has a Ph.D. in history,** is my new neighbor.

The main point here is that Carol Roth is my new neighbor. Because the other information isn't necessary for understanding the sentence, it can be set off with commas.

Hint: Do not use commas with *who, whose, which, when,* or *where* if the information is necessary for understanding the main point of the sentence.

My friend **who is a circus clown** just arrived in town.

Because the information in the *who* clause is necessary to understand which friend just arrived in town, you should not set it off with commas.

Hint: Do not use commas to set off clauses beginning with *that.*

The mall **that is downtown** has three restaurants.

PRACTICE 10: Recall/Identify Label each sentence C if commas are used correctly with the underlined words and phrases or X if they are not.

1. _____ Jacquelyn Smith, <u>who used to be a model</u>, has a line of clothing at Kmart.

2. _____ My girlfriend <u>Cheri</u>, is almost 23 years old.

3. _____ The AMC theater, <u>my favorite hangout</u>, is located on Main Street.

4. _____ Joe's leather jacket, <u>which he's had only four months</u> has a broken zipper.

5. _____ *Air Force One*, <u>the airplane</u>, used by the United States president, is the most secure aircraft in the world.

PRACTICE 11: Apply Insert commas around the interrupting words and phrases in the following paragraph.

    My favorite grandmother Gram turned 80 this year. My grandfather died last August, and we didn't want Gram living alone. She was able to take care of herself however and didn't want to go to a retirement home. Recently, we visited Rosewood which is a very popular retirement community and she was impressed with the facilities. There are group homes of course with "around the clock" care, but there are also condominiums where residents can live alone or with roommates. The entire neighborhood is monitored by security guards which is reassuring and the medical staff is always available. Gram's been there for three weeks now and said when we asked that she's never been happier.

PRACTICE 12: Write Your Own Write a sentence of your own for each of the following phrases.

1. who is very brave _____

2. which costs over $100 _____

3. however _____

4. the mayor's wife _____

5. taking the keys _____

COMMAS WITH DIRECT QUOTATIONS

Use commas to mark direct quotations.

    A direct quotation records a person's exact words. Commas set off the exact words from the rest of the sentence, making it easier to understand who said what.

Direct Quotation:	My friends often say, **"You are so lucky."**
Direct Quotation:	**"You are so lucky,"** my friends often say.
Direct Quotation:	**"You are so lucky,"** says my grandmother, **"to have good friends."**

Hint: If a quotation ends with a question mark or an exclamation point, do not use a comma. Only one punctuation mark is needed.

NOT	**"What did he want?,"** she asked.
Correct:	**"What did he want?"** she asked.

PRACTICE 13: Recall/Identify In the following sentences, circle the commas that are used incorrectly, and add those that are missing.

1. Tonya noted "I want the Kings to win tonight."

2. "If you go now" he said "don't come back."

3. "Are you absolutely sure?," David asked.

4. "That cat," Christine said "sets off my allergies."

5. Mr. Avery remarked "The paper will not be accepted late."

PRACTICE 14: Apply Add the missing commas to the following passage.

"Are you going to the game tonight?" Dirk asked Lonnie.
"Of course" she replied "I wouldn't miss it."
"But the Mets will probably be slaughtered" Dirk said.
"What difference does that make?" she questioned.
Dirk answered "I just don't want to pay money to watch them lose."
"Well, I'm a real loyal fan!" Lonnie emphasized as she walked away.

PRACTICE 15: Write Your Own Write five sentences of your own using commas to set off direct quotations.

OTHER USES OF COMMAS

Other commas clarify information in everyday writing.

Numbers: What is **2,502,500** divided by **10,522?**

A comma is optional in numbers of four digits: **4000** or **4,000.**

Dates: My great grandfather was born in December 1888 in London and died on **July 23, 1972,** in Denver.

Notice there is a comma both before and after the year.

Addresses: Ashley moved from **Chicago, Illinois,** to **15305 Jefferson Ave., Boston, MA 09643.**

Notice there is no comma between the state and ZIP code.

Letters: **Dear Alisha,**

Yours truly,

PRACTICE 16: Recall/Identify In the following sentences, circle the commas that are used incorrectly, and add those that are missing.

1. The new Honda Accord costs more than $23000.

2. Michael Finley plays basketball with the Celtics, and lives in Boston Massachusetts.

3. My five-year anniversary is June, 16 2018.

4. Jamie lives in Los Altos, California with her two kids.

5. Yours truly Deena

PRACTICE 17: Apply Add the missing commas to the following paragraph.

Norma graduated from Texas State University in San Marcos Texas on June 5 2004. There were more than 3000 people in the audience, including Norma's friends and family. Her parents drove all the way from Tulsa Oklahoma and they stayed in Texas all weekend. After the graduation ceremonies, Norma and her loved ones spent the weekend visiting the Austin area and other parts of Texas that Norma didn't get to see while attending school.

PRACTICE 18: Write Your Own Write a sentence of your own for each of the following items.

1. your date of birth

_____

2. the city and state where you were born

_____

3. your full address, including the ZIP code

_____

4. the estimated number of people who attend your school

_____

5. the amount of money you would like to make per year after college graduation

_____

CHAPTER REVIEW

REVIEW PRACTICE 1: Recall/Identify Add the missing commas to the following sentences.

1. When I was 12 years old, my father took me to Honolulu Hawaii.

2. Seth wanted more dessert but he was on a diet.

3. Although James read that book before he couldn't remember how it ended.

4. The Accord is of course the best Honda vehicle.

5. I proudly cheered as Nick my best friend scored a touchdown.

6. "We will begin discussing genetics next Tuesday" said the professor.

7. Azaleas carnations and roses are my favorite flowers.

8. The beautiful tall brown-haired model walked down the catwalk.

9. There are 300400 people in this county.

10. Craig and I started dating on August 7 2001.

REVIEW PRACTICE 2: Apply Add the missing commas to the following paragraph.

My only cat Mango is Siamese. I still remember when she was born; it was February 14 1997 Valentine's Day. There are more than 1000 different breeds of cats but the Siamese are the most strikingly beautiful. Mango is a friendly cat however unlike most Siamese. When I first brought her home my friends said "She'll be a spoiled brat" but I have come to love her.

REVIEW PRACTICE 3: Write Your Own Write a paragraph about the importance of computer knowledge. What are the benefits of computer technology? Why should we be familiar with it?

MyWritingLab™   Complete this "Write Your Own" exercise for Chapter 41 in the MyWritingLab "Activities: Your Textbook" module.

REVIEW PRACTICE 4: Editing Through Collaboration Exchange paragraphs from Review Practice 3 with another student, and do the following:

1. Circle any misplaced commas.

2. Suggest corrections for the incorrect commas.

Then return the paper to its writer, and use the information in this chapter to correct any comma errors in your own paragraph. Record your errors on the Error Log in Appendix 7.

MyWritingLab™   Visit Chapter 41, "Commas," in MyWritingLab, and complete the Post-test to check your understanding of the chapter's objectives.

Apostrophes

Add an apostrophe or an apostrophe and -s where necessary in the following sentences.

- The flight crew was surprised by the pilots rudeness when he boarded the plane.
- Its important that the car has its engine checked every 3,000 miles.
- Whats going to happen after Dominics gone?
- The mens bathroom is located on the third floor.
- James house is the third one on the left.

(Answers are in Appendix 3.)

The **apostrophe** looks like a single quotation mark. Its two main purposes are to indicate where letters have been left out and to show ownership.

Student Comment:
"I finally understand when to use its and it's! Hallelujah!"

MyWritingLab ### Understanding Apostrophes

To help you understand this form of punctuation, go to **MyWritingLab.com,** and choose **Apostrophes** in the **Punctuation, Mechanics, and Spelling** module. Next, watch the video called **Animation: Apostrophes.** Then, return to this chapter, which will go into more detail about apostrophes and give you opportunities to practice using them. Finally, you will apply your understanding of this punctuation mark to your own writing.

MARKING CONTRACTIONS

Use an apostrophe to show that letters have been omitted to form a contraction.

A **contraction** is the shortening of one or more words. Our everyday speech is filled with contractions.

I have	=	I've (*h* and *a* have been omitted)
you are	=	you're (*a* has been omitted)
let us	=	let's (*u* has been omitted)

Here is a list of commonly used contractions.

Some Common Contractions

I am	=	*I'm*	*we have*	=	*we've*
I would	=	*I'd*	*we will*	=	*we'll*
I will	=	*I'll*	*they are*	=	*they're*
you have	=	*you've*	*they have*	=	*they've*
you will	=	*you'll*	*do not*	=	*don't*
he is	=	*he's*	*did not*	=	*didn't*
she will	=	*she'll*	*have not*	=	*haven't*
it is	=	*it's*	*could not*	=	*couldn't*

Hint: Two words frequently misused are *it's* and *its*.

it's = contraction: it is (*or* it has)   **It's** too late to go to the movie.
its = pronoun: belonging to it   **Its** eyes are really large.

To see if you are using the correct word, say the sentence with the words *it is*. If that is what you want to say, add an apostrophe to the word.

    ?   I think **its** burning.
Test: I think **it is** burning.   **YES, add an apostrophe**

This sentence makes sense with *it is*, so you should write *it's*.

Correct: I think **it's** burning.
    ?   The dog wagged **its** tail.
Test: The dog wagged **it is** tail.   **NO, so no apostrophe**

This sentence does not make sense with *it is*, so you should not use the apostrophe in *its*.

Correct: The dog wagged **its** tail.

PRACTICE 1: Recall/Identify In the following sentences, circle the apostrophes that are used incorrectly, and add those that are missing.

1. Ive got to find a better job.
2. The attorney said shes working overtime on this case.
3. Theyll be glad to see you at the party.
4. It's a good thing they did'nt bring their baby to the wedding.
5. Cameron doesnt get paid until Friday.

PRACTICE 2: Apply Write contractions for the following words.

1. she + would = _____

2. did + not = _____

3. will + not = _____

4. they + will = _____

5. should + have = _____

PRACTICE 3: Write Your Own Write a sentence of your own for each of the contractions you wrote in Practice 2.

SHOWING POSSESSION

Use an apostrophe to show possession.

1. For a singular word, use *'s* to indicate possession or ownership. You can always replace a possessive with *of* plus the noun or pronoun.

the soldier**'s** rifle	=	the rifle **of the soldier**
someone**'s** house	=	the house **of someone**
doctor**'s** office	=	the office **of the doctor**
yesterday**'s** paper	=	the paper **of yesterday**

2. For plural nouns ending in *-s*, use only an apostrophe.

the soldiers' rifles	=	the rifles **of the soldiers**
the doctors' office	=	the office **of the doctors**
the painters' studio	=	the studio **of the painters**
the students' grades	=	the grades **of the students**
the brothers' boat	=	the boat **of the brothers**

3. For plural nouns that do not end in *-s*, add *'s*.

the men**'s** pants	=	the pants **of the men**
the deer**'s** antlers	=	the antlers **of the deer**
the criteria**'s** importance	=	the importance **of the criteria**

PRACTICE 4: Recall/Identify In the following sentences, circle the apostrophes that are used incorrectly, and add those that are missing.

1. The boys bicycle had a flat tire.

2. The disaster was Jennifers'fault.

3. Our two cat's water bowl was empty.

4. We knew the airlines food would be tasty.

5. Todays' temperature reached 83 degrees.

PRACTICE 5: Apply Write a possessive for each of the following phrases.

1. the feet of Charles _____

2. the guests of Dr. Blakeney _____

3. the tide of the ocean _____

4. the shirts of the men _____

5. the assignment of the students _____

PRACTICE 6: Write Your Own Write a sentence of your own for each of the possessives you wrote in Practice 5.

COMMON APOSTROPHE ERRORS

Two common errors occur with apostrophes. The following guidelines will help you avoid these errors.

No Apostrophe with Possessive Pronouns

Do not use an apostrophe with a possessive pronoun.

Possessive pronouns already show ownership, so they do not need an apostrophe.

NOT	Correct
his'	his
her's *or* hers'	hers
it's *or* its'	its
your's *or* yours'	yours
our's *or* ours'	ours
their's *or* theirs'	theirs

No Apostrophe to Form the Plural

Do not use an apostrophe to form a plural word.

This error occurs most often with plural words ending in *-s*. An apostrophe indicates possession or contraction; it does *not* indicate the plural. Therefore, a plural word never takes an apostrophe unless it is possessive.

NOT	The **clothes'** are in the dryer.
Correct:	The **clothes** are in the dryer.

NOT	She bought a case of **soda's** last week.
Correct:	She bought a case of **sodas** last week.

NOT	Get your coffee and **donut's** here.
Correct:	Get your coffee and **donuts** here.

PRACTICE 7: Recall/Identify In the following sentences, circle the apostrophes that are used incorrectly, and add those that are missing.

1. I've been to that store five time's, and I've never seen shoes like yours'.

2. My brother's are working for my father's company.

3. Sam left his' cars window's down, and it is starting to rain.

4. The soccer player's are meeting at noon.

5. The big story in the newspaper's is yesterdays flood.

PRACTICE 8: Apply Write a possessive for each of the following phrases.

1. the house belonging to them _____

2. the pants she owns _____

3. the soda you are holding _____

4. the price of it _____

5. the feet of him _____

PRACTICE 9: Write Your Own Write a sentence of your own for each of the possessives you wrote in Practice 8.

CHAPTER REVIEW

REVIEW PRACTICE 1: Recall/Identify In the following sentences, circle the apostrophes that are used incorrectly, and add those that are missing.

1. Mr. Thompson's diner serves many pasta entrée's.

2. Two plumber's came to fix the leaks.

3. I thought I picked up my purse, but it was really her's.

4. Naomi was'nt pleased with the restaurants service.

5. The rose's in my front yard havent bloomed yet.

6. Its amazing that Tricia cut her hair as short as yours.

7. His' new house is in Highland Park.

8. You've got to see Ming's new jet ski's.

9. Our high schools head cheerleader is getting a full athletic scholarship to college.

10. Marys parent's ordered four pizza's for her party.

REVIEW PRACTICE 2: Apply Add the missing apostrophes to the following sentences.

1. The trucks brakes went out while it was coming over the hill.

2. We havent heard from Ben since he left his father's ranch and headed for ours.

3. My next-door neighbors uncle is a big Hollywood actor.

4. Sarahs diet consisted of hot dogs and sodas.

5. The freeways are crowded because yesterdays fire still hasnt been contained.

6. I think its time for us to go to our house and for you to go to yours.

7. Devons kids were playing dominoes.

8. Maurice cant ever beat me at backgammon.

9. Stellas going to the game with us.

10. Both cars gas tanks are empty.

REVIEW PRACTICE 3: Write Your Own Write a paragraph about your favorite teacher. What was his or her name? What was special about this person?

MyWritingLab™ Complete this "Write Your Own" exercise for Chapter 42 in the MyWritingLab "Activities: Your Textbook" module.

REVIEW PRACTICE 4: Editing Through Collaboration Exchange paragraphs from Review Practice 3 with another student, and do the following:

1. Circle any misplaced or missing apostrophes.

2. Indicate whether they mark possession (P) or contraction (C).

Then return the paper to its writer, and use the information in this chapter to correct any apostrophe errors in your own paragraph. Record your errors on the Error Log in Appendix 7.

MyWritingLab™ Visit Chapter 42, "Apostrophes," in MyWritingLab, and complete the Post-test to check your understanding of the chapter's objectives.

Quotation Marks

TEST YOURSELF

Add quotation marks where needed in the following sentences.

- Can we go out to dinner tonight? she asked.
- Jeri screamed, Don't go in there!
- If you can't find my house, Tom said, call me on your cell phone.
- My favorite poem is The Red Wheelbarrow by William Carlos Williams.
- David said, I'll fix your car this weekend.

(Answers are in Appendix 3.)

Quotation marks are punctuation marks that work together in pairs. Their most common purpose is to indicate someone's exact words. They are also used to mark the title of a short piece of writing, such as a short story or a poem.

MyWritingLab

Understanding Quotation Marks

To understand more about this form of punctuation, go to **MyWritingLab .com,** and choose **Quotation Marks** in the **Punctuation, Mechanics, and Spelling** module. From there, watch the video called **Animation: Quotation Marks.** Then, return to this chapter, which will go into more detail about these punctuation marks and give you opportunities to practice them. Finally, you will apply your understanding of quotation marks to your own writing.

DIRECT QUOTATIONS

Use quotation marks to indicate a **direct quotation**—someone's exact words. Here are some examples that show the three basic forms of a direct quotation.

Direct Quotation: "I will not lend you the money," said the banker.

In this first example, the quoted words come first.

Direct Quotation: The banker said, "I will not lend you the money."

Here the quoted words come after the speaker is named.

Direct Quotation: "I will not," the banker said, "lend you the money."

In this example, the quoted words are interrupted, and the speaker is named in the middle. This form emphasizes the first few words.

INDIRECT QUOTATIONS

If you just talk about someone's words—an **indirect quotation**—you do not need quotation marks. Indirect quotations usually include the word *that*, as in *said that*. In questions, the wording is often *asked if*. Look at these examples of **indirect quotations.**

Direct Quotation: "I lost my job at the supermarket," said Bob.

These are Bob's exact words, so you must use quotation marks.

Indirect Quotation: Bob **said that** he lost his job at the supermarket.

This sentence explains what Bob said but does not use Bob's exact words. So quotation marks should not be used.

Direct Quotation: "The train trip took eight hours," said Kira.
Indirect Quotation: Kira **said that** the train trip took eight hours.

Direct Quotation: "Did you get the car fixed?" Mom asked.
Indirect Quotation: Mom **asked if** I had gotten the car fixed.

PRACTICE 1: Recall/Identify In the following sentences, circle the quotation marks that are used incorrectly, and add those that are missing.

1. "Help me! yelled the drowning woman."

2. "If you can't take the heat," my mom used to say, stay out of the kitchen."

3. Martina asked, "Have you found my jacket?"

4. Steffan said, My goal is to "get into the Olympics."

5. Chonda said that "she enjoyed the movie last night."

PRACTICE 2: Apply Add the missing quotation marks to the following paragraph.

When I went into the salon, my hairdresser asked, How do you want your hair cut today? I don't really know, I replied, but I brought in a couple of pictures of haircuts I like. Those are cute, she said. Do you think my hair would look good like that? I asked. Absolutely! she exclaimed. Then she set to work with the scissors. When she was finished, I looked in the mirror in horror. That's not what I had in mind, I told her. But it looks just like the pictures, she said. How can you say that? I exclaimed. The haircuts I showed you are shoulder-length, and mine is now above my ears! Well, she said, it will always grow back.

PRACTICE 3: Write Your Own Write a sentence of your own for each of the following sets of details.

1. a question asked by Claudia _____

2. a statement spoken by the manager _____

3. an exclamation spoken by Becky _____

4. an indirect question that Jared asked _____

5. a statement spoken by the electrician _____

CAPITALIZING AND USING OTHER PUNCTUATION MARKS WITH QUOTATION MARKS

When you are quoting someone's complete sentences, begin with a capital letter, and use appropriate end punctuation—a period, a question mark, or an exclamation point. You do not need to capitalize the first word of a quotation if it is only part of a sentence. Here are some examples.

Capitalize the first letter of the first word being quoted, and put a period at the end of the sentence if it is a statement. Separate the spoken words from the rest of the sentence with a comma.

"He doesn't seem very nice," she said.

He said, "Turn off the music."

If the quotation ends with a question mark or an exclamation point, use that punctuation instead of a comma or a period.

"Why do you want to know?" she asked.

He yelled, "Turn off that music!"

In a quotation that is interrupted, capitalize the first word being quoted, but do not capitalize words in the middle of the sentence. Use a comma both before and after the interruption. End with a period if it is a statement.

"Yes," said the bus driver, "this bus goes downtown."

You do not need to capitalize the first word of a quotation that is only part of a sentence.

I don't think that he will ever "find himself."

Hint: Look at the examples again. Notice that periods and commas always go inside the quotation marks.

NOT   "Yes", he said, "we're ready to leave".

Correct: "Yes," he said, "we're ready to leave."

PRACTICE 4: Recall/Identify In the following sentences, circle the quotation marks, capital letters, and other punctuation marks that are used incorrectly, and add any missing quotation marks and punctuation.

1. "Is there a doctor in the house"? the man screamed.

2. "I can't believe", she said, "That you've never seen the ocean."

3. Margarita asked, "Are you ever going to meet me for coffee"?

4. "This is the last time", he promised, "that I come home late".

5. Garrett said, "I want to take the trolley to the restaurant on the corner".

PRACTICE 5: Apply Add the missing quotation marks and punctuation to the following paragraph.

I was having car problems, so I drove to the auto shop on the corner. What do you think is wrong with my car? I asked the mechanic. I can't tell you he said, until I take a look at it myself. I replied, I'll leave it with you this afternoon, and you can tell me later today what you find out. That would be great, he said. Finally, around 4:00 p.m., he called me on the phone. Your car needs a new clutch, he said. No way! I exclaimed. Sorry, mister he calmly replied, but that's all I found to be wrong with it. I explained, But I just replaced the clutch four months ago. Well, he said, I hope you saved your receipt and warranty paperwork.

PRACTICE 6: Write Your Own Write a sentence of your own for each of the following direct quotations, punctuated correctly.

1. "No, I won't" _____

2. "How are we going to do that" _____

3. "This is the most important priority" _____

4. "Yes" "you can come to the party" _____

5. "Don't worry" "you didn't miss anything" _____

QUOTATION MARKS AROUND TITLES

Put quotation marks around the titles of short works that are parts of larger works. The titles of longer works are put in italics.

Quotation Marks	Italics/Underlining
"The Yellow Wallpaper" (short story)	*American Short Stories* (book)
"Song of Myself" (poem)	*Leaves of Grass* (book)
"My Girl" (song)	*The Temptations' Greatest Hits* (CD)
"Explore New Orleans" (magazine article)	*New Orleans Monthly* (magazine)
"Convicts Escape" (newspaper article)	*New York Times* (newspaper)
"The Wedding" (episode of TV series)	*Friends* (TV series)

PRACTICE 7: Recall/Identify Put an X in front of each sentence with errors in quotation marks or italics. Add any missing quotation marks and italics. (Use underlining for italics.)

1. ____ My favorite song by the Beatles is *Yellow Submarine*.

2. ____ When Juliet was in high school, she read Shirley Jackson's famous short story The Lottery.

3. ____ Getting through *Moby Dick* by Herman Melville took me three weeks.

4. ____ My first boyfriend recited William Blake's poem *The Garden of Love* to me on my front porch.

5. ____ The "New York Times" ran a long article called *Japan's Princess Gives Birth* about Crown Princess Masako.

PRACTICE 8: Apply Place quotation marks around the titles of short works, and underline (for italics) the titles of long works in the following paragraph.

Mark got a great job with the Chicago Tribune last summer. He is now working as the editor of the entertainment section, and he writes a column called Making a Mark. In his column, he reviews celebrity events and activities, such as concerts, hit movies, and best-selling books. For one article, he interviewed several cast members of Glee, the popular TV show. He also attended a John Mayer concert and quoted lines from the song Queen of California on Mayer's CD Born and Raised. Another article featured Nikki Giovanni, who read her poem Dream during their interview. Mark has become friends with some very interesting and well-known people, and he is now looking forward to speaking with Stephenie Meyer on the set of the latest installment of Twilight.

PRACTICE 9: Write Your Own Write a sentence of your own for each of the following items. Make up a title if you can't think of one.

1. a short story _____

2. a song _____

3. a TV show _____

4. a CD _____

5. a magazine article _____

CHAPTER REVIEW

REVIEW PRACTICE 1: Recall/Identify Add the missing quotation marks and punctuation to the following sentences.

1. Patty sang Fergie's London Bridge at the karaoke party.

2. Our next writing assignment is a critical review of Robert Browning's poem My Last Duchess.

3. You don't have to go to work today, I told Gerard.

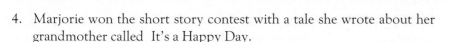

4. Marjorie won the short story contest with a tale she wrote about her grandmother called It's a Happy Day.

5. Devonne asked Where does Jack live?

6. When Princess Diana died, the Boston Globe ran an article called Too Soon.

7. The scores came in, and our coach yelled, Great job, team!

8. I can't make it to the meeting, she said, but I'll call you tonight to find out what I missed."

9. What do you want to eat for breakfast? Charise asked.

10. I submitted an article to Golf Magazine called How to Swing like Tiger Woods.

REVIEW PRACTICE 2: Apply Add the missing quotation marks, commas, and underlining (for italics) to the following dialogue.

Hurry up, I said, or we're going to be late for the Beastie Boys Concert.

I'm coming, John replied. Just hold your horses!

The write-up in USA Today said this was going to be their biggest concert ever, I told him. I asked John if he too had read that article, but he said that he hadn't.

I didn't have time to read today, he explained, because I was busy buying a CD of their greatest hits. Now, John said, I'm really excited about the concert tonight!

REVIEW PRACTICE 3: Write Your Own In paragraph form, record a conversation you had this week. Who were you talking to? What did you talk about? What were your exact words?

MyWritingLab™ Complete this "Write Your Own" exercise for Chapter 43 in the MyWritingLab "Activities: Your Textbook" module.

REVIEW PRACTICE 4: Editing Through Collaboration Exchange paragraphs from Review Practice 3 with another student, and do the following:

1. Circle any incorrect or missing quotation marks.

2. Underline any faulty punctuation.

3. Put an X over any incorrect use of italics/underlining.

Then return the paper to its writer, and use the information in this chapter to correct any errors with quotation marks and italics/underlining in your own paragraph. Record your errors on the Error Log in Appendix 7.

MyWritingLab™   Visit Chapter 43, "Quotation Marks," in MyWritingLab, and complete the Post-test to check your understanding of the chapter's objectives.

Other Punctuation Marks

Add semicolons, colons, dashes, or parentheses to the following sentences.

- Kris left for the dance Sean decided to stay home.
- We wanted to win therefore we practiced every day.
- The computer's advertised price didn't include several important parts a monitor, a printer, and speakers.
- Ramon asked the best question during the interview "Why should we vote for you?"
- Bring the jelly to a "rolling boil" a boil that cannot be stirred down.

(Answers are in Appendix 3.)

This chapter explains the uses of the **semicolon, colon, dash,** and **parentheses.** We'll look at these punctuation marks one by one.

MyWritingLab | **Understanding Other Punctuation Marks**

To learn more about other punctuation marks, go to **MyWritingLab. com,** and choose **Semicolons, Colons, Dashes, and Parentheses** in the **Punctuation, Mechanics, and Spelling** module. For this topic, watch the video called **Animation: Semicolons, Colons, Dashes, and Parentheses.** Then, return to this chapter, which will go into more detail about these marks and give you opportunities to practice them. Finally, you will apply your understanding of semicolons, colons, dashes, and parentheses to your own writing.

Student Comment:
"Even though you may want to just skip the video on **Semicolons, Colons, Dashes, and Parentheses** and go straight to the exercises, I recommend that you watch the videos. They'll save you time in the long run because they offer keys to the answers."

SEMICOLONS

Semicolons are used to separate equal parts of a sentence. They are also used to avoid confusion when listing items in a series.

1. Use a semicolon to separate two closely related independent clauses. An independent clause is a group of words with a subject and a verb that can stand alone as a sentence. You might use a semicolon instead of a coordinating conjunction (*and, but, for, nor, or, so, yet*) or a period. Any one of the following three options would be correct.

	Independent	Independent
Semicolon:	Sam never drove to school**; he** always rode his bike.	
Conjunction:	Sam never drove to school**, for** he always rode his bike.	
Period:	Sam never drove to school**. He** always rode his bike.	

2. Use a semicolon to join two independent clauses connected by such words as *however, therefore, furthermore, moreover, for example,* or *consequently.* Put a comma after the connecting word.

	Independent	Independent
Semicolon:	Traveling can be expensive**; nevertheless,** it's always enjoyable.	
Semicolon:	Brad is very smart**; furthermore,** he was offered seven scholarships.	
Semicolon:	He has trouble in math**; therefore,** he hired a tutor.	

3. Use a semicolon to separate items in a series when any of the items contain commas.

NOT	On the flight to New York, Mei Lin read a popular new thriller with a surprise ending, took a long, relaxing nap, and watched an incredibly dull movie about a rock star.
Correct:	On the flight to New York, Mei Lin read a popular new thriller with a surprise ending; took a long, relaxing nap; and watched an incredibly dull movie about a rock star.

PRACTICE 1: Recall/Identify In the following sentences, circle the semicolons that are used incorrectly, and add any commas and semicolons that are missing.

1. The car needed new front tires the old ones were quite bald.

2. Lisa's 10-month-old son didn't take a nap today however; he was very pleasant.

3. I must have lost my keys I can't; find them anywhere.

4. Our team is the strongest; and we are prepared to win.

5. Mr. Banderas teaches Spanish; writes novels; books; and short stories; and reviews movies in his spare time.

PRACTICE 2: Apply Add semicolons to the following paragraph.

When I was in junior high, my school had a big dance I dreaded it from the day it was announced. I didn't have a boyfriend I didn't have the right clothes, shoes, or hairstyle and I didn't have any money saved up for things like that. Even worse, I knew my parents felt I was too young to go nonetheless, I knew my friends would keep asking me if I was going. Finally, I thought of a good excuse: I told my friends my grandmother was having major surgery. My friends probably knew I was lying however, nobody said anything more to me about it.

PRACTICE 3: Write Your Own Write five sentences of your own using semicolons correctly.

COLONS

Colons introduce a list or idea that follows them.

1. The main use of the colon is to introduce a list or thought. Here are some examples:

Colon: Buy the following items for the trip: toothpaste, toothbrush, razor, soap, and makeup.

Colon: The fair had some new attractions: a double Ferris wheel, a roller coaster, and an antique merry-go-round.

Colon: The choice was simple: return the merchandise.

The most common error with colons is using one where it isn't needed.

2. Do not use a colon after the words *such as* or *including*. A complete sentence must come before a colon.

NOT Cook only fresh vegetables, **such as:** green beans, broccoli, and spinach.

Correct: Cook only fresh vegetables, **such as** green beans, broccoli, and spinach.

NOT We went to many countries in Europe, **including:** Spain and Portugal.

Correct: We went to many countries in Europe, **including** Spain and Portugal.

3. In addition, you should not use a colon after a verb or after a preposition. Remember that a complete sentence must come before a colon.

NOT	The movies to be reviewed **are:** *Pirates of the Caribbean* and *Superman.*
Correct:	The movies to be reviewed **are** *Pirates of the Caribbean* and *Superman.*
NOT	The box was full **of:** books, old dolls, and scrapbooks.
Correct:	The box was full **of** books, old dolls, and scrapbooks.

PRACTICE 4: Recall/Identify In the following sentences, circle the colons that are used incorrectly, and add any colons that are missing.

1. The best things about summer are: swimming, biking, and picnics.

2. The man asked me for the following items my driver's license, my Social Security number, and my credit cards.

3. We accidentally left many things at home, such as: my toothbrush, our hair dryer, and the baby's bottle.

4. I was most impressed by: the atmosphere, the prices, and the service.

5. The most expensive parts to repair were: the carburetor, the ignition system, and the fuel injector.

PRACTICE 5: Apply Add colons to the following paragraph.

> Reading is an excellent way to spend free time. A good book can do many things take you to a faraway place, introduce you to different people, and expose you to extraordinary experiences. I especially like two kinds of books science fiction and romance novels. These genres are totally opposite, I know, but they have just what I like: action, strange characters, and suspension of disbelief. When I am reading, I am in a world of my own. I escape all of my everyday problems: my difficult job, my nagging mother, and sometimes even my homework.

PRACTICE 6: Write Your Own Write five sentences of your own using colons correctly.

DASHES AND PARENTHESES

Dashes and **parentheses** both mark breaks in the flow of a sentence. A dash suggests an abrupt pause in a statement, while parentheses surround words that could actually be taken out of a sentence grammatically.

Dashes

Dashes emphasize ideas.

1. Use dashes to emphasize or draw attention to a point.

   Dash: I know what I want to be—a doctor.

   In this example, the beginning of the sentence introduces an idea, and the dash then sets off the answer.

   Dash: Money and time—these are what I need.

   In this example, the key words are set off at the beginning, and the explanation follows. Beginning this way adds some suspense to the sentence.

   Dashes: I know what I want in a husband—a sense of humor—and I plan to get it.

   The dashes divide this sentence into three distinct parts, which makes the reader pause and think about each part.

Parentheses

Whereas dashes set off material the writer wants to emphasize, parentheses do just the opposite. They are always used in pairs.

2. Use parentheses to set off information that is interesting or helpful but not necessary for understanding the sentence.

   Parentheses: When in Rome **(as the saying goes),** do as the Romans do.

   Parentheses: The senator's position on the proposal **(Senate Bill 193)** has changed several times.

3. Parentheses are also used to mark a person's life span and to number items in a sentence.

   Parentheses: Herman Melville **(1819–1891)** wrote the classic *Moby Dick*.

   Parentheses: My boss gave me three things to do today: **(1)** answer the mail, **(2)** file receipts, and **(3)** send out bills.

PRACTICE 7: Recall/Identify Use dashes or parentheses with the underlined words in the following sentences.

1. One powerful tool for student research is becoming more popular than the library <u>the Internet</u>.

2. My brother <u>the police chief</u> keeps his phone number unlisted.

3. Nick <u>head of the math department</u> hires the new teachers.

4. I signaled the oncoming car <u>by flashing my lights</u>, but it still didn't turn its headlights on.

5. Cheryl got her passport so she can <u>1</u> visit other countries, <u>2</u> go diving in all of the seven seas, and <u>3</u> photograph royalty.

PRACTICE 8: Apply Add dashes and parentheses to the following paragraph.

In high school, I volunteered to work on the yearbook. Mrs. Brady was our instructor a round lady with bright red cheeks and a strange laugh. She immediately set us to work on several things mostly after school, as we accumulated photos and news about the school's major events. I remember one lesson I learned in that class never procrastinate. If I failed to finish an assignment something that rarely happened, someone else would do it instead, and that person's work would be published instead of mine. I'll never forget my year with Mrs. Brady.

PRACTICE 9: Write Your Own Write three sentences of your own using dashes and two using parentheses.

CHAPTER REVIEW

REVIEW PRACTICE 1: Recall/Identify Add semicolons, colons, dashes, and parentheses to the following sentences.

1. We are going to the grocery store we have nothing in the pantry.

2. There are only three people I trust Krista, Tanya, and Lucy.

3. He is always home however, he doesn't ever help out around the house.

4. I bought the car in my favorite color neon yellow.

5. Put the flowers on the table outside the one by the wall, and the presents can go there too.

6. My favorite book was made into a movie *Beloved*.

7. There are many things to do today pick up the dry cleaning, vacuum the carpets, and wash the dishes.

8. The chicken coop needs to be cleaned out it is full of leaves and tree branches.

9. We will pick up Derek, Jenny, and Carmen load up with sunscreen; and go to the beach.

10. I got your favorite ice cream for your birthday fudge ripple.

REVIEW PRACTICE 2: Apply Add semicolons, colons, dashes, and parentheses to the following paragraph.

Today was an extremely windy day, so we decided to fly kites. We drove to Kite Hill a place where I went as a kid, and we climbed to the very top. We took out the kites and other necessary things masking tape, string, and ribbons. This way we were prepared to repair our kites, if necessary. The wind was perfect we couldn't have asked for better weather. There was only one thing we forgot the picnic lunch! Fortunately, Lamar remembered to pack the cooler with sodas mostly Diet Coke for something to drink when we got thirsty. After about four hours of flying kites it felt like 14, the group decided to head back home.

REVIEW PRACTICE 3: Write Your Own Write a paragraph explaining some of your five-year goals. What do you plan to be doing in five years? What do you want to have accomplished?

| MyWritingLab™ | Complete this "Write Your Own" exercise for Chapter 44 in the MyWritingLab "Activities: Your Textbook" module. |

REVIEW PRACTICE 4: Editing Through Collaboration Exchange paragraphs from Review Practice 3 with another student, and do the following:

1. Circle any incorrect or missing semicolons.

2. Circle any incorrect or missing colons.

3. Circle any incorrect or missing dashes.

4. Circle any incorrect or missing parentheses.

Then return the paper to its writer, and use the information in this chapter to correct any punctuation errors in your own paragraph. Record your errors on the Error Log in Appendix 7.

| MyWritingLab™ | Visit Chapter 44, "Other Punctuation Marks," in MyWritingLab, and complete the Post-test to check your understanding of the chapter's objectives. |

Mechanics

The mechanical aspects of a sentence are much like the mechanical features of a car, an appliance, or a clock. They are some of the smallest—yet most important—details in a sentence. In writing, *mechanics* refers to capitalization, abbreviations, and numbers. We usually take these items for granted, but when they are used incorrectly, a sentence, just like a mechanical appliance with a weak spring, starts to break down.

Following a few simple guidelines will help your sentences run smoothly and efficiently. These guidelines are explained in two chapters:

Chapter 45: Capitalization
Chapter 46: Abbreviations and Numbers

668

Capitalization

Correct the capitalization errors in the following sentences.

- According to uncle Bob, mother makes the best texas sheet cake.
- Antonio is native american.
- "the shortest path," he said, "Is down baker street."
- issa loves to go to walt disney world.
- Last year, I saw the red hot chili peppers in concert.

(Answers are in Appendix 3.)

Because every sentence begins with a capital letter, **capitalization** is the best place to start discussing the mechanics of good writing. Capital letters signal where sentences begin. They also call attention to certain kinds of words, making sentences easier to read and understand.

MyWritingLab

Understanding Capitalization

For more information about this topic, go to **MyWritingLab.com**, and choose **Capitalization** in the **Punctuation, Mechanics, and Spelling** module. From there, watch the video called **Animation: Capitalization.** Then, return to this chapter, which will go into more detail about capitalization rules and give you opportunities to practice them. Finally, you will apply your understanding of capitalization to your own writing.

Student Comment:
"When I work with
MyWritingLab, I feel in control of my learning."

CAPITALIZATION GUIDELINES

Correct capitalization coupled with correct punctuation adds up to good, clear writing. Here are some guidelines to help you capitalize correctly.

1. Capitalize the first word of every sentence, including the first word of a quotation that forms a sentence.

   My favorite city is Rome.
   "**R**ome is my favorite city," he said.
   He said, "**M**y favorite city is Rome."

   Do not capitalize the second part of a quotation that is split.

   "**M**y favorite city," he said, "is Rome."

2. Capitalize all proper nouns. Do not capitalize common nouns.

Common Nouns	Proper Nouns
person	Eleanor Roosevelt
state	Minnesota
building	Empire State Building
river	Mississippi River
airplane	*Air Force One*

   Here are some examples of proper nouns:

People:	Sarah, Julia Roberts, Tiger Woods
Groups:	Australians, Apaches, Europeans, British, Latino
Languages:	Russian, Italian, French
Religions:	Catholicism, Buddhism, Baptist
Religious Books:	Bible, Koran, Book of Mormon
Holy Days:	Yom Kippur, Kwanzaa, Easter
Organizations:	Boston Red Sox, Democratic Party, American Civil Liberties Union, Kiwanis Club, Alpha Gamma Delta
Places:	Smoky Mountains National Park, Antarctica, Louisville, Jefferson County, Madison Avenue, Highway 101, Golden Gate Bridge, John F. Kennedy International Airport

Institutions, Agencies, Businesses:	Washington High School, Baltimore Public Library, United Way, Grady Memorial Hospital, Time Warner
Brand Names, Ships, Aircraft:	Mustang, Wisk, Pepsi, USS Constitution, *Alabama, Challenger*

3. Capitalize titles used with people's names or in place of their names.

Mr. Ralph W. Gerber, **Ms.** Rachel Lorca, **Dr.** Leticia Johnson, **Aunt** Jane, **Grandpa** Bob, **Cousin** Maria, **Sis**, **Nana**

Do not capitalize words that identify family relationships.

NOT	I saw my Grandfather yesterday.
Correct:	I saw my grandfather yesterday.
Correct:	I saw Grandfather yesterday.

4. Capitalize the titles of creative works.

Books:	*The Catcher in the Rye*
Short Stories:	"Sonny's Blues"
Plays:	*Wicked*
Poems:	"My Last Duchess"
Articles:	"Two New Inns Now Open for Business"
Magazines:	*Newsweek*
Songs:	"Cheeseburger in Paradise"
Albums or CDs:	*Jimmy Buffett's Greatest Hits*
Films:	*Lady and the Tramp*
TV Series:	*Grey's Anatomy*
Works of Art:	*The Bedroom at Arles*
Computer Programs:	Apple Works

Do not capitalize *a, an, the,* or short prepositions unless they are the first or last word in a title.

5. Capitalize days of the week, months, holidays, and special events.

Monday, July, Presidents' Day, Thanksgiving, Cinco de Mayo, Mardi Gras

Do not capitalize the names of seasons: *summer, fall, winter, spring*.

6. Capitalize the names of historical events, periods, and documents:

the French Revolution, the Jurassic Period, World War II, the Depression, the Battle of Bunker Hill, the Magna Carta

7. Capitalize specific course titles and the names of language courses.

   Economics 201, Philosophy 101, Spanish 200, Civilizations of the Ancient World

   Do not capitalize a course or subject you are referring to in a general way unless the course is a language.

   my economics course, my philosophy course, my Spanish course, my history course

8. Capitalize references to regions of the country but not words that merely indicate direction.

   If you travel north from Houston, you will end up in the Midwest, probably in Kansas or Nebraska.

9. Capitalize the opening of a letter and the first word of the closing.

   Dear Dr. Hamlin, Dear Sir,

   Best wishes, Sincerely,

   Notice that a comma comes after the opening and closing.

PRACTICE 1: Recall/Identify Underline and correct the capitalization errors in the following sentences.

1. The irs is auditing aunt Joan.

2. Debbie and Sue bought their mother a bottle of chanel's coco perfume for mother's Day.

3. In our History class, we are studying the great wall of china.

4. This Winter, emilio will visit uncle Luis, who lives somewhere in the south.

5. David Bowie's song "changes" is a classic from the seventies.

PRACTICE 2: Apply Fill in each blank with words that complete the sentence. Be sure to capitalize words correctly. (You can make up titles if necessary.)

1. In my _____ class, we had to read _____.

2. Blanca bought a new truck, a _____.

3. _____ should be in charge of the charity drive.

4. I wish I could get tickets to see _____ in concert.

5. We are going to _____ for our vacation.

PRACTICE 3: Write Your Own Write five sentences of your own that cover at least five of the capitalization rules.

CHAPTER REVIEW

REVIEW PRACTICE 1: Recall/Identify Underline and correct the capitalization errors in the following sentences.

1. In April's edition of *people* magazine, LeAnn rimes talks about her love of Country music.

2. We decided to get married even though he's a member of the demo cratic party and I am a member of the republican party.

3. Raphael was born on October 31, 1972—he was a halloween baby.

4. Many Fathers, Sons, and Brothers fought against each other in the american civil war.

5. Ernesto's uncle has a beautiful statue of the buddha in his garden.

6. I watch *late night with Seth Meyers* for entertainment.

7. Christy can speak both english and spanish.

8. We celebrate both christmas and kwanzaa.

9. My Father used to drive me around town in his 1968 ford mustang convertible.

10. The spider said to the fly, "welcome to my home."

REVIEW PRACTICE 2: Apply Fill in each blank with words that complete the sentence. Be sure to capitalize words correctly.

1. Over the weekend, I watched my favorite movie, _____.

2. In history, we are studying the _____.

3. I was born on _____.

4. Ashley wears nothing but _____ clothes.

5. Fred and _____ both plan to major in _____.

6. He has an unusual accent because he's from _____.

7. If you travel _____ on Highway 101, you will eventually reach Santa Cruz.

8. My favorite relative, _____, will visit soon.

9. Every summer, we go to _____ to fish.

10. Even though she's a _____ and I'm a _____, we are still the best of friends.

REVIEW PRACTICE 3: Write Your Own Write a paragraph about the most unusual person you've met or the most unusual place you've visited. What made this person or place unique?

MyWritingLab™ Complete this "Write Your Own" exercise for Chapter 45 in the MyWritingLab "Activities: Your Textbook" module.

REVIEW PRACTICE 4: Editing Through Collaboration Exchange paragraphs from Review Practice 3 with another student, and do the following tasks:

1. Circle any capital letters that don't follow the capitalization rules.

2. Write the rule number next to the error for the writer to refer to.

Then return the paper to its writer, and use the information in this chapter to correct any capitalization errors in your own paragraph. Record your errors on the Error Log in Appendix 7.

MyWritingLab™ Visit Chapter 45, "Capitalization," in MyWritingLab, and complete the Post-test to check your understanding of the chapter's objectives.

Abbreviations and Numbers

Underline and correct the abbreviation and number errors in these sentences.

- He earned two million three hundred thousand dollars last year.
- My cat had 5 kittens.
- Sherril moved from England to the U.S.
- Mister Johnson always drinks hot chocolate in the mornings.
- I work for the Internal Revenue Service.

(Answers are in Appendix 3.)

Like capitalization, **abbreviations** and **numbers** are also mechanical features of writing that help us communicate what we want to say. Following the rules that govern their use will make your writing as precise as possible.

MyWritingLab

Understanding Abbreviations

To expand your understanding of this topic, go to **MyWritingLab .com,** and choose **Abbreviations and Numbers** in the **Punctuation, Mechanics, and Spelling** module. From there, watch the video called **Animation: Abbreviations and Numbers.** Then, return to this chapter, which will go into more detail about abbreviations and give you opportunities to practice them. Finally, you will apply your understanding of abbreviations to your own writing.

Student Comment:
"I thought I already knew everything there is to know about **Abbreviations and Numbers,** but **MyWritingLab** brought new information on this topic to my attention and clarified a few items I was confused about."

ABBREVIATIONS

Abbreviations help make communication precise and accurate. Here are a few rules to guide you.

1. Abbreviate titles before proper names. *full name*

   Mr. Michael Charles, **Mrs.** Marschel, **Ms.** Susan Deffaa, **Dr.** Frank Hilbig, **Rev.** Billy Graham, **Sen.** Diane Feinstein, **Sgt.** Arturo López

   Abbreviate religious, governmental, and military titles when used with an entire name. Do not abbreviate them when used only with a last name.

NOT	We thought that **Gov.** Peterson would be reelected.
Correct:	We thought that **Governor** Peterson would be reelected.
Correct:	We thought **Gov.** Richard Peterson would be reelected.

   Professor is not usually abbreviated: **Professor** Mya Belle is teaching this class.

2. Abbreviate academic degrees.

   B.S. (Bachelor of Science)
   R.N. (Registered Nurse)

3. Use the following abbreviations with numbers.

   a.m. or **A.M.**   **p.m.** or **P.M.**   **B.C.** and **A.D.** or **B.C.E.** and **C.E.**

4. Abbreviate *United States* only when it is used as an adjective.

NOT	The **U.S.** is in North America.
Correct:	The **United States** is in North America.
Correct:	The **U.S.** Senate will consider this bill today.

5. Abbreviate only the names of well-known government agencies, businesses, and educational institutions by using their initials without periods.

   FBI (Federal Bureau of Investigation)
   NBC (National Broadcasting Corporation)
   USC (University of Southern California)
   ACLU (American Civil Liberties Union)

6. Abbreviate state names when addressing mail or writing out the postal address. Otherwise, spell out the names of states.

   Maria's new address is 7124 Funston Street, San Francisco, **CA** 90555.
   Maria has moved to San Francisco, **California.**

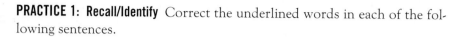
PRACTICE 1: Recall/Identify Correct the underlined words in each of the following sentences.

1. <u>Prof.</u> Smith said that I was a wonderful writer.

2. The <u>United States</u> economy has many markets.

3. When I can't sleep, I watch <u>Music Television</u>.

4. Last night, <u>sergeant</u> David Montgomery devised the winning strategy.

5. Candice moved to 237 Bella Avenue, Houma, <u>Louisiana</u> 79337.

PRACTICE 2: Apply In each sentence, write either an abbreviation or the complete word, whichever is correct.

1. We were caught speeding at 10 _____ (p.m., post meridiem).

2. Alisha will be attending _____ (CSU, California State University) and will get her _____ (B.A., bachelor of arts) degree in English.

3. Darryl and Pat are visiting relatives in Orlando, _____ (FL, Florida).

4. We moved to the _____ (U.S., United States) when I was four years old.

5. _____ (Sen., Senator) Matthews always has a kind word.

PRACTICE 3: Write Your Own Write a sentence of your own for each of the following abbreviations.

1. Mr. _____

2. a.m. _____

3. ABC _____

4. A.A. _____

5. U.S. _____

NUMBERS

Most writers ask the same questions about using **numbers:** When should a number be spelled out, and when is it all right to use numerals? The following simple rules will help you make this decision.

1. Spell out numbers from *zero* to *nine*. Use figures for numbers 10 and higher.

   I have **three** dogs.
   My mother-in-law has **19** grandchildren and **11** great-grandchildren.

   Do not mix spelled-out numbers and figures in a sentence if they refer to the same types of items. Use numerals for all numbers in that case.

   NOT   I have **three** dogs, **18** goldfish, and **two** canaries.
   Correct: I have **3** dogs, **18** goldfish, and **2** canaries.

2. For very large numbers, use a combination of figures and words.

   The state's new budget is approximately **$32 million.**
   Computer sales for the company reached **2.1 million** units.

3. Always spell out a number that begins a sentence. If this becomes awkward, reword the sentence.

   Thirty-five people died in the crash.
   Approximately **412,992** people live in Mobile, Alabama.

4. Use figures for dates, addresses, ZIP codes, telephone numbers, identification numbers, and time.

   On August **1, 1965,** my parents moved to **215** Circle Drive, Santa Fe, NM **71730.**
   My new telephone number is **(555) 877-1420.**
   My Social Security number is **123-45-6789.**
   My alarm went off at **5:00** a.m.

5. Use figures for fractions, decimals, and percentages.

   To make the dessert, you need ½ cup of butter and **16** ounces of chocolate.
   His blood-alcohol level was **0.09.**
   Over **5 percent** of Californians are of Hispanic background.
   Notice that *percent* is written out and is all one word.

6. Use figures for exact measurements, including amounts of money. Use a dollar sign for amounts over $1.

   The room measures **9** feet by **12** feet.
   She bought gas for **$4.05** a gallon today—**25** cents more than yesterday.

7. Use figures for the parts of a book.

   Chapter 10   page **12**   Exercise **8**   questions **1** and **7**
   Notice that *Chapter* and *Exercise* are capitalized.

PRACTICE 4: Recall/Identify Underline and correct any errors with numbers in each of the following sentences.

1. On August third, 2001, sixteen dogs escaped from the pound.

2. The park, which measures approximately two thousand square feet, will cost five thousand dollars to landscape.

3. Mr. Thompson's old telephone number was three, nine, nine, four, two, zero, nine.

4. Almost twenty-five percent of my income comes from sales.

5. The earthquake that hit at six forty-five last night measured 6.0 on the Richter scale.

PRACTICE 5: Apply Fill in each blank in the following sentences with numbers in the proper form.

1. Please read Chapter _____ , and answer questions _____ through _____ .

2. I   have   _____   pencils,   _____   bluebooks,   and _____ note cards; I am ready for this test.

3. _____ percent of my time is spent doing homework.

4. Christmas is on _____ every year.

5. He made $ _____ million last year.

PRACTICE 6: Write Your Own Write a sentence demonstrating each of the following rules for numbers.

1. Spell out numbers *zero* through *nine*. Use figures for numbers 10 and higher.

2. For very large numbers, use a combination of figures and words.

3. Always spell out a number that begins a sentence.

4. Use figures for dates, addresses, ZIP codes, telephone numbers, identification numbers, and time.

5. Use figures for fractions, decimals, and percentages.

CHAPTER REVIEW

REVIEW PRACTICE 1: Recall/Identify Circle the abbreviation errors, and underline the number errors in each of the following sentences. Some sentences contain more than one error.

1. According to Prof. Gleason, there is a process to writing.

2. At exactly 7:00 post meridiem, everyone will jump out of his or her hiding place and yell, "Surprise!"

3. The crew will need explosives to blast the twenty-nine-ton boulder.

4. Gen. Brevington's retirement banquet will be held on January twenty-nine, 2013.

5. Only 2 of the 8 children remembered their permission slips.

6. Of all the people polled, only ten percent were in favor of the new law.

7. 9 days from now, Columbia Broadcasting System is airing a special on former United States President Bill Clinton.

8. You can receive an associate of arts degree from your local community college.

9. The answers to questions four and five are in Chapter 21.

10. After winning the lottery for two million five hundred thousand dollars, Janene moved to Beverly Hills, CA.

REVIEW PRACTICE 2: Apply Correct the errors in Review Practice 1 by rewriting the sentences.

REVIEW PRACTICE 3: Write Your Own Write a paragraph explaining the quickest route from your house to your school. Use numbers and abbreviations in your paragraph.

MyWritingLab™ Complete this "Write Your Own" exercise for Chapter 46 in the MyWritingLab "Activities: Your Textbook" module.

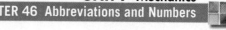
REVIEW PRACTICE 4: Editing Through Collaboration Exchange paragraphs from Review Practice 3 with another student, and do the following:

1. Underline all abbreviations, numbers, and figures.

2. Circle any abbreviations, numbers, or figures that are not in their correct form.

Then return the paper to its writer, and use the information in this chapter to correct any abbreviation and number errors in your own paragraph. Record your errors on the Error Log in Appendix 7.

MyWritingLab™ Visit Chapter 46, "Abbreviations and Numbers," in MyWritingLab, and complete the Post-test to check your understanding of the chapter's objectives.

8

Effective Sentences

At one time or another, you have probably been a member of a team. You may have actively participated in sports somewhere or been a part of a close-knit employee group. Or maybe you have taken part in classroom discussion groups or special projects that required cooperation with your peers. Whatever the situation, teamwork is important in many everyday situations. To be a good team member, you must perform your individual duties with others in mind.

Sentences, too, require good teamwork to be successful. Each word, phrase, or clause has to express its own meaning but must also work together with other words, phrases, and clauses toward the common goal of communicating a clear message. In this unit, three chapters will help you write successful sentences that work in harmony with each other to say exactly what you want to say in the best way possible:

Chapter 47: Varying Sentence Structure
Chapter 48: Parallelism
Chapter 49: Combining Sentences

Varying Sentence Structure

TEST YOURSELF

Turn each of the following pairs of sentences into one sentence that is more interesting.

- I work too much. I am tired.
- My cat is very lazy. She sleeps more than 14 hours a day.
- He enjoys reading. He likes mysteries.
- I live in an old house. My family has lived here for generations.
- My brother loves to eat. He will eat anything.

(Answers are in Appendix 3.)

Reading the same pattern sentence after sentence can become very monotonous for your readers. This chapter will help you solve this problem in your writing. Look at the following example.

I have always loved animals. I am about to get my own dog for the first time. I am ready to be responsible enough to take care of it. I am excited about this new phase in my life. I got a part-time job. I can't wait to get my own dog.

This paragraph has some terrific ideas, but they are expressed in such a monotonous way that the readers might doze off. What this paragraph needs is variety in its sentence structure. Here are some ideas for keeping your readers awake and ready to hear your good thoughts.

MyWritingLab **Understanding Varying Sentence Structure**

To find out more about this topic, go to **MyWritingLab.com,** and choose **Varying Sentence Structure** in the **Usage and Style** module. For this topic, watch the video called **Animation: Varying Sentence Structure.** Then, return to this chapter, which will go into more detail about sentence variety and give you opportunities to practice it. Finally, you will apply your understanding of sentence variety to your own writing.

ADD INTRODUCTORY WORDS

Add some introductory words to your sentences so they don't all start the same way.

> **For as long as I can remember,** I have always loved animals. **Now** I am about to get my own dog for the first time. I am ready to be responsible enough to take care of it. I am excited about this new phase in my life. **To pay for my new friend,** I got a part-time job. I can't wait to get my own dog.

PRACTICE 1: Recall/Identify Underline the sentence in each pair that could be turned into an introductory word, phrase, or clause.

1. Misty had a terrible stomachache. It was late last night.

2. We went to the river. We skipped over the rocks.

3. We went to McDonald's for breakfast. We saw our friends.

4. The sunsets are beautiful. It was spring.

5. He is afraid of dogs. He was bitten by a dog once.

PRACTICE 2: Apply Rewrite the sentences in Practice 1 by turning each sentence you underlined into an introductory word, phrase, or clause.

PRACTICE 3: Write Your Own Write five sentences of your own with introductory elements.

REVERSE WORDS

Reverse the order of some subjects and verbs. For example, instead of *I am so excited,* try *Am I ever excited.* You can also add or drop words and change punctuation to make the sentence read smoothly.

For as long as I can remember, I have always loved animals. Now I am about to get my own dog for the first time. I am ready to be responsible enough to take care of it. **Am I ever excited** about this new phase in my life. To pay for my new friend, I got a part-time job. I can't wait to get my own dog.

PRACTICE 4: Recall/Identify Underline the words or phrases you could reverse in each of the following sentences.

1. I am happy to know you.

2. All the ingredients went into the pot.

3. The cat jumped out of the hat.

4. The children were happy.

5. The strange creature appeared out of nowhere.

PRACTICE 5: Apply Rewrite the sentences in Practice 4 by reversing the words you underlined.

PRACTICE 6: Write Your Own Write five sentences of your own with subjects and verbs reversed.

MOVE SENTENCE PARTS

Move around some parts of the sentence. Experiment to see which order works best.

For as long as I can remember, I have always loved animals. Now I am about to get my own dog for the first time. I am ready to be responsible enough to take care of it. Am I ever excited about this new phase in my life. **My part-time job can help me pay for my new friend.** I can't wait to get my own dog.

PRACTICE 7: Recall/Identify Underline any parts of the following sentences that can be moved around.

1. To bake these cookies, you will need 2 cups of flour.

2. Finally, I knew the truth.

3. I was very full after lunch.

4. You will find your shoes underneath your bed.

5. If you enjoyed the film, you will probably like the book.

PRACTICE 8: Apply Rewrite the sentences in Practice 7, moving the words you underlined.

PRACTICE 9: Write Your Own Write two sentences of your own. Then rewrite each sentence two different ways.

VARY SENTENCE TYPE

Use a question, a command, or an exclamation occasionally.

For as long as I can remember, I have always loved animals. **Have you?** Now I am about to get my own dog for the first time. I am ready to be responsible enough to take care of it. **Am I ever excited about this new phase in my life!** My part-time job can help me pay for my new friend. I can't wait to get my own dog.

PRACTICE 10: Recall/Identify Identify each of the following sentences as a statement (S), a question (Q), a command (C), or an exclamation (E).

1. _____ When is the meal being served

2. _____ Did you see that object flying in the sky

3. _____ Bring me a glass of iced tea and a bowl of grapes

4. _____ First do the prewriting exercises

5. _____ I just hate it when that happens

PRACTICE 11: Apply Complete the following sentences, making them into questions, commands, or exclamations. Then supply the correct punctuation.

1. Wow, I can't believe _____

2. At the first intersection _____

3. Why is _____

4. Hand me _____

5. Did you hear _____

PRACTICE 12: Write Your Own Write two statements, two questions, two commands, and two exclamations of your own.

CHAPTER REVIEW

REVIEW PRACTICE 1: Recall/Identify Underline the words or groups of words that have been added or moved in each revised sentence. Then use the following key to tell which rule was applied to the sentence:

1. Add introductory words.
2. Reverse the order of subject and verb.
3. Move around parts of the sentence.
4. Use a question, a command, or an exclamation occasionally.

    1. Eat your peas. You aren't finished with dinner yet.

        ____ You aren't finished with dinner until you eat your peas.

    2. He did what?

        ____ What did he do?

    3. You went to the store around the corner. You bought some milk and bread.

        ____ At the store around the corner, please buy some milk and bread.

    4. To the park went he.

        ____ To the park he went.

    5. The fireflies flew. They flew all around us.

        ____ All around us, the fireflies flew.

    6. I believe that was mine.

        ____ Hey, that was mine!

    7. How many times a day do you brush your teeth?

        ____ You brush your teeth how many times a day?

    8. You are amazing!

        ____ Are you amazing or what?

    9. Out of the darkness came a terrible noise.

        ____ Out of the darkness, a terrible noise came.

    10. Carl does enjoy a good hamburger every now and then.

        ____ Every now and then, Carl does enjoy a good hamburger.

REVIEW PRACTICE 2: Apply Vary the structure of the following sentences with at least three of the four ideas you just learned.

A good teacher should be encouraging toward students. He or she should understand when a student is having problems and spend some one-on-one time together. The teacher should then help the student identify problems and give helpful instruction to solve the problems. A good teacher never makes fun of a student.

REVIEW PRACTICE 3: Write Your Own Write a paragraph about a good deed you have performed. What made you decide to do what you did? Try to use each of the four ways you have learned to make sentences interesting.

MyWritingLab™ Complete this "Write Your Own" exercise for Chapter 47 in the MyWritingLab "Activities: Your Textbook" module.

REVIEW PRACTICE 4: Editing Through Collaboration Exchange paragraphs from Review Practice 3 with another student, and do the following:

1. Put brackets around any sentences that sound monotonous.

2. Suggest a way to vary each of these sentences.

Then return the paper to its writer, and use the information in this chapter to vary the sentence structure in your own paragraph. Record your errors on the Error Log in Appendix 7.

MyWritingLab™ Visit Chapter 47, "Varying Sentence Structure," in MyWritingLab, and complete the Post-test to check your understanding of the chapter's objectives.

Parallelism

Underline the parts in each of the following sentences that seem awkward or unbalanced.

- Tony enjoys hockey, football, and runs.
- My mom and dad give money to help the homeless and for building new homes.
- I finished high school, started college, and I am beginning a new job.
- I love the mountains because they're cool, clean, and feel refreshing.
- Listening to music, watching television, or to read a book are good ways to relax.

(Answers are in Appendix 3.)

When sentences are **parallel,** they are balanced. That is, words, phrases, or clauses in a series start with the same grammatical form. Parallel structures make your sentences interesting and clear.

MyWritingLab

Understanding Parallelism

To improve your understanding of this topic, go to **MyWritingLab .com,** and choose **Parallelism** in the **Sentence Skills** module. From there, watch the video called **Animation: Parallelism.** Then, return to this chapter, which will go into more detail about parallelism and give you opportunities to practice it. Finally, you will apply your understanding of parallelism to your own writing.

Student Comment:
"I usually understand what I'm assigned from the reading alone. However, I just didn't get **Parallelism. MyWritingLab** helped me grasp this topic."

PARALLEL STRUCTURE

Following is a paragraph that could be greatly improved with parallel structures.

My brother Ricardo was not excited when he was called in to work at the hospital today. He had been looking forward to this day off—his first in three weeks. He was planning to work out in the morning, swimming in the afternoon, and going to a movie in the evening. Instead, he will be helping the patients, assisting the nurses, and will aid the doctors.

Words and phrases in a series should be parallel, which means they should start with the same type of word. Parallelism makes your sentence structure smoother and more interesting. Look at this sentence, for example.

NOT   He had planned to **work out** in the morning,
               swimming in the afternoon, and
               going to a movie in the evening.

Parallel: He had planned to **work out** in the morning,
               swim in the afternoon, and
               go to the movies in the evening.

Parallel: He had planned on **working out** in the morning,
               swimming in the afternoon, and
               going to the movies in the evening.

Here is another sentence that would read better if the parts were parallel:

NOT   Instead, he will be **helping** the patients,
               assisting the nurses, and
               will aid the doctors.

Parallel: Instead, he will be **helping** the patients,
               assisting the nurses, and
               aiding the doctors.

Parallel: Instead, he will be helping **the patients,**
                    the nurses, and
                    the doctors.

Now read the paragraph with these two sentences made parallel or balanced.

My brother Ricardo was not excited when he was called in to work at the hospital today. He had been looking forward to this day off—his first in three weeks. He had planned to work out in the morning, swim in the afternoon, and go to a movie in the evening. Instead, he will be helping the patients, the nurses, and the doctors.

PRACTICE 1: Recall/Identify Underline the parallel structures in each of the following sentences.

1. Scott plans to hide in his cabin, do some fishing, and work on his novel.

2. The car needs new windows, tires, and paint.

3. Georgia believes that she is the most wonderful person in the world and that she deserves everyone's love and attention.

4. They camped under the stars, swam in the cool lakes, and enjoyed the fresh air.

5. Because of the pouring rain, extreme cold, and bitter wind, we decided to stay inside.

PRACTICE 2: Apply Make the underlined elements parallel in each of the following sentences.

1. He will wear only clothes <u>that have designer labels</u> and <u>they are expensive</u>.

    _____

2. <u>Regular exercise</u>, <u>drinking plenty of water</u>, and <u>eating lots of good food</u> will help keep you healthy.

    _____

3. Deidra went to the mall <u>to get a bite to eat</u>, <u>to do some shopping</u>, and <u>will visit friends</u>.

    _____

4. Please do not <u>tap pens</u>, <u>talk to others</u>, or <u>eating food during the exam</u>.

    _____

5. On his trip, he <u>took pictures of mountains</u>, <u>fed animals</u>, and <u>some enjoyable people</u>.

    _____

PRACTICE 3: Write Your Own Write five sentences of your own using parallel structures in each.

CHAPTER REVIEW

REVIEW PRACTICE 1: Recall/Identify Underline the parallel structures in each of the following sentences.

1. Football, basketball, and hockey are all competitive sports.

2. Because of the terrible weather, the horrible traffic, and the missed bus, we didn't make our flight.

3. When I'm in love, the sun always shines, the stars always sparkle, and the moon always glows.

4. Marilyn went to the city's annual air show because she wanted to see the jet planes and because she wanted to try the interesting foods.

5. The biting mosquitoes, barking dogs, and burning sun made me miserable.

6. Please feed, bathe, and change the baby before I get home.

7. If Harvey cleans the house, does his homework, and begs for forgiveness, he may get out of his punishment.

8. I believe that people should be treated fairly and that everyone should get a second chance.

9. He was suspended because he fought, cheated, and disrespected others.

10. Today Mother paid the bills, balanced the checkbook, and washed the car.

REVIEW PRACTICE 2: Apply Complete each of the following sentences with parallel structures.

1. I enjoy _____, _____, and _____ in the summer.

2. Because of _____ and because of _____, Miriam didn't go to the movies.

3. You can be successful in college if you _____, _____, and _____.

4. Even though Jeremy _____, _____, and _____, he still can't find the problem.

5. _____, _____, and _____ are essential items when hiking.

6. She cooks foods that _____ and _____.

7. My favorite foods are _____, _____, and _____.

8. If I have to hear her _____, _____, and _____ one more time, I'm going to scream.

9. The instructor has already explained _____, _____, and _____.

10. If you _____, _____, and _____, you just might survive boot camp.

REVIEW PRACTICE 3: Write Your Own Write a paragraph about the best holiday you've ever had. What was the holiday? Why was it the best? Use two examples of parallelism in your paragraph.

MyWritingLab™ Complete this "Write Your Own" exercise for Chapter 48 in the MyWritingLab "Activities: Your Textbook" module.

REVIEW PRACTICE 4: Editing Through Collaboration Exchange paragraphs from Review Practice 3 with another student, and do the following:

1. Underline any items in a series.

2. Put brackets around any of these items that are not grammatically parallel.

Then return the paper to its writer, and use the information in this chapter to correct any parallelism errors in your own paragraph. Record your errors on the Error Log in Appendix 7.

MyWritingLab™ Visit Chapter 48, "Parallelism," in MyWritingLab, and complete the Post-test to check your understanding of the chapter's objectives.

49

Combining Sentences

Combine each set of sentences into one sentence.

- My brother is taking tennis lessons. He takes his lessons from a professional player.
- The baby is crying. She's hungry.
- It's too hot outside. Let's go for a swim.
- We moved overseas when I was 11 years old. I learned much about different cultures.
- I like to travel. Africa has many interesting animals and plants. I want to go to Africa.

(Answers are in Appendix 3.)

Still another way to add variety to your writing is to combine short, choppy sentences into longer sentences. You can combine simple sentences to make compound or complex sentences. You can also combine compound and complex sentences.

Student Comment:
"For this topic, I would tell fellow students to take their time, focus, and read carefully. The mistake I made was not reading each question-and-answer set word for word."

MyWritingLab Understanding Combining

To help you understand this subject, go to **MyWritingLab.com**, and choose **Combining Sentences** in the **Sentence Skills** module. Next, watch the video called **Animation: Combining Sentences.** Then, return to this chapter, which will go into more detail about sentence combining and give you opportunities to practice it. Finally, you will apply your understanding of combining sentences in your own writing.

SIMPLE SENTENCES

A **simple sentence** consists of one independent clause. Remember that a clause has a subject and a main verb.

In the following examples, notice that a simple sentence can have more than one subject and more than one verb. (For more on compound subjects and compound verbs, see Chapter 27.)

    s   v

I have several very good friends.

    s   v   v

I have good friends and enjoy being with them.

      s   s v

Martin and Louis are good friends.

      s   s v   v

Martin and I do interesting things and go to interesting places.

PRACTICE 1: Recall/Identify Underline the subjects once and the verbs twice in each of the following sentences. Then label the simple sentences SS.

1. _____ Most cats don't like the water, but most dogs do.

2. _____ Tommy and I like listening to the same types of music and watching the same types of shows.

3. _____ I feel that our luck is about to change.

4. _____ We left quickly because of the smell.

5. _____ We have pictures of the family throughout the house.

PRACTICE 2: Apply Make simple sentences out of the sentences in Practice 1 that are not simple.

PRACTICE 3: Write Your Own Write a simple sentence of your own for each of the following subjects and verbs.

1. Jessy and Miguel _____

2. we're eating and drinking _____

3. the playful kittens _____

4. looking and listening _____

5. the hot pan _____

COMPOUND SENTENCES

A **compound sentence** consists of two or more independent clauses joined by a coordinating conjunction (*and, but, for, nor, or, so,* or *yet*). In other words, you can create a compound sentence from two (or more) simple sentences.

Simple:	I can swim fast.
Simple:	I am a good long-distance swimmer.
Compound:	I can swim fast, **and** I am a good long-distance swimmer.

Simple:	She has a very stressful job.
Simple:	She works out at the gym three times a week.
Compound:	She has a very stressful job, **so** she works out at the gym three times a week.

Simple:	My parents are leaving for Hawaii on Tuesday.
Simple:	They won't be here for my birthday party.
Compound:	My parents are leaving for Hawaii on Tuesday, **so** they won't be here for my birthday party.

Hint: As the examples show, a comma comes before the coordinating conjunction in a compound sentence.

PRACTICE 4: Recall/Identify Underline the independent clauses in the following sentences, and circle the coordinating conjunctions.

1. I am not sick, and I feel fine.
2. You cannot bring food or drink in this building, but you can eat in the cafeteria.
3. We try not to gossip, for we know the damage loose lips can cause.
4. I do not like raspberries, yet I do like raspberry pie.
5. Christy likes fast cars, so she is going to buy a sports car.

PRACTICE 5: Apply Combine each pair of simple sentences into a compound sentence.

1. I am leaving. I am late for an appointment.
2. Quickly, move out of the way. The angry elephant is going to charge us.
3. We usually take a month-long vacation. We are always happy to return home.
4. This food has been sitting out all day in the hot sun. It smells awful.
5. I have a lot of cousins. I haven't met them all.

PRACTICE 6: Write Your Own Write five compound sentences of your own.

COMPLEX SENTENCES

A **complex sentence** is composed of one independent clause and at least one dependent clause. A **dependent clause** begins with either a subordinating conjunction or a relative pronoun.

Subordinating Conjunctions

after	because	since	until
although	before	so	when
as	even if	so that	whenever
as if	even though	than	where
as long as	how	that	wherever
as soon as	if	though	whether
as though	in order that	unless	while

Relative Pronouns

that	which	who	whom	whose

You can use subordinating conjunctions and relative pronouns to make a simple sentence (an independent clause) into a dependent clause. Then you can add the new dependent clause to an independent clause to produce a complex sentence that adds interest and variety to your writing.

How do you know which simple sentence should be independent and which should be dependent? The idea that you think is more important should be the independent clause. The less important idea will then be the dependent clause.

Following are some examples of how to combine simple sentences to make a complex sentence.

Simple: Myra has a large collection of DVDs.

Simple: Myra watches the same few films over and over.

Dep

Complex: **Even though** Myra has a large collection of DVDs,

Ind

she watches the same few films over and over.

This complex sentence stresses that Myra watches the same films over and over. The size of her collection is of secondary importance.

Ind

Complex: She has a big collection of DVDs,

Dep

though she watches the same few films over and over.

In the previous complex sentence, the size of the collection is most important, so it is the independent clause.

Simple: The winner of the lottery was Laura.

Simple: Laura is my cousin.

Ind   Dep

Complex: The winner of the lottery was Laura, **who** is my cousin.

This complex sentence answers the question "Who won the lottery?" The information about Laura being the cousin is of secondary importance.

Ind   Dep

Complex: My cousin is Laura, **who** won the lottery.

This complex sentence answers the question "Who is your cousin?" The information about winning the lottery is secondary.

PRACTICE 7: Recall/Identify Label the underlined part of each sentence as either an independent (Ind) or a dependent (Dep) clause.

1. _____ <u>Although I was tired</u>, I still went to school.

2. _____ Here is the furniture <u>that you ordered</u>.

3. _____ <u>Trish moved to the coast</u> because she likes the beach.

4. _____ My doctor is Janet Woo, <u>who is also my mom</u>.

5. _____ If we cannot study at your house, <u>then let's study at the library</u>.

PRACTICE 8: Apply Finish each sentence with a clause, and label the new clause either dependent (Dep) or independent (Ind).

1. ____ Whenever John's face turns red, _____

2. ____ _____ because he forgot to call home.

3. ____ Maya's mother, who _____, is a great cook.

4. ____ I like the blue one, _____

5. ____ He climbed the mountain _____

PRACTICE 9: Write Your Own Write five complex sentences, making sure you have one independent clause and at least one dependent clause in each.

COMPOUND-COMPLEX SENTENCES

If you combine a compound sentence with a complex sentence, you produce a **compound-complex sentence.** That means your sentence has at least two independent clauses (to make it compound) and at least one dependent clause (to make it complex). Here are some examples.

Simple: My cousin likes scuba diving.
Simple: He is planning a trip to Hawaii.
Simple: He is excited about diving in Hawaii.

                                 Ind   **Ind**
Compound-Complex: My cousin likes scuba diving, **so** he is planning

                                         Dep
            a trip to Hawaii, **which** he is very excited about.

Simple: She bought a new house.
Simple: It has a pool and a spa.
Simple: It doesn't have a garage.

                             Ind   **Dep**
Compound-Complex: She bought a new house, **which** has a pool and

                                Ind
           a spa, **but** it doesn't have a garage.

Simple: Today's weather is very bad.
Simple: The rain could make it difficult to drive.
Simple: This could delay your departure for home.

Ind   Ind

Compound-Complex: Today's weather is very bad, **and** the rain could

Dep

make it difficult to drive, **which** could delay your departure for home.

Hint: Notice that we occasionally have to change words in combined sentences so the sentences make sense.

PRACTICE 10: Recall/Identify Underline the clauses in each of the following compound-complex sentences. Then identify each clause as either independent (Ind) or dependent (Dep).

1. Whenever I travel, I set an alarm clock, and I arrange for a wake-up call.

2. Sandy likes Anthony because he is nice, but she also likes Mark.

3. After they fought, they decided to make up, and now they are inseparable.

4. The traffic, which is usually bad around noon, is very heavy today, so you'd better leave soon.

5. We went to the Virgin Islands because we love the sun, yet it rained the whole time.

PRACTICE 11: Apply Expand each sentence into a compound-complex sentence.

1. The boy likes oranges and pears.

_____

2. The box was very heavy, but he lifted it anyway.

_____

3. Jill says that she will never fly in a plane.

_____

4. John will be 21 soon.

_____

5. I am watching videos on YouTube and getting some rest.

_____

_____

PRACTICE 12: Write Your Own Write five compound-complex sentences of your own.

CHAPTER REVIEW

REVIEW PRACTICE 1: Recall/Identify Underline the independent clauses in each sentence. Then label the sentence simple (SS), compound (C), complex (CX), or compound-complex (CCX). The following definitions might help you.

Simple (SS)	= one independent clause
Compound (C)	= two or more independent clauses joined by *and, but, for, nor, or, so,* or *yet*
Complex (CX)	= one independent clause and at least one dependent clause
Compound-complex (CCX)	= at least two independent clauses and one or more dependent clauses

1. _____ Casey and Floyd have left the building.

2. _____ Even though he is quiet, he is very friendly.

3. _____ Marcy and David are boyfriend and girlfriend, and they are going to the prom together.

4. _____ The dog and cat ate my dinner last night.

5. _____ Mrs. Glancy is my close friend, and she visits me often.

6. _____ Marc is happy because Sheila is here, and he wants to ask her on a date.

7. _____ The folders are in the desk drawer.

8. _____ The dog needs to be fed, and he needs a bath.

9. _____ The gifts, which you bought yesterday, have been wrapped, and they are ready to be delivered.

10. _____ Because her alarm didn't go off, she was late for work.

REVIEW PRACTICE 2: Apply Combine each set of sentences to make the sentence pattern indicated in parentheses. You may need to change some wording in the sentences so they make sense. The list of sentence types in Review Practice 1 may help you with this exercise.

1. Antoine bikes in the morning. He wants to stay in shape. He goes to the gym every weekend. (compound-complex)

2. I like to play in the mud. I always get dirty. (compound)

3. You should leave now. You should be at your appointment 15 minutes early to fill out paperwork. (complex)

4. Penny brought a stray dog home. Penny loves animals. Her mother wouldn't let her keep it. (compound-complex)

5. I slammed the car door on my thumb. I broke it. (complex)

6. I love to chew gum and pop bubbles. I can't chew gum in class. (complex)

7. The little girl lost her doll. She has looked everywhere for it. She is crying. (compound-complex)

8. The sun is shining. The birds are singing. (compound)

9. The reports are missing. I need them now. (compound)

10. It is October. The leaves are turning brown and falling from the tree. (complex)

REVIEW PRACTICE 3: Write Your Own Write a paragraph about your fondest wish. What is it, and why do you wish for it?

MyWritingLab™　Complete this "Write Your Own" exercise for Chapter 49 in the MyWritingLab "Activities: Your Textbook" module.

REVIEW PRACTICE 4: Editing Through Collaboration Exchange paragraphs from Review Practice 3 with another student, and do the following:

1. Put brackets around any sentences you think should be combined.

2. Underline sentences that are incorrectly combined (for example, ones with a weak connecting word or no connecting word).

Then return the paper to its writer, and use the information in this chapter to combine sentences in your own paragraph. Record your errors on the Error Log in Appendix 7.

MyWritingLab™　Visit Chapter 49, "Combining Sentences," in MyWritingLab, and complete the Post-test to check your understanding of the chapter's objectives.

Choosing the Right Word

Choosing the right word is like choosing the right snack to satisfy your appetite. If you don't select the food you are craving, your hunger does not go away. In like manner, if you do not choose the right words to say what is on your mind, your readers will not be satisfied and will not understand your message.

Choosing the right word depends on your message, your purpose, and your audience. It also involves recognizing misused, nonstandard, and misspelled words. We deal with the following topics in Unit 9:

Chapter 50: Standard and Nonstandard English
Chapter 51: Easily Confused Words
Chapter 52: Spelling

50

Standard and Nonstandard English

TEST YOURSELF

Label the following sentences as correct, incorrect, or slang.

- You shoulda seen Claudia's new hairstyle. _____
- Where are my friends at? _Incorrect_____
- Your new bike is tight! _____
- Randy was enthused about his date. _incorrect._____
- Christina Aguilera's new video rocks. _slang_____

(Answers are in Appendix 3.)

Choosing the right words for what you want to say is an important part of effective communication. This chapter will help you find the right words and phrases for the audience you are trying to reach. Look, for example, at the following sentences. They all have a similar message, expressed in different words.

I want to do good in college, being as I can get a good job.

I be studying hard in college so I can get a good job.

I'm going to hit the books so I can rake in the bucks.

I want to do <u>well</u> in college so I can get a good job.

Which of these sentences would you probably say to a friend or to someone in your family? Which would you most likely say in a job interview? Which would be good for a college paper?

The first three sentences are nonstandard English. They might be said or written to a friend or family member, but they would not be appropriate in an academic setting or in a job situation. Only the fourth sentence would be appropriate in an academic paper or in a job interview.

Understanding Standard and Nonstandard English

To expand your understanding of this topic, go to **MyWritingLab.com,** and choose **Standard and Nonstandard English** in the **Usage and Style** module. From there, watch the video called **Animation: Standard and Nonstandard English.** Then, return to this chapter, which will go into more detail about levels of English and give you opportunities to practice them. Finally, you will apply your understanding of standard and nonstandard English to your own writing.

STANDARD AND NONSTANDARD ENGLISH

Most of the English language falls into one of two categories—either *standard* or *nonstandard*. **Standard English** is the language of college, business, and the media. It is used by reporters on television, by newspapers, in most magazines, and on Web sites created by schools, government agencies, businesses, and organizations. Standard English is always grammatically correct and free of slang.

Nonstandard English does not follow all the rules of grammar and often includes slang. Nonstandard English is not necessarily wrong, but it is more appropriate in some settings (with friends and family) than in others. It is not appropriate in college or business writing. To understand the difference between standard and nonstandard English, compare the following paragraphs.

Nonstandard English

I was <u>stoked</u> to find out I would be getting a $300 refund on my taxes. My first thought was to <u>blow it</u> on a trip, maybe <u>somewheres</u> like Las Vegas. But none of my <u>friends was enthused</u> by that. Then I thought <u>being as I</u> watch television <u>alot,</u> I would buy a new Smart TV. My brother got <u>hisself</u> one last year. Then <u>it hit me,</u> hey, I'm <u>gonna</u> need some money to buy new <u>duds</u> for my job. Alright, I decided, I <u>gotta</u> buy clothes with the <u>dough,</u> <u>irregardless</u> of what I'd like to do with it.

Standard English

I was thrilled when I found out I would be getting a $300 refund on my taxes. My first thought was to spend it on a trip, maybe somewhere like Las Vegas. But none of my friends was enthusiastic about that. Then I thought that since I watch television a lot, I would buy a new Smart TV. My brother got himself one last year. Then I realized that I am going to need some money to buy new clothes for my job. All right, I decided, I have to buy clothes with the money, regardless of what I'd like to do with it.

In the rest of this chapter, you will learn how to recognize and correct ungrammatical English and how to avoid using slang in your writing.

NONSTANDARD ENGLISH

Nonstandard English is ungrammatical. It does not follow the rules of standard English that are required in college writing. The academic and business worlds expect you to be able to recognize and avoid nonstandard English. This is not always easy because some nonstandard terms are used so often in speech that many people think they are acceptable in writing. The following list might help you choose the correct words in your own writing.

ain't

NOT	My economics professor **ain't** giving us the test today.
CORRECT	My economics professor **isn't** giving us the test today.

anywheres

NOT	Belinda buys her clothes **anywheres** she can find them.
CORRECT	Lashawn buys her clothes **anywhere** she can find them.

be

NOT	I **be** so happy.
CORRECT	I **am** so happy.

(For additional help with *be*, see Chapter 31, "Verb Tense.")

being as, being that

NOT	Emilio will not get to go home over the weekend, **being as** he has to work.
CORRECT	Emilio will not get to go home over the weekend **because** he has to work.

coulda/could of, shoulda/should of

NOT	He **could of** earned a better grade on the test if he'd studied.
CORRECT	He **could have** (or **could've**) earned a better grade on the test if he'd studied.

different than

NOT	She is **different than** us.
CORRECT	She is **different from** us.

drug

NOT	She **drug** the mattress across the room.
CORRECT	She **dragged** the mattress across the room.

enthused

NOT	Mary was **enthused** about the wedding.
CORRECT	Mary was **enthusiastic** about the wedding.

everywheres

NOT	My dog follows me **everywheres** I go.
CORRECT	My dog follows me **everywhere** I go.

goes

NOT	Then Lorie **goes,** "I'm leaving without you."
CORRECT	Then Lorie **said,** "I'm leaving without you."
CORRECT	Then Lorie **said** that she was leaving without me.

hisself

NOT	Jackson made **hisself** a cheeseburger.
CORRECT	Jackson made **himself** a cheeseburger.

in regards to

NOT	We received a letter **in regards to** your complaint.
CORRECT	We received a letter **in regard to** your complaint.

irregardless

NOT	**Irregardless** of how long you study French, you'll never speak it like a native.
CORRECT	**Regardless** of how long you study French, you'll never speak it like a native.

kinda/kind of, sorta/sort of

NOT	The room smells **kinda** sweet, **sorta** like vanilla.
CORRECT	The room smells **rather** sweet, **much like** vanilla.

most

NOT	**Most** everyone accepted the invitation.
CORRECT	**Almost** everyone accepted the invitation.

a.9.

must of

| NOT | I **must of** lost my purse at the party. |
| CORRECT | I **must have** lost my purse at the party. |

off of

| NOT | Billy jumped **off of** the back of the truck. |
| CORRECT | Billy jumped **off** the back of the truck. |

oughta

| NOT | Sometimes I think I **oughta** watch less television. |
| CORRECT | Sometimes I think I **ought to** watch less television. |

real

| NOT | My boyfriend was **real** mad when I left him. |
| CORRECT | My boyfriend was **really** mad when I left him. |

somewheres

| NOT | Your jeans are **somewheres** in that pile of clothes. |
| CORRECT | Your jeans are **somewhere** in that pile of clothes. |

suppose to

| NOT | You were **suppose to** turn that paper in yesterday. |
| CORRECT | You were **supposed to** turn that paper in yesterday. |

theirselves

| NOT | They helped **theirselves** to the food in the buffet line. |
| CORRECT | They helped **themselves** to the food in the buffet line. |

use to

| NOT | I **use to** have a truck. |
| CORRECT | I **used to** have a truck. |

ways

| NOT | Curt's car broke down a long **ways** from home. |
| CORRECT | Curt's car broke down a long **way** from home. |

where . . . at

| NOT | **Where** is the nearest bakery **at?** |
| CORRECT | **Where** is the nearest bakery? |

PRACTICE 1A: Recall/Identify Underline the ungrammatical words or phrases in each of the following sentences.

1. Do you know where the children are at?

2. Then John goes, "There is no way I'm going to touch that."

3. Our production of *Romeo and Juliet* is kinda like the original, but sorta modern.

4. I coulda stayed at home instead of sitting here listening to this boring lecture. *Could have*

5. Justin was suppose to mail the invitations.   *supposed*

PRACTICE 1B: Correct Correct the ungrammatical words and expressions in Practice 1A by rewriting the incorrect sentences.

PRACTICE 2: Apply Underline the ungrammatical word or words in each phrase, and change them to standard English.

1. Anywheres I go   _____ *Anywhere*

2. She drug it   _____ *dragged*

3. We are a long ways   _____ *way*

4. He made hisself   _____ *himself*

5. Being that Susan   _____ *Be*

PRACTICE 3: Write Your Own Write five sentences of your own using the grammatical words and phrases you chose in Practice 2.

SLANG

Another example of nonstandard English is **slang,** popular words and expressions that come and go, much like the latest fashions. For example, in the 1950s, someone might have called his or her special someone *dreamy.* In the 1960s, you might have heard a boyfriend or girlfriend described as *groovy,* and in the 1990s, *sweet* was the popular slang term. Today your significant other might be *hot* or *dope.*

These expressions are slang because they are part of the spoken language that changes from generation to generation and from place to place. As you might suspect, slang communicates to a limited audience who shares common interests and experiences. Some slang words, such as *cool* and *neat,* have become part of our language, but most slang is temporary. What's in today may be out tomorrow, so the best advice is to avoid using slang in your writing.

PRACTICE 4: Recall/Identify Underline the slang words and expressions in each of the following sentences.

HW

1. Stevie Wonder rocks!   *awesome*

2. "Wassup?" I yelled to my homies.   *What's up.*

3. This party is poppin'.   *loved*

4. My mom tripped out when I got my tattoo.   *was mad*

5. Stewart is zoning on the video game.   *zooming*

so staring.

PRACTICE 5: Apply Translate the following slang expressions into standard English.   *Talk to other person*

1. Talk to the hand _One doesn't want to hear what the person who is saying_   *Don't talk to me*

2. hella good _Very good._

3. flyboy _a member of the air force_   *Popular*

4. right back atcha _Same to you_

5. a wannabe _lacking in self confidence and is looking for guidance_   *just try to be like sb. awesom*

PRACTICE 6: Write Your Own List five slang words or expressions, and use them in sentences of your own. Then rewrite each sentence using standard English to replace the slang expressions.

CHAPTER REVIEW

REVIEW PRACTICE 1: Recall/Identify Underline the ungrammatical or slang words in the following sentences.

1. You really need to chill out.

2. He ain't going to know what's going on.

3. I was so enthused when I won the contest.

4. He's really jammin' to the music.

5. Hey, stop buggin' me.

6. Oops, I fell off of the ski lift.

7. He's no different than you or me.

8. She thinks she's all that.

9. You oughta take art lessons.

10. Sandra is really hot.

REVIEW PRACTICE 2: Apply Correct any nonstandard English in each of the following sentences by rewriting the sentences.

1. I be wide awake and can't sleep.

2. Irregardless of them, Rufus is talking to hisself.

3. Tony's making big money at his new job.

4. Those singers are bad.

5. My girlfriend was real mad when I forgot Valentine's Day.

6. In regards to your question, I don't have an answer.

7. Watcha doin'?

8. Who are the real peeps in this investigation?

9. Jane could of found extra blankets if you were cold.

10. You are solid, man.   honest

REVIEW PRACTICE 3: Write Your Own Write a paragraph on how you spend your free time. Do you spend it with your friends or alone? What do you do and why?

MyWritingLab™   Complete this "Write Your Own" exercise for Chapter 50 in the MyWritingLab "Activities: Your Textbook" module.

REVIEW PRACTICE 4: Editing Through Collaboration Exchange paragraphs from Review Practice 3 with another student, and do the following:

1. Underline any ungrammatical language.

2. Circle any slang.

Then return the paper to its writer, and use the information in this chapter to correct any nonstandard or slang expressions in your own paragraph. Record your errors on the Error Log in Appendix 7.

MyWritingLab™   Visit Chapter 50, "Standard and Nonstandard English," in MyWritingLab, and complete the Post-test to check your understanding of the chapter's objectives.

51

Easily Confused Words

Choose the correct word in parentheses.

- Miranda couldn't (choose, chose) a college.
- (It's, Its) time to leave for the show.
- I can't (hear, here) with all this noise.
- (Weather, Whether) you go or not, I still want to attend.
- (Who's, Whose) responsible for this mess?

(Answers are in Appendix 3.)

Some words are easily confused. They may look alike, sound alike, or have similar meanings, but they all play different roles in the English language. This chapter will help you choose the right words for your sentences.

Student Comment:
"**Easily Confused Words** was the most helpful topic for me in MyWritingLab because I always get confused by **their, there,** and **they're.**"

MyWritingLab **Understanding Easily Confused Words**

To find out more about this topic, go to **MyWritingLab.com,** and choose **Easily Confused Words** in the **Usage and Style** module. From there, watch the video called **Animation: Easily Confused Words.** Then, return to this chapter, which will go into more detail about word choice and give you opportunities to practice it. Finally, you will apply your understanding of word choice to your own writing.

EASILY CONFUSED WORDS, PART I

a/an: Use *a* before words that begin with a consonant. Use *an* before words that begin with a vowel (*a, e, i, o, u*).

> **a** bill, **a** cat, **a** zebra
> **an** artichoke, **an** Indian, **an** occasion

accept/except: *Accept* means "receive." *Except* means "other than."

> Mary will not **accept** the gift.
> Everyone went **except** Harry.

advice/advise: *Advice* means "helpful information." *Advise* means "give advice or help."

> My mother usually gives me very good **advice.**
> My parents **advise** me when I'm trying to make an important decision.

affect/effect: *Affect* (verb) means "influence." *Effect* means "bring about" (verb) or "a result" (noun).

> She hopes speaking out won't **affect** her chance at promotion.
> I believe that changes in the law will **effect** positive changes in society.
> The weather had a bad **effect** on his health.

already/all ready: *Already* means "in the past." *All ready* means "completely prepared."

> I have **already** taken that class.
> We had packed the car and were **all ready** to go.

among/between: Use *among* when referring to three or more people or things. Use *between* when referring to only two people or things.

> The students discussed the issues **among** themselves.
> I can't decide **between** the two dresses.

bad/badly: *Bad* means "not good." *Badly* means "not well."

> That meat is **bad,** so don't eat it.
> He felt **bad** about the accident.
> He was hurt **badly** in the accident.

beside/besides: *Beside* means "next to." *Besides* means "in addition (to)."

> She sat **beside** him at lunch.
> **Besides** sleeping, I can think of nothing else I want to do.

brake/break: *Brake* means "stop" or "the part that stops a moving vehicle." *Break* means "shatter, come apart" or "a rest between work periods."

> She didn't **brake** soon enough to avoid the other car.
> The **brakes** on my car are not dependable.
> I watched the limb **break** off the tree.
> Can we take a **break**?

breath/breathe: *Breath* means "air." *Breathe* means "taking in air."

> Take a long, slow **breath.**
> The air we have to **breathe** is unhealthy.

choose/chose: *Choose* means "select." *Chose* is the past tense of *choose*.

> Please **choose** an answer.
> He **chose** the wrong answer.

PRACTICE 1: Recall/Identify Underline the correct word in each of the following sentences.

1. I can (advice, advise) you on what courses to take.

2. The little boy behaved (bad, badly) when his father left.

3. We were (already, all ready) to leave the house when she realized she didn't have her purse.

4. (Among, Between) the three of us, we should have enough money to buy lunch.

5. The cold water took my (breath, breathe) away.

PRACTICE 2: Apply Complete the following sentences with a correct word from Part I of this list (above).

1. I _____ you to be on my team last year.

2. _____ for the humidity, we had a wonderful trip.

3. We have to keep the secret _____ you and me.

4. Corkey was a _____ dog; he chewed up my shoes.

5. Take my _____ and bring a jacket.

PRACTICE 3: Write Your Own Use each pair of words correctly in a sentence of your own.

1. a/an _____

2. breath/breathe _____

3. affect/effect _____

4. already/all ready _____

5. beside/besides _____

EASILY CONFUSED WORDS, PART II

coarse/course: *Coarse* refers to something that is rough. *Course* refers to a class, a path, or a part of a meal.

> This pavement is **coarse.**
> My **course** in math is very interesting.
> The **course** they chose was difficult.
> I will prepare a four-**course** meal.

desert/dessert: *Desert* refers to dry, sandy land or means "abandon." *Dessert* refers to the last course of a meal.

> It is difficult to live in the **desert.**
> He **deserted** his family.
> We had strawberry shortcake for **dessert.**

Hint: You can remember that dessert has two *s*'s if you think of *strawberry shortcake.*

does/dose: *Does* means "performs." *Dose* refers to a specific amount of medicine.

> My sister **does** whatever she wants.
> Children should have only a small **dose** of cough syrup.

fewer/less: *Fewer* refers to things that can be counted. *Less* refers to things that cannot be counted.

> There are **fewer** cotton fields than there used to be.
> She has much **less** free time now that she has a new job.

good/well: *Good* modifies nouns. *Well* modifies verbs, adjectives, and adverbs. *Well* also refers to a state of health.

> Bill looks **good** in his new suit.
> I'm afraid I didn't do **well** on the test.
> Kate isn't feeling **well** today.

hear/here: *Hear* refers to the act of listening. *Here* means "in this place."

> My father can't **hear** as well as he used to.
> **Here** is the book you asked for.

it's/its: *It's* is the contraction for *it is* or *it has*. *Its* is a possessive pronoun.

> The teacher said **it's** important to answer all the questions.
> The dog chased **its** tail.

knew/new: *Knew* is the past tense of *know*. *New* means "recent."

> I thought everyone **knew** I had a **new** boyfriend.

know/no: *Know* means "understand." *No* means "not any" or is the opposite of *yes*.

> We all **know** that we have **no** hope of defeating the other team.
> **No,** I didn't realize that.

lay/lie: *Lay* means "set down." (Its principal parts are *lay, laid, laid*.) *Lie* means "recline." (Its principal parts are *lie, lay, lain*.)

> He **lays** brick for a living.
> He **laid** down the heavy sack.
> She **lies** down at 2 p.m. every day for a nap.
> I **lay** in the grass.

(For additional help with *lie* and *lay*, see Chapter 30, "Regular and Irregular Verbs.")

loose/lose: *Loose* means "free" or "unattached." *Lose* means "misplace" or "not win."

> Hal's pants are too **loose**.
> If I **lose** another $10, I'm going to quit gambling.

passed/past: *Passed* is the past tense of *pass*. *Past* refers to an earlier time or means "beyond."

> John **passed** by his old house on the way to school.
> It is interesting to study the **past.**
> The dog ran **past** me and into the street.

PRACTICE 4: Recall/Identify Underline the correct word in each of the following sentences.

1. We (passed, past) Edward on the freeway.

2. I think you have made a (good, well) choice.

3. With her second job, Marsha has (fewer, less) time to spend with her friends.

4. (It's, Its) going to be a beautiful day.

5. I cannot (loose, lose) this ring; it was given to me by my grandmother.

PRACTICE 5: Apply Complete the following sentences with a correct word from Part II of this list (above).

1. The restaurant served peach cobbler for _____.

2. How do you like my _____ car?

3. Mike _____ not want to go to the concert with us.

4. This business _____ will benefit me on the job.

5. I am not feeling _____ today.

PRACTICE 6: Write Your Own Use each pair of words correctly in a sentence of your own.

1. fewer/less _____

2. knew/new _____

3. hear/here _____

4. it's/its _____

5. lay/lie _____

EASILY CONFUSED WORDS, PART III

principal/principle: *Principal* means "main, most important," "a school official," or "a sum of money." A *principle* is a rule. (Think of *principle* and *rule*—both end in *-le*.)

My **principal** reason for moving is to be closer to my family.

Mr. Kobler is the **principal** at Westside Elementary School.

My **principal** and interest payments vary each month.

He lives by one main **principle**—honesty.

quiet/quite: *Quiet* means "without noise." *Quite* means "very."

The house was **quiet.**

I am **quite** happy with my new car.

raise/rise: *Raise* means "increase" or "lift up." *Rise* means "get up from a sitting or reclining position."

The state is going to **raise** the tax on cigarettes.

Jane can **rise** slowly from her wheelchair.

set/sit: *Set* means "put down." *Sit* means "take a seated position."

Set the vase on the table.

I don't like to **sit** at a desk for long periods of time.

(For additional help with *sit* and *set*, see Chapter 30, "Regular and Irregular Verbs.")

than/then: *Than* is used in making comparisons. *Then* means "next."

My mother is younger **than** my father.

I took piano lessons; **then** I took guitar lessons.

their/there/they're: *Their* is possessive. *There* indicates location. *They're* is the contraction of *they are*.

Their house burned down last year.

Too many people are living **there.**

They're all going to London.

threw/through: *Threw*, the past tense of *throw*, means "tossed." *Through* means "finished" or "passing from one point to another."

The pitcher **threw** the ball.

I am **through** with dinner.

My brother and I rode **through** the forest on our bikes.

to/too/two: *To* means "toward" or is used with a verb. *Too* means "also" or "very." *Two* is a number.

> I went **to** the store **to** buy some bread.
> I bought some artichokes **too,** even though they were **too** expensive.
> My mother has **two** sisters.

wear/were/where: *Wear* means "have on one's body." *Were* is the past tense of *be*. *Where* refers to a place.

> Can you **wear** shorts to school?
> **Where were** you yesterday?

weather/whether: *Weather* refers to outdoor conditions. *Whether* expresses possibility.

> No one knows **whether** the **weather** will get better or worse.

who's/whose: *Who's* is a contraction of *who is* or *who has*. *Whose* is a possessive pronoun.

> **Who's** going to decide **whose** car to take?

your/you're: *Your* means "belonging to you." *You're* is the contraction of *you are*.

> **Your** attention to details proves **you're** a good worker.

PRACTICE 7: Recall/Identify Underline the correct word in each of the following sentences.

1. Janene was (quiet, quite) pleased with your work.

2. (Your, You're) the best choice for this task.

3. Please (set, sit) here and wait for the doctor.

4. (Who's, Whose) planning on going to tonight's game?

5. Our (principal, principle) is retiring at the end of the year.

PRACTICE 8: Apply Complete the following sentences with a correct word from Part III of this list (above).

1. After the performance, the audience _____ flowers at the performer's feet.

2. Beatrice's _____ reason for quitting her job was the pay.

3. Finish your homework, and _____ you can watch television.

4. _____ are you going dressed like that?

5. Why did you _____ shorts in the winter?

PRACTICE 9: Write Your Own Use each set of words correctly in a sentence of your own.

1. raise/rise _____

2. their/there/they're _____

3. your/you're _____

4. set/sit _____

5. who's/whose _____

CHAPTER REVIEW

REVIEW PRACTICE 1: Recall/Identify Underline the correct word in each of the following sentences.

1. Your influence is having a positive (affect, effect) on people's lives.

2. (Who's, Whose) that girl with Paul?

3. Jade needs to stand (hear, here) when her name is announced.

4. (Your, You're) the one for me.

5. There are many different plants that grow in the (desert, dessert).

6. Sydney (choose, chose) the smallest puppy of the litter.

7. The picture has come (loose, lose) from its frame.

8. Please sit (beside, besides) me during the ceremony.

9. Your counselor gave you good (advice, advise), and you should take it.

10. Over (their, there, they're) is the house where I grew up.

REVIEW PRACTICE 2: Apply Complete the following sentences with a correct word from all three parts of the list.

1. We _____ each other when we were children.

2. Contestants should send in _____ photographs of themselves.

3. The _____ outside was so nice that we decided to walk.

4. If you leave now, you will _____ up our happy home.

5. The crowd was so _____ that you could hear people breathing.

6. Quantitative analysis is the most challenging _____ I have ever taken.

7. Jeffrey did not _____ the phone ringing.

8. I laughed so hard that I couldn't catch my _____.

9. Because of our uninvited houseguests, we have _____ food in the house.

10. Faith has _____ donated to the cause.

REVIEW PRACTICE 3: Write Your Own Write a paragraph explaining the qualities of a good friend. What are the qualities, and why do you think they are important? Try to use some of the easily confused words from this chapter.

MyWritingLab™ Complete this "Write Your Own" exercise for Chapter 51 in the MyWritingLab "Activities: Your Textbook" module.

REVIEW PRACTICE 4: Editing Through Collaboration Exchange paragraphs from Review Practice 3 with another student, and do the following:

1. Circle any words used incorrectly.

2. Write the correct form of the word above the error.

Then return the paper to its writer, and use the information in this chapter to correct any confused words in your own paragraph. Record your errors on the Error Log in Appendix 7.

MyWritingLab™ Visit Chapter 51, "Easily Confused Words," in MyWritingLab, and complete the Post-test to check your understanding of the chapter's objectives.

52

Spelling

Underline and correct the misspelled words in the following sentences.

- What is your new addres?
- Turn left on the third avenu.
- I was using the wrong calender when I made out the scheduel.
- The dealer delt me a good hand.
- Please get all the items on the grocry list.

(Answers are in Appendix 3.)

If you think back over your education, you will realize that teachers believe spelling is important. There is a good reason they feel this way: Spelling errors send negative messages. Misspellings seem to leap out at readers, creating serious doubts about the writer's abilities in general. Because you will not always have access to spell-checkers—and because spell-checkers do not catch all spelling errors—improving your spelling skills is important.

Student Comment:
"Everything's repeated in **MyWritingLab,** and I need that because my memory is short."

MyWritingLab **Understanding Spelling**

To improve your understanding of this topic, go to **MyWritingLab. com,** and choose **Spelling** in the **Punctuation, Mechanics, and Spelling** module. From there, watch the video called **Animation: Spelling**. Then, return to this chapter, which will go into more detail about spelling rules and give you opportunities to practice them. Finally, you will apply your understanding of these rules to your own writing.

SPELLING HINTS

The spelling rules in this chapter will help you become a better speller. But first, here are some practical hints that will also help you improve your spelling.

1. Start a personal spelling list of your own. Use the list of commonly misspelled words on pages 726–730 as your starting point.

2. Study the lists of easily confused words in Chapter 51.

3. Avoid all nonstandard expressions (see Chapter 50).

4. Use a dictionary when you run across words you don't know.

5. Run the spell-check program if you are writing on a computer. Keep in mind, however, that spell-check cannot tell if you have incorrectly used one word in place of another (such as *to*, *too*, or *two*).

PRACTICE 1A: Recall/Identify Underline the misspelled words in each of the following sentences. Refer to the list of easily confused words in Chapter 51 and to the list of most commonly misspelled words in this chapter as necessary.

1. "We want to go to," cried the children. *too*

2. The baloon floated away in the breeze.

3. With John's promotion came a better salry.

4. This vacation has had a relaxing affect on my attitude.

5. It was an akward situation when the bride wouldn't say, "I do."

PRACTICE 1B: Correct Correct the spelling errors in Practice 1A by rewriting the incorrect sentences.

PRACTICE 2: Apply Fill in each blank in the following sentences with hints that help with spelling.

1. Use a _____ to look up words you don't know.

2. You can always use the _____ on your computer, but you should remember that it cannot catch confused words—only misspelled words.

3. Start a _____ to help you remember words you commonly misspell.

4. Study the list of _____ in Chapter _____.

5. Try to avoid all _____ English.

PRACTICE 3: Write Your Own Choose the correctly spelled word in each pair, and write a sentence using it. Refer to the spelling list on pages 726–730 if necessary.

1. concieve/conceive _____

2. absence/absense _____

3. vaccum/vacuum _____

4. library/libary _____

5. delt/dealt _____

SPELLING RULES

Four basic spelling rules can help you avoid many misspellings. It pays to spend a little time learning them now.

1. **Words that end in -e:** When adding a suffix beginning with a vowel (*a, e, i, o, u*), drop the final -e.

    achieve + -ing   =   achieving

    include + -ed   =   included

    value + -able   =   valuable

    When adding a suffix beginning with a consonant, keep the final -e.

    aware + -ness   =   awareness

    improve + -ment   =   improvement

    leisure + -ly   =   leisurely

2. **Words with ie and ei:** Put *i* before *e* except after *c* or when sounded like *ay* as in *neighbor* and *weigh*.

c + ei	(no c) + ie	Exceptions
receive	grieve	leisure
conceive	niece	foreign
deceive	friend	height
neighbor	relief	science

3. **Words that end in -y:** When adding a suffix to a word that ends in a consonant plus -y, change the y to *i*.

    happy + -er   =   happier

    dry + -ed   =   dried

    easy + -est   =   easiest

4. **Words that double the final consonant:** When adding a suffix starting with a vowel to a one-syllable word, double the final consonant.

big + -est	=	biggest
quit + -er	=	quitter
bet + -ing	=	betting

With words of more than one syllable, double the final consonant if (1) the final syllable is stressed and (2) the word ends in a single vowel plus a single consonant.

begin + -ing	=	beginning
transmit + -ing	=	transmitting
excel + -ed	=	excelled

The word *travel* has more than one syllable. Should you double the final consonant? No, you should not, because the stress is on the *first* syllable (**tra´** *vel*). The word ends in a vowel and a consonant, but that is not enough. Both parts of the rule must be met.

PRACTICE 4A: Recall/Identify Underline the spelling errors in each of the following sentences.

1. It's not like we're commiting a crime.

2. The boundarys have been clearly marked.

3. You are so wierd.

4. Our bagage was lost somewhere in New York.

5. The facilitys are near one another.

PRACTICE 4B: Correct Correct the spelling errors in Practice 4A by rewriting the incorrect sentences.

PRACTICE 5: Apply Complete the following spelling rules.

1. When adding a suffix beginning with a vowel to a word that ends in -e, _____.

2. With words of more than one syllable, _____ the final consonant if (1) the final syllable is _____ and (2) the word ends in a single _____ plus a single _____.

3. Put *i* before *e* except after _____ or when sounded like _____ as in *neighbor* and *weigh*.

4. When adding a suffix starting with a _____ to a one-syllable word, _____ the final consonant.

5. When adding a suffix to a word that ends in a consonant plus -y, change the _____ to _____.

PRACTICE 6: Write Your Own Make a list of words you commonly misspell. Then choose five of the words, and use each correctly in a sentence.

MOST COMMONLY MISSPELLED WORDS

Use the following list of commonly misspelled words to check your spelling when you write.

abbreviate	aluminum	baggage
absence	amateur	balloon
accelerate	ambulance	banana
accessible	ancient	bankrupt
accidentally	anonymous	banquet
accommodate	anxiety	beautiful
accompany	anxious	beggar
accomplish	appreciate	beginning
accumulate	appropriate	behavior
accurate	approximate	benefited
ache	architect	bicycle
achievement	arithmetic	biscuit
acknowledgment	artificial	bought
acre	assassin	boundary
actual	athletic	brilliant
address	attach	brought
adequate	audience	buoyant
advertisement	authority	bureau
afraid	autumn	burglar
aggravate	auxiliary	business
aisle	avenue	cabbage
although	awkward	cafeteria
calendar	condemn	disappear
campaign	conference	disastrous
canoe	congratulate	discipline

canyon	conscience	disease
captain	consensus	dissatisfied
career	continuous	divisional
carriage	convenience	dormitory
cashier	cooperate	economy
catastrophe	corporation	efficiency
caterpillar	correspond	eighth
ceiling	cough	elaborate
cemetery	counterfeit	electricity
census	courageous	eligible
certain	courteous	embarrass
certificate	cozy	emphasize
challenge	criticize	employee
champion	curiosity	encourage
character	curious	enormous
chief	curriculum	enough
children	cylinder	enthusiastic
chimney	dairy	envelope
coffee	dangerous	environment
collar	dealt	equipment
college	deceive	equivalent
column	decision	especially
commit	definition	essential
committee	delicious	establish
communicate	descend	exaggerate
community	describe	excellent
comparison	description	exceptionally
competent	deteriorate	excessive
competition	determine	exhaust
complexion	development	exhilarating
conceive	dictionary	existence
concession	difficulty	explanation
concrete	diploma	extinct
extraordinary	height	knife
familiar	hesitate	knowledge
famous	hoping	knuckles

fascinate	humorous	laboratory
fashion	hygiene	laborious
fatigue	hymn	language
faucet	icicle	laugh
February	illustrate	laundry
fiery	imaginary	league
financial	immediately	legible
foreign	immortal	legislature
forfeit	impossible	leisure
fortunate	incidentally	length
forty	incredible	library
freight	independence	license
friend	indispensable	lieutenant
fundamental	individual	lightning
gauge	inferior	likable
genius	infinite	liquid
genuine	influential	listen
geography	initial	literature
gnaw	initiation	machinery
government	innocence	magazine
graduation	installation	magnificent
grammar	intelligence	majority
grief	interfere	manufacture
grocery	interrupt	marriage
gruesome	invitation	material
guarantee	irrelevant	mathematics
guess	irrigate	maximum
guidance	issue	mayor
handkerchief	jealous	meant
handsome	jewelry	medicine
haphazard	journalism	message
happiness	judgment	mileage
harass	kindergarten	miniature
minimum	patience	rhythm
minute	peculiar	salary
mirror	permanent	satisfactory
miscellaneous	persistent	scarcity

mischievous	personnel	scenery
miserable	persuade	schedule
misspell	physician	science
monotonous	pitcher	scissors
mortgage	pneumonia	secretary
mysterious	politician	seize
necessary	possess	separate
neighborhood	prairie	significant
niece	precede	similar
nineteen	precious	skiing
ninety	preferred	soldier
noticeable	prejudice	souvenir
nuisance	previous	sovereign
obedience	privilege	spaghetti
obstacle	procedure	squirrel
occasion	proceed	statue
occurred	pronounce	stomach
official	psychology	strength
omission	publicly	subtle
omitted	questionnaire	succeed
opponent	quotient	success
opportunity	realize	sufficient
opposite	receipt	surprise
original	recipe	syllable
outrageous	recommend	symptom
pamphlet	reign	technique
paragraph	religious	temperature
parallel	representative	temporary
parentheses	reservoir	terrible
partial	responsibility	theater
particular	restaurant	thief
pastime	rhyme ↔ rhythm	thorough
tobacco	vacuum	weird
tomorrow	valuable	whose
tongue	various	width
tournament	vegetable	worst
tragedy	vehicle	wreckage

truly	vicinity	writing
unanimous	villain	yacht
undoubtedly	visible	yearn
unique	volunteer	yield
university	weather	zealous
usable	Wednesday	zoology
usually	weigh	

PRACTICE 7A: Recall/Identify Underline any words that are misspelled in the following sentences.

1. This steak and lobster dinner is incredable.

2. You shouldn't condem others for doing what you do.

3. Valentine's Day is in Febuary.

4. How long have you been writting that novel?

5. I know you will suceed in college.

PRACTICE 7B: Correct Correct any spelling errors you identified in Practice 7A by rewriting the incorrect sentences.

PRACTICE 8: Apply Cross out and correct the spelling errors in the following paragraph.

I was eating a plate of spagetti when the phone rang. It was my nieghbor. He said, "The big fight is begining in 15 minutes, and my television screen just went out." He then beged me to let him come over and watch it at my house. So I told him that was fine. He neglected to tell me, however, that he wouldn't be alone. He and seven of his rowdy freinds invaded my house, ate my spagetti and drank my soda, and left a catastrophy behind. I think the next time I have a party, I'll have it at his house.

PRACTICE 9: Write Your Own Write a complete sentence for each word listed here.

1. appreciate _____

2. laundry _____

3. marriage _____

4. excellent _____

5. opposite _____

CHAPTER REVIEW

REVIEW PRACTICE 1: Recall/Identify Underline the misspelled words in each of the following sentences.

1. I'm trying to catch the rythm of this music.

2. You ate my desert.

3. This essay shows improvment.

4. Ramona is a genuis with figures.

5. The firy-hot peppers made my eyes water.

6. Most teenagers want their independance.

7. If we stick to the scedule, we should make it home before tomorow.

8. Breath deeply, and put your head between your legs.

9. My family lives in seperate states.

10. Dr. Murphy rides his bycicle to work every day.

REVIEW PRACTICE 2: Apply Correct the spelling errors in Review Practice 1 by rewriting the incorrect sentences.

REVIEW PRACTICE 3: Write Your Own Write a paragraph explaining how to become a better speller. Are there any hints that may help?

MyWritingLab™ Complete this "Write Your Own" exercise for Chapter 52 in the MyWritingLab "Activities: Your Textbook" module.

REVIEW PRACTICE 4: Editing Through Collaboration Exchange paragraphs from Review Practice 3 with another student, and do the following:

1. Underline any words that are used incorrectly.
2. Circle any misspelled words.

Then return the paper to its writer, and use the information in this chapter to correct any spelling errors in your own paragraph. Record your errors on the Spelling Log in Appendix 7.

MyWritingLab™ Visit Chapter 52, "Spelling," in MyWritingLab, and complete the Post-test to check your understanding of the chapter's objectives.

Appendix 1: Critical Thinking Log

Circle the critical thinking questions you missed after each essay you read. Have your instructor explain the pattern of errors.

Reading	Content	Purpose and Audience		Essays			Number Correct
Describing							
Matthews Brooks Treacy	1 2 3	4 5 6		7 8 9 10			
Paul Martinez	1 2 3	4 5 6		7 8 9 10			
Narrating							
Lynda Barry	1 2 3	4 5 6		7 8 9 10			
Alice Walker	1 2 3	4 5 6		7 8 9 10			
Illustrating							
Matt Huston	1 2 3	4 5 6		7 8 9 10			
France Borel	1 2 3	4 5 6		7 8 9 10			
Analyzing a Process							
Brian O'Connell	1 2 3	4 5 6		7 8 9 10			
Sarah Adams	1 2 3	4 5 6		7 8 9 10			
Comparing/Contrasting							
Yi-Fu Tuan	1 2 3	4 5 6		7 8 9 10			
Tony Cohan	1 2 3	4 5 6		7 8 9 10			
Dividing/Classifying							
Tracy Cutchlow	1 2 3	4 5 6		7 8 9 10			
Marion Winik	1 2 3	4 5 6		7 8 9 10			
Defining							
World Freerunning Parkour Federation	1 2 3	4 5 6		7 8 9 10			
Daniel Hernandez	1 2 3	4 5 6		7 8 9 10			
Analyzing Causes/Effects							
Maria Konnikova	1 2 3	4 5 6		7 8 9 10			
Stacey Colino	1 2 3	4 5 6		7 8 9 10			
Arguing							
Warner Todd Huston	1 2 3	4 5 6		7 8 9 10			
Cary and Chapman	1 2 3	4 5 6		7 8 9 10			

Legend for Critical Thinking Log	
Questions	**Skill**
1–2	Literal and interpretive understanding
3–6	Critical thinking and analysis
7–9	Analyzing sentences
10	Writing essays

Appendix 2A: Your EQ (Editing Quotient)

A good way to approach editing is by finding your EQ (Editing Quotient). Knowing your EQ will help you look for specific errors in your writing and make your editing more efficient.

In each of the following paragraphs, underline the errors you find, and list them on the lines below the paragraph. The number of errors corresponds to the letters in each paragraph.

The possible errors are listed here:

apostrophe	end punctuation	pronoun agreement
capitalization	fragment	Spelling
comma	fused sentence	subject-verb agreement
comma splice	modifier	verb form
confused word	pronoun	

1. Many people seem to have a telephone permanently attached to one ear [a]people have several phone lines going into their homes. [b]And cell phones hanging off of their belts. People are talking on their cell phones in restaurants, in cars, and even in public bathrooms. When they go home, they go online to check email. [c]While the second line is ringing off the hook. Why would someone want to be available every second of the day? This rushed society will eventually have to slow down, [d]people can't live at this pace for long.

   a. _____

   b. _____

   c. _____

   d. _____

2. Recently, a major computer software company was accused of being a monopoly. That is, it seemed to be trying to control the whole software industry. The company, [a]reality software, sells many different types of software at reasonable prices. [b]Which results in the company selling more products than its competitors. Reality Software also signed contracts with [c]Computer Manufacturers that allow the manufacturers to install Reality programs on computers before they are sold. The courts, which guard against monopolies, say this is unfair to consumers, [d]buyers should be able to choose their software. It is also unfair to other software companies. [e]Because they are not given a fair chance to sell their products.

   a. _____

   b. _____

   c. _____

   d. _____

   e. _____

3. Public speaking is a valuable tool no matter what career path a [a]person take. At some point in every career, if a person is going to advance, [b]they will have to speak to a group. In fact, the higher up the career ladder a [c]person climb, the more public speaking

will be required. It is good preparation, therefore, to take a public speaking course in college, [d]a public speaking course not only teaches the skills involved in making a presentation but also builds a person's confidence.

a. _____

b. _____

c. _____

d. _____

4. Anyone who thinks a surprise birthday party takes a lot of time and work should try planning a wedding. Until a person plans his or her own wedding, [a]they can't fully understand all the details that must be considered. [b]Too my way of thinking, long engagements aren't to find out how compatible the couple is. [c]There to allow enough time to find a place to hold the reception. [d]On the date you want. [e]Plus a good caterer and music. Even the smallest detail must be considered, such as whether guests should throw rice [f]birdseed [g]or confetti at the happy couple after the ceremony.

a. _____

b. _____

c. _____

d. _____

e. _____

f. _____

g. _____

5. A famous author once said that his messy handwriting, [a]almost kept him from becoming a writer. [b]Struggling to be legible, the pages were impossible to read. No matter how hard he tried, his handwriting would become rushed and scribbled. He would write wonderful novels that only he could read, [c]for his twenty-third birthday his wife bought him a typewriter. He then began to write books. [d]That people all over the world have read. If he were alive today, he could write on a computer.

a. _____

b. _____

c. _____

d. _____

6. Everyone has heard the term "best [a]freind." What is a best friend? Some people [b]beleive that their oldest friend is [c]they're best friend. Yet a best friend can be someone from college or even someone who is family. [d]Such as a brother or sister. No matter who qualifies as a best friend, two [e]facts is true: A best [f]freind is someone special and trustworthy. People may wonder how they could get along without their best friend? [g]Most people couldn't.

a. _____

b. _____

c. _____

d. _____

e. _____

f. _____

g. _____

7. If I had my way, I would require every college student to take a course in geography. It is [a]embarassing how little the average American knows about [b]his own country, to say nothing of other countries. For instance, do you know the capital of [c]virginia? Can you name all the Great Lakes? On which continent is [d]greece? If you can answer these questions[e] you are one of very few people. People think geography is boring[f] but it isn't. [g]Its fascinating to learn about the world we live in.

a. _____

b. _____

c. _____

d. _____

e. _____

f. _____

g. _____

8. I believe that fast-food restaurants should change [a]there names to "fast food sometimes, but at least faster than a sit-down restaurant." When I go through the drive-up window at a fast-food [b]restaraunt, it is because I am in a hurry and want to get something to eat quickly, [c]however, sometimes it would be quicker for me to go home and cook a three-course meal. I do not understand what could take so long. I pull up to the intercom, order my food, [d]procede to the window, and wait. If fast food always lived up to its name [e]I would be able to get food fast.

a. _____

b. _____

c. _____

d. _____

e. _____

9. Doing the family laundry used to be a chore for me[a] but now I am a pro. First, I sort the clothes according to colors or whites. Before I learned this basic rule, my poor brother had to wear pink underwear from time to time. Next, I put the clothes in the washing machine,[b] and add detergent. If I'm doing whites [c]I also add bleach. I close the lid, turn the dial to hot wash and cold rinse, and push the "start" button. I allow the washing machine to do [d]it's work while I read a magazine. When it's time to put the clothes in the dryer, I pay attention to the drying instructions on the tags. Once I neglected this

step, and my favorite pants ᵉshrinked. When the dryer has done its work, I remove the clothes immediately so they do not become ᶠrinkled.

a. _____

b. _____

c. _____

d. _____

e. _____

f. _____

10. It's fun to watch a person with ᵃtheir animals. For instance, the lady down the street takes her dog for a walk every morning. The dog is a tiny rat terrier, ᵇit is really cute. The lady puts a little leash on the dog. ᶜTo keep him from running away. Even though the ᵈdogs legs are short, he can run ᵉreal fast. The dog seems so happy during his walks. He jumps and yips. The lady and her dog are a good pair ᶠthey enjoy walking with each other and keeping each other company.

a. _____

b. _____

c. _____

d. _____

e. _____

f. _____

Appendix 2B: Editing Quotient Answers

Use the answers below to score your EQ. Mark the answers that you missed.

1. a. *fused sentence or end punctuation*

   b. *fragment*

   c. *fragment*

   d. *comma splice or end punctuation*

2. a. *capitalization*

   b. *fragment*

   c. *capitalization*

   d. *comma splice or end punctuation*

   e. *fragment*

3. a. *subject-verb agreement*

   b. *pronoun agreement*

   c. *subject-verb agreement*

   d. *comma splice or end punctuation*

4. a. *pronoun agreement*

   b. *confused word*

   c. *confused word*

   d. *fragment*

   e. *fragment*

f. comma

g. comma

5. a. comma

b. modifier

c. comma splice or end punctuation

d. fragment

6. a. spelling

b. spelling

c. confused word

d. fragment

e. subject-verb agreement

f. spelling

g. end punctuation

7. a. spelling

b. pronoun

c. capitalization

d. capitalization

e. comma

f. comma

g. confused word or apostrophe

8. a. confused word

b. spelling

c. comma splice or end punctuation

d. spelling

e. comma

9. a. comma

b. comma

c. comma

d. confused word or apostrophe

e. verb form

f. spelling

10. a. pronoun agreement

b. comma splice or end punctuation

c. fragment

d. apostrophe

e. modifier

f. fused sentence or end punctuation

Appendix 2C: Editing Quotient Error Chart

Put an X in the square that corresponds to each error you made. Then record your errors in the categories below to find out where you might need help.

	a	b	c	d	e	f	g
1							
2							
3							
4							
5							
6							
7							
8							
9							
10							

Fragments 1b _____ 1c _____ 2b _____ 2e _____ 4d _____

4e _____ 5d _____ 6d _____ 10c _____

Fused sentences and comma splices 1a _____ 1d _____ 2d _____ 3d _____ 5c _____

8c _____ 10b _____ 10f _____

Subject-verb agreement 3a _____ 3c _____ 6e _____

Verb forms 9e _____

Pronoun errors 7b _____

Pronoun agreement 3b _____ 4a _____ 10a _____

Modifiers 5b _____ 10e _____

End punctuation 1a _____ 1d _____ 2d _____ 3d _____ 5c _____

6g _____ 8c _____ 10b _____ 10f _____

Commas 4f _____ 4g _____ 5a _____ 7e _____ 7f _____

8e _____ 9a _____ 9b _____ 9c _____

Apostrophes 7g _____ 9d _____ 10d _____

Capitalization 2a _____ 2c _____ 7c _____ 7d _____

Confused words 4b _____ 4c _____ 6c _____ 7g _____ 8a _____

9d _____

Spelling 6a _____ 6b _____ 6f _____ 7a _____ 8b _____

8d _____ 9f _____

Appendix 3: Test Yourself Answers

Here are the answers to the Test Yourself questions from the beginning of each chapter in the Handbook (Part IV). Where are your strengths? Where are your weaknesses?

Chapter 25: Parts of Speech (p. 492)

adj *n* *v* *adv* *adj* *n* *adj* *adj* *n* *adj*
Professional basketball is definitely this nation's best spectator sport. The talented

n *v* *prep* *n* *adv* *adv* *pro* *n* *adv* *v* *n*
players move around the court so quickly that the audience never has a chance

prep *v* *adj* *int* *pro/v* *adv* *v* *adj* *adj* *n* *adj* *n*
to become bored. Boy, I'll never forget that Saturday night last February

conj *pro* *adj* *n* *v* *pro* *prep* *v* *adj* *n* *prep* *n*
when my favorite uncle took me to see the Spurs game against the Trailblazers.

pro *v* *adj* *adj* *n* *prep* *n* *conj* *n* *v* *adj*
It was an important home game for San Antonio, so the arena was packed. The

n *v* *adv* *prep* *pro* *prep* *n* *conj* *pro* *v* *prep* *conj*
Spurs were behind throughout most of the game, but they pulled through and

v *prep* *adj* *n* *prep* *adj* *adj* *n* *int* *pro* *v* *adv* *v* *adv*
won with a three pointer in the last few seconds. Wow! I have never seen so

adj *n* *prep* *pro* *n* *conj* *v* *prep* *n* *prep* *pro* *n*
many people on their feet and screaming at the top of their lungs.

Chapter 26: Phrases and Clauses (p. 507)

<u>Using the computer</u>, [I got most <u>of the research</u> done <u>for my report</u>].

<u>To be totally confident</u>, [I checked <u>for spelling and grammar errors</u> twice].

[Susan lives <u>in the gray house at the end of Maple Avenue behind the bank</u>].

[Magdalena <u>will be a great attorney</u>] [because she argues so well].

[You <u>don't understand the math concept</u>], [so I <u>will keep going over it with you</u>].

Chapter 27: Subjects and Verbs (p. 513)

<u>You</u> <u>are</u> my best friend.

<u>Hang</u> up your clothes. (<u>You</u>)

<u>They</u> really <u>wanted</u> to be here tonight.

<u>He</u> <u>made</u> a sandwich and <u>put</u> it in a brown paper bag.

<u>Susie</u> and <u>Tom</u> <u>went</u> to the dance.

Chapter 28: Fragments (p. 520)

_____ I wanted to go to the gym yesterday.

___X___ Whose tie doesn't match his suit.

___X___ Giving up his seat for an elderly woman.

_____ Paul asked for the most popular menu item.

___X___ While the captain was away from the cockpit.

Chapter 29: Fused Sentences and Comma Splices (p. 530)

The rainstorm washed out my garden,/I had just planted spring bulbs.

When we cleaned the house, we found the TV remote control/it was between the sofa cushions.

People in authority are often criticized and seldom thanked.

The kids didn't find all of the Easter eggs during the hunt,/when we finally found them, they were rotten.

You should ask Aubri to cut your hair/she's been cutting mine for four years.

Chapter 30: Regular and Irregular Verbs (p. 538)

___X___ The pipe <u>has bursted</u>.

_____ Sim <u>reacted</u> to the scene calmly.

_____ I <u>bought</u> my car at an auction.

___X___ We <u>had hid</u> in the basement.

___X___ Sorry, I <u>eated</u> all the cookies.

Chapter 31: Verb Tense (p. 548)

___X___ Jean always <u>laugh</u> when I <u>tell</u> that joke.

_____ Mark <u>jumped</u> over the hurdle and <u>crossed</u> the finish line.

___X___ I <u>had spoke</u> to the sales clerk about a discount.

___X___ Students <u>ain't allowed</u> to bring food and drink into the computer lab.

___X___ My two cats <u>be playing</u> in the sunshine.

Chapter 32: Subject-Verb Agreement (p. 560)

_____X_____ Neither the <u>shorts</u> nor the <u>shirt</u> <u>fit</u> me.

_____ <u>Chips and dip</u> <u>is</u> my favorite snack.

_____X_____ There <u>were</u> a large <u>storm</u> last night.

_____X_____ <u>Some</u> of the soil, along with the fertilizer, <u>are</u> for the orchard.

_____ <u>Cotton and silk</u> <u>are</u> more comfortable than wool.

Chapter 33: More on Verbs (p. 571)

_____I_____ George raced across the field and catches the ball.

_____P_____ The old record was broken by Justin.

_____P_____ That painting was done by a famous artist.

_____I_____ In the future, we may live on Mars, and we have produced our food in greenhouses.

_____I_____ First, the baker prepares the dough, and then she will cut out the cookies.

Chapter 34: Pronoun Problems (p. 577)

The ball was ~~their's~~ to begin with.   *(theirs)*

Tom told Valerie and ~~I~~ the most exciting story.   *(me)*

James can type a lot faster than ~~me~~.   *(I)*

Those ~~there~~ running shoes are Kim's.

~~Me and~~ Julio are going to the movies tonight.   *(Julio and I)*

Chapter 35: Pronoun Reference and Point of View (p. 587)

<u>It</u>ˣ says to schedule <u>your</u> own appointments.

Millie and Tanya were planning to go to Las Vegas, but <u>her</u>ˣ car broke.

<u>I</u> created a backup plan because <u>you</u>ˣ should always be prepared for the unexpected.

<u>You</u>ˣ know <u>they</u>ˣ are covering up evidence of alien beings.

Jimmy forgot the answers to questions 1 and 10, but <u>he</u> remembered <u>it</u>ˣ the next day.

Chapter 36: Pronoun Agreement (p. 594)

Somebody left <u>his</u> light on in <u>his</u> car.

A judge must put aside <u>her</u> bias.

<u>Each</u> of the children needs <u>their</u> permission slip signed.

<u>None</u> of the fans could keep <u>their</u> voices quiet.

A motorcyclist must take care of <u>her</u> gear.

Chapter 37: Adjectives (p. 602)

The kites were very <u>colorful</u>.

She has the <u>worstest</u> <u>hair</u> color that I have ever seen.

We were <u>more</u> <u>busier</u> <u>this</u> week than <u>last</u> week.

He is the <u>oldest</u> of the <u>two</u> brothers.

The <u>Ford</u> Mustang is <u>more better</u> than the <u>Nissan</u> Sentra.

Chapter 38: Adverbs (p. 611)

The pants fit me <u>too</u> <u>loose</u>, so I returned them to the store.

Tori was<u>n't</u> <u>never</u> <u>so</u> happy as after she won the lottery.

When Madeline returned from Paris, she said she had a <u>real</u> good time.

We <u>happily</u> made more ice cream when our first supply ran out.

I wanted <u>so</u> <u>bad</u> to win the race, but I could<u>n't</u> catch up.

Chapter 39: Modifier Errors (p. 621)

<u>After studying together</u>, his grades really improved.

<u>Before doing the laundry</u>, the car needed to be washed.

<u>To get a good job</u>, the interview must go well.

The professor told the class he was retiring <u>before he dismissed them</u>.

I wrote a letter to the newspaper <u>that complained about rising power bills</u>.

Chapter 40: End Punctuation (p. 629)

How are we going to get there*?*

That's amazing*!*

Get me a Pepsi, please.

This will never happen to me*!*

Can you make your own dinner tonight*?*

Chapter 41: Commas (p. 635)

We drove to the beach, and we had a picnic.

Before I eat breakfast, I take a multivitamin.

"This is my favorite restaurant," said Matt.

Email, though, makes corresponding easy and fast.

They were married on February 14, 2004, in Las Vegas, Nevada.

Chapter 42: Apostrophes (p. 646)

The flight crew was surprised by the pilot's rudeness when he boarded the plane.

It's important that the car has its engine checked every 3,000 miles.

What's going to happen after Dominic's gone?

The men's bathroom is located on the third floor.

James's house is the third one on the left.

Chapter 43: Quotation Marks (p. 653)

"Can we go out to dinner tonight?" she asked.

Jeri screamed, "Don't go in there!"

"If you can't find my house," Tom said, "call me on your cell phone."

My favorite poem is "The Red Wheelbarrow" by William Carlos Williams.

David said, "I'll fix your car this weekend."

Chapter 44: Other Punctuation Marks (p. 661)

Kris left for the dance; Sean decided to stay home.

We wanted to win; therefore, we practiced every day.

The computer's advertised price didn't include several important parts: a monitor, a printer, and speakers. *(or —)*

Ramon asked the best question during the interview—"Why should we vote for you?" *(or :)*

Bring the jelly to a "rolling boil" *(*a boil that cannot be stirred down*)*.

Chapter 45: Capitalization (p. 669)

According to <u>u</u>ncle Bob, <u>m</u>other makes the best <u>t</u>exas sheet cake. *(Uncle, Mother, Texas)*

Antonio is a <u>n</u>ative <u>a</u>merican. *(Native American)*

"<u>t</u>he shortest path," he said, "<u>I</u>s down <u>b</u>aker <u>s</u>treet." *(The, is, Baker Street)*

<u>i</u>ssa loves to go to <u>w</u>alt <u>d</u>isney <u>w</u>orld. *(Issa, Walt Disney World)*

Last year, I saw the <u>r</u>ed <u>h</u>ot <u>c</u>hili <u>p</u>eppers in concert. *(Red Hot Chili Peppers)*

Chapter 46: Abbreviations and Numbers (p. 675)

He earned <u>two million three hundred thousand dollars</u> last year. *($2,300,000)*

My cat had <u>5</u> kittens. *(five)*

Sherril moved from England to the <u>U.S.</u> *(United States)*

<u>Mister</u> Johnson always drinks hot chocolate in the mornings. *(Mr.)*

I work for the <u>Internal Revenue Service</u>. *(IRS)*

Chapter 47: Varying Sentence Structure (p. 683)

Answers will vary.

Chapter 48: Parallelism (p. 689)

Tony enjoys <u>hockey</u>, <u>football</u>, and <u>runs</u>.

My mom and dad give money <u>to help the homeless</u> and <u>for building new homes</u>.

I finished high school, started college, and I am beginning a new job.

I love the mountains because they're cool, clean, and feel refreshing.

Listening to music, watching television, or to read a book are good ways to relax.

Chapter 49: Combining Sentences (p. 694)

Answers will vary.

Chapter 50: Standard and Nonstandard English (p. 704)

You shoulda seen Claudia's new hairstyle. *(Incorrect)*

Where are my friends at? *(Incorrect)*

Your new bike is really hot. *(Slang)*

Randy was enthused about his date. *(Slang)*

Christina Aguilera's new video rocks. *(Slang)*

Chapter 51: Easily Confused Words (p. 712)

Miranda couldn't (choose, chose) a college.

(It's, Its) time to leave for the show.

I can't (hear, here) with all this noise.

(Weather, Whether) you go or not, I still want to attend.

(Who's, Whose) responsible for this mess?

Chapter 52: Spelling (p. 722)

What is your new adress? *(address)*

Turn left on the third avenu. *(avenue)*

I was using the wrong calender when I made out the scheduel. *(calendar, schedule)*

The dealer delt me a good hand. *(dealt)*

Please get all the items on the grocry list. *(grocery)*

Appendix 4: Revising an Essay

Revising Peer Evaluation Form A

Use the following questions to evaluate your partner's essay in a particular rhetorical mode. Then, continue your evaluation with the standard revision items in Revising Peer Evaluation Form B. Direct your comments to your partner. Explain your answers as thoroughly as possible to help your partner revise.

WRITER: _____   PEER: _____

Describing

1. Is the dominant impression clearly communicated?
2. Does the essay use objective and subjective descriptions when needed?
3. Does the essay draw on all five senses?
4. Does the essay show rather than tell?

Narrating

5. What is the essay's main point? If you're not sure, show the writer how he or she can make the main point clearer.
6. Does the writer use the five Ws and one H to construct the essay? Where does the essay need more information?
7. Does the writer develop the essay with vivid details? Where can more details be added?
8. Does the writer build excitement with careful pacing?

Illustrating

9. What is the essay's main point? If you're not sure, show the writer how he or she can make the main point clearer.
10. Did the writer choose examples that are relevant to the main point? If not, which examples need to be changed?
11. Does the writer choose examples the reader can identify with? If not, which examples need to be changed?
12. Does the writer use a sufficient number of examples to make his or her point? Where can more examples be added?

Analyzing a Process

13. Does the writer state in the thesis statement what the reader should be able to do or understand by the end of the essay? If not, what information does the thesis statement need to be clearer?
14. Does the writer know his or her audience?
15. Does the remainder of the essay explain the rest of the process? If not, what seems to be missing?
16. Does the writer end the process essay by considering the process as a whole?

Comparing and Contrasting

17. Does the writer state the point he or she is trying to make in the thesis statement?
18. Does the writer choose items to compare and contrast that will make his or her point most effectively? What details need to be added to make the comparison more effective?
19. Does the writer use as many specific details and examples as possible to expand the comparison?
20. Is the comparison developed in a balanced way?

Dividing and Classifying

21. What is the overall purpose for the essay, and is it stated in the thesis statement? If not, where does the essay need clarification?
22. Did the writer divide the general topic into categories that don't overlap?
23. Did the writer clearly explain each category?
24. Does each topic fit into a category?

Defining

25. Did the writer choose a word or idea carefully and give readers a working definition of it in the thesis statement?
26. Does the writer define his or her term or idea by synonym, category, or negation? Is this approach effective? Why or why not?
27. Does the writer use examples to expand on his or her definition of the term or idea? Where does the definition need more information?
28. Does the writer use other rhetorical strategies—such as description, comparison, or process analysis—to support the definition?

Analyzing Causes and Effects

29. Does the thesis statement make a clear statement about what is being analyzed? If not, what information does it need to be clearer?
30. Did the writer choose facts and details to support the topic sentence? What details need to be added?
31. Does the writer confuse coincidence with causes or effects?
32. Does the writer include the real causes and effects for his or her topic? What details are unnecessary?

Arguing

33. Does the writer state his or her opinion on the subject matter in the thesis statement? What information is missing?
34. Who is the intended audience for this essay? Does the writer adequately persuade this audience? Why or why not?
35. Does the writer choose appropriate evidence to support the thesis statement? What evidence is needed? What evidence is unnecessary?
36. Does the writer anticipate the opposing points of view?
37. Does the writer find some common ground with opponents?
38. Does the writer maintain a reasonable tone?

Revising Peer Evaluation Form B

After applying the specialized questions in Revising Peer Evaluation Form A to your partner's essay, use the following questions to help you complete the revision process. Direct your comments to your partner. Explain your answers as thoroughly as possible to help your partner revise.

WRITER: _____ PEER: _____

Thesis Statement

1. Does the thesis statement contain the essay's controlling idea and an opinion about that idea?
2. Does the thesis appear as the last sentence of the introduction?

Basic Elements

3. Does the title draw in the readers?
4. Does the introduction capture the readers' attention and build up effectively to the thesis statement?
5. Does each body paragraph deal with a single topic?
6. Does the conclusion bring the essay to a close in an interesting way?

Development

7. Do the body paragraphs adequately support the thesis statement?
8. Does each body paragraph have a focused topic sentence?
9. Does each body paragraph contain *specific* details that support the topic sentence?
10. Does each body paragraph include *enough* details to fully explain the topic sentence?

Unity

11. Do all the essay's topic sentences relate directly to the thesis statement?
12. Do the details in each paragraph support the paragraph's topic sentence?

Organization

13. Is the essay organized logically?
14. Is each body paragraph organized logically?

Coherence

15. Are transitions used effectively so that paragraphs move smoothly and logically from one to the next?
16. Do the sentences move smoothly and logically from one to the next?

Use Appendix 6 to check for grammar and usage errors in your essay.

Appendix 5: Revising a Research Paper

Research Paper Peer Evaluation Form

Use the following questions to evaluate your partner's paper. Direct your comments to your partner. Explain your answers as thoroughly as possible to help your partner revise.

WRITER: _____ PEER: _____

Writing an Essay with Sources

1. Did the writer choose a subject that is neither too broad nor too narrow?
2. Did the writer find sources that are relevant, reliable, and recent to support the thesis?
3. Do you see any problems with plagiarism in the writer's paper?
4. Does the writer incorporate sources and document properly? Check the writer's sources and documentation format—in the paper and at the end.

Thesis Statement

5. Does the thesis statement contain the essay's controlling idea and an opinion about that idea?
6. Does the thesis appear as the last sentence of the introduction?

Basic Elements

7. Does the title draw in the readers?
8. Does the introduction capture the readers' attention and build up effectively to the thesis statement?
9. Does each body paragraph deal with a single topic?
10. Does the conclusion bring the essay to a close in an interesting way?

Development

11. Do the body paragraphs adequately support the thesis statement?
12. Does each body paragraph have a focused topic sentence?
13. Does each body paragraph contain *specific* details that support the topic sentence?
14. Does each body paragraph include *enough* details to fully explain the topic sentence?

Unity

15. Do all the essay's topic sentences relate directly to the thesis statement?
16. Do the details in each paragraph support the paragraph's topic sentence?

Organization

17. Is the essay organized logically?
18. Is each body paragraph organized logically?

Coherence

19. Are transitions used effectively so that paragraphs move smoothly and logically from one to the next?
20. Do the sentences move smoothly and logically from one to the next?

Use Appendix 6 to check for grammar and usage errors in your research paper.